RJG07181828
SIT ON OUR HANDS OR   180718
UGA USED G USED:GOOD   456
ABBOTT, RO Rtl: **15.00**

Location _U-gon-A_

[ ] _____ Bent

[ ] _____ Bumped

[X] _____ Creasing to Cover   [ ] _____ Edge Wear

[X] _miro_____ Shelf Wear [ ] _____ Sunned

[ ] Spine Creased [ ] Remainder Mark

[ ] _____ Foxing

[ ] _____ Soiling

[X] No Marks in Text [ ] _____ Underlining

[ ] Pages Yellowed   [ ] _____ Highlighting

[ ] Weak Hinge(s)   [ ] _____ Marginal Marks

[ ] _____ Tear(s) to DJ   [ ] _____ Shelf Wear to DJ

Notes _____

_____

_____

_____

_____

*This sticker is removable.

Sit on Our Hands,
or Stand on Our Feet?

WEST Theological Monograph Series

Wales Evangelical School of Theology (WEST) has produced a stream of successful PhD candidates over the years, whose work has consistently challenged the boundaries of traditional understanding in both systematic and biblical theology. Now, for the first time, this series makes significant examples of this ground-breaking research accessible to a wider readership.

Sit on Our Hands,
or Stand on Our Feet?

Exploring a Practical Theology of
Major Incident Response for the Evangelical
Catholic Christian Community in the UK

ROGER PHILIP ABBOTT

WIPF & STOCK · Eugene, Oregon

SIT ON OUR HANDS, OR STAND ON OUR FEET?
Exploring a Practical Theology of Major Incident Response for the Evangelical
Catholic Christian Community in the UK

Wipf & Stock
An Imprint of Wipf and Stock Publishers
199 W. 8th Ave., Suite 3
Eugene, OR 97401

www.wipfandstock.com

ISBN 13: 978-1-61097-670-1

Manufactured in the U.S.A.

I dedicate this work to
Marion, James, Chloe, Johnny, Anna, and Naomi,
in the prayerful hope and wish that what I have achieved,
through their patient support and the help of so many casualties
of traumatic incidents, might now serve to help those who have to
respond when disaster strikes in the future, as inevitably
in this poor fallen world it will, until Christ returns.

Contents

Contents

Acknowledgments

THE FULFILLMENT OF THIS book has been an enormous challenge for two main reasons: first, because re-entering academia after thirty-one years in church pastoral ministry has involved a steep learning curve in methodologies, presentation, and writing; second, because of personal and family trauma which have presented my family and me with the most torrid personal struggles we have ever had to engage with hitherto. Any degree of success I may have achieved, therefore, must acknowledge the help given to me by others. Without their encouragement, support, and practical advice I could not have succeeded.

In particular, I want to acknowledge the very practical and fulsome support and encouragement to embark upon and sustain this research given by my family, especially to Marion, for becoming breadwinner for the four years the research has taken, and being the caring, patient wife and bearer of my many lows and highs. The patient encouragement given by my primary supervisor at Wales Evangelical School of Theology (WEST), Dr. Eryl Davies, has been an enormous stimulus, and he has provided wise guidance and the necessary self-belief for the project. His reading of drafts, and his judicious commenting, has given confirmation to my thoughts as well as kept me from straying from the research path on strategic occasions. I thank Dr. Neil Messer, formerly at University of Wales Lampeter (UWL), for his approachability and the many helpful leads he has given. Staff at both UWL and WEST libraries have been enormously productive of literature sources and in recovering information for references and citations. I thank the Rev. Philip and Mrs. Jenny Eveson, Dr. Frederick Hodgson, and Dr. John Manton for their willingness to proofread the many pages of text and footnotes, and for their patient assistance in such tedious, but necessary work. The contribution of fellowship and interest by fellow scholars at the Kirby Laing Institute for Christian Ethics, Cambridge, under the guidance of Dr. Jonathan Chaplin, has been more significant than they could ever know. They have provided the necessary research community for me to share and hone my thinking in. A project of this nature could never be completed without the significant IT skills that I lack! Therefore, I want to thank my friend, Dr. Matthew Newton, of University of Leicester IT Services, for his willingness to give of his time and skills to patiently guide me to resolve computer glitches, matters of style, formatting, and final presentation of the dissertation. So many others have made valued contributions that have sustained me and given leads and helpful comments from time to time. It would take too long to acknowledge them all individually, but my thanks go to them no less than to those named. Though all these have helped, there will remain errors in both thinking and presentation for which I take sole responsibility.

I want to acknowledge the help of Almighty God for all he has enabled me to achieve with this research. His incredibly gracious, thrilling, and, albeit at times, strange providence has enabled me to engage in this project, and he has helped me so much to challenge myself with the necessary intellectual, theological, and ethical engagements it has required. I thank him for sustaining me in health and strength and for comforting me in facing the enormous emotional depths this kind of project inevitably exposes any researcher to. I thank him for bearing with my rages and my heartbreaks as I have attempted to address the salient theological and ethical factors in examining my own narrative and that are relevant for all those who have been hit by a major incident and for those who respond.

Therefore, finally, I want to acknowledge the help given to my project by all who have been struck by disasters large and small.

1

Aims and Definitions

PURPOSE

MY OVERALL PURPOSE FOR this research has been to explore a practical theology of major incident response for the Evangelical catholic Christian community, which cultivates Christian personal and community identity through the development of character in serving God's redemptive practices in a response of Christian pastoral care. My emphasis is significant. My aim has not been to explore a theology whose primary purpose is to explain major incidents. In fact I do not believe there is such a theology. I do not present a theology of major incidents, but of major incident response. Nor is my exploration for those who are responded to, only secondarily so; it is not part of the theological "grab bag" that Christian responders carry with them to use for the benefit of casualties. It is more a part of the Christian's engaged practical theological apprenticeship prior to, and during, a response. My research represents the role of the practical theologian, who empowers the church community's legitimation and contribution in major incident response, and who encourages individual Christians, whose callings into particularly relevant professions, whose natural skills and/or professional training, could find them placed in a major incident responding status (paid or voluntary), doing their work, unhesitatingly, as unto the Lord.*[1] I explore

---

1. *All Scripture references and quotes are taken from the New King James Version unless indicated otherwise.

See Eph 6:6–7; Col 3:23. (Please note: For my definition of a major incident, and other significant definitions, see below, pages 6–13). I use the term "professional" in the sense of one who has been trained to perform their role well, not in the sense of one who is paid financially to do their role. This distinction is important because it leaves room for recognizing that Christian volunteers/amateurs can carry out a truly

the theological basis as to why Christians should respond, and what they have to undergird that response with theologically, so they may respond with spiritual integrity to situations that will tax their comfort and confidence to the extreme.[2]

AIMS

First, I aim to construct a methodology that will facilitate this exploration robustly, taking into account my evangelical presupposition of the authority of the Old Testament and the New Testament (chapter 3).[3]

Second, I aim to compose my own prefigured narrative of my response as an Evangelical Christian pastoral carer to the Kegworth/M1 aircrash, to provide a concrete context of discordance for evaluating my practical theological exploration (chapter 4).[4]

Third, I aim to explore selected doctrinal themes to theologically configure my own pastoral carer's experience by engaging with evangelical and other theological traditions (chapters 5–10). Major incident response aims for a seamless approach, or "Integrated Emergency Response" (IER).[5] This is because it is now increasingly recognized that

---

professional response, even though they may not be paid financially for it. Equally, it allows for the fact that those who are paid professionals in, for instance, the police, fire and rescue, ambulance services, or who are among the general responding public at a scene (as bankers, road sweepers, airline pilots, etc.), but who are also Christians, can provide a professionally skilled Christian service/ministry, equal to paid clergy/chaplains. Vanhoozer, on the other hand, implies a "professional" is someone who performs their role because they are paid for doing so, whereas an "amateur" performs "for the love of it"—that is, for love of God (*The Drama of Doctrine*, 441–42). The context of his implication is that the church functions, canonical linguistically, as a community of amateurs—out of love for God. There is no essential difference between Vanhoozer and me: he is thinking *financially*, whereas I am thinking *skillfully* in our definitions. Both of us would agree on the church's motive as vocational, not remunerational.

2. Scheib cautions against the dangers of pastoral care providers being distracted from their central role by the crisis-driven approach that can dominate trauma response. She reminds that the key role of the Christian pastoral carer is to help provide a theological basis for the deeper issues that underlie responses to traumatic crises (Scheib, "'Make Love Your Aim,'" in Swinton and Payne, eds., *Living Well and Dying Faithfully*, 8).

3. Hereafter as OT and NT.

4. The Kegworth/M1 aircrash, of January 8, 1989, forms the context of my own personal experience, herein utilized as a prefigured narrative for my research. Hereafter I refer to this as Kegworth/M1.

5. This is a concept that has been an aim of much of the work of the Human Aspects Group (HAG), of the Emergency Planning Society, which has held a number of

"turf war" represents what Koenig has called "the greatest obstacle."[6] An IER implies one that is not confused by unnecessary bureaucracy, duplication, or dispute. Therefore, not only will pastoral care teams be of an ecumenical nature, they will also be multifaith in makeup. This is a great challenge to me personally because of my background and experience as a Christian pastor. I have, for most of my Christian life, held to a more conservative, Reformed, theologically Evangelical position, and this has been the controlling influence in my ministry as a pastor through the years. My ecclesiological perspective has produced other challenges in regard to working ecumenically. In major incidents, faith representation has to be authorized by some kind of accreditation. This requirement means only pastoral carers from within one or other of the recognized denominational bodies or NHS chaplaincy services (Anglican, Church of Wales, Church of Scotland, Church of Ireland, the Roman Catholic Church, or Free Churches within Churches Together in England and Wales), may gain accreditation. Those in the "Independent" tradition—even if affiliated with the Evangelical Alliance (EA), the Fellowship of Independent Evangelical Churches (FIEC), or to Affinity—may well not gain accreditation as things stand.[7]

workshops and conferences in the UK that have brought together both providers and receivers of services, to share and discuss their experiences of disasters, with a view to improving service provision. One of our aims has been to try and ensure that needless duplication by service providers is eradicated, together with delays in being passed from one service to another. For information about the aims and work of the HAG, see the EPS website, online: http://www.the-eps.org/. The term "integrated emergency response" is used in the government guidance document for the Civil Contingencies Act: UK Cabinet Office, "Emergency Preparedness," 59. Also 1.31 states, "the Act is intended to streamline an Integrated Emergency Management process: Anticipation; Assessment; Prevention; Preparation; Response; Recovery, by focusing upon assessment and preparation."

6. Koenig, *In the Wake of Disaster*, 105–6.

7. By 2008 the FIEC had become recognized as an authorizing agent for both the HM Prison Service and HM Armed Forces' chaplaincy. By early 2009 the situation regarding accreditation for NHS chaplaincy was in the process of change, to embrace churches outside of "Churches Together in England and Wales." The Rev. Debbie Hodge, Secretary for the Healthcare Chaplaincy Free Churches Group, provided me with the following statement: "The Free Churches Group through the Health Care Chaplaincy Steering Committee have forwarded a proposal to the Dept of Health regarding the accreditation of Free Church Chaplains (ministers/pastors of churches who are members of the Free Churches Group) and the wider Christian community—the 4th Constituency (ministers/priests/pastors whose churches are not members of Churches Together in England or Free Churches Group). The aim is for there to be an open and transparent system that gives accreditation to Christian ministers/pastors or

Fourth, I aim to bring conclusions from my configurative process alongside national/local emergency planning systems to provide a potential refiguration for future responses (chapter 11). This will ensure my research, as a practical theology, is earthed in the actual world of major incident response and is engaging with that world and not merely running along an irrelevant parallel track. However, my aim is certainly not primarily to influence emergency planners; it is to influence the Evangelical Christian community. From the way disaster response systems work in today's more secular, multifaith world, some communities/Christians may feel responding requires compromises of conscience they cannot afford, and will therefore conclude this is a prohibited area for them. However, a theological praxis that expounds to congregations publicly on the possible reasons for a disaster, but has not motivated a practical response itself, has not helped give credence to Evangelicals in this field. I suspect a focus upon static doctrine may anaesthetize our hearts as Evangelicals, and, ironically, cause us to lose that living mind of Christ which produces wisdom. My methodology and focus lies therefore in exploring a wisdom not simply a doctrine of major incident response.

I have three research questions that give shape and focus to my dissertation:

- What legitimates the Evangelical community responding to major incidents?

- What can a theologically informed community contribute to major incident response?

- What kind of Christian community is best placed to make such a response?

The theologizing of disasters represents a challenging and developing field for Evangelicals as theologians and Christian communities worldwide are forced to think through the theological and pastoral minefields of disasters and how to respond. More traditional philosophical theodicies are being challenged by recent practical, narrative, and liberation theological models.[8] The interface between theology and the sciences

---

priests, assuring the employing NHS Trust of their accountability to their church, recognition for this ministry, their commitment to work ecumenically, to keep up to date with health care chaplaincy. The Department of Health is funding this work through the Secretary for Free Church Chaplaincy at Churches Together in England" (email correspondence from Rev. Debbie Hodge to Rev. Roger Abbott, January 29, 2009).

8. For a traditional evangelical view see Davis and Wall, eds., *Christian Perspectives*.

is leading some to explore ways for utilizing social- and neuro- scientific methodologies in practical theology.[9] Others are looking at valid forms of pastoral contribution that supplement psychology and psychiatry as therapeutic inputs to disaster response.[10] Some are seeking to bring together the positive contribution of the geological and medical sciences with theology, to provide for disaster mitigation. They argue for the need to move from being cultures of reaction to disasters to becoming cultures of prevention.[11]

DEFINITIONS

Before proceeding, my research title demands some working definitions and clarification. Most immediate is what is meant by evangelical catholic community, and what constitutes a major incident response?

Vanhoozer is right to differentiate between the use of "Evangelical" to describe a historic socio-cultural segment of the Christian community and "evangelical" as defining a theology.[12] "Evangelical" is highly relevant to the research project because it represents the historical socio-culture I belong to, which has given shape to my prefigured drama.[13] It has been

---

Other views are represented by Anderson, *The Shape of Practical Theology*; Anderson, *Spiritual Caregiving*; Hauerwas, *Naming the Silences*; Graham, Walton, and Ward, *Theological Reflection*, represents a predominantly feminist perspective. See also Walton, "Speaking in Signs," 2–5; Chester, "Theology and Disaster Studies," 319–28.

9. Swinton and Mowat, *Practical Theology*. Nancey Murphy and John Cooper have been key Christian thinkers in regard to contributions from neuro-science (Murphy, *Bodies and Souls*; Cooper, *Soul & Life Everlasting*). See my discussion between these two interlocutors in chapter 6 below.

10. Koenig, *In the Wake of Disaster*; Wong, "Compassionate and Spiritual Care"; Weaver, "Psychological Trauma," 385–408. For critical voices on such attempts, see Sloan, *Blind Faith*, and Shuman and Meador, *Heal Thyself*.

11. Taylor, "Value Conflict Arising from a Disaster." Taylor makes the point, "At issue is the validity of using moral transgression as the cause of natural disasters and of expecting atonement, when a tenable and well-attested scientific alternative explanation is available." Also see Chester and Duncan, "Geomythology, Theodicy." The interesting thing is that both authors are making the basic point how important it is to take into account the spiritual beliefs of people affected by disaster and the valid role for faith representatives therefore.

12. Vanhoozer, *Drama of Doctrine*, 25–26.

13. The term "evangelical" is employed on a case basis, specific to context. That is, "evangelical" is employed when referring to the evangelical constituency/individual generically. "Evangelical" is employed to refer to the conservative sub-group within evangelicalism.

most succinctly defined socio-historically in Bebbington's *Evangelicalism in Modern Britain*. He concludes that "conversionism, activism, biblicism and crucicentrism form the defining attributes of Evangelical religion."[14] Evangelical theology conforms to this fourfold criterion. This theology is scrutinized in my research by the real-life contexts of disasters and by a wider theological interrogation. It warrants scrutiny, in my view, because it has been found wanting, in some respects, by the spiritual and emotional extremities of suffering found in disasters; but, also, I hope it is biblically big enough to withstand the scrutiny and yet elastic enough to be capable of constant reformation and development through learning from life's contexts and from other forms of theology. By evangelical I mean a theology that Webster defines as, ". . . one which is evoked, governed and judged by the gospel."[15] Vanhoozer's argument for an evangelical theology being rooted and bounded in the canon of Scripture is therefore included.[16] I want to explore an evangelical theology. In other words, I want to explore a theology that is evangelical in the above nature, but is not one that is necessarily assumed in the Evangelical socio-cultural sense.[17]

For theology to be true theology it must be biblical and catholic. That is, it must be generous in dialogue with other theologies, but non-reductively, centripetally inclined to the gospel and bounded by the canon in the interests of truth and wisdom that is centrifugally generous to transcultural ecumenical unity.[18] Within such boundaries it must be inclusive of the Christian community worldwide and in the past.[19]

14. Bebbington, *Evangelicalism in Modern Britain*, 1–17. See also Stackhouse, *Evangelical Landscapes*, chapter 10.

15. Webster, "The Self-Organizing Power," 69.

16. Vanhoozer, *Drama of Doctrine*, 22. I use the term "Scripture" in its capitalized form when referring to the Christian canonical Scriptures of the OT and NT. For all other references I use the uncapitalized form—"scripture."

17. For that would be to endorse a cultural-linguistic approach (Lindbeck), placing final authority in the interpretive community, not in *sola scriptura*. Equally, I am not attempting to provide a "new" theology that is defiant of evangelical tradition. On the significance of the church, tradition, and the Holy Spirit, see Vanhoozer, "Jesus, Spirit, Church," in *The Drama of Doctrine*, chapter 6.

18. And also to interfaith friendship (see chapter 10 below).

19. I am indebted to Vanhoozer for this perspective on catholicity. Vanhoozer, *Drama of Doctrine*, 27–30. By "non-reductively" he means a theology that refuses to be reduced under any single theological or literary form. See also O'Donovan's comments on catholicity in *The Desire of the Nations*, 169–72. Zizioulas argues, "only in the Church has man the power to express himself as a catholic person." This is because through regeneration the Christian becomes an authentic person without falling into

My focus is also upon the Christian community. By this I mean the church; but not as an institution or a denomination. I mean historic communities of Christians who are covenanted together in a common commitment to a tradition of lived *sola scriptura*.

The evangelical catholic Christian community possesses enormous divinely endowed human resources for pastoral care in major incidents.[20] Many will be persons who are responding agents in roles that are not directly religiously pastoral. I encourage recognition of their roles and skills as providentially appointed, and their response as also theologically informed, legitimated, servicing the overall pastoral benefit of those responded to. However, my research takes into account, particularly, the role of the community's pastoral leaders and carers.[21] This does not endorse clericalism, but bespeaks realism. In a major incident it will be accredited pastoral carers who will have the requisite formal authorization to respond, and who will be designated the particular role for religious and spiritual care. The Christian community can also provide resources of space and caring staff theologically supported for the traumatic scenes they will encounter from those using that space.

My research also explores a theology of major incident response. There are different definitions put forward in the literature and by different authorities for a major incident.[22] Because of its generic authority,

---

the individualism, separation, and death of human nature. In the Greek Orthodox tradition the Church becomes a partaker of the divine nature, which is shared among all believers (Zizioulas, *Being as Communion*, 57–58).

20. A fact that has been recognized in: UK Department for Communities and Local Government, "Key Communities, Key Resources," 5-41.

21. These may be referred to in emergency plans generically as faith leaders/representatives, or as clergy/chaplains (to include hospital chaplains). However, lay members of the community can be accredited where their pastoral skills are commensurate with the needs within a major incident. Taking all this into account, and to avoid any misunderstanding toward a clericalism, I will use a generic term when referring to such pastoral care responders—pastoral carers—unless otherwise specified. I use the term "carer" to mean one who engages in "caring practices," which are "concrete, if imperfect, ways in which the church bears witness to the divine love through which it is called into being and sustained." While these practices are humanly expressed, they are "gifts of the Spirit for the life of the church and the world" (Scheib, "Make Love Your Aim," in Swinton and Payne, eds., *Living Well and Dying Faithfully*, 33).

22. Starting with that definition set out in Allen, "Disasters: Planning for a Caring Response," 3. This definition, in turn, had been taken from the Association of Chief Police Officers Emergency Procedures Manual. By 2004/5 the terrorist threat had become a serious cause of a major incident being called. See also NHS Management Executive, "Emergency Planning in the NHS" for a different definition of a major incident for the Health Service context.

form, and succinctness, the best contemporary, authoritative definition for the UK context is that given by the Civil Contingencies Act 2004 (CCA 2004).[23] It describes an "emergency" as, "An event or situation which threatens serious damage to human welfare in a place in the UK, the environment of a place in the UK, or war or terrorism which threatens serious damage to the security of the UK."[24]

This definition is explained in greater detail within the legislation. An incident has to be formally declared as an emergency or major incident when the various criteria laid down in the act and the guidance notes are fulfilled. Though the CCA 2004 definition includes both war and terrorism, these represent delimited areas for my research and are complex fields, with massive literature.[25] However, I realize that casualties from theaters of war (e.g., in Afghanistan and Iraq) are arriving in the UK in various states of traumatization. Also, pastors may encounter localized immigrant populations, traumatized by war or genocide in the countries from which they have fled. Since there is a strong likelihood of terrorist acts affecting the UK and UK nationals abroad, where my theological exploration shows relevant pastoral implications, I give brief attention to contexts of terrorist activity.

One might question limiting the definition of a disaster to this particular technical form because it omits incidents of individual or small group traumatization. The definition provided by Raphael recognizes the import of this point: "overwhelming events and circumstances that test the adaptational responses of community or individual beyond their capability, and lead, at least temporarily, to massive disruption of function for the community or individual."[26] Indeed, an interesting exception

---

23. In the wake of the World Trade Center incident ("9/11") however, the act includes war and terrorism.

24. UK Cabinet Office, "Emergency Preparedness." There is also a helpful short version entitled, "Civil Contingencies Act 2004: A Short Guide (Revised)," which can be downloaded from the same address. See also UK Department for Culture, Media and Sport, "Humanitarian Assistance in Emergencies," 13. This also makes it clear that the terms emergency and major incident are now used interchangeably.

25. For a single work edition that seeks to cover all kinds of major incidents from the perspective of trauma, including "the manmade disaster of war" see Raphael et al., eds, *Individual and Community Responses*.

26. Raphael, *When Disaster Strikes*, 5 (emphasis mine). Ursano et al., also acknowledge it in their definition of traumatic events and disasters. See Ursano et al, "Trauma and Disaster," in Raphael et al., *Individual and Community Responses*, 5, as does Ripley in *The Unthinkable*, xviii–xx.

to incidents involving large numbers of casualties, and one that preceded CCA 2004, concerns the murder of two young girls in the Cambridgeshire town of Soham. This concerned only two young people, their families, the accused, and the affected school, but because the incident generated intense media attention the statuary authorities were overwhelmed, and it was declared a major incident. So, while major incidents usually involve great numbers of people being injured or bereaved, it is not always the case. For example, CCA 2004 includes serious damage to the environment, as in flooding or biological, chemical, or radiological contaminations that need not involve many people or large areas of space. Even though my selective focus is upon major incidents, I accept that my methodology, and aspects of the explored theology, will have application also to individual cases of trauma response, for example road traffic incidents, industrial accidents, even homicides.

Finally, I need to define what I mean by response. There may be many aspects to the way(s) Christians respond to a major incident; some of these aspects will be determined by their specific roles. My concern in this research lies specifically with the pastoral aspect(s) Christian theology constructs. Thus, I distinguish these from the role of counseling. I will refer to the pastoral aspects as "pastoral care," and to those who practice them as "pastoral carers." Broadly speaking, pastoral care may be defined by the following parameters:[27] pastoral care involves creating a relationship(s) for the purpose of giving Christian support in time of trouble, and fostering spiritual growth, "with a view to ensuring and enabling faithful participation in God's redemptive practices in, to and for the world" that is transformative.[28] This care should be derived from a serious theological basis of a canonical linguistic theodramatic configuration.[29] Such care is located within the evangelical catholic Christian community, yet is sensitive to, and respectful of, the individual spiritual choices of the recipient, and has no proselytizing agenda.[30] Pastoral care

27. I acknowledge gratitude to David Lyall for the basic framework of these parameters, though I have adapted his specific terms to suit my evangelical position and my version of a practical theology, which I define in chapter 3 below. (See Lyall, *Integrity of Pastoral Care*, 12.)

28. Swinton and Mowat, *Practical Theology*, 6.

29. The concepts of "canonical-linguistic" and "theo-drama" are integral to my methodology. For their meaning see chapter 3 below, pages 49–51, 69.

30. Bewes argues that proselytizing involves unworthy motives, unworthy methods, and an unworthy message to meet the desired "conversionist" result. It is when the other is made to suffer by refusing what is offered. (Bewes, "Why Christians Are

enjoys a freedom to draw upon the traditional resources of the Christian community, in terms of such things as Scripture, prayer, sacrament, and fellowship, to address the needs of victims.[31] Pastoral care may take on a more intense pastoral counseling relationship, but this may require additional counseling skills and certainly needs to be distinguished from the pastoral care responses given in the immediate and mid-term periods, when formal counseling is generally ill-advised.

These aims and definitions set out the purpose, parameters, and imply the delimitations, of this research project. This will, hopefully, prevent misunderstanding in what follows.

To give some perspective on the need for my research, I next survey the research literature.

Not Proselytizers," included in "Sharing Hope in Crisis," The Billy Graham Rapid Response Team, 2008). Stackhouse defines proselytism when he judges, "It is vocationally unethical, then, to exploit authority in one role (teacher, physician, judge) to try to influence others in another—namely, as a religious advocate." (Stackhouse, *Making the Best of It*, 335). The joint policy statement of the College of Health Care Chaplains, the Scottish Association of Chaplains in Healthcare, and the Association of Hospice and Palliative Care Chaplains, defines proselytizing as "spiritual abuse" when it states: "Spiritual abuse is the imposition of a chaplain's values and belief on those in their care, proselytism, and a failure to respect their spiritual interests," ("Health Care Chaplains: Code of Conduct").

31. Lyall states these needs must be determined by the recipient. My own experience as a responder revealed that, certainly during the immediate impact stage, casualties are not always good at recognizing their needs; just as they are not so in the case of necessary emergency medical care. There has to be a level of dependency upon the—more detached—professionalism of the responder in the immediate stages of a response. While this enhances the vulnerability of casualties, it also enhances the professional responsibility of the responder. (For the meaning of "professional" in this research see my earlier discussion. It need not amount to the "arrogance" Lyall suggests (Lyall, *Integrity of Pastoral Care*, 54).

2

Literature Review

A REVIEW OF THE literature exposes a significant gap in research of major incident response from a practical theological perspective, thus establishing the vacant ground for my project. My extensive bibliography betrays an enormous deficiency in research for the particular area of major incident response for Christian responders.[1] The breadth of literature consulted has been necessitated for identifying and confirming research aims and questions, for developing a methodology to guide the research, and for exploring theological themes salient to major incident response. Throughout my dissertation I have interacted with my bibliography, reviewing and citing from it extensively, and critiquing where necessary.

My limited literature review demonstrates how the field has moved and changed, what key influences have been involved, and the gaps in, and validity of, my chosen area of research. I review literature in ascending chronological order, under the following categories:

a. Extant research work that relates to Christians and major incident response, revealing severe research limitations.

b. Research work that attempts to reconcile theological study with social science methods. This is a vexing area in current debate between Christians and the secular world.[2] However, since so much of major incident research is dominated by social science there is need

---

1. This literature would more often than not be identified by key words into the databases, such as: "faith communities," "faith representatives," and "spirituality." These more generic terms dominate over the use of terms specific to the Christian religion.

2. For example, see Biggar, "Saving the Secular"; Knight, "Christ, Religion"; Spencer, "Doing God"; Wilson, "The Return of the Sacred."

to demonstrate a serious attempt at reconciliation, or respected parallel working, in the field of contemporary trauma response.

c. National and local government legislation and guidance, and commentaries upon these to reveal what emphasis, or lack of it, is given to the role of pastoral carers in national systems of major incident response.

EXTANT RESEARCH

In regard to Christian theological specificity to major incident response, there is no evidence of research that I have discovered at PhD level (either in the UK, Europe, or the US), and none at all directly regarding pastoral care.

Christian Perspectives on Disaster Management presents a distinctly Evangelical approach to disaster response from Davis and Wall. In fact this joint production is the earliest UK source I know of approaching an evangelical theology of major incident response.[3] A two volume work, it is designed mainly for natural disasters occurring in the developing world. Volume 2 is a trainer's guide and incorporates basic management strategies common at the time of writing. The first volume sets out a brief theology of disaster response with an introduction and four sections—Christian dimensions, attitudes, knowledge, and skills. The material under Christian dimensions and attitudes is the most relevant to this research. Their aims for the Christian dimensions are:

> Through the power of the Holy Spirit to strengthen each participant's concern to advance God's kingdom and help others who are vulnerable to potential hazards or victims of past disasters. Also to strengthen biblical understanding and knowledge of how disasters relate to our Christian faith and practice.[4]

They address theological questions pertaining to disasters, such as, why is there suffering, and why do disasters occur? Their material is standard conservative theodicy teaching. It is for the benefit of the Christian, and there is virtually nothing said about the non-Christian. Both authors are practitioners more than theologians, and this reflects the uncritical standard content of the work; from a purely practical point of view the disaster management strategies they set out are helpful. Their theology/

3. Davis and Wall, eds., *Christian Perspectives*.
4. Ibid., 5.

theodicy has been criticized justifiably by both Eyre and Chester as supportive of the "good disaster" theory. Considering this is the only extant disaster management manual from an Evangelical perspective, it highlights a grave weakness and gap in evangelical pastoral and practical theology in the disaster field. The gap is all the more alarming considering the existence of a clear literature-based case for the involvement of spiritual care in major incident response.

"Pastoral Ministry Following a Major Disaster" provides a response from a volunteer chaplain to the bombing of the Alfred P. Murrah building in Oklahoma City on April 19, 1995.[5] This was an act of homeland terrorism by a white U.S. citizen on U.S. citizens. This research reflects upon the theological implications raised by the tragedy, studies grief effects, and seeks to develop a guide for clergy/chaplaincy response. It provides a limited primary source for my research. Williams describes the events of the bombing and the effects upon the people involved, as well as the clergy response. He reflects upon providential and pastoral aspects and upon the issue of grief and the various theodicies traditionally available. He reveals some of the enigmas of a disaster when he notes that some found their prayers were wonderfully answered in being saved from the disaster, while others, equally spiritual people, died. He concludes that God is all loving and that it "was not God's plan that the Alfred P Murrah Building be blown up at 9:02 a.m. on April 19th, 1995." Having described the interviews with clergy that formed a part of his research, Williams reflects positively on the value of stress debriefing, a point that is more controversial in the UK policy of treating trauma than in the U.S. He concludes by providing a helpful major incident response guide for pastors, based upon the model of the Church World Service's holistic disaster cycle: the need to prepare, educate, prevent, mitigate, respond and integrate. In my view, Williams follows existing liberal models of theological and pastoral thought and presents no new theological and pastoral conclusions, from any evangelical perspective at least.[6]

5. Williams, "Pastoral Ministry," n.p. Again I am indebted to Norman Williams for sending me a hard copy of his dissertation, and references are taken from that copy. Williams is pastor of First Christian Church in San Bernardino, California. He is also a chaplain in the California Air National Guard, ranking as colonel. In this incident 168 people died (18 of whom were children) and 490 were treated in a hospital.

6. He also reveals how the U.S. systems of disaster response differ from those in the UK, especially regarding faith community responders as accredited chaplains.

"The Hazards of One's Faith: Hazard Perceptions of South Carolina Christian Clergy" researches the influence of clergy and their theology upon community disaster response.[7] Using a survey, the author researched how biblical orientation influences hazard perception and response among clergy in South Carolina. Two research questions were posed: do clergy of different denominations view hazards differently (with geographical location, past experience or theological persuasion explaining these differences), and do differences exist between clergy of different denominations about hazard mitigation?

Whereas hazards were once viewed religiously by most people as "acts of God," today there is an inclination to explain these naturally. However, in the southern states of North America there remains a religious interpretation of a distinctly Christian nature. Mitchell observes that to some Christian groups environmental disasters are ominous of Christ's second coming and final judgment. While Christian groups in the U.S. are renowned for their active response to disasters, little attention has been given to hazard perception and mitigation. Levels of perceived control/ loss of control as significant influences on how disasters and mitigation measures are perceived were studied. Mitchell gives a brief summary of different denominations covered by the research, with research methods involving a survey of population and use of questionnaires. From the results, factors driving hazard perception were identified. Geographic location, past experience, theological persuasion, biblical orientation, and hazard concern were investigated, but few links were found. Clergy were grouped into four categories: Evangelical, Liturgical, Pentecostal/Holiness, and Reformed. The Evangelical and Pentecostal/Holiness clergy tended to view hazards as indicators of the second coming of Christ, and literalistic readings of Scripture could drive perceptions of hazards that were threatening.[8] This being said, however, Mitchell concludes that "Overall, the theological differences noted between clergy of various denominations do not appear to have any bearing on the types of hazard considered threatening."[9] With regard to mitigation preferences, Mitchell wondered if religious belief would affect hazard awareness or the range of acceptable responses. He concluded, "Overall, there is no evidence to suggest that clergy of a particular faith tradition prefer one mitigation

7. Mitchell, "Hazards of One's Faith," 25–41. Again note the U.S. context. No equivalent research of this kind has been done in the UK as far as I know.

8. Ibid., 37.

9. Ibid., 38.

strategy over another."[10] Yet, he noted with some surprise, out of 227 respondents only four mentioned prayer as an appropriate action to reduce loss from a hazard. Thus, he concluded that neither theological orientation nor prayer drive hazard adjustments.[11] Yet, it was also noted that most members of congregations take the views of their clergy seriously, and nearly 50 percent of the clergy used references to hazards as illustrative material and metaphors in their teaching material and sermons. Finally, it is thought, "religious beliefs inform what we consider to be valuable and should be investigated further to understand how it inspires our decisions to protect our valuables and ourselves."[12] Mitchell provides a useful piece of research with natural environmental hazards in mind, which are rarely experienced in the UK. Nevertheless, this research, using a variety of theological persuasions among the clergy, is not without relevance to the situation involving clergy responding to disasters in the UK and to those affected by incidents abroad, which may well involve the kind of natural disasters Mitchell's work has in mind.[13] The conclusions indicate theological reflection and conviction seem to figure only slightly in people's sense of hazard perception and mitigation.

"A Complex Organizational Adaptation to the World Trade Center Disaster: An Analysis of Faith-Based Organizations" presents the findings of Sutton's research project following the World Trade Center disaster of "9/11," the first major attack against the U.S. since Pearl Harbor.[14] The purpose of her research was to identify how unintended and unknown consequences from a disaster test the capacity of faith-based organizations to adapt to the emergency. While literature shows that organized behavior responses in disasters have received extensive attention in sociological research, Sutton has focused specifically upon faith-based organizations, an area little researched so far. She started the research using the Disaster Research Center Typology, useful for analyzing organizational adaptation.[15] However, because of limitations,

10. Ibid., 38.

11. Ibid., 38.

12. Ibid., 39.

13. For example, the 2004 Indian Ocean tsunami and the UK flooding of 2001, 2005, and 2009.

14. Sutton, "Complex Organizational Adaptation," 405–28.

15. The DRCT was a typology for research purposes developed in the U.S. by Dynes and Quarantelli in the 1980s. It provided an original model for focusing on *organizational* responses to crises, not individual ones, researching how organizations

it needed to be expanded to account for emergent behaviors. Her methods focused mainly on help provided by the Manhattan faith-based services, consisting of the Presbytery of New York City, the Church World Service, and the Presbyterian Church's Disaster Assistance. The Temple of Understanding was an inter-faith group that was included. Twenty-four qualitative interviews were conducted with representatives from ten faith-based organizations, and the data analyzed. Certainly existing structures proved useful for assisting in the disaster relief effort, but there was very limited capacity for adaptation. Those who benefited most were members of their own communities. However, even at this level there is a need for emergency management to include faith-based organizations and congregations into their plans. The greatest capacity for adaptation in emergency conditions seemed to be the faith-based affiliates of the American Red Cross: Childcare Aviation Incident Response (CAIR) and the Spiritual Care Aviation Incident Response (SAIR). Both teams were mobilized for the 9/11 attacks and had a role in teaching local churches, as well as in setting up units in the Family Assistance Center. The American Red Cross defines spiritual care as "a sustaining care that draws upon a person's own inner religious and/or spiritual resources" and in "its fundamental sense is service to others, including the religious/spiritual; emotional; social and, at times, physical care of those *entrusted in the midst of crisis.*"[16] Therefore, because the SAIR team was responsible for screening religious professionals to ensure compliance with its charter, such could provide prohibitive challenges for many Evangelicals if a similar system were replicated in the UK. Sutton's research also identified that the faith element involved in recent terrorist activity and emergencies requires the enlisting of faith-based organizations.[17]

"The Church and Disaster: the Role of the Church in Relation to Mass Emergency and Disaster Situations" explores the role of the UK church (clergy and congregation) in responding to disasters, in regard to victims and other responding agencies.[18] Horner uses two case studies: the Lockerbie murders (1988) and the sinking of the Solway Harvester

---

function under stress. This required the convergence of collective and organizational behavior theories. It became apparent early on that this typology needed to be adaptable to disaster situations. (See Webb, "Individual and Organizational Response.")

16. Sutton, "Complex Organizational Adaptation," 13.

17. Ibid., 18.

18. Horner, "The Church and Disaster."

(2000).[19] Using these, he applied the "pastoral cycle" tool, which involves considering incidents in terms of experience, exploration, due reflection, and response, all of which provide learning for the next incident.[20] He defines his terms, states the characteristics of a disaster, and gives consideration to the psychological aspects—including post-traumatic stress disorder (PTSD) and abnormal bereavement. He also summarizes various legal aspects before focusing on the church's response. His case studies are built up around interviews with responding clergy and others, from which information is gathered and analyzed. He gathers additional information from a limited amount of literature as well as from actual visits to the sites of memorials. Horner considers how the churches became involved, who got involved, what resources were employed, where they were deployed to and when. He also considers the relationships with other agencies involved. From this he highlights lessons to be learned and a number of theological issues that come to light. He has a chapter that focuses upon theological areas, such as theodicy, the problem of evil, justice, forgiveness, the prophetic dimension, and civic theology. Conducted from a liberal perspective, it lacks theological specificity and does not address practical aspects of the emergency-planning framework within which Christian responders are required to work. My own research seeks to consider the multifaith issues more concertedly. Above all, I seek to give focus to evangelical theology and to the challenges it is likely to be faced with under current statutory systems.

A research project that focuses upon the Kegworth/M1 air disaster and a terrorist bombing on the Shankhill Road, Belfast, is relevant to my review because the researchers specifically took into account Christian clergy as one of their four groups for research. "An Empirical Study into the Psychosocial Reactions of Staff Working as Helpers to those Affected in the Aftermath of Two Traumatic Incidents" is the first empirical study of psychosocial impacts on four groups of professional responders (social workers, ambulance personnel, accident and emergency nurses, and clergy), and their design was to create a training program "to meliorate

19. On the Lockerbie murders, see appendix 1. The *Solway Harvester* was a fishing vessel that sank off the Isle of Man in 2000, with the loss of seven lives.

20. The NYDIS uses the term, "Disaster Management Continuum" and includes the following phases: Planning and preparedness; Mitigation; Response; Recovery; Evaluation. Practical theology has used "branch" and "cycle" models (Herrmann, "Disaster Response Planning and Preparedness: Phases of Disaster"). For a summary of these, and his own preferred "cycle" model, see Emmanuel Larty, "Practical Theology as a Theological Form," in Woodward and Pattison, eds., Blackwell Reader, 128–34.

any negative reactions that may be experienced by the helpers."[21] They focus on how post-traumatic syndrome studies in the latter half of the twentieth century have disclosed problems, particularly affecting so-called "third level victims," namely responders. The authors make a brief review of the post-traumatic stress disorder research literature, concluding there is a paucity of research on secondary traumatic stress for the benefit of responders. They then describe and discuss the responses to the two incidents, drawing attention to the particular differences, which hinged mainly around the issue of responder preparation. They note that, for instance, all the clergy responding to Kegworth/M1 were doing so for the first time, whereas in the Shankhill Road incident 90 percent of clergy had responded previously, and 67 percent of those clergy had been trained for response. Also, the Shankhill response clergy had a long-term involvement in the local community to pursue, whereas the Kegworth/M1 clergy response was comparatively short.[22] However, in both cases there was recognition of little training for self-coping. They conclude there is a major need for training in all aspects of trauma work, especially if responding organizations are to avoid adverse litigation moves from responders who incur lasting damage to their health. This is a valid piece of research that exposes the importance of good training. Their work also reveals the developing litigation fears, resulting from the transport and stadium disasters during the 1980s and 1990s, entering emergency planning and training awareness. In the U.S., litigation processes and courts awarded large financial compensations.

"Responses of Clergy to 9/11: Posttraumatic Stress, Coping, and Religious Outcomes" examined post-traumatic stress, religious coping, and nonreligious coping in relation to positive religious outcomes, among U.S. clergy, in regard to their awareness of the 9/11 event.[23] Findings were based upon a mailed survey of 814 active, ordained ministers in the Presbyterian Church (USA). They concluded that clergy are as likely to become traumatized by such an event as are the public. Thus, a religious perspective gives no immunity against traumatization. However, religion

---

21. Gibson and Iwaniec, "Empirical Study," 851–70.

22. I think this observation regarding Kegworth/M1 clergy is too general, since my own response lasted for above two years, and my response was not limited to the local community.

23. Meisenhelder and Marcum, "Responses of Clergy to 9/11," 544–47.

provides a pathway to positive religious coping through looking to God and prayer, and this can be associated with positive religious outcomes.[24]

"Pastoral Care During Major Traumatic Events: Implications for Pastoral Care for Emergency Responders and Their Care-Givers" supplies a useful primary source for demonstrating there is relevance for theology in major incident response.[25] Chenard qualitatively researched how theological and ontological questions raised by victims of major traumatic events led pastoral care providers to reformulate their models of care both for victims and providers. Her primary research was based on open-ended interviews with the Canadian police and chaplains involved. The findings from these interviews were subjected to the traditional pastoral care models to see if such were sufficiently helpful or whether they needed to change. Overall, she concluded that traditional pastoral models are beneficial but need to expand and be flexible enough for the peculiarities of major incidents. She highlighted the importance of narrative formation and listening as significant for victim care. Bonding is intense, and, to be of use, pastoral carers need to become a part of that response. She concludes that a model of flexibility, nonintrusiveness, and ongoing care is best, where the ministry of presence is of greatest value, rather than attempting to answer theological questions that no one is asking, at least in the early days. In fact, she argues that theological and ontological issues should be left until later when they become relevant or helpful to rescuers. While I would differ greatly in my theological position with Chenard, I found her thesis insightful.[26] Her research, however, was conducted within the Canadian context, where, as in the US, the role of clergy acting as volunteer chaplains in emergency response is formalized very differently than in the UK.

"Spiritual and Emotional Care Resource" reflects work by an American organization: World Church Service.[27] It exemplifies, again,

24. The concept of religion, however, was of a generic nature, though from a liberal Christian perspective.

25. This was based on Chenard's personal experience, working as a volunteer chaplain at the scene of the Swiss Air 111 disaster off the coast of Nova Scotia, September 2, 1998. (Chenard, "Pastoral Care," n.p.) I am indebted to Dr. Chenard for sending me an electronic version (PDF) of her work.

26. She has an interesting focus on *acedia*, or "compassion fatigue," a concept developed in theological and moral terms by Thomas Aquinas, but here reflected upon in terms of frontline responders and the rigors they are exposed to by their work. See below, 231-32.

27. Sage, "Spiritual and Emotional Care Resource," n.p.

how more aware U.S. church resources are to the challenges of major incidents than in the UK.[28] Sage argues for two possible responses being provided for responding chaplains: that of the Christian World Church Service providing training and awareness building for chaplains about the effects of major incidents, or the possibility of the same organization sending in a specialist team (Spiritual and Emotional Care Resource) to work with an affected faith community, if they request that. Sage recognizes that chaplains are being regarded (at least in the U.S. context) as first line responders, alongside the police, ambulance, fire, and rescue services. Therefore they should have appropriate training for such a challenging role. He also identifies that, in the case of faith representatives, their role may well stretch from the immediate to the long term response periods, thus risking responders "burning out" and even leaving the ministry altogether. Sage notes the need for involving the social sciences and theology in order to prepare chaplains, both in terms of disaster training and preparedness and appropriate interventions after a disaster response has taken place.

In "Remembering: Community Commemorations after Disaster" Eyre discusses rituals and commemorative responses to disasters from a mainly anthropological and sociological point of view.[29] Her aim was to explore the key issues associated with the nature, meaning, and purpose of community remembrance following disasters. She focused upon the ways in which disasters are commemorated in communities by rituals, memorials, and religious services. Her conclusion is that social support is vital to the grieving process through the spontaneous expressions of grief, often fueled and facilitated by the media, through the processes of body recovery, identification, and religious aspects. Relevant to my research, she observes that initial expressions of grief are often accompanied by increased attendance at religious places in the immediate aftermath of communal tragedy, and latent religious beliefs can become important

28. This is also evident from reading Harding, *NYDIS Manual*. Of note in the U.S. context is the inclusion of guidance to individuals, families, and church communities to create their own disaster plans. This is due to the more frequent occurrence of natural disasters within the U.S. In the UK context the government did distribute leaflets giving guidance in the event of terrorist activity, following 9/11. Possible increased flooding potential, coupled with increasing floodplain housing development, and possible global warming outcomes, could lead to similar mitigation measures being encouraged in the UK also.

29. Eyre, "Remembering," n.p. I am indebted to Dr. Eyre for sending me an electronic copy of this paper.

and overt at such times.[30] Eyre focuses upon the significance of silence in commemoration of disaster, the helpfulness or otherwise of public memorial services (with the delicate diplomacies involved), anniversary events, establishing permanent memorial sites, and the influence these can all have on survivors being able to move forward. Also, she identifies,

> Future studies might focus on the dynamic relationship between the focus of religion [*sic*] secularization and modernity in relation to the changing nature of rituals after disaster and particularly on the impact of political contexts where religious ideologies are seen as playing a part in uniting or dividing communities in disaster and its consequences.[31]

In "Literature and Best Practice Review and Assessment" Eyre reviews the disaster literature, both nationally and internationally, and gives an assessment of best practice.[32] For my research it is a useful resource, since it details the available literature on major incident response over the past forty years or so. Her purpose is to consider the best practice for the bereaved and injured in the light of CCA 2004. In part 1 she considers the nature of types of emergency events, the communal dimensions, and has an insightful section on the myths about the behavior and needs of those caught up in emergencies. Part 2 looks at the emotional impacts and the reactions to disasters and the trauma aspect of disaster in particular. Part 3 addresses the meeting of human needs, and the different types of provision at each stage of the disaster response. Part 4 reviews the various forms of humanitarian response available to date, focusing especially on the Humanitarian Assistance Centre concepts already in existence. Part 5 looks at the common pitfalls arising in psycho-social planning and response. Finally, the report is rounded off with a list of recommendations for best practice. Significantly for my research, she identifies no theological research at all. There is no mention of the research literature from Swinton and Mowat (UK) or from Weaver, Koenig, and Ochberg (U.S.).[33] Yet, her report confirms that government legislation

---

30. Ibid., 14. This was most notably demonstrated in Sweden following the Estonia ferry disaster in 1994, in which many Swedes perished, and Sweden threw open the doors of the national churches.

31. Ibid., 33. For my contribution to the issue of religious ideologies uniting or dividing communities see my new model for interfaith relations in chapter 10.

32. Eyre, "Literature and Best Practice Review."

33. Swinton and Mowat, *Practical Theology and Qualitative Research*; Mowat and Swinton, "What Do Chaplains Do?" Also, Koenig, *In the Wake of Disaster*; Weaver, Koenig, and Ochberg, "Posttraumatic Stress," 847–56.

and recommendation does see a key role for the faith communities and their representatives. However, she makes no reference to them in her key points, which is, for me, a shortcoming in her report and does not reflect the importance of the evidence she highlights from the literature reviewed.[34] In "Community Support After Disasters" Eyre aims to consider lessons learned from the events of 9/11 in New York and New Jersey upon psycho-social community recovery.[35] While largely about mental health and psychological issues, her report is of some significance to me in that she includes her meeting with representatives of the New York Disasters Interfaith Service (NYDIS), which, she states,

> grew out of 9/11 after clergy and faith-based agencies responded to Ground Zero and assisted in the rescue, relief and recovery efforts. From this reactive and improvised approach the faith communities realised that better planning and preparedness was needed, and have since developed a communication network of faith-based disaster service agencies. This coalition now coordinates faith-based readiness, response and recovery activities in New York City.[36]

Eyre's work is significant in terms of social science and a sociological view of religion. However, it betrays a lack of awareness of theological and pastoral perspectives in the field.

The extant research evidences a predominance of attention upon chaplaincy and the U.S. context. From this there is limited transference to the UK context, in which there has been a paucity of practical theological research, Horner's being the only research that qualifies for that discipline, but carrying very limited scope and reflection. In the U.S., chaplaincy is privatized and more professionalized, and there is also a stream specific to major incidents.[37] There is no equivalent system in the

34. In email communication with me, Eyre's explanation for omitting key point references was due to the absence of evidence based research studies, which, she concedes, also applies to the role of psychology as well. However, this touches on the conflict between methodologies that exists between the social sciences and the humanities—a controversial issue Sloan has addressed in his *Blind Faith*.

35. Eyre, "Community Support," n.p. (PDF copy sent to author by Dr. Ann Eyre, 2006.) This project was a result of her being awarded a Winston Churchill Traveling Fellowship, which enabled her to travel in New York and New Jersey in June and July 2006.

36. Eyre, "Community Support"; Harding, *NYDIS Manual*.

37. On the training and professionalization of chaplains in the U.S. see Sloan, *Blind Faith*, 226–28. Professionalization is an issue being taken up in the UK by the College

UK.[38] Furthermore, the U.S. context builds upon a far greater degree of religiosity than in the more secular UK that my own research seeks to address. I also note the widespread use of religion as a generic concept. However, the extant research literature demonstrates the key influence of the 9/11 terrorist event, and researchers have been eager to harvest constructive results and lessons from it as early as possible.

RESEARCH METHODOLOGY LITERATURE

Studies in trauma response have combined sociology, social science, and mental health, with religious and spiritual perspectives and methodologies. Methodologies, therefore, have tended to be dominated by social science, revealing another key influence being the pressure upon chaplaincy, from largely secular emergency planning departments and the NHS, to justify their role with an evidence base.

Of critical importance to this research is the ethical sensitivity required, even though no specific data is being collected from victims of major incidents as such.[39] The exploration of a practical theology for major incident response is itself a sensitively ethical domain. Therefore, Trauma Research Methodology provides a helpful guide, which, though often considering issues outside of my remit, nevertheless provides useful advice for aspects of my research—in particular, chapters on searching the traumatic stress literature, emotional issues, and ethical aspects are salient.[40] "Doing Better than the Media: Ethical Issues in Trauma Research" addresses the ethical discipline required in trauma research.[41] Raftery compares trauma researchers with journalists, and observes that both have the capacity to traumatize and be traumatized. He helpfully

---

of Healthcare Chaplains (CHCC) in response to pressure from the Department of Health and NHS's call for professionalization requirements.

38. The Billy Graham Association's Rapid Response Teams are deployed to disaster scenes for chaplaincy work. They now have an agenda for creating such teams here in the UK, in conjunction with local evangelical churches. (Munday, "Ministry to a Pluralistic Community.")

39. This has been why, hitherto, I have hesitated to utilize my own experience at Kegworth/M1 for research purposes. I include it in this research with great care, therefore. See chapter 4 below.

40. Lerner, "Searching the Traumatic," 1–21; Armstrong, "Emotional Issues," 174–87.

41. Raftery, "Doing Better."

sets out criteria to ensure academic institutional polices are appropriately ethical.

More controversial has been the research regarding trauma and spirituality and religion. A lead in this, from a religious perspective, has been the work done by the Duke Medical School, with Harold Koenig and Andrew Weaver. "A Systematic Review of the Research on Religion and Spirituality" is a systematic review of research on religion and spirituality in the *Journal of Traumatic Stress* during the period 1990–99.[42] Of limited value to my research because of the wide difference in the way clergy are perceived in the UK compared with the U.S., nevertheless, their work stems from the fact that research results claim there were significantly and consistently high rates of religious commitment in the U.S. in the period between the mid-1960s and the 1990s, and also that studies concluded religious and spiritual interest has positive effects upon recovery from traumas. Weaver, et al., state the purpose of the study, the methods and the results, and he reflects upon issues like spiritual growth from trauma, and the place of the clergy. They conclude, "Our analysis revealed that significantly greater attention has been given to religion/ spirituality during the last half of the past decade, *with no-research articles leading the change in this direction*."[43] They also conclude that while more traumatologists are studying the role of spirituality in trauma, it is important that the faith community recognize and study the role of trauma in affecting spiritual health, and how this should impact on pastoral practice.[44]

Counseling Survivors of Traumatic Events: A Handbook for Pastors and Other Helping Professionals has limitations for my research because of its American context.[45] However, there is some benefit to be found from the authors' professional experience in the fields of health care chaplaincy, nursing, and psychology, respectively. They are keen to highlight the key roles that clergy in the different faith communities have in trauma response. They claim people in traumatic situations are most likely to

42. Weaver, et al., "A Systematic Review," 215–28. See also Weaver, Koenig, and Ochberg, "Posttraumatic Stress," 847–56, for a similar emphasis. The authors are specialists in the field of psychiatry and psychology as well as having interest in religion and the role of clergy in trauma response.

43. Weaver, et al., "A Systematic Review," 14.

44. Ibid., 16.

45. Weaver, et al., *Counseling Survivors*. See also Weaver's earlier paper, "Psychological Trauma."

contact clergy first. Therefore, this work aims to inform clergy how to identify the symptoms of trauma—especially post-traumatic stress disorder—and how to refer people on to other professional agencies. They also state what clergy can do to educate their church communities in best practice for helping the traumatized, recognizing that such people need the supportive aid of a caring community, not just of an individual. They present a number of cases, which are not relevant to my research, and finish with a section on the clergy's unique advantage in responding to a crisis, in which they teach how clergy can identify the different types of crisis. *In The Wake of Disaster: Religious Responses To Terrorism and Catastrophe* is another work of disaster awareness from the U.S. context.[46] Koenig addresses issues of emergency planning, religion and coping with disaster, the role of the faith community and faith based organizations, how to prepare them for their roles, and the possible obstacles they may face. It is another example of Koenig's attempt to combine a social science and pastoral theology in providing an evidence base for major incident response, and it is useful from a practical perspective. However, religion is treated generically, and pastoral involvement is viewed therapeutically.

Crucial to the literature on research integrating social and medical science and spirituality and religion is *Blind Faith: the Unholy Alliance of Religion and Medicine*.[47] Sloan, a professor in behavioral medicine, argues a potent case for the separation of the practices of religion and medicine in health-care settings. He argues robustly against the research methods and results presented by Koenig, et al., of the Duke Medical School, in support of the connection between healing and generic spirituality. Sloan's complaint is not with the importance of religion, but with pseudo-scientific methodologies and their spurious conclusions being presented in medical journals and recommended in medical training. In particular, he firmly rejects, on moral and ethical grounds, the alliance between religion and science as a part of medical practice. Alleged scientific research projects concluding on health-care benefits from such religious practices as prayer and attendance at places of worship does an ill service to both medical and religious practices. This unholy alliance holds out falsely grounded hopes to the vulnerably sick and traumatized, alleging a scientifically proven connection between healing and religious practice. However, Sloan wholeheartedly endorses the role of chaplaincy

---

46. See also Koenig, *In the Wake of Disaster*.
47. Sloan, *Blind Faith*.

in health-care settings—as a parallel discipline to that of medicine; a specialty in its own right, reserved for professionally trained chaplains— under a different, though no less respectable, methodology to medicine. In my view, Sloan has sounded a needed alarm in the field of medical and trauma research to those who succumb to the pressure to ally religion to medicine in medical practice. He also thereby gives due warning to the church/chaplains engaging in such an alliance in a bid for credibility in the health-care settings today.

STATUTORY LEGISLATION AND GUIDANCE LITERATURE

As the above literature indicates, much of the extant research has been conducted in the U.S. context, while presenting lessons that can be relevant for the UK based context. However, my research explores a theology for major incident response for Christian responders under current UK statutory legislation and national and local government guidance.

The "*Civil Defence Act*, 1948" (CDA) composed the primary postwar legislation in the UK existing up to the current "Civil Contingencies Act 2004."[48] Its purpose was to provide legislation to local and police authorities for civil defense during the postwar threat and emergent Cold War contexts. It also was to serve during peacetime incidents and during the terrorist "Troubles" in Northern Ireland. This act was devised for largely administrative and technical purposes, with no focus upon real human aspects or spiritual/religious needs.

Key influences in the development of new legislation and practice were an increase in civilian emergencies (largely transport and event based), most notably during the "Decade of Disasters" (1980–90), and consequent calls for a greater focus upon welfare and human aspects of response. Thus, a working party was commissioned in 1989, chaired by Lord Allen, with terms of reference set by the Department of Health that focused upon the work of social service departments and other agencies in providing social and psychological help during and after disasters.

---

48. "Civil Defence Act, 1948." Online: http://www.opsi.gov.uk/acts/acts1948/pdf/ ukpga_19480005_en.pdf. The act states, civil defence "includes any measures not amounting to actual combat for affording defence against any form of hostile attack by a foreign power or for depriving any form of hostile attack by a foreign power of the whole or part of its effect, whether the measures are taken before, at or after the time of the attack." I am grateful to Paul Hickling, Resilience Team Officer for the Local Resilience Forum, Leicestershire and Rutland, for his furnishing me with information and references (email communication on September 7, 2009).

"Disasters: Planning for a Caring Response (Parts 1 and 2)" collates lessons learned from a wide range of agencies, and resources available, including those of the faith communities.[49] This proved a strong springboard for further guidance being issued on major incident response, including "The Needs of Faith Communities in Major Emergencies: Some Guidelines," now revised under the direction of the Home Office's Cohesion and Faiths Unit, but originally developed during the 1990s.[50] After an introduction and glossary, the document helpfully summarizes the specific needs and beliefs of some faith groups. There is a chapter on the grieving and healing process that results from major incidents, locating the role(s) likely to be specific to pastoral carers—namely at the scene, in the hospitals and local community, at funerals and memorial services, and at anniversaries. There is a useful appendix setting out the specific requirements of many faith groups, regarding such things as language, diet, dress, physical contact, medical treatment, acts of worship, and attitudes to dying and death. This is a significant contribution to research for it claims to set out the government's position on, and regard for, faith groups, and their key role in major incident response. It is somewhat isolated, however, when it is compared to many other government documents and the plans of other statutory agencies. It does not concern itself with theological issues, but is intended as a guidance and reference document for responders in general. It could be argued that its later inclusion in the Home Office's Cohesion and Faiths Unit has a political edge, to ensure it conforms to the secular agenda of government policy. However, it could also be an indication of the centralizing intention of national government that developed during the opening of this century, also stimulated by preparations for celebrating the millennium and by the foot-and-mouth crisis of 2001. Major incident response became centralized in the Civil Contingencies Secretariat (CCS) in the Cabinet Office. This was due to calls for a greater level of unified national response structure. (Such calls would soon be put under further pressure by the terrorist dimensions of the 9/11 events in the US, when the whole dynamics of major incident response became much more focused upon human aspects). In "Working Together: Co-operation between Government and Faith Communities" we have a review following the successful

49. Allen, "Disasters: Planning for a Caring Response (Parts 1 and 2)."

50. Blears and Goggins, "Needs of Faith Communities." This was initially published as "Guidelines for Faith Communities when Dealing with Disasters" following a series of ecumenical meetings of which I was an invited member during the 1990s.

collaboration between faith communities and government departments at the time of the millennium and golden jubilee celebrations in the UK.[51] This review set out the government's enthusiasm for collaboration with faith communities and highlighted ways of overcoming problems. While this review was directed more to the issues of securing government funding (a vexed issue for Christian agencies and churches),[52] and not specific to major incidents, nevertheless it is helpful in identifying the government's position. Of note is the explicit requirement for a wide representation of the Christian constituency to be consulted, and for the Church of England not to be accorded privileged status.[53] The document is helpful in introducing the role of the Inter Faith Network for the UK, a significant body in the multifaith area of major incident response.[54] The review also sets out the roles of churches in acts of worship and memorials of national significance. It is a very fair work, which for all its emphasis upon multifaith collaboration, nevertheless fully recognizes the significant theological differences and sensitivities involved, which should not be fudged.[55]

In March 2003 the Home Office announced details of intention to enhance "key generic capabilities" to allow the UK to respond to emergencies. The Civil Contingencies Secretariat would manage this. As mass fatalities is a key feature, "Guidance on Dealing with Fatalities in Emergencies" is an important document, since it sets out the protocols for handling mass fatalities nationwide and affecting UK citizens abroad.[56] Provoked by the 9/11 attacks, the government became concerned about major incidents of a catastrophic proportion. Emergency planners are encouraged to invite all organizations that might be involved in such events to contribute to the planning process. This clearly could/should involve the faith communities. The various categories of mass fatality are set out—natural causes, major transportation and crowd related accidents, hostile acts, contamination/pollution, structural failure, industrial and health related, including chemical, biological, radiological, or

51. UK Home Office, "Working Together." This was ordered under the then Home Secretary, Rt. Hon. David Blunkett, MP.

52. Especially for those who work evangelistically and are open to being construed as proselytizing.

53. See UK Home Office, "Working Together," 2.2.38.

54. See website for details: http://www.interfaith.org.uk/.

55. UK Home Office, "Working Together," 4.3.13.

56. UK Home Office and Cabinet Office, "Guidance on Dealing with Fatalities."

nuclear incidents ('CBRN). It also stresses that incidents may well be multinational, multicultural, and multireligious in their aspects. The various statutory roles are set out (police, coroner, etc.). The document is important in providing awareness about the awful dimensions major incidents can assume in terms of fatalities and the problems that may arise. Explicit reference is made to religious organizations and their significant role, albeit in generic terms. The purpose of this guidance is to ensure a response that respects the dignity of the dead. The guidance is realistic about potentially gruesome scenes and the inherent dangers responders face and the precautions they need to take. Great care is advised in respect of care for the bereaved and the viewing of their deceased.[57] A section is given over exclusively to "Faith, Religious and Cultural Considerations" (4:32-48) in which it is made very clear that discussions should be held at an early stage in planning with religious leaders concerning the needs of those in that community who may be involved in a mass fatality incident, including the organizing of testimonials and memorials.

Thus the "Civil Contingencies Act 2004" and "Emergency Preparedness," the accompanying guidance document, seemed inevitable.[58] The latter is not legislative, but guidance for applying the CCA 2004. Neither categories (1 and 2) specified in the act make mention of faith roles.[59] However, the guidance advises relevant voluntary sector agencies should be consulted, and may be invited to attend meetings with category 2 responders.[60] For the purposes of the CCA 2004, churches/pastoral carers would come under the voluntary sector. The act and guidance devolves key duties upon both regional and local resilience forums, and these forums decide how pastoral carers are included in emergency plans. It is helpful in revealing the ambivalence with which national government views the pastoral carer role in major incident response, and gives

57. Responders are referred to the previous document Blears and Goggins, "Needs of Faith Communities," 46. For a somewhat fuller guide to faith, and non-faith, needs, see also, NHS Education for Scotland (NES), "A Multi-Faith Resource for Healthcare Staff."

58. UK Cabinet Office, "Civil Contingencies Act 2004 (Contingency Planning) Regulations 2005."; "Civil Contingencies Act 2004: A Short Guide (Revised)."

59. Even though it is recognized pastoral carers may provide a frontline service at an incident, it is a voluntary one and, therefore, not a statutory role. Only statutory agencies are included under category 1 responders.

60. It was by such an invitation that I was invited to join the Leicestershire and Rutland Local Resilience Forum, category 2 group, from early 2008.

a secondary thrust, therefore, to my research project, to demonstrate a theology that gives a role worthy of respect and enhanced validation.

In the light of the CCA 2004, following the 9/11 terrorist assault and the 7/7 bombings, the concept of what is now termed a humanitarian assistance centre (HAC) has become focal to emergency planning. The details of such centers are set out in "Humanitarian Assistance in Emergencies: Non-Statutory Guidance on Establishing Humanitarian Assistance Centres."[61] This guidance document has been produced under the joint aegis of the Department for Culture, Media and Sport (DCMS) and the Association of Chief Police Officers, with contributions also from Disaster Action and from the Local Government Association (LGA). It is designed as guidance principally for emergency planners and Local Resilience Forums (LRF), to ensure that sites for humanitarian assistance centers are identified by all local authorities in contingency measures for a major incident. A humanitarian assistance centre is a "one-stop-shop" where affected relatives and friends, and also survivors, can access the humanitarian assistance available following a major incident. The document gives guidance on the multi-agency nature of responders and the kind of assistance they should seek to provide in such a center. It details the purpose and the planning stages for it and then the response phase. Direction is given on considering the needs of the various communities that are involved, how the center is to be publicized, how data is collected, and what organizations should be involved. There is little concerning the clergy, other than the oblique references to "assistance in respect of individual and diverse requirements—including multifaith and cultural support" and to the importance of regarding faiths in diversity issues. It reminds local authorities that they are to "have regard" to faith communities and faith representatives. Given the measure of importance that other literature seems to place upon the role of pastoral carers this guidance is very disappointing, and, unless users of the center specifically request it, the role may be omitted altogether.

Significantly, two more recent documents seem to indicate a greater level of explicit recognition of the importance of pastoral carer roles. The first is "Key Communities, Key Resources."[62] In contrast to other muted

---

61. UK Department for Culture, Media and Sport. "Humanitarian Assistance."

62. UK Department for Communities and Local Government, "Key Communities," 5–41. This was published by the Department of Communities and Local Government—a department set up in 2006, and the document is the most recent in terms of official government departmental thinking on faith issues.

government documents reviewed above, this is a major advance on earlier material, and it identifies and describes the benefits of the UK faith communities for major incident response. It readily acknowledges, "Faith communities are increasingly recognised as significant partners in working for the common good in their localities" on account of their size and nature; their buildings, plant, human resources; their economic resources and volunteer base; and, not least, their historic contribution of instinctive response to crises. It seeks to contextualize the faith communities' contribution in the CCA 2004, and is intended to aid emergency planners and faith communities working together in integrated emergency management. Using case studies and general research knowledge, this guidance document represents a sea change in government, explicitly of the positive historic contribution that faith communities make to emergency situations. The guidance is never patronizing, always courteous, sensitive, and ethical toward faith issues, and, above all, takes faith communities seriously. It actually encourages theological thinking, but not consensual thinking.[63] This document is the result of a working group set up by the Faith Communities Consultative Council, consisting of representatives from Roman Catholic, Methodist, and Anglican Christian denominations, also with representation from the Jewish, Muslim, Hindu, Sikh faiths, and involving the Inter Faith Network for the UK. A second significant document is "Planning for a Possible Influenza Pandemic: A Framework for Planners Preparing to Manage Deaths."[64] This refers extensively to pastoral carers because of their likely role in the event of "excess deaths," for attending to the dead, for care of the sick, dying, and the grieving and fearful.[65] National policyholders and business and faith communities were consulted and are seen as key players in the event of a pandemic. Ministers of religion are encouraged to study this document.[66]

63. The precise wording is, "Encourage faith communities to think theologically through the issues. It may be that their scholars can come to a position through study of their sacred scriptures and traditions which can, if not entirely accepting what must happen, at least seek to understand it. This is especially important for the 'not business as usual' scenarios described above. Emergency planners should also consider how they support faith communities in organising a theological seminar to deal with this." (UK Department for Communities and Local Government, "Key Communities, Key Resources," 37.)

64. UK Home Office, "Planning for a Possible Influenza Pandemic." See also, UK Department of Health, "Pandemic Flu."

65. "Faith community representatives" is the document's preferred term.

66. UK Home Office, "Planning for a Possible Influenza Pandemic," 4, n.1.

With the official declaration by the World Health Organization of a flu pandemic in the early summer of 2009 and the fears of mass fatalities in the UK during the winter of 2009–10, the added edge was given to my research by this document. It is envisaged that, eventually, normal processes for disposal of the dead will become overwhelmed. A worst-case scenario was planned for, in which 50 percent of the UK population was predicted susceptible to the virus in a 12–15 week single wave. The predicted deaths from such would have been 750,000.[67] Therefore, business continuity planning would have become critical, especially for those services needed for dealing with excess deaths (coroners, funeral services, crematoriums, burial services, faith centers, registration, medical). The document stipulated local faith leaders should be invited to consultations.[68] Faith representatives will need to work with the other services, within the restrictive practices applied in such a pandemic, but always seeking to maintain a dignity of service as much as possible. Extensive guidance is given regarding working under such conditions.

Also of future significance for major incidents in the UK are the impending Olympic Games in 2012. The projected increased student population for the 2012 Olympic Games and the increased risk of a major incident have stimulated the publishing of "Emergencies Planning and Management: A Good Practice Guide for Higher Education Institutions." This is a jointly funded work by the Association of University Chief Security Officers and the Higher Education Funding Council for England.[69] Reference is made to the role of chaplaincy in higher education institutions in the event of a major incident, but it is only slight and advisory.[70] Given the higher education institutions' feed into national and international business and politics, emergency planning and training, and the tragic precedents of mass shootings, it is surprising that education institutions have been so slow in rising to the necessity of emergency planning.[71]

67. Ibid., 13.

68. Ibid., 17.

69. Association of University Chief Security Officers, "Emergencies Planning and Management," 1–190.

70. Ibid. In regard to: training (116); health (159); Emergency Management Team actions (160, 166).

71. Principally, the shootings at Columbine High School (1999) and Virginia Tech University (2007) in the US; the Tuusula High School (2007) and Kauhajoki College (2008) in Finland.

CONCLUSION

In most of the above literature, reference is made to the role of faith providers only in a generic sense. There is little theological reflection or focus upon the role of specifically Christian, let alone evangelical, faith responders. This very significant gap in research, throughout the whole postwar period to date gives added prominence to the call for my research project. Nevertheless, there is significant proof of an acknowledgement of the generic role of faith providers in regard to trauma response, especially in the U.S., but even in the UK government literature, which provides a challenging province for my research.

For achieving my purpose and aims, and for progressing my research in a gap readily identified by the literature, I have developed a particular methodology, which I enunciate next.

3

Methodology

PRACTICAL THEOLOGY

PRACTICAL THEOLOGY IS NOTORIOUSLY short on definition; or, at least, is sufficiently embryonic to permit considerable flexibility of construction.[1] It is often allied with the social and human sciences, and has been dominated by both liberal and postmodern constituencies, with little take-up by the evangelicals.[2] It is the aspect of significant engagement with the practical realities of living prior to the interpretive processes of Scripture that is appealing about practical theology. Living contexts can address the revealed scriptural text in the belief that those revealed texts have themselves emerged from real life (often traumatic) contexts, for the purpose of configuring today's discordant contexts for refiguring future responses. This key core aspect is enormously attractive to me as an evangelical researcher.[3] The traumatic nature of major incident contexts calls for an inductive method wherein the contemporary context of tragedy and trauma interrogates the Scripture, and then Scripture interrogates these contexts in a *praxis*.[4] Thus, in this research

---

1. See Stone, "Word and Sacrament."

2. For an avowed evangelical attempt, from the Charismatic Pentecostal constituency, see Cartledge, *Practical Theology*.

3. In particular, I have found professors Ray Anderson (Fuller, California) and John Swinton (Aberdeen, Scotland) helpful, albeit with both carrying a distinctly Barthian bias. See Anderson, *The Shape of Practical Theology*; Swinton and Mowat, *Practical Theology*. For while Swinton especially shows interest in the social sciences for the qualitative aspect of practical theology as a research approach, both authors endorse the priority of Scripture, central in evangelical tradition.

4. Donald Schön uses the concept of "reflective practitioner" in his work about professional development (Schön, *Reflective Practitioner*. Graham, et al., endorse this

project, I have sought understanding in interpreting scriptural texts by beginning with the traumatic contexts of major incidents, rather than assuming an understanding of those texts prior to those contexts, anticipating an applied theology can be superimposed onto them. Practical theology also recognizes the appropriateness of other disciplines with which theology should engage, such as the philosophical, social, clinical, and human sciences.[5] Through such *praxis* it is hoped that truth can be discovered and more rightfully applied, where "*praxis* includes the effect of the Word as well as a presentation of it."[6] Through my construction of a methodology, combining the mimetic theory of Paul Ricoeur and the canonical linguistic narrative approach of Kevin Vanhoozer, I have pursued this research with an evangelical practical theology where *sola scriptura* has remained the ascendant authority, but one's capability to interpret the scriptural texts has been tested and modified by the contribution from other disciplines and by my personal experience of a major incident response. Furthermore, the Christological center to the theodrama has been safeguarded and has ensured I have avoided the pitfall Graham's postmodern approach to practical theology has been criticized for, namely: "commending practice as the guiding criterion of Christian theological identity as something entirely antinomian, spontaneous," and led by the spirit of the age.[7] Nonetheless, the discordances of major incidents have been permitted to interrogate my interpretation of that drama, to configure my narrative for the refigured benefit of others. Overall, I am supportive of Swinton's definition of practical theology, therefore: "Practical theology is critical theological reflection on the practices of the Church as they interact with the practices of the world, with a view to ensuring and enabling faithful participation in God's redemptive practices in, to and for the world."[8] Further elaboration of my practical theology comes out in the rationale given below.

---

move toward a more reflective *praxis* in theological method. (Graham, et al, *Theological Reflection*, 4. Also, Lyall, *Integrity of Pastoral Care*, 170–81.) Major incident response, of course, requires technical rationality and expertise, but the development of skills "on the job" of reflective practice are even more essential.

5. O'Donovan judges that the practice of enriching theology with concepts borrowed from the social sciences has produced mixed results. The principle of borrowing is not a problem provided what is borrowed can be "well metabolized into the system of theological intelligibility." (*Desire of the Nations*, 16.)

6. Anderson, *Shape of Practical Theology*, 50.

7. See Graham, et al, *Theological Reflection*, 198.

8. Swinton and Mowat, *Practical Theology*, 6.

My own theological position is that of an evangelical who accepts that Christianity is more than a set of propositions, but is propositional nonetheless.[9] I am a theistic foundationalist, accepting the *sensus divinitatis* and scriptural revelation as universally accessible, owing to common grace providing a level of epistemology that is necessary for sustaining human understanding and communication.[10] However, I contest the concept of foundationalism propounded by liberalism's conception of a universal reality and rationality that is accessible to human reason independent from divine revelation.[11] I have reservations concerning the postmodern non-foundationalism of George Lindbeck and Hans Frei, but I do seek to appropriate critically important aspects of their work that are consonant with the evangelical commitment to the authority of the centrality of Christ and the cross of the Christian canon.[12] The importance of

9. Vanhoozer expands the concept of propositionalism, helpfully, to include doctrine as a form of stage-direction for the church's performance of the gospel. (*Drama of Doctrine*, 18. See also pages 276–78.)

10. Plantinga speaks of theistic foundationalism in preference to strong foundationalism (in Helm, *Faith and Understanding*, 186–87). Helm describes Calvin's *sensus divinitatis* as that which gives to all people an awareness of God's existence (idem, 179–84). Helm traces Plantinga's use of the *sensus divinitatis* to disprove *strong* foundationalism, but he believes Plantinga's interpretation of Aquinas to be wrong regarding the role of external proofs, on the basis that Plantinga believed the proofs were *necessary* as well as *sufficient* for belief in God's existence. Strong foundationalism is the belief that basic beliefs need to be evident to the observer or to their senses (idem, 184). For a discussion on Calvin's ideas being foundational/non-foundational, see Helm, *John Calvin's Ideas*, 240–45.

11. I also contest, and seek to avoid, liberalism's, and not just a little of contemporary Evangelicalism's, pursuit of an existential anthropology under the guise of theology. In other words, the focus upon questions that are, essentially, about me: my welfare, happiness, and flourishing, more than about God. Theology is primarily about the study of God, and only secondarily about humans, but not forgetting that the focus of God's wisdom is upon the "sons of men." (Prov 8:31). See also my reference to God as a Trinity of perichoretic self-denial, in chapter 8, p. 199–202.

12. I utilize aspects of Paul Ricoeur's philosophical hermeneutics as a balance to the Yale School's anti-foundationalism. Though these figures are representatives of narrative approaches to theological methodology, they represent two distinctly opposed schools: Ricoeur the Chicago School, and Lindbeck and Frei, the Yale School. Frei accused Ricoeur of relegating history behind fiction, the biblical text behind a universal hermeneutic, and the literal sense of the text behind the ideal sense (a concept developed from Ricoeur's practice of creative imagination). For a discussion on the purported/real distinctions between these two schools within narrative methodology, see Vanhoozer, *Biblical Narrative*. He concludes that both schools are deficient by imposing on the Bible literary forms that do not fit the Bible, and do not allow for the biblical narrative's own claim to inspiration.

the Christian interpretive community over that of the outside world, and the primacy of intratextuality over extratexuality in their hermeneutical method, are also significant.[13] Given the interactions this research project involves, I am concerned to explore the right for Christian theology to operate from canonative authority, rather than deferring to a liberal theology that secular systems largely operate with—a case postliberalism has argued much more forcefully than has Evangelicalism hitherto.[14] Postliberalism's emphasis upon truth being validated by the doing of the text is of great relevance to a research project that explores the *praxis* of a Christian's response to major incidents.[15] Evangelicals should acknowledge the postliberal reminder that Scripture gives priority to living above knowing. Inerrancy follows from a faithful doing (as well as a reading) of the text.[16] Therefore, it is doubtful if a valid theology can be constructed prior to real engagement in the drama of doing the faith.[17]

13. For a good discussion of foundationalism, see Rodney Capp, "How Firm a Foundation: Can Evangelicals be Non-Foundationalists?," in Philips and Okholm, eds., *Nature of Confession,* 81–92; Groothuis, *Truth Decay.* Vanhoozer rejects the postliberal insistence that the Scriptures are the products of the Christian communities alone, in favor of his priority and normativity of the scriptural canon.

14. Postliberals would argue the reason for this is because of the influence that modernism has had upon evangelical theology. Frei and Lindbeck have argued that cognitive propositional Evangelical theology is as modernist as liberal theology is. See George Hunsinger, "What Can Evangelicals and Postliberals Learn from Each Other? The Carl Henry–Hans Frei Exchange Reconsidered," in Philips and Okholm, eds., *Nature of Confession,* 134–50. Hunsinger argues that Abraham Kuyper and Herman Bavinck were nearer to Frei than Henry because they had less call for extrabiblical systematization for their doctrines of inerrancy than Henry had. He judges that Frei's actual position, of "ad hoc minimalism" may well be nearer the *sola scriptura* principle than that of Henry's "systematic consubstantiation" (Hunsinger, *Disruptive Grace,* 352). Vanhoozer has been the most convincing evangelical proponent of biblical authority, but he acknowledges the postliberal contribution and the detrimental effects of modernism upon Evangelical theology (*Drama of Doctrine,* 26).

15. I understand postliberalism is principally about theological methodology— essentially a "throat clearing" exercise (Jeffrey Stout), and, therefore until completed and conclusions firmly identified—if such is possible in a postmodern context—it is of limited value. It still leaves much to be desired in the realms of authority, revelation, and evangelism. It is a research project pioneered by the late Hans Frei, and George Lindbeck, of Yale Divinity School.

16. See 2 Tim 3:16–17, "All Scripture is given by inspiration of God, and is profitable for doctrine, for reproof, for correction, for instruction in righteousness that the man of God may be thoroughly equipped for every good *work*" (emphasis mine). The repetition of the purposive, "for" προς—indicates the goal/destiny or purpose of (Arndt and Gingrich, eds., *Greek-English Lexicon,* 717).

17. Jonathan R. Wilson, "Toward a New Evangelical Paradigm of Biblical Authority," in Philips and Okholm, eds., *The Nature of Confession,* 157. Hauerwas somewhat

I conclude, therefore, a particular theological approach most suited to my research project is that of practical theology. However, I interact also with systematic, biblical, and narrative forms, with which my practical theology functions. I therefore proceed to present a rationale for this conclusion.

Rationale

My research has a narrative, situational, and operational base to it. Major incident response is operational and is my starting point and context for exploring theology. Practical theology is operation centered and facilitates this kind of exploration.[18] A lead narrative method would prove too subjective and limited in scope, though it cannot be neglected in view of the impact upon the narrative of the responder the response has. A systematic or biblical theology approach is too static and lacks the necessary flexibility and capacity to be interrogated by the profound cognitive dysfunction, and emotional shock, of major incidents, but neither can they be neglected because of the kind of scriptural foundationalism I endorse.[19]

---

decried the arrival of "practical theology" onto the academic curriculum, in view of the fact that "theology, to be Christian, is by definition practical" (Hauerwas and Willimon, *Resident Aliens*, 164).

18. Hiltner distinguishes between "operation-centred" (practical theology) and "logic-centred" (systematic, biblical, and historical theology) branches of theology (Seward Hiltner, "The Meaning and Importance of Practical Theology," in Woodward and Pattison, eds., *Blackwell Reader*, 28–29). See also Swinton and Mowat, *Practical Theology*, 6. Note also their emphasis upon practical theology being a communal exercise. Scheib's definition is similar ("Make Love Your Aim," in Swinton and Payne, eds., *Living Well*, 31–33).

19. O'Donovan's critique of the "reflecting upon *praxis*" concept of practical theology is a necessary warning. He argues that this is theological reasoning ordered to action, reasoning that must comport with our actions in the world, and such actions are prior to reflection, so that it is our practical engagements that yield the wisdom we seek. Thus, "Our action becomes the predetermining matrix for whatever God may say to us, ensuring that we hear nothing from him but the echo of our own practical energies" (O'Donovan, *Desire of the Nations*, 13–14). I believe that the practical context is the place where reflection must begin—because every part of Scripture has come out of a particular practical/political context—but that the context must bear scrutiny and interpretation by the authoritative canon of Scripture, which, in turn, can benefit from the light shed upon it by the context. I want, thereby to hear the echo of the voice, and work of God in Scripture (configuration), not my own practical energies (prefiguration). In this way a canonical linguistic approach can overcome the sociological embeddedness of a liberation theology approach. As O'Donovan explains,

My research interacts with the world (e.g., with secular human sciences), not just with the church. Major incident response and emergency planning systems are based upon secular, modernist philosophical systems. Campbell argues a path between Thurneysen's primacy of word, and church, based foci, and Hiltner's veer toward the contributions of social science and psychology.[20] Campbell criticises Thurneysen as too church-focused and affirms that practical theology has scope for both church and world contexts. Thus, Campbell claims,

> In an age when destruction seems ever closer at hand . . . it seems that some branch of theology must be concerned with matters which directly affect human well-being in whatever future awaits us. This appears to be a task especially suited to a recreated 'practical theology', one which treads a difficult path between practical relevance and theological integrity.[21]

This interaction makes practical theology attractive to my engagement with major incident response.[22]

My research assumes a presupposition of canonical authority that might seem more suited, therefore, to a biblical or systematic approach. However, I needed a discipline that could engage Scripture in dialogue with the complex, and often changing, situations and discourses of major incidents, for which there are often no direct scriptural rules. In practical theology the Bible, liturgies, and theology are taken as primary.[23] The exposure to multiple definitions and the vagueness of this discipline allows for such forms where Scripture is foundational. Thurneysen's Barthian focus was on the primacy of the word of God, as a way of bringing coherence to practical theology, and I utilize a model that sees practical theology providing an immensely interesting and useful instrument for my

---

"The 'political hermeneutic' is discovered and explored in a particular context of discipleship; yet it does not belong only to that context. Nor is it the context that imposes it in the first place. It belongs to the Scriptures, and is imposed by the exercise of reading the Scriptures" (*Desire of the Nations*, 22).

20. See Lyall, *Integrity of Pastoral Care*, 25–27, 31–32.

21. Alastair Campbell, "The Nature of Practical Theology," in Woodward and Pattison, eds., *Blackwell Reader*, 86.

22. Peter Holmes, "Spirituality: Some Disciplinary Perspectives," in Flanagen and Jupp, eds., *Sociology of Spirituality*, 27.

23. Woodward and Pattison, "An Introduction to Pastoral and Practical Theology," in Woodward and Pattison, eds., *Blackwell*, 8.

research, but it must be founded on God's revelation in his word.[24] The postliberal revival of the text focus is welcome, but it must not separate the text from the reality (historicality) the text is addressing and assuming, or this could risk deification of the text.[25] Reality is not only found in the text, but also behind the text, even though the text is the appointed meeting place for us engaging with the reality. The text does not create the ontology; it speaks it and signposts it.

Main Approach

Of the many forms of practical theology, I have selected that developed by Kevin Vanhoozer, expounded best in his *The Drama of Doctrine: A Canonical Linguistic Approach to Christian Theology*, in which he effectively draws upon the similarities between drama and theology.[26] My main reason for this choice is because Vanhoozer argues convincingly the retention of the *sola scriptura* principle that is a presupposition of my research, while, equally convincingly, challenging other aspects of theological thought in a direction my own thinking has been exploring in recent years, especially under the testing contexts of my church pastoral work. Particularly attractive is the concept of *sola scriptura* affirming the Spirit-inspired canon as normative but regarding the Christian message and life as a Spirited-practiced theodrama, which combines the necessity of both word and action—doctrine as performance.[27] This connects with my design to pursue the Christian's response to major incidents as an adventure in order to bring out the constructive transformative aspects of responding to such dramatic scenarios. Furthermore, canonical linguistic theology avers the importance of doctrine, not as static cognitive proposition but as theodramatic direction, incorporating cognition,

24. On Eduard Thurneysen's *A Theology of Pastoral Care*, see Campbell, "Nature of Practical Theology," in Woodward and Pattison, eds., *Blackwell Reader*, 30.

25. Stone draws attention to this as an aspect of his critique of Brueggemann, and cites the accounts of the resurrection as a case in point (Stone, "Word and Sacrament," 444–63).

26. Vanhoozer, *Drama of Doctrine*. He also appeals to cartographical and musical analogies, as does Stephen Crites in his "The Narrative Quality of Experience," in Hauerwas and Jones, *Why Narratives*, 65–88.

27. Vanhoozer, *Drama of Doctrine*, 266–78. For Vanhoozer, canonization amounts to the providence of God put into writing by the Holy Spirit (*Drama of Doctrine*, 231). Mathewes speaks of the Christian Midrashic form of this cycle (Mathewes, *Theology of Public Life*, 103). Swinton and Mowat stress the concept of Christianity as faithful performance being at the heart of practical theology (*Practical Theology*, 4–5).

affection, and volition, where interpretation is communicative action while apprenticed to Christ in the contemporary, situational context of the theodrama.[28] Doctrine is central to the Spirited performance of the Christian as a "reflective practitioner."[29] It provides the instruction for directing our participation in the theodrama, in which the Triune God is the playwright, Jesus the principal actor, the Holy Spirit the director (who uses Scripture to direct), and pastors/elders are the assistants.[30] Doctrine provides a "fitting participation" that "helps the Christian to think, act, and feel in evangelically appropriate manners in particular situations."[31] It also creates the social demarcation of our involvement, thus ensuring the missionary identity of the Christian community is maintained.

In the canonical linguistic method the theologian becomes the dramaturge, whose task "is to study the playscript and prepare it for performances that truthfully realize its truth."[32] He or she is the conscience of the church, which does the work of dramaturgy by the twin interpretative practices of *scientia* (exegesis) and *sapientia* (wisdom).[33]

28. In canonical linguistic theology, doctrine has meaning prior to being taken up by the community (contra Lindbeck's cultural-linguistic theology), but the doctrine is incomplete until it is acted upon by the community. Lindbeck's valuable contribution, however, was to emphasize the point that truth must be self-involving. That is, "Valid performance (the proper kind of self-involvement) is thus a condition for the possibility of cognitive truth. Cognitive truth in the sense of correspondence with reality is not an attribute religious utterances can have when considered in and of themselves." Barth, however, was not prepared to go this far. He believed there is a plane upon which truth remains valid even when the social and moral context of its form of delivery was contradictory. There are contexts when the truth sits in judgment upon the social and moral action, making *it* invalid rather than the truth itself. Even when the social situations may falsify the truths the semantic features of divine revelation retain their "objective superiority" (Hunsinger, *Disruptive Grace*, 307, 310, 312). Wolterstorff also contests Lindbeck's (and Frei's) view. He argues Lindbeck gives priority to the reader-performer over the author-playwright. (Wolterstorff, *Divine Discourse*, chapter 10, cited in Vanhoozer, *Drama of Doctrine*, 165–66).

29. Vanhoozer, *Drama of Doctrine*, 103. The theodrama is Trinitarian based, (*Drama of Doctrine*, 41–44), and the Holy Spirit is the director who inspires our practice through his regenerative and promptive work (idem, 226–31). See also, Schön, *Reflective Practitioner*.

30. Vanhoozer, *Drama of Doctrine*, 244.

31. Ibid., 103–4.

32. Ibid., 247.

33. For Vanhoozer, Aristotelian *scientia* is understood as that which "proceeds from the 'first principles' that are intrinsic to some aspect or area of reality." In the Thomistic sense it is God's science, his knowledge of himself shared with us. Vanhoozer is careful to distinguish this concept of science from the modernist empiricist conception, while

Canonical linguistics is a science of Scripture by exegesis, attempting to understand God's communicative action, centered in Jesus Christ, taking into account historical, literary, and canonical contexts. However, the purpose of theology is not only to arrive at exegeted propositional information, but also to construct a practical wisdom. Such *sapientia* provides the resources for transposing the canonical theodrama for contemporary audiences, so that we know what to do in any given situation today through ensuring that canon and context fit in a Christo-centric fashion that promotes in the Christian the mind of Christ, the ultimate aim of the canonical linguistic method.[34] This approach avoids the static, doctrinaire tendencies of systematic and applied theology, while retaining the authority and normativity of the scriptural canon. It has a suitable fit to the contemporary cultural, social, and traumatic contexts of major incident response with the emphasis upon *sapientia* as the critical feature above dogmatic propositional principles or the relativity of personal experience. It endorses a virtue-based phronetic theology: that is, a theology that produces character that "deliberates well." It is about engaging in spiritual practical reasoning, which "involves forming judgments about what to do in situations for which there is no guaranteed theory, method, or technique,"[35] while all the time not losing the broader, theodramatic perspective. In canonical linguistics, faith seeks nothing less than a performance understanding, which is Scripture-authorized and which instructs the Christian/church in a *mimesis* of Christ.[36]

However, Vanhoozer's sympathy with narrative is significant to his approach, and, therefore, some exploration of forms of narrative is important.[37]

---

affirming his view is nonetheless scientific in the classical sense. This point contributes to my argument for the compatibilism of the different methodologies utilized in the theological and scientific communities referenced in my research. Vanhoozer laments that most Evangelicals owe more credibility to the modernist concept than to the Thomist sense, thus resulting in an analyzing of what God has said rather than participating in the life of God the canonical text demands (*Drama of Doctrine*, 268).

34. Vanhoozer, *Drama of Doctrine*, 256–63.

35. Ibid., 325.

36. Ibid., 102, 408–9. This mimesis is enacted symbolically in the Lord's Supper. It is creative of performance, not simply a memorizing of the past Eucharistic event.

37. Ibid., 93–95, 282–84, 339–440.

NARRATIVE

What Is Narrative?

Narrative is a term, essentially from the literary world,[38] applied to a variety of genres of storytelling, and to a way of understanding or perceiving reality through a particular language.[39] Stroup, acknowledging narrative can mean different things to different people, describes it as a "literary form in which a person's life-story comes to expression."[40] A narrative will, generally speaking, presuppose a story, or stories, which have been shaped by the author to form a plot with a process of movement.[41] It may be biographically or autobiographically narrated, but will assume both narrator and reader. It may be historical or fictional.[42] It is regarded as a significant form of reflection and communication because humans are fundamentally storytelling beings.

My interest in narrative stems from the view that it has a very practical bearing upon behavior, including intentions and actions, and is highly formative of both personal and community character and identity. It is also important for intelligibility, since actions flow from a human agent's motives, passions, and purposes—each act finding its intelligibility in the context of a narrative.[43] Behavior presupposes intentions, beliefs, and settings. We all have social and historical identities that are a part of who we are, and these are all aspects of our narrative formation.[44] Vanhoozer judges, "Narrative, for instance, enables us to experience and reflect on

38. With roots going back through ancient history, but given classical form by Aristotle in his *Poetics* and his concept of the *muthos*, a crafted composition of both fictional and historical elements.

39. I use "language" here in the Wittgensteinian sense of language games being at the heart of interpreting texts of a literary genre. Each narrative has its own peculiar language, which needs to be learned before the narrative can be understood. The sense of a word is dictated by its particular use and context.

40. Stroup, *Promise of Narrative Theology*, 89.

41. Paul Ricoeur refers to stories being formed out of *events*, or *incidents*. He calls this "emplotment" (Ricoeur, "Life in Quest of Narrative"). Movement in a plot may be in various directions—past through present to future; future through present to past; or any combinations thereof. Such movements may work to different concepts of time, combining linear and constructed/configured timescales. It must be said there is not always consistent use of terms among narrative scholars.

42. Or, in Ricoeur's case, a mixture of both.

43. MacIntyre, *After Virtue*, 209–10. I discuss the significance of passions in chapter 9.

44. Ibid., 213, 221.

the temporal connectedness of human existence and personal identity unlike any other framework of literature (or thinking)."[45] In terms of responding to major incidents and trauma, do such events/actions determine Christian responders to a disabling victimhood, or can they have transformative and empowering impacts upon them? This will be largely answered by the narrative we construct out of the effects events had on us at the time (present) and the way these affect our memories of the past, which will, in turn, affect perception of our future.[46]

Narrative has been reflected down through Christian history in the abundant use of storytelling and personal spiritual biography/testimony, not merely illustrative of theological propositions, but as a form of theological intelligibility in itself. It has firm roots in the Christian evangelical tradition, with, for example: St. Augustine's *Confessions*, John Bunyan's *Pilgrim's Progress*, and C. S. Lewis' *The Chronicles of Narnia*. From a theological perspective, narrative has the capacity to relate systematic, propositional theology to the reality of life, to actualize and humanize the theological exercise.

As a form of theological reflection narrative can take two forms: constructive and canonical. Constructive narrative is my dominant approach in narrating my own experience as a Christian responder to a major incident. However, as I will argue that the plot giving configured coherence to that narrative is based on the communicative practices of God in Christ, a conversation between a constructive narrative theory of *mimesis*, developed by Paul Ricoeur and the canonical linguistic narrative approach, developed by Kevin Vanhoozer, will service my utilizing of both constructive and canonical narrative forms.

Constructive Narrative

This is the art of constructing our own narratives out of our histories and stories, to give meaning, coherence, and purpose to our lives.[47] Though its antecedents go back to Aristotle, through Augustine, it has lately been

45. Vanhoozer, *Is There a Meaning?*, 342.

46. One of the problems in post-traumatic stress disorder is a casualty's inability to place the separate traumatic events into a coherent narrative within the total life story. Hence the images, smells, and sounds recur through uncontrollable memories to persistently retraumatize the casualty. (See Van der Kolk, et al., eds., *Traumatic Stress*; Kinchin, *Post Traumatic Stress Disorder*.

47. Hauerwas states: "If we are to understand how Christian convictions help us form our lives truthfully that narrative nature of our lives must be recognized" (*Community of Character*, 90).

foregrounded, in 1941, by H. Richard Niebuhr's "The Story of Our Life" in his *The Meaning of Revelation*. More recently, constructive narrative was given significant thrust in an article by Stephen Crites, in 1971, entitled "The Narrative Quality of Experience." Crites argued, phenomenologically, the "formal quality of experience through time is inherently narrative."[48] He meant that cultures are shaped by human narratives, and these contribute to the formation of human identity. This process happens through the interplay of three forms of narrative: the sacred, which consist of untold, almost unconscious and deeply embedded stories, which are articulated by many mundane stories constructed from memory, which, when told, contribute to human consciousness of experience in which past, present, and future take on coherence.[49] MacIntyre's concept of selfhood resonates with this: "a concept of a self whose unity resides in the unity of a narrative which links birth to life to death as narrative beginning to middle to end."[50] Clearly, memory and imagination also have a significant role to play in constructive narrative. Without memory there is no narrative or history; without imagination there is no future. Memory and imagination imply some concept(s) of time.[51] Given that both these suffer limitations from a sinful state throws doubt upon any claim to a narrative history being completely true. Susceptibilities to distortion and delusion will need to be factored in, since all constructed narratives are created to impress particular readers/audiences in various ways. Thus, truthfulness and sincerity are essential for narrative formation and relations. These are notoriously awkward factors for those who respond to major incidents. Those who have been traumatized in particularly humiliating ways may tend to edit their narrative toward an impression that is more positive, thus endangering them to living with

48. Niebuhr, "Story of our Life," 21–44; Crites, "Narrative Quality," 65–88. Crites' thesis has been applauded but also criticized as "maddeningly imprecise" and unverifiable other than by illustration and allusion. (See Graham, et al., *Theological Reflection*, 61.)

49. Fodor confirms similarities between Crites' process and that of Ricoeur's mimetic theory. (See Fodor, *Christian Hermenuetics*, 11.)

50. MacIntyre, *After Virtue*, 205.

51. Augustine, *Confessions*, book XI, chapters 13–28. There are severe implications for the traumatized whose experiences/injuries result in amnesia, where the "lack of integration of traumatic memories is thought to be the pathogenic agent leading to the development of complex biobehavioural changes, of which PTSD is the clinical manifestation" (Bessel A. Van der Kolk, "Trauma and Memory," in Van der Kolk, McFarlane, and Weisaeth, eds., *Traumatic Stress*, 286).

two narratives: the more repressed, humiliating one that haunts them in private, and the public edition they hide behind. Those whose response has been mundane may place a "spin" on their narrative that gives more dramatic quality. In both cases the elements of illusion may play a perfectly understandable role, where memories are too painful to be exposed in their reality.[52] I will need to be aware of these dangers in the way I compose my own narrative of responding to Kegworth/M1.[53]

Paul Ricoeur's Theory of Mimesis

I explore a narrative theory of the French philosopher, Paul Ricoeur, called *mimesis*.[54] The term is derived from Aristotle's *Poetics*, and describes a form of life through imitation, or representation, that is not a mere static copying of another, e.g., the imitation of a piece of art, but is creative imitation—imitation of action in such a way that transfigures daily life.[55] It is a mediating process between the temporality of narrative and the timelessness of emplotment, between time and narrative.[56]

---

52. Hauerwas comments, "The kind of character the Christian seeks to develop is a correlative of a narrative that trains the self to be sufficient to negotiate existence without illusion or deception" (*Community of Character*, 132).

53. My initial reading of Vanhoozer raised in my own thinking the vulnerability to hypocrisy his theodramatic approach could allow. However, he convincingly addresses this quite explicitly in *The Drama of Doctrine*, 364–69. Lyall explains Ricoeur's (and Donald Capps') concern over this possibility to illusion and the threat to pastoral integrity it poses (Lyall, *Integrity of Pastoral Theology*, 53–55).

54. Ricoeur, *Time and Narrative*, vol.1, chapter 3. Because my interest in Ricoeur is largely confined to his theory of mimesis, I have sought to gain understanding of this theory more from experts on Ricoeur than my own reading of Ricoeurian primary sources. Most of his reflections on mimesis are, however, found in his *Time and Narrative*, vol. 1, chapters 1–3, which I have read. My secondary sources have given me light on how his wider philosophical thinking impacted upon his theory of mimesis. Donald Capps has used Ricoeur's concepts of hermeneutics to construct his approach to pastoral theology. From Ricoeur, Capps understands that as we read and interpret texts in order to understand them, so we should read and interpret actions in order to understand them. (See Capps and Browning, *Pastoral Care and Hermeneutics*; Lyall gives a summary of Capps' interpretation of Ricoeur in his, *The Integrity of Pastoral Care*, 50–55.) Capps makes no reference to mimesis, and has only one passing reference to *Time and Narrative*.

55. Ricoeur saw mimesis as praxis, not mere imitation. (See Ricoeur, *Time and Narrative*, vol. 1, 34–35.) For a good introduction to the way Ricoeur envisaged mimesis working, see Fodor, *Christian Hermenuetics*, chapter 5.

56. Ricoeur, *Time and Narrative*, vol. 1, 52, 70.

Ricoeur's theory of *mimesis* is attractive to my exploration for a number of reasons:

First, because of Ricoeur's trauma-formed life. Born in Valence, near Lyons, France in 1913, he was bereaved of his mother when he was just seven months old. His father took care of him and his elder sister Alice until the father was taken away from home when he was mobilized for World War I. He was killed in action in 1915, whereupon the grandparents took over the parental role. Living in Rennes, Paul was raised in a strict Protestant home, attuned to reading, bible study, and regular churchgoing. In 1928 his grandmother died, followed by his grandfather in 1933. Soon after, his sister died of tuberculosis. Some consolation followed with his marriage to Simone in 1935, with whom he had five children. However, during his military service in World War II he was made a prisoner of war from 1940–45. Thus, the first half of Ricoeur's life of ninety-two years was steeped in trauma of some kind. Though he never claimed to be a theologian, his experiences of suffering and grief were focal motivations in his philosophical pursuits, and he always remained close to theological reflection in his philosophical work.[57]

Second, because of Ricoeur's concept of imaginative thinking, or creative imagination. This thinking is both supernatural and super sensible. It entails both thinking and feeling that is sometimes within, and sometimes over, the boundary of reason. It has close synergy with the epistemology offered by the bible—the knowledge of faith as expounded, and illustrated by Hebrews 11, summarized in verse 1, "Faith is the substance of things hoped for, the evidence of things not seen." Ricoeur endorses thinking, and feeling, of what already is, to show what the situation can be; for Ricoeur possibility is also a part of reality.[58] Such a process can help me conflate seemingly contradictory contributions of

---

57. "In the final analysis, narratives have action and suffering as their theme" (Ricoeur, *Time and Narrative*, vol. 1, 56). Vanhoozer queries whether Ricoeur developed a general philosophy of hermeneutics that found its real home in biblical hermeneutics, or whether he fitted interpreting the Bible into his general hermeneutic. Even though ambiguity lies at the heart of Ricoeur's philosophy, where his method veered from one side of reason to the other, Vanhoozer's conclusion is that "Ricoeur's philosophy approximates in style and content the theological virtues of grace, hope and love" (Vanhoozer, *Biblical Narrative*, 249, 287). See also David Stewart, "Ricoeur on Religious Language," in Hahn, ed., *Philosophy of Paul Ricoeur*, 423–42.

58. See Fodor's focus on imagination in his, *Christian Hermenuetics*, chapter 5. Vanhoozer argues the church should imitate the gospel, not as wooden replication, but as the gospel life should be *in our time* (*Drama of Doctrine*, 376–80, 404, emphasis mine).

liberal and postliberal thinking and navigate the awkward path between Niebuhrian realism and Barthian idealism, along a "third way" of possible impossibilities. This is the expansiveness that Ricoeur's concept of creative imagination/mimesis facilitates. It is the expansiveness the Scriptures offer me as well.[59]

Third, because of Ricoeur's view of humans as possibility laden, and the implications this has for creating identity through facing events as part of a project. This resonates with the concept of life as a drama/adventure of faith, from the biblical perspective.[60] This is the perspective that the Hebrew Christians were taught as a way of interpreting their sufferings, in Hebrews 11. While they are by no means identical, there are similarities between Ricoeur's view of humans as possessing a surplus of possibility (to be explored and effected by *mimesis* and *poiesis*) and the life of faith.[61] In both cases we are much more than we are; especially, as it was for Ricoeur, and is for the Christian, where evil, suffering, and eternity are figured. There is hope through the creative reshaping of time. However, in Ricoeur there is circumstantial evidence that this process was conceived as a process theology, where God never determines our lives, but merely encourages us in a direction he would prefer towards possibilities we have to create. If this was Ricoeur's position, then I distance myself from this aspect of his theology, though his process of mimesis need not depend upon a process theology per se.[62]

Fourth, because the theory of mimesis resonates with my overall practical theological approach. Mimesis represents an attempt to develop coherence and meaning out of contingent and discordant contexts and events (often of suffering) that appear incoherent, lacking purpose and meaning. Jervolino can conclude, "The concrete, temporal, and historical existence of these acting, suffering human beings is the true point

59. Mathewes conceives a similar trajectory in his reflection upon the Christian doctrine of *hope*. He believes Reinhold Niebuhr's realism to be dangerously stoic, liberation theology to be dangerously messianic, and Yoder's pacific waiting to be dangerously dichotomist. In contrast to these, he esteems Augustinianism to provide a hope that is imaginative, yet realistically patient. See Mathewes, *Theology of Public Life*, 238–60.

60. And thus, with Vanhoozer's theodramatic approach.

61. Hence the title of chapter 5 in Vanhoozer, *Biblical Narrative* is "Narrative: the 'substance' of things hoped for."

62. Vanhoozer discusses this possible stance of Ricoeur's, in his *Biblical Narrative*, 213–16.

of reference for Ricoeur's work."[63] However, mimetic activity is never a static exercise, for those who refigure then form another basis for prefiguration, recommencing the cycle. This cyclical dynamic fits with my practical theological interrogative approach.[64]

Fifth, because Ricoeur did not believe in working within a single discipline, but very much within an interdisciplinary conversation, which is the process I favor. Though I principally employ canonical linguistic and systematic approaches, I also utilize the fields of narrative, biblical, historical, and philosophical theology as well.

Sixth, because mimesis is a theory within Ricoeur's interest in time and narrative, integrating Aristotle's *muthos* and Augustine and Heidegger's reflections on time with Kant's on imagination.[65] As such it provides a practical theological hermeneutic and pastoral tool for working with my own prefigured experience of responding to a major incident, facilitating theological interaction to form a configured narrative that converses with Christian evangelical catholic readers/responders to help refigure future *praxis* in the field of major incident response.[66] Ricoeur's intention was to create coherence, identity, and change in action, especially in the events of suffering, with a configurative process that is both

63. Domenico Jervolino, "The Depth and Breadth of Paul Ricoeur's Philosophy," in Hahn, ed., *Philosophy of Paul Ricoeur*, 542. Mimesis is about *action*, not event, and is thus concerned with *doing*, as a significant aspect of knowing. See Karl Simms, *Paul Ricoeur*, 62–65.

64. Ricoeur was sensitive to the charge of his mimetic theory being *merely* circular. He did not deny its circularity, but insisted such was never meaningless, because each time the cycle was completed the point at which it met was at a different altitude each time (Ricoeur, *Time and Narrative*, vol. 1, 72; Fodor, *Christian Hermeneutics*, chapter 5.) Vanhoozer refers to the importance of the *dramaturgical circle* that is a key aspect of the *scientia* of his canonical linguistic approach, in which participation in the subject matter of the text is essential to the textual interpretation. See Vanhoozer, *Drama of Doctrine*, 248; also, Mathewes, *Theology of Public Life*, 103.

65. Fodor, *Christian Hermeneutics*, 184. Augustine's reflections upon time in *Confessions*, book 11 and Aristotle's *Poetics* were the animating forces for Ricoeur's theory of time and narrative. See Ricoeur, *Time and Narrative*, chapters 2 and 3.

66. Ricoeur favored the use of fiction over history in the process of configuration. He believed this gave the process greater freedom to configure the *possibility* within human beings. In my process I prefer theodrama as the equivalent to Ricoeur's fiction, with the caveat that this does not imply the theodrama is fiction. However, I agree with Ricoeur and Frei that Scripture cannot be defined as history either. It is more configured/refigured historicity.

in and outside of time.[67] For Ricoeur, narrative is transformative.[68] Meaning, as well, can only come through narrative action.[69]

Seventh, because Ricoeur's work was ultimately pastoral in nature. By this I mean his purpose was to facilitate discovery of human identity through the process of interpretation of the contingent events of life, especially those involving suffering and impairment by evil. His intention was to facilitate hope and to give human beings a reason for living that was greater than the point of death. In this latter sense Ricoeur is said to have completed the work that Heidegger left incomplete at the boundary of human mortality and death.[70] My purpose is also supremely pastoral in nature. To explore a configured theological narrative that can contribute to the pastoral care of Christian responders to major incidents, which involve living "deaths" (severe injuries) and actual fatalities, I want to explore a theology of pastoral enabling that sustains pastoral care as an adventure of faith, to give faith and hope during a prolonged period of response when despair, incoherence, and incompetence could dominate the responder.[71]

Mimetic Cycle—Ricoeur's mimetic theory comprises three modes for mediation between time and narrative. In summary these are: a stage of practice; a mediating role of emplotment; and a process of reading. Ricoeur summarized these as: $mimesis_1$—prefiguration; $mimesis_2$—configuration; and $mimesis_3$—refiguration. It is by this mimetic process Ricoeur theorized humans could explore their full possibility in a passionate way that combined submission to suffering (*pascha*) with the discovery of meaning and hope.[72]

---

67. See Taylor, review of *Time and Narrative*, 380–82.

68. Ricoeur seemed to replace the concept of reference with that of refiguration, which was synonymous with transformation (Fodor, *Christian Hermeneutics*, 15–19). Fodor argues Ricoeur interrogated the concept of reference, or subject, which the Enlightenment view regarded as static. It is only by the mimetic process that the subject can read truth with any accuracy, through virtuous transformation.

69. Pellauer, *Ricoeur*, 71; Fodor, *Christian Hermeneutics*, 208.

70. See Fodor, *Christian Hermeneutics*, 199–200, 202–5.

71. Ricoeur claimed, "The whole history of suffering cries out for vengeance and calls for narrative" (*Time and Narrative*, vol. 1, 75). He referred to such adventures as "projects."

72. On "hope" see Ricoeur, *History and Truth*, quoted in Fodor, *Christian Hermeneutics*, 91.

I implement this theory as a methodology for my research in the following way:

Mimesis₁—For Ricoeur's theory, "'Mimesis₁' is the entire set of presuppositions required for the possibility of any narrative at all. The possibility of emplotment, of constructing a story, is rooted in our 'preunderstanding' of the world of practical action."[73] It assumes a prefigured knowledge of things such as intention, purpose, motive, act, consequence, and effort, and that we understand the symbolic nature of many actions and their place in culture and institutions.[74] This is the stage where I relate my personal story(ies) of responding to Kegworth/M1, as an Evangelical Christian responder, already situated in my own culture and traditions, and as one who had certain presuppositions about compassionate pastoral response, the Bible, the church, the world, suffering and evil, salvation, eschatology, and ecumenical and interfaith relations. So, I asked questions of my experience as a Christian responder such as: What actions did I do? Why did I do those actions? What did they achieve? What regrets have I been left with as a result? What theological/ethical questions did those actions pose? What assaults upon my identity did they make? What levels of incoherence have they left? As my memories mingled with my expectations, this mode disclosed a significant discordance about life in major incident response: life was turned upside down/inside out. I appeared to have "lost the plot."

Mimesis₂—Mimesis₂ is the stage where configuring my narrative really begins. It is the process of taking the prefigured data and configuring it, from memory and imagination, through the exploration of salient theological themes, into a narrative that could afford meaning and purpose for my response, which gives me identity as a Christian responder. Thus, mimesis₂ is an attempt to mend discordance through a process of emplotment. The plot is essential because it is "the necessary mediation between the individual events, incidents, accidents, characters, etc., on the one

---

73. Charles E. Reagan, "Words and Deeds: The Semantics of Action," in Hahn, ed., *Philosophy of Paul Ricoeur*, 341. Also, Fodor sees these as "the opaque depths of lived experience" (*Christian Hermeneutics*, 190).

74. I take Ricoeur's point that action is distinguished from physical movement in that action implies goals and motives (Ricoeur, *Time and Narrative*, vol. 1, 55. Also, Dornisch, "Ricoeur's Theory of Mimesis," 310).

hand and the story taken as a whole on the other."[75] Mimesis$_2$ is where narrativization has a

> function which, above all else, plays a mediating role, whether between individual events or incidents and the story as a whole; or whether as a synthesis between the unity of a plot and the heterogeneity of factors such as pitiable and fearful incidents, sudden reversals, recognitions, violent effects, etc., resulting finally in concordant discordance as an essential characterization of emplotment.[76]

It is where I find help in regaining the plot, not by simply moving the existing pieces of the jigsaw into a new order, but where new pieces of the jigsaw are introduced.[77] The genius of Ricoeur's theory is that it approximates the wisdom of a biblical approach.[78] Both encourage two important dynamics:

First, a configuration of time that is not time-bound in a normal chronological sense. Mimesis$_2$ permits a movement between chronological time and the act of *poiesis*, where time is configured by the plot to form a kind of fictitious time, but which also includes chronological and cosmic dimensions. It links what was to what may be. The retention of a link between fictitious time and a positivist connection was Ricoeur's unique emphasis in narrative.[79] These configurations of time "present a certain picture of the way the world is, but also a picture of the way the world should be, or should become."[80] The narrative created is one of a new situation/story, which has learned from the benefit of combining the past (memories, traditions, etc.) and imaginative new insights (wisdom). Ricoeur likens this to psychoanalysis, where "together the analyst and

---

75. Vanhoozer, *Biblical Narrative*, 93.

76. Jervolino, "Depth and Breadth," 541.

77. An interesting illustration could be of an unmade jigsaw puzzle, where some pieces are missing, and some are grubby and discolored, so they are almost incomprehensible. The process of mimesis2 would help restore the messy and incomprehensible pieces of the narrative to their true image—thus enabling us to see where they are *meant* to fit into the narrative to give meaning; then the process may provide the missing pieces—information we never had before.

78. Making it compatible with canonical linguistics' emphasis upon *sapientia* and *phronesis*.

79. Fodor, *Christian Hermeneutics*, 210.

80. Wisse, "Narrative Theology," paragraph 5. Lyall, in interpreting Capps' engagement with Ricoeur, makes the point that written texts and meaningful action have creative capabilities (Lyall, *Integrity of Pastoral Care*, 52).

patient construct a narrative which redescribes the patient's past in terms of some forgotten possibility, thus allowing him a new understanding."[81] Mimesis2 enables the composition of paradigms and ideas that, on the one hand are products of the imagination, yet which could be transformative when actioned.[82]

Second, there is an opportunity for multidisciplinary theological reflection—for bringing in the contributions of systematic, biblical, philosophical, and historical theology to the configuring process.[83]

I reflect, therefore, theologically upon my prefigured response to Kegworth/M1, to explore if a canonical linguistic theology can contribute to this process of configuration in such a way as gives greater coherence and purpose, and whether this process creates a virtuous identity for evangelical Christian responders.[84] I argue that the central plot to the theodrama is the incarnate Jesus Christ, in his life, death, and resurrection, and that a configured narrative should be read around that center—that it is only in a salvific relationship with Jesus Christ as Lord that virtuous identity can give greater coherence and purpose for the responder. I explore through this perspective of the centrality of Christ, certain doctrines that are most salient to major incident response for Christian responders. These are: evil, trauma, grace, compassion, reconciliation and justice, and ecumenical and interfaith friendship.

Mimesis$_3$—In this mode, narration must interact with readership in a process of refiguration.[85] Where mimesis$_2$ mediates between time and narrative, mimesis$_3$ brings the process down to earth again by mediating

81. Taylor, review of *Time and Narrative*, 382. A similar psychotherapeutic interest in Ricoeur accounts for Capp's pastoral care model.

82. Kathleen Blamey, "From the Ego to the Self," in Hahn, ed., *Philosophy of Paul Ricoeur*, 580. This process must allow for mutability and adaptation. Vanhoozer raises the question as to how Ricoeur could judge between what possibilities were possible and what were impossible, because they were unattainable by impaired human nature. Ricoeur's answer to this was the test of *praxis*—pragmatic testing, mainly through testimony (Vanhoozer, *Biblical Narrative*, 23–25, 257–65).

83. Dornisch concludes that Scripture is a "configuration of human action," and historical and systematic theology "partake of the structure of configuration as developed in Ricoeur's theory" (Dornisch, "Ricoeur's Theory of Mimesis," 313).

84. Identity, for Ricoeur, is virtue based. For this reason I remain the same person through time, even when aspects of me might change. It is my virtue that maintains my true identity—*ipse*, not *idem*. *Ipse* is my narrative identity, which can encompass both change and sameness. For implications regarding eschatology, see chapter 9 below.

85. Ricoeur, *Time and Narrative*, vol. 1, 70–87.

narrative and time.[86] It is the process where the reader of the configured narrative actualizes the narrative back into the realities of life for the future. Dornisch comments, "The intersection of mimesis$_2$ and mimesis$_3$ is the act which makes the . . . theology live. This is the process which is the constant challenge for those who wish . . . scripture, or theology to be other than dead letters or sedimented paradigms."[87]

I conclude my dissertation, therefore, by interacting my configured narrative with applicability and serviceability by conversing with my *aporias*, the Civil Contingencies Act 2004 and accompanied guidance, along with the secular culture of major incident planning, as well as reflecting from a practical theological perspective, to evaluate as a reader, if this methodology does hold out hope for a future *praxis* for Evangelical Christian responders to major incidents.

Critically, I want to distance myself from certain aspects of Ricoeur's underlying philosophical framework regarding his perspective on biblical authority and inspiration, which would expose me to liberal universalizing assumptions I am resolved to resist. These have been exposed most forcibly by the opposing Yale School and by Hans Frei in particular. Frei's criticism of Ricoeur's philosophical theology is precisely because it is that—philosophical, not biblical. He accuses Ricoeur of imposing a universal framework of natural theology/philosophy onto the gospel narratives as a hermeneutical method, whereby the issue of biblical inspiration and authority is essentially bypassed because the biblical text is primarily ignored as a controlling hermeneutical factor.[88] Furthermore, as an aspect of this universal framework, Ricoeur assumes a natural gracing of the world of all humankind under the love of God, and the Jesus referent is of allegorical value only, and the gospels are parables of the kingdom of God. Frei insisted, after Barth, that there is no foundational truth prior to a revelation of God in Christ. Vanhoozer judges Frei's critique of Ricoeur's view of the biblical text and its authority as largely

---

86. "Narrative has its full meaning when it is restored to the time of action and of suffering in mimesis3" (Ricoeur, *Time and Narrative*, vol. 1, 70).

87. Dornisch, "Ricoeur's Theory of Mimesis," 317.

88. Vanhoozer thinks this point is a moot one. He is not sure if Ricoeur actually believed biblical hermeneutics best served up a universal approach or if he first developed his universal and then fitted biblical hermeneutics into it. Fodor also judges Ricoeur's philosophical hermeneutical system "vitiates the traditional designation of biblical hermeneutic as a special, if not unique, enterprise . . ." (*Christian Hermeneutics*, 260–61).

valid.[89] It is on account of these issues exposed and criticized by Frei that I am uncomfortable with employing Ricoeur's doctrine of Scripture for my research exploration.[90] I am also suspicious of Ricoeur favoring a process theology at the back of his concept of human "possibility." However, as a tool for a constructive narrative mimesis holds huge potential.

Canonical Narrative

Scripture is a significant factor in my exploration, in terms of the emplotment/drama, configuration, and refiguration of my pastoral carer's narrative. Jesus Christ, as set out in the canonical theodrama, is the central figure in the plot that also serves coherence for an identity of compassion and hope through the development of character for the Christian responder.[91] Therefore, some consideration of canonical narrative is important.

Cultural-Linguistic

A possible form of canonical narrative could be the cultural-linguistic approach. This started as story Barthianism, pioneered from Karl Barth, and then further developed by George Lindbeck and Hans Frei, and is now popularized more pastorally by Stanley Hauerwas.[92] They argued much of the Bible is in narrative form, and even that which is not, is narrative based.[93] Furthermore, God has revealed himself narratively, not ontologically.[94] We have the revelation of God in the stories of Israel

---

89. Yet Comstock argues that Frei was not without foundations in his own claim to nonfoundationalism. See Comstock, "Truth or Meaning." He argues Frei's foundationalism resides in two assumptions: first, that narrative is autonomous; second, that the Bible's narratives are self-referential.

90. Or, indeed, Frei's later ideas on the doctrine of Scripture, which tended to subject *sola scriptura* to the role of tradition.

91. Hauerwas and Willimon, *Resident Aliens*, 53–60.

92. Barth, *Word of God*; Lindbeck, *Nature of Doctrine*; Frei, *Eclipse of Biblical Narrative*; Hauerwas and Jones, eds., *Why Narrative?*; Hauerwas, *Naming the Silences*.

93. Hauerwas and Willimon, *Resident Aliens*; Hauerwas, *With the Grain*. For Hauerwas, "the Bible is foundationally a story of a people's journey with God" (*Resident Aliens*, 55). There are other literary forms in the Bible: prophecy; wisdom; didactic; apocalyptic, but he argues these all arise out of narratives. So, narrative is foundational to all other forms of theology. Vanhoozer describes the Scriptures as a "drama of redemption," involving five acts: creation; the election, rejection, and restoration of Israel; Jesus; the Holy Spirit; and the consummation of all things (Vanhoozer, *Drama of Doctrine*, 2–3).

94. Thus, even the internal communication within the Godhead is conveyed in

and Jesus, told and lived through the early Christian community: a revelation of God-in-action more than God-in-being.[95] The central thesis of canonical narrative is that the Christian life is vested in the story of the life, death, and resurrection of Jesus Christ, whose story fulfills the story of Israel, as this configuration has been composed by the Christian community.[96] For the Yale scholars the gospels are the narrative key to understanding the rest of the Scriptures.[97] The Scriptures are God's story in Jesus Christ, narratively configured from the real events concerning Jesus, by the human authors.[98] Therefore, the narrative is given in the context of a Christian community (the church), which is both formed by, and is the former of (and interpreter of), the narrative, and one needs to be a part of the church in order to understand it.[99] This teaching of the

---

linguistic narrative form (Gen 1:26). This is not to imply that there is no propositional revelation intended.

95. Hence the metaphor of drama is apt. This is not to relegate the concept of the propositional to the redundant, but merely to set it in perspective in doing theology. The Apostle John states that God is "light" and "love" (1 John 1:5; 4:8). This is timeless proposition, even though it is a truth exhibited narratively in other parts of the Bible. For a stern defense of the validity of a propositional approach to revelation and the Bible, see Henry, *God, Revelation and Authority*, vol. 3, chapters 25–27. In a notable debate between Henry and Hans Frei, encapsulated by George Hunsinger, Frei accuses Henry of being a liberal in terms of his dependence upon a universal reason (Hunsinger, *Disruptive Grace*, 338–60). Also Philips and Okholm, eds., *Nature of Confession*, 134–50. Vanhoozer, however, believes Henry was appealing only to the universality of the *imago Dei* and to the Spirit's sanctifying work in countering the *noetic* effects of sin (*Drama of Doctrine*, 87, n. 32). See also Carson, *Gagging of God*, 163–72, where Carson recognises the Bible cannot be reduced to propositional revelation, but neither can it be omitted as insignificant. Also, see Helm, "Propositions and Speech Acts"; also his "Revealed Propositions." For a denial of the propositional approach see Wiles, "Scriptural Authority."

96. The use of "story" should not be taken to imply lack of historical or truthful validity to the events in the story. It will inevitably, though, imply a certain concept of how such events, even if they happened, are interpreted and crafted by authorial intent. By "historical" we should also include historiography—the shaped form of narrated events. "Pure" history is impossible; it is always someone's story.

97. This is in contrast to the Ricoeurian view of the scriptural text needing to be interpreted by a philosophical hermeneutic outside of the text, and that applies to interpreting any literary texts (Fodor, *Christian Hermeneutics*, 260–61).

98. I stress the importance in my view of the historical nature of the events behind the gospel narratives; the "stories" out of which the narratives have been configured under the Holy Spirit. I wish to distance myself from the stance Murphy rightly exposes, in her critique of narrative theology, that narrative makes God a story by reducing him to the narrative. See Murphy, *God Is Not a Story*.

99. Reformed theology has referred to the *perspicuity*, or clarity, of Scripture.

church, takes the key form of *habitus*, a way of living, as well as, if not more than, propositional exposition.[100] In short, narrative theology is, "the process through which individuals and communities seek to embody and act out the story of God told in Jesus."[101]

Certainly, narrative theology has become a part of the postliberal reaction to Enlightenment liberalism's consuming focus upon cognitive perception of reality. Whereas the latter proclaimed a universal reason accessible to all reasoning people and relegated religion to the realms of the archaic, and behavior to ethics, postliberalism has triumphed the overarching "reason" of the Bible, accessible to those who are figuring their own narrative into the narrative of Jesus.[102] For narrative theology, the issue is not the necessity of fitting the Christian worldview into an Enlightenment liberal epistemological framework, but the necessity of understanding the world from the epistemology of the Scriptures. This is necessary not only in a broad cultural sense but also in a community and personal context. Community and personal meaning become rooted in the biblical text and the world it reveals.[103]

Canonical Linguistic

Another form of narrative could be that of the canonical linguistic approach, as set out above.[104] While this has a great deal of sympathy and similarity with the cultural-linguistic form, it has distinct differences, most notably, in the belief that narrative cannot be the central key to understanding the Bible. Narrative is but one of a number of literary forms

---

Grudem defines this to mean, "the Bible is written in such a way that its teachings are able to be understood by all who will read it seeking God's help and being willing to follow it" (*Systematic Theology*, 108).

100. See Vanhoozer, *Drama of Doctrine*, 254–56.

101. Graham, et al., *Theological Reflection*, 105. Also, Hauerwas and Willimon, *Resident Aliens*, 55. For Lindbeck the truth statement is only actually true when it has been performed/actuated by the individual/community. For Lindbeck the form of life (of the church) was the semantic vehicle through which scriptural utterances must pass for them to become valid. In this concept he diverged quite radically from Barth. Barth regarded Christ as the primary Word, and the Scripture forms the vehicle of semantic correspondence (Hunsinger, *Disruptive Grace*, 317).

102. On the concept of "figuring in," see Loughlin, *Telling God's Story*, 42–46.

103. Thus, Hauerwas can aver, "the Bible is the product of the church's process of canonization, but there is no hearing of God's word apart from a people who are struggling to listen truthfully for God's word . . ." (*Resident Aliens*, 128).

104. See above, 40–42.

operating in the formation of the canon. Vanhoozer, therefore, argues a far greater holistic view of Scripture is required. He thus contends for the concept of drama being more suited, in view of the fact that it can encapsulate all of these literary forms.[105] Furthermore, and equally important, Vanhoozer opposes the reductive perspective of the Scripture story/plot being composed ultimately by the church. He argues for the principle of *sola scriptura*, and for a strong view of biblical inspiration, the Holy Spirit utilizing the personalities of the human authors.[106] His focus is upon the significance of doctrine rather than narrative, although narrative forms make an important contribution toward the construction of the doctrine.

In order to weigh up the merits of both these forms of canonical approach I provide some critical focus.

Critical Focus

From a description of these narrative approaches, it is important to critically focus on certain specific aspects that test these as methodological contributions for a practical theology in the evangelical tradition. These aspects are: Scripture and authority; propositional/systematic theology; engagement with the world; community focus; virtue ethics; character, identity, coherence, and meaning.

Scripture and Authority—There is much in some narrative theology that is attractive to the Evangelical tradition of *sola scriptura*, due to an emphasis upon the Bible as a significant source of authority and upon textual commitment by way of plain sense and intratextual disciplines, whereby different genres of Scripture crisscross in their interpretative capacity.[107] However, this *sola scriptura* focus needs to be distinguished

105. Even so, Hauerwas could make a strong appeal to the Christian life (especially within the context of the Christian community as a colony) being a great *adventure*. See also *Resident Aliens*, chapter 3, where he makes a pointed comment, concerning the role of the clergy, "We want the clergy to see how much better it is to be part of an adventure than merely to be 'a member of the helping profession'" (58–59).

106. Ricoeur, however, placed little importance upon the intentions of human authors on the basis that these are largely unknown. The purpose of the text is to also interpret the reader and to open up a world, hitherto unseen, by polysemic and metaphoric meanings. That is, to be able to distinguish between the ostensive and world-disclosive meanings of the biblical text. See Capps and Browning, *Pastoral Care and Hermeneutics*, 16–17, 20–25.

107. The "plain (or literal) sense" method refers to a more literal interpretation of the text, as against the allegorical (Ricoeur), or indeed literalistic (evangelical fundamentalist) method. This does not suggest that every single word/statement of Scripture

from the tradition-based authority of the linguistic turn of much narrative theology.[108] Indeed, Vanhoozer and Murphy argue that a key problem with story Barthianism is it grounds the formation of the church in the impersonality of a common language, rather than in Christ and the Spirit, and human witnesses to the resurrected Christ upon whom the Spirit comes, and the Scriptures testify to.[109] Thus, the story itself takes precedence over the tellers of the story and their mobilizing personalities. Story Barthianism thus not only fails in its own agenda of non-foundationalism, it also loses the *sola scriptura* principle. A healthy emphasis shared by both forms is upon immersing oneself in, or giving oneself up to, the literal textual world of the Scriptures, where *we* take our place within the biblical narrative.[110] To achieve this we must give ourselves to a faithful Christocentric reading of the Bible within a Christ-formed community. It is not just to reading; there is need to consume the text so we may "grow in the strength and shape of Christ."[111] This means so much more than a mental/rote learning of Scripture; it means to live one's life as an enactment of the world of the Christocentric biblical text. This fits well with the Pauline endorsement that, "All Scripture is given by inspiration

---

must be taken literally, but, rather, the text presents its own sense (which may include the need for allegorical or typological interpretation at certain points where the text/context gives plain/literal indication of such a need). For a fuller discussion on the literal sense, see Vanhoozer, *Is There a Meaning?*, 303–35. Also, *Biblical Narrative*, chapter 7; Murphy, *God is Not a Story*; Fodor, *Christian Hermeneutics*, 285–87. Vanhoozer also makes the comment about sola scriptura in respect of Ricoeur's method: "Ricoeur's principle of intertextuality gives new meaning to the methodological principle of sola scriptura, as well as to the theology of correlation" (*Biblical Narrative*, 201). Also see his *Drama of Doctrine*.

108. Fodor believes the phrase and concept—linguistic turn—was first coined by Gustav Bergmann in his *Logic and Reality*, 177. The phrase was then given wider circulation by Richard Rorty in his editing of *The Linguistic Turn*. Rorty believed philosophical problems can be solved "either by reforming language, or by understanding more about the language we presently use" (3).

109. This "turn" is summed up by Loughlin, when he states, "The location of biblical inspiration is not the text itself, but the life of the community in which the text is read and celebrated" (*Telling God's Story*, 114). See also Hauerwas, *Community of Character*, 63–64.

110. Loughlin, *Telling God's Story*, 133; also Walton, "Speaking in Signs," 2–5. Fodor concludes that Hans Frei "is certainly to be commended for his unrelenting stress on Jesus' unsubstitutable identity and its adequacy for faith as conveyed by the biblical text alone" (*Christian Hermeneutics*, 274).

111. Loughlin helpfully bases this concept of consuming the text on Rev 10:9–10. See *Telling God's Story*, 139.

of God, and is profitable for correction, for instruction in righteousness, *that the man of God may be complete, thoroughly equipped for every good work.*"[112] It also has synergy with the NT concept of union with Christ as expounded in passages such as John 15, Rom 6 and Eph 1, with the recurring theme of "abiding in Christ," and being "in Christ" in such a way that is an objective status to be worked out in a subjective living.[113] Particularly challenging to some more apologetic Evangelical foci on the authority of Scripture is the premodern emphasis postliberalism/Radical Orthodoxy places upon inspiration and authority being vested in the life-action of the text-bound community of the Holy Spirit. Traditional references to inspiration and authority, such as 2 Tim 3:16 and 2 Pet 1:20–22, locate these concepts in such community contexts, as well as the context of the inspiring Spirit.[114] This is a suitable balance, both to modernity's (and the post-Reformation) concept of the right to private judgment, or to objectifying Scripture in such a way that kills the life of it by making the process of inspiration a test of orthodoxy more than the wisdom it propounds.[115] Hauerwas reminds us, "The proper object of theology is not stories but God. Our task is not to try to show how stories save but how God saves."[116] Vanhoozer draws upon the use of mimesis as used by the Apostle Paul in Eph 5:1—"Be imitators of me"—and suggests the church's role is one of creative imitation as "a non-identical participation

112. 2 Tim 3:16 (emphasis mine). The Pauline endorsement is given in the context of both warning the Christian community against the deceit of intrusive unfaithful lives (2 Tim. 3:9) and the exhortation to follow Paul's "manner of life," (v. 10), and the exhortation to "live godly in Christ Jesus." (v. 12). The context presents an emphatic focus upon *habitus*.

113. Vanhoozer approves the strength in Lindbeck's focus upon living the text, but sets forth his own "postconservative, canonical linguistic theology and a directive theory of doctrine that roots theology more firmly in Scripture" (*Drama of Doctrine*, xiii. See also pages 392–96).

114. See also Hauerwas, *Community of Character*, 63–64.

115. On the inappropriateness of private judgment, see Vanhoozer, *Drama of Doctrine*, 233. This point about the danger of killing the life revealed by the text must not be confused with the Pauline text that is often appealed to by those defending a non-propositional approach to revelation—2 Cor 3:6, "for the letter kills, but the Spirit gives life." For a robust riposte to such an appeal, see Henry, "A Theistic View of Language," in *God, Revelation and Authority*, vol. 3, 395. I agree with Vanhoozer that the term, and concept of, "wisdom" (Col 4:5, which, in turn, emphasizes the necessity of wisdom to Christian pastoral mission—"toward those who are outside") is the best linguistic conception for bridging the "ugly ditch" between theory and practice (Vanhoozer, *Drama of Doctrine*, 13–14).

116. Hauerwas, *Community of Character*, 68.

in the missions of the Son and the Spirit."[117] Thus, the authority of Scripture lies equally in its right to authorize the kind of community (and/or, in this research context, the kind of responder) the Christian/church must be to be faithful, namely creative imitators of Christ.[118]

Yet for all Frei's emphasis upon the authority of Scripture, the gospel seems inaccessible and unknowable for the unbeliever. The only way to understand the text is to know Jesus. Yet to know Jesus, one needs the text. Thus, Frei seems exceedingly ambiguous over the Scriptures having an accessible, universal appeal to the unbeliever.[119] There is a kind of Biblically legitimated circularity in the arguments of Barth and Frei, that we cannot make sense of the Scriptures until we first make sense of ourselves, but for this we need to first immerse ourselves in the scriptural narrative world. The circularity is resolved, in a way Frei fails to do in my view, by acknowledging the autonomous work of the Holy Spirit, made explicit in the narrative itself, to reveal the message.[120] It is this work that gives the text autonomy.

Even so, debate has been concerned with whether the biblical textual narratives are historical or true. For Frei, historicality was not

117. Vanhoozer, *Drama of Doctrine*, 401.

118. Hauerwas, *Community of Character*, 68. Stackhouse is right, therefore, to warn that community has potential for both good and evil—depending on what the community stands for. See Stackhouse, *Making the Best of It*, 176–78.

119. See Comstock, "Truth or Meaning," 124–5; Fodor, *Christian Hermeneutics*.

120. This is the kind of argument the Apostle Paul uses to counter the worldly philosophical attractions upon the Corinthian Christian community, in 1 Cor 2. Paul distinguishes between human wisdom, (v. 4–6), and wisdom of God (7) revealed by the Spirit to gift the apostolic community with the "mind of Christ" (v. 16). This was to be preached in dependence upon the autonomous Spirit's ability to demonstrate the wisdom and transformative power of the gospel in lives that are transformed through faith (1 Cor 2:1–4). On the significance of the "mind of Christ" as the *telos* of God's communicative practice in canonical linguistic theology, see Vanhoozer, *Drama of Doctrine*, 254–56. Also Ricoeur acknowledges that circularity between narrative and temporality in his mimetic process is healthy not vicious. However, he is also wise to the charge of his theory of mimesis being a circular tautology. He counters this by arguing his theory is much more than "dead tautology," however. See Ricoeur, *Time and Narrative*, vol. 1, pgs. 3, 54, 71–76). The subjectivity of the cycle needs to be balanced by the objectivity of a structural analysis of the text prior to its interpretation (Capps and Browning, *Pastoral Care and Hermeneutics*, 25–26). Circularity has been a criticism made against narrative theology, by Murphy. Her thesis is that certain narrative forms (notably by Karl Barth, Hans Frei, and Robert Jenson) fail to fulfill their own agendas by reducing God to a story of our own making, thus imprisoning the free and unpredictable being of God, and his love, within "overdependence on words, narratives, and stories in theology" (Marsh, review of *God is Not a Story*, 338–40).

unimportant, but the internal world of the narrative had priority. He argued passionately against the need for any extratextual referent. For Frei, the Scripture narratives are history-formed, but their being true was deemed an unnecessary issue in view of his concept of the autonomy and self-referentiality of the text. But this could make the truth value of the text inaccessible to the public.[121] Ricoeur countered this with a specific attempt to make the narratives publicly intelligible under a universal philosophical hermeneutic, and arguably at the expense of their historicality. They were symbolic references for structuring reconfiguration to manifest the possible that is always available to us via imagination. Comstock's argument in favor of Ricoeur's nuance, affirming the definite distinction between Frei and Ricoeur's approaches, nevertheless confirms for me the value of conflating aspects of both Frei and Ricoeur, as well as rejecting some, in my use of narrative as a methodology.[122] Vanhoozer, however, argues for the universality of the canon lying in the Christotopical nature of what God was doing in Christ, namely, that "the history of Jesus Christ is significant for all times and places."[123]

Hauerwas and Ricoeur have invited the charge of relativism/fideism and thus how they can judge the biblical narrative has any more authority than that of any other sacred text.[124] Ricoeur and Frei are both open to the criticism that they impose onto the biblical narrative an anachronistic literary form that ignores the biblical claim to divine authorship and inspiration, and thus to a divine narrator.[125] Hauerwas struggles to

---

121. Fodor argues Frei's position exposes him to two possible, equally unacceptable, alternatives: either one abolishes all apologetic conversation with unbelievers, or one attempts to force every aspect of the non-textual world into the framework of the biblical text. He concludes the former creates the stigma of isolation, while the latter creates the "ugliness of imperialism" (*Christian Hermeneutics*, 273). Fodor goes on to criticize Frei's referential ambiguity over the narrative Jesus and the actual life of Jesus. Though Frei argues in favor of the former, he cannot completely omit reference to the latter in order to distinguish between the meaning and the truth of the narrative as a meaningful thing. Even so, Frei believed the scriptural narrative contained no true referent without itself. The narrative defined reality (Fodor, *Christian Hermeneutics*, 280–1, 297).

122. See Comstock, "Truth or Meaning."

123. Vanhoozer, *Drama of Doctrine*, 347–48. He calls these "concrete universals," in contrast to abstract universals, because they are embedded in particular situations. These may be concretized in different cultures, contra Lindbeck's cultural-linguistic form. A "Christotope" is a place where Christ makes himself present.

124. See Graham, et al., *Theological Reflection*, 106.

125. Vanhoozer, *Biblical Narrative*, 177–78. Of Frei, Fodor judges, "The literary and

explicate why the Scriptures are right intrinsically, rather than becoming right for me because I will them to be. Therefore, Hauerwas, Frei, and Ricoeur's interpretations of the inspiration and authority of Scripture lack the objective nature the Evangelical tradition emphasises, and the text indicates, of the role of the Holy Spirit inspiring the revelation.[126] My point is an appeal for an acknowledgment of reasonableness from within the human sphere of intelligibility assumed by Spirit-inspired Scripture, without which all reasoning would be impossible, or at least restricted to some form of Gnosticism.[127] Lucie-Smith comments usefully upon the inevitability of embeddedness in one's specific tradition (as per Hauerwas) and yet the need (and possibility of) a disembodiment: the need to "reflect on tradition and keep a critical distance from it," to be a "divided self."[128]

---

historical conventions distinguishing 'history' from 'realistic narrative' in nineteenth-century England . . . are not transferable to those governing textual composition in first-century Palestine" (*Christian Hermeneutics*, 284).

126. Even so, Vanhoozer argues that Lindbeck's classic hermeneutic of reading the OT in the light of the NT, Christologically, is what led to the formation of the church as the authoritative interpretive community, "which conquered the empire in defiance of the normal laws of sociological gravity: non-violently, despite persecution, and without special economic, social, cultural, or ethnic support" (George A. Lindbeck, "Scripture, Consensus, and Community," in Neuhaus, ed., *Biblical Interpretation in Crisis*, 78.

127. A point I take up again in my exploration of common grace, in chapter 7 below. Vanhoozer describes this in terms of a theologically informed prolegomena (*Drama of Doctrine*, 6, n. 16). See also Lucie-Smith, *Narrative Theology*, chapters 2 and 5. He discusses the less credible attempt of Hauerwas to argue for a rationality of plausibility through a believable character. But the criteria for a believable character are "internal to the narrative itself" (Lucie-Smith, *Narrative Theology*, 39–40). Also, Carson, *Gagging of God*, 102–5). Starting from opposite poles, the later MacIntyre and Rawls, while taking into account the specificity of traditions, acknowledge a universal perspective of reason and rationality (echoes of Eccl 3:11), as does Habermas in his belief in the inherent rationality implied in communicative act. Vanhoozer nuances this assumption with a "local rationality of diverse literary forms"(Jürgen Habermas, "What is Universal Pragmatics?" in *Communication and the Evolution of Society*, quoted in Vanhoozer, *Is There a Meaning?*, 344–45). It is in this difference between acknowledging an external, as well as internal, criteria for rationality that MacIntyre and Hauerwas, so often at one, differ. For H. Richard Niebuhr the "external" history was essential for checking the "internal" (as noted above), but, with his more Enlightenment liberal presuppositions. See also Wallace's discussion of the naming of God prior to a real knowledge of God, in Wallace, "Can God Be Named?"

128. Lucie-Smith, *Narrative Theology*, 133, 134. Smith reminds us of how the early MacIntyre drew similar criticism regarding his view of all traditions having only relative perspectives on truth. However, the later MacIntyre, reviewing his understanding

Many narrative theologians, for all their emphasis upon the inspiration and authority of Scripture, acknowledge there are many errors and contradictions within the text, and have an aversion to verbal inspiration. This is based chiefly on the argument that verbal inspiration must imply a "dictation" theory.[129] However, Evangelical scholars have long seen this as a "man of straw," and have argued strongly for a divine verbal inspiration that is fully concomitant with the involvement of the human personalities and characters of the Scripture authors.[130] My assumption of divine inspiration leads me to concur with Vanhoozer's argument that the biblical text (as with any text) is controlled by authorial intent, where "the author is not only the cause of the text, but also the agent who determines what the text counts as."[131] It must be also added that Lindbeck's and Hauerwas' insistence upon the Bible being under the exclusive interpretive "ownership" of the church begs the questions: "Which church, and with what narrative?" Hauerwas' response, illustrated by his own leanings toward Roman Catholicism, tends towards a spiritual elite/*magisterium* that would lead inexorably toward an elitist empowerment he himself

---

of Aquinas, comes to accept a meta-history being granted by God, in terms of a natural theology. McGrath refers to this as "tradition transcendent reality" (McGrath, *Open Secret*, 249). Vanhoozer, in the context of achieving creative understanding from both scriptural text and present contexts, advocates this distancing (or "outsidedness"). See Vanhoozer, *Drama of Doctrine*, 352. On Ricoeur's concept of critical distance, see Capps and Browning, *Pastoral Care and Hermeneutics*, 30–34.

129. For example, see Loughlin, *Telling God's Story*, 115. Loughlin, nevertheless, makes the useful point about inspired *reading* being as—or, in his case, more—significant than the *writing* of Scripture in regards to Scripture's authority and infallibility. For many Barthian narrative theologians it is the existential encounter with the divine through the reading of Scripture that constitutes revelation more than the original givenness of the word to the authors.

130. For instance, Vanhoozer steers a careful course around the "rocks" of the dictation theory of inspiration. He argues for the Spirit's sanctifying of the human communicative practices, not stultifying human agency or personality (Vanhoozer, *Drama of Doctrine*, 226–29). See also Carson, *Gagging of God*, 152–63. In a "fallen" world then even language is susceptible. What Lucie-Smith refers to as the "alienation of language" is salient (*Narrative Theology*, 138). He judges, "as we know the whole, and alas, we cannot, defeated as we are by the contingency of language, which is contrasted with the absoluteness of truth." But, appealing to Augustine, he concludes there is the stabilization provided by the word of God, and so, "Thus one can be led astray by the vacuities of language, but one can also be cured by the Word of God" (140). See also Henry, "A Theistic View of Language," in *God, Revelation and Authority*, vol. 3, chapter 23.

131. Vanhoozer, *Is There a Meaning?*, 228.

deplores.[132] He seems to leave no room for a Martin Luther, whose radical reformative theology began with his own private spiritual struggle with God, and for which he was accused of novelty by the Roman Catholic magisterial establishment.[133]

Frei has also been criticized, for his rigid confinement of reality to the text in a way that obscures the world the text is signposting or assuming, without it being explicit in the actual text.[134] But the point Frei stresses is: all we know of Jesus Christ is narratively contained to the biblical text. Jesus Christ is a narratively configured person. Also, Scripture narratives reveal truth in a specific context, and their composition has been for a specific contextual purpose. Scripture is creative narrative; the utilizing of different stories to form purposeful narratives that, in the purposes of divine providence and inspiration, combine to form a total narrative of which Jesus Christ is the center. Thus, Barth's concept of the Bible being a nonfictional novel need not be so inaccurate to an Evangelical perspective.[135]

Overall, I conclude, therefore, that Vanhoozer's canonical linguistic approach is the most suited to the Evangelical practical theological exploration I wish to make, safeguarding the principle of *sola scriptura* the cultural-linguistic form confuses.

132. However, Vanhoozer rightly draws attention to the many possible interpretations of Hauerwas concerning the authoritative place and role of the interpretive community (Vanhoozer, *Is There a Meaning?*,173). Hauerwas seems ambiguous in many respects. See Stackhouse, "In the Company of Hauerwas."

133. Canonical linguistic theology however, does take such incidents into account. Vanhoozer argues that in his work on canonical linguistics, "the canon alone has final authority in theology (*sola scriptura*), even when it sometimes goes *against* the tradition of its interpretation" (*Drama of Doctrine*, 330). See also Glenn Tinder's astute judgment that, in final terms, determining the direction of God's leadership is the responsibility of the individual, and must not be surrendered to any other leader or group (Glenn Tinder, *The Political Meaning of Christianity: An Interpretation*, quoted in Stackhouse, *Making the Best of It*, 178, n. 9).

134. On this point see Fodors' discussion in *Christian Hermeneutics*, 269–73. He believes "Frei is careful to point out that he is not denying the difference between meaning as the sense of the story and meaning as something outside the story—that to which the story refers. But he is saying that, in terms of Christian self-description, the distinction is complicated" (272).

135. Hunsinger prefers an (equally suitable) alternative analogy: "As the ultimate author of Scripture, God is more like an artist than a photographer" (*Disruptive Grace*, 356).

Pʀᴏᴘᴏsɪᴛɪᴏɴᴀʟ/Sʏsᴛᴇᴍᴀᴛɪᴄ Tʜᴇᴏʟᴏɢʏ—Relating to systematic theology, the issue is not an "either/or." All theology needs to be systematic or else it is incomprehensible.[136] It is also hard to conceive of something being systematic that is not, in some way, also propositional and doctrinal in what it says. Even if we concede that narrative is basic to biblical revelation and truth, the question remains: for what purpose has God chosen to reveal himself in this narrative way? Is it just to tell us a story, or a history? Surely telling a story or giving a history is for an intelligible purpose, which can be stated only in a propositional form. The communicative matter of the text can only be propositional, or it cannot communicate.[137] Analysis of such propositions will lead to doctrine. I thus concur with Vanhoozer when he judges, in prefacing his form of canonical narrative, "Christian doctrine is necessary for human flourishing; only doctrine shows us who we are, why we are here, and what we are to do."[138] The issue for my research purposes is whether narrative, as a genre, contributes to forming a coherent system of theology. My Evangelical assumption for this research is that the Bible is divinely inspired and infallible. This is based upon a foundation, itself from within Scripture, though not confined there, of God revealing himself coherently through acts and words, in the various corpora of the Bible, that are comprehensible and logical to humans.[139] I concur with Carson that a quality of logic is therefore necessary, not on an Enlightenment basis, but as "the substratum of any communication, whether between two individuals or two ages . . . regardless of the literary genre in which the communication is embedded."[140] I will argue later that this is sustained by God's common grace/Christological natural theology.[141]

---

136. D. A. Carson, "Unity and Diversity in the New Testament," 65–95 in Carson and Woodbridge, eds., *Scripture and Truth*.

137. Vanhoozer, *Is There a Meaning?*, 229.

138. Vanhoozer, *Drama of Doctrine*, xiii.

139. This is not the same as saying that all humans will understand this revelation. John 3:1–21 stresses the need for regeneration by the Holy Spirit as necessary to correct understanding. 1 Cor 2:10 also speaks of the necessity of the Holy Spirit for the recognition and personal appropriation of this revelation. Yet, Rom 1:18–21 gives indication of human capacity to willfully repress/refuse to acknowledge divine things that can actually be clearly seen (v. 20).

140. D. A. Carson, "Unity and Diversity in the New Testament," in Carson and Woodbridge, eds., *Scripture and Truth*, 80. See also Henry, "A Theistic View of Language," in *God, Revelation and Authority*.

141. See more on common grace in chapter 7.

The "narrative turn" in theology came about during the second half of the twentieth century, from the traditional use of the Bible for developing a metaphysical system to a narrative for a more ambiguous representation. This followed the philosophical linguistic turn from referential use of language to the use of texts, which passed over into the use of Scripture in a move from a traditional systematizing of doctrines, composed referentially, to narrative readings and theological reflection.[142] This turn came about during an era when much scholarship questioned the legitimacy of any claim to a unitary systematic theology. However, attempts have been made to explore the use of combining the referential and narrative approaches to systematic theology. This has been through the method of mimetic prefiguration, configuration, and refiguration.[143] Wisse argues provided a proposition is not always confused with an assertion then propositional and narrative contributions to systematic theology may have synergy where narrative helps "earth" more abstract propositions where there may be more ambiguity with such propositions that equates with the ambiguity of narrative theology.[144] I want a situation-sensitive, as well as systematic, theology, and referential propositional theology can collaborate with narrative theology to nuance specific aspects of a doctrine that different narratives disclose (e.g., the effect of the resurrection on different players' fears). Doctrinal propositions can help to fill in the gaps that ambiguous narratives invariably leave.

WORLD ENGAGEMENT—The narrative school's critical focus on Christian engagement with the non-Christian world confirms to me the value of including this discipline in my methodology for my research. I conclude this because I explore the legitimacy, or otherwise, of the Christian community responding to major incidents. Responding requires interaction

142. For more on the "linguistic turn," see Vanhoozer, *Drama of Doctrine*, 9–12. The origins of the linguistic turn impacting theology came with Lindbeck's, *Nature of Doctrine*, in 1984. See also above page 59 nn. 108, 109.

143. Yet Vanhoozer claims Ricoeur would never even think of writing a systematic theology, because he believed the work of interpretation never ends (*Biblical Narrative*, 5).

144. Wisse, "Narrative Theology." Also Helm, "Revealed Propositions." Vanhoozer, in the context of making promises, discusses the argument of John R. Searle that assertions must be distinguished from propositions. It is the performance indicator ("illocutionary force") that shows how the proposition is to be taken (*Is There a Meaning?*, 210). He also argues for a distinction between an assertion and proposition in his *Drama of Doctrine*, 278–91.

with key secular agencies and institutions involved in emergency planning and response.

The twin poles adopted by scholars are: that Christian engagement with the world is both legitimate and crucial if the Church is to realistically carry out her God-given mandate to be a witness to the world by being in the world, albeit not of the world; or, the belief that the Church should withdraw from the world and concern herself with the theology and ethics of her own community exclusively. This issue is critical to my research and I address it in detail under my exploration of grace later.[145] At this stage I am concerned to adopt a methodology that will help me explore it critically, and narrative contributes to this, even though it is the most hotly disputed aspect of the discipline, because of the polarization outlined.

Taking into account this critical analysis of narrative approaches, I therefore conclude that a nuanced narrative theology is a valid methodology for engagement with the world of major incident response.

Virtue Ethics and Character—Because the Christian community is defined and formed by the canonical theodrama, and because she needs to be a community of holiness to do that textual work in order to "be herself" in the world, then she must be a virtuous community. Cultural and canonical linguistic theologies understand truth to be actions under the ethics of virtuous living by the church. For example, for Hauerwas theology is ethics.[146] Alasdair MacIntyre's contribution to narrative is emphatic in regard to the role of virtue in narrative. In asking "What is the right thing to do in this situation?" he believes liberalism raises the wrong basic moral question. The Christian should be asking, "What kind of person do I need to be to identify, and then carry out, the right action?" Whereas liberalism enabled a separation between life and practice, and thus, for example, between the kinds of person one is ordinarily and how one functions as a skilled professional, MacIntyre argues that a virtuous life removes an artificial distinction Hauerwas esteems to be non-Christian.[147] This philosophical and theological collaboration between MacIntyre and Hauerwas echoes the scriptural focus upon the

---

145. See chapter 7, 155–94.

146. Stroup, *Promise of Narrative Theology*, 77.

147. MacIntyre, *After Virtue*, 216; Hauerwas, *Community of Character*, 126–27. See also Schon, *Reflective Practitioner*.

good "works" (Jas 2:18) and "fruit of the Spirit" (Gal 5:22–23) that is essential to the life of the truth-formed community.[148]

My research explores how a canonical linguistic theology can help recreate a coherent narrative for a Christian responder, one that develops a Christ-minded compassionate character and gives a hopeful identity. Canonical linguistic theology's direct concern with such a profile makes it a significant methodological contribution. In both narrative and canonical linguistic theology, virtues are essential to character formation, which, in turn, is essential to one's identity and purpose in life. Thus, a narrative is as good as the character it generates. The Bible links trauma with character formation via the use of the word δοκιμος—tested, approved, and thus character formed.[149] The word is used in explaining the purpose of trials, invariably in very traumatic situations for the early Christian communities.[150] Character, for my purposes, "is the correlative of narrative that trains the self to be sufficient to negotiate existence without illusion or deception" and that leads one to see life as a gift, not a right.[151] Virtues are the skills responders in the evangelical tradition need to fulfil the moral task of a response. These are developed into character through experienced living, not by technique or professional training as such. They are learned in the hard business of engaging with contingent circumstances.[152] Thus, "an ethic of virtue always gains its intelligibility from narratives that place our lives within an adventure."[153] A community of virtue is the context in which such a character is trained and developed, both in regard to intentions and actions. Narrative reminds responders that they can, and will sometimes fail in that community pro-

---

148. See also Wright, *Use of the Bible*, 11.

149. Χαρακτηρ is only found once in the NT, in Heb 1:3, where it is used entirely differently than our modern psychological concept where character is developed by a will that "seeks to conform to principles." Χαρακτηρ refers to one on whom God has stamped his being, supremely his own Son. (See H. Haarbeck, "δοκιμος" and J. Gess, "Χαρακτηρ" in Brown, ed., *New International Dictionary of New Testament Theology*, 808-811 (hereafter referred to as *NIDNTT*); also vol. 2, 288–89.

150. 2 Cor 8:2; James 1:2; 1 Pet 1:7.

151. Hauerwas, *Community of Character*, 132, 135.

152. Loughlin, *Telling God's Story*, 70.

153. Hauerwas, *Community of Character*, 115. Ricoeur seems to follow Aristotle in placing character beneath action; or character is formed by action (*Time and Narrative*, vol. 1, 36–37, 46–47). Vanhoozer prefers the term "drama" to "adventure" but also emphasizes the dramatic, participatory concept that doctrine should effect in us (*Drama of Doctrine*, 16, also chapter 12).

cess as they learn. [154] Narrative is not about a "success story," but about a graced story of hope.

IDENTITY, COHERENCE, AND PURPOSE[155]—The essence of canonical linguistic and narrative theology is the pastoral contribution, which is central to my research purpose. The very nature of a major incident is traumatic, and trauma has the tendency to shatter one's identity, the self-hood of "who I am," by shattering so many assumptions about one's life and the world as a safe place. Because the narrative of trauma is incoherent there seems no purpose to what has happened amid a victim's discordance. Responders cannot effectively respond without an, albeit incomplete, always developing, coherence in their personal and community narrative; for them to do so would be like jumping into the sea to rescue a drowning person when they cannot swim.[156] Theology can help form narrative identities that enable the traumatized to "move on."[157] The intertextual approach means "the Bible intersects the 'autobiographical text' or life of the reader," so that the "biblical narrative figures and transfigures the reader's own historicity."[158] Narrative will not change the events, but it changes the way we perceive their reality. For Hauerwas, the Jesus narrative shaped community is the sphere where such perceptions and consequent identities are formed.

Canonical and narrative theology define identity differently to the world, where identity tends to be something we choose for ourselves. For Vanhoozer and Hauerwas it is something we are graciously gifted by the life, death, and resurrection of Jesus. Identity is formed by understanding who Jesus is and the difference this makes to one's life. The NT affirms

---

154. Loughlin also states that character is formed through the engagement with contingent circumstances, and reminds that the Hebrews narrative is so uniquely realistic in that the "heroes" invariably failed at certain (sometimes critical) junctures (*Telling God's Story*, 70–77).

155. By identity here I mean qualitative identity. This should not be confused with Murphy's concept of numeric identity (as in her discussion of the identity of a person after resurrection vis-a-vis that prior to resurrection). See Murphy, *Bodies and Souls?*, 132–45.

156. In his advocacy of a theology of the cross, I note Swinton uses the analogy of someone jumping down a well (John Swinton, "Why Me, Lord?" in Swinton and Payne, eds., *Living Well*, 126.

157. Graham, et al., *Theological Reflections*, 66.

158. Vanhoozer, *Biblical Narrative*, 199.

being united to Christ does create a transformed identity.[159] Thus, following Calvin, Christian identity comes through knowing ourselves and knowing God—in whatever order.[160] All true knowledge of our self requires knowing God, and knowing God is academic unless it discloses a true knowledge of self.

A final word of warning about becoming overenamored with the narrative approach deserves to be heard for pastoral reasons. Walton warns that the redemptive power of narrative cannot guarantee healing and release. Traumatic incidents will invariably withstand resolution by narrative because their pain and discordant notes will not succumb to narrative coherence. Sometimes we have to live with an incoherent narrative, and pastoral care must facilitate coming to terms with such.[161] Ricoeur recognized this in his insistence that narrative required balancing with the biblical genre of wisdom, by which the incoherence of life amidst tragedy is exposed, and for which lament forms the incomplete solution.[162] Thus, narrative is a resource, not a panacea, and is unreliable when used on its own, and is severely limited without the accompaniment of a canonical linguistic approach.

CONCLUSION

I conclude I have constructed a robust narrative methodology, combining *mimesis* and canonical linguistics, that holds exciting potential for this practical theological exploration, in three related parts, which focuses the necessary interaction between the traumatic realities of a major incident and relevant theological themes integral to a Christian pastoral response. The mimetic exploration can now commence.

---

159. Rom 6:17–18; Gal 2:20—the identity remains that of oneself, but one's previous identity is transformed through union with Christ's crucifixion. We should note the role of doctrine accorded to this transforming work as well, and be careful not to leave all to narrative, albeit that doctrine is formed out of narrative. From the perspective of a canonical linguistic theology's contribution to identity, see Vanhoozer, *Drama of Doctrine*, 392–96.

160. Calvin, *Calvin: Institutes*, vol. 1, 1:1.

161. Graham, et al., *Theological Reflection*, 74–76; Walton, "Speaking in Signs."

162. According to Wallace, "Can God be Named?"

PART 1

Mimesis₁—Prefiguration

MY RESEARCH INTEREST ARISES from the significant personal context of responding to a major incident. "Articulated subjectivity"
is inevitable in this project.[1] Since this subjectivity plays a large part in
motivating my interest, it is significant for me to narrate that experience
as a context for my research. However, both prior to and after my own
experience, there were many other major incidents involving pastoral
carers, which provide a wider contextual narrative to my project.[2]

Part 1 of this dissertation is a narrative of my own prefigured narrative to a major incident.[3] It involved me responding to a major air disaster,
which happened on the M1 motorway, near to the village of Kegworth,
on the borders of Leicestershire, Derbyshire, and Nottinghamshire, as a
flight attempted an emergency landing at the East Midlands Airport. The
incident happened on the evening of January 8, 1989, and my involvement, for the purposes of this research, lasted for two years.

I utilize Ricoeur's hermeneutical interpretive narrative theory of
mimesis1 as the method for this prefiguration. That is to say, I recount my

1. "Articulated subjectivity" is a term used by Robert Jay Lifton (an American
psychiatrist who studied war victims) to refer to the use of self as an investigative
instrument (*Home From the War*). Also, Judith Armstrong has stated, "Your research
will be an expression of who you are because there is a profound connection between a
researcher's personality and his or her research" (Armstrong, "Emotional Issues," 175).
See also Jackson, *Priority of Love*, xi; Plude, "Coping With Disaster."

2. For a summary of these see below, Appendix 1, pp. 373–78.

3. I can judge it as prefigured because I had never responded to a major incident
before, nor had I been involved in any emergency planning for such. My response
was, thus, simply on the basis of what I knew at the time. My prefiguration comes
from knowing how people in the real world behave based on our day-to-day experience, because narrative is always based on some basic grasp of reality. See Simms, *Paul
Ricoeur*, 84.

experience/actions as a Christian responder from the perspective of actions already configured at a pre-narrative level, and naming these, relating them to motive, cause, or reason, and even evaluating them as good or bad.[4] Because the events of the response period are etched upon my memory so clearly still, I believe I can recount my experience as near to the perspective of that period, without overmuch additional hindsight.[5]

What makes mimesis1 so appropriate as my methodology is the invitation it gives to state my experience in terms of my actions, as it happened, taking into account the "routinely acquired skills of perception and self-consciousness and pre-understanding of the human experience of time" and my presuppositions.[6] Ricoeur proposed mimesis1 should expose the *aporias* of lived experience to which narrative configuration responds. It displays discordance rending concordance (à la Augustine).[7] Therefore, I present my prefigured experience and understanding in response to the structural questions—What did I do? Why did I do it? Who did I do it for? How did I do it? With whom did I do it? What hindered it?—narratively, only to the extent that "minimal narrative appears most simply in a sentence indicating the action of a subject in a particular situation."[8] I also take into account the cultural symbols of these actions and acknowledge the temporality of the experience that makes it in need of configuration into a meaningful narrative for readers to refigure into that which can give greater wisdom to future responders. I structure my account under the different stages of response and relate the salient aspects under different categories of involvement.[9]

---

4. I am grateful to Dr. David Pellauer for clarification on this point of what to include in a prefigured account (email communication on September 9, 2009). One needs to remember that the mimetic process is cyclical, so each prefigured narrative may well have come about as a result of someone's prior refiguration thereby rendering a prefigured account as, inevitably, narrival to a point.

5. The sources of my prefiguration are, principally: my own memories, supplemented by notes (including a few personal diary entries) I made at the time, together with the official reports, other news articles I either read or authored, and notes taken from the inquest, etc.

6. Head, *Cambridge Introduction*, 11.

7. Taylor, review of *Time and Narrative*.

8. Dornisch, "Ricoeur's Theory of Mimesis," 310. The questions are suggested by Ricoeur, in his "Time and Narrative: Threefold Mimesis" in *Time and Narrative*, vol. 1, chapter 3.

9. Gibson gives some indication of these stages in respect to her taxonomy of crises. See Gibson, *Order from Chaos*, 46–51.

4

A Prefigured Response

IMPACT STAGE

Initiating Response

WHEN I FIRST RECEIVED news of the aircrash incident, during the Sunday evening of January 8, 1989, at around 9 p.m., my initial reaction was hesitation.[1] I was sure there must be systems in place already for controlling the response, and accredited pastoral carers would know who they were and when and how to respond.[2] Yet, I felt deeply uneasy about doing nothing. As a pastor it was instinctive to try and do something to help in such distressing situations, but hesitation has been a feature of my life, out of fear of rejection or of interfering. Furthermore, I was a part of the conservative Evangelical culture—which did not readily get its hands dirty with such incidents and the liberal ecumenical cohabitation they assume response systems would necessitate. It was a culture of detachment, not involvement. By this hesitation, I lost perhaps two hours of response time, and the opportunity for more constructive involvement at the immediate post-impact stage.[3] I was concerned about

1. The providential coincidence of being informed by a church member who was looking after the children of a nurse in the Leicester Royal Infirmary Accident and Emergency Dept, was not lost on me. This nurse was being sent with the A & E "flying squad" to the scene. The plane (a Boeing 737-400 series), crashed onto the northern embankment of the M1 motorway, near the village of Kegworth, at precisely 2024.43 hrs, at an air speed of 115 knots (Trimble, "4/1990 Boeing 737-400, G-OBME").

2. At this stage I was not officially accredited, in terms of being formally included in the emergency plan call-out procedure. At this stage (1989) emergency planning procedures were far more primitive than they are today, when, at least in theory, more details have been mapped out.

3. In offering my services to subsequent major incident responses—for example,

possible compromises of doctrine and ecclesiology through involvement. However, my instincts overtook these cultural influences, and I decided to take the initiative and contact the airport authorities to offer my services as a pastoral carer. My offer was accepted, and I was instructed to proceed directly to the incident scene. At the temporary incident control room in Kegworth village, I received the necessary authorization for being taken directly to the crash site.

Though general recommendations from emergency plans today strongly indicate that no one should respond to an incident until they are officially instructed to do so, I believe my instinctive response during this initial phase was justified, though it is hard to disentangle, or prioritize, my motives of that evening. The initiative I believe was right in view of the clergy call-out system being delayed until the early hours of the following day.[4] It raises the questions: Why is there the instinct to respond? Is this an especially Christian instinct? Why did I really take that initiative that went against my theological culture? How should I balance the natural hesitation to respond—thereby risking delay—with any natural lust for adventure and opportunism?[5] How should we read the coincidences of life around such times? Can these phenomena be given coherent clarification, theologically?

Actual response

At the scene the chief incident officer (CIO)[6] informed me there was little he felt I could do, but I was welcome to remain, observe, and mingle, if I wished. I accepted this offer and spent the remaining four hours or so (until around 2:30 a.m.) watching the process of extraction and rescue of the injured, and the recovery of the dead from the broken fuselage. The

---

the Hillsborough stadium disaster, the London bombings ("7/7"), I experienced the same hesitation. In the case of "7/7" this was educated far more by my awareness of how systems had developed, and the awareness that terrorist related incidents would make accreditation essential as I assumed at the time.

4. Though I was not to know this until during the official clergy debrief, which took place three weeks or so later.

5. I had recognized these as features within my own character long before Kegworth/M1.

6. Who in this instance was a senior police officer, which is usually the case, though not necessarily so. In the case of Kegworth/M1, as with most incidents, it was regarded as a potential scene of a crime. Furthermore, because of the Northern Ireland dynamic, the terrorist element could not be ruled out given that there were military personnel onboard the flight.

former were evacuated by RAF CASEVAC helicopter and road ambulances to the receiving hospitals, and the latter to the temporary mortuary.[7] I have great regrets over the decision to not involve myself that evening. I was shocked by the scenes I witnessed but admired the great many responders already working together harmoniously. I so wanted to be part of that team, to do something useful. Yet, I felt so useless.[8] I did not take any more initiative to secure more profitable involvement that evening, for fear of being an interference. Later I was to learn that just being there at the scene provided some useful credibility for me as a pastoral carer. However, the sense of uselessness coupled with some anger at the CIO's immediate negative response to my offer stayed with me for a long period afterward. This increased in the following months as I learned there had been passengers (some were committed Christians) still trapped in the fuselage awaiting extraction as I looked on.[9] I also regret my own inertia at not mingling more with rescue personnel, who I could have been of some pastoral value to. Why did I not do that, given the strength of my initial instinct to be of help? Should I have been more persistent with the CIO? Since the response, numerous friends have suggested that had I become more involved in the casualty recovery and evacuation of that night, and witnessed the scenes of carnage inside the aircraft, I may not have been able to be as useful as I was in the aftermath. This may well be true in view of the fact that I was the only clergy person at the scene who continued as a pastoral carer through the ensuing response stages. Yet, such counsel did little to assuage my regret. Why? This experience has created an *aporia*, which I explore being clarified by configuration.[10]

7. CASEVAC refers to casualty evacuation, and is a service provided by the military for extreme emergencies in both war and peacetime contexts. The receiving hospitals were the Derbyshire Royal Infirmary, the Queen's Medical Centre, Nottingham, and the Leicester Royal Infirmary. A few casualties were later transported to other centers for specialist treatment for their injuries. The temporary mortuary was set up in a hangar at the East Midlands Airport, Castle Donnington, just a mile or so away from the crash site.

8. Responders came from among the public traveling on the motorway, from the village of Kegworth, from the police, fire, and ambulance services, from the military, the AA, Mountain Rescue, RNLI, and Cave Rescue services, etc. Of the 126 passengers and crew on the flight, 39 died at the scene, with a further eight dying from their injuries later. Seventy-four were seriously injured.

9. I later received an apology from the police for this decision, which went some way to mitigating my sense of grievance.

10. Ricoeur did not claim that configuration will resolve the *aporia*, only that it may help clarify it (Taylor, review of *Time and Narrative*, 381).

Immediate Post-Impact

Work with the Bereaved

The day after the crash I was invited to report to the East Midlands Airport, where I was deputed to the adjoining Donnington Thistle Hotel complex, where relatives and friends of the bereaved were being ushered.[11] There I was given further accreditation by the police and authorized to move freely within the cordons and among all involved. I was given no formal instructions but left to my own initiative. On entering the designated lounge area, I introduced myself to two men who, I discovered, had traveled up from London during the night. Once they were assured of my credentials, they spoke to me freely. One told of his fear that his wife had died in the crash; the other already knew that his wife and two young sons had perished.[12] These men were colleagues together in business, and in the next day or so introduced me to another mother and adult son who had lost a son (and brother) who had also worked for the same company.

I worked as a chaplain to these persons and to their wider families as they joined us through the week. I decided my primary role was to represent Christ as a compassionate presence and listener. Over the seven days or so they visited the hotel, I became a close confidante and advisor.[13] I was invited by one of these men on one occasion to pray openly in the hotel lounge with him and with his relatives. They joked that they wanted a Roman Catholic priest, but all they could get was an Evangelical pastor! This man's remaining son, who had been away on an overseas school trip, soon joined the group.[14] I will never forget the meeting between him—now bereft of his mother and brothers—and his father, in the hotel

---

11. Many of these were flown in on special flights from Northern Ireland, by British Midland, the concerned aircraft company carrier, because the crashed flight had been a shuttle service between London Heathrow and Belfast International Airport, Aldergrove.

12. At this time I had two children who were of similar ages to the sons who died, and this fact gave me some empathy with these cases. Both cases involved children who were either bereaved or killed.

13. I am very careful to stress that I was never their *counselor*. Though there were some Samaritans present on the first day after the crash, and social workers that remained throughout, there were never any professional counselors, as such, present. No attempt was made to engage in counseling as far as I knew.

14. In other words, had he not been on that trip he would have likely been on the flight that crashed.

lobby. Witnessing that meeting, also hearing the deepest sobbing from a mother that punctuated the already profoundly somber atmosphere of the lounge area, brought home to me the overwhelming grief dynamic that distinguishes a major incident from others. It is the corporate grief over sudden deaths that haunts you. Death becomes super-horrible, utterly indiscriminate, and totally uninvited and unexpected, at the end of an incoherent, heterogonous trail of events.

Part of my role became liaison/advocacy work, as I would be asked to liaise between the relatives/friends and the investigative agencies when they had no energy or heart left to do it themselves. Of particular struggle to the families was the apparent lack of information coming from the investigative agencies, especially concerning where their deceased were, the condition they were in, and when they could be viewed. This was an awkward time for me as I tried to be an advocate for the bereaved while understanding the difficulties the authorities were having in formally identifying the dead prior to permitting viewing by relatives.[15] They assumed I could respond with some accuracy to their questions concerning the circumstances of the aircraft crashing, and, in particular, that I could confirm their deceased did not suffer prior to dying. I found responding wisely to such persistent questioning very harrowing, especially in regard to my three families, as the investigation proceeded, reasons for which I will return to below. This role led to me accompanying these families as they viewed their deceased, in a designated room, tastefully set out, adjoining the temporary mortuary. These were intensely emotional sessions for all concerned, though somewhat satisfying to the bereaved.[16] Another harrowing aspect of my role was when I accompanied one man to where the recovered personal effects had been taken, in Leicester. These were in a large pile on the floor of a room, and the poor man had the job of sifting his way through it all until, item by item, he recovered as much as he could identify. On the journey back to the airport he begged me to stop on the hard shoulder, at the site of the crash. He climbed up the embankment to the spot where his beloved wife and sons had perished.

15. I was informed at one stage of concern over the visual state of some of the deceased. As it turned out, the bodies at Kegworth/M1 were all relatively intact compared with some other major incidents around that time, e.g., Lockerbie (December 1988).

16. Each family was offered and accompanied by a pastoral carer, social worker, and detective. For a recent academic research study on the disputed therapeutic value of viewing the body of a deceased following a traumatic death, see Howarth, "Viewing the Body."

That was important for him, and I was happy to oblige despite the technical illegality of such a maneuver.

A further detail to my role during the first week of response, was to assist with a colleague, in the debriefing of the airport fire and rescue service "watch" that had responded to the crash scene. Theirs had been an extraordinary feat, since they had to negotiate dense traffic to be confronted with a fuselage split in two places, with aviation fuel spilling from the underwing tanks, as members of the public were responding to the injured and dying, both inside and outside of the aircraft. Had this fuel become vaporized, ignition would have certainly resulted in an all-consuming inferno. The response of the watch prevented that happening, at no small risk to them. Following their duty, they did not return to work for some days. When their next duty came, they returned to the fire station to find other investigative agencies were using their staff mess as a site for sorting identifying items, such as intimate personal effects belonging to the casualties. They were deeply distressed by this and their senior officer called for a visit from the pastoral care team. We listened as, one by one, various crew members told their stories of what they had done and how they were feeling about it. At the end I was asked to pray for the assembled gathering. A sequel to this was I initiated opportunities for the watch to visit the receiving hospitals and meet again the patients they had helped rescue; a visit they found greatly rewarding for their own healing, given the gratitude of the casualties. Again I judged that initiative to be a sound one, befitting my role.

Work with the Injured

Mainly this took place following the departure of the bereaved from the Thistle Hotel, just over a week after the crash. I decided to focus upon survivors in the Leicester Royal Infirmary (LRI). The reason for this choice was because it was the hospital I was most familiar with from my church pastoral work. But there was another reason. While I was working at the Thistle Hotel the man bereaved of his wife and sons asked me if he could make a visit to that hospital, to visit some survivors. He wanted to set his own losses in the perspective of so many surviving the crash. I had some reservations about this request but did not voice them or contest the request. I obtained consent from the nursing staff for such a visit and accompanied the man. By the time we had arrived back at the Thistle Hotel I think we both felt it had been a mistake, for the man himself and for the survivors. It exposed the potential for conflict and misunderstanding between the bereaved and survivors in major incidents.[17] It reinforced to the man that he was bereaved while others survived, and it made the survivors feel guilty about surviving. It was also while I was on this visit that the staff requested I met a young, bereaved casualty, who they feared was becoming severely depressed. This man's situation again exposed the indiscriminate nature of the incident. His recently wed wife had perished beside him while he had been saved by the quick actions of a passing motorist. He poured out his story to me as I sat and listened. I then prayed with him, and promised to return. This became the first of many visits to this man, including attending the surrogate thanksgiving service for his wife, in a hospital side ward, while the funeral service was taking place in her European home town. I also visited several other men, all with various degrees of serious injury, one with life-threatening injuries, and offered support to their visiting relatives and friends. I continued my regular visits until the last patient went home, three months after the crash.

In respect of the bereaved patient: he once asked me if I could discover who the person was who had saved his life, a man he called his "angel." I was able to do this, through police sources, and to arrange a meeting between the "angel" and his wife (who also had given valuable assistance to the injured at the scene) and the man in hospital. This meeting was judged to be of value to all parties.

Throughout my experience in visiting both bereaved and survivors I never encountered any hostility toward God, or to my role as a Christian carer. I discovered, from the military police, there was a member of the military who had been injured and was at the LRI. He was from my native Cornwall so I chose to visit him, a visit he later expressed great appreciation for in a letter to me. He also acknowledged that whereas he had not been a religious man, the events of the crash had led even him to think and pray.

A further facet I must record is the experience of working with victims in such an ecumenical context.[18] The pastoral care team was ecumenical in nature, involving pastoral carers from the Roman Catholic, Anglican, United Reformed, Baptist, and Evangelical Free Church traditions. Though I feel now I could have done so much more in terms of social grace with other pastoral carers, I nevertheless held each of them

17. I quickly learned there are different dynamics in working with the bereaved and with the survivors.

18. In this particular incident the casualties were mainly, not exclusively, Protestant or Roman Catholic. I do not recall whether a few may have been of other faiths.

in highest esteem for being there. This ecumenical response challenged my separatist cultural presuppositions into increasing shame—a challenge I now feel very grateful for. This shame was reinforced just some weeks after the incident when I attended a meeting of pastors in London. During the usual discussion session a pastor asked what we should make of these disasters; what was God telling the nation, and what should we think of the many liberal ministers who were responding and delivering "wishy-washy" sermons in the memorial services?[19] The chairman of the fellowship knew I was present and invited me to respond. I simply said that I had felt responding to the aircrash to be a great honor, as it also had been to work with the "liberals." I concluded by saying, "At least they were there, when many Evangelicals were not," and sat down. Little was said on the matter after that.

Longer Term Post-Impact

For many months, even years, after a major incident, the processes of investigation, litigation, medical treatment, physical and emotional recovery, and even spiritual transformation, carry on regardless of the fact that the public soon forgets and moves on until the next newsworthy crisis. My role as a pastoral carer was not for the short-term. There are five particular periods I feel warrant recording, due to the discordance they left:

Private Reflection

Some weeks after the crash I received a visit from a police detective who was interviewing responders as a part of the investigation process. I mention this because, up until then, I had resolutely focused on the needs of "my" families. I had not imbibed much general detail about the incident as a whole. I was dealing with just a few pieces of the jigsaw. That interview resulted in me being given a much larger and detailed picture of the magnitude of the crash. As I lay in bed later that evening, the events overcame me emotionally, and for the first time in my involvement I silently wept. This occurred again the next day as I was trying to work in my church study, only this time in an even greater degree of emotional collapse—in that privacy, I too sobbed, and I felt so tired. As a traumatized responder, I felt the need to talk about Kegworth/M1, but found

---

19. Kegworth/M1 occurred during the so-called "Decade of Disasters" in the UK, when many major incidents had already taken place. See below, [xref].

few people seemed to have the heart or patience to listen (more than once). However, after having done the talking, I always felt, "What did that achieve? What difference did doing that make?" This lasted for more than a year after the crash. For the same period I found myself anticipating another imminent lurid incident and constantly thought about how I would handle it better.[20]

Work in Northern Ireland

I was invited to attend two memorial services for the incident in Belfast, Northern Ireland. There are three reasons why I refer to these:

First, because they highlight a peculiar dynamic of fear that punctuated my response. This was the fear of flying. Prior to Kegworth/M1 I had never flown in my life, and flying used to invade my worst dreams. When I received the official invitation to fly across to Belfast from the East Midlands Airport, it resurrected my worst fear as never before. Strangely, this haunted the few weeks between the invitation arriving and my flight. It provoked more fear in me than anything the incident response had created, for by then I knew in some detail what could really happen when a plane crashes. Yet, I could not refuse to go. Two things in particular helped me accept the invitation, in fear and trembling. The first was the fact that many of the bereaved and survivors had dared to fly home to Belfast. The second was the value of prayer. I shared my fears with God in prayer, and I also shared them openly with my church and asked them to pray for me as well.

Second, while in Northern Ireland I was accommodated by one of the businessmen I have referred to. There I was introduced to his extended Roman Catholic family and work colleagues, to many of whom (quite unknowingly) I had become somewhat of a "hero." Again, this figures in my account because I found the love and respect offered me from this Catholic family to be emotionally overwhelming and deeply spiritually humbling for me. On the second visit I was able to help a Christian family who had lost a wife/mother and teenage son/sibling in the crash. They had made the decision not to view his body, but wanted to know more of the details concerning the crash from my being there on the night and involved with the response over the following year.

Third, I had the option, when attending the memorial service, of joining the official procession of civic dignitaries and clergy at the

20. Soon after Kegworth/M1 a fire chief told me this was exactly how his own colleagues were feeling after their response to that incident.

commencement of the service. I made a deliberate choice not to join this, preferring to sit with the people I was serving. I struggled then, and still do, with the official pomp of such occasions, and apparent preferential focus in the seating arrangements given to political dignitaries over victims and their families, and even responders. Yet, my concerns have to be weighed against the benefit victims gain from knowing that the nation cares, as represented in the presence of civic dignitaries.

Work at the AAIB

On two occasions the Air Accidents Investigation Branch (AAIB), in Farnborough, Hampshire, invited the bereaved, survivors, and myself, to meet members of their investigation team, to be brought up to date with the investigation ahead of any public announcements, and to view the recovered wreckage of the aircraft. These were incredibly emotional events, yet equally helpful for the attendees. They provided valuable information and explanation to satiate the appetites of the bereaved and survivors for understanding of what happened to cause the crash. Even so, the investigation exposed more starkly the extremely complex, contingent causals of major incidents, especially transport incidents.[21] The investigations and inquiries could find no signs of terrorism, engineering malpractice, or airline operator blame.[22] It was all terrible "bad luck." Can theology provide anything for pastoral care responders to help supply some understanding, or coherence, for such things?

A Cosmic Dimension

After eighteen months or so following the crash, a popular evangelical magazine published an article in which the author purported to have had a vision, around the time of the crash, in which his attention was drawn to the influence of malevolent spiritual forces having some bearing on the confusion, which he alleged took place in the cockpit of the aircraft as an emergency landing was being effected. Also, his attention was drawn to a

---

21. In this particular incident: How does a single freak fan blade shear causing an engine failure—that, ordinarily, is manageable but for the confusion caused by smoke in the cockpit and analogue warning dials that are too small to read in a crisis, leading to experienced pilots shutting down the wrong engine of an airplane carrying no few Christians, and a generic hierarchical airline culture that hindered passengers and cabin crew communicating with the flight deck—all fit into a conceptuality of divine love, providence, and human freedom?

22. For a detailed account of the possible causes of Kegworth/M1, see Trimble, "4/1990 Boeing 737-400, G-OBME."

wooded copse area beyond the western end of the airport perimeter. The author asked some friends to investigate the copse, which they did, and he claims they discovered evidence of satanic worship having taken place there recently.[23] Using this information he prophesied that satanic forces had a key bearing on the cause of the crash through confusing the pilot and copilot, and provoking them to argue as to which engine they ought to close down, resulting in them shutting down the wrong engine. In his article the author made allegations concerning the alleged confusion that just did not tally with my own understanding from the Air Accidents Investigation Branch's official report of what had taken place, including cockpit voice recordings.[24]

Work at the Inquest

I worked with the bereaved and survivors' group created from Kegworth/M1, prior to the inquest, to be held at Prestwold Hall, some two miles northeast of Loughborough, during May, 1990. I was asked to be a chaplain at the inquest with the role of being a presence for those attending in whatever capacity, but principally for the people I had been helping already.

However, I also had a problem of my own to prepare for. At some stage during the months after the crash, I came to learn from the investigation that the deceased of one of the persons I was helping had not died at the scene as they had presumed. They had been evacuated alive, albeit unconscious and critically injured, to one of the receiving hospitals where they died after maybe two hours. However, they had not been identified at the point of rescue. Knowing how the bereaved believed the loved one had died at the scene and had felt it pointless going to any of the receiving hospitals to look for them, I then learned that a different account would come out at the inquest. I endeavored to investigate, as much as I could, the actual circumstances of this death, so that I could prepare the family for hearing the inevitable at the inquest. However, the coroner was adamant he could not release information either to me or to the family prior to the inquest. I deeply regretted I could not reveal what I suspected to be the truth about this person's death to the family until they heard it in detail from the pathologist's evidence at the coroner's

23. The author did not live anywhere near the East Midlands area, where the crash occurred.

24. For the article, see the editorial in *Prophecy Today* 6, (September/October 1990).

court. It left me feeling I had failed that family in an ethically significant way.[25] The inquest also heralded another problem for me, which again stemmed from details that had been communicated to me by a member of the public who had responded to the scene of the crash. They had heard someone calling out for their mother as they were dying, having been extracted from the aircraft. They felt confident in identifying that person as being one of the two children who had died, of a man I was helping. I shared this possibility with the man, but subsequent inquiries proved these details may well have been wrong, and the child who cried out may have been the child of another mother who also died at the scene. This raises again the problems information demand places upon responders in the "fog of disaster," when even intrepid media reporters cannot guarantee reporting the events accurately. It also exposes the temptation for a responder to indulge his/her egotistical lust for being "in the know" of significant details about a person that others are unaware of, and being the first to reveal them. I regretted profoundly my part in this particular debacle, and it is something I sought forgiveness for, both from God and from the father concerned.

Work with the Memorial Garden

A small plaque was erected early on, in honor of those who died and those who responded, on a road bridge crossing the motorway, just north of the crash site. Its size and site, however, were never adequate. In the spring of 1990 I read in a newspaper concerning a local landowner trying to adjust his initial offer of some land to be for a *temporary* memorial only, a condition utterly unacceptable to the victims' group. I got in touch with their spokesperson in Northern Ireland and offered to act as advocate and mediator again for the group, which was accepted. I quickly contacted the chairperson of Kegworth Parish Council to discuss possible alternative sites. Before too long we all agreed upon a site in the village cemetery. I was able to negotiate, through a friend at a local quarry, a *gratis* donation of a huge lump of local granite, to be the centerpiece of the memorial site. It was eventually laid on the top of soil taken from the crash site when the M1 was widened at that site. Kegworth Parish Council then arranged to have the rock embedded with a plaque inscribed with the names of

---

25. I regret it even more now, having learned that the coroner could well have been more helpful and obliging towards my ethical dilemma as a pastoral carer. Happily, the family did not hold it against me and understood the impossible position I had been placed in, when I explained it to them afterwards.

the deceased, another plaque honoring those who responded, and one inscribed with the words of Romans 8:28. I attended the consecrating of the garden in an ecumenical service.

The "Angel"

After 1990, my involvement with the response to Kegworth/M1 continued intermittently, usually as a result of one or another of the bereaved and survivors telephoning for a talk or from the media contacting me for information at anniversaries. There is one particular case that warrants recording that happened some years after the crash. This concerned the "Angel" and his wife, who responded to the crash as they were traveling home on the motorway. Both had become involved in saving the lives of different people that night, and afterwards they simply continued their journey home. Some years later the wife contacted me in some distress over the state of her husband and the effect he was having upon their marriage and family life. By this time I had some understanding of post-traumatic stress symptoms, and I was able to put them in touch with an experienced consultant psychiatrist, the sequel to which was a successful treatment program and full recovery for the man, his wife, and their marriage. This crisis, which concerned non-Christians, emphasized to me the intensely spiritual dynamics to trauma, a persuasion the whole of major incident response often impressed on me. It also proved the value of pastoral carers working in tandem with experts in the human and clinical science disciplines. I explore the coherence for this in my configuration below.

CONCLUSIONS

My prefigured narrative left me with numerous *aporias*, which can be summarized by the following discordant questions:

Why had this awful tragedy happened?[26]

Why did sudden death come as such an evil for the bereaved, irrespective of their religious beliefs? Why was death so indiscriminate and seemingly unfair?

---

26. This question became increasingly acute as the investigation advanced. In fact it took two further incidents, where engines of the same type failed in similar fashion, thankfully without further incapacitation of, or damage to, the aircraft or passengers concerned.

How could such traumatized people forgive God, or any other persons implicated with blame?

How should pastoral care respond to concerns about the postmortem status of the deceased?

Why is viewing the deceased so important for many, even if it is just a body part?

What possible role can theology serve for Christian responders in the midst of such tragedy where the empirical reality tests propositional theological dogmatics beyond its limits?

What wisdom can theology help create for enabling Christian pastoral carers respond to the spiritual crises, and theological *aporias*, victims encounter?

What help can theology be in helping Christian responders recover from the traumas they have seen, smelled, and heard, with an enhanced sense of identity and purpose?

Is there a theology that legitimates Evangelicals working ecumenically, and even in interfaith friendship?

How can the Christian community train and prepare pastoral carers for responding?

This level of discordance provides the basis for the next part to my dissertation —namely, the application of mimesis$_2$ as a process for exploring a theology for configuration, with the use of a canonical linguistic approach, for some coherence of understanding and personal identity.

Part 2

Mimesis$_2$—Configuration

RICOEUR'S THEORY OF MIMESIS embodied his philosophical outlook: centering upon the human being as hopeful and as surplus of possibility, rich with a project-forming capability for which language and texts are the means.[1] Mimesis$_2$ is the method of creating a reality out of what is already and what is possible. This mimetic mode mediates, by configuring temporal practical experience into something meaningful for future action, through emplotment.[2] Cognition, along with imagination and affection, become means for invention and discovery of the possible in time and eternity. For Ricoeur it was important to live in two worlds: the empirical world, which is actually supplanted by the possible world. Actuality is both what is, and what if. The essence of a thing is discovered through exploring its possibilities through the medium of imagination and feeling.[3] Illusion is avoided in the refigurative process by ensuring

---

1. The NT states this as, "the substance of things hoped for" (Heb 11:1), and "it has not yet been revealed what we shall be" (1 John 3:2).

2. Ricoeur, *Time and Narrative*, vol. 1, 53.

3. Vanhoozer, *Biblical Narrative*, 20. Ricoeur's focus upon fiction as equally significant as history has exposed his theory to the possibility of illusion and make-believe. Vanhoozer's response to this vulnerability is to insist the scriptural canon is the measure against which what is real and possible should be decided. This is based upon the central fact of God's breaking in, in revelation, revealing possibility through promises, metaphors, and parables, serving a link between God's actions in the past and future possibility (*Biblical Narrative*, 104–8). For the idea of illusion in philosophical free will conception, see Saul Smilansky, "Free Will, Fundamental Dualism and the Centrality of Illusion," in Kane, ed., *Oxford Handbook,* 489–505. By illusion Smilansky does not

one adheres to the language of praxis. Theologically accounted, configuration is a facet of the *imago Dei* by which we are enabled to create our possibility through creative language, particularly deployed by special grace. This resonates with the biblical concept of the development of character through the constructive interpretation of life experience by faith. Though there are suspicious Pelagian aspects to Ricoeur's philosophical theology, his concept of imagination seems to equate with Augustine's two cities and the biblical concept of regeneration as new creation (2 Cor 5:17) and faith (Heb 11:1), wherein the believer comes to realize things can become actual that before seemed impossibly unreal in an empirical sense.[4] I explore whether we can configure a new reality out of the dismal empirical experiences of a major incident.

To configure my experience of major incident response (MIR), I utilize Ricoeur's mimesis$_2$ but now engage Vanhoozer's canonical linguistic approach to respond to the fundamental aporias, categorized under the research questions: What legitimation do pastoral carers have for responding Christianly? What doctrinal formulations help configure the pastoral carer's contribution to major incident response? A related question that must run parallel to these is: What kind of person do I need to be to respond to the questions of incoherence and discordance that major incident response throws up? Thus, my thesis is: in order to contribute Christianly in MIR, I need to be a canonically configured sort of person, because the primary issue in MIR is not how can I answer all the questions of incoherence and discordance, but how can I be the kind of person that is best placed to live with these issues, to operate the theological theodrama responsibly toward others? How can theology configure a series of different, discordant microstories into a single concordant narrative? In perspective, this is drawn together by Paul's affirmation in Rom 8:28 "And we know that all things [all the discordant micronarratives] work together for good to those who love God, to those

---

mean that we should induce illusory beliefs, or that we should live with beliefs we believe are illusory. Rather, he means illusory beliefs are already in place and these can work positively. He argues these are necessary to prevent determinism destroying innocence or threatening responsibility, a sense of value, or remorse and integrity.

4. This also resonates with the two realities Hart thinks the Christian should see at the same time: the reality of the beautiful and yet broken world as it is, and the "world [of creation] in its first and ultimate truth" (*Doors of the Sea*, 60). Taking this into account we can say actuality is also what *will be*. Zizioulas sees the regenerate person as something that separates humans from their created limitation (*Being as Communion*, 54).

who are called according to His purpose [the concordant metanarrative or theodrama]."[5] This draws upon the need for Vanhoozer's focus upon the primacy of *sapientia*, or canonical wisdom, more than propositional knowledge/information. It also establishes the plot to be God with us in Jesus Christ. It is the "mystery of godliness" that forms the meaning to all other aspects of the theodrama.[6]

For Ricoeur, mimesis₂ represents the mediating process that transfigures the one side of the text to the other by way of configuration.[7] The genius of Ricoeur's theory accords well with the biblical concepts of transformation, which promise freedom from an imprisonment of victimhood—that is, "This is what happened to me, therefore I cannot be other than tragically, irreversibly, disabled," becomes, "This is how what has happened has helped enable me."[8] The genius of Vanhoozer's theory is that it provides the canonical linguistic interrogation of transformative doctrines that hold the potential for this *eucatastrophic* configuration.[9]

I proceed through the process of mimesis₂ by exploring the following theological/doctrinal themes: evil and suffering; trauma; grace; compassion; reconciliation and justice; ecumenical and interfaith friendship. I have made this selection on the basis of what addresses most the aporias my prefigured narrative has exposed and what relates to a legitimate and contributive response. It is selective, not exhaustive, given the limitations imposed on PhD research projects. A notable omission is the doctrine of providence that, I have concluded after extensive research work, possesses massive literature, is hugely controversial, but is inconclusive, even among evangelicals, for major incidents where any one of a multiple of factors may be significant. I do, however, give brief reflection upon the most controversial aspect of the doctrine—theodicy. Even though my project is for the benefit of the evangelical catholic Christian community, I do not include ecclesiology in my selection. While there can be

5. The context is that of the aporia of persecutory sufferings of the Roman Christians.

6. See Matt 1:23, "Immanuel . . . God with us"; 1 Tim 3:16, "God was manifested in the flesh . . ."

7. Ricoeur, *Time and Narrative*, vol. 1, 53.

8. Jesus implied such a transformative purpose to his messianic work in Luke 4:18–19.

9. A *eucatastrophe* is a cataclysmic event with a beneficial effect (2 Cor 5:19) (Vanhoozer, *Drama of Doctrine*, 38). J. R. R. Tolkien described it as a term, "for a spectacularly good thing happening to spectacularly bad people" (quoted in Yancey, *Soul Survivor*, 6).

conflicts within emergency planning regarding which should be the lead agency for faith community response, in reality a distinct ecclesiology plays no crucial part in a response by the Christian traditions within the UK. Indeed, my focus seeks to dilute the emphasis upon any particular church tradition, by the inclusion of the concept of catholicity. However, I am comfortable that my choice of themes has both rigorously tested my methodology and helped configure my narrative for constructive refiguration.

5

Legitimation—Evil and Suffering

LEGITIMATION

ONE OF THE DISCORDANT issues within my own narrative is that of theological and systemic legitimation. This accounted for my initial hesitation: Why should I respond? Why did I feel that compulsion, as a pastor, to take the initiative? Was that adventurism, humanitarianism, or something more profoundly rooted in a distinctly Christian wisdom? In the interests of configuration, I explore the following questions: What is the theological perspective given by the theodrama upon major incidents? And, in parallel: What kind of person should I be to interpret such a perspective sapientially? There are three theological themes I explore, which respond to these questions: evil and suffering; the theology of trauma (inclusive of death and bereavement); and divine grace. I found each of these basic to the pastoral care I proffered at Kegworth/M1. They also overlap configuring the contribution Christian responders can make, but for now I will only explore aspects that relate to legitimation.

EVIL AND SUFFERING

The canonical theodrama emplots God's eucatastrophic response to the catastrophe of evil and to issuant suffering. The theodrama commences with an embodiment of evil (the serpent) tempting Adam and Eve into disobedience, fueling their own lust for autonomy from God's goodness, blinding them to the liberty they already possessed.[1] This delusion

---

1. See Gen 3:1–6. Freedom, in a theodramatic sense, is my will delighting in and "freely" choosing the will of God (John 8:34–36). For the purposes of mimesis2 it makes little difference whether one interprets Gen 1–3 as historical narrative or as poetic symbol/*muthos*. For Ricoeur's mimesis2 the use of fiction was justifiable in order

precipitates an experience of shame and pain in regards to their intra-
and inter-relational perception.[2] Pain, blame, expulsion, punishment,
and alienation become consequences,[3] added to which are guaranteed
the pains from life in a cursed world—from both animate and inanimate
nature.[4] Yet, hard on the heels of such evil and tragedy comes the proto-
evangelical Christological "seed(s)" of hope, configuring the Christocentric emplotment for the rest of the drama.[5] The ensuing theodrama is a
configuring of this incursion of evil and suffering into God's "very good"
creation and of God's response to it. This response is processed through
a community of God's covenant people (Israel/Judah) as a precursor
and antitype to the very Son of God himself entering the cosmic and
human fray. He comes as the savior from sin and healer from suffering.[6]
His response is supremely care-full and pastoral, a paradigm for pastoral
care, which Christ mandates the new covenant spirited community to
continue.[7] In theodramatic terms, Jesus is God incarnate, and in him we
understand how God responds to evil and suffering because he is God's
response.

---

to explore the possible. My concern at this stage, in my interpretation of the drama
of the fall, is simply to draw out the fundamental theological issues being revealed
therein.

2. See Gen. 3: 7–13. It is difficult to estimate to what extent guilt was a factor in
the experience described in Gen 3. The response of Adam and Eve gives indication of
shame (the desire to cover themselves) from knowing the difference between good
and evil. But there is no spontaneous acknowledgement of guilt made. Watts discusses
the significant role of the emotions in the experience of sin more in terms of shame
than guilt, though he recognizes there is overlap in the definitions. He suggests the real
significance of the fall lies in the shame it caused from the state of alienation rather
than from individual sins (Frazer Watts, "Shame, Sin and Guilt," in McFadyen and
Sarot, eds., *Forgiveness and Truth*, 53–69).

3. For the Hebrew Bible's exile motif commencing in Genesis 3, see Lorek, *Motif
of Exile*, 63–69.

4. See Gen 3:14–18. This is how the Genesis narrative was interpreted in the NT
Pauline perspective, also Rom 8:18–23. The context of suffering in Romans chapter
8 also shows the relevance of creation and fall theology to the suffering contexts of
major incidents.

5. See Gen 3:15. In canonical linguistic terms, it is legitimate to take into account
the interpretation of the "seed" motif, as it is progressed through the promise to Abraham (Gen 22:18) and interpreted by the Apostle Paul, in Gal 3:16, to be Christ. Lorek
acknowledges that, however vaguely, some kind of return to Eden is implied in the
promise of victory of the woman's seed over the serpent (Lorek, *Motif of Exile*, 69).

6. See Matt 1:21 and Luke 4:18–21 respectively.

7. See John 10:11–18, and hence such statements as John 16:7–15; 20:21–23.

My thesis here is: because major incidents are, essentially, events of evil as pathology, a holistic response will always be deficient and dangerous if evil, and its consequent suffering, are not correctly identified, recognized, and addressed theodramatically in Christian pastoral care. I demonstrate this by a theological exploration of evil, suffering, and also trauma.

Evil

Attempts to define evil have been various: from the dualistic theories of Manichaeism and Zoroastrianism positing good and evil as ontological opposites, to the theory of evil as privation of good (the Patristics and later Augustine). However, Kelly defines evil eco-theologically as, "the deliberate imposition of suffering by a human being upon another sentient being."[8] But, there are severe limitations with this definition, not least the fact it is anthropocentric and suspiciously subjective.[9] While the problem of evil and suffering can be made to disappear by simply defining God and evil differently, as some other religions do, theocentrically, and theodramatically, evil must be defined more objectively in relation to God as revealed in the canonical text.[10] Stackhouse cites Alvin Plantinga's "not the way it's supposed to be" because it falls short of God's standard, as fundamentally defining evil. In this case, Kelly's definition also falls short because of its restriction of evil to the acts of human beings. By Plantinga's definition, the acts of another "sentient being" (say a lion) tearing apart a human being can be classed as evil, as a dysfunction of creation, as could the nonsentient actions precipitated by geophysical movements, climate change, and meteorology (earthquakes, tsunamis, floods, famines).[11] Evil is that rebellion that, in Christian tradition, angels attempted in the heavenly realms, thus resulting in their earthly residence, and which the first humans engaged in, soon after creation.[12]

---

8. Kelly, *Problem of Evil*, 3. Thus, he includes the animate creation, not just humans.

9. It also does not take account of the biblical concept of sins of ignorance. We can carry out evil even when we are not deliberately doing so, either out of ignorance or a hardened heart. In light of Job 1–2, it also implies God to be evil.

10. See Stackhouse, *Can God Be Trusted?*, 15–16. His chapter 1 develops this thesis further. He also refers to the tendency to define evil subjectively (42).

11. Ibid., 43.

12. See Rev 13:7.

It is that which evangelical Christian doctrine avers every human being has engaged in ever since.[13]

Swinton defines evil from the distinctively theological perspective of the redeeming purposes of God.[14] He asserts four presuppositions:

1. We live in God's creation.

2. The world is not the way it should be.

3. In Christ we discover God re-creating the world.

4. Christians wait in hope for that re-creation to be complete.

Taking these by faith, and exercising "eschatological imagination,"[15] Swinton proposes, "If God is the creator, and if in Christ God is working towards the redemption and re-creation of fallen creation, then evil is defined as everything that stands against God and his intentions for the well-being and transformation of human beings and God's creation."[16] Including systems in this definition is important to safeguard against modernist, individualistic definitions; it engenders a balancing view that societal and corporate contributions and culpability are equally important.[17]

---

13. See Rom 3:23. Rev 13:7, taking into account Christian tradition, has appealed to the descriptions of Lucifer in Isa 14, and to the king of Tyre in Ezek 28, as symbolizing the fall of the devil. Yet there is no explicit connection made in either Old or New Testaments to affirm this connection categorically. The theodrama's relative silence over the fallen angels, advises great caution on our part in trying to fill in where the canon is silent, for fear of distorting the drama.

14. Wright also states that the central evidence for evil as a fact of life lies not primarily in human experience but in the testimony of the New Testament to Jesus, in terms of his temptation (Luke 4:1–13), his ministry of exorcism (Mark 1:21–28; 5:1–20), and in terms of his own death, "as an overcoming of 'the prince of this world.'" (John 12.31)." He states, "The redeeming work of Christ is understood against the backdrop of the reality of evil, and the negative presupposition of the positive work of redemption cannot be omitted without changing radically the nature of Christian faith" (Wright, "Reality and Origin of Evil," 4–7).

15. "Eschatological imagination," means Christians recognizing the way the world is at present is not what it will become in its eschatological outcome; thus recognizing the "what if" possibility dimension, in Ricoeurian terms. Eschatological imagination is a significant aspect of a configurative approach.

16. Swinton, *Raging with Compassion*, 55.

17. See Swinton, *Raging with Compassion*, 52–56. Walter Rauschenbusch overstated the corporate when he suggested individuals are led into sin by society, because original sin is corporate (Robbins, *Methods In The Madness*, 43). See Brueggemann, "Theodicy in a Social Dimension"; Hall, *God and Human Suffering*, 82–89.

Others have attempted to distinguish between natural and moral evil. Natural evil is not directly caused by humans; for example: earthquake, tsunami, avalanche, flooding, and hurricane. Moral evil is caused directly by human action, or inaction, deliberately or otherwise; for example: terrorism, faulty construction, irresponsibility, and dereliction of duty. While this division may serve as a helpful general guide, it is problematic in a complex, messy world.[18] Reflecting upon the Asian tsunami (2004), Hicks acknowledges,

> It is noticeable that the distinction between moral and physical evil is often blurred even in secular thought. When the tsunami of December 2004 struck, it was quickly pointed out that many of the deaths could have been prevented had an early warning system been used; no such system was in place because the vulnerable countries were too poor to set one up, so, in a sense those who were responsible for the unfair distribution of the world's resources and technology were morally responsible for the deaths.[19]

In fact, natural disasters are rarely completely natural. They are often preventable but for political and socioeconomic processes that encourage and sustain a disparity between rich and poor.[20] However, human fac-

---

Interestingly, Wright reflects upon a new nihilism in the form of postmodernity, creating a "no blame" culture (*Evil and the Justice of God*, 14). This is becoming increasingly recognized in litigation terms relating to major incidents, as charges of "corporate manslaughter" can be brought against corporate bodies considered culpable. In July 2007 the Corporate Manslaughter and Corporate Homicide Act 2007 gained royal assent and came into force in April 2008 (Masonis, "Corporate Manslaughter Act."

18. But it is certainly better than the more emotionally-laden definition of Kelly, which judges a situation as being evil or good depending on whether it hurts or pleases. By such a measure, for instance, the long periods of Joseph's imprisonment in Egypt could be judged as entirely evil, whereas Joseph, with his big view of providence, could judge it otherwise: "But as for you, you meant evil against me; but God meant it for good . . ." (Gen 50:20a), even though from a human perspective evil lay behind much of his experience. Similarly the sufferings and death of Jesus could be interpreted as entirely evil, and yet Peter (and Jesus) viewed it otherwise (albeit after a considerable struggle), (Mark 8:31, 32; Acts 2:23). This raises the possibility of certain events being both evil and good, depending on the perspective. Such a perspective challenges those who insist predestinarian theologies lead inexorably to God being culpable of evil. For example, see Jackson, *Priority of Love*, 78, n. 21.

19. Hicks, *Message of Evil and Suffering*, 70, n. 30.

20. Chester, "Theology and Disaster Studies." This conclusion leads Chester to endorse a Marxist liberation theology approach. The tension between human and divine responsibility is carried in Dyson, *Come Hell or High Water*, 179–201, and by

tors aside, all evil is ultimately moral in nature, by virtue of a moral God ultimately deciding that evil will occur, as Isa 45:7 suggests.[21] Thus, Hicks writes,

> Though the biblical writers would have been well aware of the distinction between a moral act and a physical act, the biblical approach to evil does not divide into two clear categories. There is a simple reason for this: the Bible does not accept our Enlightenment concept that the world functions as a non-moral machine . . . An earthquake or a storm is a moral act, since God or the devil causes it, or, at the least, is morally responsible for it.[22]

There are certain aspects to the canonical doctrine which warrant exploration and interrogation, so as to clarify what we mean by evil, and how it relates to suffering and to major incidents; these are: evil and ontology; cosmic evil; and evil and original sin.

Evil and Ontology

Pertinent to the understanding of evil is the question of ontology. Is evil something substantial? Does it have an independent existence? Did God

---

Rothstein, "Seeking Justice," and Steinfels, "Scarcely Heard Question." See also, Chadwick, *The Victorian Church*, 490; Bosher, *Social and Institutional Elements*, 132–40, 177; Dynes, "Noah and Disaster Planning." Bryan Walsh's comment, regarding the most recent major earthquake in Haiti is poignant: "The catastrophic death toll was a result not so much of the earthquake's strength but of Haiti's history of corruption, its shoddy buildings and ultimately its poverty" ("Picking Up the Pieces," 64. See also, 72). For the idea of nature having "clean hands," see Lance Marrow, "Evil," quoted in McCann, *Theological Introduction*, 94.

21. I further elaborate on the pastoral context of this verse below, p. 99. Augustine viewed natural disasters as consequences of the human sinful will (see Evans, *Augustine on Evil*, 97–98).

22. Hicks, *Message of Evil and Suffering*, 69–70. The "moral" *and* "natural" tragedies to befall Job and his family (chapters 1 and 2) are the result of permission granted to the satan by God. Interesting anecdotal cases where victims failed to acknowledge this moral dimension in any divine sense, are highlighted in the study by Kroll-Smith and Crouch. In these cases religious leaders aided the affected communities in their belief that God had nothing to do with the disasters, only human failure. See Kroll-Smith and Crouch, "Chronic Technical Disaster." See also how Rothstein and Steinfels address the same dilemma, concerning Hurricane Katrina (2005) in Rothstein, "Seeking Justice," and Steinfels, "Scarcely Heard Question." The so-called "nature-nurture" debate concerning evil behavior also makes the natural—moral evil distinction very fuzzy. Undoubtedly, our behavior is influenced by our genetic factors and by social influences, but these also, in turn, are aspects of fallen nature.

create evil? On face value, Yahweh's statement could give an affirmative answer—"I form the light, and create darkness, I make peace and create calamity; I, the LORD, do all these things."[23] The context is of Yahweh's explicating the career of Cyrus and his place in the divine purposes, to refigure pastoral comfort for the Jews during future traumatic events.[24] This comfort came from knowing that all that was happening, both good and chaotic, was under the sovereign control of Yahweh. The King James' Authorized Version has been misleading, with its translation as: "I make peace and I *create evil.*"[25] For it is not evil *per se* that was in mind, rather the events of evil.[26] Nevertheless, the Hebrew term for creation is used by Yahweh [*br'*], suggesting that Yahweh creates the traumatic events (or sanctions them for his good purposes, at least); in which case, is there any real distinction between him willing and creating the events? Young's view is that Yahweh creates light and peace, and darkness and calamity are the opposites of these; but, he concludes, "in the very context, then, we are compelled to admit that the word includes all evil, moral as well as calamities."[27] He is then anxious to affirm the passage does not teach God as the author of sin, and he falls back onto systematic theology to confirm the Bible teaches a *decretum absolutum*—that God ordains all things that come to pass, and yet God never authors sin. Thus, for Young, "God included evil in His plan, and has foreordained its existence."[28] Young's view raises two possible issues: that evil has an existence; that God foreordains all evil events. There is a fundamental pastoral implication to these issues, namely, how can it be legitimate for the Christian to respond transformatively to events that God has himself ordained to be as they are?[29] Calvin notes the equation rests between peaceful and evil *events*, not righteousness and evil. Thus, rejecting the notion of God creating evil, he makes the interesting distinction between God authoring the "evil" (events) of just punishment (i.e., the Persians being used to punish Judah's sin),

23. Isa 45:7.

24. Motyer, *Prophecy of Isaiah*, 356.

25. Emphasis mine.

26. That is, things of which evil is adjectival.

27. Young, *Book of Isaiah*, 200. *br* always has God as its subject, and never indicates the material from which God creates (Eugene Carpenter, *br* in VanGemeren, ed., *New International Dictionary*, vol. 3, pg. 548. The New International Version translates the Hebrew *ra* as "disasters." Thus, calamitous events form the context.

28. Young, *Book of Isaiah*, 201.

29. This question has moral implications for reconciliation and justice as well. See chapter 9 below.

but not the "evil" of guilt.[30] This poses a helpful distinction, in fact. It shows that God's own pastoral response to the traumas of the exile was to confirm that he had authorized the use of evil for disciplinary (therefore transformative) purposes, of which he was in complete control. He fore-ordained for good something he never created.[31] This concept suffuses the pastoral care given by the prophets, Jeremiah and Ezekiel, in their response to these traumas.

Saint Augustine, who formerly embraced the Manichean view, be-came persuaded, as a Christian, of two key convictions regarding evil: that God was indeed sovereign; that evil was nothing. In his *Confessions,* Augustine wrestled with the problem and origins of evil. He concluded that evil arises from perversion of the human will, not from any sub-stance of its own, because a good God can only create good. Since God cannot create evil, evil does not have an existence as such.[32] On the other hand, God, as sovereign, has control over evil.[33] In coming to this conclu-sion Augustine was in a line with the patristic and the medieval fathers' perspective. His view of evil, as nothing/unsubstantial negativity, has been propounded in the context of trauma in more recent times by Karl Barth and David Bentley Hart, to whom I now turn in regard to the issue of ontology and evil.

Karl Barth—*das Nichtige*

Barth's exposure to evil at first hand, from the first and second World Wars, was highly influential and motivating for his conception of evil.[34]

30. Calvin, *Calvin's Commentaries*, Isaiah 45:7. Helm points out how Calvin could appeal to the distinction between the evil of the punishment and the evil of the fault. God could be the author of the former, but never of the latter (Helm, *John Calvin's Ideas*, 107.

31. God's providential activity is omni-causal but not solely-causal. Since this is the created order then both causals are free and responsible. Libertarians, of course, insist there are no causes of free actions, or nondeterministic causes are only event-related—that is, limited to events such as beliefs and desires. (For a consideration of free agency that concludes for philosophical compatibilism, see Randolph Clark, "Libertarian Views: Critical Survey of Noncausal and Event-Causal Accounts of Free Agency," in Kane, ed. *Oxford Handbook*, 356–87.) See also Webster, "On the Theology of Providence." Also, Calvin, *Institutes*, 1:7.9).

32. Augustine, *Confessions*, 7, chapter 9–16. Augustine eventually concluded that evil was not a substance but a perversion of a rebellious will (ch. 16). See also Evans, *Augustine on Evil*, chapter 1.

33. Evans, *Augustine on Evil*, 97.

34. McDowell, "Much Ado about Nothing," 321. McDowell judges Barth became more positive and prophetically hopeful between 1922 and 1945. McDowell also adds

However, his exposition of that concept has been dubbed "notoriously untranslatable."[35] *Das Nichtige* is expounded in Barth's *Church Dogmatics* as "God and Nothingness."[36] Nothingness is that which is resistant to God's will, and alien to his creation; not, "preserved, accompanied, or ruled by the almighty actions of God like creaturely occurrence."[37] It is the "chaos" out of which the creation arose.[38] Since God can create only that which is good, then evil is "nothingness." It is the break between God's creature and the Creator by virtue of a human choice to resist the divine will. In fact, a key statement in Barth's exposition of evil as nothingness is:

> It is the antithesis which is only comprehensible in correlation with creation not as an equilibrating but an absolute and uncompromising No. For it is in opposition, primarily and supremely to God Himself, and therefore necessarily and irrevocably to all His works and creation. Yet God Himself comprehends, envisages and controls it.[39]

For Barth, evil was both something and nothing. Evil is something in the sense that it is existentially very real, powerful, damaging and dangerous, as opposition to God's creation: "as negation nothingness has its own dynamic, the dynamic of damage and destruction with which the creature cannot cope."[40] Barth confirmed, "Nothingness is not nothing."[41] It is not nonexistent, but nor is it a necessary determinant of being or creaturely existence. In fact, the creature does not have access to evil except in terms of awareness of God's attitude toward it of wrath and judgment. Thus, "Nothingness is that from which God separates Himself and in face of which He asserts Himself and exerts His positive will."[42] It is that to which his elective will is opposed.[43] In conclusion: "that which

---

the Cold War as an influencing factor on Barth ("Nothing Will Come of Nothing").

35. Mangina, *Karl Barth*, 100.

36. Barth, *Church Dogmatics*, 3/3, section 50. Mangina prefers the translation "nihil," resonating with annihilation and nihilism (Mangina, *Karl Barth*, 100). Bromiley and Torrance also acknowledge this (*CD*, 3/3, 289, n. 1).

37. Barth, *Church Dogmatics*, 3/3, 289.

38. Gen 1:2.

39. Barth, *Church Dogmatics*, 3/3, 302.

40. Ibid., 310.

41. Ibid., 349.

42. Ibid., 351.

43. Ibid.

God renounces and abandons in virtue of His decision is not merely nothing. It is nothingness, and has as such its own being, albeit malignant and perverse."[44] It is something; it is a Nothingness.[45]

Evil is nothing in the sense that it has no created substance or elective purpose or value.[46] It has no relation to God other than opposition. It is the attempt to defraud God of his honor and right, at the same time robbing the creature of its salvation and right.[47] It is "mere" (in the most pejorative, not minimalist, sense) privation of the good (*privatio boni*) because it is an issue that is, primarily, God's affair, since it contests his honor most of all. It is so serious, therefore, that it must be denied all substance before God, even though it has its own curious existence. It is nothingness in the sense that evil is so abhorrent an antithesis to God that it must not be granted any "oxygen" that would give it prominence, even in infamy. For this reason Barth judged theodicy could amount to evil intent, because it implies evil is so prominent a problem for humans that even God must justify himself for its existence.

Furthermore, Barth was adamant it was only possible to really know of nothingness from the perspective of the revelation of Jesus Christ. This is because it is in the coming of Jesus Christ into the world (incarnation,

---

44. Ibid., 352. Yet "being" must not be understood ontologically. Barth also regarded evil as parasitic.

45. Stackhouse disagrees with Barth. He thinks Barth suggests evil is more than the abstraction he (Stackhouse) believes it to be. I am not convinced Stackhouse is right in his interpretation of Barth. I think Barth emphasizes the fact of evil *not* being nothing, but rather it *is* nothingness, in order to emphasise the reality of evil. See Stackhouse, *Can God Be Trusted?*, 202, n. 1. Stackhouse concludes evil is only an abstract quality, a concept that has no real existence, which can be discussed only as if it were a thing, and only in relation to things that are qualified by the abstraction (*Can God Be Trusted?*, 41). However, Barth's precise meaning of "das Nichtige," it must be said, is notoriously unclear. In email conversation with me concerning his interpretation of the term, Stackhouse responded: "It seems to me that he [Barth] is gesturing toward a *tohu wabohu* or 'chaos,' a Nothing*ness* rather than merely nothing. But, again, even the experts disagree, so I simply acknowledge what *might* be his view along the way to making my more general point of the several versions of nothing and evil that are out there" (in email conversation, September 2009). McGrath also describes Barth's "Nothingness" as "A mysterious power . . . which has its grounds in what God did *not* will in the act of creation." It is a "Nothingness" that threatens to reduce to nothing. McGrath points out critics of Barth's idea of evil think he lapses into "arbitrary metaphysical speculation," where the biblical narrative is central (Alister E. McGrath, "Theodicies: The Problem of Evil," in McGrath, ed., *Christian Theology*, 233).

46. Barth, *Church Dogmatics*, 3/3, 361.

47. Ibid., 353.

cross, and resurrection) that true nothingness is revealed. There is no natural awareness of sin other than to misunderstand and misinterpret it.[48] Createdness can only reveal the positive and negative aspects of our nature, enabling some discernment of good in ourselves and a greater bad in others.[49] Thus, no natural law can reveal sin to us.[50] There is no self-awareness of sin in human nature, only in the revelation of Jesus Christ.

> In plain and precise terms, the answer is that nothingness is the "reality" on whose account (that is, against which) God Himself willed to become a creature in the creaturely world, yielding and subjecting Himself to it in Jesus Christ in order to overcome it. Nothingness is thus the "reality" which opposes and resists God, which is itself subject to and overcome by His opposition and resistance, and which in this twofold determination as the reality that negates and is negated by Him, is totally distinct from Him.[51]

It follows that in Jesus Christ sin cannot be diluted to a natural imperfection or even to disobedience of law. Real sin is man's repudiation of love and the command of God in Jesus Christ. It is resistance to the "merciful and patient and generous will" of God.[52]

> Sin is when the creature avails itself of this impossible possibility [of falling away from the grace of the Creator] in opposition to God and to the meaning of its own existence. But the fault is that of the creature and not of God. In no sense does it follow from what God is in Himself. Nor does it result from the nature of the creation. It follows only from the incomprehensible fact that the creature rejects the preserving grace of God.[53]

---

48. Ibid., 2/2, 165. Barth considers the Pauline claim in Rom 1:32 ("who, knowing the righteous judgment of God, that those who practice such things are deserving of death, not only do the same but also approve of those who practice them") means the natural understanding (the "Night"), while "it understands quite clearly the meaning of its direction and of its goal," yet it insists on pursuing it approvingly. Thus, for Barth there can be no convincing light of understanding of sin's sinfulness apart from God's light. (See Barth, *Epistle to the Romans*.

49. Barth, *Church Dogmatics*, 3/3, 306. Also 308.

50. Contra Kant. (Barth, *Churhc Dogmatics*, 3/3, 312–14.)

51. Barth, *Church Dogmatics*, 3/3, 305. Yet this reality is only a quasi-reality (McDowell, "Much Ado about Nothing," 326).

52. Barth, *Church Dogmatics*, 3/3, 308.

53. Ibid., 2/1, 503–4.

Evil, then, is human surrender to nothingness, even though it may include surrender to an alien adversary. Evil is the highest stupidity and cognitive and affective vacuousness, which has never had any place in the choice, will, or decree of God, but which has gate-crashed into created life.[54] Evil denaturalizes us. It is the evil it is because it is the ultimate insult (a defiant no!) to God's love. However, it is also that over which God exercises sovereign control and which he has utterly defeated in the cross and resurrection of Christ.[55]

It is important, however, to distinguish evil as nothingness from Barth's concept of a negative, shadowy aspect to creation. Creation has a twofold aspect—of light and darkness, positive and negative. These simply refer to the distinctive differences between God and humans. In this sense even the negative is a positive facet of creation, part of the "very good."[56] This seems to suggest Barth recognized (in a kind of common grace he would have been reluctant to acknowledge) certain neutral features to creation, which can still serve in a positive way to praise the Creator.[57] It was important, for Barth, that one does not confuse this concept of shadow, or negative facet of creation with evil, so that God is never interpreted as creating evil in any way.

Das Nichtige was never a theodical concept for Barth. He abhorred theodicy because it gave an unwarranted existence and prominence to evil. For Barth, it was utterly inappropriate to think of defending/justifying God, for such would imply the problem of evil was God.[58] Barth regarded theodical attempts as hangovers from liberalism and rationalism. However, evil is too great an absurdity to be resolved by either words (theodicies) or systematic formulations (dogmatics). Evil is resistant to systematization, because it is an alien presence, antithetical to all God has made and willed. Theodicy domesticates evil more than trivializes it. Evil can be considered, therefore, only under certain claims: that God's

---

54. Ibid., 3/3, 304. Also McDowell, "Much Ado About Nothing," 327.

55. I address the divine response to evil in terms of reconciliation and justice. See chapter 9 below.

56. See Gen 1:31. Barth, *Church Dogmatics*, 3/3, 295–97.

57. Barth appealed to the music of Mozart as an example of this. Though Mozart was not a Christian, and could live a frivolous lifestyle, yet his music comprehends and expresses much that is good and positive. (*Church Dogmatics*, 3/3, 297–99). This seems to compute with a good that is recognized, but without real reference to God.

58. Whereas the focus upon evil as a "problem" smacks of Enlightenment atheological attempts to haul God to account, for Calvin (as for Barth), the existence of God as the righteous and good Creator was a chief premise.

holiness and omnipotence are respected, we think and speak with joy, and that this power of nothingness be rated as low as possible in regards to God, and as high as possible in regards to ourselves.[59]

Barth was clear that humans had no right, reason, or freedom to sin, and there was no foreordination to sin either.[60] Therefore, when they did sin it was as a consequence of their choice to do so.

Even so, Barth's *das Nichtige* has been criticized for becoming a theodicy in the end. Hick argued that *das Nichtige* is a something, as an aspect of the good, the *O felix culpa*—a happy fault—that is necessary for revealing the light of God's glory.[61] Barth does seem to refute this, but, nevertheless, the problem of why God permits evil is left as "an unresolved mystery expressed in paradoxical terms."[62] Others have raised the protest that if evil is nothing, then how can it be so real, so devastating, warranting such a response from God in terms of the incarnation, cross, and resurrection? However, Barth never implied that "nothing" meant insignificant or minor. On the contrary, he insisted evil causes great harm, and is so powerful that human nature can only be overwhelmed by it. This is why it takes the gracious response of God himself, in Jesus Christ, going to the cross in human flesh, to die and rise again, to be the only adequate solution to evil. This is what legitimates the response of the Christian community to evil—evil as a waste of time and life, an insult to God for which we are entirely to blame.

David Bentley Hart—*The Doors of the Sea*

Just five days after the 2004 Asian tsunami, Hart wrote an article for *The Wall Street Journal*, reflecting theologically on that tragedy. Though, he confessed, silence would have been a more appropriate response, he felt provoked to write by the opportunism of some of the secular press promoting their anti-theistic theses. Such was the response to his article from different quarters—not least from a spectrum of Christians—he was persuaded to expand his thoughts into book form. *The Doors of the Sea* is

---

59. Barth, *Church Dogmatics*, 3/3, 295. See also McDowell, "Much Ado about Nothing," 320. McDowell preferred to call Barth's theological reflection, "mythopoetic."

60. Barth, *Church Dogmatics*, 2/2, 171–72.

61. Hick, *Evil and the God of Love*, 135–36. Barth's refutation comes in *Church Dogmatics*, 3/3, 353.

62. Barth, *Church Dogmatics*, 3/3, 367; McDowell, "Nothing Will Come of Nothing." In *Church Dogmatics*, 2/2, 170, Barth states, "God wills evil only as He wills not to keep to Himself the light of His glory but to let it shine outside Himself."

an apologetic work, countering the anti-theistic claims that this tragedy placed the nonexistence of God beyond dispute, but also responding to certain Catholic and Calvinistic critiques of Hart's views that he found alarming.

Fundamental to Hart's argument is his antipathy toward any attempt at reducing God to a "finite ethical agent, a limited psychological personality, whose purposes are measurable upon the same scale as ours, and whose ultimate ends for his creatures do not transcend the cosmos as we perceive it."[63] Hart sympathizes with the challenge to Christianity posed by the rebellious quest of Dostoyevsky's Ivan Karamazov.[64] In the figure of Ivan, Hart sees a profound and prophetic shadowing of the response of the "rebel" Jesus Christ, who "is Himself the truest 'rebel' entering human history with a divine disregard for its internal economies, disrupting it in fact at the deepest level by sowing freedom with an almost profligate abandon among creatures who—with very few exceptions—are incapable of receiving it."[65] For Hart, Ivan's argument provides a "spiritual hygiene" from the semi-Hegelian theology of nineteenth-century Protestantism, which preferred a more realized, social eschatology, to the final, biblical sort. Whereas Voltaire argued that suffering is not morally intelligible, Dostoyevsky argued that it would be worse if it was.[66] Evil defies intelligibility.

This conclusion brings us to the core of Hart's theological argument. He judges that Christians should not oblige the sceptics' demand for rationalizing God and evil, because, "Christian thought, from the outset, denies that (in themselves) suffering, death, and evil have any ultimate value or spiritual meaning at all." These are simply "cosmic contingencies, ontological shadows, intrinsically devoid of substance or purpose, however much God may—under the conditions of a fallen order—make

63. Hart, *Doors of the Sea*, 13.

64. Dostoyevsky, *The Brothers Karamazov*. Hart has confirmed that his own book is an endorsement of Ivan's rebellion against the traditional nineteenth-century Christian view that all suffering, including that of children, will be seen, in the end, to have been purposeful, good, and necessary. Hart's clear focus upon the suffering of children indicates his sympathy with such a rebellion. See, "Where Was God?," 26–29.

65. Hart, *Doors of the Sea*, 43. In the subsequent interview, Hart has clarified what he meant by this: "Still, the pathos of his [Ivan's] protest is, to my mind, exquisitely Christian—though he himself seems not to be aware of this: a rage against explanation, a refusal to grant that the cruelty or brute natural misfortune or evil of any variety can ever be justified by some 'happy ending' that makes sense of all our misery and mischance" (Hart, "Where Was God?," 26–29).

66. Hart, *Doors of the Sea*, 44.

them the occasion for accomplishing his good end."[67] For God to need evil to achieve his purposes would render him less than God. God is an ontologically free being, and therefore incapable of evil. Hart takes the patristic, Augustinian (and Barthian) view that evil is a privation of the good, "a purely parasitic corruption of created reality, possessing no essence or nature of its own."[68] Thus, to pursue the "problem" of evil for total explanations, via schemes of natural theology, feeding into a theodicy, encourages granting evil an ontology it does not warrant.

Whence, then, according to Hart's theology, come evil and suffering? Christianity has the only answer—from within the human will: "Evil is born in the will: it consists not in some other separate thing standing alongside the things of creation, but is only a shadow, a turning of the hearts and minds of rational creatures away from the light of God back toward the nothingness from which all things are called."[69] Echoing Barth, Hart insists this must not imply evil is illusory or unreal; it emphasizes that rather than being a substance, evil is more a kind of "ontological wasting disease," which eats away at the beauty of God indwelling his creatures and "toward the deformity of nonbeing."[70] For Hart, evil can have no place in God's determinate purpose for his creatures. If it did, this would amount to a deterministic fatalism.

In conclusion, I am persuaded that Barth and Hart make an essential point: evil is non-ontological; it is a *privatio boni*, and yet it has undoubted reality and has awful, overwhelming power to affect both the fallen cosmos, all earthly life, and, supremely, human nature. Evil is evil because it is never the outcome of God's intention, action, or plan. The theodrama does not require a brutish Actor who needs evil to glorify his "perfect and irresistible might."[71] Evil is only ever the outcome of the rejection of divine love and goodness and beauty. I agree with Holland's biblical theological conclusion that,

> sin is essentially relational. The breaking of God's law is the symptom of the problem. Man has declared himself to be a lover—a covenant partner—of the one who is at war with Yahweh ... Sin is betrayal. It is the rejection of Yahweh and the embracing

67. Ibid., 61.

68. Ibid., 73.

69. Ibid.

70. Ibid.

71. Ibid., 30. In this, Hart strikes out against the unnecessary arguments of Edwards, Piper, et al., that evil has been created to service the glory/beauty of God.

of other gods. Thus, Adam was not merely disobeying Yahweh but was forming a new relationship with the one who challenged God. In NT terms, Adam's relationship is a relationship with Satan himself.[72]

Evil is the ultimate waste—a ghastly cognitive and affective insulting vacuum, for overwhelming that the theodrama declares it required God to enter this world in his Son, Jesus Christ. By his light he exposes the darkness of evil, the waste, the meaninglessness, the nothingness that is not nothing.[73] God's response to the non-ontological nothingness of evil is the beautiful ontological Son, who is the church's beauty for her own response.[74] It is only in Christ that this broken world will be eventually restored to the beauty, "conformed to [God's] infinite love for his Son in the joy and light of the Spirit."[75] Given the "ineradicable triumphalism" that is at the heart of the theodrama, "a conviction that the will of God cannot ultimately be defeated and that the victory over evil and death has already been won," then here is sure legitimation for the Christian community's response to such an outrageous insult to God and the *imago Dei* that evil is.[76]

Cosmic

For Augustine, evil's origin and force, lay with the fall of angelic beings. These brought sin into the world through their interaction with human beings so as to cloud human vision by distortion of the truth.[77] This cosmic dimension to the concept of evil is more contentious because Western modernism has rationalized such discernment and psychologised it. More recently, Nigel Wright has contested the traditional perspective of evil—with reference to the devil, the Adamic fall, and humans falling prey to evil through temptation as a part of the good against evil drama—by claiming, "it is by no means clear that there is a solid biblical basis for it."[78] Instead he ventures his concept of non-ontological realism, wherein

72. Holland, *Commentary: Letter to the Romans*.

73. See John 3:16–21.

74. See Matt 5:14–16.

75. Hart, "Where Was God?," 26–29. The ἀποκατάστασις of Col 1:20.

76. Hart, *Doors of the Sea*, 66. See also my exploration of hell as the ultimate triumph over, and eradication of, evil in chapter 9.

77. For a more detailed commentary on Augustine and the angelic darkness, see Evans, *Augustine on Evil*, 98–111.

78. Wright, "Reality and Origin of Evil," 5.

the devil is conceived non-ontologically and mythologically, as a product of sinful human society. Evil is godlessness, and the devil is not a being but a power, "which takes on the appearance of agency and intelligence and chaotically wars against God."[79] But Wright is wrong to suggest the traditional perspective comes from a view of evil being ontologically vested in a devil creature. A non-ontological definition of evil can easily reside within the traditional view. For the theodrama, the cosmic dimension is integral to its view of reality.[80] Hart argues evil is reinforced in its operations within a fallen cosmos (κοσμος as distinct from κτισις) by the activity of spiritual forces, which are divinely permitted to unleash power in creation. He is clear:

> In the New Testament, our condition as fallen creatures is explicitly portrayed as a subjugation to the subsidiary and often mutinous authority of angelic and demonic 'powers', which are not able to defeat God's transcendent and providential governance of all things, but which certainly are able to act against him within the limits of cosmic time.[81]

Hart advocates strong belief in a fallen creation that is victim to vicious spiritual forces under the permissive will of God. To this degree he argues a "provisional" cosmic dualism is latent in the New Testament, which is never an ultimate one.[82] Thus, God's ultimate will can at least be temporarily resisted by an autonomous force of defiance, or hidden by virtue of our corruption, but, nevertheless, his ultimate purpose for good remains a divine victory.[83] Such a focus can balance what can be an unnecessary overprotective zeal, foreign to the theodrama, but obsessive in some propositional, systematic approaches, to protect the absolute sovereignty of God over each eventuality. Hart can locate some responsibility for the Asian tsunami, therefore, in the realm of evil cosmic forces when

---

79. Ibid., 7.

80. For similar demythologized views of the cosmic, see Anderson, *Spiritual Caregiving*, 128–44, with regard to mental health. Also Murphy, *Bodies and Souls*, 142–44. For a contrasting view, see O'Donovan, *Desire of the Nations*, 93, 151–52.

81. Hart, *Doors of the Sea*, 65.

82. Ibid., 62.

83. Ibid., 63. Dan 10:13, where an unidentified angelic messenger relates having been delayed for twenty-one days by a Persian prince, would seem an instance of this resistance. (Compare Rev 12:7.)

he concludes, this is "to say that he who sealed up the doors of the sea might permit them to be opened again by another [master]."[84]

However, major incidents will never be events where everything, or anyone, involved is completely evil.[85] For instance, common grace theology should cause Christians to exercise caution in designating the causes of major incidents as entirely demonic. Never, theodramatically, are the powers of evil allowed to exercise absolute and unmitigated evil, even if this world is described as darkness, and lying under the sway of the wicked one.[86] Mouw shrewdly reminds us, "We have a tendency to dehumanize and supernaturalize the enemy so that we're dealing with absolute radical evil. The tendency then is, if we can see our enemies as satanic, then we no longer have to acknowledge their humanness."[87] Every perpetrator of evil has something of common grace about him or her, and that means respect owed to people "goes further than respect for what people do. Their bearing the image of God will mean respect for the opponent, even respect for the deviant, the wicked, in as much as he or she has the capacity for reflecting God, as if in some respect at least, they were family."[88]

In conclusion, the canonical theodrama displays this cosmic dimension, and, as Hart strongly argues, we cannot omit this aspect from our perspective on major incidents, while accepting the possibility that used wrongly it can over-egg the drama into a cosmic fiction. Wright is largely correct to judge, "that in describing the world's condition the Bible

84. Hart, *Doors of the Sea*, 63. Alvin Plantinga also argues that this permissiveness is a *possibility* that is at least *compatible* with the Free Will Defense theodicy, if not necessarily true (*God, Freedom, and Evil*, 58–59).

85. See the discussion on the doctrine of "irresistible compassion" (chapter 8). The eighteenth-century philosopher, David Hume, maintained that "absolute, unprovoked, disinterested malice has never, perhaps, place in any human breast" (David Hume, *An Inquiry Concerning the Principles of Morals*, quoted in Fiering, "Irresistible Compassion," 210).

86. That the theodrama has such a perspective seems clear from such statements as Eph 6:12; Col 1:13; 2 Thess 2:7; and 1 John 5:19, in the sense of these statements being interpreted with the plain text perspective I have enunciated.

87. Mouw, *He Shines*, 51; Larsson makes the point about demonization/satanization and dehumanizing of the enemy, in the context of religious violence (*Understanding Religious Violence*, 107).

88. Mark Elliott and Adrian Papa, "Conclusion: Some Considerations of a Theological Nature," in Mark Elliott, ed., *Dynamics of Human Life*, 230–31. Calvin had made this clear in the *Institutes*, 3:7:6. See also my exploration of innocence/innocents, in chapter 9.

does not offer a narrative about a fall of angels but of human persons. It is from this that sin and death are said to have come into the world (Rom. 5:12)."[89] The Word becomes flesh not spirit, and he works redemption in the earthly, not the heavenly, realm. This world represents the main arena for the theodrama, ensuring that our coherent view of evil must come from a perspective that places responsibility for evil firmly at the feet of human nature; passing the buck to spiritual beings is disallowed.[90] However, Wright is wrong in making this the exclusive focus, as significant tracts of Scripture remind us.[91] Cosmology in Scripture is never appealed to in order to deflect human culpability, yet it is referenced in order to give explication to the extraordinary powers that lie at back of certain world events, and which sometimes aggravate an already sinful condition.[92] O'Donovan makes the point that cosmic evil can be a significant

89. Wright, "Reality and Origin of Evil," 6.

90. Gen 3:13. Even so, this does not deny the guilt of such evil spirits or protect them from divine judgment, as Jesus' exorcisms demonstrated. Demonic exorcism from repenting sinners was not incompatible with human guilt.

91. Holland argues that this cosmic enslavement of humanity to Satan is fundamental to OT theology and subsequently equates precisely with the theology of Paul in the NT. In fact he states explicitly the synonymy of sin/death and Satan, in his commentary on Rom 7:2–3, (see *Contours of Pauline Theology*, chapter 5). Also Holland, *Commentary: Letter to the Romans*. The Hebrew שָׂטָן. Śātān can be used in the Old Testament to refer to one charged with challenging the actions of others (e.g., in a court of law, Zech 3:1–2), or the actions "of a foe bent on overthrowing the king" (2 Sam 19:23 [Eng. 22]; 1 Kgs 5:18 [Eng. 4]; 11:14, 23, 25) (Hartley, *Book of Job*, 72, n. 7). Hartley and Vriezen also mention a possible origin for the role was Persian court officers who policed and challenged any possible ill intentions toward the king (Vriezen, *Outline of Old Testament Theology*, 70–72). They also conclude that what is said of "the satan" in Job 1 and 2 foregrounds the later development in the New Testament of Satan as a personal, fallen angelic being, opposing God. Tate, reviewing some key Old Testament texts referring to "satan" concludes that there is no "Satan" in the Old Testament, but what is there prepares for such a development in the New Testament, as well as continuing the theme of human evil of the Old (Tate, "Satan in the Old Testament"). Caldwell, on the other hand, argues that "the satan" is not a malevolent being but one whose role is to challenge "sham and false pretensions," being jealous for the honor of the king (Caldwell, "Doctrine of Satan").

92. For an example, see Dan 10:13. For a commentary upon Augustine (in many ways the father of the non-ontological view of evil) and his focus upon angelic darkness as a reality at back of the fall of the Christian Roman empire to pagan invaders, see Evans, *Augustine on Evil*, 98–111. Considered in the wider context of Paul's theology and ethics of his letter to the Ephesians, the focus upon cosmic agencies that St. Paul insists Christians should be alert to, in Eph 6:11–12, is never intended to subtract human responsibility for the ethical failings he warned his readers about previously (for example, Eph 4:22—5:5). Even so, he insists the cosmic dimension must remain a

presence on account of the church's presence, which often leads her to be a suffering presence.[93] Cosmology serves as backcloth to the drama, as if it should be assumed and in need of little explication. Today, in Western modernist culture at least, that assumption is not present; therefore it requires the Christian community to bring to light a dimension to major incidents that is needed to give a coherent configuration.[94] My prefigured account of the satanic coven story, and discerning any truth in it, may gain hermeneutical configuration by a more serious attention to this cosmic aspect.[95]

Original Sin

From the perspective of the theodrama, major incidents are never morally neutral contingencies. They are evil, not because they are necessarily consequences of the sins of anyone in particular, but because they are ugly, vacuous intrusions into a world designed by God for beauty, peace, and holy joy, for which pain and suffering were never ordained, and for the restoration of all things they will make no contribution.[96] In the sense that sin affects our relationship with God and each other, we may regard evil (and suffering) as significant ingredients to the pathology of a major incident, because evil, "indicates the religious and theological dimension of all pathology, even those which it might be tempting to handle in secular or profane terms," precisely because,

> every verse of the Bible . . . is permeated by an undergirding consciousness of living in and through the great and dynamic drama of relation with God, which permeates all dimensions and aspects of life in such a way as to render problematic any firm distinction between sacred and profane.[97]

---

significant reality to a Christian understanding of life in this world. Only a reductionist perspective would conclude otherwise. See also, Stackhouse, *Can God Be Trusted?*, 51–52.

93. See O'Donovan, *Desire of the Nations*, 178–80.

94. See Hicks, *Message of Evil and Suffering*, 118, 142.

95. My problem in this lies with certain aspects of the article concerned that report conflicts within the cockpit that voice-recorder data do not supply, according to the official AAIB report, and also with the author's claim to be offering a prophetic perspective.

96. See Rev 21:3–4. All evil (in this case, exposed in evil acts) will be cast out, in fact (21:8; 22:15).

97. McFadyen, *Bound to Sin*, 222–23.

It is this religious and theological contribution to the pathological consequences of a major incident that legitimates a response from the Christian community offering the communicative practices of the theodrama. The loss of her ability to speak of such pathologies in relation to God, currently "represents a serious, concrete form of the loss of God that is a general characteristic of contemporary, Western culture."[98] It is the controversial doctrine of original sin that provides the profoundly deep diagnosis of the pathology of evil and suffering that makes the theodrama so configurative, because it roots sin less in our particular acts of behavior, but more in a systemic and structural disorder in our human nature that affects our identity and underlies our actions.[99] McFadyen's theological contribution here is helpful. He contests the view that God has no explanatory power in relation to reality, including its pathological aspects. In this he provides a perspective that, wrongfully, Hart decries.[100] McFadyen argues secular ways of speaking of such aspects,

98. Ibid., 4.

99. Ibid., 17. This is very different from Galen Strawson's thesis, wherein he argues that there is no such thing as moral evil, ultimately, since every "free" choice has a previous cause, a process of ever increasing regressive choices back to our heredity and environmental contexts over which we had no control or responsibility. He concludes: "Maybe one way to put it is this: People in themselves aren't evil, there's no such thing as moral evil in that sense, but evil exists, great evil, and people can be carriers of great evil. You might reply, Look, if they're carriers of evil they just are evil, face the facts. But I would have to say that your response is in the end superficial. After all, we don't call natural disasters evil" (Strawson, "The Buck Stops—Where?"). For an extended discussion on the corporateness of the Pauline theology of sin, see Holland, *Contours of Pauline Theology*, chapter 5. Yet, Holland rejects the traditional view of a *nature* that is *inherently* evil, where evil is something passed on by sexual generation. Rather, the problem lies in a broken covenantal status we are born into, which we inherit, in our union with Adam. Holland's reactive stance over the term "nature" lies in his conviction of its embeddedness in Western Christian thinking in sustaining an unbiblical substance dualism in the traditional concept of Christian anthropology. I maintain such a dualism is not in my thinking at this point. See Holland's "Excursus: The Anthropology of Paul," in his *Commentary: Letter to the Romans*, chapter 8. I am thinking of evil and the natural human being (i.e., in Adam). While I agree with Holland on the corporate, covenantal values of the biblical terminology, an anthropology that speaks of a human nature does not have to conflict with Holland's interpretation. While Holland is reluctant to go any further than the biblical terms permit, for fear of sliding over into unbiblical (Greek) thought, in my view it is inevitable that non-Hebraic conceptualities can become incorporated in attempting to understand what is, and is not, meant by "nature."

100. Hart, *Doors of the Sea*, 32–35. Hart betrays his more Orthodox Pelagian credentials by his attention to the Pauline focus upon cosmic powers at the expense of, an equally Pauline, attention to original sin.

and addressing these, via criminology, medicine, sociology, social science, and psychology, are always inadequate. The theological content is essential to a comprehensive evaluation of a major incident.[101] The anthropology of the theodrama understands our human nature is subject to a profound disruption at the very heart of our being that destroys our freedom to avoid sinning, and this pre-personal status determines "our situation before God *already* as one of guilt, prior to and independently of anything we do or will."[102] By this Augustinian approach, human beings would experience the devastation of a major incident within their corporate union as fallen, guilty sinners.[103] Canonically, the state of original sin consists of a forensic/covenantal imputation, coupled with an inexorable moral corruption.[104] Since the evil is universal, so, by God's grace, is the salvation provided in Christ.[105] McFadyen takes the Augustinian theory and tests it against the real life traumas of child abuse and the Holocaust, and concludes it provides the sapiential biblical contribution to the understanding of traumas, which secular disciplines lack. In as much as secular discourse has become pragmatically atheistic in our culture, then withholding this theodramatic understanding of evil, with its stark empirical basis, will risk a substantial misdiagnosis of the pathologies involved, and the requisite pastoral response—for example, whether that response should be medico-therapeutic or Christocentric.

This exploration of evil, wherein I conclude it is non-ontological, cosmic, and yet inherently rooted at the heart of a pathologically distorted human will, which plunges the individual into a corporate culpability much bigger than any one individual, legitimates the Christian

---

101. McFadyen, *Bound to Sin*, 11. See also, Swinton and Payne, eds., *Living Well*, xii–xviii, where they suggest "we do medicine in a theological context rather than doing theology in a medical context."

102. McFadyen, *Bound to Sin*, 28 (emphasis author's). Holland would affirm human nature as "fallen," and sinful, by virtue of the corporate union with Adam, not by virtue of a distinctive sinful ontological nature, though he would aver our natures inevitably sin because they are in covenantal alienation from God. Holland's summary of the work on corporate solidarity by J. A. T. Robinson, in his *The Body: A Study in Pauline Theology* is extremely useful. See Holland, *Contours of Pauline Theology*, 89–108.

103. Holland would eschew the use of "guilty," though not of "fallen."

104. Hence Grudem prefers the terms "inherited sin" and "inherited corruption" (*Systematic Theology*, 494).

105. See Rom 5:12–21.

community's theodramatic response.[106] Without such pastoral care, a response to a major incident stands to be seriously deficient and denies the holistic duty of care owed.

Suffering

Suffering is the experience of pain that can be physical and/or spiritual in nature and usually prolonged.[107] The precise relationship to evil however is morally and theologically complex.[108] Yet, in the theodrama, suffering emerges most obviously out of the enactment of evil in its primal sense: that is, consequential to the rebellion of Adam and Eve against God.[109] But the theodramatic connection between evil and suffering is more profound than simply a primal cause and effect. Provided we do not lose

106. In the classic—Augustinian—concept of original sin there is the belief that this is passed on, from generation to generation *via* either a biological, sexual transfer and/or *via* a forensic/judicial reckoning. Holland rejects the biological view in preference of each individual being born into a status—in Adam—wherein all are born into a broken covenantal non-relation with God; all are born into alienation from God. It is this state of alienation/exile, wherein all are in captivity to Satan that renders all inexorably vulnerable to sinning (Holland, *Contours of Pauline Theology*, chapter 5).

107. For the important distinction between suffering and trauma, see below p. 121.

108. For instance, Hall's idea of *integrative suffering* argues positively for suffering; or, "the stuff out of which some types of human suffering are made," being integral to the original creation (*God and Suffering*, 54). From indicators in the Genesis account, Hall argues suffering is integral for the development of life, which would not be life without this dimension. Without loneliness (Gen 2:18), limits (2:16–17), temptation (2:36), and anxiety (3:1–5), their positive antitheses, and thus full human potential of creation's "good," could never be realized. Hall's contention is: there are "forms of suffering which belong in God's intention, to the human condition. Not all of what we experience as suffering is totally absurd, a mistake, an oversight, or the consequence of sin." This is just part of Hall's conviction that, "almost any form of human suffering could become the occasion for integration and growth in fullness of humanity. Even when the suffering is very severe—even when it brings about death, degradation or disillusionment—it may be or become the occasion for greater immersion in and understanding of life" (*God and Suffering*, 57). There are echoes in Hall's position of the "soul making" defense propounded by Irenaeus, and now developed in John Hick's *Evil and the God of Love*. Hick has been criticized for encouraging acquiescence toward evil's presence in the world. Hall, however, is making it clear he does not view suffering, in the integrative sense, to be evil. Hall may have a valid pastoral point, namely, that evil has conscripted pain for its malicious purposes. Hall's point may have bearing on the New Testament concept of suffering as a means of maturation (Hall, *God and Human Suffering*, chapter 2).

109. Augustine distinguished between the evil we do and the evil we suffer. God can only have implication in the second, in terms of his inflicting punishments. See Evans, *Augustine on Evil*, 114.

sight of the reality of the fall, we can allow that suffering may be judged *tragic*, but not all is evil. While it can be argued that Scripture portrays suffering as *conscripted* by evil, this does not mean that each case of suffering is a consequence of the evil of the suffer*er* or someone else.[110] This point is important for pastoral care, as the book of Job highlights with its case against the theology of cause and effect represented by Job's friends. We need to steer a course that resists the instinctive bias of conservative religious natures to judge our sufferings by our sins. Hall's reminder is valid that many in the third world encounter extreme suffering from exposure to catastrophe and deprivation they have never chosen, but that has been forced upon them by the choices of a Western world that basks in relative ease from suffering.[111] Equally, in many major incidents in the UK people suffer as a result of the evil, malicious, or mistaken choices of others, or from purely natural causes from a creation subject to futility that is groaning as it awaits final redemption.[112] The point is salient when Hall suggests, "Perhaps there could be no more responsible act on the part of the church in today's world than that it should seek in imaginative, concrete, and contextually pertinent ways to explore its theological tradition of sin."[113] The primal evil of Adam and Eve resulted in a judgment with massive implications for the whole of the animate and inanimate creation, where degrees of suffering become a feature of life that has no necessary immediate and contextual connection with the sins of the sufferer.[114] Yet there is a connection of sorts, as the doctrine of original sin exposes. Carson judges, "At the most basic level, suffering is to moral evil what cause is to effect; yet suffering itself is so tied to the fallen order that it too is rightly thought of as evil, and experienced as such."[115] According to the doctrine of original sin, that tie is closer than is naturally perceived,

110. In the case of Jesus—who had no sin, yet he suffered.

111. See Hall, *God and Human Suffering*, chapter 3. Also, Redmond, "Natural Disasters"; Ripley, *Unthinkable*, 87–90.

112. See Rom 8:20–21.

113. Hall, *God and Human Suffering*, 90. In fact, "It is not easy to know what Jesus called for his hearers to repent from; he speaks often of sinners, but rarely of their sins" (Volf, *Exclusion and Embrace*, 115).

114. It is generally accepted that the significance of the words of the divine "curse," in Gen 3:14–19 are meant to include more than Adam and Eve. They signify an impact of cursedness upon the whole of creation, and this becomes the rationale for the theodrama, concluding in a new heaven and a new earth in which there is no evil (Rev 21:1, 4).

115. Carson, *How Long?*, 45.

for it teaches that suffering is not just a fact of life, where the innocents have to suffer irrespective of their righteousness, but that there are no "innocents" in a fallen world, where all are born with inherited sin. We all carry the pathology of evil and inexorable suffering in our fallen natures, of which death is the universal proof. None can escape the "effluence" from the fall, on account of the relational corporateness that binds the human race, not by our freedom but "through the dynamics of God in creation and salvation."[116] This corporate connection between evil and suffering supplements humanity's moral connection, and, thus, a sense of culpability with every incident of suffering even though, as an individual, one may not be a perpetrator or victim of a particular incident. If original sin is taken into account then our solidarity with those who suffer in a disaster lies not only in our createdness, even less with sinfulness, but more significantly in our fallenness.[117] Those not directly involved in a disaster cannot morally disconnect themselves from those who are involved, and who suffer, as if there were no such connection; there is, when evil is brought into the perspective, and herein lies a further, significant moral, legitimation for a Christian response.[118]

However, a more existential reason for a Christian response relates to the lament factor the theodrama itself explicitly includes in its enactment of reality, and is, therefore, integral recognition of the incoherence in evil to which the central actor (Christ) responds, and the director (the Holy Spirit) guides the church. Christ enters into that incoherence himself and saves out of it.[119] Such lament suffuses the canonical records, sufficiently identifying the gospel as "good news" because it responds to such seeming unjust incoherence.[120]

116. McFadyen, *Bound to Sin*, 248. So much of the philosophical discussion on human freedom and responsibility focuses upon the individual, so that we deny responsibility for external influences, such as heredity or environment. A theodramatic perspective gives attention also to moral responsibility in heredity, in the concept of our being "in" Adam. Eco-theology provides a perspective on individual and corporate responsibility for environmental issues as well. "In Adam" sin theology provides resonance with our corporate solidarity as a created human race. Thus, as Barth reminds us, our life is a gift we owe each other, as well as from God. See Barth, *Church Dogmatics*, 3/ 4. We all share in differing levels of sickness and disability and dependence, therefrom (Shuman and Meador, *Heal Thyself*, 105–7).

117. That is, in our shared, corporate pathologies.

118. See also Carson, *How Long?*, 48.

119. See Matt 27:46, where Christ utters the lament of the psalmist (Ps 22:1).

120. On lament, see chapters 8 and 9.

Christ's full integration with suffering also presents the theodrama with a distinctive contributive response to suffering. It teaches an embracing of suffering, rather than a therapeutic escape. This is what makes Christian particularism so problematic for the generic conception of religion that is current within a modernist health care setting. The concept of "health" from an evangelical Christian perspective is very different from that of the medical utilitarianism within the contemporary NHS. The Hebraic concept of *shalom* constitutes good health from a theodramatic perspective. *Shalom* is holistic, but primarily indicative of enjoying a right relationship with God. Thus, from a Christian perspective it is possible to be in good health while still embracing suffering, and even death, in Christ.[121] Thus, Swinton is right when he speaks of Christianity's response to the tragedy of suffering being such that it can prevent suffering becoming evil.[122] Suffering is not evil *per se*, but it can become such. The alternative is to ensure it works to develop character.[123] This is what gives poignant legitimation to a theodramatic response to major incidents.

CONCLUSIONS

I conclude from this exploration that evil exists as a pathological reality we should not ignore, precisely because it has no created ontology, meaning, or purpose. It originates within the human race's corporate rejection of the loving and beautiful Creator, in an act of human defiance and disgrace, and consequent fall. Evil is a vacuous waste that is the ultimate insult to God's glory and loving goodness, and which has precipitated divine punishment, expulsion, and alienation. Evil is perpetuated through our corporate union with Adam, wherein all humans are born into the cursed state in relation to God; this is inherent and pathological, rendering all inexorably vulnerable to committing sinful acts and to the demonic. Indeed, the whole created cosmos lies under that curse, rendering it vulnerable too, and, thus, ensuring suffering is inevitable. Evil and suffering, therefore, are central causals to the *aporetic* nature of my prefigured narrative, and have considerable configurative value. Evil

121. Shuman and Meador, *Heal Thyself*, 108–9.

122. Swinton, *Raging with Compassion*, 61–68.

123. See Harak's discussion of Hauerwas' theology on character being the outcome of actions and affections, though, in Harak's judgment, Hauerwas places too much stress upon actions at the expense of passions. How we receive our sufferings will have a formative bearing on our character (Harak, *Virtuous Passions*, 46–47).

alienates and blinds me to any divine *telos*, deceives me by its illusions of significance, and exposes me as a body/soul to catastrophic vulnerability, whereby I must suffer. In a major incident evil and suffering come to light most in the acute pathology of trauma—a particular experience of evil and form of suffering that I explore next.

6

Legitimation—Trauma

TRAUMA

AN EXPLORATION OF TRAUMA is essential to my configurative process for at least three reasons:

First, the aporias exposed in my prefigured narrative are the casualties of trauma and evil, which make such incidents "major."[1]

Second, in Western culture, trauma constitutes a frightening threat to our pathological narcissism.[2]

Third, our view of trauma *vis à vis* a theological anthropology will help adjudicate on the legitimacy of a Christian pastoral response and the nature of that response.

In this chapter, I explore the nature of trauma, theologically, by comparing an empirical evidence-based approach with that of a canonical linguistic approach that interacts with neuroscientifc and theological anthropological explorations.

Therefore, my thesis is: a canonical linguistic practical theology of trauma requires the theodrama for pastoral configuration for the maturation of a virtuous character. The primary concern, therefore, is not with therapeutic health care purposes.

---

1. Trauma makes up a key ingredient of the "serious damage to human welfare" element in my definition of a major incident. For the CCA 2004 definition, see chapter 1, p. 8.

2. Shuman and Meador, *Heal Thyself*, 78–80. The authors reflect upon US culture, but the resemblance to UK culture is similar in many respects. Both cultures share a trend toward narcissism.

General Observations

Trauma, understood differently according to context, is a term that is integral to disaster response. It can describe a physical injury: *traumatology* is a recognized field of emergency medicine and orthopedic surgery.[3] However, the term *trauma* in my research, generally speaking, refers to the psychosomatic, social, and spiritual impacts pastoral carers respond to, and often incur themselves in the process.

It is important, in regard to major incidents, to distinguish between *suffering* and trauma, because, for some people suffering can be a routine way of life, which a major incident intrudes into traumatically.[4] Bridgers also distinguishes between a crisis, which assumes the individual will be able to reverse their temporary emotional paralysis within weeks, and a trauma, which is more biologically and psychologically overwhelming, shattering integrity and inducing powerlessness and estrangement.[5] Koenig extends defining trauma to include "a sense of *spiritual disorientation or loss of faith*."[6] This is helpful because it includes the spiritual dimension that is central to the nature of my research. Additionally, trauma can be experienced directly or vicariously, and it can kill.[7]

As well as the trauma from direct injury or from witnessing an incident, there is also that which bereavement and grief brings—in particular, scenarios involving traumatic loss and death, most starkly, facing one's own or witnessing (or learning of) someone else's sudden and/or violent death. Furthermore, major incidents can precipitate a bereavement of limbs, faculties, employment, relationships, independence, property, pets, hobbies, and locality while the victim remains alive.[8] There is

3. Using religious metaphor, at least one expert in the field of traumatology considers that the science of traumatology itself will hold the answers to resolving all traumas. See, Valent, "Traumatology at the Turn."

4. I am grateful to Jack W. Munday, director of the Billy Graham Rapid Response Team, for drawing my attention to this distinction. He exemplified it with reference to the context of the Haiti earthquake (2010), where the disaster superimposed its traumata upon an already poverty-stricken society in which suffering for many people was already a way of life/normal (Munday, "Ministry to a Pluralistic Community.")

5. Bridgers, "Resurrected Life," 62. See also, Ganzevoort, "Scars and Stigmata," 19.

6. Koenig, *In the Wake of Disaster*, 142 (emphasis mine).

7. I address the problem of compassion fatigue further, in chapter 8. See, Purves, *Search for Compassion*, 12; Palm, et al., "Vicarious Traumatization." Also, on vicarious stress, "secondary stress," or "compassion fatigue," see Figley, ed., *Compassion Fatigue*; William O. Sage, "Faith Community."

8. Loss of locality may be caused by catastrophic damage by earthquake, tsunami,

appropriate grieving for such survivor bereavements that pastoral carers may help facilitate.[9] Major incidents create complicating factors in the grief and bereavement process. These are: sudden, violent loss; the "lottery" of life and death; the absence of a body or presence of only body parts; mass fatalities and grief; body recovery and identification procedures complicating funeral arrangements;[10] the "ripple effect";[11] the public spectacle of, and repeated exposure effect from, inquests, inquiries, repeated media coverage,[12] memorials and rituals for mass fatalities; and in the case of criminal dimensions, there are issues about justice and forgiveness. In particular, the suddenness of the incident—without due warning or preparation, the overwhelming power, often involving multiple casualties and multiple agencies—make major incident grief distinct. Collective grief and/or public tragedy are incredibly overwhelming and contagious.[13] Perception of suffering is another factor. If the deceased is

---

flooding, fire, disease, or nuclear/radiological/biological pollution (e.g., Chernobyl [1986]). See The Chernobyl Forum 2003–2005, "Chernobyl's Legacy," 32–42. On community displacement, Kroll-Smith and Crouch conclude, "A principal victim of the chronic technical disaster is the existential community" ("Chronic Technical Disaster," 29). Long-term, albeit temporary, displacement due to flooding, can also result in traumatic effects, as happened in the floods in Cumbria (2001, 2005, and 2010) and Hull and Doncaster (2007).

9. On the roles of church and of the Christian organization Farm Crisis Network during the foot-and-mouth epidemic of 2001, in which farmers lost their livestock, livelihoods, self-esteem, and contact with the community, see Mort, et al., "Psycho-Social Effects"; Carruthers, "Farming Families in Crisis."

10. See Ellen and Shackman in their *Building Resilience*. For the general effects of exposure to mass fatalities, see Robert J. Ursano and James E. McCarroll, "Exposure to Traumatic Death: The Nature of the Stressor," in Raphael, et. al., eds., *Individual and Community Responses*.

11. The "ripple effect" refers to the spreading impact of a major incident. The impact of the actual incident first impacts the immediate victims, then spreads to responders (general public, professional rescue services, volunteers), then to witnesses, spectators in the vicinity, the local community, and family and friends (Roberts and Ashley, eds., *Disaster Spiritual Care*, xv). The BBC even spoke of "Grappling with Global Grief" following 9/11 (Lane, "Grappling with Global Grief"); Kathleen M. Wright and Paul T. Bartone, "Community Responses to Disaster: The Gander Plane Crash," in Raphael, et al., *Individual and Community Responses*, 267–84.

12. On research into the effect of media coverage on audiences, see Plude, "Coping with Disaster." Her ongoing research is investigating the impact of vicarious traumatization via media coverage. She notes the media taking the place of religion as an authority figure. See also Ellen and Shackman, *Building Resilience*; Harrison, "Your Disaster, Our Story."

13. See Doka, "What Makes a Tragedy Public?" Within ten years following

perceived to have suffered much in the course of dying, this increases the grief. For rescue workers, though, traumatic stressors built up prior to the event due to anticipation, especially among the less experienced, are salient.[14] Allied to trauma is the pathology of post-traumatic stress disorder (PTSD), a clinical syndrome first formally identified as an anxiety disorder in the standard psychiatric diagnostic work of the American Psychiatric Association, *The Diagnostic and Statistical Manual of Mental Disorders* (DSM-III) in 1980.[15] There are other mental health disorders that can follow a major incident, such as depression and anxiety. I mention PTSD because it is the most severe pathology specific to trauma.[16]

A Theological Perspective

In order to make a viable assessment of legitimation for a pastoral response, it is necessary to explore some theological configuration of trauma.[17] From this perspective it becomes possible to assess if it legitimates a particular response from the Christian community without which a response to human beings as victims of disaster could be a failure in a duty of care.

That there is an existential synergy between trauma and spirituality/religion seems established from the literature, though there is significant debate about whether this synergy can be interpreted exclusively through a clinical, and/or even human, science discipline, or by a distinctly separate theological and pastoral perspective.[18] To respond to this debate, I

Kegworth/M1, I had been present at the deaths of both my parents (on separate occasions). Yet the physical and emotional effects I experienced were distinctly different between the major incident and the deaths of my parents.

14. Robert J. Ursano and James E. McCarroll, "Exposure to Traumatic Death: The Nature of the Stressor," in Raphael, et al., *Individual and Community Responses*, 47–51.

15. *The Diagnostic and Statistical Manual of Mental Disorders* (DSM-III).

16. Figley identifies Secondary Traumatic Stress as a parallel set of symptoms, provoked by traumatic causes from proximity to the primary victim(s), essentially the same as in PTSD. This affects those impacted secondarily (Figley, "Compassion Fatigue as Secondary Traumatic Stress Disorder," in Figley, ed., *Compassion Fatigue*, 1–20).

17. So that we can respond pastorally to mimetic questions, such as: Who am I that I should feel traumatized in this way? Why am I reacting like this? Is my reaction appropriate? How should I configure my reactions in such a way as develops character and virtue?

18. My prefigured narrative also gives at least my own anecdotal case history evidence of this synergy. But, as I was already a practicing Christian at the time, this

engage in a critical comparison between two practical theological collaborative approaches to evaluating trauma. These are: an existential empirical evidence-based approach and a canonical linguistic approach. I explore both as ways of exploring an underlying theodramatic assumption: human beings are "fearfully and wonderfully made."[19]

Existential Empirical Evidence-Based Approach

To my knowledge there have been no academic scientific studies in the UK that have addressed links between major incidents, trauma, and specifically spiritual/religious impacts.[20] Even so, desires for a scientific, evidence-based case for the spiritual/religious dimension in trauma care are understandable given contemporary health care's empiricist ethos. Therefore, a burgeoning movement has developed within the U.S. context, of theological and medical professionals whose research projects claim an empirical evidence base for introducing spiritual/religious care into the role of health care and, more specifically, into trauma care. There are demands from the UK NHS for an empirical evidence base to undergird

---

synergy cannot be assumed to exist with all victims of major incidents. The literature seems to suggest that those with a predisposition to spirituality/religion tend most to find that religion helps. For a helpful discussion on the relative value (and controversial nature) of recognizing the modern/postmodern distinction between spirituality and religion, see Beardsley, "When the Glow Fades." Her study on the interface between spirituality and religion comes from within the NHS chaplaincy context. She herself argues the distinction is highly contested, and, in my view, both her cases of multidisciplinary nonreligious rituals seem syncretistic, and are highly controversial from an evangelical perspective, even though the shifting meaning of "spirituality" may seem to open up more connections with other health professionals. This seems credibility at a cost too high. For an extensive discussion of the ambivalent research history of the debate over religion's benefits to health, see Levin and Schiller, "Is There a Religious Factor in Health?" Note the bibliography gives indication of the huge literature contributing to this debate. Their review, published in 1979, reveals research in this disputed field has gone on for two hundred years, producing a vast literature (some previously undisclosed until their review). The literature has only increased since 1979. Shuman and Meador point to a medical database search for items on "religion" recording over 4,000 items, over two hundred of which were published after 1999 (*Heal Thyself*, 20, n. 4).

19. Psalm 139:14. For a discussion of the Hebrew text and an argument for translating "wonderfully" as "distinguished," thereby identifying the unique covenantal status, see Collins, "Psalm 139:14."

20. There have been two studies which have reflected concertedly on trauma from a theological perspective, but which have not purported to be of the scientific empiricist sort. These are, Ganzevoort, "Scars and Stigmata" and McGrath, "Post-Traumatic Growth."

all forms of modern health care provision, placing pressure upon hospital chaplaincy to engage in such research here.[21] However, there is a distinction to be made between studies in the U.S. and those in the UK. In the U.S. there seems to be more concern to produce an evidence base for placing spiritual care into the hands of clinical staff (doctors and nurses), whereas in the UK it is hospital chaplaincy that is under pressure to produce evidence justifying its own practice within the NHS.

There are psychosocial studies which have been carried out to evaluate basic connections between trauma and spirituality/religion.[22] These studies do find there are connections between trauma and spirituality/religion. These findings are summarized as follows:

Trauma's Negative Impact on Spirituality and Religion

Trauma tends to impact negatively upon one's spirituality or religion by bringing us face to face both with "human vulnerability in the natural world and with the capacity for evil in human nature."[23] Trauma arising from major incidents creates a crisis of *telos* and shatters cherished beliefs that life is fair and orderly. Terror can supplant faith. Decker argues that trauma shatters our innate self, because, "we operate under the illusion

21. Darzi's report for the NHS includes, "We therefore need to pursue evidence-based interventions that support people to make healthy choices and prevent ill health" ("NHS Next Stage," 37, 52). Shuman and Meador argue that (certainly in the U.S. context of health care) the focus upon the individual patient, as a consumer of medicine and religion, is a product of the "consumerist forces of late modern culture" (*Heal Thyself*, 26).

22. A selection of research includes: Gibson and Iwaniec, "Empirical Study"; Taylor, "Spirituality and Personal Values"; Smith, "Exploring the Interaction"; Zinn-bauer and Pargament, et al., "Religion and Spirituality"; Furman, et al., "Comparative International Analysis"; Weaver, et al., "Systematic Review"; Weaver, "Psychological Trauma"; Harold G. Koenig, "Religion and Coping with Stress in Disaster," in *In the Wake of Disaster*, 29–42; Weaver, Koenig, and Ochberg, "Posttraumatic Stress"; Drescher and Foy, "Spirituality and Trauma Treatment"; Decker, "Spirituality and Trauma Treatment"; Wong, "Compassionate and Spiritual Care." See also Avgoustidis, "Are Psychiatric Preconceptions?" Evans argues, from studies in cancer care, that the patient's ability to be a healer should be harnessed. She maintains, "The human spirit may help a patient develop the will to be well," but she concedes that the faith involved in this is more significant than the object of that faith. This highlights a real theological problem from the point of view of Christian particularism, a problem Shuman and Meador are highly critical of (See *Heal Thyself*). Also, Abigail Rian Evans, "Healing in the Midst of Dying: A Collaborative Approach to End-of-Life Care," in Swinton and Payne, eds., *Living Well*, 165–87.

23. Herman, quoted in Weaver, "Psychological Trauma," (draft copy, emailed to author, n.p.).

that we have an agreement with an omnipotent force which guarantees our invulnerability to sudden change."[24] Traumatic events shatter the link between individual and community and so create a crisis of faith.[25] In their report, Ellen and Shackman were persuaded that "Some people question or lose their religious faith . . . Where faith is questioned or abandoned, this can cause isolation from a person's usual faith-based support networks and can cause conflict within families."[26] From her nursing perspective, Smith draws on Parlotz' studies and concludes,

> In summary, the effect of trauma on spirituality is manifold. It can include feelings of emptiness and abandonment, doubt in religious beliefs, pervasive cynicism, guilt and shame, betrayal of strongly held world views, loss of meaning and purpose, and a general sense of isolation and despair.[27]

Trauma also affects spirituality and religion negatively as it touches essential human aspects like dignity.[28] Disasters are degrading and humiliating. Incidents tend to be overwhelming in force, exposing the fragility and weakness of the human physique and psyche in rescued and rescuer alike. The damage wrought pays no respect to age, race, status, gender, or religion. It humiliates casualties: exposing nakedness, disabling, even dismembering, causing incontinence, and ensuing dependence upon others for life-saving extraction, evacuation, hospitalisation and rehabilitation.[29] Incidents remove homes, possessions, communities, and self-respect,

24. For a symptom list of spiritual disease on account of trauma, inclusive of: reconsidering core tenets of religious beliefs, questioning justice and meaning, feeling a need to be cleansed, feeling guilty, etc., see Roberts and Ashley, eds., *Disaster Spiritual Care*, xx.

25. Weaver, "Psychological Trauma," 1.

26. Ellen and Shackman, *Building Resilience*, n.p.

27. Smith, "Exploring the Interaction," 234.

28. For a significant study of the place of dignity in regards to care for the dying, see Daniel P. Sulmasy, "More than Sparrows, Less than the Angels: The Christian Meaning of Death with Dignity," in Swinton and Payne, *Living Well*. Also, see Nussbaum, *Upheavals of Thought*, 368–86.

29. Issues like unethical body recovery and handling can further traumatize the bereaved. For the importance of ethical body handling, see relevant sections in UK Home Office and Cabinet Office, "Guidance on Dealing with Fatalities," 25–26, 34, and the whole of Section V, 3:69–80, 3:100–112. Examples of defective procedures, which caused additional anguish for relatives, were found to have taken place following Lockerbie (1988), Hillsborough (1989), and the "Marchioness" (1989) disasters in particular.

bringing dependence upon disaster funds and other forms of charitable aid. They humiliate relatives and friends by traumatizing and bereaving and catastrophically changing life.

Spirituality and Religion's Negative Impact on Trauma

Spirituality and religion can have a negative effect upon trauma. This arises, chiefly, in regard to the issues of guilt and shame, society's defensive response, loneliness, and disintegrated belief.

Guilt and Shame

Major incidents create guilt and shame by their capacity to disempower. The catastrophic forces unleashed in a major incident can overwhelm human physical prowess, emotion, and intellect. Also, the levels of resultant disability can lead to self-stigmatization, leading to antisocial behaviors and self-activated social isolation.[30] There are the *sequelae* stemming from survivor guilt and guilt from irrational thoughts of personal culpability.[31] Guilt/shame may arise from the interpretations of events clergy and religious peers can impose. For example, Smith notes that in the response to the 9/11 incident, "some religious officials claimed the attacks were a punishment for the sins of the nation" and such outcries, "only served to re-enforce guilt, fear, blame, and anger."[32] Thus, "Religious and spiritual

30. Alternatively, in the case of a failed attempted terrorist suicide mission there may be guilt and shame imposed by the failure and by perceived theological/ideological transgressions.

31. It was once anecdotally reported to me that an engineer—who worked for a subsidiary to an aircraft manufacturer, upon hearing that a certain aircraft had crashed, causing multiple fatalities—had become tormented by the thought, *what if* one of the bolts he had help manufacture had been the one identified as a suspected fault responsible for the crash?

32. Similar outlooks were presented after the Waco fire, the Oklahoma and London bombings, the "Marchioness" river boat, 9/11, and the Asian tsunami. But this carried on an historical trend in Evangelical tradition, e.g., Thomas Vincent's writing on the great plague and fire of London (1665–1666) being a judgment on London's sins, though he, at least, remained in London, offering succor throughout the disaster (*God's Terrible Voice*). John Wesley and George Whitefield declaimed on the Lisbon earthquake (and tsunami) of 1755 being an act of divine judgment against popery (Whitefield, *Whitefield at Lisbon*, 19–32; Wesley, *Serious Thoughts*, 1–13). See also Chester's commentary on the *institutional* complicity of the Inquisition, in Chester, "Theodicy of Natural Disasters." Exceptionally, however, C. H. Spurgeon, under the influence of his own personal experience of trauma at the Royal Surrey Gardens Music Hall tragedy in 1856, pastored sensitively when he preached a sermon following a rail crash in the Clayton Tunnel, near Brighton, which killed 23 and injured 126 people, just five years later. Many Christians were inclined to think this crash happened as an

beliefs change from a possible source of healing to another weapon in an overwhelming onslaught."[33] Such negative impacts from spirituality and religion can actually complicate post-traumatic stress (PTS) into the disorder, PTSD. Taylor recounts negative influences from fundamentalist Christians (rescue workers as well as clergy) who believed disasters to be judgmental, such beliefs having already been embedded into the culture by nineteenth-century missionaries.[34] This trajectory, from sin to suffering and injury to guilt and shame, is condemned by Anderson who affirms, "such a theology only serves to further 'disable' a person's coping power and adds an additional burden of guilt and shame."[35] Despite human resilience, guilt can be further fortified, and recovery hindered, by the formation of an unrealistic Jesus role model.[36] It is because of the weakening effect of trauma upon the human being that ideal role models may prove counterproductive to healing.

SOCIETY'S DEFENSIVE RESPONSE—Society's defensive response in blaming the traumatized can exacerbate the trauma, since "society's reactions seem to be primarily conservative impulses in the service of maintaining the beliefs that the world is fundamentally just, and that people can be in charge of their lives, and that bad things only happen to people who deserve them."[37] Trauma represent real threats to the three basic human assumptions about life: that life is meaningful, benevolent, and caring and loving[38] Thus, the urge to control one's life is compelling, and, "By

---

act of divine judgment for those traveling on a Sunday. Thus, Spurgeon's first point was, "let's take heed that we do not draw the rash and hasty conclusion from terrible accidents, that those who suffer by them suffer on account of their sins" (Spurgeon, *Park Street and Metropolitan Pulpit*, 482). Islamic condemnations can outdo those of Christians at times, such as the condemnatory proclamations to the survivors in Banda Aceh, Indonesia, following the Asian tsunami, and the Iranian earthquake of 2003, in Bam. See "Iranian Cleric Blames Quakes on Promiscuous Women."

33. Smith, "Exploring the Interaction," 235.

34. Taylor, "Spirituality and Personal Values," 112–15. Even more contemporarily, Dyson reflects, in respect of Hurricane Katrina (2005), "But in the theological arena where interpreters fought over God's design for the disaster, conservative Christians battered the victims of Katrina all over again," because New Orleans was deemed a place where God was mocked (*Come Hell or High Water*, 180).

35. Anderson, *Spiritual Caregiving*, 147.

36. Decker, "Spirituality and Trauma Treatment."

37. Van der Kolk, et al., eds., *Traumatic Stress*, 35.

38. Ganzevoort, "Scars and Stigmata," 29.

assigning blame, an illusion of safety and preventability can be maintained. It fosters a sense of control,"[39] as Job's friends evidenced.

LONELINESS AND DISINTEGRATED BELIEF—McFarlane and Van der Kolk argue that only a minority of traumatized victims seem to escape the notion that their ordeals are meaningless. For so many, it is meaninglessness that brings one of the most painful aporia. Meaninglessness invites a sense of godforsakenness and betrayal by fellow human beings, often resulting in loneliness and disintegrated belief. Pastoral carers' ignorance and naiveté can also exacerbate these. As Weaver implies,

> At the same time that more traumatologists recognize and study the role of spirituality in recognizing, recovering from, and being inspired by trauma, *it* is important that the faith community recognize and study the role of trauma in the spiritual health and practice of people of faith.[40]

Weaver's research (in the U.S. context) claims many people are more likely to seek out clergy than mental health workers, yet many clergy are underskilled in recognizing the symptoms of post-traumatic stress and in making referrals to other professionals.[41]

Trauma's Positive Impact on Spirituality and Religion

The research literature indicates trauma recovery can also be positive where there is a strong spiritual presence and focus. Sheehan and Kroll evaluate,

> Since humans appear constitutionally designed to seek meanings for the events in their lives or to impose meaning on them, it is not surprising that they will often use a religious framework in this constant endeavour. Providing a meaning for the otherwise incomprehensible circumstances of personal tragedy is one of the major functions, raison d'être, and appeals of religion.[42]

39. Doka, "What Makes a Tragedy Public?" 7. See also Nussbaum's reflection that, "the very magnitude of an accidental grief sometimes prompts a search for someone to blame, even in the absence of any compelling evidence that there is a reasonable agent involved." This is because "blame is a valuable antidote to helplessness" (Nussbaum, *Upheavals of Thought*, 29, n. 19).

40. Weaver, et al., "Systematic Review," 16 (emphasis mine).

41. In my experience of the UK context, most people would not seek out clergy. On referrals see also, Collett, et al., "Faith-Based Decisions?"

42. W. Sheehan and J. Kroll, "Psychiatric Patient's Belief in General Health Factors and Sin as Causes of Illness," quoted in Avgoustidis, "Are Psychiatric Preconceptions?" 18.

Koenig judges that trauma gives rise to many theological questions and spiritual needs that personal faith can help meet.[43] In their respected work on traumatic stress, Van der Kolk, et al., see an essential role for spirituality and religion in the recovery process. As well as recognizing the therapeutic value of religious ceremonies, they affirm religion provides a purpose by placing suffering in a larger context of a commonality of suffering and a transcendence of any embeddedness in their personal suffering.[44]

Wong distinguishes between spiritual and religious help, noting that there is,

> empirical evidence that existential coping is distinct from religious coping. The former, similar to Puchalski's concept of spiritual coping, emphasizes acceptance of a bad situation and finding positive meaning and purpose in the midst of suffering. The latter focuses not only on God as the source of help, strength, and comfort, but also God as a person with whom we can relate and communicate.[45]

Meisenhelder and Marcum's research survey of clergy responses to 9/11 found there was a high degree of increased positive religious coping in clergy response to those attacks that led them to conclude that suffering produces religious growth when the association applies to the most dedicated of followers.[46]

Post-traumatic growth can also result when victims feel empowered and dignified. All too easily the traumatized can take on an identity that renders them vulnerable to further victimization, and this dissipates energy and curtails the chances of recovery.[47] Eyre highlights certain myths

43. Koenig, *In the Wake of Disaster*, 115.

44. McFarlane and Van der Kolk, "Trauma and its Challenge to Society," in Van der Kolk, et al. eds., *Traumatic Stress*, 25. See also Anderson, *Spiritual Caregiving*, 103; Ripley, *Unthinkable*, 91–92.

45. Wong, "Compassionate and Spiritual Care," n.p. Wong strongly supports Viktor Frankl's concept of logotherapy, based upon Frankl's own experiences in the concentration camps during the Second World War. Frankl insisted that healing needed to take place at the spiritual level as much as the physical. While it is difficult to consider Frankl's ideas specifically Christian, Wong's version seems more overtly sympathetic to Christianity in its basis.

46. Meisenhelder and Marcum, "Responses of Clergy to 9/11," 553.

47. McFadyen, *Bound to Sin*, 236. Volf notes, there is "the paradoxical and pernicious tendency of the language of victimization to undermine the operation of human agency and disempower victims . . . and to imprison them within the narratives of their own victimization" (*Exclusion and Embrace*, 103).

extant in emergency planning and which are detrimental to major incident response.[48] One such myth is: victims of incidents (individual or communal) are rendered helpless and hapless. Eyre reports the opposite is often the case. Victims have enormous resilience and resourcefulness—especially during the early "honeymoon" period—that, in themselves, make positive contributions to recovery.[49] Gibson therefore warns, "Helpers can not take away the stress and they should not take 'control' from the person." She advises, "Any help given must seek to reinforce the individual's own coping mechanism in such a way that they adapt for current and future demands. Help which substitutes for the person's coping mechanisms the alien ones of the helper will have no long-term validity."[50] Trauma, complicated by oppression, can stalk the powerless.[51] In the aftermath of major incidents, the traumatized can feel oppressed by their protests not being taken seriously, feeling politically silenced and thereby losing their voice, and by being smothered by compassion.[52] There is a "grace of empowerment" which frees responders from the need to control. Pastoral carers armed with a theology of grace have great resources to re-establish a sense of empowerment and self-worth for the traumatized.

Many of these researchers claim an evidence base for the generic functions of religion/spirituality in recovering from trauma and illness and facing death. Koenig, Weaver, and Eyre, admit, however, there has been little published research on the topic in the mental health literature.[53]

---

48. Eyre, "Literature and Best Practice Review." Ripley concurs on the resourcefulness, yet she claims that paralysis is a common feature unless there is strong leadership. For an example in the benefit of empowerment see her references to the leadership heroism of native Cornishman, Rick Rescorla during the 9/11 incident (Ripley, *Unthinkable*, 203–10).

49. Also, Desmond Tutu recalls the resilience of the "ordinary people" (black South Africans) in the ability to keep their composure in the wake of terrible experiences during the apartheid period. This composure lasted right up to and after their testifying at the Truth and Reconciliation Commission. See Tutu, *No Future Without Forgiveness*, 82.

50. Gibson, *Order from Chaos*, 34.

51. Bridgers, "The Resurrected Life," 61–80. It must be said that since the 1990s and the emergence of the charity Disaster Action, representing bereaved and survivors, there has been a very effective "voice" for the traumatized. For Disaster Action see their website: http://www.disasteraction.org.uk/.

52. Bridgers, "The Resurrected Life," 64–67. Also, Volf, *Exclusion and Embrace*, 103.

53. Weaver, et al., "Systematic Review," 13. Also, Weaver, et al., *Counseling Survivors*,

Critique

Utilizing social-scientific empiricist methodologies to understand trauma as a psycho-spiritual pathology is controversial and has been called into question from scientific and from theological-philosophical perspectives. Shuman and Meador major on this aspect in fact. They argue that the "contemporary rapprochement" between medicine and health produces a new, and false, religion.[54] Richard Sloan, a professor in behavioral medicine, has written a severe critique of the generic approach. Though he does not have trauma studies particularly in mind, nevertheless he is concerned with the empiricist claims being put forward to justify the health care benefits of spirituality/religion. He argues the research methods employed in the principal projects are seriously flawed from the point of view of scientific empirical research methodology, and amount to trivializing the theological.[55] In addressing three questions—Do the efforts to link religion and health represent good science? Do they represent good medicine? Do they represent good religion?—Sloan concludes in the negative on all three. He challenges the claims for a voluminous research literature that demonstrates positive health benefits for religiously involved people, on the basis of poor quality criteria enlisted and the resultant evidence. His work challenges whether there is empirical medical evidence for traumatization requiring, and benefiting

---

385–408. Roberts and Ashley, also comment on the lack of research material available (*Disaster Spiritual Care*, xxv).

54. This "religion," or, in fact, religiosity, is designed on the basis of its helpfulness above truthfulness; one where the deity, "is often invoked as a means to achieve variety of ends that are determined more by forces of the broader culture than by any one historic religious tradition" (Shuman and Meador, *Heal Thyself*, 7). See also Churchill, "Dangers of Looking."

55. See Sloan, et al., "Religion, Spirituality, and Medicine"; Sloan, et al., "Should Physicians Prescribe?" Koenig, et al., responded to this *Lancet* paper the same year, with "Religion, Spirituality, and Medicine: A Rebuttal to Skeptics." (I am grateful to Dr. Koenig for sending me a hard copy of this paper.) Nearly ten years later Sloan published his book, *Blind Faith: the Unholy Alliance of Religion and Medicine*, in which part 2, in particular, deals with methodological flaws. He makes no specific reference to studies in traumatology or disasters as such. Nevertheless, I discern similarities of methodology in the relevant trauma research literature as Sloan critiques in his work. Many of the studies he criticizes are also used to justify the health benefits of spirituality/religion on trauma. For instance, Koenig appeals to an array of such research (Koenig, *In the Wake of Disaster*, 29–42). According to one reviewer of Shuman and Meador, *Heal Thyself*, the authors "argue that to operate within the confines of an empirical trial, a god would need to be automated and reproducible, and therefore could not be God" (Plevak, review of *Heal Thyself*).

from, a spiritual/religious pastoral response, so that this dimension can justifiably be made a part of the role of clinical practitioners in health care.[56] Sloan also judges the social-scientific empiricist approach to be bad theology in view of its capacity to trivialize the transcendent.[57] On the other hand, he does not question that there is a significant spiritual/religious aspect to health problems and he endorses the role of suitably trained chaplains in the health care system for addressing this. The basis for such involvement, however, does not lie with scientific empiricism or the practice with medical clinicians, but lies with theology and pastoral carers.[58] Koenig, et al., would argue differently however, judging that there is an empirical base to the religious benefits to health. If it is established that religion/spirituality is linked to health behaviors, and the primary task of the physician is "to cure sometimes, to relieve often, to comfort always," then, "to comfort always" may include the support and recognition of what the patient finds comforting, inclusive of religious beliefs and practices as a primary way of coping with medical illness and the stresses associated with it.[59]

Apart from the debate over the methodologies and interpretation of evidence for religion as a health care resource, another immediate concern is that these methodologies employ a generic concept of religion/spirituality.[60] Where studies make reference to Christianity (as tends to

56. However, Shuman and Meador believe that Sloan, et al.'s *Lancet* is too dismissive of the large research literature's evidence, and mistakenly denies that the social and behavioral aspects of religion are not as constitutive as the non-empirical aspects. They stress the need for caution in this fraught area of research. (*Heal Thyself*, 24–25).

57. See Sloan, *Blind Faith*, chapter 13.

58. Lysaught has also helpfully discussed the tensions within modern health care's demand for an empirical evidence base for justifying hospital chaplaincy (in the U.S.), wherein "Faith perspectives must accommodate themselves to modern medicine if they are to gain permission to operate within its jurisdiction." She argues cogently against trends to make Christian practices health care *instruments*. In fact, the application of empiricist scientific methodologies to the practices of prayer for the sick, for example, could well show very little by way of materialist healthcare benefits (Therese Lysaught, "Suffering in Communion with Christ: Sacraments, Dying Faithfully, and End-of-Life Care," in Swinton and Payne, eds., *Living Well*, 61–67). This point is driven home by most of the contributors in Swinton and Payne's book. Swinton suggests, "Perhaps we should move our focus away from the medicalizing research, which is fascinated by whether or not prayer can heal, and begin to explore the possibility that prayer as it is made manifest in the practice of lament might have much more clinical utility" (137, n. 45).

59. Koenig, et al., "Religion, Spirituality, and Medicine," 123–31.

60. Shuman and Meador make a very clear critique of the generic concept of religion. See *Heal Thyself*, 37–40.

be the case more in U.S. research), then such loose criteria as church attendance, meditation, and prayer can be employed. The religious criteria tend to be predominantly Protestant/Catholic, and thus relate, presumably, to Christian forms of religion, from which results are extrapolated as generically applicable. From a public health care point of view, using such ambivalent evidence to conclude the superior value of Christianity as a health resource would seem ethically highly suspect.[61] There is stark resistance in the research methods to particularism or to defining Christianity by doctrinal or doctrinally related practices.[62] Faith as a human activity is considered to be more significant than the objects of such faith. This is a dangerous assumption because faith is central to the development of our identity.[63] In assessing Christianity as a therapeutic discipline, it would be highly questionable that it could be scientifically proven to be such, given its ambivalence toward physical health and given the self-denial motif so fundamental to Christianity.[64] Therefore, social-science empiricist methods assume a measurement that is highly questionable from a Christian particularist perspective.[65]

61 Sloan addresses this very point in his *Blind Faith*, 256–57. See also Levin and Schiller's exploration of the connection between religion and health, in "Is There a Religious Factor?" Levin and Schiller give attention to the extensive research literature of H. King, et al., who represent an exception to the tendency just mentioned. They propose a greater usage of Allport's concept of "interiorized" religiosity being employed—that is, the concept of religion as something involving interior belief. In response to Sloan, et al., Koenig, et al., admit, "Religion is not a single homogenous construct where different religious measures all assess the same thing. The many aspects of religion, which include public ritual observances, private devotional practices, as well as attitudes, beliefs, and feelings, make it difficult to study" ("Religion, Spirituality, and Medicine").

62. Levin and Schiller refer to this aspect of religion (generically) as "interiorized" as alternative to "institutionalized" religion.

63. Shuman and Meador, *Heal Thyself*, 34–35. Theology thus becomes neutralized, so faith can fit any religion/belief system whatsoever. On the influence upon human identity (a core aspect of Ricoeurian mimetics) see Shuman and Meador's reference to Giddens' work, in *Heal Thyself*, 77.

64. See Mark 8:34, where the "cross" did not have a tradition of good health for its victims. Also see 10:29–30 for reference to distinctly physically unhealthy "persecutions" being an assured promise of a spiritually healthy Christian discipleship. Also, the description of the Apostle Paul's regular lifestyle experiences in his missionary work would not correspond with best practice in health care. (See his shipwreck disaster and sequel in Acts 27–28; also 2 Cor 4:8–11; 6:4–10; 11:24–33.)

65. Thus, Shuman and Meador comment: "For the inordinate human propensity to . . . prioritize the immediate benefits of being religious over the requirements of faithfulness, many of those same traditions have a name: idolatry" (*Heal Thyself*, 21).

From a more theological, anthropological perspective, Drane has looked critically at the concepts of spirituality *vis-à-vis* religion that are now utilized in Western research and that are employed so generically in much trauma literature. His thesis is: spirituality, especially in therapeutic claims, is now being globalized as a form of Western imperialism, through the marketing of things so diffuse as discipline, enthusiasm, or lifestyle. Thus, he comments, "Indeed, the spiritual can often be presented as a form of psychological therapy with no apparent connection to any recognizable faith tradition."[66] Certainly, much of the existential empiricist approach would evidence this. It is quite patronizing, reductionist, and dislocated from religions and their cultures by a Western repackaged approach. Drane concludes that trying to define spirituality in ontological terms is "a lost cause" because "the language of spirituality is now being used so widely, and to indicate such disparate entities and experiences . . ."[67] Yet, in secular health care today there is a demand for a distinction between spirituality and religion, so that spirituality is interpreted as personal, existential, inclusive of nontheistic beliefs and experiences, whereas religion is more directly theistic, institutional, doctrinal, and formal. Religion is more related to institutional practice, while spirituality is more akin to personal being. Furman, et al., identify someone as religious if they belong to a faith group, accept the beliefs, ethics, values and doctrines of that group, and participate in the ceremonies and rituals of that chosen group. However, they consider spirituality an essential quality of a person that is deemed sacred and basic to a person's search for meaning or a moral framework in life. It may also embrace their perceived encounters with the transcendent, whatever they might understand by that. It might mean their involvement in support groups that may, or may not be religious, and it might involve engagement in behaviors such as prayer and meditation.[68] Their study concluded (albeit in the U.S. context) that religion and spirituality are popularly considered different concepts, but not fully independent of each other and different groups tend to identify themselves in differing ways. Thus, as Drane concludes, "religion can be categorized within the scope of things that are now regarded as 'spiritual', though the reverse is not also invariably

66. Drane, "Globalization of Spirituality," n.p.

67. Ibid.

68. Furman, et al., "Comparative International Analysis," 816. See also, Roberts and Ashley, eds., *Disaster Spiritual Care*, xvii–xviii.

the case, for everything that is now regarded as 'spiritual' is not necessarily 'religious.'"[69] Whenever the spiritual/religious practice approach to trauma slides into a generic agenda for redefining spirituality and religion nebulously, to suit its own anti-particularistic ends, this approach must inspire caution. It is worth remembering the term "spirituality" did not exist in Christian vocabulary in the modern sense until the late eighteenth and early nineteenth centuries, but even then, "it is one of those invaluable words of which the meaning seems obvious until one attempts to define it."[70] Zinnbauer, et al., accepting the above historical evolution of the term "spirituality," helpfully argue retaining a close connection between spirituality and religion, to prevent concepts of spirituality becoming too ephemeral.[71]

I conclude that the existential empirical evidence-based approach has limited value in its configurative ability to understand trauma. While allowing for some degree of legitimation in its results, despite Sloan, et al.'s, critique, the concepts are so generic as to be unsafe for evaluating a Christian understanding of trauma. I certainly resist any approach that seeks to turn Christianity into a medical utility. One suspects the underlying, formative, cultural/ideological agenda to the existential empirical evidence-based approach may be blasphemous, in that it turns into techniques those essential practices within the theodrama that are designed for relationship with God.[72]

Canonical Linguistic Approach

My canonical linguistic approach places a high priority upon a doctrinal interpretation of trauma, contra the empiricist approach. Interpretations are highly significant with trauma, because often the interpretation of

---

69. Drane, "Globalization of Spirituality," n.p.

70. Gordon S. Wakefield, "Spirituality, Christian," in McGrath, ed., *Blackwell Encyclopedia*, 626–33. Denying it has Christian origins, Carson traces the emergence of the concept of spirituality in a Christian sense from the nineteenth-century Catholic pursuit of perfection, pursued by an elite (*Gagging of God*, 555–57). For a thorough sociological discussion, see Guiseppe Giordan, "Spirituality: From a Religious Concept to a Sociological Theory," in Flanagen and Jupp, eds., *Sociology of Spirituality*, 161–80.

71. Zinnbauer, et al., "Religion and Spirituality," 563.

72. By practices I am thinking of things such as: prayer, meditation, reading of Scripture, acts of worship, fellowship, etc. On the distinction between "practices" and "techniques," and the domestication of God in a culture of the logic of exchange, see Shuman and Meador, *Heal Thyself*, 90–93.

events is more significant than the events themselves.[73] This reminds us that trauma is predominantly an emotional/passionate encounter, which means it is a holistic encounter.[74] Yet many would consider doctrine to be potentially dangerous to medical outcomes, particularly where negative beliefs are judged to produce potential negative health outcomes. The canonical linguistic method suggests that the particular objective doctrine (*sola scriptura*)—as cognitively and affectively understood and practiced—is crucial to defining authentic experience.[75] Christian doctrine contributes prophetically to interpreting the experience of trauma, therefore, and responding appropriately to it pastorally. The difficulty, as Murphy judges, is that Scripture does not present us with a conclusive anthropology; therefore some engagement with other disciplines is important.[76]

Given trauma's strong neurological constitution, neuroscience is a fast developing field which offers potentially interesting philosophical and theological perspectives on human anthropology and functionality, and pastoral responses thereto—not least in regards to the effects of cranial trauma, and/or pharmacological treatments on religious experience and commitment.[77] It also has relation to issues of identity and

---

73. Bessel Van der Kolk and Alexander C. McFarlane, "The Black Hole of Trauma," in Van der Kolk, et al., eds., *Traumatic Stress*, 4–6.

74. Harak's argument is significant in making this point. He rejects the Cartesian/Enlightenment model of the primacy of cognitions over passions as both scientifically and theologically indefensible. Passions [trauma] have distinct body signatures (*Virtuous Passions*, 7–26).

75. The utilitarian concepts of religion, under the existential empiricist view, consider the actual experience of a belief to be the essential aspect. Thus, "a good religion is one that corresponds to a good experience, where what makes for a 'good experience' is to be defined first of all—and perhaps even only—by the experiencing subject, according to her desires" (Shuman and Meador, *Heal Thyself*, 38). Where Shuman and Meador prefer the cultural-linguistic concept of doctrine as the learned language of a particular cultural community, I prefer the canonical linguistic concept of doctrine as a learned grammar from *sola scriptura*.

76. Murphy, *Bodies and Souls*, chapter 1. I concur, equally, with Calvin, when he judges that knowing oneself is as much a part of sound wisdom as knowing God, but that it is impossible to know oneself without first contemplating God (*Institutes*, I:I, 1–2).

77. Hasker raises these issues as problematic for Cartesian dualism. See Hasker, "On Behalf of Emergent Dualism," in Green and Palmer, eds., *In Search of the Soul*, 97. For the neurological aspects of trauma, and psychobiological abnormalities, see Bessel A. Van der Kolk, "The Body Keeps the Score: Approaches to the Psychobiology of Posttraumatic Stress Disorder," in Van der Kolk, et al., eds., *Traumatic Stress*, 241. Van

postmortem existence.[78] Brain mapping and the possibility of identifying neuroanatomical mediators of religious experience are possibilities fast emerging, thus bringing the disciplines of neuroscience and practical theology to work collaboratively in the interests of holistic care.[79] So, as a representative traumatized person, the following questions are salient: What am I? Why do I become traumatized? Why do I react intuitively in spiritual/religious ways?

Two significant Christian approaches that explore anthropology combining neurophilosophy with philosophical theology are those of Nancey Murphy's non-reductive physicalism, and John Cooper's holistic dualism.[80] Both have theological credentials for working within Scripture as inspired revelation, which serves my mimetic canonical linguistic methodology with much less modernistic hubris than the existential empiricist, or even biblical, theological approaches, as it engages with contributions of science and the experiences of trauma.[81]

---

der Kolk highlights the essential roles of brain chemistry on emotions and cognitions and perceptions. The possible chemical impact of trauma upon memory, given the significance of memory in things like identity, is salient. On the related pharmacological treatment of trauma, see Jonathan R. T. Davidson and Bessel Van der Kolk, "The Pharmacological Treatment of Posttraumatic Stress Disorder," in Van der Kolk, et al., eds., *Traumatic Stress*, 510–24. PTSD has opened the door to the scientific investigation of suffering (Bessel Van der Kolk and Alexander C. McFarlane, "The Black Hole of Trauma," in Van der Kolk et al., eds., *Traumatic Stress*, 5).

78. On eschatology see below, 254–60.

79. On the prospects of neuroscientific research and development in relation to religion, see Koenig, et al., *Handbook of Religion and Health*, 470–1. Sloan is highly critical of *Handbook*, in view of both methodological inadequacies and massaging of other research study information. See Sloan, *Blind Faith*, 130–40. Shuman and Meador believe Sloan's criticisms in this regard are too dismissive (*Heal Thyself*, 24).

80. Murphy, *Bodies and Souls*. For a helpful review of the taxonomy of mind-body positions, see Green and Palmer, eds., *In Search of the Soul*, in which Murphy's own article states her position. See her "Non- Reductive Physicalism" (115–51).

81. As an alternative canonical linguistic approach I gave considerable consideration to a biblical theological study of the OT figure of Job and the phenomena of traumatization as explicated by the Joban narratives. Factors which influenced me against pursuing that approach were: 1. It would present an anthropology, and eschatology, which would have to carry the limitations of the OT perspective, thereby lacking the developments that occur within the OT and more significantly in the NT. 2. It is highly debatable if the Bible gives us a definitive and conclusive anthropology anyway. 3. It would not take into account the, largely, verifiable evidence provided by the contemporary scientific fields, which, given my definition of a practical theological approach, I am bound to take into account, albeit subject to the controlling canonical linguistic

Nancey Murphy—*Non-Reductive Physicalism*

Murphy's is one contribution to the scientific empirical, canonical linguistic discussion on why and where trauma impacts us as human beings. As a philosopher/theologian she does argue for theological specificity, albeit from a physicalist perspective.[82] She is attempting to build on a facet of anthropology where she feels the Bible lacks clarity, and where most Christians have been influenced by culture.[83] She is convinced that the NT writers were not intending to teach anything metaphysical with their references to the soul, but simply that they saw humans as psycho-physical unities.[84] Postmortem existence, therefore, is vested in the resurrection, not in the Platonic concept of immortality of the soul. The human self is a distinctly corporate, social personality, the image of social Trinitarian relations.[85] Forms of Christian living should reflect this in the social and political relations of this life.[86] With such anthropology, Murphy challenges the traditional Augustinian stress upon the inward spiritual life. Such "liberation" from historic-cultural ignorance allows Christians today to utilize new scientific developments to clarify their views.[87]

As an anthropological physicalist, Murphy once concluded that "it is still possible to claim that there is a substantial mind and that its operations are neatly *correlated* with brain events . . . It follows, then, that no amount of evidence from neuroscience can prove a physicalist view of the mental."[88] She later argues that Scripture's lack of clear teaching on the nature of the human being permits the significant contribution of contemporary neuroscience that shows "all of the capacities once attributed

---

sola scriptura principle. For these reasons, therefore, I have opted for the discussion between Murphy and Cooper.

82. As a philosophical theologian who opposes the classic concept of foundationalism, see her *Beyond Liberalism*, cited in Vanhoozer, *Drama of Doctrine*, 292, n.79. Also, see her reflections on the doctrines of God, Christology, and Trinity, salvation and history, in Murphy, *Bodies and Souls*, 23–30.

83. Murphy, however, believes the NT is clear that humans are psychophysical entities (*Bodies and Souls*, 22). For similar theological views, see also *Out-of-Body*, chapter 10; Walters, *Why Do Christians?*

84. Murphy, *Bodies and Souls*, 22.

85. Ibid., 24.

86. Ibid., 28.

87. Ibid., 37.

88. Nancey Murphy, "Nonreductive Physicalism: Philosophical Issues," in Brown, et al., eds., *Whatever Happened?*; Cooper, *Body, Soul*.

to the mind or soul now appear to be (largely) functions of the brain."[89] Murphy contends the development of modern physics has created an insoluble problem for traditional dualistic concepts of mind-body inter-action, and that neuroscience now provides the "most decisive scientific contribution."[90] All human capacities once attributed to dualistic concep-tions of human nature can be scientifically demonstrated to be monistic processes involving the brain, the rest of the nervous system, and other bodily systems interacting with the socio-cultural world.[91] Modern biol-ogy reduces the "soul" to a life principle that comes into being when, as a non-vitalist emergent property, it becomes complexly organized to self-maintain, grow, and reproduce. Thus, what distinguishes humans from other animals is their evolved capacity for language and sophisticated reason, and a will for the goods only a language user can have.[92] These capacities are all developed within the brain. Significantly, however, Mur-phy rejects human nature as a product of Cartesian reductive physical-ism—that is, where every capacity can be reduced to a micro-causation of our basic subatomic makeup, developing upwards through a hierarchy of complex systems.[93] She proposes a concept of non-reductive physi-calism. That is, human nature is also a macro-causation of higher level socio-cultural and linguistic interactions, working downwards (super-veniently) and in a cycle with the bottom-up atomic structures (which remain unaltered).[94] Our whole is not simply the sum of our atomic parts, but those parts are also working with the whole, a concept devel-oped within psychology in the 1970s.[95] Thus, God is able to influence

89. Murphy, *Bodies and Souls*, 5. Murphy concludes there is no such thing as *the* definitive biblical view of human nature (39). She does not rule out dualism conclu-sively, though (22).

90. Ibid., 56.

91. Ibid.

92. Ibid., 67.

93. She lists these as a "bottom-up" hierarchy, commencing with the leptons, quarks, neutrons, and proteins of physics; ascending through the atoms, molecules, and macro-molecules of chemistry; into the cells, tissues, organs, organisms, and ecosystems of biology, with a transfer to life occurring via an evolutionary process between macro-molecules and cells (Murphy, "A Non-Reductive Physicalist Account of Human Nature."

94. This could be understood as a mimetic like process, in Ricoeurian terms, as the lower level actions are revised and redirected (reconfigured) by the higher level actions (social, environmental, political, theological, etc.).

95. By Donald Campbell, "'Downward Causation.'" Also, Van Gulick's "Who's in Charge Here?"

our natures through this process of top-down causation and also at the quantum level, where she sees God working in all quantum events. These involve a combination of natural and divine causality. Thus, God not only sustains but also governs all that nature does.[96] This process, while being a physical one, requires a theological interpretation of the science, however. The divine influence thus equips us as human beings, distinguished from animals by virtue of our capacity for moral relationships and communication with God.

Murphy's thesis has been criticised by Jaegwon Kim, who argues that it is impossible to conflate physicalism and non-reductive approaches; one must have one or the other. Mental states cannot cause mental states because they are not *causa sui*. For a mental state to happen, it requires a physical event to cause it. So, macroscopic beliefs and desires cannot cause mental states and influence microscopic neurological particles, as in Murphy's top-down fashion. All epiphenomenal incidents have previous physical causes, almost *ad infinitum*, like an infinite number of onion skins to peel back. Kim's thesis is that all mental events ride on more basic causal interactions of the most basic subatomic particles.[97] In critique of Kim's thesis, Teed Rockwell argues Nancy Cartwright's concept of emergence could provide for the possible existence of an alternative pluralist approach, where macroscopic physical patterns (e.g., mind) emerging out of the microscopic physicalist processes, may then be able

96. Murphy, *Bodies and Souls*, 131; Robert John Russell, "Quantum Physics and the Theology of Non-Interventions: Objective Divine Action," in Clayton, ed., *Oxford Handbook*, 151–52. See also Robert Kane, "The Contours of Contemporary Free Will debates," in Kane, ed., *Oxford Handbook*, 3–41; Benjamin Libet, "Do We have Free Will?" in Kane, ed., *Oxford Handbook*, 551–64. Conceiving of God acting at the quantum level may give credence to major incidents being viewed as events of chance. There is nothing discernibly self-evident about providential care at the level of human experience, which is the reason events can appear to us fortuitous. Calvin acknowledged this, in *Institutes*, I: VI, 9. However, Helm suggests that Calvin would only have agreed to some events inconsequential to human beings being "chancy" (*John Calvin's Ideas*, 94, 106–7). Ripley described this as, "the whimsy of the devastation" ("How to Survive a Disaster." It is a pity that Hill, in his exposition of Calvin's thought, while placing stress upon Calvin's opposition to fortune and chance, does not also mention Calvin's due deference to these in terms of how incidents may *appear*. See Hill, *Suffering*, 49–52.

97. See Kim, *Supervenience*. Hasker believes Kim's argument is correct, so that Murphy cannot escape the charge of causal materialism ("On Behalf of Emergent Dualism," in Green and Palmer, eds., *In Search of the Soul*, 87–89). See also Strawson, *Freedom and Belief*; Hookway, review of *Freedom and Belief* by Galen Strawson.

to influence the way the microscopic works.[98] David Siemens has prof-fered a critique of non-reductive physicalism, maintaining it is deeply problematic for explicating the doctrine of the incarnation. Since, by non-reductive physicalism, the human soul is a physical product of the body, it is difficult to conceive of how such can be joined to the spiritual substance of the Son of God.[99] Murphy predicts criticism on this point, and responds with her support of James Dunn's Spirit Christology, where the Holy Spirit is seen as the divine aspect of the person of Christ.[100] Alan Gijsbers posits possible ethical problems with a physicalist perspective, in that anthropological monism can lead to ethical perspectives on the human being and what constitutes life.[101] The ethical issue has been high-lighted, in the context of major incidents, by the landmark case of Tony Bland, a casualty of the Hillsborough Stadium disaster (April, 1989). Bland, a seventeen-year-old teenager, suffered crushing injuries that left him severely brain damaged, leading to him entering an extreme coma-tosis known as Persistent Vegetative State. The neurological damage was such that his eyes were open at times and there remained a rudimentary brain stem function. The cerebral cortex, essential to normal conscious activity, was irretrievably damaged. In this state, Bland lasted for three years before a high court and then appeal court application by his parents and a doctor led to his artificial feeding system being switched off and he was left to die. Given a potential for high levels of cerebral damage from major incidents, such ethical dilemmas could well be those long term pastoral carers need to address.[102] More problematic for the physicalist is what happens when traumata prove fatal. What form, if any, does post-mortem existence take? How can the person who has died be the identical person who is resurrected, by the non-reductive physicalist conception? Murphy's answer would lie in the concept of identity. The issue here is not that of qualitative identity.[103] It is numerical identity, which becomes

---

98. Rockwell, "Physicalism, Non-Reductive." The whole debate is summarized and discussed in Torrance, "Developments in Neuroscience."

99. Siemens, "Neuroscience, Theology." Goetz also raises this point ("Substance Dualism," in Green and Palmer, eds., *In Search of the Soul*, 34, n. 3).

100. Murphy, *Bodies and Souls*, 24–26.

101. Gijsbers, "Dialogue."

102. For a reflection on this case from a Christian perspective, see Wyatt, *Matters of Life and Death*, see index on "Tony Bland."

103. As in the Vanhoozer and Ricoeurian sense.

a controversial issue in the monist–dualist debate.[104] Murphy maintains that human identity consists of a neurobiological combination of higher and lower levels of body, memories, self-consciousness, and moral character (virtue), and God.[105] Virtue is formed by moral practice, inclusive of "top-down" interventions that train the neural networks in character traits. Also significant are social relationships. Yet holistic interdependence of these aspects of identity is essential in both the present and the resurrection life. There can be no real relationship outside of the body: "embodiment is necessary for social life."[106] Yet we should conceive of our bodily identity as that which gives structural support to bearing one's memories, character, habits, etc., which for the moment happens to be a spatio-temporal formation of material stuff. However, this will be a transformed body at the resurrection. At the same time, our resurrected memories will also be transformed/sanctified, so that they do not constitute painful memories. In this sense, at the resurrection it is possible that God creates a transformed body into which he places our memories, consciousness, and character, so that the person who "awakes" knows themselves to be themselves.[107] However, the nature of this transformed material stuff is unknown to us.[108]

104. Loughlin defines "identity" as: "that which must be so if a person is to be the same person through time" ("Persons and Replicas," 307). We might add—and into eternity, as well, though eternity need not mean absence of time.

105. Marsh refers to "memory traces" being "held by God during the interim period until the uniting of these with a new and glorified resurrection body" (Marsh, *Out-of-Body*, 214). Loughlin questions the validity of memory, since memories can be fallible and open to distortion ("Persons and Replicas," 308; see also Murphy, *Bodies and Souls*, 134). They can also be forgotten/erased by cranial trauma in particular, and/or by traumatic shock. See Hasker's reference to *visual agnosia* in "On Behalf of Emergent Dualism," in *In Search of the Soul*, 97–98. Amnesia and dysfunctional memory loss are key aspects of trauma. See references to amnesia and memory in Van der Kolk, et al, eds., *Traumatic Stress*. Kihlstrom, however, argues that studies conclude traumatic memory loss is not as common as is often made out, but can be found in cases of PTSD especially (Kihlstrom, "Trauma and Memory Revisited.")

106. Murphy, *Bodies and Souls*, 139–40. It is this belief that is potentially problematic for those who interpret the Apostle Paul's spiritual experience ("whether in the body or out of the body," 2 Cor 12:3) in dualist terms. Clearly, as the apostle was referring to an experience, the precise nature of which he was unclear about, this statement cannot be at all definitive. However, it certainly places a concept of being out of the body firmly into the frame of discussion. Paul would not have mentioned the possibility if he not believe such a thing was possible.

107. Murphy, *Bodies and Souls*, 132–37.

108. Ibid., 142.

A non-reductive physicalist perspective would, therefore, view trauma as a psycho-physical reaction and response, in that the major incident would have impact upon an entirely physical human body/soul in ways that are the function of material brain chemistry.[109] However, the chemistry will be of a non-reductionist nature. That is, the chemical reactions within the brain will act in a top-down, as well as bottom-up, manner. Emergent macroscopic entities, such as consciousness and person, socio-relational (including our relations with God) and environmental aspects, will interact in a cycle with the microscopic actions of subatomic particles to play a part in forming the traumatic effects experienced.

John Cooper—*Dualistic Holism*

In his original work, John Cooper concluded a position of holistic dualism was the only view consistent with the teaching of Scripture.[110] His biblical anthropology is determined, crucially, by what happens to the human being after death and prior to the resurrection of the body, the

---

109. For a discussion on the relationship between cerebral pathology and religious experience, and their moral measurement, see Helminiak, "Neurology, Psychology." Helminiak refers to studies on Temporal Lobe Epilepsy, a neurological pathology associated with what can be vivid religious experiences. He reviews the research and concludes that such religious experiences can be accounted for in purely neurological terms. What Helminiak, and other related studies, do not seem to discuss is the relevance of the direct work of the Holy Spirit in interacting with the human being, even if that interaction is of a physicalist nature. Dr. William Sargant propounded a similar thesis in his 1957 publication, *Battle for the Mind*. Sargant concluded, after studying the experiments of Pavlov's dogs, that religious, political, and social conversions could be explained in terms of induced conditioned reflexes of brain chemistry. Dr. Martyn Lloyd-Jones, critically reviewed Sargant's book in *Knowing the Times*. In his review Lloyd-Jones fully agreed with Sargant that conditioned reflexes do work, but only when a person has been placed into an abnormal state of mind already by their circumstances (e.g., by the horrific trauma of war). Lloyd-Jones agreed that human responses are the products of brain functionality—but that is why what is presented to the brain is of such crucial importance that it must be truth (*Knowing the Times*, 70). This being said, Lloyd-Jones' address gives a concerted critique of Sargant's thesis, mainly on the basis of Sargant's failure to recognize the high cognitive value in the scriptural historical accounts and theology of conversion, and the distinctive work of the Holy Spirit. My reason for citing these works is because Sargant and Lloyd-Jones both acknowledge the undisputed reality of brain chemistry upon human reactions and brainwashing (Sargant, however, it seems to me was arguing as a reductive physicalist at this point).

110. Cooper, *Body, Soul*. Joel B. Green broadly identifies William Hasker, J. P. Moreland, and Stewart Goetz also as holistic dualists ("Body and Soul, Mind and Brain," in Green and Palmer, eds., *In Search of the Soul*, 13).

so-called intermediate state.[111] His later edition of *Body, Soul, and Life Everlasting*, however, reflects subsequent thinking by contemporary neurophilosophy, and he has adjusted his own position accordingly.[112] He now concedes dualistic holism is an equally suitable term. The difference is subtle. Whereas in his first edition, the emphasis was upon the dualist/ separatist aspect, the contemporary focus lies on the holistic/unified aspect.[113] Cooper's more recent position concedes William Hasker's emergent-dualism could be consistent with traditional Christian eschatology. The person, in the form of consciousness, may emerge, from the basic electro-chemical reactions that subserve life, while remaining ontologically distinct from the body/brain matter—though still dependent upon it—and survive death by virtue of divine sustainment.[114]

Cooper's argument is more specifically, though by no means exclusively, theologically argued, than Murphy's.[115] His first chapter sets out traditional Christian anthropology and the various objections raised against it. Cooper, sympathetically, rejects the long-standing traditional Augustinian, Calvinistic, Cartesian dualism, for its exaggerated concessions to Platonic dualist thought.[116] He concedes that Hobbesian materialism and the dual aspect monism of Spinoza, posed philosophical challenges to the traditional view. These were later supplemented by the emerging sciences of brain physiology, psychology, and psychiatry, that, directed by Darwinian theory, produced evidence for mind being a product of brain state, thereby displacing need for the soul. On the back of such science came the higher critical school of biblical theology, seeming to undermine traditional dualism from a biblical perspective. Historical

---

111. Cooper, *Body Soul*, 191.

112. Cooper, *Body, Soul,* (2000 edition).

113. Cooper's adjustment/concession is not a recognition of physicalism, though, simply that recent forms of emergentism come closer to his holistic dualism.

114. Cooper makes this concession to his original dualist arguments in his 2000 edition of *Body, Soul,* xxvii, 221, n. 27. See also Hasker, *The Emergent Self*; William Hasker, "On Behalf of Emergent Dualism," in Green and Palmer, eds., *In Search of the Soul*, 75–113. Palmer thinks Hasker, in turn, is influenced by Cooper's exegetical work ("Christian Life and Theories of Human Nature," in Green and Palmer, eds., *In Search of the Soul*, 199, n. 15). Hasker uses the analogy of an emergent magnetic field continuing to exist even after the electro magnets have been turned off.

115. Cooper sees a lot more revelation, where Murphy hears silence from the canon.

116. Cooper, *Body, Soul*, 10–15, 94–95. Cooper is less critical of Thomist dualism, with its more Aristotelian focus upon form-matter.

theology traced the contaminative effects of Greek/Hellenistic dualism upon Hebrew holism, which led to the traditional view becoming (heretically) orthodox, and in need of acute surgery. Finally, Cooper argues that a contemporary focus upon orthopraxis has exposed the traditional view as culpable for Christians and non-Christians endorsing unethical cultural and ecological attitudes and practices. These challenges to traditionalism have led contemporary consensus opinion more in the direction of monist anthropology. Cooper responds by arguing that a (theodramatic) Christian anthropology must also be consistent with an eschatology that unequivocally teaches some kind of continuation of the postmortem existence of a person.[117] He favors, and argues for, holistic dualism, because, "the Hebrew view of human nature strongly emphasizes living a full and integrated existence before God in this world, but that, unquestionably, it also includes belief in continued existence after biological death."[118]

Regarding OT Christian anthropology, Cooper relies upon Wolff's *Anthropology of the Old Testament* as the undisputed scholarly source. His accomplished review of key Hebrew anthropological terms leads him to conclude that the OT view leaves little room for dualism, as moods, mind, personality, and character traits are all depicted in terms of organic functionality.[119] OT anthropological terminology is frequently synecdochaic, meaning, at very least, Hebrew anthropology "affirms the functional unity of some entity in its totality."[120] But, it is not monistic materialism, since human being consists of two stuffs/elements—dust and life-force, that together "amount to a mutually irreducible duality which God puts together to get one person," separate from which neither stuff has functionality.[121] The "dust" and "breath" interaction at creation (Gen 2:7), while not sustaining the traditional body-soul dualism, nevertheless implicates some kind of functional dualistic distinction of "sourc-

---

117. Murphy's argument that the Bible is largely silent/ambiguous in regard to the intermediate state seems exposed by Cooper, in my view. In Murphy's view we need to either give up, or at least to finesse, the traditional intermediate state view (Murphy, *Bodies and Souls*, 23).

118. Cooper, *Body, Soul*, 37. Helm comments on Calvin's dualism, his indebtedness to Renaissance Platonism, and his strident rejection of the Aristotelian concept of form that Aquinas endorsed in his own anthropology (Helm, *John Calvin's Ideas*, 129–35).

119. Cooper, *Body, Soul*, 38–43.

120. Ibid., 45.

121. As in Gen 2:7 and Ezek 37. Cooper, *Body, Soul*, 48.

es or ingredients."[122] This is functional holism. The OT concept of the *rephaim* in *sheol* also contributes a dualist dimension, which forbids monistic annihilation, since the concept necessitates postmortem survival in some form. *Sheol* is a general postmortem resting place, a state largely of inertia though capable of occasional rousing in recognizable form and identity, as in the case of the appearance of Samuel.[123] Thus, there remains a distinctly recognizable postmortem identity, which is what is left after either the removal of flesh and bones, or, it is the life-force in the form of an ethereal/quasi body.[124] Cooper relates the structures for this back to the *nephesh-ruach* conflation in Gen 2:7, which could be interpreted biblically, but not platonically, as "soul," which formed the "dust" into a body with which it is a whole. Similarly, *nephesh* can be used to infer postmortem survival.[125] This concurs with what, at least, are intimations of resurrection life in hopeful statements as: "But God will redeem my soul from the grave, for he shall receive me," and the explicity of "Your dead shall live; *Together* with my dead body they shall rise."[126] From the OT data, inclusive of holistic emphases and dualistic intimations, Cooper concludes, "all capacities and functions belong to the human being as a whole, a fleshly-spiritual totality."[127]

The Intertestamental (IT) data, in Cooper's view, provides evidence of an anthropological conceptual development, in that ideas of a postmortem life, an intermediate state, and a resurrection of the body, emerge sufficiently to make a monistic anthropology theologically impossible.

---

122. Gen 2:7 states, "And the Lord God formed man of the dust of the ground, and breathed into his nostrils the breath of life; and man became a living being." Cooper maintains that the OT Hebrew terminology (*nephesh, ruach, basar, qereh, leb*) produce no conclusive adjudication on the debate, other than leaning toward a functional holism. Murphy argues the *nepesh* vocabulary takes us to more relational concepts of being (*Bodies and Souls*, 23–26).

123. See 1 Sam 28. Also, see the *rephaim* are roused to greet the king of Babylon (Isa 14:9–10) (Cooper, *Body, Soul*, 58–59).

124. Cooper, *Body, Soul*, 68–69.

125. As in Pss 16:10; 49:15; 139:8.

126. Ps 49:15. Also Ps 16:10, "For you will not leave my soul in Sheol," and Isa 26:19 respectively. Whereas Cooper regards the latter text as explicit of bodily resurrection, Motyer is more ambivalent, and acknowledges those who interpret it as meaning a national resurrection (*Prophecy of Isaiah*, 218, and also n. 2). Young points out while the noun is singular (of the nation), the verb is plural (of individuals); thus, he concludes on the side of resurrection of the individual (*Book of Isaiah*, vol. 2, 226–27).

127. Cooper, *Body, Soul*, 70.

The striking exception to such dualist concepts was the belief in annihilation held by the Sadducees.

Regarding the NT data, Cooper acknowledges that it presents no systematic anthropology, but employs multiple synecdoches and synonymies. NT evidence of dualism is slim, therefore, until one addresses the question of postmortem existence and, thus, eschatology. For Cooper, the adjudicating factor is which personal eschatology is taught in the NT, the writers of which, he insists, worked with at least a core of OT holistic dualism. Three hermeneutical alternatives present themselves: an intermediate state (dualism); immediate resurrection (dualism/monism); and extinction and subsequent recreation (monism).

Cooper proceeds, cautiously against prejudgment, to examine non-Pauline texts that are central to biblical anthropology. He explores possible NT dualist anthropological terminology as: "spirit;"[128] death as "giving up the spirit;"[129] and "soul,"[130] concluding these only *probably* point towards dualism. Then he explores the time of the resurrection—whether immediate or future;[131] the "God of the living" assertion, in respect of the dead Abraham, Isaac, and Jacob;[132] the transfiguration event giving indication of a postmortem, intermediate existence of Moses and Elijah;[133] the rich man and Lazarus, where the reference to *Hades*, as against *Gehenna*, can only imply an intermediate state;[134] Jesus and the thief on the cross, and the promise of an imminent place in paradise;[135] and, the whereabouts of Jesus between Good Friday and Easter Sunday. His provisional conclusion is: "The facts that persons survive physical death and that they are resurrected in the future together entail an intermediate state."[136]

Taking into account the extensive amount of extant scholarly contribution on Pauline anthropology, Cooper makes a chronological and contextual study of key Pauline texts where references, and context,

128. See 1 Pet 3:19–20; Heb 12:23.

129. See Matt 27:50; John 19:30.

130. See Rev 6:9–11; Matt 10:28.

131. See Luke 20:35; John 5:28–29; 11:23–24. He concludes the latter text is more decisive than the others, though.

132. See Luke 20:38.

133. See Matt 17:1–13; Mark 9:2–13; Luke 9:28–36.

134. See Luke 16:19–31. Jesus was also loosed from death in Hades (Acts 2:27, 31).

135. See Luke 23:42–43.

136. Cooper, *Body, Soul*, 133.

have relevance to postmortem existence.[137] He concludes in favor of a holistic postmortem survival in an intermediate state over the immediate resurrection, and extinction and subsequent recreation alternatives. By holism, Cooper means: "human beings are single entities all of whose capacities and functions are interrelated and integrated as a systemic unity." By dualism he means: "humans consist of the conjunction and interaction of two totally different substances each with its own distinct set of functions."[138] Functional dualism means, "a holistic entity could conceivably be constituted out of any number of metaphysical substances or principles." So, one or more of these constituted entities could exist temporarily without the other(s), albeit weakened and incomplete.[139]

Provided we assume his agreement with Hasker's emergent-dualism, I consider that Cooper's case is robustly made from both biblical and theological perspectives. His methodology of giving primary focus to biblical theology, but cautiously testing his conclusions philosophically, is persuasive, if not entirely conclusive. The choice of texts is focused, and the exploration is initially cautiously provisional, but cumulatively effective and thorough, as it sources the best extant scholarly works. From his theological and exegetical study, Cooper configures an anthropology of dualistic holism, which sees human nature as a supratemporal embodied soul, a holistic configuration of a physical body and nonphysical identity, where, in death, the identity is able to survive, albeit in an unnatural form. It is this identity that ensures there is precise continuity between the same person from life through death into resurrection. Trauma, therefore, is a holi- dual- istic phenomenon, which impacts upon the human being as a body-soul, revealing an intuitive existential consciousness in regard to God, meaning, purpose, and eschatology.

Discussion

The comparison of Murphy and Cooper makes an interesting contribution to Christian anthropology in the interests of a practical theology of trauma. Significant *sapientia* is contributed by the non-reductive physicalist perspective by highlighting the biomedical dimension to traumatic pathology, provided the non-reductive element is a fundamental proviso to engaging with Murphy's thesis, allowing sufficient contingency for

137. Cooper, *Body, Soul,* 134. The Pauline texts Cooper selects are: Acts 23:6–8; 1 Thess 4:13–18; 1 Cor 15; 2 Cor 5:1–10; 12:1–4; Phil 1:21–24.

138. Cooper, *Body, Soul,* 43.

139. That is, as *rephaim*/the functionally weak (Cooper, *Body, Soul,* 55–56).

divine mystery.[140] It is wise and compassionate to acknowledge this fact for a Christian pastoral response if pastoral care is to remain focused, unnecessary foci avoided, and if potential conflicts between medical and pastoral contributions are to be minimized. Traumatic shock, cranial-cerebral injury, and pharmacological treatments, can produce psycho-somatic sequelae in victims of trauma, which can be confusing for all concerned.[141] It is important that pastoral carers recognize the possibly significant physiological dimensions to such and do not attempt futile, if not damaging, Platonic dualist theological "cures" when pharmacy or clinical surgery may be a necessary recourse.[142] Except that in such cases sapiential pastoral care may be necessary to steer the patient through the existential disruption and discomforts that drug treatment programs can involve—cognitive and affective disorientation, nightmares, etc.—and/or postoperative care may require. More complex are near death experiences—not unknown in major incidents—and out of the body states.[143] A compassionate holistic approach, however, can be highly contributive in bringing spiritual comprehension, and comfort, to the injured and assurance to their loved ones.[144] The comparison is also useful for emphasizing the importance of the body/mind for physically traumatized victims. Pastoral carers, facing persons with horrific physical injuries, can all too readily resort to spiritual applications that overlook the bereavement encountered in the physical damage experienced and the social implications physical injuries can have. Murphy's non-reductive physicalism serves a necessary purpose in retaining a pastoral focus upon the person as a physical being, traumatized severely by the damage incurred to their

140. I insist life is as much a divine mystery as a biological chemistry.

141. For an indication of the possible prevalence of cranial trauma in the Haitian earthquake disaster (January 12, 2010), see Etienne, Powell, and Faux, "Disaster Relief in Haiti."

142. Cooper has a helpful, brief section, reflecting on such complex states (See *Body, Soul*, 212–15).

143. E.g. 2 Cor 12:3. For a comprehensively researched project into out-of-the-body and near-death experiences, explicable in terms of recovery of severe antecedent insults to the brain, see Marsh, *Out-of-Body*.

144. People can live without up to half their brain and remain the same person. Yet, "In fact, people often change personality. But we do not think that they are different people, though we may say: 'She's a different person.'" In the same way a person may change in terms of their physique—through surgery, etc.—but they remain the same identity as a person. (Sydney Shoemaker and Derek Parfit, *Reasons and Persons*, cited in Loughlin, "Persons and Replicas," 314).

limbs and organs, including the brain. In the end, though, as Hasker has argued, Murphy's theory suffers from causal reduction, because her higher levels remain ontological products of the micro-levels.[145] Cooper's holistic-dualist perspective presents a credible form of emergence more closely tied to my canonical linguistic method, and, therefore, represents a more biblical and theological contribution to the anthropology of trauma. His dualism certainly responds to the argument from antecedent soulism employed by Goetz.[146] This also devotes explanation to the postmortem problematic that Murphy's non-reductive physicalism has less success in addressing.

Even so, Murphy's theory challenges an Evangelical preoccupation with the soul/spiritual that can be all too often implicated in the Christian community's failure to provide ongoing social and pastoral support for the severely injured, even more so when they are rendered mentally impaired by their injuries. There are people who legitimately depend upon their physique for their livelihood and professional development, for whom physical trauma can involve extreme post-traumatic distress, which can be exacerbated by imprudent platonic dualistic interpretations of texts.[147]

CONCLUSION

The biblical literary genre evidences traumatization as an integral part of the theodrama, and of its Christological emplotment.[148] Canonical narratives present a catalog of trauma. These include: the narrative and poetic

145. Hasker, "On Behalf of Emergent Dualism," in Green and Palmer, eds., *In Search of the Soul*, 88–89.

146. Who also quotes Cooper approvingly. See Goetz, "Substance Dualism," in Green and Palmer, eds., *In Search of the Soul*, 33–60.

147. E.g., the athletes, actors, and models involved in the Marchioness river boat disaster. See 1 Tim 4:8, "For bodily exercise profits a little [interpreted as "not a lot"], but godliness is profitable for all things, having promise of the life that now is and of that which is to come." Or 1 Pet 3:3, "Do not let your adornment be merely outward [interpreted as "Do not get hung-up about your looks."] . . . rather let it be the hidden person of the heart."

148. The drama emplots the lament of Ps 22 firmly on the lips of a traumatized Son of God (Matt 27:46), and Jesus' healing and suffering ministry is founded in the Suffering Servant of Isa 53. (Matt 8:17). Isaiah 52:13—53:12 describes both the pastoral/ missiological role of Israel, as the covenant people, as a typological foreshadowing of the redemptive role of Jesus Christ (as interpreted by Philip the evangelist, in Acts 8:30–35).

accounts of the fall of the human race, of the Noahic flood, the Genesis patriarchs, the Exodus from Egypt, Israel's wars, and the exile into Babylon. There is also the wisdom of Job and the Psalmists giving voice to existential trauma. In the NT, there is the gospels' focus upon Jesus' sufferings and crucifixion and the destruction of Jerusalem in AD 70, the persecution of the early church (Acts), and the pastoral care expressed in the apostolic letters.

I also conclude that trauma is a set of physical reactions and responses within the human being to situations of perceived overwhelming shock and horror that then impact intuitively, and passionately, upon a person as a divinely created body/soul. The existential empirical evidence-based approach may give scientific evidence of trauma as a physico-spiritual pathology, but it can be relied upon only as a methodology in developmental progress for empirically demonstrating humans as intuitively religious/spiritual. Certainly it should not be used as a test of particularist Christian benefits to health care.[149] It requires a theological approach which collaborates with the psycho-medical perspectives to substantiate a credible pastoral understanding of trauma.[150] I conclude a canonical linguistic holistic concept of human anthropology sees trauma as a bio-spiritual dualist-holism, and an experience fully consistent with an anthropology that is divinely psychosomatically "hard-wired."[151] Such seems to offer configurative potential for Christian pastoral carers with its focus upon the interpretive and pastoral nature of doctrine upon science.

149. To do so would risk any particular religion that could "prove" its health care benefits above other religions becoming a health technique (Shuman and Meador, *Heal Thyself*, 26).

150. From a research, academic perspective there should be no grounds for rejecting this approach as inferior to the empirical approach. Ricoeur's hermeneutical method (mimesis) assumes a level of universal connection, as previously stated. See chapter 3, above, pp. 54, 62. My methodology invites a compatible mutuality of research methodologies, not a conflation of them, that is, a working as respected parallel rather than conflated disciplines, a point Sloan also makes (*Blind Faith*. 263–67). This allows Christians today to utilize new scientific developments to clarify their views, where possible (Murphy, *Bodies and Souls*, 37; Harak, *Virtuous Passions*, chapter 1).

151. This is the Thomistic view, that the passions are hardwired within the body/soul. Thus, the "fight or flight" response within traumatic situations is a spontaneous, intuitive reaction, where the emotions require appropriate moral training to be the right reaction for the right time. See Aquinas, *Summa Theologica*, question 44, where he describes the physical stimulus the bodily effects from fear give to a fight or flight reaction. Also, Harak, *Virtuous Passions*, 71–73, 87). Shuman and Meador recommend that a combination of clinical and religious interest factors are important for holistic responses (*Heal Thyself*, 29).

However, the evolutionist substrate of the emergentism of both Murphy and Cooper will be deeply problematic for the creationist beliefs of some Evangelicals, for whom Hasker may offer some hope.[152] I conclude the virtue of wisdom, therefore, is essential for a Christian responder: one who knows themself through knowing God and who learns to orientate even the passions of trauma by loving and delighting in God. Such a work requires an engagement with divine grace, to which exploration I turn next in terms of a bridge between the legitimation and contribution the evangelical catholic Christian community has for MIR.

152. Hasker believes his theory of emergence need not require an evolutionary base, however ("On Behalf of Emergent Dualism," in Green and Palmer, eds., *In Search of the Soul*, 79). Goetz argues substance dualism is not dependent upon a Darwinian evolutionism ("Substance Dualism," in Green and Palmer, eds., *In Search of the Soul*, 39). In terms of a Greek Orthodox perspective, Zizioulas would seem, while allowing for biological evolution, nevertheless to adhere to a view of regenerate humanity, that transcends the biological hypostasis, in eucharistic communion with the Church (*Being as Communion*, 60–61). While, he insists, the biological and the reconstituted substances (*ousia*) of regenerate human nature are not separated, or the biological denied, in this life, yet the biological must be hypostatized in terms of a new mode of ecclesial existence, formed by the Eucharist. This gives an ecclesial perspective on the way we view and incorporate others even in the exclusivity of love for one person. Hence, Zizioulas sees this as a particular transcendent dimension to marriage (63).

7

Legitimation/Contribution—Grace

M Y PREFIGURED NARRATIVE GIVES evidence of the following discordant features: first, I encountered many examples of humanitarian kindness and self-sacrifice exhibited by non-Christians that were, at times, quite overwhelming for me. Given my enculturation by a particularist Christianity with doctrines of original sin, total depravity, and Christian righteousness, these experiences were severely challenging. Second, at Kegworth/M1 I experienced a sense of close bonding with members of all the responding agencies working in the Thistle Hotel and LRI, inclusive of working respect and sympathy for each other, irrespective of any faith or unbelief. This created a discordance with the influence of certain aspects of my Evangelical culture which had formed reservations about close social interaction with non-Christians and about levels of integration a Christian should permit in working partnerships with secular agencies. Throughout my involvement I could not remove the inner hope that my witness would issue in conversions to Christ, in view of the gospel I had to offer shattered lives. Here were areas of life requiring further reflection if my theodramatic performance was to connect with reality in major incident response. Furthermore, in what lay the real authority for me to respond—the secular major incident response systems or my pastoral vocation?[1] Additionally, the severity of the issues of trauma, life, and death that confronted me at Kegworth/M1 thrust upon me the self-examination as to whether I was the kind of Christian that had a worthy contribution to make—a dilemma of virtue.

---

1. The dilemma I experienced with initial hesitation in responding was due, mainly, to this issue of authority/legitimation, and, to a lesser extent, the fear of being regarded an interference.

GRACE

My canonical linguistic approach to configuration regards doctrine as theodramatic direction, integrating experience with canonical text and propositions. Thus, for configuring my *aporias* at this point, I explore the doctrine of grace and, in particular, the classic Reformed aspects of special and common grace. Grace is the exciting heart of the gospel, which influences how we should view God, ourselves, and others. Given its centrality in Evangelical rhetoric and confessionalism, my discordant experience exposed a need to explore this doctrine more fully in the areas of trauma and divine and human interaction in this world.

In this chapter I will argue that a Reformed doctrine of grace provides an important clarity both to the case for a coherent legitimation and contribution, and serves as a significant bridge between these two aspects of my overall configurative exploration. I shall also explore the case that special grace provides a rationale for Christian responders partnering with unbelievers because of dimensions it adds to humanitarianism, to Christian exclusivity, and to the missiological aspect of the Christian's love of God in the redemptive drama. My thesis here is that special grace does legitimate levels of partnership between Christian and non-Christian responding communities, and also makes a unique contribution to the roles of Christian responders, not least for pastoral carers. I present an exploration of the doctrine of common grace as being a significant aspect of a special grace perspective, which illuminates a graced humanitarianism. This should sustain a high level of discerning cooperation between responding Christians and non-Christians, and Christians should not be at all surprised by experiences of overwhelming kindness from human beings, or of a close human bonding in a traumatizing context, nor by God's own gracious responses to this humanitarianism. Over and above this, special grace provides a Spirited life of compassion and redemptive mission, which only Christians can bring to major incident response.[2]

Special Grace

I explore the doctrine of special grace, since this delineates the distinctiveness of the Christian responder offering a Christian, and not just a humanitarian, response. By special grace I mean an aspect of divine grace that is displayed specifically in Jesus Christ effectually for salvific/

---

2. These are explored more fully under the chapters below: compassion; reconciliation and justice; and ecumenical and interfaith friendship.

redemptive purposes and specific to the Christian life.[3] Here, a canonical linguistic configuration clarifies such hesitation as I gave evidence of in my prefigured account, and promotes an unhesitating, confident proactivism.[4]

There has been a move to recast practical theology's attempt to formulate the church's relation and witness to the world as "public theology," in preference for it being an ecclesial discipline. In exploring contributions of special grace to partnerships between Christian and non-Christian, I utilize a conversation between two interlocutors who have reflected on this attempt theologically, who have close resonances with the Evangelical perspective, yet who arrive at contrasting conclusions on what God can bless, or what can be seen as a part of his redemptive activity in the world. Professors Stanley Hauerwas and John G. Stackhouse Jr. have a suitable fit with my methodology:[5] Hauerwas represents the "radical," cultural-linguistic approach, in his *Resident Aliens* works; Stackhouse follows a canonical linguistic approach, in his *Making the Best of It*. My reasons for this engagement are: *first*, they each address *the* focal issue here, which is not a canonical justification of a divinely proffered specialty of justifying grace, but a canonical and ethical evaluation of Evangelical Christian communities who have appropriated this grace relating to the secular *polis*—a theology of cultural and ethical relationship from a special grace perspective.[6] *Second*, Hauerwas and Stackhouse represent

3. It could be termed equally, "salvific or redemptive/persevering grace." It is not a second type of grace, but the dimension to God's grace that is ultimately salvific/redemptive/persevering, not just temporarily kind and/or restraining. In email correspondence with me on July 18, 2007, Brian Brock indicated he is uncomfortable with the terminology of special and common grace for fear it suggests two kinds of grace. I make it clear that I do not imply two kinds of grace, but one, operating on two different levels or planes.

4. By "proactive" I must be careful to clarify that I am *not* endorsing a response that ignores emergency plans in operation at the time (via a call-out system). Rather, I mean a proactivism on the part of the Christian community that actively seeks involvement during the planning and pre-response period; a proactive attempt to get involved with major incident plan exercising and, thus, attempting to become a party to the call-out system.

5. Stanley Hauerwas, is a professor of theological ethics at Duke University. He denies being either a theological or ecclesiological liberal or conservative. But his radical perspective includes exclusivist aspects that resonate with Reformed Evangelicals. John G. Stackhouse Jr. is the Sangwoo Youtong Chee Professor of Theology at Regent College, Vancouver, British Columbia, an evangelical establishment.

6. Since we are considering relationships, then the *ethics* of grace is significant. The theodramatic approach for configuration is also concerned with relationships more

different neighborhoods within the Christian kingdom; yet both argue from a special-graced doctrinal, theodramatic perspective. *Third*, H. Richard Niebuhr and Karl Barth are two significant theological ethicists of the twentieth century. Stackhouse and Hauerwas are nuanced contemporary exponents of these two significant actors and make good foils for one another. In *Making the Best of It*, Stackhouse reflects upon and explores a particular stream of Niebuhr's church typology, in a bid to create an Evangelical (Niebuhrian) new realism.[7] His theology represents the direction my own thinking was evolving at the time of Kegworth/M1. Hauerwas' theological and political enemies are the Niebuhr brothers, and he raises several potent challenges to Niebuhrian thinking. *Fourth*, both authors reflect pastorally upon the issues of evil and suffering in the context of their theologies.[8]

At least one alternative interlocutor could have been selected, in the form of Oliver O'Donovan. I judged that his key work on political theology was too focused upon the politics of rulership, government, and the church's relationship to these.[9] Valuable though his contribution is, he addresses a thesis for the church's mission via a context of Christendom that does not currently exist.[10]

Hauerwas and Stackhouse address more immediate contexts. However, O'Donovan's concept of Christendom, or the Christian nation, warrants reflection in the interests of the integration of imagination and fiction in the mimetic process of configuration, even though he accepts that the era of Christendom is past, so that the contemporary separation

---

than abstract propositions (Vanhoozer, *Drama of Doctrine*, 77).

7. I acknowledge that both authors write with the American context in mind, but they also point out that their arguments and conclusions have relevance to other cultural and social contexts.

8. For their particular focus on these issues, see Stackhouse, *Can God be Trusted?* and Hauerwas, *Naming the Silences*.

9. O'Donovan's key work on political theology is his *The Desire of the Nations*. His focus on the redemption of society (chapter 7) is concerned, mainly, with the key features of a liberal society from the perspective of his concept of Christendom ("the idea of a professedly Christian secular political order, and the history of that order in practice" [195]). I briefly critique his idea of the Christian nation in chapter 9 below, p. 326–28.

10. This is not to fall guilty of the charge that Stackhouse is adamant O'Donovan must *not* be accused of, namely, that he is "merely an apologist for Christendom" (Stackhouse, *Making the Best of It*, 326, n. 11). It is simply judging that O'Donovan is on the more idealist, Hauerwasian side of the spectrum.

of church and state means the state does not feel obliged to offer deliberate assistance to the church's mission.[11] On the other hand, he argues, canonically, in favor of the church believing in her post-incarnational status as: subject to, and authorized by, the ascended King Christ, to be commissioned to challenge the state in the hope that her witness to rulers will, in turn, influence their rule, which, in turn, will create a Christian framework for a healthy and hopeful society. This raises the question: if such a phenomenon did, under God's providence, happen again, could this be a status which could be deemed consistent with the canonical theodrama?[12] Is O'Donovan's thesis biblically realistic, and, even under the most favorable conditions to the church, would it be the best? I conclude that O'Donovan's thesis is compelling, and is not inconsistent with Stackhouse, but does not advance on Stackhouse's more recent thought.[13]

---

11. O'Donovan, *Desire of the Nations*, 244. His accounting for the demise of the Christendom era is set out in chapter 7. O'Donovan believes that Christendom was the product of the church's faithful witness by which the rulers were converted and thus had subsequent positive impact upon society through their rule of law. Contributions as diverse as the Age of Revolution, the Evangelical belief that rulers were dispensable, the desire by the formers of the U.S. Constitution to free the U.S. church from the Anglican centralism in Great Britain, and the Puritan focus upon the privatization of faith, led to a separation of connection between rulers and Christianity. O'Donovan believes the church gave away more than she realized. Thus, "Excluding government from evangelical obedience has had repercussions for the way society itself is conceived." Society no longer was driven by a moral purpose (*Desire of the Nations*, 246). It seems, theoretically, obvious that under conditions of Christendom then there would be much firmer endorsement of the Christian community's contribution to major incident response. However, there remains a fear, given human nature, of inter-church rivalry or denominational domination developing. This would be less likely under a politics of a "principled pluralism," which I endorse. See chapter 10, below, p. 331–38.

12. O'Donovan believed such did come about providentially, not by right (*Desire of the Nations*, 224).

13. Hence the many points of agreement with O'Donovan that Stackhouse references (See Stackhouse's index, under "O'Donovan"). Mathewes, who also is in large agreement with O'Donovan, challenges him over his concepts of rule and authority. Mathewes encourages a greater degree of faith in politics, without making politics a faith. Thus, he makes a theological criticism of O'Donovan's view that the only choices lie between delusional modern concepts of anarchically individualistic liberal democracy and of a premodern picture of power. Mathewes argues for a concept between the two extremes. For Mathewes it is O'Donovan who is too ideal. Mathewes reminds us that the church is no more an ideal institution on earth than any other. He concludes, "Construals of our current condition and our ultimate aim should differ from each other more dramatically than O'Donovan's account allows" (*Theology of Public Life*, 182–87).

Stanley Hauerwas

Stout refers to Stanley Hauerwas, John Milbank, et al., as representing "new traditionalism."[14] However, Hauerwas is more commonly registered with the narrative school's cultural-linguistic theological approach. This association, together with his emphasis upon the Christocentric gospel exclusivity of the Christian community as a "colony" in an alien world, makes his perspective exclusively special-graced. His *Resident Aliens: Life in the Christian Colony*, and the sequel, *Resident Aliens: Exercises for Christian Practice* (which responds to specific criticisms of his position) address a legitimation and contribution of special grace to social interaction with the world from a Barthian idealist perspective.

Hauerwas expresses an acute reaction toward the realist liberalism of Reinhold Niebuhr and, in particular, H. Richard Niebuhr's *Christ and Culture*.[15] In fact, he views Richard Niebuhr's contribution to be the greatest hindrance to an accurate assessment of the Christian community's position in the world, because it underwrites a pluralistic theology for liberal democracy. Therein, the church becomes the servant of the state, inexorably suppressing its particularities in the interests of participating responsibly in culture, by utilizing a grain of universal generic religious awareness in the populace for making a Christian contribution of state servanthood credible.[16] For Hauerwas, nothing has contributed more to the demise of Christianity as this surrendering to modernism's terms for phrasing the important questions.[17] Where Niebuhr argued for Christ and culture, Hauerwas pleads for Christ and the church being the most effective response to the world.[18]

---

14. Stout, *Democracy and Tradition*, 2.

15. Hauerwas, *Resident Aliens*, 31–32, 39–41; Niebuhr, *Christ and Culture*. Hauerwas' critique of Reinhold Niebuhr is found in chapters 4 and 5 of Hauerwas, *With the Grain*. Stackhouse has little sympathy with Hauerwas' position, on the other hand. In regard to Hauerwas' perception of the Niebuhr brothers, he saw little difference between them both, regarding their concepts of Christianity and culture—they were both liberals, even though both brothers are often labeled as neo-orthodox. Gilkey sees them as neo-liberals (Langdon Gilkey, *On Niebuhr: a Theological Study*, cited in Stackhouse, *Making the Best of It*, 94, n. 34). Also in Niebuhr, *Moral Man*, xx.

16. Hauerwas, *Resident Aliens*, 41.

17. Ibid., 20. Hauerwas thought Reinhold Niebuhr a functional atheist because of the way he sold out the Christian church to the world and encouraged the lust for Constantinian power.

18. By the judgment of Stout, Hauerwas goes beyond Barth with his emphasis upon the centrality of the church, and criticizing Barth on this point for his concession

In what follows, I explore a Hauerwasian special graced theology of legitimation for, and contribution to, major incident response by addressing the key (theodramatic) question he would ask in approaching major incident response.[19] This is not, what should we do? but, what should we be? In reply, Hauerwas utilizes the vocational question: What kind of Christ-formed church community do we need to be in order to help the world understand itself as the world needing redemption?[20] The issue is not whether we shall live as Christians in this world, but, "now that God has entered this world as Jesus the Christ, how then shall we live?"[21] His answer is: as a special graced responding community that is:

An "Alien" Colony

The church consists of resident aliens whose purpose is not to prop up the old regime of a Christianity subsumed into the world, but to enter into the adventure of being church today, as aliens whose commonwealth is in heaven.[22] Hauerwas wants the Christian to be part of a gospel church adventure rather than merely being a member of the helping professions, "running errands for the world."[23] Therefore, a Christian response needs to resist being judged "by how well or ill the church's presence in the world works to the advantage of the world."[24] Disciples who are aliens are ill at ease in the world, working to agendas that are, in the world's eyes, often alien. Because, for the secular world the individual's rights have become sacrosanct, idolatrously taking the place of God,

---

to liberalism. Barth can allow for the possibility for God working in the world if he so chooses (Stout, *Democracy and Tradition*, 155–6). However, Hauerwas is critical of Barth, in that "Barth seems too willing to leave the world alone." (That is, not to enter into too much critique of the world). For Hauerwas it is the church's duty to critically engage with the world, by separation, in order to expose the world's failing, by challenging its "false notions of science, morality, or art on theological grounds" (*With the Grain*, 202–3).

19. Therefore, in what follows I shall refer only to Hauerwas, even when citing the jointly authored *Resident Aliens* works. This intends no disrespect for Willimon, but retains the focus upon Hauerwas' theology.

20. Hauerwas, *Resident Aliens*, 94.

21. Hauerwas, *Where Resident Aliens Live*, 102.

22. Hence, Hauerwas appeals to texts such as Phil 3:20 and 1 Pet 1:1; 2:9. The "church" in Hauerwas' thinking is "a socio-political, ethical and epistemological necessity . . . and these three dimensions of [the church's] existence are ultimately one in its witness" (Gay, "A Practical Theology," n.p.).

23. Hauerwas, *Resident Aliens*, 58–59, 94.

24. Ibid., 30.

then responsibilities once resting with the church have been hijacked by the "welfare" state—pointedly, responsibilities in healing and public welfare.[25] Thus, the church becomes judged by how useful we are as a "supportive institution" and our clergy as members of a helping profession.[26] Biblically, the church has its own reasons for being, hidden within its own mandate and not found in the world. We are not "chartered by the Emperor."[27] The primary social focus of alien disciples, therefore, lies within the "confessing church's" own community.[28] Contra the charge of sectarianism, the Hauerwasian issue is not whether the church should be in the world or not, but in what form it should be in the world, and for what purpose.[29] Existing as a political alternative to secular society, the

25. Ibid., 34. They argue that Troeltsch's liberalism presented a deterministic sociology, so that the way the world is, is the way it has to be. Thus, in the liberal approach the world sets the agenda (Hauerwas, *Resident Aliens*, 68). The perspective of the church is quite different—"We believe the sociological reality of the church is to be a gathered people separated from the world so that the world may know it is the world" (Hauerwas, *Resident Aliens*, 68).

26. This view is at the very heart of contemporary debates within the NHS regarding the legitimacy of NHS funded hospital chaplaincy. I dispute whether the church should be instrumentalized for public health care purposes, as health care is currently understood within the NHS. In this respect, I have enormous respect for the Hauerwasian model.

27. Or, in my research context, Her Majesty's Government/NHS (Hauerwas, *Resident Aliens*, 39).

28. Following Yoder's categorization of types of church, Hauerwas endorsed the "confessing church" model as a radical alternative to the *activist church* (a "liberal" constituency, concerned with building a better society through social change, not church reformation), or the *conversionist* church (a "conservative" constituency, concerned with transformation of the individual's inner life of sin, via repentance). A *confessing church* rejects both the inner transformative and the social transformative models in preference for the "congregation's determination to worship Christ in all things" (Hauerwas, *Resident Aliens*, 45). On the primary social focus of the church, also see, Hauerwas, *Community of Character*, 10. The church is a social ethic.

29. Hauerwas, *Resident Aliens*, 43. O'Donovan insists Hauerwas cannot be justly charged with sectarianism, but he does think Hauerwas is wrong to link Christendom with a blanket conclusion that every historic instance of the church and the state being linked must imply an acquisitive Constantinian lust for power on the church's part. He argues there have been times when Christian rulers have become subject to the reign of Christ and, at the same time, been very aware of the dangers inherent in their position. He believes it can be right to believe the angelic powers (Christian rulers) can submit to the rule of Christ—but, this should never be assumed to be a permanent right (O'Donovan, *Desire of the Nations*, 215–16). Hauerwas seems to accept this view in his later reflections. See Hauerwas, *With the Grain*, 221, n. 33).

church's "alien" discipleship gives the telos for decision making. It defines who Christians are, and what they do, and why.

Christocentrically Biblical

Hauerwas praises Barth for his reassertion of the primacy of biblical language.[30] Natural theology, therefore, has no place in the church's theology.[31] The church's special-graced Christology is known by her story-formed character.[32] There is an intense focus upon the Bible and ethics from Barth's Christocentric perspective, that is, from the perspective of the justification offered by grace through the life, death, and resurrection of Christ. Only conversion to Christ can deliver from "the distorted thinking of a crippled intellect."[33] It is this emphasis which makes the church radical for major incident response. The church knows Jesus, whereas the world does not.[34] Therefore, a Christian responder will have a unique Christocentric perspective upon what has happened and upon what constitutes best practice from the church community. Special grace provides, in the scriptural revelation, the narrative needed to provide "the basis for a self appropriate to the unresolved and often tragic, conflicts of

30. Hauerwas, *Where Resident Aliens Live*, 21. For Hauerwas, languages are not collections of words, but, as per MacIntyre, practices (59). Hauerwas states, "Rather the 'political' question crucial to the church is what kind of community the church must be to be faithful to the narratives central to Christian convictions" (Hauerwas, *Community of Character*, 2).

31. Hauerwas could only conceive of natural theology in the sense he interpreted the Niebuhrian, liberal, interpretation to be. Stackhouse believes Hauerwas' interpretation of Niebuhr to be wrong here. See Stackhouse, *Making the Best of It*, 37, n. 45, where Stackhouse accuses Hauerwas of caricaturing Niebuhr.

32. Hauerwas, *Community of Character*, 37. For Hauerwas' view on the moral authority of Scripture, see *Community of Character*, chapter 3. O'Donovan sees Christology as the key to the proclamation of the kingdom. Christ is both mediator and priest, who unites God and God's people by his ontological and eschatological Christology. Through this emphasis upon Christ's death and resurrection we enter a new realm (O'Donovan, *Desire of the Nations*, 123–28).

33. Kenneth Surin, *Theology and the Problem of Evil*, cited in Hauerwas, *Naming the Silences*, 50. See also Mathewes' discussion of an Augustinian conversionist approach as the necessity for resolving the bondage of the will, by a reorienting of humans' loves back to God (*Theology of Public Life*, 122–23). For Hauerwas, conversion seems to coincide with baptism. His sympathy with Catholic theology's doctrine of baptismal regeneration comes out at these points. For his conversionist focus upon baptism, see *Resident Aliens*, 52.

34. Hauerwas, *Resident Aliens*, 28.

this existence."[35] Hauerwas challenges the concept of there needing to be a special relationship between Christianity and some form of liberal democratic social system.[36] Rather than a Niebuhrian liberal absorption of the church into the world, there needs to be a radical configuration of the church by the gospel in a way that may contradict the world's view of itself.[37] Liberalism believes access to truth is denied, whereas, for Hauerwas, truth is gifted in Christ, by special grace. Pastoral confidence in this biblical base should lead to a greater exposure of the world to the truth of the gospel from fearless pastoral responders.[38]

A Servant Of, and Then For, the Church

Hauerwas abhors the individualism of modernist liberalism.[39] Christians only gain their identity and purpose in relation with God in Christ, and each other, in the community of the church. The church is the epistemology for the world. Only, then, as servants of the church can Christian responders, serving for the church, serve the world effectively. Hauerwas argues, "the Christian life means, in baptism, to put oneself in the context of other lives than can make us more than we could ever be by ourselves,"[40] and, "the political task of Christians is to be the church rather than to transform the world."[41] Priorities must be in place, therefore. But this is

35. See also Hauerwas, *Community of Character*, 149. Hauerwas bases this on the statement of St. Paul, in 1 Cor 15:10, "But by the grace of God I am what I am, and His grace toward me was not in vain; but I labored more abundantly than they all, yet not I, but the grace of God *which* was with me."

36. Hauerwas, *Community of Character*, 4.

37. Hauerwas, *Resident Aliens*, 28, 83. By "getting into bed" with the secular culture, Christians may fail "to challenge the moral presuppositions of our polity and society" (Hauerwas, *Community of Character*, 73).

38. Hauerwas, *Resident Aliens*, 168–69. Hauerwas admits that *Resident Aliens* represents "a manual for missionaries who have been on furlough for the longest time but are now ready to go back into the fray" (*Where Resident Aliens Live*, 27). Yet, for Hauerwas, missionary evangelism was not so much by verbal confrontation as by the Christian community living out her special graced-ness (*Community of Character*, 105). O'Donovan would endorse Hauerwas' concept of the church confronting the world (as would Stackhouse), even accepting that such confrontation may lead to martyrdom; *but*, it may also lead to a converted citizenship or, when rulers are converted, to a Christian nation that in turn will facilitate the church's mission.

39. Hauerwas, *Where Resident Aliens Live*, 102.

40. Ibid., 112.

41. Hauerwas, *Resident Aliens*, 38. Hauerwas believes that "the church in its profoundest expression is the gathering of people who are able to sustain one another

not a decision for withdrawal from the world. Hauerwas does not see this as a sectarian stance; rather it is a necessary exclusivity for an effective witness to the world, for two reasons: first, because the church must learn and understand her own language, determined by the holiness of God before she can speak to the world; and, second, the world cannot know itself to be the world without the presence of the colony of resident aliens in her midst to identify the world's true needs.[42] The church helps, on the church's own terms, with responders who have learned that what equips them best for responding are the virtues of character the community instills in them.[43]

Faithfully Effective

Hauerwas believes that God has promised that when Christians are faithful then their lives will not be without effect.[44] Faithfulness means serving the faith as it has been revealed in Jesus Christ.[45] He pleads for a renewed and disciplined confidence from the church in its gospel agenda in the world. To this end he rejects the concept of the church's mission being to transform individuals' hearts or to modify society. The church's primary faithfulness is to be manifest in "the congregation's determination

---

through the inevitable tragedies of our lives" (Hauerwas, *Community of Character*, 108). For an example of this in practice by the Mennonite Amish community of West Nickel Mines, Pennsylvania, following a tragic kidnapping and shooting incident in a school, which resulted in five dead and five seriously injured children, see Kasdorf, "To Pasture."

42. Hauerwas, *Community of Character*, 50. Mathewes, on the other hand, argues that an "other worldly" engagement by Christians with the world permits Christians to feel more at ease in the world because their level of expectation from the world is commensurably limited. Therefore, "we can care for the world as much as we do only if the source of our caring is not simply the world itself" (*Theology of Public Life*, 37).

43. Hauerwas, *Resident Aliens*, 61, 83. Also, Hauerwas, *Community of Character*, 85. This has important implications for Christian responders whose remit is outside of the specifically pastoral care realm, because, for Hauerwas, it is not so much *what* we do (though that is by no means unimportant), but *how* we do it—that is, how virtuously we do it (113).

44. Hauerwas, *Community of Character*, 106.

45. In such a stance Hauerwas would argue he is being neither liberal nor conservative, but radical. His point makes quantifying, and qualifying, effectiveness by modern health care criteria impossible, in my view. Certainly, the benefits of Christian pastoral care may not be evident, or assessable, until even years after the major incident, because the criteria Christians work for include eternal not simply temporal measurements (2 Cor 4:16–18).

to worship Christ in all things."[46] To this extent, such faithfulness trumps effectiveness. But, such a dualism is actually false: faithfulness to this priority is a sure way to effectiveness, because, "For the church to set the principle of being church above other principles is not to thumb our noses at results. It is trusting God to give us the rules, which are based on what God is doing in the world to bring about good results."[47] Faith and faithfulness are synonymous. By faith we are incorporated into God's story; we find out who we are, and what our alien purpose is. Our faithfulness may seem odd therefore, but it is essential to the church's mission. Her oddness appears most in her ethics, as revealed in the Sermon on the Mount.[48] Such are the church's ethics, which are largely incomprehensible to the world. Whereas Enlightenment ethics are more about what is right for "me" (the individual), the ethics of the Sermon on the Mount are about revealing what God is like, and, therefore, what the church should be like so she may witness to the world for God.[49] Looking at the world from this ethical perspective, we are able to grab hold of the world wisely.[50] The world needs the church to know it needs redeeming, so a Niebuhrian, accommodationist, approach gives the world less and less to disbelieve.[51] For Hauerwas, an exclusivist approach to cooperation with the world's agencies is essential, because the true enemy in the cosmic battle the church is involved in is the world's capacity to coerce the church into cooperation.[52] The church lives in the world (and cooperates) on her own terms.[53]

---

46. Hauerwas, *Resident Aliens*, 45

47. Ibid., 46.

48. See Matt chapters 5–7. Hauerwas, *Resident Aliens*, 74–75, 94. In the *Resident Aliens* volumes Hauerwas focuses upon *ethics*, but in his *A Community of Character* he makes it clear he prefers to stress the importance of *virtues*. The difference being: ethics are concerned with quality of actions, and virtues with quality of character for performing suitable actions. For O'Donovan the Sermon on the Mount provides the law of the new Christian community.(*Desire of the Nations*, 180).

49. Hauerwas, *Resident Aliens*, chapter 4.

50. Ibid., 87.

51. Ibid., 94.

52. Hauerwas, *Where Resident Aliens Live*, 34. For Hauerwas, the Christian community is built upon trust in God not coercion (*Community of Character*, 84).

53. Hauerwas, *Where Resident Aliens Live*, 48. O'Donovan offers a significant observation when he rejects the concept of the church as "a kind of service-agency (inevitably clerical) which puts itself at the disposal of a multitude of rulers" (*Desire of the Nations*, 162). Akin to Hauerwas, O'Donovan argues that through the royal ascension

Holy

Hauerwas rejected the liberal univocal concept of "morality." Different traditions and communities have different concepts of morality. For the Christian tradition, morality means spiritual growth in holiness and grace as a gift, not as an autonomous right.[54] Christian responders are converted to Christ, and they lead holy lives. For, without grace and conversion then it is impossible to gain answers to the question of evil— "Only faith in Christ makes possible the cleansing of our vision."[55] These holy lives will be strictly disciplined, both individually and corporately, resistant to tolerance and inclusivism.[56] This Christ-centred holiness is expressed most significantly in the church's worship, which is, in turn, her witness to the world. It is in her communal worship that the church learns to see in the right direction ethically.[57] It is also how her practices are discerned and directed.[58] The special-graced community has the valuable contribution of a virtuous character to offer. This is cultivated by being a member of a truthful community in which destructive histories are escaped. The contributive value of such goods exceeds that which any professional, technical training programs can make.[59] Of particular significance to major incident response is the virtue of patient hope, where "patience is training in how to wait when there is no way to resolve our moral conflicts or even when we see no clear way to go."[60]

This, I propose, would be Hauerwas' virtuous character of a major incident-Christian-responding community.[61]

---

of the resurrected King Jesus, Christians, as citizens of the kingdom of heaven, are authorized to teach and impact upon the secular by her influence and with a divinely endowed confidence, since the church is free from all other lordships (*Desire of the Nations*, 161–66).

54. See 2 Pet 3:18.

55. Hauerwas, *Where Resident Aliens Live*, 80–81; Hauerwas, *Community of Character*, 130. Also, Hauerwas, *Christian Existence Today*, 42; Hauerwas, *Naming the Silences*, 50.

56. Hauerwas, *Resident Aliens*, 63. It is worth noting that Hauerwas considers the closest analogy to such a disciplined way of life he would endorse, in the church community, is that of the U.S. Marines' training camp regime (Hauerwas, *Where Resident Aliens Live*, 74–76).

57. Hauerwas, *Resident Aliens*, 95–97.

58. Hauerwas, *Where Resident Aliens Live*, 18.

59. Hauerwas, *Community of Character*, 126.

60. Ibid., 127.

61. It is important to note that the Anabaptist/Mennonite Church community in

John G. Stackhouse Jr.

Stackhouse's work is a selective revision of H. Richard Niebuhr's *Christ and Culture*.[62] Whilst Niebuhr was not an Evangelical, Stackhouse is.[63] Stackhouse's explication of Niebuhr's typology of ways Christians can relate to culture, and his development of a new realism, presents a special grace perspective on the relationship the evangelical catholic Christian community can have to the multi-agency world of major incident response.[64] Stackhouse says that his work represents theology as a "reflection upon any subject that is conducted with primary reference to the special revelation given to us in the person of Christ and in the Scriptures . . ." *Making the Best of It* is a theology of culture "shaped by what God has revealed about it."[65] Stackhouse's approach resonates with both canonical and cultural-linguistic schools (thus with Vanhoozer and Hauerwas), most notably, his belief that the Bible is a narrative story that follows the basic plot of creation, fall, redemption and consummation, where historicity is vital for faith in God, and for understanding our own part in God's plan.[66] His canonical linguistic approach combines the theodramatic principles of *sola scriptura* and doctrine as communicative action.[67] He employs a (Protestant) Christian tetralectic of Scripture, reason, tradition, and experience.[68] These combine in a conversation within a hermeneutical spiral to bring greater coherence to our understanding of the truth. Yet, even with Scripture and the indwelling Holy Spirit, we need to avoid binary thinking, and engage in only proportional conclusions, given our

---

the U.S. does have a system for disaster response. See the Mennonite Disaster Service website: http://www.mds.mennonite.net/; also Mennonite Disaster Service, "Early Response Team Manual."

62. Niebuhr, *Christ and Culture*.

63. Niebuhr was more a Christian theological ethicist, while Stackhouse is a theologian.

64. Niebuhr's typology consists of: Christ against culture; Christ of culture; Christ above culture; Christ in paradox with culture; Christ transforming culture (Stackhouse, *Making the Best of It*, 22–30).

65. Stackhouse, *Making the Best of It*, 5.

66. Ibid., 183–205.

67. Ibid., 193.

68. Note, each of these is also essential to Vanhoozer's canonical linguistic theological approach as well, particularly in regard to Scripture and tradition (*Drama of Doctrine*, 233–36). Hauerwas' main problem with this tetralectic would be the referent of reason and maybe even individual experience, that is, personal experience aside from the church community.

lack of full information, our fallibility and weaknesses. Thus, "the solitary Christian [and community] draws together her findings from Scripture, tradition, and reason, and experience in a hermeneutical spiral that she hopes will eventuate in knowledge sufficient for her to know God better and to do his will in the world."[69]

In summary, Stackhouse constructs a theology that forms a hybrid of Niebuhr's "Christ in paradox with culture" and "Christ transforming culture."[70] His thesis is:

> Under the general providence of God, who has ordained and who continues to supervise the structures and powers of earthly life, and particularly institutions such as family and government, Christians are to participate in, and contribute to, non-Christian or sub-Christian societies while (somehow) maintaining their ultimate allegiance to Christ.

And, in so doing, under special grace, bring about some transformations within those societies.[71]

In what follows, I attempt to explore a "Stackhousian" special graced theology of legitimation for, and contribution to, major incident response.

Again, the key question he would ask in approaching major incident response concerns not what we should do, but what we should be. Thus, Stackhouse utilizes the vocational question, who are we, for Jesus Christ, today?[72] His answer is: a special graced responder of:

Realism

Christians inhabit the space between Eden and the New Jerusalem and must be careful not to allow the idealism of Eden or the apocalypticism for the New Jerusalem to cloud their judgment of life in the messy world

---

69. Stackhouse, *Making the Best of It*, 176.

70. Ibid., 41. After some explication and analysis of Niebuhr's typology (part 1), and then some consideration of particularly helpful theological influences upon Stackhouse, from C. S. Lewis, Reinhold Niebuhr, and Dietrich Bonhoeffer (part 2), his actual theology is presented in part 3 of the book.

71. For the quote, see Stackhouse, *Making the Best of It*, 26. I have attempted to summarize, overall, Stackhouse's thesis.

72. Stackhouse, *Making the Best of It*, 7. Even asking "What would *Jesus* do?" is invalidated by the fact that we are not living in light of Jesus' earthly life, but in light of his resurrection, of the Holy Spirit's enabling of "greater works" (John 14:12), and of the vast cultural gap between then and now (*Making the Best of It*, 190–91). Having the mind of Christ, Christ's *habitus* for today's traumatic contexts, is the key.

of the in between.[73] Therefore, we must resist oversimplifying ethics.[74] Biblical worldview realism can be more real than our Evangelical eyes are prepared to admit. Special grace should grant the Christian a clearer view of this reality, an epistemological precedence over the world's view of itself, and a central axis in the person of Christ for guiding critical choices.[75] This realism enables clarity in regard to both the good and the evil aspects of societies. Fundamentally, creation is good, not evil. Special grace enables the Christian to qualifiedly revel in the goodness of the world and in the hope of transformation. Culture is a cohabitation of good and evil, which, qualifiedly, takes place not just in the world, but in our own hearts.[76] On the one hand, grace enables us to discern the sin within as well as the sins without. Ambiguity and ambivalence inhabit the fallen human realm; thus, we shall expect to work with less than best assumptions and results.[77] On the other hand, grace also hopes in the transformative value of the gospel for good as it is lived out and voiced by the communicative actions of Christians, in a concomitant realism about life in the Spirit.[78] We may see that grace has equipped us to navigate the world, and to negotiate with the world, so that good things happen and bad things do not.[79] Thus, "We are not to stand on the sidelines wringing our hands over situations in which we have refused to invest ourselves and invoking God's miraculous power to achieve what our disobedience has not."[80] We imitate Christ's involvement with reality.[81]

73. Mathewes calls apocalypticism "a form of eschatological meteorology." He believes Christians can provide a necessary balance between the dangers of apocalypticism and passivism as they live "during the world" (*Theology of Public Life*, 39, 159).

74. Stackhouse, *Making the Best of It*, 162.

75. Ibid., 167. Stackhouse cites Yoder's claim that the church precedes the world epistemologically and axiologically (ethically).

76. Stackhouse, *Making the Best of It*, 187.

77. Ibid., 265.

78. See Rom 8:27–28; Gal 5:16–25. With the Roman's statement it is important to understand the Pauline assurance of the providence of God working all things together for the good of Christians (v. 28) in the context of the Spirit's intercessory work (v. 27).

79. Stackhouse, *Making the Best of It*, 273.

80. Ibid., 274.

81. Ibid., 166.

Shalom

The key special grace contribution to transforming the non-Christian world is the work of shalom.[82] For Stackhouse, shalom is rooted originally in the creation commandments to love God and our neighbor—in being truly human. However, the fall has created an emergency situation for which the covenant of redemption commands love and the Great Commission (Matt 28:18–20). These special graced redemptive commands now serve the creation ones as "[emergency] measures for an emergency situation." Shalom is a provision unique to special grace, practically rooted as it is in Christ.[83] It provides the singular achievement where all involved only benefit.[84] Evaluating/auditing shalom requires a theology broad enough to envelop everything that contributes to the flourishing of creation and the divine pleasure, and also fine enough to see how particular tasks contribute to the whole. The implications of shalom for the empowering and encouragement of every responding agent and agency to a major incident are enormous. Major incident response requires such a vast array of skills, and Stackhouse is helpful in endorsing the divine deployment of particular modes of calling to accomplish particular purposes.[85]

Love/Grace

Special grace gives a unique motivation to offer love on the basis that a Christian has received love in the form of grace from God—that is,

82. Stackhouse defines *shalom* as "A condition in which each individual thing is fully and healthily itself and in which it enjoys peaceful, wholesome, and delightful relations with God, with itself, and with all the rest of creation" (*Making the Best of It*, 49).

83. Stackhouse, *Making the Best of It*, 222. The driving force for the shalomic principle is the eschatological and apocalyptic vision of the church (Rev 21:1—22:5). Without this vision it is impossible to resist the "relentless conformist pressures of our culture." In this Stackhouse concurs precisely with O'Donovan (see O'Donovan, *Desire of the Nations*, 285). However, this conception must not be understood in dispensationalist terms—terms that Stackhouse firmly rejects (*Making the Best of It*, 194).

84. Stackhouse, *Making the Best of It*, 204–5.

85. Thus, specialties and specialists should be acknowledged and respected to avoid the peril of the "turf war" so endemic in major incident response. To endorse specialties/specialists is not to endorse elitism, or, in the case of pastoral carers, a clericalism. It is simply to recognize God's gifting of certain persons to do particular works in the interests of promoting *shalom* as well as recognizing the reality of major incident plans requiring a category of faith responders who have been suitably trained and accredited. See Stackhouse, *Making the Best of It*, 242–49.

unmerited love.[86] Therefore, either humanitarianly, or, through a Christian community, the Christian works out of the creation commandments to take dominion over the earth, and the great commandment to love God and one's neighbor.[87] So, "There is nothing we can justify doing if it means not loving God above all else and with all that we are. There is nothing we can justify doing if it means not loving our neighbor as ourselves."[88] Thus, responding to human need is unavoidable, irrespective of the cost. Grace means "our mission is to get things done, not to avoid getting dirty, or bloody in the process . . . we must recognize that loving God and one's neighbor in this troubled and troubling world often entails dirt and blood."[89] We are to show love and to discern it wherever we can.[90] However, there is a particular love the Christian community is to experience among its own members, which is consequentially missional and evangelistic.[91] There is an exclusivist love the evangelical catholic Christian community should be showing to be a blessing to the whole world.[92]

Vocation

Special grace provides a Christian culture of neither withdrawal from nor conquest of public life, but rather of perseverance in it. This culture inspires a vocational relationship with the world for the Christian.[93] Such a concept of vocation has different facets: *first*, it is rooted in Christological

---

86. It is unique because of its definition: "the act of going beyond the strict requirements of justice, beyond satisfying some standard of correct behavior, to seeking the welfare of the other, to acting so as to benefit the other beyond his or her just deserts" (Stackhouse, *Making the Best of It*, 212). This is why I am happy to use the term grace as synonymous with love.

87. Gen 1:26–28; Matt 22:37–40; Stackhouse, *Making the Best of It*, 209–16. See also Mathewes' reflection on divine love providing a resolution to the egotistical infection of human nature's capability to love aright. He claims, "But a way has been made available to us, in Christ: we should love this world because God loves it, and in the way that God loves it—which is a depth of love so great that God enters the world in the person of the Son. But we must love the world in God, by participating in God's love of it" (*Theology of Public Life*, 84).

88. Stackhouse, *Making the Best of It*, 210.

89. Ibid., 211.

90. Ibid., 215.

91. See John 13:34–35.

92. Stackhouse, *Making the Best of It*, 217. It is at this level that the Hauerwasian model can be very positive.

93. Stackhouse, *Making the Best of It*, 7.

discipleship and mission.[94] So, the Christian's priority is to attend to Jesus by increasing in the knowledge and loving obedience of God and believing God will provide all that is necessary to achieve this.[95] Out of this, the witness of Christians loving comes a vocation to work for shalom in the world. This could be controversial for major incident response if it meant only voicing the gospel in acts of proclamatory evangelism. Though evangelism in this sense cannot be abandoned, for by it, principally, the world is transformed by the Holy Spirit; yet, this is not all the Christian aims for under the Great Commission. So, second, a holistic view of vocation is encouraged, involving one another, and then humanitarianly serving the world in the creation of shalom.[96] Special grace reveals a divine vocation to be a Christian in every mode of life, public as well as private, religious as well as secular. So, any Christian within the responding agencies can do their particular work to the glory of God, as a part of their mission. Their divinely endowed skills serve the great commission.

Wisdom

Sapiential development is integral to the canonical linguistic approach to configuration, and it is integral to major incident response. However, Stackhouse recognizes that Christians do not have a monopoly upon wisdom because grace "rains down intelligence on the just and the unjust … such that non-Christians frequently have better ideas than Christians."[97]

94. Luke 24:48; Acts 1:8. Stackhouse, Mathewes, and O'Donovan all believe civic involvement to be a theological task that is integral to Christian mission in the world.

95. Stackhouse, *Making the Best of It*, 166. Ken Myers argues strongly for culture being neutralized by common grace, and therefore it being important for Christians to work within cultures, not trying to create new "Christian" cultures. See Myers, "Christianity, Culture," n.p. O'Donovan insists the church is not at liberty to withdraw from mission, but such withdrawals have taken place when the church and state have become unified. In such times the church ceased to challenge the state's rulers, a weakness, he believes, in all secularly/religiously neutral states (*Desire of the Nations*, 212–3).

96. Stackhouse helpfully reminds us that we are human before Christian (*Making the Best of It*, 234). Mathewes reflects upon the potential "zealot" dimension to a conversionist approach. He argues that, with due maturation, "Conversion does not draw humans out of the world; rather, it puts them more fully, and more properly, *into* it" (*Theology of Public Life*, 123). O'Donovan, however, reflects on the early Palestinian zealot movement and concludes that the reason Jesus did not espouse it was due to his view of the cosmic dimension being of greater importance than the humanly political—upon the spiritual forces that were preventing Israel from living before the world as they should (O'Donovan, *Desire of the Nations*, 95).

97. Stackhouse, *Making the Best of It*, 167. Intriguingly, Hauerwas also recognizes

However, indwelt by the Holy Spirit, the Christian worldview should enable seeing reality more clearly. In a context of suffering, special grace gifts the sincerely prayerful asker with wisdom.[98] Responders can then wisely utilize the tetralectic of Scripture, tradition, reason, and experience to explore what to do in their situation.[99] Wisdom will also direct to the most effective forms of Christian relation with our neighbors and society, and, most controversially, in major incident response, when to speak the gospel and when not.[100] Capps reminds us, in his Ricoeurian fashion, that texts and actions leave their mark, and can have unintended consequences, for good or ill.[101]

Faith

Special grace grants salvific faith, not just in the moment of justification, but for a life of faith that, essentially, means a life of trustful hope in God's providence and love.[102] This involves not just believing in remarkable things being possible, and God being able to achieve such things in the teeth of our own great weakness and fear within a major incident, it also means trusting that God can use Christians even when they cannot work perfection and they make mistakes.[103] As Stackhouse comments:

> "Our way of life" is to be performing good works, so we need
> not be paralyzed by our inability to discern with certainty what
> to do in a difficult situation or to foresee all of the consequences

there can be a valid contribution by the world (*Resident Aliens*, 100). Whereas for Hauerwas this is a concession, for Stackhouse it is fundamental to his graced worldview.

98. Jas 1:5. This assurance comes in the context of the early Christians' experience of trial and suffering where critical, difficult decisions were essential.

99. Stackhouse, *Making the Best of It*, 224.

100. More recently, the Billy Graham Association's "Rapid Response Teams" information tends to focus upon the opportunities disaster contexts have given for leading people to Christ. See Munday, "Ministry to a Pluralistic Community."

101. Cited in Lyall, *Integrity of Pastoral Care*, 51–52.

102. See also the focus upon the priority of love and critical hopeful citizenship, wherein Christians maintain a basic estrangement from the world to remain prophetic critics of it in a spirit of hopeful charity, not a "spectatorial sneering," in Mathewes, *Theology of Public Life*, chapters 2 and 5. He concludes, "Public life for Christians, then, when properly undertaken, inevitably leads to contemplation of the mysteries of providence, sovereignty of God, and the cultivation of the holy terror that is integral to true piety" (259–60).

103. Stackhouse reflects upon the possibility of the miraculous as an aspect of possibility, though he judges God "normally works in normal ways" (*Making the Best of It*, 270–74).

of our actions. We trust that God will show us what he wants to show us in order for us to respond as he wants us to respond.[104]

However, for Stackhouse, faith/faithfulness must also equate in some measure with effectiveness. Good results demonstrate the integrity of our works of faith.[105] This, in turn, should stimulate a constant reviewing of relations, policies, and methods. Faith should leave an audit trail of good practice.

Friendship

Special grace should make us friendly.[106] How can *shalom* be worked in any other way? By Stackhouse's thinking this principle would be relevant at two levels for major incident response: interagency cooperation and professionalism. While Stackhouse stresses the need for ethical clarity in the differentiation between agencies, he states,

> What keeps this differentiation from devolving into sheer fragmentation, however, and even a kind of low-grade civil war of various sectors and groups encroaching on each other's turf . . . is the underlying purpose of the cultural mandate. Each sector of society, and the groups and individuals within those sectors [whether emergency planning, rescue, healthcare, law enforcement, investigation, pastoral care] maintains a central concern to . . . increase shalom—and will therefore welcome and cooperate with others who have the same concern.[107]

Special grace should give a sharp focus on the reality of common grace humanitarianism that bridges differentiation.[108] It articulates a morality that seriously addresses the deep challenge of pluralism today.[109] But, special grace should give a discerning focus on the common *telos*

104. Stackhouse, *Making the Best of It*, 292. This would shed encouraging light on my aporetic experience of trying to "investigate" the case of the dying boy crying out (see chapter 4, [**xref**]).

105. He appeals to Matt 25:14–30.

106. Matt 18:21–35.

107. Stackhouse, *Making the Best of It*, 230–31.

108. Stackhouse's position here would accord with Jeffrey Stout's conclusion, in his *Democracy and Tradition*, which is summarized in Stahlberg's review article: "then they should work to unearth those values *wherever they see them lying dormant* . . ." (202, emphasis mine).

109. Mathewes, *Theology of Public Life*, 116. See chapter 10 for my exploration of ecumenical and interfaith friendship in this regard.

of the response for each agency—the *shalomic* purpose, and this should guide and temper the focus upon technical professionalism so that each responder ensures professionalism serves the human good, not the less ethical ends of mere technical functionality.[110]

Holiness

Special grace provides a golden thread of holiness, woven through the lives of Christian responders, because special grace is, above all, redemptively holy. Christian responders' lives will not be perfect, and, indeed, they must be alert to any such pretentiousness within themselves, but they will have a heart for holiness and a grace that forgives the lack—in themselves and others.[111] Stackhouse helps navigation of this tension by recommending,

> Thus we will need to exercise a holy shrewdness, a spiritual prudence about what—in a world bristling with problems and crying with needs—we should do. We need to keep our minds on the big picture, recognizing all the while that such awareness often entails interrupting our plans to care for the wounded stranger by the side of the road. We must be true to our vocations and be wise in their fulfilment. We will remember that we are not called to root up all the weeds . . . And we will be willing to overlook minor issues to focus on major ones and to sacrifice lesser goods for greater ones—a principle that is very hard to accept for binary-minded Christians, those who think that compromise always involves tolerating a certain amount of evil (which it usually does) and therefore must always be avoided (which is the way to get very little accomplished in the real world). Again, God tolerates a certain amount of evil and does not try to fix everything at once. We should therefore be more godly and less fastidious. And we can do so because we hope in the God who one day will make all things new.[112]

---

110. This point is significant in view of a criticism that was made about the response of the statutory emergency services in their response to the London bombings of July 7, 2005. See "Addressing Lessons from the Emergency Response to the 7 July 2005 London Bombings."

111. See also Reinhold Niebuhr, "The Christian Church in a Secular Age," in Brown, ed., *Essential Reinhold Niebuhr*, 87–92.

112. Stackhouse, *Making the Best of It*, 294–95.

In Stackhousian terms, as Christian responders, our calling is to make the best of it; to be a voice neither for capitulation nor isolation, but for perseverance toward transformation and ultimate consummation.

Discussion

From my review of these interlocutors there are some points of convergence worth noting. These are: primacy of virtues; Christian particularity; canonical integrity; Christocentricity; faith; wisdom; and holiness. Significantly, however, there are points of considerable divergence, such as: realism-idealism; individual-community; boundaries of discipleship; and vocation in the world. Some brief discussion of these is salient.[113]

Convergence[114]—Both parties to this discussion place the cultivation of virtue before that of performance/technical ability or action. Of primary importance to defining the effectiveness of major incident response for Christian responders, and especially pastoral carers, is the virtuous life. It is the unique contribution of God's special grace that, by the indwelling Spirit, nurtures such a life.[115] There is a level of agreement upon the centrality of the Bible in the formation of virtue as the guidance for good action. There is also a level of convergence in terms of particularity. Both

---

113. It is worth noting that neither party is a slave to their preferred forebear. Hauerwas is critical of Barth at certain points (notably in his *With the Grain*, chapter 6), and Stackhouse states explicitly that he is not providing an apologetic for H. Richard Niebuhr, or any others who have influenced him (*Making the Best of It*, 161).

114. Hauerwas makes no reference to Stackhouse, and Stackhouse refers to Hauerwas only dismissively. He refers to *Resident Aliens*, as "an irresponsible reading of Niebuhr . . . theologically, ethically, and hermeneutically" (*Making the Best of It*, 37, n. 45).

115. Or, in terms of Gal 5:22–23, the Spirited life. The use of virtue, as a term, owes more to Aristotle than to scriptural rhetoric of "fruits of the Spirit." See H. G. Link and A. Ringwald's comment on, "*aretē*, virtue" in Colin Brown, ed., *New International Dictionary of New Testament Theology*, vol. 3, 927–28. For the Spirit's work see, Rom 8:1–17; compare 2 Pet 1:5–7. Virtue is not the only capability, however. It is possible for Christians to have high levels of virtue and yet be disqualified from responding because of physical or psychological factors that would expose them and/or casualties to high levels of risk if they responded. Also, there may be certain cases where the Christian is in a low level of virtue (due to a rebellious backsliding), but because of their employed role as a responder they have no choice but to respond. We would not wish to undermine the value of their technical proficiency in such cases, nor the fact that God can sovereignly use them for spiritual good. While effectiveness should be a measure of faithfulness to truth (as both Hauerwas and Stackhouse maintain), a level of effectiveness can also be achieved in unfaithfulness as well at times. The OT prophet Jonah is a case in point (Jonah 3).

parties consider that an adherence to a distinctly Christian spirituality is essential, for which redemptive faith in Christ's life, death and resurrection, and eschatological return is vital. The importance of conversion, faith, and holiness is important for both parties as well. Both would argue that the formation of wisdom is essential to good responding, and that special grace grants a Spirited insight into the Scriptures for such.[116] They also agree that faithful working of the truth will lead to effectiveness that can be audited—special grace works, it has an evidence base, when assessed by the narrative methodologies of theological testimony.[117]

DIVERGENCE—There is, however, significant divergence between Hauerwas and Stackhouse. Regarding the primacy of virtue, it should be noted that Hauerwas' concern is on the virtuous community, whereas Stackhouse's is inclusive of the individual person.[118] But the fundamental divergence is over their views of the world and what relationship the Christian/church should cultivate with the world. Hauerwas rejects the Niebuhrian concept, and "realist" application, of natural theology, which he judges is both liberal and favors liberal democracy—Hauerwas' chief enemy.[119] Stackhouse, interpreting Richard Niebuhr somewhat differently and more favorably, believes Hauerwas' interpretation of Niebuhr is wrong, both factually and theologically.[120] There is fundamental divergence over the moral nature of the world. Whereas Hauerwas creates a dualism, between church and world, Stackhouse considers there to be a basic goodness within the fallen creation, commensurate with God's priority of creative and redemptive love. From this basis he enunciates a compelling evangelical theological legitimation for Christians relating to, and even partnering with, the world at certain levels of mutual respect

116. This emphasis accords also with the sapiential focus of the canonical linguistic approach of Vanhoozer.

117. Hence, the purpose of the testimony of Heb 11.

118. For Hauerwas there is no authentic individuality outside of the church community.

119. Hauerwas' chief target for criticism in regard to natural theology is Reinhold Niebuhr (see Hauerwas, *With the Grain*, chapter 5).

120. Hauerwas was guilty of caricaturing Niebuhr by implying Niebuhr creates an either/or polarization of church and culture. O'Donovan would also show distance from Hauerwas on this point. He acknowledged that none of us can reflect without the influences of liberalism. Liberalism is a Westerner's fate, which does deserve some respect insofar as it has served the church well, if qualifiedly so (O'Donovan, *Desire of the Nations*, 229). Jeffrey Stout, David Ford, and Nigel Biggar would all concur with O'Donovan on this point.

and love, based upon the creation commands to love. However, these relations are always to be kept under the careful governance of a Christocentric canonical perspective. Admittedly, Stackhouse's position suffers from a history of considerable periodic failure when the church has indeed "sold out" to secularism while she has been attempting a secularized discourse.[121] To this extent Hauerwas serves as a necessary check on this realist stance.[122] Nevertheless, realism allows for Christians to work for the shalom of humanity by levels of partnership with humanitarian agencies in a way that Hauerwas would seem to forbid as compromising and ineffective for the church's true mandate, that only an actual alienation of the Christian, into the church community, can be effective. It is precisely this Hauerwasian strength which is his greatest weakness. Hauerwas' position continually begs the question, *What church?* Into which church community should we retreat, when each church community is already embedded into a culture? The fact is that churches differ hugely in theology and ethics. Some of these would not consider some others even to be churches.[123] Hauerwas is just not being real at this point. For Stackhouse

121. O'Donovan makes a similar point. Prochaska argues that historically this happened especially in the late nineteenth and early twentieth centuries when Christian voluntary charitable movements became subsumed under the state (*Christianity and Social Service*, chapter 1 and pages 75–76). I am grateful to Jeffrey Stout for this distinction between "secularism" as an ideology, and "secularization" as a form of ethical discourse. Stout argues compellingly for such a distinction in his argument against a resentment of the secular (by Radical Orthodoxy proponents) for the secularization of ethical discourse. He argues all societal voices are to have a legitimate place, and the opportunity of "thick" discourse so there can be an attempt to prevent the misunderstanding and caricature (something Stackhouse believes Hauerwas is guilty of with regard to H. Richard Niebuhr), and Stout would argue Hauerwas needs democracy to prevent. In fact, Stout argues, Hauerwas makes some of his forceful points while benefiting from a liberal democracy he hates (*Democracy and Tradition*, 119). Stout defines "secularized" as, "The fact that participants in a given discursive practice are not in a position to take for granted that their interlocutors are making the same religious assumptions as they are" (*Democracy and Tradition*, 97). Also see Coffey, "Secularisation," n.p.

122. O'Donovan does too, somewhere in between Hauerwas and Stackhouse. He gauged the church must never be too much at home in this world—she is, after all, a martyr church. However, she must be willing to honor the martyrs by taking advantage of the positive influences they had upon repentant aspects of the *saeculum* (*Desire of the Nations*, 215).

123. On the other hand Hauerwas makes the valid rejoinder that there are also great differences between the various claims to universal natural law principles, and this makes the approach of modernism equally unsafe. (Stout, *Democracy and Tradition*, 145).

(and for Hauerwas' critics in general) Hauerwas represents an unnecessary, sectarian, tribalism.[124] This is dangerous because it encourages in the church a hubris that could deafen her to the critical contribution to learning and wisdom the world has to offer the church.[125] There is an important difference between believing that Christ is the truth and that the Hauerwasian church of Christ is the truth. It will also deafen the ears of an insulted world to anything the church may have to warn her about herself.[126] Nevertheless, Hauerwas presents a case for the church entering into partnerships with a stronger requirement that her terms be heeded—that she is not chartered by the state.

Both parties are strong on Christian discipleship, but diverge strongly over its boundaries. Hauerwas argues for the vocation of discipleship to be separatist, within the "resident alien" life of the church, witnessing only by the internal life of the church. While it would be wrong to underestimate the value of this Hauerwasian principle (and I do not believe Stackhouse does), yet Stackhouse argues more convincingly for the legitimate extension of the vocation of discipleship into the world itself. Therefore, Stackhouse's strength is in his emphasis upon Christian vocation in the real world and the holistic nature of that vocation.[127]

---

124. Hauerwas responds to criticisms of his theological stance being sectarian, fideistic, and socially irresponsible in his *Christian Existence Today*, as does Willimon in the *Where Resident Aliens Live* volume. Stout, who believes Hauerwas has some very important emphases, believes he does his cause a massive disservice by caricaturing liberal democracy and demonizing it to the extent he does.

125. Not only does this view risk a spiritual hubris in the church, but also an uncharitableness. Stout accuses Hauerwas of offending the "vocation of charitable interpretation" (*Democracy and Tradition*, 157).

126. Hence Stout can accuse Hauerwas of "[leaving] the world outside the modern church in a doubly darkened condition" (*Democracy and Tradition*, 154). One sensitive area, where the willingness to learn is now significant, is that of terrorism. An additional aspect to this dimension is the deep concern for human rights and humanitarianism that terrorists can feel. The work of Rai serves to highlight this in respect of the London bombings of 2005 (*7/7: The London Bombings*).

127. Also from within the U.S. context, Mathewes usefully argues a similar case based on an Augustinian exposition. Mathewes argues the case for Christians entering fully into a faithful, hopeful, and charitable citizenship. He argues it is possible for Christians to be faithful both to their church and civic communities, while acknowledging the need to guard against the enemies of Constantinianism and totalitarian theocracy. For him, civic involvement for the Christian is theological, a part of Christian liturgy, or service (*Theology of Public Life*, 146).

Conclusion

From this discussion of Hauerwas and Stackhouse, I conclude the following practices and virtues are provided uniquely by a contribution of special grace to major incident response: holy lives, converted and committed to Christ in a holistic discipleship of compassion and mercy, within the graced church community primarily, but overflowing in a vocation to the world in community and individual humanitarian partnerships, at shalomic levels that do not require a diminution of a distinctly Christian contribution essential to the context of that partnership. A response should come out of the Christian community, not simply from isolated individuals. Accreditation of, and by, that community of individuals should be positive, supportive, and pastoral in nature. While the calling to make disciples of all nations is to be at the heart of every Christian community, the inner compulsion to form a conversionist agenda needs to be gracefully and sapientially restrained. Nevertheless, responders will possess a discernment of the issues from within traumatic contexts which can be best addressed from a distinctly spiritual perspective, and have the wisdom to address these themselves, as pastoral carers, or refer to those who have more time and/or expertise.[128] Special grace theology can also make a sapiential pastoral contribution in the construction of national civic and local church memorial services and through the routine practice of worship.[129]

God in Christ shows us "distance from a culture must never degenerate into flight from that culture but must be a way of living in a culture."[130] This interlocution reveals a central issue of dispute between key players who, I believe, have genuine compassion over suffering and who are convinced they have a responding role to play in the world.[131]

128. On the dilemma of referring to Christian and/or non-Christians, see Collett, et al., "Faith-Based Decisions?" 119–27.

129. One person who has been able to do this from an Evangelical constituency is the Rev. John Mosey, whose daughter died in the Lockerbie murders (1988). Mosey has been involved in the creation and delivery of memorial liturgy and preaching at a number of the Lockerbie memorial services. He has shared something of the theological and pastoral sensitivity required in such roles. I experienced something of this in my role in the creation of the memorial garden for Kegworth/M1 (See Appendix 2.)

130. Volf, *Exclusion and Embrace*, 50. Stout suggests, "From Barth's point of view, the issue is whether the church maintains a proper recognition of the distance between the human social practices it embodies and God's freedom to act graciously wherever and however he sees fit" (*Democracy and Tradition*, 155).

131. There is no indication that those espousing a Hauerwasian position feel any

The root of this dispute lies in the different concepts of "distance" the parties feel they should place between the world and themselves. Theologically this is rooted in differing interpretations of grace, and in the concept of common grace in particular.

Common Grace

Common grace is a theological observation intelligible only from the Christological perspective of special grace, and, as such, is an integral aspect to the theodrama.[132]

Major incident response, besides being a realm of great trauma and evil, also represents a theater of the good, the heroic, and selfless acts of bravery, where people have even laid down their own lives to comfort, if not actually save, others.[133] In some incidents it is remarkable that

less compassion towards major incident contexts, or respond any the less, even if their response is less open. (Witness the way in which the Mennonite Amish community have responded to their traumas, or how some of the Ulster families responded to their traumas from Kegworth/M1, where some felt they wanted separation from the ecumenical aspects, or the distinctly Roman Catholic or Protestant aspects of that ecumenism.)

132. For this perspective, see Wells, *Above All*, 251–57. This is also McGrath's view in his nuanced form of natural theology (or a theology of nature, since nature requires being seen through the lens of Christ). There is no departure, therefore, from the theodrama, which controls my methodology, in giving consideration to common grace. I am still adhering to the principle that, "the gospel, God's saving Word/Act wrought in the person and work of Jesus Christ—must shape theology's method, not vice-versa." If Scripture presents a "canonical atlas" with a diversity of maps "that variously render the way, the truth, and the life," then Jesus Christ is always the orientation of north. Our place in the plot is measured by the way our actions fit onto the biblical map (Vanhoozer, *Drama of Doctrine*, 35, 294–99). The doctrine of common grace I explore is always orientated north. It is a Christological common grace.

133. For instance, Channel 4, as a part of commemorating the London bombings (7/7) produced two documentary programs, reflecting a spiritual theme (though not religious as such). This was further expressed in the titles for the programs—"The Miracle of Carriage 346" that was concerned with the arbitrary, remarkable, escapes from death or serious injury some passengers had. Also, "7/7: The Angels of Edgware Road," that focused upon fellow passengers (traumatized and injured themselves) who were able to give life-saving care to the injured prior to the emergency services arrival at the scene in the tunnel at Edgware Road tube station. Yet both programs dwelt exclusively upon how this miraculous, and angelic, human response reaffirmed faith in *human* nature. So, Wong, "Compassionate and Spiritual Care," 3, reflects on the work of medical staff in containing the SARS (Severe Acute Respiratory Syndrome) outbreak in Hong Kong in 2004. 299 people died and 7 million residents lived in fear. Wong states, "The only bright spot throughout the ordeal was the courage and compassion of frontline healthcare professionals. They worked long hours and risked

so many survive while others perish.[134] Unbelieving survivors can be incredibly resourceful and non-Christian rescue and medical staff can be extraordinarily compassionate and caring. The massive operational resources and equipment the emergency services possess is largely the product of non-Christians.[135] Much of emergency planning and response expresses philanthropic resources between human beings, but also God's specific gifting of unbelievers.[136] Major incidents, therefore, can combine both terrible evil and extraordinary good.[137] Such ironies need accounting for theologically.

I am also sensitive to a problematic tension that exists among Christians regarding non-Christian altruism being esteemed as good.[138]

---

their own lives to serve the sick and contain the illness. With their heroic efforts they demonstrated the indispensable role of compassionate and spiritual care." See also Ripley's account of Cornishman, Rick Rescorla, at the World Trade Center during 9/11 (*Unthinkable*, 203–10).

134. This observation was made by those responding to the Kegworth/M1 incident, in view of the total devastation that could have taken place if the aircraft's spilling fuel had vaporized and caused an explosion upon impact. Given the speed of impact and the structural damage to the fuselage, some have considered it a "miracle" that only 47 souls perished. However, it is this feature to common grace that creates the aporias, since it gives the impression that divine favor seems so random—and thereby unfair. Common grace and theodicy can seem in conflict therefore. This tension needs to be worked through in the minds of responders.

135. I had the privilege of seeing this firsthand when I worked as chaplaincy volunteer in the emergency department of a major UK acute hospital, in 2006–7. See also "Show Issue" for an array of resources available for the emergency services and related agencies. An example would be the work of London's Helicopter Emergency Medical Service (HEMS), which, on the day of the July 7 London Bombings in 2005, "flew 26 missions and along with the services rapid response cars, carried 32 trauma trained doctors and paramedics to the four locations . . . Compared to previous major incidents around the world, the scenes were cleared of patients in an unprecedented time scale" ("Show Issue," S65).

136. What better summary of this capacity to develop enhanced emergency response equipment and service than the statement of Calvin: "There are at hand energy and ability not only to learn but also to devise something new in each art or to perfect and polish what one has learned from a predecessor . . . *Hence, with good reason we are compelled to confess that its beginning is inborn in human nature.* Therefore this evidence clearly testifies to a universal apprehension of reason and understanding *by nature implanted in men.* Yet so universal is this good that every man ought to recognize for himself in it the peculiar grace of God" (Calvin, *Institutes*, vol. 2, 2:14, emphases mine). Calvin believed in this specific gifting as a feature of common grace (*Calvin's Commentaries*, Genesis 4:20, 21, and *Institutes*, vol. 1, 11:12).

137. This was the case in my prefigured narrative.

138. This was the salient issue in the lapsarian disputes between Abraham Kuyper

Johnson expresses this when he asks if there is a "sound biblical and theological rationale for paying respectful and discerning attention to the perspectives on the non-Christian as we work out our theology of the practice of ministry?"[139] Common grace is that vital theological rationale.

Theological Explications

I explore the doctrine first, in mainly biblical and systematic theological disciplines.

Explications of Biblical Theology

On the one hand, we have biblical statements affirming no human goodness. Jesus stated, only God is good.[140] But that is not the only concept of goodness when used elsewhere in Scripture. Christians can overcome evil with good; they can also do good to all; they are created in Christ Jesus to do good works and are accounted as devilish without them.[141] Thus, God is good absolutely, and Christians are good relatively. Also, non-Christians can be "full of good works," can show "unusual kindness," and can achieve a blamelessness concerning righteousness under the moral law.[142] Jesus assumed human nature to be evil and yet also naturally disposed to do good.[143] So, there are levels of goodness.

A study of texts within Paul's letter to the Romans reveals a tension between affirmations of human unrighteousness, and the recognition that human nature is capable of willing and performing good acts at certain levels.[144] Despite overwhelming biblical argument for humanity's

and Hermann Hoeksema. See Bolt, "Common Grace"; Bavinck, "Common Grace." I also draw attention at this point to Coakley's Harvard Divinity School research project, demonstrating from game plan theory, that divine cooperation in the process of evolution shows altruism, sacrifice, and even forgiveness to be consistent with the evolutionary process. She avers, "The fear, then, often expressed by the Vatican, that the embracing of Darwinism somehow encourages hostile competitiveness or individualism has to be severely modified. At the very least, and in advance of any ascription of religious meaning to the phenomenon, evolution at significant junctures favors cooperation, costly self-sacrifice, and even forgiveness . . ." (Coakley, "God and Evolution," n.p.).

139. Johnson, "Spiritual Antithesis," 79.

140. Mark 10:18.

141. See Rom 12:21; Gal 6:10; Eph 2:10; and Jas 2:19–20 respectively.

142. See Acts 9:36; Acts 28:2; and Phil 3:6, respectively.

143. See Matt 7:11.

144. I have selected Romans because Paul presents his case for total unrighteousness, and weakness, most strongly in that epistle. He makes his strongest affirmations

incapacity to save itself, and therefore the need for total renewal by the grace of God in Christ, I concur with Ridderbos that,

> It is in harmony neither with the teaching of Jesus nor with that of Paul to deny zeal for the law or desire for the good to every man outside of Christ, or to consider such impossible to him. It is likewise not in harmony with the reality to which Paul, without fear of being wrongly understood, appeals with a certain degree of self-evidentness (Rom. 2:14ff.).[145]

Along with Rom 2:14–15, there is evidence for this conclusion from the argument concerning the "righteous" and "good" man in Rom 5:7, and also from what the "I" of Rom 7:7–25 is able to achieve.[146] Some further examination of these texts and their contexts is helpful to an explication of common grace theology.

What Paul states in Rom. 2:14–15 could suggest not all Gentiles belong to the "given over" status that is true of some Gentiles who display ungodliness and unrighteousness in their suppression of the truth (Rom 1:18).[147] The argument, in summary, is: though all Gentiles have a natural awareness of law, some Gentiles are possessed with a peculiar sensitivity that shows awareness of law naturally, and this enables them to perform good deeds similar to the Jews who have the revealed law.[148] Their con-

---

of human hopelessness before God therein. It is an epistle where his pastoral theology is foremost, addressing the contexts of sin and suffering in particular. See Olsen, "Romans 5–8."

145. Ridderbos, *Paul*, 128.

146. Whether one interprets these Romans' passages in the traditional sense of referring to the individual, or in the sense of Holland's corporate Israel, makes no difference to the point I am making about common grace.

147. Gathercole reports Augustine, Melanchthon, and Luther holding to this view, though Augustine later changed his view ("A Law unto Themselves," 28, and n. 3, 4, 5). Helm concludes Aquinas and Calvin based their belief in natural law on Rom 2:14–15 (*John Calvin's Ideas*). Bavinck doubts that this rebellion (Rom 1:18) is even a conscious one on the part of human nature, so much as an unconscious and unintentional, but inevitable, slide into guilt. He describes the eventual state as one where "The aerial of their hearts can no longer receive the wavelength of God's voice although his voice surrounds them on all sides" (Bavinck, "Human Religions," 48). However, it seems to me that the state of being *given up (παρεδωκεν)* (vv. 24, 26, compare v. 28) by God does result in very conscious and deliberate behavior in view of what Paul states in Rom 1:32, "who, *knowing* the righteous judgment of God," (emphasis mine). This conscious deliberateness is the state of judgment, not the basis for it.

148. For Sanday and Headlam the number of Gentiles Paul intends in v. 14 seems unspecified, though it implies *some* rather than all or most (*Critical and Exegetical*

sciences both restrain them from committing evil and constrain them to do good. They know and achieve aspects of the law behaviorally by the constraint of their natures (φυσις) because of what is imprinted on their hearts (καρδιας) and enacted by conscience (συνειδησις).[149] What is more, Paul can appeal to this as self-evident because life can "show" it. Thus, not all of life may be as morally dismal as Rom 1:24–32 displays.[150]

Though the above is a majority view among scholars, in my view Gathercole has effectively argued against this being the right exegetical interpretation.[151] Appealing to the immediate context he argues that the Gentiles concerned were regenerate Christians, hence their ability to "do the things of the law" (Rom 2:14), even though they did not have the law by nature. Gathercole cites Achtemeier and Maerten's case for φυσει qualifying identity rather than behavior.[152] He concludes that in

---

Commentary, 59). The authors note that historically there has been a great reluctance by Christian theologians to support the literal force of Paul's statements, preferring to limit the number of law abiding Gentiles to a "favoured few among the heathen who had extraordinary divine assistance." Rationalists, on the other hand, take it to include works capable of salvation (*Critical and Exegetical Commentary*, 60). I cannot see why either represents the only tenable position. Hodge takes the view that Paul intends all Gentiles, not some (Hodge, *Commentary on the Epistle to the Romans*, 54–55). It is hard to see any other meaning than that all Gentiles are in mind here, though not all Gentile behavior reflects equal levels of success in living by this natural law. Hahn regards the situation of Gentiles keeping the law without hearing the OT law as hypothetical however. (H. C. Hahn, "Conscience," in Colin Brown, ed., *NIDNTT*, vol. 1, 350).

149. Murray, *Epistle to the Romans*, 71–72. Elliott rightly points out the fallibility of conscience because it too is subject to the fall, but suggests that conscience is an aspect of common grace. He also reminds us that Bonhoeffer rejected the use of conscience in moral reasoning and decision making because of such unreliability (Elliott, ed., *Dynamics of Human Life*, 16). Gathercole argues (convincingly) for an "internal trichotomy" being at work in the regenerate Gentile, of heart, conscience and thoughts working positively in conjunction with the Holy Spirit. He avers, "Thus, the accusing and defending thoughts are features of the regenerate Gentiles in 2.14–15, while contrasting starkly with the Gentiles of Rom. 1.18–32" ("A Law unto Themselves," 27–49).

150. See Macleod, *Behold Your God*, 128–29. However, the "dismal" impression given in Rom 1:24–32 represents God's judgment on the Gentiles' rejection/repression of the *sensus divinitatis* that their created natures were endowed with (Rom 1:19–20). On natural theology and *sensus divinitatis*, see Helm, *John Calvin's Ideas*, 209–46. Helm avers Calvin did not entertain a doctrine of suppression, however (*John Calvin's Ideas*, 235).

151. Gathercole, "A Law unto Themselves."

152. Achtemeier, *Romans*, 45; P. Maertens, "Une étude de Rm 2.12–16," cited in Gathercole, "A Law unto Themselves," 36.

the context, "although Paul is talking *about* Gentiles in these verses, he is not talking *to* them."[153] In my view Gathercole does not refute the notions of natural law *per se*, merely that such notions cannot be gleaned from Rom 2:14–15. Barth believed Paul had Gentile converts to Christianity in mind here—those already encompassed in the covenant and upon whose hearts the law will be written.[154]

In Romans 5:7 the Apostle Paul refers to the "righteous" and to the "good" man. While some commentators think these are synonymous terms, the prevailing view is that they do not identify the same person.[155] One view is: the "righteous man" is probably someone who respects the moral law, who strives to keep the rules of the law, and who does right in that dutiful sense. The "good man" however, goes further than that. He has a deeper level of love for the law and its value. In Morris' words, "There is a warmth of good feeling and generosity about his actions."[156] It is the good man more than the righteous man that inspires another person to "even dare to die" for him because there is something particularly inspiring and worthy about such a man's goodness, or, he commanded a social hold on the respect and dutifulness of a beneficiary.[157] Thus, among these three persons there are different levels and kinds of good.

In Romans 7:18 there is another statement that would lead one to question any good in human nature whatsoever. Paul confesses, "For I know that in me (that is, in my flesh) nothing good dwells." It seems as categorical as Rom 3:12. Indeed, the context argues the utter incapacity of human nature to achieve salvation through doing good. It shows

---

153. Gathercole, "A Law unto Themselves," 48.

154. Barth, *Church Dogmatics,* 1/2, 304; 2/2, 242, 604; 4/1, 33, 369, 395.

155. For a contrary view, see Murray, *Epistle to the Romans,* 167–68.

156. Morris, *Epistle to the Romans,* 223.

157. A helpful review of literature concerning the six possible interpretations of the "good man" is given in Clarke, "Good and the Just." Clarke argues the case for the distinction of the "good man" from the "righteous man" lying in the contemporary Roman culture of patronage, where élite social benefactors commanded dutiful respect in return for their "good" works toward their beneficiaries. He suggests that same meaning is attached to Paul's use of "good" in Romans 7 as well. Martin, on the other hand, citing Clarke's study, rejects his interpretation in favor of his own exegetical argument that the "good man" is, in fact, a reference to God. He argues that the deity in contemporary secular, as well as biblical, usage, referred to god as "The Good" (Martin, "*The Good* as God." None of these possible interpretations denies the concept of righteousness/goodness in the human being.

that human nature is "wretched" and "dead" in such an ambition.[158] But, again there is some qualification required of this seemingly absolute statement. Paul explains that there is an aspect of the "I" of which this is true, namely his flesh (σαρξ); that is, "human nature in its weakness," or "man's existence apart from God," which has "a drive that is opposed to God."[159] However, Paul testifies that he also has a will (θελω), which is capable of desiring not to do evil and of wanting to do good.[160] He thus testifies of a war between what is true of his mind (νουσ) and his flesh (σαρξ), which the flesh inexorably wins. Though Paul's point is to prove the total weakness of human nature's capacity to save itself, and the total dependence upon Christ alone for salvation (Rom 7:24–25), my point is: his case would not exist if human nature did not have some capacity for willing good and for achieving some level of good, albeit worthless for salvific purposes.[161]

Given the moral impact of the Adamic fall and humanity's being dead in sin, there would seem to be two possibilities for human goodness: either this capacity for good remains as a part of the created human nature, the *imago Dei* divinely preserved and sustained, or it is a capacity donated by God at specific times, thus causing actions to take place that override the will of the person acting. I believe the former possibility is the only one justified. In other words, humans are capable of varying levels of good as God exercises a providential restraint from evil on their nature. In Rom 1:18–32, Paul describes both the reason for divine wrath being manifest against all human ungodliness and unrighteousness (18–23), and the manner of that wrath being manifest, namely through God "giving up" such people.[162] This implies some levels of prior restraint or preservation. A biblical theology of divine restraint is provided through

158. Rom 7:24, exemplified by Paul's own narrative.

159. Guthrie, *New Testament Theology*, 174; A. C. Thiselton, "Flesh" in vol. 1 of Colin Brown, ed., *NIDNTT*, 675. Ladd defines σαρξ in ethical terms at this point, as, "human nature, man viewed in his entirety apart from and in contrast with the righteousness and holiness of God" (*Theology of the New Testament*, 472).

160. See Rom 7:15–16; Rom 7:19.

161. See also Phil 3:6b. There is extensive debate whether Paul was testifying as an unregenerate or regenerate person. On the basis that this debate remains inconclusive, after so many generations, I conclude there is at least *a* validity in my assuming, for the purposes of exploring common grace, that Paul was harking back to his experience as *un*regenerate. Thus, he was referring to his capabilities while in an unregenerate state (hence "wretched man," v. 24).

162. See also Rom 1:24, 26, 28.

the NT in 2 Thess 2:6–11; 1 Tim 2:1–4; Rev 20:1–3.[163] Such retention of the *imago Dei* by restraint is not human nature's desert or boast. The self-evident bondage of the will, and the force of human moral gravity propelling humans away from God, suggest that divine justice would be vindicated by a full visitation of wrath (Rom 1:18).[164] That life generally shows something very different under divine restraint is due to the gracious disposition of God towards humanity. It is a grace that is common to all.[165]

The purpose of addressing these texts, and their contexts, has been to highlight a theological recognition of human capacity for substantial levels of goodness according to Christian anthropology.[166] In respect of exploring an evangelical theology of major incident response, my fear is that the impact of the weighting of Paul's arguments establishing salvific hopelessness for Jews and Gentiles, and therefore the emphasis upon Adamic depravity, has produced a Reformed anthropology that has been too dualistically, and moralistically, applied.[167] It is uncomfortable with the notions of "good" or "spiritual" non-Christian others, provoked by

163. See Calvin, *Institutes*, 2.3. For a discussion on identifying the agent(s) of restraint (political agents, Christian missionaries, God, etc.), see Ridderbos, *Paul*, 521–26; Guthrie, *New Testament Theology*, 807–9. O'Donovan also speaks of the role of divine common grace as a restraint in his concept of political theology. He asserts, the "common grace of God, rather than his saving purposes, forms the foundations of secular society." Outside of that retainer the secular can be a "beast," exercising one last attempt to overwhelm the church (*Desire of the Nations*, 149, 156–57). However, the features of the secular, formed by common grace, owe their roots to the special grace of God in the lives of rulers, and within public society, during such times (usually previous eras) when special grace has been operative in a bigger way.

164. On the significance of divine wrath and justice, see chapter 9.

165. Kreider stresses this element of divine restraint and mercy as a key aspect of Jonathan Edwards' famous/infamous sermon, "Sinners in the Hands of an Angry God," which has received so much criticism for its focus upon divine wrath and eternal judgment ("Sinners in the Hands"). Kreider refocuses our attention from the concept of an angry God (though he does not distract attention from the fact that God is angry with the sinner) onto "the other major category of divine attributes," namely, God's mercy, compassion, patience, and love. He equates Edward's "mere pleasure" with God's grace. Concluding, "The fact that He has not destroyed sinners under His wrath was, for Edwards, compelling evidence for His gracious character" (263).

166. Myers, "Christianity, Culture," 4; Stackhouse, *Making the Best of It*, 183–85.

167. My concern is with how Christians, who do not have the divine status (or full perspective), and who are therefore limited in their capacity to see everything as God sees, use this weighting to view their fellows and relate to them at a common level. I believe this has had particular negative impact upon ecumenical and interfaith relations (see chapter 10).

those whose enthusiasm for such possibilities would believe these "good" people capable of salvation apart from personal faith in Christ alone.[168] In my view this reaction is invalid and unethical. Confronted by empirical observation of human goodness, we have been too quick to decry this goodness from the salvific perspective of God, and thereby failed giving it the canonical recognition of being a level of goodness.[169] My belief is that while we should hold to salvation through faith in Christ alone on account of the Adamic Fall, we must not lose sight of humanitarian aspects the apostle Paul averred to be self-evident, that humans can be capable of immense kindness, heroism, self-denial and good. This is a grace common to all humanity, sustaining a humanitarianism that enables and benefits all by way of giving and receiving.

It is important that common grace theology does not veer only towards the good that human nature can achieve when endowed with such grace. Equally important is the great good that God does for all human beings when none deserve it.[170] Thus, we might define common grace theology as a continuing disposition of God toward all humans, preserving and restraining aspects of the *imago Dei*.[171] It explains the continuing relationship between God and *imago Dei* in humanity, which though it has become corrupted by the sin of Adam, and the union with him, nevertheless is preserved from total extinction by the grace of God.[172] Because such grace can enable humans to develop and improve the welfare of life to varying degrees, it risks being reduced to humanistic excellence and natural goodness, and can therefore produce a secular hubris.[173]

168. See Pinnock, *Wideness in God's Mercy*.

169. I concur with Barth when he states, "He [God] is the fullness, measure and source of all goodness, and therefore of what may be called good in human action" (*Church Dogmatics* 3.4.4). For that very reason what God pronounces "good" we should not pronounce as not so good as to be evil. Biggar refers to the "humane" liberalisms of eminent contemporary philosophers such as Jürgen Habermas, John Rawls, and Jeffrey Stout, who stand in a tradition that reaches back to J. S. Mill, Immanuel Kant, and John Locke ("Saving the Secular," 5).

170. See Matt 5:45.

171. It is important to point out that such a view differs from the Wesleyan/Arminian concept of prevenient grace. Prevenient grace is more a divine endowment of the Holy Spirit through the grace that flows from Calvary (Cox, "Prevenient Grace").

172. See Gen 1:26; Gen 3; Rom 5:12; and Gen 9:11–17 respectively.

173. In fact, an absence of a sufficient contemporary common grace emphasis in Reformed anthropology *encourages* a secular challenge precisely because there is so much self-evident goodness in the natural world for secularists to appeal to. Reformed theology has, in my view, used an appeal to the spiritual "blindness" factor of the

Explications of Historical and Systematic Theology

Historically, the formal doctrine of common grace emerged from a clash between what is termed the *antithesis*—namely Reformed Christianity's view of human nature being totally depraved, able to respond positively to God by virtue of divine regeneration alone—and the empirical observations of, for example, social development, human kindness, selfless heroism, and civic benevolence.[174] Though Calvin strongly supported the total depravity view of human nature, realism compelled him to conclude, "in man's perverted degenerate nature some sparks still gleam." And, therefore, "When we so condemn human understanding for its perpetual blindness as to leave it no perception of any object whatsoever, we not only go against God's word, but also run counter to the experience of common sense."[175] Kuyper observed,

> It is not exclusively the spark of genius or the splendour of talent, which excites your pleasure in the words and actions of unbelievers, but it is often their beauty of character, their zeal, their devotion, their love, their candor, their faithfulness and their sense of honesty. Yea . . . not unfrequently you entertain the desire that certain believers might have more of this attractiveness.[176]

Common grace theology responds to moral dilemmas, such as "Why do good things happen to bad people?"[177]

---

non-Christian as an excuse for its failure to sufficiently acknowledge a common grace work in human nature. It also accounts for the prevalence of *traditional* natural law rhetoric, which is unfortunate, given McGrath's revision, in *The Open Secret*, which is synonymous with a Christological common grace.

174. Johnson, "Spiritual Antithesis"; Mouw, *He Shines*.

175. Calvin, *Institutes*, 2:2.12. Calvin makes another appeal to common sense in 1:15.6. The problem with major incidents is that they shatter common sense in many ways. Yet, common sense can only seem shattered if one already possesses some conviction on what should be sensible. Part of the *abnormality* of traumatizing events is their distinction from the sensible. Common sense is a product of common grace.

176. Abraham Kuyper, quoted in Johnson, "Spiritual Antithesis," 76. See also Berkouwer's citing of Kuyper in *Man: The Image of God*, 153.

177. See the observations of Job in Job 21:7–16, and the psalmist, in Ps 73:6–9, for theodramatic expressions of this dilemma. Johnson, "Spiritual Antithesis," 73. Johnson judges this question "virtually turns inside out the title of Rabbi Harold Kushner's twenty-year-old best-seller," which was entitled, *When Bad Things Happen to Good People*. Also Mouw, *He Shines*, 3.

Controversially, in systematic theology, common grace has inter-sected with natural law and general revelation. Calvin argued strongly for the idea of a general revelation made known to all humans (the *sensus divinitatis*), and that is comprehensible as well, and common grace is that part of general revelation that is concerned with revealing God's favor to all, restraining sin, stimulating civic goodness, and providing humankind with a basic level of cognition and affection to make communication comprehensible. For Calvin, natural law was a legitimate concept pro-vided it was nuanced by the belief that the fall had substantially affected its "naturalness." As Helm suggests, "so we may say that human nature, though intact, is disordered by sin." However, since the fall has not de-humanized the human race, it remains, "Man's nature is intrinsically religious, intrinsically orientated to the knowledge of God, which was or-dered in unfallen mankind, but became perverted (not extinguished) in fallen mankind."[178] Helm claims Abraham Kuyper and Herman Bavinck rejected the coupling of common grace with natural law, and their view influenced later Reformed thought. They feared such linkage would risk a Roman Catholic understanding and/or Enlightenment autonomy. Helm concludes their thinking, however, was based upon a caricature of Aquinas and Calvin.[179] Stump argues that Aquinas' virtues, being dif-ferent from Aristotle's, are infusions of grace, not natural. From this she maintains that only Christians are truly virtuous. Cottingham responds that this is counterintuitive, and he resolves the issue by maintaining that virtue is inherently present in every human, as an infusion of grace but without belief in that grace being necessary for being virtuous.[180] In re-solving this controversy, much depends on how "natural" is understood. If it means an autonomous moral law that is universal to human nature and accessible independently of gracious, supernatural revelation, then Kuyper, et al., have a point. It has been this understanding that, once stripped of its metaphysical origins by Enlightenment hubris, has led to the contemporary secular concept of a neutral reason.[181] The danger

178. Helm, "Natural Law," n.p.

179. Helm, *John Calvin's Ideas*, 383–84.

180. Cottingham argued this in his conference paper, "Philosophy and the Moral Virtues."

181. Helm argues that Calvin and Aquinas had the same ontological view on natural law, but different epistemological concepts. Aquinas had more acceptance of natural law being accessible to human reason without special revelation, whereas, "For Calvin, though those without benefit of special revelation know that there is a natural

is this abstracts nature from grace and destroys the contingency of the created order to God.[182] However, I believe a common grace theology does not have to equate with either Kuyper's dualism or Catholic semi-Pelagianism. Natural law as common grace is wholly sustained by God, taking into account total human unrighteousness, and is entirely a gift of God's grace to corrupt humans, but non-salvific.[183] Bavinck went beyond this by insisting that natural law rests upon God's revelation alone.[184] He asserted, "The life and being are no longer 'natural'. Rather, they are the fruit of a supernatural grace to which man no longer has a self-evident claim (Gen. 8:21, 22; 9:1–17)."[185] In doing this he, and the Dutch Calvinists, became too reactionary to Roman Catholic concepts, which may also account for certain reactions by contemporary Reformed theologians to the work of Vandrunen, who has begun exploring and developing a Reformed version of natural law.[186]

McGrath proposes a form of natural theology that is firmly rooted in distinctly Christian, Trinitarian, incarnational, and redemptive foundations. He rejects much of the traditional Enlightenment concept of natural theology, and yet his perspective provides a way for natural sciences and theology to interact with each other respectfully, (something Enlightenment natural theology effectively scuppered by evolving a secularism devoid of a Christian reason).[187] McGrath's view also involves a far

---

law and have some sense of its content, nevertheless what that moral law is can as a result of the Fall only be known clearly through a reasoned understanding of special revelation" (*John Calvin's Ideas*, 372–73). Kloosterman argues for a level of subordinacy of natural theology to the Mosaic Decalogue, which Helm avers Aquinas and Calvin did not support ("A Biblical Case," n.p.; Helm, *John Calvin's Ideas*, 372–73).

182. Russell Hittinger, "natural law," in McGrath, ed., *Blackwell Encyclopedia*, 398–402; A. F. Holmes, "Natural Law," in Atkinson and Field, ed., *New Dictionary of Christian Ethics*, 619–21; Anderson, "Barth and a New Direction." Barth saw this contingency as existing between God in the humanity of Christ and the created order.

183. Thus, I concur with Helm when he argues, "'common grace' and 'nature' are complementary descriptions of the same phenomenon; they are not at odds with each other, and so they are not to be set in opposition to each other" ("Natural Law").

184. Bavinck wrote his work on common grace to counter a revival of Roman Catholic teaching under Pope Leo XIII.

185. Bavinck. "Common Grace," 40.

186. Helm, "Natural Law"; Vandrunen, *Biblical Case*. See also Kloosterman, review of *A Biblical Case*. The same author enlarged his critical review in his "A Biblical Case." Vandrunen responded in his "Vandrunen In The Hands." I am grateful to Prof. Helm for informing me of Vandrunen's work.

187. On this interaction see: Richard Roberts, "Social Science and Christian

more holistic anthropology than classical views, incorporating not just human intellect but also the emotions as valid ways of "seeing" the world. McGrath states that his theology could also be referred to as a "theology of nature."[188] Whereas classical Enlightenment natural theology involved theology originating from nature itself, distinct from the Creator himself, McGrath argues for a theology derived from the Christian revelation of God that provides a lens through which further revelation in nature is disclosed. Without this distinctly Christian revelation then nature's secrets would lie hidden. For him natural theology is about discernment, and seeing nature through a certain specific kind of lens. It comes out of a Christian theology of nature, which discloses God. Thus, such a lens leads to truth, beauty and goodness being readily acknowledged as existent within nature, but not salvifically so.

Thus, the triune God has revealed himself in a very gracious way for those encountering the most awful suffering and trauma of major incidents. Commenting on the Luke 13:1–9 incidents, Green states the reasons others had escaped the fate of the Galileans and Jerusalemites was "not because of their relative sinlessness or goodness but because of God's temporary clemency."[189] In other words, every human being is in a state where they are vulnerable to catastrophic events as a part of their fallen state under divine judgment. The fact that there are not more such events is due solely to temporary clemency, an aspect of common grace.

Thought," in McGrath, ed., *Blackwell Encyclopedia*, 608–16; McFadyen, *Bound to Sin*, 54. Postliberalism has had to acknowledge this as well, even though it focuses priority upon the intratextual hermeneutic of the Christian community. See also Wolterstorff's "reversal of conformation" which asks, "but is the relation of the Church theologian to the non-theological disciplines exclusively that of melting down gold taken from the Egyptians? Isn't some of the statuary of the Egyptians quite ok as it is? Does it all reek of idolatry? Isn't there something for the church theologian to learn from the non-theological disciplines?" (*What New Haven*, 2). See also, Swinton and Mowat, *Practical Theology*; Mowat and Swinton, "What do Chaplains do?" See also Mowat's discussion of how NHS chaplaincy can respond to the NHS' demands for evidence-based research to substantiate the role of chaplaincy in a modern health care service (Mowat, "Potential for Efficacy"). For a postmodern critique of the whole relationship between the methodologies of the social sciences and theology, see Milbank, *Theology and Social Theory*. Milbank and Hauerwas played up the distinctives between social science and theological narrative methodologies because, in their view, narrative theology is committed to *witness*, not explanation (Hauerwas, *With the Grain*, 146).

188. McGrath, *Open Secret*, 256.

189. Green, *Gospel of Luke*, 513.

CONCLUSION

The doctrine of grace is crucial to both the legitimation for, and contribution to, major incident response for the evangelical catholic Christian community. The doctrine, inclusive of both common and special forms of grace, exhibits the priority of divine love, which forms the heart of the theodramatic response of gospel grace to the disaster of the fall and the sequelae of human evil. Common grace must not be construed independently of special grace, for it finds its roots, and perspective, in the covenant of redemption. God is disposed to show a certain favor to all humans, for it is out of that fundamental redemptive love, which is his ontology, he has resolved to save through his Son all who will receive him.[190]

From biblical, historical, and systematic theological perspectives, common grace provides a valid explanation for the self-evident phenomena of human and divine goodness more than I prefigured. Biblically and apologetically, therefore, nothing is gained from Christians denying the reality of human goodness. Unregenerate human beings are capable of exhibiting great acts of humanitarian compassion, heroic self-sacrifice, and skill. Furthermore, such common grace legitimates levels of partnership, for humanitarian planning and care for the welfare of human beings, between Christian communities and non-Christian agencies, provided these do not demand Christian language and doctrine become so thin that they lose any substantial Christocentricity on a response through being "chartered by the state." Responders will contribute most when they are virtuously gracious people/communities, possessing and outliving the divine largesse of grace. Hence, every moment of common grace represents God's call to embrace the special grace in Christ. Even the most tragic incidents are never devoid of the liberal distribution of divine grace feeding the human *appetitus*.[191]

This exploration of special and common grace unearths a closely related theological theme: compassion, which also flows out of both special and common grace, and to which I turn next.

190. See 1 John 4:16 and John 1:12 respectively. On God's ontology of love, and its implications for human love, and the social disaster that can ensue when love is misdirected (as happened in the Roman Empire), see Mathewes, *Theology of Public Life*, 230–38. Also, see Jackson, *Priority of Love*.

191. *Appetitus* here refers to the sense of natural gravity infusing the natural world that draws us after God. See Harak's consideration of this aspect of Thomist theology, in his *Virtuous Passions*, 61–67.

8

Contribution—Compassion

M Y PROCESS OF MIMETIC configuration now moves on in a doctrinal exploration of theological contribution for the Christian community's response to major incidents. Again, I assume that a credible practical theology should give priority to *sola scriptura*, and to theodramatic mimesis, where character comes before action; virtue precedes practice. Having explored the priority of grace, I proceed to compassion, as this lies at the heart of the graced response of God in Christ to the suffering world, according to the theodrama.[1] Compassion, therefore, is the inevitable, though undeserved, outcome of divine grace.[2] As such, it forms a crucial basis for humanitarian responses to tragedy. My prefigured narrative reveals an overwhelming encounter with the compassion of so many different people: from members of my own family, my church com-

---

1. Confirmed by the words of the *Benedictus*, Luke 1:78, δια σπλαγχνα ελεους Θεου ημων, literally, "through compassionate mercies of our God." Green judges that the strategic location of this statement, at the very center of vv. 76–79, suggests that what God does in bringing salvation "springs fundamentally from his compassion" (Green, *Gospel of Luke*, 118–19). Swinton believes there is a sense in which suffering defines the gospel because it sits at the heart of Christ's compassionate experiential response ("Why Me, Lord?" in Swinton and Payne, eds., *Living Well*, 107).

2. Fiering, "Irresistible Compassion," 195–218. Tonya Armstrong states that the *imago Dei* provides the basic building blocks of compassion, upon which the (special) salvific grace of God develops a distinct Christian compassion ("Practicing Compassion for Dying Children," in Swinton and Payne, eds., *Living Well*, 158). The Reformed, Calvinistic faith would, as I have done, distinguish between special and common grace. However, for Arminian theology compassion is an aspect of the prevenient grace that enables every person to turn to God in Christocentric faith and repentance. I would not wish to imply in my research that an Arminian view will necessarily lead to any less compassion being expressed than from the Reformed view. From a Barthian perspective, "A natural theology that does not have at the center a cross sunk deep into human flesh will not find transforming love at the center of human moral action" (Anderson, *Shape of Practical Theology*, 157).

munity, but also, from many non-Christians. Additionally, my response experience tested my own levels of compassion towards, principally, the bereaved and survivors in their excruciating sufferings, toward fellow Christian and non-Christian responders, and toward myself. Was my response an ego trip—a lust for adventure—or one of genuine compassion? Was my contribution theologically rooted in an experience of God's compassionate response to me in Christ? Does such compassion advance upon other humanitarian forms?

My thesis in this chapter is: compassion originates within a Trinitarian ontology of perichoretic self-dispossession, which is common graced to all human nature but made accessible to an enhanced degree by special grace through the incarnate Son of God. Jesus Christ embodies divine compassion, and through salvific union with him the Christian recipient of divine compassion discovers their own ontology of self in relation to non-self.

COMPASSION: DEFINITION

Initially, some definition is required. Nussbaum states, "To put it simply, compassion is a painful emotion occasioned by the awareness of another person's undeserved misfortune."[3] This does not fit a Christian definition, or the Christ paradigm, where divine/human compassion is also actively displayed toward the guilty and blameworthy, and which Christians are called to show to fellow humans.[4] More helpfully, Purves suggests, "At the common level, then, compassion is understood to be sympathetic awareness of another's distress, with a desire to alleviate it in some way."[5] This makes the definition for a Christian pastoral response to a major incident more specific and proactive.[6] Tonya Armstrong concludes, compassion is the recognition and internalization of the suffering of another,

3. Nussbaum, *Upheavals of Thought*, 301.

4. Nussbaum distinguishes between compassion and mercy, where mercy is for the blameworthy, however. See *Upheavals of Thought*, 365–68.

5. Purves, *Search for Compassion*, 15. Also D. L. Parkyn, "Compassion" in Atkinson and Field, eds, *The New Dictionary of Christian Ethics and Pastoral Theology*, 244 (hereafter referred to as *NDCEPT*).

6. Thus, in this case the character necessary for compassion includes a proactive dynamic. There is no such thing as a virtue of compassion that does not feel compelled to act. In fact Oliver Davies argues that compassion is not a virtue *per se*, but it represents the structure that provides for virtuous action (*Theology of Compassion*, 18). In his thesis that passions are ethical, Harak maintains every virtue is directly related to a passion (*Virtuous Passions*, 3).

but also exceeds the dimensions of pity, empathy, and mercy, because it reveals a profound commitment to a caring response to the suffering of another.[7] In other words, "Compassion is not caring from a distance. It has a face-to-face quality, and something of the sense of presence and involvement."[8] Compassion demands a certain flexibility, therefore, a freedom from presuppositions and rules, so that it can be governed by the needs of the victim and respond accordingly. In a Christian sense, compassion has an inner compulsion that presses one to go beyond the realms of ethical duty and cultural convention. Because there is also a high level of risk involved, and it involves self-denial in the interests of relieving the suffering, compassion is not mere compliance.[9] Arguing from the Good Samaritan parable, Keller stresses that awareness of one's duty is not enough. The priest and the Levite possessed all the biblical knowledge, all the ethical principles, and all the ethnic affinity with the man in the road. It was not enough, whereas the Samaritan had none of these things, but he had compassion. "It was enough!"[10]

A more precise focus on what compassion is will come from an exploration of theological and pastoral perspectives.

COMPASSION: THEOLOGY

Biblical

Though the Old Testament Psalms exalt God on account of his compassion, most modern scholars look to the person and work of Christ to find that point convincing.[11] God is most exegeted in Jesus; but, it is equally

7. Armstrong, "Practicing Compassion for Dying Children," in Swinton and Payne, eds., *Living Well*, 147–48.

8. Purves, *Search for Compassion*, 125. Nussbaum acknowledges this but rightly qualifies in cases where no practical avenue of help is available. See *Upheavals of Thought*, 335.

9. Armstrong emphasizes the aspect of risk is central to Christian compassion because of the kenotic dimension of a Christocentric self-denial inherent in it ("Practicing Compassion for Dying Children," in Swinton and Payne, eds., *Living Well*, 156). For the important distinction between compassion and compliance, see Batson, et al., "Compassion or Compliance."

10. See Luke 10:30–37. See Keller, *Ministries of Mercy*, 13.

11. Pss. 78:38; 86:15; 111:4; 112:4; 145:8; Matt 9:36; 14:14; 15:32; 18:27; 20:34. God's people found him to be compassionate in their experience, just as he had conditionally promised (Luke 7:13; 10:33). In each of the NT cases the Greek σπλαγχνιζομαι is used. This word derives from the root σπλαγχνα, meaning "inward parts, entrails," and this refers to the seat of human emotions. See "σπλαγχνα" in *NIDNTT*, 2:599–601;

the case that we should understand the person and character of Jesus in the light of what is already revealed of God in the Old Testament.[12] Thiselton concludes, of all the options, in the light of the "wider context of Johannine thought," εξηγεομαι probably refers to the Logos giving "an accurate, clear, and full revelation of God."[13]

The narrative of the shipwreck disaster recorded in Acts 27 tells of a near loss of life of the 276 persons aboard (v. 37) but for a divine, gracious, intervention, communicated through the special-graced Paul (vv. 21–26), which spared the lives of all.[14] The sequel, in Acts 28, reveals a common-graced response by the barbarian islanders showing "unusual kindness" to the survivors (v. 2). This whole disaster is intriguing for its theological content. The apostle Paul interpreted the event as a "disaster" (27:10, 21).[15] It clearly involved forces of nature, in the combination of threatening wind and sea conditions (27:4, 13–14, 20). But the disaster was also a result of precipitate human error (vv. 9–12, 21), and the consequences were prevented from being worse only by virtue of the grace of God (v. 24). Even so, those involved suffered the psychosomatic effects of their traumatized state (v. 33) and were made additionally vulnerable, post-impact, by virtue of the consequent exhaustion and traumatization, the rain and cold (28:2). Relief came from the response of the barbarian

---

"σπλαγχνιζομαι" in Arndt, *Greek-English Lexicon*, 770. On his regret over OT-NT dualism, see Fretheim, *Suffering of God*, xv. Hunsinger maintains Karl Barth's concept of eternity arising out of the Trinity makes such a dualism theologically improper. Barth's analogous relationship between the three *hypostases* of the Trinity and the three forms of eternity (beginning, middle, end), and their perichoresis, means they cannot be played off against each other (Hunsinger, *Disruptive Grace*, 208).

12. John 1:18, "The only begotten [μονογενης] Son, who is in the bosom of the Father, He has declared [εξηγησατο] *Him*." Recent research has focused on the roots of the Johannine concept of the μονογενης lying in the Old Testament idea of Israel being the "firstborn" son of Yahweh (Exod 4:22; Jer 31:9). Thus, as it was in Israel's exodus that God demonstrated his compassion supremely, this has been exceeded by that revealed in Jesus Christ. See Ra, "Investigation of the Influence," chapters 1–4. Morris, however, warns that μονογενης derives etymologically from γινομαι not γεναω (*Gospel According to John*, 105). For Weinandy also, the defining moment in Israel's history was the exodus because there Yahweh showed that he is primarily experienced, and known, as a God capable of establishing imminent and intimate relationships, and he does it at his own initiative (*Does God Suffer?*, 43).

13. See A. C. Thiselton, "Explain" in Brown, ed., *NIDNTT*, vol. 1:573–76.

14. There is some discrepancy between the manuscripts, so that some suggest a figure of, or about, 76 persons.

15. The Greek, ὑβρις—events that cause injury, abuse, humiliation, hardship—is an apt descriptor.

"natives" (NKJV) or "islanders" (NIV). That is, from Luke and Paul's perspectives, the responders were non-Christian, non-Greek, uncivilized, superstitious pagans, yet who showed "unusual kindness" (v. 2) and who could extend three days of generous hospitality to the casualties and donate provisions for their ongoing journey (v. 10).

Systematic

Perichoresis

Of particular interest is Oliver Davies' work, exploring a systematic theology of compassion.[16] Davies' exploration links compassion to the divine ontology in a theologically intriguing manner. He maintains that compassion is the most intensive form of intersubjectivity because it involves the sufferings of another, which are not my own, becoming the cause of my actions as if those sufferings were my own. Thus, it involves me putting myself at risk for the other knowingly.[17] At the heart of compassion, therefore, is a voluntary kenosis, configured ontologically in God himself, refigured in the compassion of God to Israel and in the incarnate Son.[18] Through union with Christ, such configured compassion can also be refigured in the Christian's narrative.[19]

Within God's Trinitarian ontology, Davies argues, there is a perichoresis which is fundamentally kenotic.[20] That is, an essential aspect of the relationship between the *mia ousia* and the *treis hypostasis* of the immanent Trinity is a conceiving of self only in relation to another.[21]

16. Davies, *Theology of Compassion*.

17. Ibid., xix, 9.

18. I use the language of mimesis here guardedly. Vanhoozer expresses his uncertainty regarding the suitability of mimesis for describing other than human actions (email conversation between Vanhoozer and author, September 16, 2009).

19. "Configured" is my term; "Refigured" is Davies' own term (*Theology of Compassion*, 9).

20. On the significance of perichoresis, including the Christological and humanitarian implications, see Egan, "Toward Trinitarian *Perichoresis*"; Harrison, "Perichoresis in the Greek Fathers"; Marshall, "Participating"; Tipton, "Function of Perichoresis." Also, Prestige, *God in Patristic Thought*, chapter 14.

21. Prestige suggests *ousia* "tends to regard internal characteristics and relations, or metaphysical reality," while *hypostasis* "regularly emphasizes the externally concrete character of the substance, or empirical objectivity" (*God in Patristic Thought*, 188). See also Barth's conception of perichoresis as a key aspect of the Trinity as *ousia*, *hypostases*, and *perichoresis*, and how this controls his concept of eternity as duration, temporal time (past, present, and future), and simultaneity (Hunsinger, *Disruptive*

Therefore, there is an ontological self-dispossession within the Godhead that provides the structure for compassion as expressed through the incarnate Christ and which is fundamental to Christian personhood, discipleship, and community.[22] Perichoresis balances the tension between the unity of the *mia ousia* and the *differentia* of the *treis hypostasis*. There is a mutual indwelling which is true of the Trinity, but also of the union between Christ and his people.[23] Davies argues this divine kenotic ontology is revealed, strategically, in the OT theodrama, in the revelatory words of Yahweh to Moses: "I AM WHO I AM,"[24] which are framed by a context of God's compassionate works for his covenant people. Contra Western tradition's interpretation of this as an ontological statement of God's "necessary and eternal existence, freed from any contingency or constraint," Davies prefers a rabbinic interpretation, which draws a connection between the divine naming and God's creative speech, the *Memra*.[25] This rabbinic usage draws together "the notion of divine utterance as theophany, divine creativity, divine compassion . . . and the theme of divine presence with and for Israel."[26] The Hebrew etymology adds to the dynamics of compassion by *rhm* (compassion) linking with *rehem/ raham* (womb), and the way this metaphor carries the image of kindred

---

Grace, 189–203). Hunsinger states, *perichoresis* is, "The three divine 'persons,' each of whom is fully God, coexist simultaneously *in mutual self-giving*" (*Disruptive Grace*, 196, emphasis mine). See also, McGrath, *Christian Theology*, 251–52.

22. Luke 1:78 ("tender *mercy* of our God." Yet the Greek word is σπλαγχνα, which translates as compassion, not ελεος, which, as mercy, has more of a juridical dimension); Phil 2:5–8; Matt 16:24–25; 20:26–28; Phil 2:1 (σπλαγχνα και οικτιρμοι), respectively.

23. As expressed by Jesus, in John 17:21–23.

24. See Exodus 3:14. Similarly in Exodus 33:12–13 Yahweh is directly associated with compassion (מ רח *rhm*). See Davies, *Theology of Compassion*, 240–4; Mike Butterworth, "רח מ" *rhm* in VanGemeren, ed., *NIDOTTE*, vol. 3, 1093–95. Kaiser judges *yhwh* was "not so much an ontological designation or a static notion of being (e.g. I am that I am"), it was rather a promise of a dynamic, active *presence*" (*Towards an Old Testament Theology*, 107). Fretheim points out that though the divine name was used prior to the specific naming, in Exodus 3 and 6, finding its original home has been impossible. Fretheim suggests the divine name (*yhwh*) is probably most accurately translated as "I will be who I am/I am who I will be," which essentially means, "I will be God for you." God will be faithful to his relationship with his covenant people (Terence Fretheim, "Yahweh," in VanGermern, ed., *NIDOTTE*, vol. 4, 1295–1300).

25. "The *Memra* is a theological motif, found only in the Targumim, which means the "word" or "utterance" of God" (Davies, *Theology of Compassion*, 241).

26. Davies, *Theology of Compassion*, 242.

bonding and tender care toward vulnerability.[27] Rather than compassion being a static, ontological attribute of God, these Hebraic and rabbinic aspects suggest compassion is a relational dimension of the Godhead.[28] In the NT, the term σπλαγχνα is used of Jesus' compassion.[29] This conveys a deep psychosomatic, visceral meaning ("innards"), echoing *rhm*. Thus, Jesus is the compassion of Yahweh.[30]

From this interpretation, Davies suggests that compassion is a relational attribute of the Trinity, demonstrated through the Son's incarnate life and death, to be further expressed through the relationships within the church and between the church and the world to which she witnesses.[31] Thus,

> in σπλαγχνα natural affection is refigured by divine self-giving and becomes the foundation of the new life that is the spirit of the church. Compassion in this sense then represents the transformation of humanity by the supremely compassionate act of God in the incarnation. God is πολυς σπλαγχνος, and by *becoming* compassion in the flesh, God has summoned his people likewise to become compassion within the community of the church, whose mutuality re-enacts, through participation, the original mutuality of Father, Son, and Spirit.[32]

Compassion, then, is to be prioritized in view of its revelatory significance. With roots going back to God's self-naming and his hypostatic self-communication, such revelation can only be received and appropriated in a relationship of compassion.[33] Weinandy also roots God's passions in the Trinity, where God is *actus purus*: God cannot be more

---

27. As in Isaiah 49:1, "Can a woman forget her nursing child, And not have compassion on the son of her womb? Surely they may forget, Yet I will not forget you."

28. See also Purves, *Search for Compassion,* 68–70. Weinandy argues that the persons of the Trinity are defined by their relationships. In this sense the Father, Son, and Holy Spirit are pure verbs (*Does God Suffer?* 118).

29. See Matt 8:2; 14:14; 15:32; Mark 1:41; 6:34.

30. Luke 1:78, "the tender mercy of our God." This would follow, also, from the perichoresis between the members of the Trinity.

31. See 2 Cor 6:12 ("affections"); Phil 1:8 ("affection"); Phlm 7, 12, 20 ("heart") respectively. Weinandy also believes these relationships reveal who God is (*Does God Suffer?*, chapter 3). In explaining the similar view of Maximus the Confessor, see Harrison, "Perichoresis in the Greek Fathers," 65. See also Harak, *Virtuous Passions,* 83–84.

32. Davies, *Theology of Compassion,* 248–49.

33. Ibid., 251.

pure than he is in his actions.[34] God's passionate love to all creatures is based on this immutable Trinitarian relationship. Though ontologically distinct, yet he relates passionately to his creatures because, as Trinity, he is their creator. Central to Weinandy's thesis is his insightful point:

> We clearly perceive now the awesome truth that because creatures, especially, human persons, are in the act of creation related to the persons of the Trinity as they are in their subsistent relations, and so are related to each person of the Trinity in a specific manner, they are assumed into the very mystery of the Trinity itself. Thus the act of creation mirrors, though imperfectly, the unchanging processes within the Trinity.[35]

The canonical linguistic configurative and refigurative implications from this theology are immense. The self-dispossessive divine ontology encourages not simply a knowing of God but a way of relating to God and to an other. Therefore, through relating to God we come to know ourselves, and others, through an ethical dispossession of ourselves in responding to the suffering other as if their sufferings were ours, as God has done in Christ to us.[36] In so doing we "align our 'being' with God's 'being,'" and, thus, performatively, this is "to participate in the ecstatic ground of the Holy Trinity itself. It is to activate God's image in us in accordance with Lev. 11:44: 'be holy, for I am holy,' an image that will only ultimately be renewed, refigured and transfigured, through our own rising with Christ from the tomb."[37] Compassion is, thus, virtue laden.

Impassibility

The issue of God's compassionate response to suffering is controversial in contemporary theological and Christological discussion.[38] It is integral

---

34. *Actus purus* is a term from scholastic philosophy that refers to God's attributes and his operations/actions being identical and absolute. He does not need any "trigger factors" in order to act purely.

35. Weinandy, *Does God Suffer?*, 142.

36. The so-called "passion narratives" could more realistically be termed the "trauma narratives."

37. Davies, *Theology of Compassion*, 352. See also page 8.

38. Significantly, Weinandy believes that a key reason for the nineteenth and twentieth centuries' review of divine impassibility in favor of passibility was due to the suffering brought on by the Industrial Revolution and the two World Wars, including the Shoah. This inspired a generation of scholars, including Bonhoeffer and Moltmann, to address this aching disparity. For them it seemed only a suffering God could exhibit true compassion, because only such a God could really help. Weinandy's contention

to the divine impassibility/passibility debate. Weinandy, in his defense of the *impassibility* of God, insists the OT reveals a God of great compassion, the most defining experience for Israel being the Exodus, where, by his own initiative, God forged a relationship based on compassion. Traditional theology has interpreted such references to divine passion anthropomorphically. Weinandy concurs, qualifiedly, while maintaining that God is impassibly Wholly Other. For him, it is the wholly otherness of God, not the capacity to suffer, that is the basis for God's great compassion:

> I believe that the singular passion of God's love, compassion, mercy, forgiveness, anger, etc., as witnessed in the Hebrew Scriptures, demands that his passionate love, compassion, mercy, forgiveness, anger, etc., be that of Wholly Other, for these passions themselves arise out of and testify to his total otherness.[39]

These passions can be explained in terms of super-humanness rather than anthropomorphisms.[40] God's compassion is unique to him, and does not model ours, yet ours resonates with his.[41] Frame also acknowledges Scripture reveals God having emotions, but these are not the same as our emotions.[42] Hart, endorsing divine impassiblity, reflects

---

is that such a conception of God in fact alienates God from humanity, because "The sufferer stands alone in his or her suffering before a suffering God, who is himself a helpless and impotent victim." Passibilists pander to a spirit of victimhood—to a "God who authenticates and justifies their self-pity" rather than one who authentically goes to the root of the problem and redeems from sin (Weinandy, *Does God Suffer?*, 261, 281).

39. Weinandy, *Does God Suffer?*, 62. Hunsinger also rejects the common mistaken conclusion that Barth's ontological otherness of God—as indicated in his use of "wholly other"—prevents God's immanence. He argues Barth actually affirms the divine presence is so pervasive, multiform, and rich that it represents "the triumph of God's freedom in immanence" (quoted in Hunsinger, *Disruptive Grace*, 199).

40 Weinandy, *Does God Suffer?*; Gavrilyuk, *Suffering*. Both authors respond to the prevalent contemporary view among scholars, that patristic theology soon fell victim to Hellenistic philosophy, which demanded the impassibility of God from a specifically Hellenistic perspective. Gavrilyuk's conclusion is: "The theory of Theology's Fall into Hellenistic Philosophy must be once and for all buried with honours, as one of the most enduring and illuminating mistakes among the interpretations of the development of Christian doctrine" (*Suffering*, 46).

41. Seth and Helm, commenting on Warfield, make the point that we should not deny in God what we recognize as the source of dignity in ourselves. (See Andrew Seth quoted in Warfield, "Imitating the Incarnation," 571; Helm, "B.B. Warfield").

42. Frame, *No Other God*, 184. Also. Gavrilyuk, *Suffering*, 60.

upon the death and trauma caused by the Asian tsunami (2004), and concludes God's *apatheia* is not divine indifference but an aspect of his ontological love. That is, his love and pathos do not require stimulating from without, but are perfectly satisfied from within the divine ontology. In Hart's words,

> We are not necessary to him: he is not nourished by our sacri-
> fices or ennobled by our virtues, any more than he is diminished
> by our sins and sufferings. This is a truth that may not aggran-
> dize us, but it does, more wonderfully, glorify us: for it means
> that, though he had no need of us, still he loved us when we were
> not. And this is why love, in its divine depth, is apatheia.[43]

Compassion should also be rooted in economic and social Trinitari-anism.[44] Thereby the Christian partakes in Christ's ministry to the Father, in the power of the Spirit, for the sake of the world.[45] Compassion *per se* cannot be attributed to the ontological Trinity, for there is no context of suffering that adheres to that aspect of Trinitarian life; nevertheless, as I argue, Trinitarian life does form the structure for compassion to emerge. It is relevant to add the point, however, that in the covenant of redemption we must never conceive of a Trinitarian disjunction, such as Chalke and Mann have implied in their caricature of the doctrine of penal substitution. Their comments are particularly relevant in view of the claim that their own interpretation of the lost message of Jesus is more compassionate that the penal alternative.[46]

Since God is immutably compassionate, it is not surprising that compassion is at the very heart of Christology. We do not have to wait for the incarnation to judge if God is compassionate, but in the light of

43. Hart, *Doors of the Sea*, 77. This contrasts with Fretheim's argument for "reciprocity," arising out of his "organismic" concept of relating to God. In this he considers God is also dependent upon the world, through his own sovereign choice (*Suffering of God*, 35). Prestige clarifies on *apatheia* as God's will being determined from within him rather than being swayed from without. Thus: "If it were possible to admit that the impulse was wrung from Him either by the needs or by the claims of His creation, and that thus whether by pity or by justice His hand was forced, he could no longer be represented as absolute; He would be dependent on the created universe and thus at best only in possession of concurrent power" (Prestige, *God in Patristic Thought*, 7).

44. Armstrong appeals to the Father-Mother relationship within the economic Trinity, demonstrated through the interaction of the Son and Holy Spirit ("Practicing Compassion," 153).

45. Purves, *Search for Compassion*, 133.

46. See Chalke and Mann, *Lost Message of Jesus*.

the OT revelation it would be alarming if the Son of God was not. God does not learn compassion through becoming human and experiencing suffering; he becomes human and experiences suffering because he already is strongly compassionate. So, Weinandy can rightly judge, "To make God less than wholly other does not make him more personal, loving and compassionate, but rather he would be less personal, loving and compassionate."[47] What comes to light in the incarnation is immutable compassion in a human nature, and this is why we have the human form of compassion in Jesus of Nazareth that we do.[48] Frame judges: "His [God's] experiences as a man are truly his experiences, the experiences of God."[49] The suffering to which God directs his compassion is suffering that God has experienced and known firsthand, as one of us. Thus, divine impassibility and the experience of human suffering are locked in together.[50]

Passibility

Fretheim, in his defense of the passibility of God, makes the point that even anthropomorphisms are meant to communicate something close to the metaphor used.[51] For Purves, God's solidarity with suffering amounts to vulnerability: "God's compassion requires us to understand God now in terms of God's vulnerability and willingness to suffer with us." Fretheim focuses upon this divine vulnerability as a feature of the passible God he argues for.[52] Fretheim and Purves are among a growing number of scholars calling for a revolution in the understanding of God's nature, "in which we no longer understand God to be an unchangeable, unaffected being who loves us in distant untouchability," but one who is now changed by the experience of suffering.[53]

47. Weinandy, *Does God Suffer?*, 54.

48. See also Crisp, "Problems with Perichoresis." Crisp argues that the divine nature of Christ interpenetrates his humanity, by virtue of his omnipresence, but never vice versa.

49. Frame, *No Other God*, 190.

50. Weinandy, *Does God Suffer?*, 206. Weinandy argues that the passibilist position effectively locks God out of human suffering.

51. "The metaphor does not stand over against the literal. Though the *use* of the metaphor is not literal, there is literalness intended in the relationship to which the metaphor has reference" (Fretheim, *Suffering of God*, 7). See also Carson, *How Long, O Lord?*, 187; Weinandy, *Does God Suffer?*, 59.

52. Fretheim, *Suffering of God*, 75.

53. Purves, *Search for Compassion*, 16.

Conclusion

I conclude that divine compassion can be accounted for theologically from an impassibility that renders God invulnerable. Hunsinger argues in favor of Barth's impassibilist concept, when he avers the triune God does not need the world for self-actualization. God is eternally already totally actual in the perichoretic relations between the three divine hypostases.[54] In his argument for the impassibility of God, Gavrilyuk states, "Many believers would find it immoral and openly offensive to their piety to expect God to be a perpetual sufferer, while at the same time they deeply cherish God's love, mercy, and compassion."[55] A Christian spirituality encompasses a holistic union with Christ, and should reflect God's compassion to the world in him. Thus, "Spirituality has as its goal the living out of one's faith, one's identity, in the world."[56] Working with casualties, in union with Christ, ensures that the language of compassion we use is that of spirituality and theology rather than the language of social work and psychotherapy.[57] Such casualties place a call for Christians who will respond like Christ when,

> He took no account of self. He was not led by His divine impulse
> out of the world, driven back into the recesses of His own soul
> to brood morbidly over His own needs, until to gain His own
> seemed worth all sacrifice to Him. He was led by His love for
> others into the world, to forget himself in the needs of others,
> to sacrifice self once for all upon the altar of sympathy. Self-
> sacrifice brought Christ into the world. And self-sacrifice will

54. Hunsinger, *Disruptive Grace*, 196.

55. Gavrilyuk. *Suffering*, 12. Gavrilyuk argues for the term "impassibility" being used as a "apophatic qualifier." That is, it describes what God is *not* more than what he is (*Suffering*, chapter 4). It is interesting that Nussbaum—as a non-Christian philosopher—recognizes that true deity does not require a sense of vulnerability in order to be compassionate. What is required is omniscience. Contra Aristotle, she does not consider divine vulnerability to be ontologically inherent for a deity to have compassion, other than being "vulnerable to upset in the person of another," whereas this would be necessary in a human (see Nussbaum, *Upheavals of Thought*, 319, 324–25.). Davies in *A Theology of Compassion* speaks of the "risk" within outworkings of perichoresis, but these are limited to the vulnerability of being human, not divine. They are the risks of faith, of giving oneself over to another (Christ). In fact, the Trinitarian perichoretic relationships of mutual, interpenetrative passion make the passibilist position an affront to the divine-human relationship.

56. Purves, *Search for Compassion*, 109.

57. Ibid., 132. See also Weinandy, *Does God Suffer?*, 251, 258.

lead us, His followers, not away from but into the midst of men. Whenever men suffer, there will we be to comfort.[58]

Thus, compassionate major incident response is self-dispossessive, which, though mimetically Trinitarian, has certain potential health risks for humans.[59] It is the giving away of oneself for the plight of another, without the certainty of reciprocation.

COMPASSION: ANTHROPOLOGY

Major incidents precipitate expressions of immense humanitarian compassion, to such a degree that this phenomenon can challenge the faith of Christian responders who hold to orthodox beliefs concerning human nature as fallen, totally depraved, and egocentric. Also, so self-evident is this element of compassion in human nature that it has provoked debate challenging what additional benefit religion can give by way of an enhanced level of response.[60] Howard Murphy argues it was a nineteenth-century revolt against the orthodox Calvinistic dogmas of election, reprobation, and vicarious atonement, with their emphasis upon natural depravity, that accounted for the demise of evangelical faith and the climax of rational liberalism in the UK, far more even than Darwin's evolutionism. He traces how three figures, two of whom were convinced Evangelicals, gave up their faith altogether, on the basis that they found such Evangelical doctrines were out of touch with the clear observations on human goodness and unethical in their dismal view of life. Such pessimism seemed contrary to the philosophical meliorism of that time.[61] However, Murphy's argument needs to be balanced by those of Prochaska and Bowpitt. Both argue a case for evangelical theology

58. Warfield, "Imitating the Incarnation," 574.

59. On self-care, see chapter 8 below, 228–33.

60. From Acts 28:2 it is difficult, from both the words used and the context, to judge whether the "unusual kindness," shown by the barbarians, was unusual because Paul and Luke, as Christians, did not expect such a high level of kindness from non-Christians or because the level of kindness was such that it would exceed even that normally shown by anyone, Christian or not. One suspects the former is more accurate.

61. Murphy, "Ethical Revolt." Meliorism is "the belief that the specific conditions which exist at one moment, be they comparatively bad or comparatively good, in any event may be bettered. It encourages intelligence to study the positive means of good and the obstructions to their realization, and to put forth endeavor for the improvement of conditions" (James Dewey, *Reconstruction in Philosophy*, quoted in Robinson, "Critique of Meliorism," 178).

and *praxis* having had very significant positive influence in social welfare during the eighteenth and early nineteenth centuries, precisely because of the emphasis upon a *praxis* of compassion inherent to that theology.[62] In 1969, Rokeach's research (in the U.S.) addressed three questions, one of which was: Does going to church incline people to be more compassionate toward others? He concluded that adherence to Christian values or to church attendance did not result in more social compassion. In fact, religious institutions were, "at best, irrelevant, and, at worst, training centers for hypocrisy, indifference, and *callousness* . . ."[63] Christenson revisited Rokeach's research with a similar project, which presumed Rokeach's conclusion—that more frequent resort to religious worship and related values will produce less compassion than in those who attach less importance to such values. He found that his "findings did not indicate a clear pattern concerning moral integrity and social compassion issues."[64] However, "those who attached greater importance to the value of helping others were clearly more sensitive to others and more willing to help them."[65] Batson, et al., also found religion's success in promoting pro-social behavior to be inconclusive. They concluded that those who show high doctrinal orthodoxy, and have an intrinsic end in mind, tend to offer what they consider to be appropriate help, whereas those with a strong quest orientation were more responsive to the wishes of the person seeking aid.[66] Both Christenson and Batson's research was carried out in the 1970s and in the U.S., and, therefore, must not be assumed to contradict the findings of Prochaska, as his analysis of Christianity and social service in the UK covers a period of two hundred years. It does indicate, however, how social science quantitative research in the 1970s might have subsequently influenced perception of the validity for a Christian involvement in major incident response systems. In 1983 Horton Smith argued that social science and religious research are separated by their own topical specialization boundaries, so neither really benefits from respected access to each other's research. For this reason he concluded

---

62. Prochaska, *Christianity and Social Service*; G. Bowpitt. "Evangelical Christianity." Bebbington argues similarly, only he extends evangelical dominance into the latter part of the nineteenth century too (*Dominance of Evangelicalism*, 235–49). See also, Forsyth. *Justification of God*, 124.

63. Milton Rokeach in Christenson, "Religious Involvement," 218 (emphasis mine).

64. Christenson, "Religious Involvement," 225.

65. Ibid., 225.

66. Batson, "Religion as Prosocial."

that in contemporary voluntary action research, the religious tends to be neglected because it is not so susceptible to social science research methods. He pleads for a mutual recognition of each other's research.[67]

Fiering's aim has been to trace the eighteenth-century assumption, "that men irresistibly have compassion for the sufferings of others and are equally irresistibly moved to alleviate that suffering."[68] He argues that the notion of "irresistible compassion" that sprang from optimistic observation of human nature in the eighteenth century, gave rise to a secular sanctification of compassion, again in reaction to the seventeenth-century view dominated by Calvinism, with its belief that human nature was only guided by self-interest, self-love, and self-pity. The Cambridge Platonists led a reaction that saw compassion rooted in human nature.[69] Whereas the secularists believed compassion was natural, others considered it either in the form of a natural theology or of common grace.[70]

67. Smith, "Churches Are Generally Ignored." In more recent research Milbank's (and much of Radical Orthodoxy's) objection to Christianity's surrender to the "superiority" of the secular sciences has some validity when he argues that the logic of Christianity involves the interruption of history by Christ and the church, and these should interpret all other events. Because these are social events, they can legitimately, by the intratextual Christian narrative, interpret other social practices. See Milbank, *Theology and Social Theory,* 388. For a critical response to Milbank's general resentment of the secular, see Stout, *Democracy and Tradition,* 100–107. Stout argues that rather than society's infection by secularism, as an ideology, being the responsible factor for the modern secularization of society, it was more the secularized attempt to deal with an increasing religious plurality of discourse in society, for which the nuanced liberal democracy Stout espouses would be a more effective control than Milbank's blank resentment. Stout concludes, "So we must at least entertain the possibility that secularized political discourse in modern democratic societies can to some large extent be disentangled from the antireligious animus of some of its ideological defenders" (*Democracy and Tradition,* 102–3).

68. Fiering, "Irresistible Compassion," 195–218. He argues that such a concept was developed out of Puritan theology and advanced by such moral philosophers as Francis Hutcheson (who had been influenced also by Malebranche). Hutcheson cut right across the traditional assumption that good actions were always the products of intellect, and he argued that such actions can be, and often are, the products of passions created by God and which are irresistible and irrepressible. See Fiering, *Moral Philosophy,* 198–206.

69. The Cambridge Platonists were a group of seventeenth-century English thinkers, based in Cambridge University, and supporters of the philosophies of Plato and Plotinus. They shared a theological background but believed in the compatibility of faith and reason. They had an optimistic view of human nature and supported human autonomy. See Sarah Hutton, " Cambridge Platonists."

70. Which, Fiering records, was indeed Hutcheson's belief (*Moral Philosophy,* 206).

Studies have reflected on the evidence of great compassion expressed within other religions, most notably Buddhism. In regard to the Asian tsunami of 2004 CAFOD reported Ven. Dr. Nagoda Thero, a Buddhist monk, claiming, "Within hours of the tsunami, Buddhist monks went to the survivors and fed, clothed and sheltered them—sometimes in their thousands. It didn't matter what faith they were: we only saw their humanity!"[71] Cobb applauds the previous work of Keenan in exploring the benefits of reflecting on Christianity with the aid of an Eastern philosophical interest, because of the greater focus on compassion perspective, over against the traditional influence of Greek philosophy.[72]

These studies make a point that is too often overlooked in the interests of loyalty to conservative Evangelical orthodoxy: namely, compassion is not unique to the Christian. Also, sometimes traditional theology has been guilty of fuelling a lack of compassion that has been shamefully inconsistent with the nature of God. If we place compassion within the province of common grace, we should have no difficulty accepting that unbelievers can manifest compassion to a high degree, sometimes putting Christians to shame.[73] Arguably, it has been the concept of irresistible compassion that has formed the vocabulary of words such as "human," "humane," and "humanitarianism." Accepting compassion under the aegis of common grace need not mean that belief in human nature as unrighteous is at all undermined, but it should provide a healthy and realistically balanced effect upon the psychological impact the doctrine of original sin (and the related teachings on total depravity, election, reprobation, and atonement) can have upon churches impatient to defend conservative Evangelical theology against any shift towards a social gospel.[74] This impatience may have colored how Evangelical responders have

71. Reported by the Catholic Agency for Overseas Development (CAFOD) website.

72. Cobb, "Response to Mahayana Theology." Before Cobb, Kearsley had noted, "Commentators have seen in the influential third-century Greek writer Plotinus an affinity with Hindu thought and Islamic mysticism, and so there are some common roots in apparently different world views" ("Impact of Greek Concepts").

73. Johnson, "Spiritual Antithesis," 76. See also Berkouwer's citing of Kuyper in, *Man: The Image of God*, 153.

74. Fiering notes the conservative Evangelical New England pastor–theologian Solomon Stoddard, in the context of reflecting upon man being a natural lover of self, had to recognize people are "sometimes ruled over by a spirit of compassion. Men that are devoted to themselves, are so over-born sometimes with a spirit of Compassion, that they forget their own interest . . . There is no man so void of compassion, but

been perceived by those who control response systems, and such impatience may have led to their exclusion, on account of their generic reputation in relation to compassion. However, the experience of special grace for the Christian believer, providing the most compelling of instincts for Christians expressing compassion, makes the paucity of Evangelical response to major incidents shameful, given the emphasis upon the general humanitarianism that infuses contemporary emergency planning and response.[75]

I conclude that a theodramatic anthropology can accept both total unrighteousness and human compassion, as mutually compatible, if understood in terms of a doctrine of grace. With reference to his thesis concerning the self-dispossession within the Godhead, Davies argues that this principle is found outworked throughout humanity, and if it were not so, "most human societies could not keep at bay the violent and selfish tendencies of the human spirit."[76]Also, because there is common grace operative throughout humanity, Christians are beholden to recognize it and glorify God for it by respecting compassion wherever, and in whomever, it is found.

COMPASSION: DOING CHURCH AND WORSHIP

Taking into account the Hauerwasian and Stackhousian foci on grace a canonical linguistic theological approach suggests, the environment in which Christian compassion should be best discovered is the church. This is not to suggest that Christians, as individuals, cannot show compassion

---

upon some occasions [it] will prevail upon him. The seeing or hearing of the miseries of others, will extort acts of compassion, and they will be under a necessity to deny themselves, and relieve them" (Fiering, "Irresistible Compassion," 204).

75. Though, arguably, this can be an unconscious, if not indirect, humanitarianism. Our experience working on the Human Aspects Group showed that certainly up until the 9/11 attacks in 2001, or even the 7/7 bombings in 2004, then there was a severe lack of research interest in the human aspects of emergency response compared to the interest in the more technical and logistical aspects. Response agencies were more concerned that they got their equipment and their professional roles right than how the specifically human aspects of the incidents were cared for. Although this has changed in recent years with a much greater focus being given to human aspects (of which compassion is one), yet it was a criticism of the 7/7 response. (See HMG report, "Addressing Lessons"). A concerted attempt to address the human aspects of major incidents is the guidance document produced by the Emergency Planning Society, "Responding to Disaster."

76. Davies, *Theology of Compassion*, 21. See also his comments from Lanctantius on page 235.

on their own. Clearly they can and do. However, in terms of a significant Christian pastoral contribution to major incident response, then the Christian community must be a significant contribution. In that community, God should be found in both the individual skills/gifts of detailed pastoral care, and a community of grace whose communal friendship and worship can provide the secure and supportive environment within which traumatized persons can recover.[77] It is important to emphasize that no proselytizing agenda is in mind here. One is not suggesting that traumatized persons need to first become members of a church, or to become professing Christians even. I take into account my focus upon grace, and the church's witness under grace to the world. Therefore, I am thinking of the community being willing to embrace traumatized persons, irrespective of their faith/non-faith, and to welcome them into the care of that environment, to encounter all the humanitarian resources of grace she has to provide.[78]

Davies maintains that the church is the sphere in which the kenotic speech of the Trinity is vocalized in the world through the Holy Spirit. By preceding the Father-Son speech, the Spirit shapes the world to receive the ecclesial forms of public witness, prophecy and preaching, and Christian faith, "in which Christ is the object of our affirmation, is expressed in discipleship, where the suffering other becomes the object of our compassionate affirmation."[79] Compassion is first formed within

77. Zizioulas' focus upon the church as a form of divine being is interesting here. He believes God can only be known by being in *relationship* in the church. God cannot be known, as God, in any other way, because God cannot be God outside of relationship (hence the Trinity). Ecclesial being and the being of God are organically bound. For Zizioulas this is realized most in the eucharistic practice that transcends localism and universalism. See Zizioulas, *Being as Communion*. The point of the church needing to be a virtuous community is also highly significant. The Hauerwasian concept of the relationship between health and community is essential. Wendell Berry commented, "the community—in the fullest sense: a place and all its creatures—is the smallest unit of health and . . . to speak of the health of an isolated individual is a contradiction in terms" ("Health as Membership," quoted in Shuman and Meador, *Heal Thyself*, 12). This must make Hauerwas' point—the church as a distinctive community revealing the world to be the world—important.

78. Apart from civic memorial services, examples of pastoral care for the wider community have included: providing space for private prayer and/or reflection; "drop-in" centers for advice and conversation; arrangement for, and management of, donations of food, furniture, and clothing.

79. Davies, *Theology of Compassion*, 275. See John 16:7–11. The Spirit's work is to operate within the world in such a way as its life (including traumas) prepares it to listen, kenosis not being something human nature is naturally disposed to acquire.

the Christian community, and prioritized within her particular Christian bonds: "It is those who share our faith who first arise within the relation with Christ as the object of our compassionate love."[80] The Trinitarian self-dispossessing is expressed within the body of Christ as self-denying mutuality. This form of divine speech is then witnessed into the world not just by words, "but also in what they do, as the deepening visibility through embodiment of what has been revealed."[81] The church's massive resource of truth is theodramatically performed within the world, and, "what is performed publicly is a compassionate and dispossessive truth which can itself only be authentically communicated through compassionate and dispossessive existence."[82] This becomes the church's role in the pastoral theodrama for major incident response: to manifest a "theatre of dispossession" which, "can challenge and unsettle its audience simply by displaying an alternative existence, inviting them to reflect critically upon the character of their own lives and experience."[83]

There are certain aspects of the church's theodramatic dispossessive performance that are particularly compassionate components for major incident response. There are three important messages that should inhabit such components: "You *can* grieve for as long as necessary," "We *will* listen for as long as it takes," and, "We *are* here for you, for as long as you need."

Worship

The church's liturgies and Orders of Service are a significant aspect of a compassionate response, particularly within private funeral and public memorial services.[84] Such occasions can provide opportunity for the sur-

---

80. Davies, *Theology of Compassion*, 275.

81. Ibid., 276. The prioritizing of compassionate assistance in this way is endorsed by Gal 6:10.

82. Ibid., 278–79. In true Vanhoozerian language Davies, says, "The recitation of the Christian poem is akin to taking part in a theatrical performance, in which the stage props are real objects, the scene settings are real places, but the script shared among the actors is the unfolding and realization of a divine narrative . . . Thus, the church in this respect is itself a field or performance, a bodily acting out of the truth of the revelation, in a kind of theatre of dispossession" (279).

83. Ibid., 279.

84. The Hauerwasian and Stackhousian approaches would, I suspect, differ over the practicalities of this point. I suspect the Hauerwasian approach would not endorse public memorial services, where the state, either in the form of a government department (e.g., the Department of Culture, Media, and Sport) or the state church

vivors to give thanks and to reflect more seriously upon their experience in the light of the bigger picture of God and their life, and can assist the bereaved in gaining comfort and meaning, even transformation.[85] Both can know a community supporting them in serious prayer, and/or being helped to verbalize their needs before God, or just be silent where they cannot speak. Integral to the church's worship (and witness) is her engagement with God in prayer, on her own and the world's behalf.[86] Her prayers for the casualties of major incidents are intrinsic to her response.[87] Prayer is the foundation of power for every other ministry of response she makes.[88]

I suggest certain essential dimensions in the interests of compassionate forms of worship.

Thanksgiving

Christian grieving finds comfort in great thanksgiving.[89] Every life possesses something for inspiring thanksgiving, but in the case of the

---

arranges a service designed for the bereaved, survivors, families and friends, and the responding agencies, and attended also by national and local civic dignitaries. The Stackhousian approach may see such an arrangement as a part of making the best of it, an aspect of the church's public theology and witness, though some Evangelicals will be uneasy with the ecumenical (and certainly any interfaith) participation and aspects to the worship. I was happy to attend such services following Kegworth/M1, though I made a decision not to officially "process" with other clergy, but to sit with the families I had helped.

85. See Eyre's identification of this in "Remembering: Community Commemorations."

86. Yet, note the conclusions regarding prayer and hazard perception in Mitchell's research, in chapter 2, pp. 14–15. For a helpful contribution on the importance of prayer in the context of living well in preparation for dying faithfully, see Allen Verhey, "The Practice of Prayer and Care for the Dying," in Swinton and Payne, eds., *Living Well*, 86–106. In particular, Verhey recommends Christian responders should be prayer-formed people, operating out of a prayer-formed community (93). The prayer-formed person will evidence the virtues (reverence, humility, gratitude, care, and hope), which are "formed in simple attentiveness to God, and they spill over into new virtues for dying and caring for the dying in daily life" (93). Prayer is identity disclosing and forming. Intercessory prayer, both for and with, traumatized persons is the particular engagement of the Billy Graham Rapid Response teams in disaster areas.

87. For example, Paul's thanksgiving and intercessory prayers in Acts 17:35; 28:8.

88. See O'Donovan, *Desire of the Nations*, 188–90.

89. See 1 Thess 4:13–18. However, thanksgiving must be distinguished from death denying practices of worship. Scheib's reminder of the central focus of funeral services needing to be the deceased's *death* is important. She also points out the regrettable declension in modernity's capacity to face up to the reality of death, through the

Christian this is more so, whether in the living or dead. Thanksgiving for cases of survival needs to be very sensitively handled in the presence of the bereaved, in compassionate corporate acts of worship. Regarding the deceased, one sensitive approach can be giving due acknowledgment to the dead in the liturgy, and, in the case of the redeemed dead, to engage in some measure of fellowship with the saints gone before, being thankful that we are not alone. Here is where Evangelicals can afford to learn from other traditions. Traditionally, the Christian church has held to concepts of the *communio sanctorum*—"Communion of the Saints."[90] Far more developed within Roman Catholic and Eastern Orthodox than in Evangelical traditions, this refers to the Spirited, Christocentric union that exists between all believers in the "pilgrim" and "heavenly" churches. Catholic and Orthodox belief is that the lives of (particularly) the heroically faithful in the heavenly church exchange spiritual goods with those in the pilgrim church.[91] This benefit is obtained through the pilgrim church's veneration and invocation of the saints who, in turn, intercede for the saints on Earth.[92] Evangelical tradition resists this belief in the main.[93] From the Reformed perspective, Calvin was only prepared to very loosely speculate upon the possibilities of how the two churches related to one another. He saw no Scriptural basis for the intercessory/protective powers of the heavenly saints or for the practice of the invocation of the saints. In his section on the "communion of the saints," Calvin

---

increased diversion from funeral services toward memorial services as celebrations of life, but which can be devoid of meaning in the light of death. See Scheib, "Make Love Your Aim," 30–56. On these same tendencies see also, Walters, *Why Do Christians?*

90. See Scheib, "Make Love Your Aim," 33, 44–56. See Nicetas' discussion of the patristic origins of this term. He argues it was probably used first in creedal form by Bishop Niceta of Remesiana (ca. AD 338), and was most likely an addition to the Western creed. Niceta understood the term in an abstract, not concrete, sense. He probably used the concept in his ordinary catechetical ministry as a missionary (Nicetas, *Niceta of Remesiana*, lxxvi–lxxxiii).

91. Letham describes how the physical design and layout of the Orthodox Church buildings and the liturgy is meant to symbolize that worship constitutes the meeting place of the heavenly and pilgrim church (Letham, *Through Western Eyes*, 69).

92. According to Letham, *Through Western Eyes*, 148–52, "veneration" (προσκυνεισις) was distinguished from "worship" (λατρεια).

93. For an Evangelical-Catholic dialogue's conception of the *communio sanctorum*, see Brown, "Communion of Saints." See also Buckley, "Invocation of Saints." What is less clear is exactly how we are to pray for one another, and whether "one another" includes the members of the heavenly church.

makes no mention at all of relations with the heavenly church.[94] In fact he believed, "when the Lord withdrew them from our company, he left us no contact with them [Eccl. 9:5–6], and as far as we can conjecture, not even left them any with us."[95] Even if we argue that there is a Spiritual union between those in heaven and upon Earth, yet, "but if any man contend that . . . it is impossible for them to cease to keep the same love toward us, who has disclosed that they have ears long enough to reach our voices, or that they have eyes so keen as to watch over our needs?"[96] Leaving aside these controversial aspects, there is a focus that Catholic/Orthodox theology has given to the relations between saints on earth and those in heaven that deserves more attention from a practical theological perspective on major incident response. In particular, chapter 7 of the Vatican II document, *Lumen Gentium*. For all its reference to the intercessory work of the heavenly saints and to the pilgrim church's need of invocation for help, it affirms, "Indeed, in the early Church and through the patristic era, the phrase *communio sanctorum* had primary reference to this enduring bond between the faithful on earth and the faithful who had gone before, especially those whose witness was crowned with martyrdom."[97] But, does this mean anything more than Grudem's statement?

> The phrase "the communion of the saints" in the Apostles' Creed refers to the fact that we have in one sense a communion or fellowship with those who have died and gone into heaven, an idea that is affirmed in Heb. 12:2. This does not imply that we can be aware of them, but simply that when we worship we join in worship that is already going on in heaven.[98]

If, from an Evangelical perspective, we eliminate, on theological and scriptural grounds, the possibility of the pilgrim saints praying for the dead, or heavenly saints interceding for the pilgrim saints, or the pilgrim saints invoking the aid of the heavenly saints, it remains that a close bond of fellowship exists through their joint union with Christ, and, from this, a realistic interest and awareness between one another may exist.[99] Letham's description of the *communio sanctorum* is based on:

94. Calvin, *Institutes*, 4:1:3. He refers only to relations within the pilgrim church.
95. Ibid., 3:20:24.
96. Ibid.
97. Pope Paul VI, *Lumen Gentium*, n.p.
98. Grudem, *Systematic Theology*, 821, n. 19.
99. This bond is traditionally referenced to Heb 12:2, 18–25. Letham, helpfully,

Greeting living saints with a holy kiss is a Biblical recommendation, from the apostle Paul; the kissing of icons is the kissing of images of departed saints. We recall the words of the author of Hebrews that we are surrounded by a great cloud of witnesses (Heb. 12:1). Later, he declares that in church worship we have come to Mount Zion, to the spirits of just men made perfect (Heb. 12:18–25). We remember also the teaching of Revelation that when the church gathers for worship it joins the angels and the church triumphant in heaven around the throne of the living God and of the Lamb. We are not alone. The church is not a lecture room; we are gathered with saints present and past—and the angels too [1 Peter 1:10-12]—as we meet around the throne of God in heaven. We have access to the worship of the renewed created order, the church centrally included. We are with the saints and the angels, the apostles, prophets and martyrs—and above all with the Lamb of God once slain, now risen, and with the holy and undivided trinity.[100]

Such a concept of worship, displayed/performed, offers to be a great comfort for the Christians bereaved by a major incident.

Lament

Out of the milieu of communal prayer, Verhey expresses one form deserving particular attention: "If we retrieve lament, we may also renew our capacity for genuine compassion, for we may learn again to give the suffering a voice, to preserve for them a place in community, to be present with them."[101] The concept of lament is one that pastoral scholars have identified, and biblical ethicists and practical theologians have taken up, in the context of the churches' worship and pastoral response to trauma.[102] By facilitating lament, the church nurtures the practice of authentic grieving and, as such, can also serve as a locus and outlet for communal grief.[103]

---

responds to the argument that praying to the saints is justified by the fact that members of the pilgrim church regularly invite their fellow members to pray for them (*Through Western Eyes*, 166–71).

100. Letham, *Through Western Eyes*, 155–6.

101. Verhey, "The Practice of Prayer," in Swinton and Payne, eds., *Living Well*, 99.

102. See Hauerwas, *Naming the Silences*; Brueggemann, *Message of the Psalms*; Fretheim, *Suffering of God*; Hall, *God and Human Suffering*; Purves, *Search for Compassion*; Swinton, *Raging with Compassion*; Swinton, "Patience and Lament"; Walton, "Speaking in Signs."

103. Increasingly nowadays, local churches (including some evangelical churches) are opening their premises for centers of prayer and vigil following major incidents. Anglican parish churches have tended to do this historically, but Nonconformist

In general terms, a lament is, "a repeated cry of pain, rage, sorrow, and grief that emerges in the midst of suffering and alienation."[104] But, theodramatic lament is more than this. It is a disciplined and structured form of giving voice to suffering in the world of horrible disorientation a major incident creates. Brueggemann's work in the field of Psalmic lament is invaluable. He shows that nothing must be hidden from God in silence: "There is nothing out of bounds, nothing precluded or inappropriate."[105] Nor should we fear that God has sensitivities that need protecting. So, lament is pain, rage, sorrow, and grief being openly unleashed to the covenant God in semblance of faith, however weak. Such openness should be facilitated in funeral/memorial liturgies in the way prayers are shaped. Yet, lament, in my view, identifies a serious gap in the contemporary Evangelical church's capacity to respond effectively and compassionately to major incidents. Bridgers notes, "Those dark passages that provide the greatest depth and meaning in their [traumatised] spiritual lives, those defining events, are neither acknowledged or [sic] valued."[106] Brueggemann's diagnosis is penetrating. He acknowledges that the evangelical church's obsession with praise and thanksgiving in her worship and liturgies could be an act of evangelical defiance in the face of life's struggles. However, his judgment is actually,

> this action of the church is less an evangelical defiance guided by faith, and much more a frightened, numb denial and deception that does not want to acknowledge or experience the disorientation of life. The reason for such relentless affirmation of orientation seems to come not from faith, but from the wishful optimism of our culture. Such a denial and cover-up, which I take it to be, is an odd inclination for passionate Bible users, given the large numbers of psalms that are songs of lament, protest,

churches less so, due to them not claiming a parochial authorization. Those espousing a Hauerwasian ecclesiology would welcome non-Christians, but in submission to the church's terms.

104. Swinton, *Raging with Compassion*, 104.

105. Swinton and Payne identify lament as first and foremost a form of prayer (*Living Well*, xxi); Brueggemann, *Message of the Psalms*, 52. Day, while commending Brueggemann for his insistence that lament and imprecation be included and acknowledged in worship, criticizes his overall concept (expressed in Brueggemann, *Praying the Psalms*, 68) of the imprecatory psalms being valid expressions of pain, but ones that need to be expressed and then rejected. See. Day, *Crying For Justice*, 25–26. In regards to the point about the validity of lament I am making, each author complements the other.

106. Bridgers, "Resurrected Life," 74.

and complaint about the incoherence that is experienced in the world. At heart it is clear that a church that goes on singing "happy songs" in the face of raw reality is doing something very different from what the Bible itself does.[107]

Swinton's admission, in the light of the Omagh bombing (1998), is equally challenging:

> As I reflected on the way my church worshipped, its emphasis, its tone, its expectations, its expressed hopes, I suddenly understood clearly that there was no room in our liturgy and worship for sadness, brokenness and questioning. We had much space for love, joy, praise, and supplication, but it seemed that we viewed acknowledgement of sadness and the tragic brokenness of our world as almost tantamount to faithlessness. As a result, when tragedy hit: either directly at home or at a slight distance as in the Omagh bombing, we had no idea what to do with it or how to formulate our concerns . . . It was clear that we had few resources to enable us to resist the evil caused by such outrageous suffering as was inflicted on the people of Omagh on that terrible day. So we closed our eyes and worshipped God, or at least those aspects of God that brought us more comfort and relief."[108]

A true theology of compassion must embrace a theology and practice of lament, both for the traumatized individual and community. I concur with Purves when he concludes, "Compassion must have nothing to do with any strategy that circumnavigates lament. Religion which does that becomes a narcotic aiding in the denial or repression of suffering."[109]

A provision of lament, showing how the community brings its experience of extremity to expression in worship, is vital. Brueggemann's

107. Brueggemann, *Message of the Psalms*, 51–52. Brueggemann calls such songs, "songs of disorientation." See also, Carl Trueman, "What Do Miserable Christians Sing?" 2.

108. Swinton, *Raging with Compassion*, 92–93.

109. Purves, *Search for Compassion*, 91. The unfamiliarity of the Western church with lamentful worship contrasts with the experience I have had, over a period of twelve years, with some of the Evangelical Baptist communities in the Russian Federation, many of which have carried with them the liturgies, music, and hymnology formed in the hard years of Communist persecution. Equally, their times of "open prayer" are often punctuated by tearful, sobbing lament. McCann makes the point, from Ps. 13, that agony and ecstasy can hang together throughout life (*Theological Introduction*, 97). Ps. 88, therefore, represents a long and difficult work of lament in process.

identified structured lament means it is far more than an angst release onto God or a naked expression of anger.[110] Therefore, psalmic lament's teleological movement means it is not being unfaithful but utterly faithful. Hence,

> While we may think this [Psalmic imprecation] ignoble and unworthy, it demonstrates that in these psalms of disorientation, as life collapses, the old disciplines and safeguards also collapse. One speaks unguardedly about how it in fact is. The stunning fact is that Israel does not purge this unguardedness but regards it as genuinely faithful communication.[111]

For Brueggemann, Psalm 109 reveals that Israel understood that what is *healthily human* intersects with what is *vitally faithful*.[112] Hauerwas concurs: "It is an act of bold faith on the one hand, because it insists that the world must be experienced as it really is and not in some pretended way."[113] Lament is an integral part of a Christian's covenantal relationship with God. Therefore, faithlessness is represented by "the unwillingness to acknowledge our inexplicable suffering and pain," and, "ironically, the act of unbelief turns out to be committed by those who refuse to address God in their pain, thinking that God just might not be up to such confrontation."[114] By building lament into the liturgy of the funeral/memorial service the church assures the heartbroken, "You can grieve."[115]

---

110. Brueggemann's structure for Psalmic lament is: articulation, submission, relinquishment. There is a significant difference between defiant *unbelief* against God's promises, and a *struggle* to believe those promises when circumstances are excruciating.

111. Brueggemann, *Message of the Psalms*, 55.

112. Ibid., 86.

113. Hauerwas, *Naming the Silences*, 81.

114. Ibid., 83, 84.

115. I would argue that time for lament should be a frequent provision in the routine life of church worship, given the frequency of disasters in the world and the corporate solidarity in these I have argued for in this dissertation. Brueggemann also gives an extensive critique of the most common model of therapeutic grieving: Elizabeth Kübler-Ross' stages of denial, anger, bargaining, depression, and acceptance. See Kübler-Ross, *On Death and Dying*; Brueggemann, *The Psalms*, 94–95). Ross views death as something to be embraced as a "last home" rather than the biblical concept of a last enemy, conquered only in Christ. Grief thus becomes pathologized as a sickness to be cured by therapy, rather than a natural response to be suffered.

Preaching

In a very significant sense a funeral/memorial service throughout is an act of pastoral declaration. However, Evangelical tradition still possesses a core focus upon delivery of a spoken/preached message, and it would be churlish to deny the overall value of this aspect of her tradition. I say this even though many traumatized persons take in very little of anything that is preached on such occasions, and it would be cruel to place such a premium upon the sermon's length and complexity if it just exacerbated the traumatized state of the congregants. Nevertheless, there can be value in bringing the truth of the theodramatic narratives to bear on the events in mind, considering these narratives have themselves been forged from contexts of trauma.[116] Accepting these benefits of preaching, I am persuaded that the chief context for preaching for major incident response is that recommended by Alan Billings, when he stated, from reflecting on his own experience at the Hillsborough football stadium disaster of 1989, that it helped him

> to see more clearly than I had ever done before just how important the theological task is. The best pastoral help the Christian clergy can offer people is not that which we make available when disasters strike—the human comfort we offer is no more than any other human being would offer to a fellow human being in distress—but *the careful teaching we undertake throughout our ministries.* Unless we are helping the members of our congregations to construct that Christian framework themselves—holding together belief in God's providence and the reality of suffering—they will have no more resources to draw upon than anyone else in emergencies, because how we respond to disasters is culturally (or, in this case, sub-culturally) conditioned. *The most important pastoral work is therefore theological,* and helping a dispirited clergy whose morale is low in a more secular culture to see that [theological work] again is crucial. If the Christian framework is in place, we can talk to people and pray with people in ways which draw appropriately upon our Christian theology and experience; if it is not in place we cannot put

116. It is significant that most local and, certainly, national memorial services for disasters tend to include some sermonic content. See, for example the Orders of Service for Lockerbie and Kegworth/M1. Furthermore, the availability of electronic recording, catch-up TV, etc., can provide a facility for hearing/viewing the service after the actual live event, when more benefit can be gained from its content; but knowing it was delivered at the live event gives extra poignancy to the recording.

it there during the crisis and without it many people will have few resources.[117]

The place of robust, informative preaching is more essential to the routine normality of the church's missional context as she prepares her people to suffer/die well.

Hospitality

Because we are divinely created to not suffer alone, the theology of the Christian community in the recovery from trauma and the role of pastoral carers in facilitating this, is crucial. Trauma is often haunted by loneliness and the theodramatic response is a hospitality of friendship and presence.[118]

Friendship

"To be a friend of the [traumatized] is not an easy thing—[traumatized] people, after all, are not much fun to be around—and to be a [traumatized] friend is probably even harder."[119] The value of community support for disaster victims is widely acknowledged yet overlooked by churches.[120] Koenig judges a key factor in local church community preparedness in trauma response is their theology on helping.[121] Humanitarian helping

117. Quote from a paper delivered by the Rev. Dr. Alan Billings at a working party, in the Jerusalem Chambers, Westminster Abbey, that I attended (emphases mine). This was one of a number of meetings preparatory to the production of the publication, which is now revised as Blears and Goggins, "The Needs of Faith Communities in Major Emergencies: Some Guidelines." This focus upon the preparation given by the pastoral ministry of the church all through life, prior to any major incident, is also carried by the contributors to Swinton and Payne, eds., *Living Well.*

118. Swinton, *Raging with Compassion,* 200–205, 213–43. Shuman and Meador's appeal to the incident of Jesus' dealings with the man born blind (John 9), is compelling (*Heal Thyself,* 126–27). Yet the grandeur of the theodramatic response lies in being embraced by the company of the Trinitarian God, and by his people. On the sociality of the Trinity see also, Zizioulas, *Being as Communion.*

119. I here utilize a statement of Shuman and Meador, while substituting my "traumatized" for their "sick" (see *Heal Thyself,* 130).

120. Bridgers, "Resurrected Life" 61–80. On the validity of community see Eyre, "Community Support," 4:12.

121. Koenig, *In the Wake of Disaster,* 75; also Everley, "Pastoral Crisis Intervention." "Key Communities, Key Resources," suggests a greater willingness of government to recognize the historic and contemporary contribution of the faith communities. A lesson learned after the U.S. government's defective response to Hurricane Katrina (2005) was the U.S. government's historical neglect of formalizing the Christian community's

needs to be a built-in aspect of a theology of mission. Gospel mission need not be compromised by a theology of compassion and grace, if that mission can be performed holistically. Conservative Evangelicalism's pastoral practice has focused too narrowly upon individual spirituality to the neglect of the social/community dimension, exposing the Enlightenment modernist influence upon that constituency, causing focus upon ecclesiology in detachment from the world in which the church is called to serve. Bretherton states, "As an eschatological social practice, Christian hospitality is inspired and empowered by the Holy Spirit, who enables the church to host the life of its neighbours without the church being assimilated to, colonized by, or having to withdraw from its neighbours."[122] In today's global village people can be traumatized many hundreds of miles from their homes then repatriated in their traumatized state to urban housing estates or rural communities devoid of community heart, or they may become part of the immigrant population coming into the UK. The role of a theology of local church community can prove essential to trauma recovery, validating development of a *praxis* of friendship and community capable of responding to such casualties.[123] Swinton highlights the *ubuntu* (literally, "humanity") theology of Desmond Tutu that has developed out of an African epistemology that begins with community and then moves to the individual. In *ubuntu* theology humans are created for relationships.[124] Very often major incidents can involve whole social communities. Survivors and bereaved may find themselves plunged into these communities as total strangers, requiring food, clothing, accommodation, and compassionate care.[125] In these civic communities there may well be Christian communities for whom the challenge can be that

human resources into emergency plans. (See Fragos, "Federal Response," 63).

122. Bretherton, *Hospitality as Holiness*, 143.

123. See Bridgers' case for trauma being political as well as personal, and for discussion on the benefits of forms of a liberation theology, combining with practical and pastoral theology, working through small church communities ("Resurrected Life," 67–71).

124. Swinton, *Raging with Compassion*, 200–205. See also Tutu, *No Future Without Forgiveness*, 34–36; Battle, "Theology of Community."

125. See Spencer, *Asylum and Immigration*. This was the case after the Lockerbie murders (1988), the Kegworth/M1 aircrash (1989), the London bombings (2005), Carlisle floods (2005), and, most recently, the floods in Hull and North Yorkshire, Worcester, and Hereford (2007) and Cumbria (2009). In the aftermath of Kegworth/M1 our church offered free accommodation and companionship to relatives who came to Loughborough for the coroner's inquest.

of providing hospitable friendship. Swinton's focus on Christian communities needing to be friendly and hospitable becomes salient:

> The stranger may not know Jesus, and his belief system may stand in stark contrast to those offering hospitality in Christ's name. Our task is to be hospitable to him and to respect and seek to understand the differences that he brings; but that hospitality is offered from a position of faithful integrity and Christ-centredness. The offer of friendship is made with integrity. It is made from a position of certainty about whose we are in Christ, yet it is always open to the surprise that the stranger will bring and always hoping that the stranger, through our friendships might come to recognize Jesus as the source of all friendship. In loving the stranger and offering him friendship, we minister to God in the hope that through our friendship the stranger can recognise who he is and find reconciliation with God despite the terrible experiences he has had.[126]

Listening Presence

An additional focus of practical theology that pertains critically to hospitality, is a ministry of presence. Pastoral carers report this as their principal role, especially during the early stages, when people are too traumatized to take in theological arguments. So, "suffering is not a question that demands an answer; it is not a problem that demands a solution; it is a mystery which demands a presence."[127] Alison Hutchison, a chaplain in attendance at the Piper Alpha disaster, testifies:

> What could I possibly say to these people, what could anyone say? . . . There was very little that could be said in the face of such overwhelming grief—it wouldn't be enough—it wouldn't even be heard by people too hurt and confused. It wasn't the time for words but for care. God's grace was needed at a deeper, wordless level.[128]

Paddock summed up the significance of this ministry in his report on the Kegworth/M1 incident:

> The reason for our presence at the scene of accidents was put into mouths by a senior ambulance officer: "In a situation of

126. Swinton, *Raging with Compassion*, 241.

127. Wyatt, *Matters of Life and Death*, 73.

128. Hutchison, "Christ Within Crisis." The Piper Alpha oil rig disaster happened in 1988.

indescribable muddle and chaos and pain and fear and danger
. . . your very presence, whatever you do, will be a reassuring
symbol of order and purpose and calm and hope. You will be
of more help than you know, just by being there, not only to the
shocked and the injured, but to the young policeman or fireman
who is having his first experience of violent death. We need you
for that reason, if for no other." Some will see this as a parable of
the life of the Church in a secular society.[129]

From her response to the Swiss Air disaster off Nova Scotia in 1998,
Chenard confirmed, "The willingness of a chaplain, or a pastoral care
giver, to be amid the trauma, to walk gently and quietly alongside those
working under extremely difficult conditions, tells those workers that they
are not alone, that in fact there is a God who cares even though we may
not understand the mystery, or have the answers to all the questions."[130]

Focally linked with the ministry of presence is what Anderson calls
the ministry of *paraclesis*. Rather than the church being simply an extension of the incarnate Christ of history, the church is empowered and
authorized by the Holy Spirit ministering through the contemporary, living, resurrected Christ to the world. In this sense the church community
is not an institution tied only to a figure of the past but is dynamically
led by the Spirit ministering the resurrected Christ.[131] In *paraclesis* the
Spirit-empowered church comes alongside the suffering and traumatized
in the humanness of the incarnate Christ. As Torrance helpfully states,

Christ does not heal us by standing over against us, diagnosing
our sickness, prescribing medicine for us to take, and then going
away, to leave us to get better by obeying his instructions—as an
ordinary doctor might. No, he becomes the patient! He assumes
the very humanity which is in need of redemption and by being
anointed by the Spirit in our humanity, by a life of perfect obedience, by dying and rising again, for us, our humanity is healed
in him. We are not just healed "through Christ" because of the
work of Christ but "in and through Christ."[132]

129. Paddock, "Air Crash M1 Motorway."

130. Chenard, "Pastoral Care" n.p.; Sage, "Faith Community," 18.

131. Bretherton's concept of hospitality, as a model for morally diverse relationships, strongly places similar emphasis upon the Christian community being eschatologically empowered by the Holy Spirit (*Hospitality as Holiness*, 103–4, 143).

132. James Torrance, quoted in Anderson, *Shape of Practical Theology*, 199–200.

Kettler affirms Torrance's concept of Jesus' vicarious humanity by describing Jesus' faith, as well as his death, as vicarious.[133] The church's ministry of *paraclesis* is to affirm such a living, vicarious humanity by her Spirit-empowered presence amidst the traumatized.

Often during trauma and grieving there can be the compulsion to talk of what happened; but this can be repressed by the fear that no one will want to listen.[134] It is important that opportunities of hospitality acknowledge this by creating space for narrating and assuring that both God, and his church, will listen. In regard to major incident memorial services, these provide an opportunity for the injured and bereaved to be together for a while. Such gatherings of peers can provide a secure environment for the devastated.[135] The pastoral benefit of pastoral carers and church leaders facilitating an opportunity for the grieving to have time, both during and after a formal service, to narrate together, cannot be overstated. Also, active listening ensures we pastoral carers are attending to the actual experience of another's brokenness, and challenges us to confront our own brokenness, that then "validates the dignity of the other, and permits us to embody the compassion of God as we absorb the suffering of the other."[136] Narrative theology also provides a distinct method that can be helpful in addressing traumatization from major incidents by the use of *imagination* as one narrates one's story and weaves it into the canonical story. This focus on the value of imagination should not be overlooked, and a conservative Evangelical restrictive focus upon preaching/teaching systematic truth may make less pastoral progress with seriously traumatized victims.[137] Also, Walton reminds us that there are times when *silence* is an important part to listening, when, "those

133. Kettler, "He Takes Back the Ticket," 37.

134. As was my own experience. See chapter 4, 83.

135. The bereaved and survivors of Kegworth/M1 showed some disparity over such occasions, with some needing such gatherings of peers more than others.

136. Armstrong, "Practicing Compassion for Dying Children," in Swinton and Payne, eds., *Living Well*, 161.

137. See Graham, et al., *Theological Reflection,* chapter 3. Imagination is also a significant factor in the value of Ricoeur's mimetic process. Also Vanhoozer concurs with Ramm's view of Scripture being more than propositional revelation, and, therefore, there is appropriate room for imagination in view of its capacity to affect the self more powerfully than conceptual thinking does (Bernard Ramm, in Vanhoozer, *Drama of Doctrine,* 278–81). Also, chapter 3 in Stackhouse, *Evangelical Futures.* Swinton and Payne's *Living Well and Dying Faithfully,* is an attempt to fund pastoral imagination in the interests of improving end-of-life care (272–76).

who have experienced trauma themselves are often alien to coherent accounts of their experiences which others require them to utter."[138] Therefore, she concludes, "We will begin to learn that there are times when it is not right to make connections, supply meanings or resolutions for others. At points all we will be able to do is preserve the sanctity of their silence."[139] Pressurizing the traumatized to speak of things that to them defy speech is hardly compassionate. Funerals and memorials should provide coherent space for those who will not be able to "tell all" except to God, in silence.[140]

Through appropriately shaped worship and hospitality the church becomes a form of practical theodicy, because, though she does not verbalize a reason for evil, she, "through [her] practices and gestures of redemption, reveals in concrete, tangible forms the various ways in which God responds to evil."[141]

COMPASSION: THE COST

There is always a cost in exercising true compassion.[142] A refiguring of Trinitarian dispossession is high risk because of the relinquishment of self in the interests of another. Reflecting on Jesus' response to the blind men,[143] Purves states that compassion "asks us to go where it hurts, to enter into places of pain, to share in brokenness, fear, confusion and anguish . . . Compassion requires us to be weak with the weak, vulnerable with the vulnerable . . . Compassion means full immersion in the

---

138. Walton, "Speaking in Signs," 4. This becomes highly significant, pastorally, in those contexts where churches utilize "small groups" for fellowship and discipleship. These occasions can place pressure upon members to become "open" to sharing their life experience(s), and can, thus, be intimidating for traumatized persons. However, Bridgers states, "participating in base communities seems particularly promising for trauma survivors. Small church communities could provide a safe environment for the survivor to address issues of remembrance" ("Resurrected Life," 67–71).

139. Walton, "Speaking in Signs," 5. Also, Helm, "Evil, Love, and Silence."

140. Stanley Cohen espouses the view that denial is normal, however, and not necessarily the pathology of popular understanding (*States of Denial*).

141. Swinton, *Raging with Compassion*, 246. Eyre reflects upon a danger that civic attention to memorials can evidence, where a particular affected civic community can compete with another in their public display of grief, to see which community can keep the longest silence. See Eyre, "Remembering: Community Commemorations."

142. Davies emphasizes "risk" of exposure (*Theology of Compassion*, 8).

143. Matt 20:29–34.

condition of human being."[144] It implies going beyond the boundaries of contract.[145] The Good Samaritan shows compassionate pastoral care as: doing the right things in achieving ortho*praxis* as much as believing the right things in orthodoxy. But to do the right thing is costly in terms of our priorities, our time, and our vulnerability.[146]

It is this dimension of cost that often leads to casualties among the responders.

COMPASSION: SELF-CARE

In light of the cost to compassionate responding a component to a theology of compassion for major incident response should include compassionate self-care. In many ways this is the most complex of all the components and can be explored only summarily here. Factors in this complexity include prior/parallel life experiences and medical history; the medical/clinical aspects of psychological breakdown; the dynamics of personal spirituality and psycho-physical stressors. Addressing these fully lies outside of my pastoral domain. An important factor in self-care for Christians, and for pastors in particular, is the humility to recognize there are factors which can deeply affect their lives, and their spiritual experience that, as pastors, they do not have the skills to address appropriately. This can be of singular importance in addressing PTSD in pastoral carers who have responded to major incidents. However, a key pastoral problematic stems from kenotic selflessness being a requisite virtue for

144. Purves, *Search for Compassion*, 35. See also Puchalski, "Compassion," in Swinton and Payne, eds., *Living Well*, 192.

145. Jackson, *Priority of Love*, 12.

146. See Luke 10:30–37. In the case of the Samaritan there was the racio-emotional cost of responding to a Jew; the cost to himself of exposure to being robbed and killed; the cost of his time/prior commitments; and the financial cost of the care he offered. Illustrations of the cost can be found among some of the evicted Puritan pastors who returned to London during the Great Plague. See Vincent, *God's Terrible Voice*. Also see the accounts of the plague-stricken Derbyshire village of Eyam in 1666. Legend has it that, under the brave leadership of the Rev. William Mompesson, the villagers agreed to a self-imposed quarantine to prevent the disease spreading. Wallis claims that this narrative "history" is largely fiction, produced by poets, novelists, and local historians. This was manipulated in the nineteenth century to "fit changing literary and historical fashions" (Wallis, "Dreadful Heritage." Anderson provides a possible contemporary model based on an emergency plan for the evacuation of Los Angeles in the event of nuclear attack and concludes, "If the church is truly the body of Christ, it ought to covenant with those who will not be evacuated that it will stay and minister in solidarity with them" (*Shape of Practical Theology*, 315).

a Christian responder.[147] Issues, such as rewarding salary scales, public awareness, and recognition, are rare, and mandatory mentoring and spiritual directorship may not be built into responders' employment terms or major incident plans.[148] These can amount to significant omissions when it comes to the stresses responders are exposed to in a major incident as they encounter high levels of trauma in others. Front-line responders are recognized as particularly vulnerable to secondary traumatic stress (STS), or compassion fatigue (CF).[149]

Compassion fatigue

Figley distinguishes between "burnout" and "compassion fatigue" in the sense that the former tends to come on gradually and over a long period of time. CF is the conclusion to a cumulative effect, while its onset is more immediate and specific to secondary trauma exposure from a major incident or a series of incidents.[150] I would argue that distinction, though valid, is more complex in view of a long history of prior exposure levels experienced in pastoral service. In other words, Christian responders may be already in the early stages of burnout as they respond, and this can complicate their vulnerability to CF from the incident itself.[151]

---

147. Mark 8:34–35. On the ministry of kenotic *charis* in the context of end-of-life care, see Lysaught's referential use of the life and ministry of Joseph Cardinal Bernardin (the late Roman Catholic bishop of Chicago), in her "Suffering in Communion with Christ," in Swinton and Payne, eds., *Living Well*, 77–82.

148. Many NHS chaplaincy contracts do have mentoring and spiritual directorship attached, and major incident plans can make some provision for welfare and health and safety factors that can include risk assessments for vulnerability to secondary stress exposure. However, these are no guarantees for preventing secondary stress reactions, especially in the immediate impact phase when responders may want to commit to longer hours of work and to higher levels of traumatic exposure. Furthermore, there is a "macho" culture within some frontline responding agencies that discourages seeking professional help, because, among other reasons, it may reflect badly in their professional development portfolio.

149. Roberts, et al., "Compassion Fatigue," in Roberts and Ashley, eds., *Disaster Spiritual Care*, 217–18; Anderson, *Spiritual Caregiving*, 96–111. See also Figley, ed., *Compassion Fatigue*.

150. Charles Figley, "Secondary Traumatic Stress Disorder," in Figley, ed. *Compassion Fatigue*, 12.

151. Rogers makes the helpful point that pastors are subject to burnout at different rates, influenced by childhood experiences. Self-neglect can be a sign of unresolved past history (*Pastoral Care*, 90).

Definition

Compassion fatigue, secondary stress disorder, and vicarious traumatization, are synonymous terms for a set of symptoms that show spiritual, physical, and emotional exhaustion as a result of a caregiving, "that causes a decrease in the caregiver's ability to experience joy or to feel and care for and about others."[152] Figley defines CF as, "the natural consequent behaviors and emotions resulting from knowing about a traumatizing event experienced by a significant other—the stress resulting from helping or wanting to help a traumatized or suffering person."[153] As a term, CF must not be confused with being tired of showing compassion. It is exhaustion while showing compassion. However, if CF becomes deeply embedded then an embitterment can ensue from feeling it has been compassionate self-commitment that has brought this problem upon oneself. In other words, it has been doing what you were convinced God would have you do that has resulted in traumatizing yourself. You may then weary of showing compassion.[154]

Strategies

There are theologico-spiritual, psycho-social, and organizational, strategies that can help responders reduce their vulnerability. Appropriation of these should not be considered optional, however, in view of the fact that CF in responders risks harm to oneself and to those under care.

Theological

In regarding selfhood theologically,[155] there are themes such as legitimate self-love and the sanctity and care of the physical body as a Christian

152. Roberts, et al., "Compassion Fatigue," in Roberts and Ashley, eds., *Disaster Spiritual Care*, 209. Symptoms can include intrusive imagery and thoughts, avoidance and emotional numbing, hyper-arousal symptoms, somatization, and physical and alcohol abuse issues (Palm, et al., "Vicarious Traumatization," 73). In fact they bear great similarity to those of primary traumatic stress. Palm, et al., do not mention clergy/chaplains among the professionals they list who are vulnerable, though they aver that "indirect trauma reactions are more likely among those whose job duties require an empathetic interaction with trauma survivors."

153. Figley, "Secondary Traumatic Stress Disorder," in Figley, ed., *Compassion Fatigue*, 7.

154. I place Elijah in this category after his traumatic context on Mt. Carmel (1 Kings 19:14, "I have been very zealous for the LORD God of hosts . . . I alone am left; and they seek to take my life").

155. The *imago Dei* of Gen 1:27; 5:1; also the assumption of self-love in Lev 19:18.

emphasis.[156] Additionally, problems can arise from having theological uncertainty about the legitimation of one's role as a responder to major incidents. Therefore, being clear about this is a prime requisite prior to any involvement.[157] In part, this research is a contribution for assisting responders to refigure such certainty. My theological themes can be recruited in spiritual self-care *praxis* to reduce vulnerability to CF. Anderson's guide to "spiritual fitness," as a means of self-care, is pointed. He reminds us,

> The so-called 'burn-out' phenomenon among professing care-givers is not so much due to our over investment in one's work as to a lack of self-care. It is lack of spiritual fitness. It results from a disconnect between the inner life of the self and the social and physical boundaries within which one seeks to meet the demands placed on the self.[158]

He recommends attention being given to the needs of the soul and to forming an inner spiritual fitness that can assist in discerning between those burdens it is good and necessary for us to bear and those it is important for us to lay aside or to have support from others in bearing.[159] Letting go, or allowing others (including God) to bear those burdens with us, is vital for the mitigation of CF.[160] Preserving one's access to God, and resorting to trustworthy spiritual supporters in one's church community, is an important discipline to maintain in spiritual fitness.[161]

Chenard's discussion on the concept of *acedia* is helpful. She is careful to distinguish between *acedia* meaning spiritual weariness, as

---

156. See 1 Kings 19:5–6; Rom 12:1; 1 Cor 6:15, 19–20; Eph 5:29. Yassen refers to this as "Body Work" ("Preventing Secondary Traumatic Stress Disorder," in Figley, ed., *Compassion Fatigue*, 183).

157. For example, a recent research project has addressed the reasons for Church of England male clergy entering health care chaplaincy generally, and has drawn attention to the issue of negative motives for certain cases of chaplaincy. See Hancocks, et al., "'Are They Refugees?'"

158. Anderson, *Spiritual Caregiving*, 105.

159. Ibid., 107. Also, Verhey, "The Practice of Prayer," in Swinton and Payne, eds., *Living Well*, 102–6.

160. See Matt 11:28–30; Gal 6:2–5; 1 Pet 5:7.

161. See Anderson's quote from Bonhoeffer: "Everyone who cares for the soul needs a person to care for his or her soul. Only one who has been under spiritual care is able to exercise spiritual care . . . We need someone to intercede for us daily. Those who live without spiritual care move easily toward magic and domination over others" (quoted in Anderson, *Spiritual Caregiving*, 109).

proposed by the fifth-century desert father John Cassian, and it meaning the sins of sloth, anxiety, boredom, and depression, which CF can mimic, as understood by later scholastics, thereby inviting a negative diagnosis. Her reflection is significant:

> If those involved in the dedicated life of prayer and supplication for others found themselves suffering from weariness of spirit due to the cognitive dissonance created by a life deeply grounded in God and God's promises, a life of belief and prayer and the life seen in the 'outside world', a world of disbelief, violence and disasters; if those who daily tried to reconcile their profound spiritual belief in prayer and a God who listens to prayer became discouraged and confounded by times in the search for answers, then could not the same be true today? Are there those in our churches, synagogues and other religious institutions who are growing spiritually weary due to the constant perception that one must seek reconciliation between a faith in a compassionate, loving God and the tragedies of the world? [162]

It is important not to confuse the spiritual with psycho-physical reactions to the horrors of a major incident, as the Lord's interaction with the prophet Elijah, post the Mount Carmel incident, makes clear.[163]

Psycho-Social

Psycho-social strategies are also important for reducing risk of CF.[164] These can include good time management and boundary setting (by responders, and their managers and organizations), ensuring sufficient rest periods during the response period.[165] It is also important for responders to maintain reality with their spouses and children, to ensure they engage

162. Chenard, "Pastoral Care," n.p. See also Altschule, "Acedia."

163. See 1 Kings 19. This records Elijah's reactive suffering from the intensely traumatic competition with the Baal prophets on Mt. Carmel (1 Kings 18), and also to the relentless murderous threats from Queen Jezebel, whose prophets had been slain at Carmel (1 Kings 19). Elijah's reaction exhibits symptoms of post-traumatic stress: despair and hopelessness (v. 4); loss of appetite and overwhelming tiredness (v. 5); anger and self-pity (vv. 10, 14). The Lord's response was not primarily one of revelation, but one of meeting Elijah's need of food and rest (vv. 5–8).

164. That is, strategies that take into account the holistic anthropology I have favored.

165. On the significance of limitations and boundaries, see Yassen, "Preventing Secondary Traumatic Stress Disorder," in Figley, ed., *Compassion Fatigue*, 190–93; Roberts and Ellers, "Compassion Fatigue," in Roberts and Ashley, eds., *Disaster Spiritual Care*, 210–11. Also Worden, *Grief Counselling*, 133–40.

in diversionary activities such as physical exercise, getting adequate sleep, attending to nutrition, and having relaxation and contact with nature.[166] Employers can ensure responders are relieved of other work duties during the response duration. The use of voluntary debriefings, peer support groups, and patient, sympathetic, faith community support are also helpful to prevent a slide into isolation.[167]

CONCLUSION

I conclude that my practical theological exploration of compassion has immense configurative value for the *aporae* of my prefigured narrative, for strengthening both the legitimation of Christian responders and their contribution to major incident response. Contributively, the doctrine of compassion provides the public with a Christian pastoral care the secular does not possess yet and often secretly yearns for, if only that care was not so attached to Christ.[168] But a divinely graced compassion is fortified by having pastoral resources to offer that are rooted in the redemptive reconciliation in Christ most of all. Christian compassion emerges from the graced awareness of being reconciled to God.[169]

---

166. Yassen, "Preventing Secondary Traumatic Stress Disorder," in Figley, ed., *Compassion Fatigue*, 183–86.

167. Roberts, et al., "Compassion Fatigue," in Roberts and Ashley, eds., *Disaster Spiritual Care*; James F. Munroe, et al., "Preventing Compassion Fatigue: A Team Treatment Model," in Figley, ed., *Compassion Fatigue*, 211–13; 209–31. On the benefit of a treatment team that maintains positive and understanding, non-judgmental relations with trauma responders, they comment, "These non-exploitative relationships serve as a counterpart to the isolating effects of secondary trauma" (212). For a secular, social science perspective on the value of social and interpersonal supports, see Yassen, "Preventing Secondary Traumatic Stress Disorder," in Figley, ed., *Compassion Fatigue*, 188–90.

168. Arguably, the secular is comfortable with a civil religion, where the demands of the gospel are accommodated to the altruistic expectations of society. O'Donovan suggests, "To the extent that the Christian community is possessed by its Gospel, it will be protected against social conformity" (*Desire of the Nations*, 226). The current situation regarding the generic role of NHS Chaplaincy runs the danger of becoming governed by civil religion rather than by Christian theology, which has implications for Christian pastoral carers in major incident response, in my view.

169. See 2 Cor 1:3–7.

9

Contribution—Reconciliation, Justice, and God

RECONCILIATION, JUSTICE, AND GOD

HAVING IDENTIFIED MAJOR INCIDENTS as qualifiedly evil and traumatic, to which God responds with grace and compassion, a crucial
issue remaining is that of reconciliation conjoined with justice, for this
constitutes resolution of evil.[1] Often this can take on two strands: reconciliation with a loving and just God, which can be severely tested by major incidents; and, victims being reconciled and/or finding justice with
other human agents (and agencies) involved, which is often significant
in incidents where human culpability of some kind has been a factor.[2]
To explore the theology and ethics of both strands would be more than
my permitted research space could permit. Therefore, even though one
might conclude with Barth, that "evil is a problem before God, not God
a problem before evil,"[3] choosing to explore reconciliation and justice
with God—in large part from the perspective of the victim—is pastoral *sapientia* for two reasons: first, because the devastation wrought by a
major incident will often raise spiritual issues, even in the most strident
unbeliever, as my exploration of trauma has concluded;[4] and, second, because evil is such a vacuous absurd nothingness and God's response to it

1. Major incidents are qualifiedly evil because not everything about them is evil
necessarily. Roberts and Ashley list questioning justice and meaning as one of the
spiritual symptoms of the dis-ease resulting from trauma (*Disaster Spiritual Care*, xx).

2. As most major incidents in the UK are structure, transport, fire or flood-related,
then human culpability is invariably a causal.

3. See my exploration of "evil" in chapter 5.

4. See on trauma, chapter 5.

is overwhelmingly serious; therefore, its problematic hold upon us needs breaking with pastoral care.

The Problem

Reconciliation and justice in relation to God might seem more acute in cases of natural disaster than in the man-made kind. However, both human nature and disasters are too complex for any such clear distinction.[5] In both natural and man-made incidents there may be huge issues over how victims think and feel toward God and one another. In natural disasters, such as a hurricane, an earthquake, or a tsunami, it can seem more obvious that some divine being or force has been ultimately responsible because either there has been no discernible human aspect, or the forces of nature, such as a catastrophic overwhelming of the best flood defenses or disease control systems, have been so overwhelmingly out of proportion to any human factors. When floods, hurricanes, or tsunamis destroy livelihoods and take the lives of adults and children, natural disasters challenge confidence in the authority of Scripture and divine sovereignty over nature, or the divine will to prevent fear.[6] What God can achieve by his raw power seems unjust in the face of human weakness. Even in man-made incidents the quarrel with the divine is significant, because statements concerning his sovereignty can create moral conflicts.[7] If God's sovereign power can overrule the weaknesses and mistakes of humans, why did it not do so? How can his raw power slay innocents? Such dilemmas arose at Kegworth/M1 regarding the random manner in which fatalities were located in the plane and in dilemmas (related to the "Troubles" in Northern Ireland) regarding perceived moral discrimination among some fatalities. Christian pastoral carers will face such dilemmas in the course of their response, and they may encounter them arising within themselves. Such *aporias* are often associated with notions of innocence in victims of major incidents, hence my unorthodox practical theological

---

5. See on evil, chapter 4.

6. For example: the stilling of the storm narrative (Mark 4:35–41) depicts Jesus' disciples expressing their astonishment that even the wind and the sea obeyed him. It is implied that faith in this fact should have relieved any fear they had during the Galilee storm because his command over nature was significant of his divinity: "What is true of the God of Israel is true of him" (Lane, *Gospel According to Mark*, 178). Or, as Hendriksen comments, "But it takes deity to change the weather" (*Gospel of Mark*, 181).

7. See Steinfels, "Scarcely Heard Question"; Rothstein, "Seeking Justice."

angle of approach starting from a human anguish with God and its relation to reconciliation.[8] This risks, however, giving a disproportionate
prominence to evil, which Hart rightly discourages, when he avers,

> As soon as one sheds the burden of the desire for total explana-
> tion—as soon as one has come to see the history of suffering as
> a contingency and an absurdity, in which grace is ever at work
> but upon which it does not depend, and has come also to see
> the promised end of all things not as the dialectical residue of a
> great cosmic and moral process, but as something far more glo-
> rious than the pitiable resources of fallen time could ever yield

and the greater the relief we shall obtain.[9] So, I have chosen to focus not
on the *Why?* question of major incidents, which while legitimate as a
human response, is often met with divine silence.[10] Instead, I focus on
the *What?* questions: "*What* has God done for us in this disaster? *What*
should we do with what God has done for us? These seem to offer more
configurative value for pastoral care and are addressed most in a theology
of reconciliation and justice. I also take into account eschatological foci,
but these do not imply a diminution of pastoral practices available for
this life, merely that much of the problematic will only be fully reconciled
in final eschatological terms:[11]

> A life ordered in response to that presence [of God in the world
> in the life, death, and resurrection of Jesus of Nazareth] under-
> stands finite human life in a fallen creation apocalyptically. To
> have an apocalyptic understanding of life . . . is to abandon the
> modern obsession with controlling the course of history and to
> live *hopefully*, with the certainty that the ultimate meaning of

8. See on "Practical Theology" in chapter 3. The importance of practical theology—and of the mimetic canonical linguistic methodology I have adopted—is that
they seek to interrogate Scripture with the prefigured traumatic contexts, in order to
provide scriptural configuration for refiguration of future praxis.

9. Hart, *Doors of the Sea*, 68–69. The doctrine of providence can give some help
in interpreting disasters in the light of faith, but, even then, only by taking into account the controversial and philosophically and morally complex issue of primary
and secondary causation. The most practical and pastorally useful doctrine is that of
reconciliation and justice.

10. See Matt 27:46 [Psalm 22:1], "My God, my God, *why* . . . ? (emphasis mine). I
agree with Hans Reinders when he states, "The 'why?' question is a lament, indicating
that people long to be comforted; they are not trying to find out who did it" ("Providence and Ethics," n.p.). I am indebted to Professor Reinders for sending me a copy of
his conference paper, with permission to cite.

11. See Shuman and Meador, *Heal Thyself*, 12–13.

> history . . . is determined . . . by the cross and resurrection of
> Christ.[12]

In particular, I pastorally address a fivefold problem in relation to reconciliation and justice represented by traumatic incidents: innocence; emotions; forgiving God; theodicy; and eschatology.

Exploring Innocence and "Innocents"

The issue of evil and innocence is one that has tormented every age. Bricker, exploring whether Mesopotamian texts offer a theodicy of innocent suffering, concludes that the ancients had a resignation to evil and suffering such that, "The only proper recourse the suppliant had was not to argue and complain in the face of seemingly unjustifiable misfortune, but to plead and wail, and lament and confess, his inevitable sins and failings . . . Since there is none without guilt there is no innocent sufferer, only an ignorant one."[13]

The question of innocent sufferers is relevant when disasters seem causally unrelated.[14] It especially touches on the cases of children and the severely mentally impaired in major incidents, and "noncombatants" in acts of war and terrorism.[15]

12. Shuman and Meador, *Heal Thyself*, 17.

13. Bricker, "Innocent Suffering," 199.

14. It is the forces unleashed in major incidents, seeming so totally disproportionate to the frailty of the human being, that makes innocence seem inevitable to many today.

15. Regarding mental impairment, we should take into account contexts wherein trauma impacts upon neuro-biological aspects of the human being, and where pharmacological treatments affect behaviors. In other words, contexts where responsibility is effectively controlled by traumatized, or pharmacologically affected, brain-states. Regarding war/terrorist related incidents: by "non-combatants," I would also include any persons who would have good reason to consider themselves as illegitimate targets either by interpretation of the conventions of war or from the authoritative religious texts that religious terrorist groups may claim to operate by. Innocence is a virtue disdained in religious warfare and certain acts of terrorism, owing to the cosmic dimension to the battle religious adherents often espouse. Larsson argues that the views of cosmic battle adopted in religious warfare/violence ensure, "everyone is forced to choose sides, there are no innocents in a religious war and there are no victims, either, be they innocent or not" (*Understanding Religious Violence*, 23) because, for the adherents, religion claims priority over international rule of law. By this view there can be no compromise with evil, only war, in which all—men, women and children—are combatants (See Larsson, *Understanding Religious Violence*, chapters 2 and 6). Rai describes the terrorists' claim that in national democracies there are no innocents.

Sin, guilt, and justice have a strange synergy played out in major incidents and the trauma they inflict. Mental health professionals, Mc-Farlane and Van der Kolk, note that an underlying societal belief that bad things only happen to bad people often becomes a way of making sense of evil events in the world. They note, "society's reactions seem to be primarily conservative impulses in the service of maintaining the beliefs that the world is fundamentally just, and that people can be in charge of their lives, and that bad things only happen to people who deserve them."[16] Contrastingly, Wolterstorff, reflecting upon the death of his son in a mountaineering accident, affirmed, "to the 'why' of suffering we get no firm answer."[17] Whereas some kinds of suffering are easily seen to be identified with our sin or for chastisement purposes, not all are. For much suffering, the meaning eludes us: "Our net of meaning is too small. There's more to our suffering than our guilt."[18]

That the Bible recognizes "innocence," is clear from the fact that the term is applied freely to various people.[19] However, authorial usage of innocence needs to be balanced by the same author's awareness of inherent corruption. Job's innocence was relative, for he also acknowledged his fear that God would *not* find him innocent,[20] and he readily acknowledged that total innocence was not possible for any human.[21] In

He suggests the results of the General Election of 2005, confirming a further Blairite government in the UK, influenced the London bombers. (7/7: *The London Bombings*, chapter 20). Ahmed confirms the point when he quotes Omar Bakri Mohammed, from an interview held in April 2005 (three months prior to the London bombings), "We don't make a distinction between civilians and non-civilians, innocents and non-innocents. Only between Muslims and unbelievers" (Ahmed, *London Bombings*, 53–54).

16. Van der Kolk et al., *Traumatic Stress*, 35.

17. Wolterstorff, *Lament for a Son*, 74.

18. Ibid. He reacted very strongly to Hick's better world theory: "How do I receive suffering as blessing while repulsing the obscene thought that God juggled the mountain to make me better?" (97).

19. For examples, see Pss. 10:8; 15:5; 94:21; 106:38, where the Hebrew נָקִי (*naqi*) means, *free from, exempt, pure, innocent* (VanGemeren, ed., *NIDOTTE*, 3:152).

20. Job 9:28, "I know that you will not hold me innocent." Hartley puts this down to Job's fear of God's "seemingly capricious power" (*Book of Job*, 180).

21. Job 14:4, "Who can bring a clean thing out of an unclean? No one!" Compare 25:4, "How then can man be righteous before God? How can he be pure *who is* born of woman?" For further on Job's "innocence" see Helm's helpful, critical review of Calvin's concept of a double righteousness/justification, enunciated from Calvin's *Sermons on Job* and the *Institutes*, in Helm, *John Calvin's Ideas*, 282–9. Calvin believed Job to be

Luke 13:3 Jesus confirms that without due repentance both victims and witnesses would perish, implying innocent non-innocence on the part of both victims and witnesses. In John 9, the man born blind is challenged to believe in Jesus as Son of God and the spectators are warned of judgment.[22] Both events presage judgment, and Luke 13:1–9 certainly indicates the universality of judgment "by the recurrent use of 'all' in vv. 2, 3, 4, and 5."[23] Even so, crucial to the argument of the book of Job is Job's protest of innocence, and the fact that his suffering seemed so out of proportion to any evil he was guilty of.[24] Though he does not use the term, Jesus' refusal to link suffering to any particular sin, where religious people presumed otherwise, is stated adamantly in cases brought to his attention.[25] Early Christians could experience non-blameworthy grief and suffering.[26] Yet none of these cases were attempts at what Volf terms "the politics of the pure heart;" that is, they do not attempt to deny the need of repentance for the victim(s) of injustice as well as for the perpetrator(s).[27] This assumption of non-innocence is theological. It is rooted in original sin. That is, "we are subject to a profound pre-personal distortion at the very heart of our beings, which destroys our freedom to avoid sinning; that sin encompassed us, independently of anything we do or will."[28] This significant consideration, albeit deeply unpopular in modernist conceptual thought, suggests a different perspective to major

---

righteous, relatively, when judged by the law of God (creaturely righteousness), but unrighteous when judged by God's immaculate righteousness.

22. John 9:35–38, 39–41.

23. Green, *Gospel of Luke*, 514. Therefore, I cautiously concur with Piper's theology expressed in his *Desiring God* website articles following the tragedies of "Katrina," the Asian tsunami, and the Minneapolis bridge collapse, when he stresses this universality of judgment and need for repentance. However, I take exception to his lack of wisdom of the timing and, in some cases, the interpretation of events and wording of these messages (Piper, "Putting My Daughter to Bed."

24. See Job 31 and 7:20–21; 13:20–23 respectively.

25. See Luke 13:1–5; John 9:2–3.

26. See 1 Pet 2:19–20. Hicks also acknowledges the category of innocence with reference to the cosmic dimension as far as Christians are concerned (*Message of Evil and Suffering*, 142).

27. Volf, *Exclusion and Embrace*, 111–9. Volf goes on to conclude, "But no one can be in the presence of the God of the crucified Messiah for long without . . . transposing the enemy from the sphere of monstrous humanity into the sphere of shared humanity and herself from the sphere of proud innocence into the sphere of common sinfulness" (124).

28. McFadyen, *Bound to Sin*, 28.

incidents where the only distinctions seem between victimized and guilty parties. Thus, even where "innocents" are involved in a disaster, a human sinful state, deserving of judgment, cannot be ignored.[29] The feeling, and fear that somehow or other, I as a victim, have had some hand in what has happened to me and to others is theologically inescapable. However, I conclude "innocence" is a valid descriptor provided it is recognized relatively and never absolutely.[30] It is in this relative sense that my research uses the term because it is helpful in acknowledging that much suffering is not causally or punitively related to any particular sins of the sufferers. Yet this fact adds to the anguish of sufferers and to their sense of injustice, especially where children are involved. There is an instinctive wish for a sphere of life in this world where total innocence is still preserved. Children, especially, are seen in that sphere. Therefore, a child's suffering or death is a major cause of offense to the sacredness of life still cherished by many in a secular world. The same offense is also extended to adults who have suffered from incidents due to unrelated causes.[31] However, "innocent" in both cases, theodramatically, cannot mean personally free from all evil in every context.[32]

Thus, on the one hand a practical theology of "innocence" can afford to be liberal when caring for those who regard themselves as innocent sufferers, having a greater concern to effect comfort than to reflect

29. So, Fackre, reflecting on the 9/11 event, concludes, "Returning to our present 9/11 context, it is Christ the judge of the quick and the dead whom the suicide bomber will meet at the Great Assize, as will all of us who contributed to the circumstances that brought that day to be" ("Claiming Jesus as Savior," 15). Jackson states that forgiveness "requires . . . that one begin by acknowledging one's own complicity in this or related evils and asking for pardon" (*Priority of Love*, 159).

30. That is, there is "a noninnocent way of being innocent" (Volf, *Exclusion and Embrace*, 95).

31. In such cases the horrific event that has happened to "innocents" can appear to disqualify whatever sin they have committed in their lives otherwise. Hence a statement often heard, or written, is, "he/she never deserved to suffer/die in that way."

32. Some argue that this stands even for Jesus, because they regard him, as an infant, to be complicit in the massacre of the "innocents" under Herod. See, Aichele, "Slaughter Of Innocents." As a theodicy view on the perceived divine injustice regarding the sparing of the infant Jesus as the "innocents" were massacred, see Ericksen, "Divine Injustice?" For an interesting and, in my view, productive discussion on the idea of Jesus needing forgiveness, in view of the concept of sin being a *state* wherein we fail to glorify God (revealed most by death) rather than a breaking of divine laws, and where Jesus was "made sin" (2 Cor 5:21) but also forgiven through his resurrection, see Haddon Willmer, "Jesus Christ The Forgiven: Christology, Atonement and Forgiveness," in McFadyen and Sarot, eds., *Forgiveness and Truth*, 15–29.

theological, ontological accuracy. On the other hand, however, relative innocence must be offset against the conservative theology of "non-innocence" that pervades Scriptural anthropology. Birthed in the Christian theology of the creation and fall it means, in the words of Marjorie Suchocki, "To break the world cleanly into victims and violators ignores the depths of each person's participation in cultural sin. There simply are no innocents."[33] In his reflection on the media presentation of "truth," following the Virginia Tech killings (2007), Rittenhouse argued that,

> It is a denial of reality to ignore the truth that every U.S. resident participates in social sins that form the context for the killer's actions, and to suggest that the guilt for this crime can be apportioned without remainder among the killer, his family, the Virginia Tech administrators, the Blacksburg police, and the Virginia legislators . . . Instead of the reality disclosed by God in which all are sinners and need to repent and seek God's mercy, they choose a lie that contrasts their own absolute innocence with their designated scapegoats' absolute guilt.[34]

This solidarity in sin can be part of the presupposed worldview pastors inculcate in themselves and their congregations to enable moral judicial realism to underscore their view of what has traumatized humans in a major incident.[35] But it also underlines the inclusion of the cross of Christ in their ministry as essential, since "Solidarity in sin underscores that no salvation can be expected from an approach that rests fundamentally on the moral assignment of blame and innocence . . . Rather, the question is how to live with integrity and bring healing to a world of inescapable noninnocence that often parades as its opposite."[36] This in turn compels us to introduce (or confirm) the need of God's Messiah, Jesus Christ, and "the economy of undeserved grace" having "primacy

---

33. Quoted in Volf, *Exclusion and Embrace*, 80.

34. Rittenhouse, "What Does It Mean?" David Self shares an interview he conducted with Marion Partington, the sister of one of the victims murdered by Fred and Rosemary West in Gloucester in the 1970s. In relation to Marion being able to forgive the Wests, she spoke of the struggle she faced in view of the discovery of her own noninnocence in regard to people she needed to be forgiven by and needed to forgive (Self, "Enfolding the Dark," in McFadyen and Sarot, eds., *Forgiveness and Truth*, 159–60).

35. McFadyen points out that modern theology has different concepts of "solidarity" in regard to sin; these are based upon priorities of human autonomy in reaction to the traditional concept of original sin (*Bound to Sin*, 30–31).

36. Volf, *Exclusion and Embrace*, 84.

over the economy of moral deserts."[37] The *skandalon* of Christianity—the doctrines of original sin and the death and resurrection of Christ—are not the fundamentalist offenses they are often besmirched as being. Such an evangelical theology of innocents is more realistic than any alternatives and is therefore important to the sensitive ministries of pastoral carers who have other than mere short-term effects in mind.

Just Emotions?

Major incidents are intensely emotional events. Trauma is an emotion, or a collection of emotions. Anger, relief, despair, and elation are emotions that are felt and communicated by and to God and humans. Since victims do feel grievance with God passionately, a theology legitimating feeling and expressing this is relevant.[38] Understanding and interpreting emotions is therefore salient. For this reason, a practical theology should interact between the biblical contexts of trauma and contemporary traumatic impacts on spirituality that victims of major incidents encounter and often express (or repress) intellectually and *emotionally*. This is not to place emotions above cognitions, but it is necessary in view of morally configuring the deep emotional *aporias of trauma, such as I experienced* within my body/soul—along with others—at Kegworth/M1. Emotions are integral to the configurative process.[39] Significantly, it is in Christ that God identifies with our bodily passions, to reconcile or judge them.

Up until the nineteenth century, a distinction was made between passions and affections. Passions were wild, unruly, and affections were profound and deep-seated. The nineteenth century saw a change of language, abetted by a philosophical and religious outlook, and "emotions" became the preferred terminology, driven by the developing science of psychology.[40] As Knight states, "The Enlightenment assumed a conflict between reason and 'the passions' over the control of the will,

---

37. Ibid., 85.

38. In one sense Scripture's narration of feelings of outrage, despair, and grievance, is tantamount to legitimation. See on "Lament" in my exploration of the doctrine of compassion, in chapter 8, p. 217–20.

39. See above, p. 38, 73.

40. For a helpful discussion on the significant changes that occurred in psychological lexicology in nineteenth-century Britain and America, and how underlying religious or antireligious worldviews influenced psychologies of the affection/emotions, see Dixon, "Psychology of the Emotions."

with emotion playing the negative role."[41] Contrastingly, in concluding his consideration of free will from the perspective of neuro-philosophy, Walter states, "In summary, the traditional notion that feelings obstruct reflective and responsible decision making is not true. Emotions actually constitute a foundation for our subjective values."[42] While I concur that every religious emotion has neuro-physiological aspects to it, the actual triggers for those emotions may be spiritual and even divine revelation.[43] I agree with Edwards that religion is made up in "great part" by "holy affections." [44] Emotions are inseparable from the cognitive processes

41. Henry H. Knight III, "The Affections: Biblical Narrative and Evangelical Spirituality," in Philips and Okholm, eds., *Nature of Confession*, 194.

42. Benjamin Walter, "Do We Have Free Will?" in Kane, ed., *Oxford Handbook of Free Will*, 573.

43. See also my discussion on human anthropology as body/soul, in chapter 5, p. 136–53. For the significance in major incidents of emotions of *fear*, and their biological mechanisms, see Harak, *Virtuous Passions*; Ripley, *Unthinkable*, 55–84. For a summary of the role of the Amygdala part of the brain, see Van der Kolk et al., *Traumatic Stress*, 230. Also, in his reply to my email concerning the brain chemistry linkage between cognitions and affections, Prof. Gordon Turnbull replied: "It seems that the amygdala in the brain may hold many of the secrets you are seeking to unravel . . . The amygdala are paired organs at the front of the brain . . . part of the limbic system and closely connected with the hippocampi (involved in memory processing) . . . they act as 'sentries' and are utterly dedicated to one's survival . . . they act as a 'go-between' connecting the perceptual information that comes into the brain in the form of a 'stream' with the right type of response . . . A lot to do with 'conditioning' . . . in the Pavlovian sense . . . When a perception comes in it is recognised as 'friendly', 'unfriendly', or anything in-between by the amygdala which have been conditioned to respond by past experience . . . Perceptions arrive by one of the five sensory channels . . . through the eyes, ears, mouth, nose and touch . . . and a sample of the information runs through the amygdala . . . The amygdala are connected to the endocrine system which produces the chemical messengers in the body. . . the hormones . . . If the amygdala recognise a perception as being dangerous then they send a message to the adrenals to provide more adrenaline and cortisol which get us ready for a challenge . . . If they recognise something as safe and pleasurable then they stimulate the production of endorphins . . . So, I think that incoming information . . . which is initially sensory . . . is combined with an emotional response (adrenaline/endorphin inspired) to form a complex impression of what is going on . . . that complex is laid down as a memory once processed and memories are known to have both a cognitive and an emotional component bound together . . . The early brain mapping work evoked memories of past events and it was noted that the cognitive component was combined with an emotional component" (email communication, March 4, 2008). Professor Gordon Turnbull is consultant psychiatrist, at the University of Chester, Capio Nightingale Hospital, London and Ridgeway Hospital, Swindon,

44. See Edwards, "Treatise Concerning Religious Affections." Also Don Saliers, *The Soul in Paraphrase, Prayer and the Religious Affections*, quoted in Harak, *Virtuous*

(mind).[45] Their validity is assessed by practices revealing their roots, and, in particular, by the presence of love.[46] My thesis is: strong emotions of grief and anger should not be dismissed as irrelevant to cognitive value, and therefore should be assessed carefully.[47]

Pastorally, Calvin sent a mixed message with reference to the expostulations of Job and Jeremiah. He recommended sufferers should keep silent in view of the sovereign wisdom of God.[48] Yet at other times he could counsel, "When God permits us to lay open before him our infirmities without reserve and patiently bears with our 'foolishness', he deals in great tenderness toward us. To pour out our complaints before him after the manner of little children would certainly be to treat his majesty with very little reverence, *were it not that he has been pleased to allow us such freedom*."[49] Pouring out of emotions was permissible and advisable, "provided the bridle of obedience keeps us within due limits."[50] Certainly the rhetoric, if not also the concepts, of Calvin's advice need to be reframed if they are to be of value to people who are far less willing to regard stoical attitudes as helpful to trauma recovery today. There is Biblical precedent for a more expressive approach, as evidenced by the Joban speeches, Elijah's post-Carmel despair, the lament and imprecatory

---

Passions, 41–42. However, contra Harak, Saliers believes religious emotions are distinct from other kinds.

45. Proudfoot avers, "Edwards is aware that affections can be identified and described only by reference to a rich context of cognitive and evaluative judgments" ("From Theology to a Science," 157).

46. As in the theology of Augustine and Aquinas. See Harak, *Virtuous Passions*, 76–77.

47. Edwards, "Treatise Concerning Religious Affections," 236–37. Compare James, *Varieties of Religious Experience*. "Affections" would be interpreted positively in contemporary English culture now as romance, love, or tenderness. For a discussion of the shift from accounting for religious emotions in a theological context to a psychological phenomenological accounting, see Proudfoot, "From Theology to a Science." Proudfoot approves Edwards' view of the assessment of religious emotions by moral practice not by introspection and resists William James' view that religious emotions are to be viewed purely subjectively, irrespective of their roots, and betraying a basic religious core.

48. Calvin, *Sermons of Job*, sermon 78, (Job 21:1–6), 369.b.4, and Commentary on Jeremiah 20:13–15, though in the latter, Hill reckons Calvin "cuts Jeremiah some slack, allowing that the prophet's burden of sorrow was indeed unbearable" (Hill, *Suffering*, 243).

49. Calvin, *Calvin's Commentaries*, Ps.102:2 (emphasis mine)

50. Ibid., on Hab 1:2–3.

psalms, and Habakkuk's confusion, in the OT; Jesus' experience in the Garden of Gethsemane and on the cross, and the cry of the martyrs, in the NT.[51] These cases all display attempts at understanding the justice of God in varying degrees of human anguish that sat awkwardly with an assumed underlying theology. Such cries are intensified with their agony being shared by Jesus and incorporated into inspired holy writ and not rebuked.[52] Such precedents do not give warrant for abusive or blasphemous protests, but not all protest or anger need be such.[53]

Contemporary Reformed Christianity struggles with intensely emotional protestations because of a great stress on the cognitions, which are actually more influenced by Enlightenment thought than biblical theology. Despite Edwards' balancing theology on religious affections from the eighteenth century, it remains a common view that emotions are less stable and reasonable than rational thought processes and often should be ignored or overridden. This is deeply regrettable and has significant negative potential for pastoral carers who espouse Reformed Christianity being effective in major incident response. However, Nussbaum's philosophic ethical work on the emotions challenges such an imbalance. She sets the challenge as one where, "We will have to grapple with the messy material of grief and love, anger and fear, and the role these tumultuous expressions play in thought about the good and the just."[54] Her thesis is: emotions are the energy that drives the psychological mechanisms of a reasoning creature and "lightly complex and messy parts, of this creature's reasoning itself."[55] Thus, emotions can be essential aspects of human intelligence. They are related to our goals and influenced by early

51. See book of Job; 1 Kings 19; Pss. 3, 4, 5, 7, 9–10, 13, 14, 17, 22, 25, 88; 130, 139, 140; Habakkuk; Matt 26:36–46; 27:46; and Rev 6:10 respectively.

52. For example, regarding Jesus shedding tears as drops of blood (Luke 22:43), see Aquinas on the positive value of weeping in his "Treatise on the Passions," *Summa Theologica*, question 38.2.

53. As my exploration of lament has confirmed. (See chapter 7, p. 217–20). See also Harak, *Virtuous Passions*. Roth's theodicy (or anti-theodicy, according to Luhman, "Belief in God") comes close to this though. See also Billings, "After Tilley." Adams concludes feelings are highly relevant to the problem of evil and hell, since they are one source of information as to how bad something is for a person. She insists, "To be sure, they are not an infallible source. Certainly they are not always an articulate source. But they are *a* source" ("Problem of Hell," 326). She supports a combination of feelings and cognitions informing each other and working together.

54. Nussbaum, *Upheavals of Thought*, 3.

55. Ibid., 2–3.

attachments, the fruits of our biological neurology of cognitions, and integral to them. Nussbaum's neo-Stoical paradigm for emotions believes that our judgments, imaginations, and beliefs are objects formative for our emotions and central to eudaemonism (our sense of flourishing and well-being).[56] Though I query her underlying humanistic and evolutionary psychological base, I believe aspects of Nussbaum's thesis have weight from a biblical perspective. Hauerwas concurs with this perspective and concludes, "it is a mistake to argue whether reason or passion is more basic to human nature, since both reason and passion are essential for the development of a life of virtue."[57] Harak's interactive model argues virtue is the guide to moral passions, not mere cognitive processes.[58] Of particular value is McGrath's treatment of the theology of aesthetics and awe. There can be awe in a major incident: due to the catastrophic forces involved and their exposure of human weakness, they can create strong feelings of awe even in victims.[59] These may be highly reasonable from a theological perspective. Jesus broke down and sobbed when he looked upon Jerusalem and envisaged the destruction to be wrought in AD 70.[60] Thus, I question the Enlightenment influences on some Christian theology that reflect a dualism between cognitions and emotions that is at odds with the holistic anthropology of the Old and New Testament Scriptures. Like reason, emotion has been impacted by the fall, and is as distorted and vulnerable as every other part of humanness, including

56. Ibid., 30–75. Renata Rosaldi defines emotions as, "feeling is ever given shape through thought and that thought is laden with emotional meaning . . . Emotions are thoughts somehow 'felt' in flashes, pulses, 'movements' of our livers, minds, hearts, stomach, skin. They are embodied thoughts" (quoted in Davies, *Death, Ritual and Belief*, 16).

57. Hauerwas, *Community of Character*, 125.

58. Harak, *Virtuous Passions*. He argues passions are formed by interaction between historically formed habits through to the present, with a future relational goal in mind, by way of a holistic interactive process (40–41).

59. In the 1960s a German artist, Gustav Metzger, produced Auto-Destructive Art, as a medium through which he could expose the destructive nature of industrial societies. The background lay in the development of Nazi Germany from 1933 to 1939, when Metzger was sent to England. He was influenced as a child by the destruction of synagogues and the horrors of the Second World War. Yet, Metzger's art is designed to bring out not only the horrors of destruction, but even "beauty through terror" (Pollard, "Art Attack").

60. McGrath, *Open Secret*, 277–80. See Luke 19:41–44, εκλαυσεν (κλαιω)is expressive of violent emotion (Haarbeck, "κλαιω" in Brown, ed., *NIDNTT*, 416). Therefore, equivalent to the "sobbing" I encountered, and expressed, at Kegworth/M1.

the cognitions.[61] Irrespective of gender, emotions must not be dismissed or disdained, but heard and evaluated on equal terms with all forms of cognition.[62] Acknowledging this can be important in the reconciliation of emotions to cognitions within victims.

When Yahweh addressed Job's protest of injustice, it could seem that he forced Job into silent submission (repression) by the power of his cognitive claims—a divine "shock and awe" policy, beneath which Job buckled.[63] This would be a simplistic and grossly inaccurate reading of what was going on. Yahweh did not reprove Job for wrongdoing, nor was his design to crush Job into a repressed submission. As Hartley claims,

> Rather he addresses Job like a teacher instructing a student who fails to understand an important matter, for he wishes to open up for him new ways of understanding the created order and his wise care of that order. Yahweh seeks to temper the bitter strains of Job's lament by having Job contemplate his gracious ways in governing the world. He also hopes to persuade Job to perceive the false inferences that have led to his complaint that God fails to keep the times of judgment.[64]

In fact, the whole Yahweh and Job interaction, though dominated by Yahweh, is rich with emotional rhetoric on both sides. Job stood to lose his case by his limited reasoning, not his strong emotion.[65] This is what provoked his defective (not sinful) emotions. The position of trust (faith) Yahweh was attempting to bring him to was emotional as much as

61. On feelings as a vital part of the social construct of the self, see Anderson, *Spiritual Caregiving*, 86–88.

62. There is an issue of gender here as well, of course. Are those emotions that women display to be considered less cognitive or reasonable than those of men, given the male assumption that women are more emotional? Do the emotional outbursts of women deserve to be taken less seriously than those of men? It would be hard to justify an affirmative answer. High or low intensity and habituation of emotional expression are not necessarily indicative of high or low cognitive content.

63. See Job 38–39; Job 40:3–5; 42:1–6. This is how Potter interprets Job's case, in his divine dualism between the God of the Old Testament and the New. He lambasts the God of Job 38–39: "Can you imagine saying to a woman whose husband and two children died in the Lockerbie disaster, 'God has done this to test your faith?' Our duty is to spurn and hate such a God" ("Rebel Against the Light," 198); Also, May, "Job and Jeremiah." Contrastingly, see Elkins, "Suffering Job."

64. Hartley, *Book of Job*, 487–88.

65. See Job 42:3. "At this point it is important to restate that Job committed no sin that lead to his affliction and that he has not sinned in his lamenting. That is why Job does not confess any sin here" (Hartley, *Book of Job*, 536).

it was cognitive.[66] Volf confirms therefore, "rage belongs before God . . . not in the reflectively managed and manicured form of a confession, but as a pre-reflective outburst from the depths of the soul."[67]

Forgiving God

Is there a theology that responds to those "non-innocent innocents" who are trying to forgive God for what has happened to them? Is there a way to respond to the feelings of outrage that victims often have? Regarding forgiving God, Anderson cites this expression, from conversation with a cerebral-palsied student at her graduation: when he suggested that she might have a significant ministry to other handicapped people, she replied, "No, most of them haven't forgiven God for who they are, and I have." She was not protesting against a doctrine of divine sovereignty. She could "forgive" God because, through the process of her struggle with God, she came to realize that she could trust him. She could therefore "forgive" him because he was not guilty. But her route to discovering this was through lament.[68] The gruesome work of sorting human remains following the Swiss Air disaster brought investigating personnel to confess to supporting chaplains how their thoughts and experiences "shaped a narrative which brought both the sense of self and the meaning of God's transcendence into question."[69] The cry "Where's God?" Guinness avers, is irrepressibly "written in blood in the human story"; it is a cry for justice and divine accountability and has to be answered.[70] Psalmic lament legitimates the cry, but where is the answer that will justify God? My thesis is: while such a question is irrepressible, Christians do not believe God needs to justify himself to humans. Philosophic theodicy is, therefore, a construct of modernity, and one I largely resist, in preference for the premodern focus upon what God has done in Christ, enabling us to

66. See Job 42:5–6.

67. Volf, *Exclusion and Embrace*, 124.

68. This is my understanding of Anderson's account (see *Spiritual Caregiving*, 79). Jackson also addresses the question, "May we/must we forgive God?" in his *Priority of Love*, 163–6, in which he also refers to the benefit of lament (165). See also Haddon Willmer's discussion of Jesus as needing forgiveness, on account of being made to be sin ("Jesus Christ the Forgiven," in McFadyen and Sarot, eds., *Forgiveness and Truth*, 15–29).

69. Chenard, "Pastoral Care," 13. She points out, strangely, that no one blamed God for what happened.

70. Guinness, *Unspeakable*, 66.

overcome. The response of the Christian community to a major incident will be a mimesis of God's salvific response to evil and suffering in Christ.

Philosophic Theodicy

Since theodicy is all about the justifying of God. I conclude that the literature shows there is large rejection of philosophical (or theoretical) theodicy—the attempt to justify God's actions vis-à-vis his being, rationally and philosophically—by scholars and pastoral practitioners.[71] In his reflection upon justifying God concerning the traumas of the First World War, Forsyth gave no hope for a philosophical theodicy.[72] Reflecting on the Asian tsunami, Hart maintains that it is a hopeless agenda to pursue a theodicy for a "total explanation." He judges, "the New Testament also teaches us that . . . suffering and death—considered in themselves—have no true meaning or purpose at all; and this is in a very real sense the most liberating and joyous wisdom that the gospel imparts."[73] Surin considers theodicy to be inherently flawed, because "it requires us to be articulate, rational and reasonable in the face of that which is so often unspeakable" and concludes,

> Theodicy, it could be said, is always doomed to be at variance with the profound truth that the "problem of evil" will cease to be such only when evil and suffering no longer exist on this earth. Until that time there is much substance in the charge that the theodicist's presumption . . . only trivializes the pain and suffering of those who are victims. It is therefore necessary to stress that we are not likely to bring much comfort to the victims of suffering with a theodicy.[74]

Swinton sees severe limitations with philosophical theodicy: "The intellectual arguments of the theodicist struggle to carry the great weight

71. However, I accept the point made by Hicks when he believes that some have found possible benefits from theodic theories (*Message of Evil*, 151, 201). See also Helm's comment, "Part of a fully Christian philosophical response to evil involves identifying and rejecting the unbiblical and consequently sub-Christian conceptions of God that are rife in so many 'Christian' philosophical responses to it. For Christians, philosophy and theology should not be separated, nor should philosophy and pastoral care" ("Evil, Love, and Silence," n.p.). Also Steinfels, "Scarcely Heard Question."

72. Forsyth, *Justification of God*, chapter 8.

73. Hart, *Doors of the Sea*, 35.

74. Kenneth Surin, "Evil, the problem of," in McGrath, ed., *Blackwell Encyclopedia*, 198.

of the evil, pain, and suffering that seeks to engulf the world . . . Life is *not* fully comprehensible, controllable, or fixable. We constantly find ourselves as individuals, as communities, as nations, forced to live with unanswered questions. Where is God when it hurts?"[75] Theodicy can be a real impediment to healing because it focuses upon the event and keeps it in the memory unjustifiably. Volf avers an anti-theodicy is better, "an abandonment of all speculative solutions to the problem of suffering."[76] Even Plantinga prefaces his philosophical attempt to resolve God, freedom, and evil, with the warning that, as far as specific evil goes, "Neither a Free Will Defense nor a Free Will Theodicy is designed to be of much help or comfort to one suffering from such a storm in the soul . . . Neither is to be thought of first of all as a means of pastoral counselling."[77] Carson admits his *How Long, O Lord?* is "not even the sort of book I would give to many people who are suffering inconsolable grief."[78]

I conclude philosophic theodicy is incompatible with Christianity since it doesn't view life through the lens of Christ and the cross. It has modernist assumptions of the existence of knowledge that, separate from God himself, and accessible to humans, attempts arbitration on matters of divine justice. It also represents a flight from reality that creates more problems than it solves. Stott rightly concludes, "It needs to be said at once that the Bible supplies no thorough solution to the problem of evil, whether 'natural' evil or 'moral' . . . Its purpose is more practical than philosophical. Consequently, although there are references to sin and suffering on virtually every page, its concern is not to explain their origin but to help us to overcome them."[79]

Theodicy is not part of the theodrama, nor a work for the dramaturge. Theoretical theodicy is a creature of the Enlightenment and post-Enlightenment arrogance, provoked into existence by the demise of authoritative religion. In premodern times there was an almost universal acceptance of some form of providence doctrine. Few sought comfort in theodicy then, and I am not convinced those who seek it there now find significant answers. Philosophical theodicy is more a "spectator sport" than of real value. It provides an arena for "spectators" to major incidents

---

75. Swinton, *Raging With Compassion*, 3 (emphasis his).

76. Volf, *Exclusion and Embrace*, 138.

77. Plantinga, *God, Freedom, and Evil*, 28–29.

78. Carson, *How Long?*, 9.

79. Stott, *Cross of Christ*, 312.

to judge God; yet it provides little help to the actual sufferers. Intellectually naive though it may seem to modernity, Christianity "is not the sacrifice we make, but the sacrifice we trust; not the victory we win, but the victory we inherit. That is the evangelical principle. We do not see the answer; but we trust the Answerer, and measure by Him."[80]

Practical Theodicy—The Gospel

The word from the answerer is found in Christ and his cross and resurrection, and it is from these "particulars" a true practical theodicy in the context of reconciliation and justice is found.[81] God is found vindicated at the cross and in the resurrection. I affirm with Forsyth, therefore, Christ is God's revealed theodicy of grace, not man's discovery nor achievement. "It is not a rational triumph but a victory of faith. Christ is the theodicy of God and the justifier both of God and the ungodly. The supreme theodicy is atonement."[82] This is practical theodicy, or rather, theodrama.

The Christian community is called to this practical theodicy in major incident response, which Swinton defines as, "the process wherein the church community, in and through its practices, offers subversive modes of resistance to evil and suffering experienced by the world. The goal of practical theodicy is, by practicing these gestures of redemption, to enable people to continue to love God in the face of evil and suffering and in so doing to prevent tragic suffering from becoming evil."[83] Such "gestures of redemption" are inspired by the life, death and resurrection of the Son of God. In theodramatic terms, redemption is from the mess of the fall, sin, and judgment.

In contemporary caregiving however this theology has been questioned (especially in the hospice care context). Matthew Fox, for example, suggests the traditional fall/redemption motif holds a devastating psychological corollary, because it is built upon fear and not the psychologies of trust as the "ever-growing expansion of the human person" warrants.[84]

---

80. Forsyth, *Justification of God*, 230. See also Bray, *Doctrine of God*, 250.

81. See Shuman and Meador, *Heal Thyself*, 102. Jackson argues the emphasis should be upon the incarnation, however (*Priority of Love*, 92). See also Bray's affirmation (and its complete context): "but Christ did not come to share in our sufferings as such; he came to provide the answer to them" (*Doctrine of God*, 249–51).

82. Forsyth, *Justification of God*, 175; also Surin, "Evil, the problem of," in McGrath, ed., *Blackwell Encyclopedia*, 196.

83. Swinton, *Raging with Compassion*, 85.

84. Matthew Fox, *The Coming of the Cosmic Christ: The Healing of Mother Earth and the Birth of Global Renaissance*, quoted in Anderson, *Spiritual Caregiving*, 103.

I would not dispute that, teleologically, trust is focal to Christianity; but Fox starts with the assumption that God first needs to earn our trust. I also dispute the assumption that the fall/redemption motif does not teach trust. In theodramatic terms, human sin has caused fracture and offense in relating to God, and has brought expulsion, punishment, and alienation upon humans.[85] From this state (and its effects upon creation as a whole), in which a requisite fear is perfectly apposite,[86] redemption is essential. Only under terms of redemption can trust become viable. Trust (faith) is the key component of the justification that flows from the redemptive work. Fall/redemption and trust, therefore, are not mutually exclusive in the biblical *telos*. We would not dispute that the fall/redemption motif is capable of abuse, making use of fear as a primary factor in place of trust, but this would be an abuse of the motif not the legitimate purpose of it.

Douglas Hall does not oppose the fall/redemption motif so much as insist it is nuanced in view of Western enculturated interpretations. He rejects the motif of power and conquest presented in redemptive theories, such as the *Christus Victor* and classical ransom theories of the Reformation, which he considers are too influenced by a Constantinian, politically ascendant Christianity. For God to address evil and suffering by a stroke of his power would not be possible since such power would eliminate humans, for humans and sin are inseparable, and "There is no sword that can cut away sin without killing the sinner."[87] Hall argues strongly for a motif of weakness, vested in God becoming a human and fully identifying with human suffering, because to be human is to suffer. This is God's *modus operandi* to address the problems of suffering and evil within the human heart: a theology of the cross rather than of glory. Thus, "God incarnate and crucified bears with us and for us the 'weight of sin' that is the root cause of our suffering, and that we cannot assume in our brokenness."[88] Hall pleads for the full scandal of the weak man on the

85. Lorek, *Motif of Exile*, 17–19.

86. According to Gen 3:10, "I heard Your voice in the garden, and I was afraid . . ."

87. Hall, *God and Human Suffering*, 98. Yet, Hall does not address the Pauline concept of either the sinful/fallen nature being "killed" by the law (Rom 7:9–11), or of the believer/believing community "dying" to sin and self through union with Christ (Rom 6:8). In neither case is "killing" and "dying" seen as harmful to the human being, but quite the opposite, to be desired in the interests of dealing with sin. Surely the Holy Spirit, with the word of God, can cut away sin without slaying the sinner (in any harmful sense). Compare Heb 4:12.

88. Hall, *God and Human Suffering*, 113.

cross to be expressed as the only way for redemption, for this is God's way of dealing with sin and suffering, because "suffering is where God and human beings meet."[89] He also argues that the force of God's pain is not realized by verbal propositions but by meditation and imagination. Hall's valid nuances have particular pertinence in major incident response, where pastoral carers are caring for those who have been deeply crushed by forces of power. Power motifs stand to stir negative emotions from incidents where power has been overwhelmingly catastrophic, since if God has such power, then why cannot he eliminate suffering in a single act?[90] This is a question many sufferers could raise legitimately where the power motif becomes primary, in my view.[91]

The fall/redemption motif must go beyond the individual, however, and address large corporate, societal evils. Those who suggest addressing social symptoms is wrong warrant Hall's judgment, "Too many of the intellectuals and 'spiritual people' among us maintain our safe distance from the world by telling ourselves that we are interested only in the root causes of our late twentieth-century dis-ease. Thus, theology, preaching, the conversion of souls, and 'pastoralia' become for us fences upon which to sit, while others risk their lives and fortunes to save human bodies and the body politic."[92] This point is a justified critique of some conservative Evangelical reserve concerning, for example, disaster mitigation attempts or support for action groups crusading for corporate and political bodies

89. See 1 Cor 1:21–25. C. S. Song, quoted in Hall, *God and Human Suffering*, 117.

90. Could this have been the conflict that the Old Testament prophet Elijah wrestled with (1 Kings 18–19)? The demonstration of God's power against the prophets of Baal on Carmel (1 Kings 18) was followed by the death threat from Queen Jezebel that precipitated Elijah's retreat into the wilderness and his experience of total depression and despair in the cave. Was that brought on by a realization that God would not use his power to crush Jezebel (as well as the prophets of Baal)? Thus, Elijah's despair was a conflict about divine power. Intriguingly, God's revelation to him came *not* as a revelation of power, but as "a still small voice" (1 Kings 19:12).

91. Yet there are references to power in a pastoral context in the New Testament, Rom 1:16 (gospel is power) and Eph 1:19 (prayer for Christians to understand the power at work in them). But it is such power as works through weakness, 1 Cor 2:3–4; 2 Cor 12:9.

92. Hall, *God and Human Suffering*, 103. Chester and Hall, too, would advocate addressing corporate bodies, even by way of a nuanced form of liberation theology. See Chester, "Theology and Disaster Studies," 325. Also, "Theodicy of Natural Disasters"; Hall, *God and Human Suffering*, 100. Brueggemann argues that in the Old Testament theodicy is not wrestled with reference to God but to human structures of social injustice. See Brueggemann, "Theodicy in a Social Dimension." Also Bridgers, "Resurrected Life," 61–80.

to address issues of housing development and flooding, air and rail crash survivability, or access to legal assistance.[93]

In summary: it is the theodrama of divine reconciliation that is the answer to the *aporias* of trauma. To the question we put to God: "What have you done?" We are given a resounding answer: "This is My beloved Son, hear him!"[94] Having so heard the beloved Son, it is Christ made sin for us that has become the ministry of reconciliation in the ambassadorial mission of the evangelical catholic Christian community to a world awaiting eschatological judgment.[95]

Reconciliation, Justice, and Eschatology

Eschatological factors are salient to major incident response because of the threats from, and to, this life. Traumatic, catastrophic incidents raise cognitive and affective concerns about wrath and judgment in view of the loss of life and collapse of meaning to life. They also heighten post-mortem inquiries and assurance concerning the deceased. In the context of trauma, grief, and bereavement, these issues require enormously sensitive handling by pastoral carers. Because of the human tendency to self-blame, pastoral carers should use their theological and pastoral expertise to help sufferers assess this dimension with care and realism.[96] Theodramatically, the only resolution to the problem of suffering lies with reference to the victory of Christ's cross and resurrection; not even death can constitute a resolution.[97] Henry affirms, "Only one theological

93. See appendix 2 for an example of crusading, in the sensitive, sensible sermon preached by the Rev. John Mosey at the Act of Remembrance on the tenth anniversary of the Lockerbie disaster, December 2007, in Westminster Abbey. His sermon indicates how critical an issue justice can be for certain types of major incident where human, criminal culpability has been obvious.

94. Mark 9:7. See also Mark 12:1–11.

95. See 2 Cor 5:18–21. This mission is motivated by the awareness of all having to appear before the judgment seat of Christ (v. 10) and of the "terror of the Lord" (v. 11).

96. On self-blame see, Gray et al., "Acute Psychological Impact"; Hodder, "Exploration of Family Communication"; Nader, "Guilt Following Traumatic Events." Nader's article is a supplemental article to "Terrorism: September 11, 2001, Trauma, Grief and Recovery." However, Nussbaum points out that anger toward oneself is rarely attributable to the traumatic event itself (*Upheavals in Thought*, 29, n. 20). Pastoral carers will need to be cognizant of this in their responsible care.

97. Zizioulas argues suicide is the only, logical, choice open to the nihilistic Western philosophy of human autonomy, as it was expressed by Dostoyevsky. Since true freedom requires absence of necessity, humans cannot be truly free without relation to God. Their very existence is a necessity. Thus true freedom can only be on the basis

perspective, only one philosophical perspective, has an enduring future, a worldlife view, namely, that openly acknowledges that the future belongs to God."[98] In regard to eschatology, Shuman and Meador remind of the significance of imagination, a key aspect of mimesis, particularly in respect of apocalyptic.[99] Herein lies a theology of hope that, allowed to have its effect, maturates the virtue of hope within us.[100]

In Zizioulas' conceptuality, hope does not rest in *ousia*, but in *hypostasis*, the Spirited regenerate *person*. The gospel, through regeneration, creates a "new" person whose ontology belongs to the future.[101] They become eschatological persons/members of an eschatological community.[102] That there is both a life to live, and a hope, is also made available in the theodrama by way of the doctrine of the resurrection. Where the immortality of the soul, or any other hope vested in our natural being, is highly questionable in Christian terms, the resurrection is fundamental to theodramatic eschatology. In the theodrama this eventuates in heaven and/or hell.

Heaven

It is important to understand that the theodramatic focus upon heaven is not intended as a projection of human desires for fulfillment and happiness that cannot be fulfilled on earth.[103] Liberation theology has served as

---

that humans can be bold enough to choose not to exist. Zizioulas rightly points out that this can only lead to nihilism, which is hope-less (*Being as Communion*, 42–43).

98. Henry, *God Who Stands*, 492.

99. Shuman and Meador, *Heal Thyself*, 109–14.

100. The implications of such a theology for the controversial aspects of end-of-life care, such as euthanasia, assisted suicide, and mercy killing, are great, but my research cannot permit space for exploring such.

101. See Rom 6:4–5 that speaks of a union with the resurrected Christ already in this life, implying the believer is already a resurrected being.

102. See Heb 11:1. Zizioulas comments: "It makes man as a person always sense that his true home is not in this world, in the goods and values of this world" (*Being as Communion*, 62). This is because the regenerate person (*hypostasis*) is not dependent upon the substance (*ousia*) of this world. This is what makes Christianity possess an essential ascetic dimension for Zizioulas. Yet, it also gives a concept of person that transcends/ liberates from individualism, and even death (*Being as Communion*, 62–65). From the perspective of a quite different ecclesial camp, by Holland's thesis this principle is also worked out by the apostle Paul in his use of the baptismal motif, in Rom 6, which is describing that new status of the church community (*Contours*, chapter 7).

103. This was the view of Ludwig Feuerbach and, to some extent, Karl Marx. See McGrath, ed., *Christian Theology*, 449–50; Shuman and Meador, *Heal Thyself*, 65–70.

a salient balance against any such tendency in Evangelical history. However, Shuman and Meador have reminded us that Western culture has co-opted religion as a medical utility, to attempt producing on earth that which Scripture promises should belong to heaven.[104] The theodrama responds to two essential eschatological questions: "How then shall we live?" And, "For what shall we hope?" And it responds to these with the doctrine of heaven. But, not all see it that way.

"Paradise Syndrome"

On account of the Constantinian abuses of redemption theology and eschatology, Hall reacts against what he calls the "Paradise syndrome," and argues for recognition of pain and suffering being integrative and positive to life here and now.[105] I do not deny *some* realized eschatological justice is necessary in a world where horrific evils can exist with apparent impunity. Therefore, in his First World War context, Forsyth judged the liberal Protestant church was too soft in its prewar life, permitting little emphasis upon judgment.[106] He had no doubt that the war was a divine judgment for a nation's lack of moral righteousness and was a shock to past meliorism. He saw the events of war providing a theodicy, not requiring one: "The judgments of history, so far from calling for a theodicy are parts of God's historic and practical theodicy . . . that, with such a world, the difficulty would be to defend God if they were not there," and without "a judgment final both in future time and *present principle*, no theodicy is possible."[107] Making such an assumption in general concerning a world war is not the same as a prophetic judgment on particular incidents, which must be cautioned against. Davis and Wall pointedly comment, "We should be careful of saying any disaster is a judgment; even if it is a judgment, it should not affect our attitude of compassion to those who suffer as a result."[108] While Hall's emphasis upon the redemptive provisions for the distresses of *this* life and Forsyth's concept of war as a realized eschatology are a necessary balance for any dualistic

---

104. Shuman and Meador, *Heal Thyself*, 74.

105. Hall, *God and Human Suffering*, 146–47.

106. Forsyth, *Justification of God*, 99.

107. Ibid., 186, 200 (emphasis mine). Richard Niebuhr also made the potent evaluation of American liberal theology, that, "a God without wrath brought men and women without sin into a Kingdom without judgment through the ministration of Christ without the cross" (quoted in Philips and Okholm, eds., *Nature of Confession*, 235).

108. Davis and Wall, eds., *Christian Perspectives*, 14.

pietisms that eschew real significance for this world, standing alone they risk too much.[109] Because many injustices seem unresolved in this life, the eschatological dynamic to the theodrama is essential.

Eschatological hope, in a life to come, is irrefutable as a theodramatic feature and adds to the validity of my theology. The cross and resurrection present both a now and not yet dialectic to theology. On the cross Christ has dealt with sin, it is finished,[110] yet suffering and injustice will remain until the final judgment.[111] For now, it is the church's work to implement that victory of God in the world through her suffering love. Citing Romans 8:17–27, Hicks comments, "God has decided that the world as we know it should not last for ever, that it should not make perfect sense, that we should not feel completely at home here, that it should not ultimately satisfy."[112] Christians resorting to *future* hope in response to their own traumas is fully theodramatic.[113] Gospel grace provides an effective counter to suffering in a hope to be fully realized only in eternity. McFadyen confirms that, in this messy world, caught in the throes of the fall, "living towards a future of which it only has a foretaste, the life of faith is characterised by patient forbearance, struggle, failure, forgiveness, confession and hope."[114]

---

109. See also Billings, "Lived Question," for similar balance. Wright acknowledges the importance of redemptive resources for this life but argues for the future hope as well in good balance. See Wright, *Evil and the Justice of God*. Kübler-Ross, by contrast, ponders the Christian emphasis on postmortem hope as a form of denial of our mortality (*On Death and Dying*, 8). Rauschenbusch probingly asks "which will do more to make our lives spiritual and release us from the tyranny of the world, the thought that we may at any moment enter into the presence of the Lord, or the thought that every moment we are in the presence of the Lord?" (Walter Rauschenbusch, quoted in Robbins, *Methods in the Madness*, 58).

110. John 19:30, though Calvin and Balthasar would argue the redemptive work also required the descent into hell. See below, p. 285–86.

111. Rom 8:18, "For the sufferings of this present time . . ."; Rev 21:4, "And God will wipe away every tear from their eyes."

112. Hicks, *Message of Evil*, 157.

113. See Acts 7:54–60; Rom 8:18, 23–25; 1 Cor 15:19. Compare 1 Cor 15:20; 2 Cor 4:7–18; Phil 1:21–23; 3:20–21; Heb 11; Rev 7:14–17 for explicit reference to suffering. Wright comments, "Romans 8 is the deepest New Testament answer to the 'problem of evil,' to the question of God's justice. And it is all accomplished according to the pattern of the Exodus, of the freeing of the slaves, of the cross and the resurrection, of the powerful new life of the Spirit" (Wright, *Evil and the Justice of God*, 75–76).

114. McFadyen, *Bound in Sin*, 191.

"Instrumentalizing Virtue"

Timothy Jackson also takes an ambivalent view of heaven as an eschatological reality. He reacts to the instrumentalizing of virtue the apostle Paul seems to engage with, when he infers a virtuous life without resurrection hope is vain and pitiful.[115] Jackson insists that the priority of his strong agapic love is resistant to extrinsic motivation (that is: loving because of the postmortem benefits this incurs). Given the Johannine focus upon a full life possibility here and now, Jackson rejects the idea that a doctrine of resurrection is indispensable to Christian moral behavior. He also appeals to the Johannine concept of eternal life being here and now.[116] Therefore, epistemically, Jackson cannot believe the resurrection is morally necessary; however, morally, he believes God owes it to those who strive to live virtuously in an unjust world.[117] It may seem by this, that I should endorse Jackson's view, given my focus upon forgiving God. I do not endorse it. My focus is a pastoral one, not an epistemic or moral one. Contra Jackson, the theodrama places the resurrection at the climax of the redemptive drama, as a confirmation of the acceptance of Christ as Son of God in the complete redemptive value of his atonement and of a future judgment.[118] Its relation to virtue lies in the promissory word of God and thus in divine integrity, without which, virtue, from a Christian perspective, would be suspect.[119]

I conclude that eschatological hope is not a "syndrome" but it can be a healthy dimension to the theodramatic adventure of faith, without which all ultimate hope for justice and redemption is removed. Nor is it an instrumentalizing of virtue. It is critical to a true handling of the gospel.[120] Because we can assume life should be comfortable and comprehensible in the present, and that God should be judged by this, not

115. See 1 Cor 15:14, 19, 32.

116. For instance, see John 5:24, "He who hears My word and believes in Him who sent Me *has* everlasting life" and 11:24, "I *am* the resurrection and the life" (emphases by Jackson).

117. Jackson, *Priority of Love*, 82–89.

118. See John 14:1–3; Rom 1:1–4; 8:34; Acts 17:31 respectively.

119. See also Acts 2:22–32. The resurrection of Jesus was central to the apostle's preaching and a key to the conviction of sin and to the moral repentance, experienced by the three thousand who gladly received the word. Also from a moral-philosophical point of view it is difficult to establish the point that virtue is the best way to live, irrespective of the outcome. This is the dilemma faced in Ps 73:4–14.

120. Thus, the Apostle Paul ends his address to the Areopagites with reference to the resurrection, offensive though it was (Acts 17:31).

his future promises, when a major incident shatters this assumption and we have no future promises to trust, then nihilism becomes our only option, with all the despair and darkness it is notorious for. Hall's emphasis, that all forms of suffering have some constructive, integral benefit for sufferers in this life, is only a part of the equation.[121] Christian responders are justified in drawing attention to eschatological dimensions in their care of the traumatized, but this must be done with appropriate sensitivity, humility, and compassion. Failure to do justice to these theological themes, in general terms, amounts to dereliction of duty, since here is a dimension pertinent to the church's role in preparing people for dying and for eternal life. This forms an essential part of her ethical responsibility before God and humanity.

But the theodrama's focus upon resurrection from the dead—originating in Christ, the "first fruits"—is also upon resurrection *to* heaven.[122] The pastoral implications of the doctrine of Christ's resurrection on the doctrine of heaven are enormous for comforting the bereaved and those facing poor quality of life from injuries that will prove seriously disabling. Comforts include: the relief from suffering/disfigurement in the enjoyment of a resurrected body, the "double *nihil* of nonexistence and nonremembrance" of all things old, so that horrific

---

121. Hall objects to the heavenly emphasis of C. S. Lewis' *Problem of Pain*. He thinks Lewis places too strong a link between sin and pain, and places too much of the Christian's hope in heaven. Thus Hall prefers: "God's project, the modus operandi of which is a series of 'covenants' culminating (for Christians) in 'the new covenant in my blood,' is not to get people into heaven but to make them responsible, grateful, and joyful citizens of earth" (Hall, *God and Human Suffering*, 167). This thinking seems close to that of Stoddart's postliberal belief that the vocabulary of "heaven" and "hell" should be considered as verbs, not nouns. Thus, the issue is about "heavening" or "helling" during this life (whatever that may mean), not preparing us for literal heaven/hell in a life to come, about which Stoddart is somewhat agnostic (internet conversation between Prof. Eric Stoddart and author in July 2008). Nancey Murphy posits whether Christians through the centuries would have "devoted their attention to working for God's reign on earth" if a Neoplatonic view of the human being had not predominated for so long (Murphy, *Bodies and Souls*, 27).

122. This is not to overlook that, in some way, largely unrevealed, there will also be a resurrection of the damned (John 5:28–29), which I address in detail, below. In the context of Jackson's preference for everlasting life being largely here and now, the Johannine explicit inclusion of the resurrection, both of "those who have done good" (thus, the virtuous) and "those who have done evil," makes Jackson's contest between Johannine and Pauline perspectives utterly unnecessary.

SIT ON OUR HANDS, OR STAND ON OUR FEET?

memories no longer torment the victim,[123] postmortem recognition,[124] and the fulfillment of justice.[125] A more controversial aspect is that of understanding: will there be a perfect resolving of all the *aporias* of evil in heaven? I believe Volf has got it right. When he asks: "Will we be able to see 'sense'?" he answers, "No, the 'non-sense' of at least some suffering is eternal; all the 'work of thinking' must finally fail and evil remain a 'permanent aporias.'" He posits the only resolution will be "the *nontheoretical act of nonremembrance.*"[126] We might add, in light of my exploration of the doctrine of evil, that we shall see how vacuous this wretched nothingness was, and how glorious that such an awful *privatio* must give way to the ontological *boni* of the Lamb of God in heaven.

These aspects, and more, have been explored well by others, and I propose not to explore them further in this dissertation, since, generally speaking, there is large agreement upon the theology of heaven, to which available space in this project could add little by way of advancing knowledge. Where disagreement becomes serious is in regard to aspects of the doctrine that overlap with the doctrine of hell. In regard to this aspect of eschatological reconciliation and justice, therefore, I choose to develop my exploration much more fully.[127]

---

123. Volf, *Exclusion and Embrace*, 136. Volf roots his phrase in Rev 21:4, "And God will wipe away every tear from their eyes; there shall be no more death, nor sorrow, nor crying. There shall be no more pain, for the former things have passed away."

124. This particularly concerns relationships where deep love has been a factor—in marriage/civic partnership, in familial relations with and between children—and where unresolved problems remain. The question of whether there will be postmortem recognition, what form that will take, and what form relationships will take, become deeply important. (For example, see Jesus' reference to such, in his response to the Sadducees, in Luke 20:27–35).

125. Justice is fulfilled along two streams: the fulfillment of divine justice in regard to those who revile *him* (as in 2 Thess 2:3–8) and in regards to those actions of injustice toward his people (the church), as referenced in 2 Thess 1:4–10; Rev 6:10–11; 19–20.

126. Volf, *Exclusion and Embrace*, 134–5 (emphasis his).

127. My motivation for this choice is because the doctrine of hell is perhaps *the* most controversial in Evangelical theology, and it is the most controversial in the field of a Christian response to major incidents. Most seem agreed on a heaven of some sort; most seem agreed there is no hell of any sort, other than that which the major incident represents in itself. No research exists in regards to trauma and hell, as far as I can find.

Hell

Relevance to the Research

My thesis here is: the canonical linguistic method, employing *sola scriptura*, authorizes and provides for a Christian response, where one's key resource is the gospel of Jesus Christ and, without a doctrine of hell, that gospel is incomplete. However, exploring a theology of hell from an Evangelical perspective is hugely controversial today in any context let alone one of traumatic major incident response. Since hell is often judged as an integral part of the problem of evil, and therefore morally indefensible,[128] I need to justify including such an exploration in this research project. I do so by the following points.

First, my canonical linguistic methodological principle of *sola scriptura* requires exploration of a theme that is no mere addendum to primary claims of the Christian faith. It is integral to a biblical eschatology of final consummation, inclusive of a judgment that makes right all wrong.[129] Kvanvig concludes, "Christianity still must include an account of what would have happened to humanity apart from God's intervention in Christ if Christianity is to explain adequately the point of that intervention."[130] Hell is a consistent and focal part to the gospel, and to deny it is to undermine one's Christian foundations by trivializing them.[131]

128. See McTaggart, *Some Dogmas of Religion*; Adams, "Problem of Hell"; Marty, "Hell Disappeared," as examples of those who see the doctrine in this light. For the same reason as Van Holten, I give no credence to the view that one does not require an afterlife to make Christianity, let alone hell, coherent. I agree with Van Holten that such a view would leave Christianity severely emaciated and deeply problematic ("Hell and the Goodness of God," 39). Whatever the validity may be for McTaggart's argument, that there is no empirical evidence for the existence of hell, and, therefore, revelation must first provide a good reason for its existence. His argument is circularly hopeless. Since, in his opinion, the only one who can provide such a revelation is the same wicked God who, he judges, sends people to hell, then such a God cannot be trusted. Therefore, hell cannot exist. This is "McTaggart's dilemma." See Kvanvig, *Problem of Hell*, 10.

129. Stackhouse judges, "Only in this context does the mysterious idea of hell make any sense" (*Can God Be Trusted?*, 142). Geach affirms, "If the Gospel account [of Christ's teaching] is even approximately correct, it is perfectly clear that according to that teaching many men are irretrievably lost" (*Providence and Evil*, 123).

130. Kvanvig, *Problem of Hell*, 11, 17 (author's emphasis). Kvanvig also maintains "the doctrine of hell has a central place in any serious eschatology, and it is no longer true that this doctrine is one of the ignored aspects of eschatology" ("Hell," 413–27). See also Van Holten, "Hell and the Goodness of God," 39–40).

131. Walls, *Hell*, 6–7, 22–27. Kvanvig judges that to abandon the doctrine of hell is to abandon Christianity (*Problem of Hell*, 18).

Vanhoozer defends his priority of *sola scriptura* over the selectivity of *sola traditio* by appealing to the fact that few vocal traditionalists today support an eternal punishment view, "even though this notion figures consistently in formulations of the ancient Rule of Faith."[132] Hunsinger argues scriptural authority must decide the doctrine of eternal punishment, not rational intelligibility.[133] However one may interpret it, a doctrine of hell is unavoidable from reading the Biblical data, and arguably, from reading the NT gospels, since the most frequent use of the rhetoric of hell is found within the teaching of Jesus Himself. Not even our contemporary Western moralistic sensibilities can afford to finally arbitrate on a matter of such severity.[134]

Second, since my research is in the form of a practical theology, it is incumbent upon me to explore how the gospel resource should reconfigure pastoral care for the already traumatized in a manner that is consistent with its content.[135] The doctrine concerns the afterlife and its finality, and, therefore, the final outcome of those who have perished.[136] I am not

132. Vanhoozer, *Drama of Doctrine*, 164. Carson suggests there is considerable distance between the perspective of the reader and that of the author of Scripture (*How Long?*, 96). Kvanvig takes the view, however, that the process of arriving at a right interpretation of the doctrine of hell, even operating with a *sola scriptura* principle is not straightforward but requires "hard thinking." He cautions that, "our canons of interpretation are necessarily our own canons, and any attempt to relieve ourselves of the weighty, philosophical obligation to develop and defend such canons by appeal to 'the text' is obscurantist" (*Problem of Hell*, 21). While this serves as a necessary caution against simplistic attempts to circumvent hard thinking, it risks placing too high a premium on philosophy over *sola scriptura*.

133. Hunsinger, *Disruptive Grace*, 233.

134. See Keith's comments with regard to Augustine's attitude to the doctrine of hell and Augustine's shrewd perception that human and divine perspectives on justice may differ, but only because of a distortion by sin, "not because of any intrinsic difference between divine and human justice" ("Patristic View on Hell—Part 2," 292). Rom 9:20 indicates both an ontological and moral gap between God and humans.

135. Alastair Campbell believes practical theology should be both politically aware and theologically courageous ("The Nature of Practical Theology," in Woodward and Pattison, eds., *Blackwell Reader*, 84). Though he is opposed to the concept of hell, nevertheless Marty rightly draws attention to the fact that hell cannot be separated from the moral teaching of Christianity. Therefore to invoke the name of God in the interests of civic morality without mentioning hell is disingenuous ("Hell Disappeared").

136. On finality being involved in any adequate eschatology, which is one of the virtues of the traditional view of the doctrine of hell, see Kvanvig, "Hell," 425. Macquarrie maintains even in the case of those who do not believe in an afterlife nevertheless the language of hell can hold significant metaphorical importance (quoted in Kvanvig, "Hell," 413).

suggesting that it is the role of pastoral carers to provide a judgment on such an issue, but the doctrine is important because of the reflections the bereaved can have upon the postmortem whereabouts of their loved ones, and the seriously injured may ask of their selves. It would be pastorally irresponsible to assume that in today's secular world the injured and bereaved would not/should not think of heaven and hell as possibilities. Yet, recent studies attempt to suggest certainly that the Augustinian and Calvinistic doctrines of hell amount to toxic spiritual violence and abuse.[137]

Third, my dissertation assumes a primacy of divine goodness/love. The doctrine of hell, certainly in traditional Augustinian/Calvinistic terms, would appear to conflict with this primacy. Kvanvig explores why there can be such an abrupt transformation from God's love in regard to heaven to his anger and vindictiveness in hell. While acknowledging the necessity for displaying different attitudes, he is concerned to discover ways in which such divergent attitudes can be morally integrated, not kept segregated.[138]

Thus, I explore how divine anger can form an integrated response together with love, by way of some history of the developments within the doctrine, an exploratory evangelical formulation of the doctrine, and an exploration of how the doctrine should be handled pastorally in the context of major incident response.

A History of the Doctrine of Hell and Its Developments and Changes within Evangelicalism

Allowing for a slow process of theological development, Sheol gradually came to be understood differently, as locations for the good and for the bad, in keeping with their earthly life.[139] For the wicked it was a place of darkness reserved for outcasts. Whereas most OT scholars would see the origins of the doctrine of hell springing from the development of the doctrine of Sheol, Holland and Lorek believe it originates in the concepts of Adam's alienation from Eden into the wilderness, and the exile of un-

137. See Stoddart, "Hell"; Stoddart and Pryce, "Observed Aversion"; Stoddart, "Bespoke Theology; Purcell, "Spiritual Terrorism." E. S. Chesen is vitriolic: "The concept of hell is also useless and harmful. I suspect that those who continue to peddle this asinine idea are beyond redemption" (quoted in Kvanvig, *Problem of Hell*, 12).

138. Kvanvig, *Problem of Hell*, 109.

139. Rahner, *Encyclopedia of Theology*, 602. Cooper is more agnostic on Sheol possessing any judicial moral distinctions. For him Sheol was a place of mostly inactivity and unconsciousness that could at times become alive and conscious, as in the case of the "raising" of Samuel, in 1 Sam 28 (*Body, Soul,* 54–59).

faithful Israel. Lorek argues a motif of exile is fundamental in the Hebrew Bible. This motif consisted, invariably, of the components of expulsion, punishment, alienation, with lesser emphasis on return and remnant.[140] It is only in the NT that hell becomes developed into a distinct concept as such, where it is found in the teaching of Jesus most of all. Thus, Guthrie could conclude, "There is no way of avoiding the conclusion that Jesus firmly accepted that there was a counterpart to heaven for those who were condemned before God."[141]

More controversial is how this concept has been subsequently developed and interpreted doctrinally by the church. In the first two centuries there seems little evidence of any creedal formulation of the doctrine. Minimal eschatological references tend to focus upon resurrection of the body and a final judgment day, with considerable flexibility permitted on surrounding issues. It is with Origen (ca. AD 185–254) that we first find any concerted attempt to formalize a doctrine as such.[142] The underlying influence of Origen's Platonic cosmology was significant, supplying his assumptions of the pre-existence of souls endowed with free will, and human self-determination that God must respect. Yet, he also assumed the priority of a divine love that ensures the conquering of all that is opposed to God. Though originally all absorbed in the contemplation of God, humans were endowed with free will to self-determine their own love of God.[143] Inevitably, such souls declined immersion in the good and slipped into evil, to which God responded with various disciplinary and corrective measures in the bid to gradually persuade them to abhor the sinful and love the good. This decline was also very gradual, and sin was conceived as more a failure to make best use of the good than as outright

---

140. Holland, *Commentary*; Lorek, *Motif of Exile*. He provides a brief review of current OT scholarship that gives prominence to the importance of this motif.

141. Guthrie, *New Testament Theology*, 888. Also, see Matt 25:41—punishment for unbelief; Matt 5:29; 13:42, 50; 22:13—a place for the unrepentant; Matt 5:22; 13:42, 50; 18:19. Also 18:12; 22:13; 25:30—as a place of unquenchable fire. This later is developed in Rev 14:10; 20:10; 21:8. In the Pauline literature references are found in Rom 9:22; Phil 3:19; 2 Thess 1:9; 2:10. In the Petrine literature there is the reference to "perdition" in 2 Pet 3:7.

142. See Origen, *On the Principles*. I acknowledge my debt to Graham Keith's work on Origen and Augustine as a key secondary source for my summaries of their positions regarding the doctrine of hell. See "Patristic Views on Hell—Part 1" and "Patristic View on Hell—Part 2." Also Bauckham, "Universalism."

143. Hunsinger describes it as the wind of God's grace blowing, but human freedom navigating, each cooperating with the other (*Disruptive Grace*, 236).

rebellion, which meant Origen very much toned down the biblical concept of sin to equate it more with neglect or sloth. Thus, the measures God took were more corrective than punitive. What is more, the period for correction was extensive, postmortem, and born of God's patience, but temporary.[144] For Origen, it was unworthy of a good God to punish out of vindictiveness, and his motives could only be for the spiritual good of those concerned. Any pains encountered were simply the pains of interior anguish from experiencing the effects of one's own sins. The final outcome of these measures would be the salvation of all in an ultimate consummation of all things (*apokatastasis*).[145] Hell would be empty.[146]

Whilst Origen's universalist views lingered in the East, overall there continued to be disparities of belief, some emphasizing the punitive nature of hell's fires, interpreting them either literally or metaphorically, some pondering if punishment would actually be time-limited in some way.[147] After over four centuries of doctrinal disparity on hell, it took Saint Augustine of Hippo (AD 354–430) to construct a serious formulation of the doctrine that attempted to take the biblical revelation seriously.[148] Of critical importance in his thinking was the priority of the justice of God. Inscrutable though that justice could be, nevertheless it was such that it would resolve all interim apparent unfairness and inequalities. Central to the conviction of the retributive nature of hell was Augustine's perspective on sin. The severity of God was just because the whole human race was corporately united with Adam's rebellion and fall. This fall was without any good reason whatsoever because it was in the face

---

144. Origen seemed to allow even for a form of reincarnation to be part of the postmortem process of renewal of the soul. This owed much to his Platonic concept of the human soul. Plato taught (*Timaeus*) that all souls were created the same, only to take on distinct personality when united to a body. But he also believed in multiple reincarnations of the soul (*Republic*), which creates huge problems over antemortem—postmortem continuity of identity, since each reincarnation would give the soul a different identity. (I am grateful to Zizioulas for drawing my attention to this point, in *Being as Communion*, 28, and n. 2.)

145. Kelly, *Early Christian Doctrines*, 473–74. Hunsinger indicates that recent studies on Origen give some indication of his position on hell being more akin to the "holy silence" views of Clement of Alexandria, Gregory of Nazianzus, and Maximus the Confessor, and, more latterly, Karl Barth and Balthasar (see Hunsinger, *Disruptive Grace*, 243).

146. Possibly even of the devil and the fallen angels.

147. Bauckham, "Universalism," 49.

148. See Saint Augustine of Hippo's *Civitas Dei* and his *Enchiridion*.

of every psychological, circumstantial, and environmental advantage.[149] That original sin then multiplied into further acts of disobedience from a corrupted will. Thus, it was within God's justice to condemn all and save none.[150] God's acts of punishment on the damned, contra Origen, were primarily for the purposes of retribution, not correction.[151] Keith concludes, "Thus Augustine recognised the disintegration of the personality and the execution of a divine sentence as two distinct aspects of Hell. He did not, however, work out the link between the two."[152] In summary, we may take Hunsinger's sevenfold concept of Augustine's doctrine of hell as accurate for what became the traditional view: Hell is actual; hell is severe—consisting of the pain of loss (*poena damni*) and the pain of sense (*poena sensus*); hell is endless; hell is penal/retributive; hell is just; and hell is inscrutable.[153] Hell will be fuller than heaven.

The views of Origen and Augustine echo through the development of the doctrine of hell in subsequent centuries.[154] Interest in the doctrine of hell, by the Augustinian view, climaxed in the Middle Ages with attention focused upon portraying the torture rhetoric of hell literally and graphically.[155] Aquinas enlarged upon the Augustinian priority of justice. In particular, he expanded on the just nature of the physical and spiritual punishments of the damned, on the will and the intellect of the damned, and he explored the balancing of mercy and justice toward the damned.[156] Calvin's view was essentially Augustinian. In the *Institutes*, he reflects

149. Keith's comment is: "No theologian since the apostolic age and very few since then have ever offered such an extensive analysis both of the gravity of the first sin and of its devastating effects on man's relationship to God or even to himself" ("Patristic Views on Hell—Part 2," 294).

150. In fact, even unbaptized infants (or *in utero*) possessed original sin and deserved hell. Though in the case of little children, Augustine clearly had great struggles (Keith, "Patristic Views on Hell—Part 2," 295).

151. In the case of believers, however, Augustine allowed for both corrective and deterrent purposes of punishment. Punishments can also be demonstrative, to bring home to believers how much they owe to God's saving grace.

152. Keith, "Patristic Views on Hell—Part 2," 308.

153. Hunsinger, *Disruptive Grace*, 231–3.

154. Hence, what may seem a disproportionate focus upon them, particularly upon Origen. This is because contemporary alternatives to the traditional (Augustinian/Reformed) view are tending in an Origenist direction.

155. See Dante Alighieri, *Divine Comedy*, 477.

156. Aquinas, "Treatise on the Last Things," in *Summa Theologica*. Also see Seymour, "Hell, Justice," 72–74.

upon the sufferings of the reprobate that are described figuratively by the biblical images of darkness, weeping and gnashing of teeth, the unquenchable fire, and the undying worm. Such expressions are intended by the Holy Spirit to "confound all our senses with dread" so that we may learn how wretched it is to be cut off from God. The damned experience the full weight of God's wrath as all the good in creation turns against them. Their unhappy consciences find no rest "from feeling they are being torn asunder by a hostile Deity."[157] Calvin's most controversial contribution to the doctrine of hell was his explicit affirmation that reprobation is the concomitant of election and an act of God's will. The damned come to a deserved hell through their election of God, as from their standing in Adam, for that wickedness in Adam is the cause of their downfall.[158] For Calvin, the mystery of God's secret will behind such an anomaly is suited to his justice and glory.[159]

This Augustinian/Calvinistic view of the doctrine predominated over the Reformation and Puritan eras.[160] However, by the eighteenth century distinct changes were coming about in regard to the traditional view. Whereas, up to this point divine punishment had been conceived largely as penal and retributive, eighteenth-century Romantic thinking produced a cultural change in the nature of punishment. Punishment *per se* was being conceived as a process of deterrence or restoration, views on hell were moving accordingly more in the direction of the Origenist perspective.[161] However, Jonathan Edwards resisted this move and upheld the Augustinian view.[162] Central to Edwards' view was the glory of God.

157. Calvin, *Institutes*, 3, 25.12.

158. Calvin, *Institutes*, 3, 23.1, 3, 7–8. However, 3, 23.8 is confusing, for Calvin affirms God's will and his permission are one and the same, and thus God willed Adam's fall and the rejection of the reprobate. He argues the reason for this is hidden in God's secret will, which also affirms God's justice. However, he asserts the "evident cause of condemnation" is the "corrupt nature of humanity," and we should rather look to this, "which is closer to us—rather than seek a hidden or utterly incomprehensible cause in God's predestination."

159. Calvin asserts, "Where you hear of God's glory mentioned, think of his justice" (*Institutes*, 3.23.8). Hart reacts against this, believing God's eternally preordaining human's fates reduces God to "infinite banality" (*Doors of the Sea*, 91).

160. Trueman, "Heaven and Hell." Eternal punishment was a feature of creedal Christianity up until the nineteenth century (Bauckham, "Universalism," 48, n. 6).

161. Holmes, "Justice of Hell." See also Walker, *Decline of Hell*; Almond, *Heaven and Hell*.

162. Holmes points to the view of Wilson Kimnach, who is editing the Yale edition

If men would not glorify God by living for him in life then they would glorify him in eternal death.[163] Contra the traditional *poena damni*, Edwards believed that God is present in the pains of hell to further glorify himself.[164] Central to this concept is the justice of God, accounted for by human sinfulness and divine sovereignty. Human sinfulness is heinous because it is infinite in nature, being directed against a God of infinite status. Punishment must be accordingly, either of infinite worth (as in Christ) or of infinite duration (as in hell). God's infinite status requires us to love, honor, and obey him proportionally to his own loveliness.[165] In Edwards' scheme, God is under no obligation to stop us sinning; he may justly permit sin even where he knows it leads to damnation, and he may justly unite all humanity in union with Adam's sin.[166]

Though Edwards' view was shared and expressed by other Evangelicals in the Great Awakenings, such as John Wesley and George Whitefield, Romantic thinking was provoking the aforementioned general drift away. Bebbington argues this stemmed from changing views on the nature of God and the atonement. By the mid-nineteenth century, under the influence of a constructed moderate Calvinism of John Macleod Campbell and Thomas Erskine, who resisted the primacy of divine justice, the view of God as father of all humans, not just of believers, emerged.[167] This change had a corresponding effect upon the doctrine of the atonement. The cross event was no longer considered a propitiatory act, appeasing the retributive wrath of God over sin; instead it was an event to persuade humans of a "permanently kindly disposition of God towards men and

---

of Edwards' works, and has traced the genre of Edwards' famous sermon, "Sinners in the Hands of an Angry God," to the "hands" sermons often preached to criminals condemned to execution (Holmes, "Justice of Hell," 394). This demonstrates the complex, subtle nature of cultural and sociological influences upon theology.

163. "The usefulness of hell, and hence the existence of hell, depend on this overarching teleological theme: God glorifies himself in every part of creation" (Holmes, "Justice of Hell," 394).

164. This glory is further facilitated by God's presence in hell in the glorified saints being able to witness the torments of the damned; the so-called "vision across the abyss."

165. Holmes, "Justice of Hell," 395.

166. See Edwards, "Sinners in the Hands of an Angry God." Glenn Kreider attempts to present an ameliorative interpretation of Edward's sermon, in his "Sinners in the Hands of a Gracious God."

167. Bebbington, *Dominance of Evangelicalism*, 157.

women he had created."[168] Both these changes brought about a much softer conception of hell doctrine, even though the Evangelical Alliance sought to maintain the traditional view, in its original 1846 basis of faith.[169] Among Evangelicals, hell was accepted but not dwelt upon in any detail or with any relish. Generally, however, there was a turning away from the traditional view, and this had a compromising effect upon Evangelicals as well.[170] Alternative views, on the annihilation of the damned and conditional immortality began to emerge, contributing a reasonable basis for milder views on the fate of the lost.[171] But, as liberalism gathered increasing ascendancy through the latter half of the nineteenth and into the twentieth centuries, the doctrine of hell fell effectively silent, in general terms, even if it quietly resided in the minds of a few conservative Evangelicals.[172] Certainly, the traditional view was silenced by changes in the understanding of sin (as finite), and God (as love). These made the traditional doctrine of hell appear morally incompatible with the priority of divine goodness and love. The Calvinistic concept also appeared incompatible with human freedom, which was deemed essential to any human responsibility and divine punishment. It also failed to provide for God's final victory over evil since the damned continued in evil.

From around the 1980s there has been a revival of interest in the doctrine of hell. Initially, this had more to do with Evangelical presentations

168. Ibid., 158.

169. Hilborn, *Nature of Hell*, 136.

170. T. R. Birks, the honorary secretary of the British Evangelical Alliance, was forced to resign his position after writing his *The Victory of Divine Goodness* (1867), which presented a much more congenial perspective on hell (Hilborn, *Nature of Hell*, 4). Hilborn affirms that Birks did resign. Bebbington says that though Birks came under pressure to do so, it was decided that his views did not conflict with the EA basis of faith, so he did not resign, actually (*Dominance of Evangelicalism*, 161). Either way, this gives some indication that the changes taking place generally among Christians were influencing Evangelicals increasingly.

171. Views on reconciliationism also emerged in the nineteenth century (Saville, "Reconciliationism"). (I acknowledge gratitude to Prof. Tony Lane at London School of Theology for drawing my attention to reconciliationism, and this reference). Kvanvig also allows for a possible reconciliationism (*Problem of Hell*, 155). But his is quite different from the view(s) of T. R. Birks and of Henri Blocher, which I discuss below.

172. Such as J. C. Ryle (Anglican) and C. H. Spurgeon (Baptist). In 1996 the Doctrine Commission of the General Synod of the Church of England commented that, "Over the last two centuries the decline in the churches in the Western world of a belief in everlasting punishment has been one of the most notable transformations of Christian belief" ("Mystery of Salvation," 199).

of the softer versions of the doctrine—universalism, annihilation, and conditional immortality.[173] However, from the 1990s there have been attempts within philosophical theology to explicate versions of the traditional form, but which also attempt to address the incompatibilities I have mentioned above, most notably that between love and justice.

Taking into account this brief history, and the recent attempts by Jonathan Kvanvig, Jerry Walls, Charles Seymour, and Henri Blocher, I make my own exploration of the doctrine. My selection of these four is based upon their attempts to realign the doctrine with, broadly speaking, the traditional (evangelical) view.

How Can a Biblical Affirmation of Eternal Punishment be Compatible with the Primacy of Divine Goodness/Love and of Human Responsibility?

Referring to God's moral goodness is a task legitimated by Scripture.[174] There are things God cannot do because they are immoral as judged by his own revealed nature.[175] The OT patriarch Abraham is a case in point: God made him promises and consistently assured him of these being kept. This promissory integrity was to inform a key aspect of the faith with which Abraham was asked to follow God.[176] By such promises, his

173. For example, see John W. Wenham, "The Case for Conditional Immortality," in Cameron, ed., *Universalism*; Pinnock and Brow, *Unbounded Love*; Stott and Edwards, *Essentials*.

174. Van Holten considers the Calvinistic doctrine of hell is incompatible with God's moral goodness, because it seems to imply the premise that God does not actually want the salvation of all. God's decrees imply that only some are desired to be saved. This is the implication of the supralapsarian view, which seems to have been that of Calvin. This would conflict with Scripture statements such as Ezek 18:23; 1 Tim 2:4; 2 Pet 3:9. But the Calvinistic riposte that the Pauline statements refer only to the elect is highly questionable and seems to be special pleading given the apostle's deliberate and careful usage of the term "elect" throughout his letters.

175. Walls, *Hell*, 84. Marilyn McCord Adams argues strongly against this view. For her, the ontological gap between God and humans is so great that it is impossible to speak in terms of divine obligations ("Problem of Hell"). Her view is reviewed sympathetically, but critically, by Jackson, who argues that the divine nature is ontologically kenotic and thus God has *voluntarily* obligated himself to humans in terms of his promises. Adams, however, takes such promises only in a "as if" sense. Jackson argues that God's voluntarily obligating himself represents, "a characteristically voluntary self-sacrifice to meet us where we are" (*Priority of Love*, 72, 79). Jackson's voluntarist view should be distinguished from the perichoretic concept of Trinitarian self-denial that is significant to God's ontology. See chapter 8, above, pp. 199–202.

176. See Gen 15:1–6; Heb 11:9–12 respectively. See also Heb 6:13–18, where it is

wife Sarah is said to have "judged him [God] faithful."[177] In respect of his belief in God hearing his intercessory prayer for Lot in Sodom, a city under imminent threat of disaster, Abraham also sought consolation in the fact he believed God to be just and would not slay the righteous with the wicked, precisely because he is the judge of all the earth who does right.[178] It is justifiable, therefore, to test a doctrine of hell in terms of the revealed moral goodness of God.[179] Kvanvig is right to argue a doctrine of hell should be constructed issuant from the divine nature and the doctrines of heaven and hell should be inseparable—"the account one accepts of one constrains the kind of account one can develop of the other."[180] I therefore outline four broadly evangelical responses to the question I have posed, those of: Jonathan Kvanvig, Jerry Walls, Charles Seymour, and T. R. Birks and Henri Blocher.

JONATHAN L. KVANVIG—Kvanvig concludes that in a hierarchy of divine attributes love trumps justice, because, "at the heart of Christianity is a story of God's conforming the demands of justice and holiness to his love."[181] He bases this conclusion on his issuant composite conception of hell, where only God's love can account for the two great acts of creation and redemption.[182] Therefore, Kvanvig's contention is: the choice model of hell is more suitable to the primacy of divine love than the retributive model. He means that hell has been constructed to honor the choices of free human beings, not as the imposition of divine punishment. This does not negate punishment, merely, "the guiding motif is to explain

stated it is impossible for God to lie. See Jackson's argument that in this instance God did not promise with a view to himself, but to assuring Abraham (and his "seed") (*Priority of Love*, 80–81).

177. Heb 11:11.

178. Gen 18:25. In this context God's justice is an aspect of his moral goodness.

179. God's "goodness" is conceived in two categories in theology: 1) His moral goodness, which refers to the narrow sense of God's perfection, including the virtues of being loving, merciful, faithful, and just. 2) His metaphysical goodness, which refers to a broader sense of his perfection, namely the fullness and self-sufficiency of his being.

180. Kvanvig, *Problem of Hell*, 109–12; "Resurrection, Heaven, and Hell," 636.

181. Kvanvig, *Problem of Hell*, 119.

182. By "issuant" is meant: "any adequate account of hell must begin with an understanding of the nature of God and present the possibilities of heaven and hell as flowing from this one nature" (Kvanvig, *Problem of Hell*, 112). In favor of the primacy of love he asserts, "Justice has no hope of explaining the two great acts of God, creation and redemption, only love can account for them" (Kvanvig, "Hell," n.p.).

continued presence in hell in terms of choices instead of in terms of some simple demands of justice regarding one's earthly life."[183] Kvanvig opposes the Edwardsian view of an equal punishment on the basis of the status principle.[184] While, he argues, all sin is against God in view of God being our creator and, our being divinely sustained by degrees of intimacy, immediacy, and connectedness, yet this does not mean that all sin is equal in God's sight or deserving of equal punishment. The punishment must fit the crime by degree, and this is evaluated by intention.[185] This is compatible with the love of God, since true love risks losing the other, "and a part of loving completely requires a willingness to lose the other completely as well."[186] For Kvanvig, hell is a composite, consisting of a teleological and a mechanical component. Teleologically, hell is a journey to annihilation, but solely where there is a free choice for complete independence from God, which can only be a choice for total nonexistence. Divine love permits such a severe choice, akin to capital punishment exceeding life imprisonment. Since an argument for annihilation would depend upon "settled, rational beliefs," and, as the mechanism that enables this process is complex, dependent upon a truly free rationality, everlasting punishment in hell could remain the predominant possibility. Equally, humans being self-determining, the theoretical possibility exists for some/all in hell to repent in newfound love of God and to escape from hell.[187] Either way, because it is a consequence of free choice, neither the moral goodness of God, nor human freedom are impugned. Kvanvig's emphasis upon human freedom means he rejects Thomas Talbott's view that the only reason anyone can choose damnation is due to "interfering factors"—ignorance, deception, or bondage to desire. Talbott argues that a morally good God should intervene to overrule such influences for freely choosing damnation, because final separation is an evil that a loving God would prevent (as parents would). Kvanvig responds: "freedom

183. Kvanvig, "Hell," n.p. Punishment consists in the loss of ultimate good.

184. The "status principle" is, "guilt incurred by wrongdoing is proportional not only to the severity of actual or intended harm but also to the kind of being against whom the act is committed" (Kvanvig, *Problem of Hell*, 29).

185. For example: an action that sets out to offend God directly is more serious than one that, though offensive, has not been deliberately motivated to offend God.

186. Kvanvig, "Hell," n.p.

187. While Walls allows for some postmortem possibility of escape from hell, for Seymour this possibility is closed by virtue of the continual sinning of hell's inhabitants. Birks and Blocher also disallow escape.

is sometimes more important than the harm that might result from an exercise of freedom,"[188] as is analogous in some cases of determined, rational suicide (that is, where the person has resolved to take relief in death in preference for dying in prolonged pain). Kvanvig's view is very similar to that of C. S. Lewis' conception of hell being locked on the inside, by the choices of its inhabitants; but, he criticizes Lewis' rejection of annihilation according to Lewis' Platonic conception of existence. He argues that Lewis' view is internally incoherent because Lewis neglects the creation *ex nihilo* capacity of God that implies God can destroy anything back to nothingness also. According to Eleanore Stump, God preserves his love for the damned by ensuring their best possible welfare in hell—namely, by quarantining them, so that being isolated from the degenerative influences of others, they will not degenerate themselves any further. Kvanvig critiques this as a naïve hope given the perverse power of evil persons to corrupt others. He also critiques Stump's priority of being over freedom, so that God cannot annihilate, and thus destroy being (according to Stump's preference for the Thomist conviction that being is inherently good in some respect, no matter how evil it may become). [189]

Jerry L. Walls—Walls also responds to the increasing orthodox and Evangelical drift away from the traditional doctrine of hell, toward softer alternatives, on account of the traditional version being viewed as morally indefensible and party to the problem of evil.[190] Walls attempts to counter this drift by arguing the doctrine cannot be so cleanly extracted from a traditional Christian corpus, nor can it be decided on the basis of human phenomena or "genetic fallacy."[191] It must be resolved theologically and philosophically.

Walls also pursues an issuant approach, insisting that a morally acceptable view on hell must be related to understandings on divine foreknowledge, power, and goodness. Walls rejects as morally unacceptable the Calvinistic concept of God predetermining a human's future choices

188. Kvanvig, *Problem of Hell*, 85.

189. Ibid., 152. See also pages 120–30; Stump, "Dante's Hell." Also Aquinas, *Summa Theologica*, 1.5.1; 1.16.3.

190. Walls, *Hell*, 3.

191. By phenomena, Walls means the instinctive emotional and cognitive aversive reactions people may have toward the concept of hell. The "genetic fallacy" infers a belief is false on account of its questionable origins. For example, the argument that the doctrine of hell is rooted in the vindictive feelings of early Christians (including Jesus himself) against those who persecuted them.

absolutely, where divine foreknowledge is based on predestination. He also rejects applying the principle of double effect in this instance. He does see some value in the concept of middle knowledge, however, as a means of defending both divine sovereignty and human free will.[192] But this involves some element of risk on God's part because it implies God does not know exactly who/how many will be saved. Regarding appeals to divine, sovereign power, Walls concludes both Calvinists and universalists share similar problems, based on their mutual premise that God can save precisely who he wants. Whereas Calvinists believe God can choose for himself who to save and who to damn, the universalists deduce a good God will choose to save everyone. Walls questions the Westminster Confession's attempt at a compatibilism, where humans can choose freely because God, who effectually calls the elect, then enables that choice. Walls argues such freedom does not amount to the libertarian freedom, which the Westminster Confession seeks for its compatibilism, because the freedom it defines is the freedom God makes us willing to choose. Whereas the Westminster Confession resolves the mystery of its compatibilism by reference to the primacy of divine power and glory, this seems to collapse justice into sovereign power. However, universalism fares no better, by Walls' analysis. Hick's conviction that a sovereign God would choose to save all because evil cannot coexist with a fully good omnipotent being, runs into conflict with the concept of free will, given Hick's assumption of the free will defense in regard to the problem of evil.[193] Logical to Hick's thinking is merely the hope/possibility that God will save all, but this cannot be guaranteed if there is self-determination.

Walls equates God's goodness with his love, and so insists God's moral goodness is displayed in showing love and mercy to all creation and his wanting all people to be saved. In justifying how a good God can send some to hell, Walls explores further thinking on middle knowledge, thus, "God creates some persons in circumstances in which he knows

---

192. Middle knowledge, or Molinism (after Luis de Molina, a sixteenth-century Jesuit who developed his own alternative view to the Calvinism of his Dominican counterparts). Molina's own description of middle knowledge is that "by which, in virtue of the most profound and inscrutable comprehension of each faculty of free choice, [God] saw in His own essence what each such faculty would do with its innate freedom were it to be placed in this or in that, indeed, in infinitely many orders of things—even though it would really be able, if it so willed, to do the opposite".(quoted in Walls, *Hell*, 37).

193. See Hick, *Evil and the God of Love*.

they will choose evil and be damned."[194] But he finds it immoral that some people will be damned when circumstances are out of their control—most notably the swathes of humanity who will never have access to holiness. Walls posits, therefore, that God grants an optimal measure of grace to every person, that is, the amount that is necessary for each person to make a free choice for salvation or damnation. Such measures may differ from person to person according to their circumstances. What is more, choice may occur even at point of decease or postmortem.[195] On this concept of optimal grace, Walls concludes, "if God does everything he can to save all persons, short of destroying anyone's freedom, it may be that God can, consistent with perfect goodness, create some persons knowing they will never act in accordance with grace."[196] Such persons come to hell by a decisive act of rejecting optimal grace.

Walls responds to difficulties with compatibilism and libertarianism. In regard to compatibilism, he explores a Kierkegaardian concept of the development of self. True selfhood is measured in relation to God: "It is consciously to live in relation to God so that one becomes the sort of self, or person, that God desires."[197] But there can be a consistently increasing rejection of such a relationship, so that one becomes inured to evil and deliberately avoids the temptation to view evil as evil. Thus, by both moral weakness, and by strong determination to pursue evil, one can come to prefer hell to heaven. This concept of a distorted pleasure in evil accounts for Wall's response to the challenge of Thomas Talbott's question as to what possible motive, psychologically, a human being can have for choosing hell. By raging, the damned can convince themselves

194. Walls, *Hell*, 85.

195. Walls argues that optimal grace can only work justly if it carries over into a postmortem existence, so that those who during their earthly life missed out, can be guaranteed their fair share of optimal grace postmortem. Only thus can it be assured that God does everything possible to save all persons (Walls, *Hell*, 92).

196. Walls, *Hell*, 93. Walls' concept of "optimal grace" configures with the Wesleyan/Arminian doctrine of "prevenient grace," though he does not use that term. This, in turn, corresponds with my doctrine of common grace, with the important exception that for me common grace is non-salvific. In Wesleyan/Arminian terms the difference was one only of degree—prevenient grace could lead into salvific grace. In the Reformed view it could not without special grace. Adams rejects the concept of "sufficient" grace being universally distributed, in view of some people seeming to be so disadvantaged by no fault of their own. Of particular significance are "premature" deaths, where disasters cut off the lives of children and youths disadvantaged by the sins of others. See Adams, "Problem of Hell."

197. Walls, *Hell*, 119.

they are right to resist grace. This, of course, amounts to deception, but it is self-deception of a resolute kind.[198]

On the sufferings of hell, Walls, again, insists these are real but not penal impositions by God. They are the outcomes of living a sinful life, since there can be no happiness apart from God. Because we are psychosomatic beings, however, these sufferings are also physical, corresponding to the resurrection bodies those who come to hell will possess.

CHARLES SEYMOUR—Charles Seymour defines a generic doctrine of hell as, "The belief that it is logically and epistemically possible that some persons will experience an everlasting existence, each of whose moments is on the whole bad."[199] In his own defense of the doctrine of hell against the "argument from justice," Seymour claims that Augustine, Aquinas, and Edwards, who each worked within a primacy of justice approach, were susceptible to this "argument." He also argues that the "separationist" model (of Kvanvig, Walls, Lewis, and Swinborne) "is too humane to be considered a serious alternative," in view of the evident fact from life that humans can enjoy times of freedom from pain while still rejecting God.[200] Seymour presents his own version of a doctrine of hell that centers upon human freedom, yet retains the traditional concept of hell as a place of punishment. Where hell is deemed as reserved for those sins

198. Therefore, not that kind of deception that, on Talbott's reckoning, a good God would remove. In fact, this concept of Walls' has pastoral relevance to major incidents response that his reference to C. S. Lewis' "Big Ghost," in *Great Divorce* reminds us of. Lewis portrays the "Big Ghost" as reacting to the apparent injustice of finding a former murderer in heaven. Victims of major incidents who have suffered greatly can feel great anger toward God concerning the apparent injustice of their injured/bereaved state, and so they turn their anger toward Christianity, convinced they are right to judge God in the pejorative way they do. By Walls' account such people are "vulnerable" to the kind of self-deception that can lead them toward a settled disposition where they prefer hell to heaven—because the God they hate is where the latter is.

199. Seymour, "Hell, Justice." It is important not to confuse the "argument from justice" with arguments for the primacy of justice. The "argument from justice" consists in: all human sin is serious; it is unjust to punish sins disproportionately to their seriousness; to punish finite sins infinitely is disproportionate; to punish disproportionately is unjust; hell is infinite punishment; it is unjust to punish human sin with hell; God does nothing unjust; therefore God does not punish human sin with hell.

200. Seymour, "Hell, Justice," 76. Van Holten (who dismisses Seymour's model on the basis that it implies evil will never actually be defeated) responds by arguing this appeal to human experience is overridden by the "foremost" metaphysical claim that maintains ultimate happiness consists in being in right relationships with God ("Hell" 54, n. 62).

that have been committed in this life only, then hell's punishment is a suffering that one enters into passively. For Seymour this is the weakness of the traditional view and exposes it to the argument from justice criticism. The problem is solved, in Seymour's account, by recognizing the damned have freedom to carry on sinning in hell, thus "what is essential is that the continued punishment of the damned is proportional to their continued sin; no one in hell is merely a victim."[201] The consequent punishments in hell are both from God and from each other. The social organization of hell, therefore, would require divine management to ensure the amount of punishment experienced was apportioned according to the sins committed. Important to Seymour's defense is his view that those in hell continue to sin everlastingly, which is what justifies their being there, and being punished, forever.

T. R. BIRKS AND HENRI BLOCHER[202]—T. R. Birks became the main exponent of a so-called "fourth view" regarding hell, called Reconciliationism.[203] Interest in Reconciliationism was almost entirely confined

201. Seymour, "Hell, Justice," 78. Seymour mentions that Marilyn McCord Adams came to acknowledge this possibility (see Adams, "Problem of Hell"). Carson also believes it is possible that the inhabitants of hell continue sinning: they "continue in all that is vile, indeed in the very consummation of what is vile" (Carson, *How Long?*, 102). See also David Kingdon's belief (in Grudem, *Systematic Theology*, 1151). Both Carson and Kingdon appeal to the words of Rev 22:11, "He who is unjust, let him be unjust still . . ." However, this begs the question, where is the ultimate victory over evil, if it is allowed to be perpetuated everlastingly? Do isolation/exile represent justice? Holland argues it could, since the NT language used of hell finds its contextual meaning in the OT concept of corporate Judah's "exile." He states, "The wrath of God is being revealed 'against all godlessness and wickedness of men'. Our sin will find us out, and its consequence is not temporal separation from God but eternal exile. This is the OT model. In the Garden, Adam preferred the voice of the serpent to the voice of God, and was consequently exiled. Israel, a nation created for God to be his people, rejected his rightful claims and was eventually exiled also. While the language of hell in the Gospels is vivid and awful, we must not lose sight of the fact that this language was used in the OT to speak of God's judgement on faithless Israel. Expressions about the soul being cast into a lake of fire (Isa. 66:24) and the sinner being 'cut off' must be kept in the OT framework of judgement (Ps. 37:9). The imagery is not literal but powerfully symbolises separation from God in exile" (Holland, *Commentary*, n.p.).

202. I acknowledge indebtedness to Andy Saville for his contribution in this section, from his "Reconciliationism."

203. Birks, *Victory of Divine Goodness*. Also his reply to two critical responses: *Victory of Divine Goodness: Reply to Strictures in Two Recent Works*. Also, Blocher, "Everlasting Punishment." It is important that "reconciliation" by this view does not refer to a salvific reconciliation. It carries the sense of "reconcile" as used in Col 1:20, "And by Him to reconcile all things to Himself, by Him, whether things on earth or

to the period 1850–1915, with the exception being that of the contemporary evangelical scholar, Henri Blocher, who has since argued for a view not dissimilar to Birks.[204] Both authors seek a defense of the traditional view, but seek to respond to the annihilationist's chief criticisms: that the traditional doctrine is unjust and leaves hell flourishing with perpetual sin. The main points of Birks' view, as summarized by Saville, are: judgment brings about a solemn contrast of doom, between everlasting reward and punishment; everlasting punishment is everlastingly under the penal sentence of God, in contrast to annihilation; this punishment must be complete, so that Satan, the fallen angels, and the damned are brought to submit to Christ's judgment in passive subjection and utter humiliation under the mighty hand of God, so they do not continue to defy God by persistent sin and evil; divine goodness and some kind of mercy, as well as justice, are shown to the damned; and, such will lead the damned to glorify God as their maker and judge amid the fires of penal judgment.[205] Blocher's view is essentially the same, with two exceptions. He does not share Birks' view that Christ's atonement delivers everyone from condemnation of the curse of the law but leaves the lost to the condemnation of the gospel. Nor, in Blocher's view, does the atonement grant some degrees of mercy for the lost, so they can admire and even enjoy the glory of God in their punishment. For Blocher, God suppresses all rebellion only through inflicting retributive punishment; God's mercy and love are reserved only for the saved in heaven. Reconciliationism is an issuant model, assuming the primacy of divine goodness and sovereignty. It also responds to the question of how divine goodness and love can equate with justice in such a way that ensures that equation is fully resolved. Thus, for Birks and Blocher, the atoning victory of Christ over sin, death, and Satan is total, and facilitated by the goodness of God so that all sin and rebellion cease by the damned accepting their punishment, submitting to the lordship of the risen and exalted Christ and glorifying God's justice out of the domain of their shameful everlasting punishment in hell. Hell is empty of evil, and justice triumphs by divine goodness.

---

things in heaven." That is, there is a reconciling of God's justice with his love in Christ in the eternal punishment of the lost, as well as in the salvation of believers.

204. Yet, Blocher gives no acknowledgement of Birks' view.

205. Saville, "Reconciliationism."

DISCUSSION—With the exception of Birks and Blocher's view, the above contemporary models of the doctrine of hell are all largely philosophical theological theories. Whatever their strengths or weaknesses, they do, at least, establish a philosophical case for a doctrine of hell being a morally legitimate facet of the gospel that Christian responders employ in their pastoral care. However, from my Evangelical perspective the following questions interrogate the key assumptions of the alternative models outlined above:

> Is there a primacy that should be given to love?

> Can hell, as retributive, also be consistent with divine love?

> Is the doctrine of hell a part of the problem of evil?

> Is there a primacy that should be given to divine love?

For each of the above models, love is synonymous with moral goodness.[206] But divine moral goodness envelops a number of attributes—e.g., righteousness, love, mercy, grace, justice. Yet, these must be understood as integrated, not segregated, forms of goodness, as essential moral contributions to God's unity. Grudem makes the point that, in practice, this means we ought not to single out one attribute as more important than the others. Everything God does is consistent with all his attributes.[207] I maintain any doctrine of hell must be constructed on this principle of the unity of God's goodness, of which love is one aspect of goodness. Segregating the divine attributes always risks losing their holistic intent. A way of understanding the place of love within the goodness of God may be to distinguish "primacy" from "priority." As a noun, "primacy" can mean

206. Walls, *Hell*, 83–84. Walls takes the argument for this synonymy from John Wesley.

207. Grudem reminds us that the attributes of God are not external add-ons to his real ontology, rather they describe the unified being of God holistically; so he is "*entirely* loving, *entirely* merciful, *entirely* just, and so forth" (author's emphasis). Each attribute qualifies the others (Grudem, *Systematic Theology*, 180). Berkhof locates justice within the righteousness of God, which he equates with holiness (*Systematic Theology*, 74–76). Holmes also, appealing to Aquinas' insistence on the simplicity of God, suggests, "the game of playing off one attribute of God against another is no longer a possibility; rather we must find a way of taking every perfection of God seriously in everything we say" ("Justice of Hell," 402). This challenges the contemporary alternative models with their emphasis upon the love of God, and the conservative model, which emphasizes the justice of God. Thus, I concur with Blocher: "As people under the Word, we believe that justice and love are one in God, the same fire of holy passion" ("Everlasting Punishment," 298).

"state of the highest perfection," or "best part." In adjectival form it can mean "chief, most important."[208] In theological terminology, God's perfections are classified under his goodness. Therefore, a primacy of divine goodness is more appropriate than of love.[209] However, I maintain there is a case for a priority of love within God's goodness, in terms of it being his moral motivational priority, provided we understand it is divine love, not a human, experiential, kind. It is God's love—known only in Christ—that is prior. Hauerwas' passionate avoidance of pastoral care resorting to sentimental illusions of love, therefore, is salient. Jackson applauds Hauerwas' suspicion over the primacy of love in the sense that Hauerwas was alert to the fact that "love," understood and appropriated in human terms can be as tyrannical as "justice." Yet, Jackson also argues Hauerwas' fear of the priority of love over justice is based on an unnecessary view of love that is sentimental and sham. Hauerwas prefers an emphasis upon truth, in the sense that the gospels proffer a truthful story that enables a suffering person to confront the truth about their own situation and address it. A primacy of love, for Hauerwas, risks an escapism from facing up to the reality of one's suffering and, thereby, being disillusioned by hoping in some illusory sentimental vision of love. As Thompson explains, for Hauerwas, "the Christian story enables a narrative embrace of the tragic without premature closure, for while the story indicates its hopeful end, it also accepts that while on the journey pilgrims can get hurt. Christian love is specific in its commitment to stay with the particular sufferer."[210]

By the Edwardsian view, God's primacy is his own glory.[211] While this fits the Calvinistic Westminster Shorter Catechism well, it is open to question as to how we glorify God most.[212] Much depends upon what is meant by God desiring his own glory. Kvanvig criticizes this notion

208. "Prime," in *Oxford Illustrated Dictionary*.

209. This would not be appropriate for the Kvanvig, Walls, and Seymour models because of their rejection of any retributive aspect to punishment in hell. For them, therefore, love holds ontological priority. Hell is never about God inflicting punishment by his justice. Jackson however, recognizes that, in his *agapic* love model, love is not a monism (*Priority of Love*, 20).

210. Jackson, *Priority of Love*, 16–20. Also, Hauerwas, "Love's Not All You Need," 227; Thompson, *Ecclesiology*, 130.

211. Edwards concludes, "that a truly virtuous mind, being as it were under the sovereign dominion of *love to God*, above all things, seeks the *glory of God*, and makes *this* his supreme, governing, and ultimate end" ("Dissertation," 127, author's emphasis).

212. Question 1, "What is the chief end of man? Man's chief end is to glorify God and to enjoy Him forever." *Westminster Shorter Catechism*.

as potentially self-centered and egocentric, tantamount to divine narcissism.[213] However, it need not be if, as I have argued, we regard the Trinity as ontologically self-sacrificial.[214] Divine ontological condescension thus revolutionizes our concept of aseity and omnipotence.[215] Edward's concept of divine glory arguably, equates to God's virtuous love/benevolent being.[216] This is God's loveliness/beauty, which, in turn, consists of all God's perfections, inclusive of his righteousness. However, for Edwards, God's loveliness means, primarily, he is loveable; there is everything about God that should attract our love, because he is love.[217] This loveable beauty also accounts for the perfect justice of God in infinitely punishing sin in the unbeliever, because sin is a slight of the infinite loveliness of God.[218] By this measure, original sin condemns all humankind to being guilty of infinite sin, worthy of everlasting punishment, because it is the most heinous of sins precisely because it is the slight of God's love-liness—his priority.[219] Yet, given this priority upon love, it is difficult to reconcile

213. Kvanvig, *Problem of Hell*, 115. Edwards responded to this kind of criticism in his day by arguing: 1. It supposes an inconsiderate view of selfishness. 2. God's self-interest is consistent with his interest in the universal whole of creation. 3. God's interest in his own glory disposes him to seek the best interest of the creation ("Dissertation concerning the End for Which God Created the World," in Hickman, ed., *Works of Jonathan Edwards*, vol. 1, 103).

214. See my exploration of *perichoresis* above, chapter 8, p. 199–202. Holmes judges that the later Edwards' position stated all God's needs found perfect fulfilment in the internal life of the Trinity, a concept, Holmes concludes finds "little place in the recent philosophical theological literature" (such as that of Kvanvig, Walls, and Seymour) (Holmes, "Justice of Hell," 401).

215. Jackson, *Priority of Love*, 76 and 81 respectively

216. Edwards, "Dissertation," 122–24.

217. Edwards would agree, therefore, that all of God's perfections/goodness are inseparable from his love. Justice—as pure justice—is an aspect of divine love therefore.

218. I have also previously argued that evil represents a continuous "outrageous insult" to God's beauty. See chapter 5, pp. 107–8, 118.

219. To those who object to the *infinite* nature of the punishment arising from "unavoidable" original sin toward God, Edwards argues that if original sin renders sins blameless, then why do we blame people for sins against *us*, which we all invariably do? In so doing we show how we all actually do believe that "there is no necessity in men's acts that is inconsistent with blame." He also argues since neither allowing every particular person to stand for themselves, nor allowing Adam to act as federal representative for all humanity, is injurious to humanity then allowing the latter cannot be more injurious or unjust (Edwards, "The Justice of God in the Damnation of Sinners," In Hickman, ed., *Works of Jonathan Edwards*, vol. 2, 669–70). Seymour argues Edwards was wrong to ascribe infinitude to human sins, on the basis that beauty and love cannot be infinite qualities such as omniscience and omnipotence can be. For humans to

that with Edwards' inclusion of God being glorified in the salvation and damnation of sinners. These represent two equal yet opposite directions.

Birks and Blocher's view takes into account the glory of God in the damnation of sinners by arguing the atonement brings ultimate victory over all evil so that even the damned in hell cease to commit evil. In everlasting remorse and shame they acknowledge and admire God's glory in his just sentencing of them to their punishment, in view of the overtures of divine love they have rejected. For Blocher, at least, remorse in hell does not equal repentance nor even equate with remorse in this life. Birks' view drew the criticism that if the damned could repent of their sin then they would no longer be in hell. Blocher insists that final remorse differs from earthly remorse in that such will only be able to relate to the past not to a future that repentance always must open to. Birks argued that the damned actually receive of God's mercy in the sense that God's judgment at least delivers them from ceaselessly sinning.[220]

Scripture places a priority upon the command to love God and our neighbor.[221] Everything else of a moral nature springs from this primary divine *telos*. This is most developed in the Johannine ontological statements asserting who God is: "God is light"—affirming his moral, transparent being, inclusive of his justice and love, and, "God is love"—also inclusive of his justice.[222] In an integrated form, these contribute to God's moral goodness. Thus, we are commanded to love God and to love one another, because God has first loved us.[223] Our very existence as creatures and as objects of God's grace is due to God's love.[224] Interestingly, Jesus' high priestly prayer opens with an appeal to the Father to glorify his name by glorifying the Son, because the Son glorified the Father while

---

have infinite traits does not mean their sins are infinite (*Hell, Justice*, 74–76). However, given my exploration of evil, along the lines of Barth and Hart, then it is conceivable to regard human sin as justifying everlasting punishment. The punishment fits the crime of the origin of evil lying within ourselves, and with our status in Adam, as one of rejection of the love-liness of God. See chapter 5.

220. Saville, "Reconciliationism," 46.

221. Deut 6:5; Luke 10:27.

222. 1 John 1:5; 4:8. Zizioulas argues that love is constitutive of God's substance; that is, "it is that which makes God what He is, the one God. Thus love ceases to be a qualifying—i.e., secondary property of being and becomes the *supreme ontological predicate*" (*Being as Communion*, 46).

223. 1 John 3:23; 4:10–11.

224. In this I concur with Kvanvig, that divine love is at the origin of creation and redemption.

upon earth. The Son thus asks the Father to glorify them both together with the glory they shared before the world was.[225] But in what did that primordial glory consist? I suggest, in the mutuality of divine love, primordially within the Trinitarian communion, and, incarnationally, in that Trinitarian perichoretic love for believers and their desire for believers to share in that same love.[226] And, in what did love consist during Jesus' earthly ministry? In the fact that, "God did not send his Son into the world to condemn the world, but that the world through Him might be saved."[227] God is thus most glorified in his love—in his loving, his being loved, and in Christians manifesting God's love for one another. It is difficult to think of God having a moral priority different from that which is mandated to be humanity's greatest—namely, love.[228]

Yet, within this priority of love there is a justice aspect, which the gospel emphasis upon the cross exhibits within a penal substitutionary framework as essential to divine goodness. The Johannine and Pauline texts provide the theology for such. The Apostle John affirms: "In this is love, not that we loved God, but that he loved us and sent his Son *to be* the propitiation for our sins."[229] If "propitiation" is the correct contextual theological concept then this integrates the justice of God into the equation of love.[230] For God to love us as sinners, he also acts justly in regard to his own moral goodness, his being "light." It is on account of this aspect of his goodness that God also has "wrath," a distinguished punitive response to sin, without which his love would not be whole and his moral

225. John 17:1–5.

226. John 17:22–26.

227. I acknowledge my debt to Holmes for this point, though it fits with my own observation on the famously, related, text, John 3:16. See Holmes, "Justice of Hell," 402. Yet, in both instances the stress upon divine love is accompanied by the concepts of perishing and condemnation as a consequence of the rejection of love. God has promised eternal judgment/"perishing" to those who do not believe upon the Son. Given that the promise is made out of God's love for the world and desire to save the world/whoever believes, he cannot do other than keep that promise. To do otherwise would represent caprice or a lie.

228. 1 Cor 13:13. The fact that we are mandated to also be righteous (1 John 3:7) and holy (1 Pet 1:15–16) again indicates love is not a monism and requires holistic integration.

229. 1 John 4:10.

230. On the use of ἱλαστηριον in this context, see Leon Morris, *Apostolic Preaching*, chapters 5 and 6.

goodness would be compromised.[231] The Pauline focus on divine love is no less integrated. In Rom 3:19–26 the Apostle Paul is concluding an argument developed from Rom 1:16, namely his passion for declaring the gospel of Christ.[232] A key facet of that passion is the way the gospel of Jesus Christ addresses the goodness, or "righteousness of God" (v. 19), which, only on account of human sin, inclines God to impartial wrath (v. 1:18—2:11). The apostolic argument proceeds: confirming the righteousness of God against sin condemns both Jew and Gentile equally, so that "every mouth may be stopped, and the entire world may become guilty before God" (Rom 3:19). Thus, punishment is deserved.[233] The gospel of Christ is the resolution to the "problem" the righteousness of God poses, both for God and for sinful humans (Rom 3:21–26).[234] It is the resolution to those who have faith in Christ because the propitiatory work of Christ was a "demonstration" of righteousness that justifies both God and the believer (vv. 25–26). On this argument one might feel justified in concluding justice is the priority of God's goodness, but that would ignore the crucial primary question of what it is in God that moves him to make a response to that which his justice condemns—when judicially he could simply enact his pure justice? The answer is, his love. Since the Scriptures never indicate God having a second thought over this, I conclude the priority of divine love in the primacy of divine goodness is theologically legitimate.[235]

231. John 3:36. The Johannine theology in 1 John is overwhelmingly focused upon love integrated with justice. By the Johannine criteria, Christian love, in response to God's love, is fundamental to an authentic profession of faith in Christ. See 1 John 2:5, 10; 3:1, 10, 14, 23; 4:7–12, 16; 5:3.

232. "For I am not ashamed," is a rhetorical device for expressing the Apostle's pride, or sense of honor, in preaching the gospel. See also Morris, *Apostolic Preaching*, chapters 5 and 6.

233. Edwards stresses this point in his "The Justice of God in the Damnation of Sinners," in Hickman, ed., *Works of Jonathan Edwards*, 669: "To say that one *deserves* such a punishment, and yet to say that he does not *justly* deserve it, is a contradiction; and if he justly deserves it, then it may be justly *inflicted*" (author's emphasis).

234. That the gospel of Christ is seen by the apostle Paul as a resolution of the *righteousness* of God is conclusive from the use of the δικος cognates eleven times in Rom 3:1–26. That it is seen by Paul as also the solution to God's "problem" is the only way to understand why Paul affirms, in v. 26, that "He [God] might be just and the justifier . . ."

235. The divine covenantal moral dilemma faced by Yahweh, in relation to the sin of Israel (Hos 11:8–9) is an example of a second thought, maybe—but not really. One might argue that the book of Jonah establishes this point, where Jonah's sense

Can hell, as justice, also be consistent with divine love? The issue of penal justice is the major stumbling block in the traditional doctrine of hell for many. Kanvig, Walls, and Seymour, each make their attempt to resolve this by assumptions of libertarian freedom, the primacy of divine love, but at the expense of penal emphases. For my research, love must be consistent theologically, with God's penal justice, for the *sola scriptura* principle reveals that both are aspects of the primacy of God's goodness.

Can the Reformed doctrine of Christ's descent into hell shed any light on its reality and purpose? For Calvin the doctrine of Christ's descent into hell was obvious from Scripture, and to ignore it would omit much of the benefit of Christ's death. He rejected the Thomist notion of the descent being an announcement of redemption as already accomplished for the OT imprisoned patriarchs. The descent was necessary in order for Christ's redemption to become complete. For Calvin, in addition to Christ's death there had to be his experience of appeasing the wrath of God by experiencing the forsakenness of the Father and everlasting death.[236] For Holmes, this *descensus* represents "the full display of both the *poena sensus* and the *poena damni*, which the saints are depicted in the Revelation as gazing upon."[237] In viewing the slain Lamb of God, the saints have the greatest vision of the glory of God in hell, a vision of love. More recently Hans Urs von Balthasar has propounded a version of the Reformed view, contra the traditional Catholic doctrine.[238] For Balthasar, more than the shed blood of Christ is needed for redemption. There is also need for the second death in hell, where Christ surrenders his deity to a completely passive humanity, experiencing God's wrath on sin. By Trinitarian perichoresis the Son completely defers to the Father's wrathful abandonment. In this way the Christ configures sin so it is absorbed into the Trinitarian life of love. Balthasar's skew on the Calvinistic doctrine is that he conceives of Christ continuing to suffer alongside the

---

of morally superior justice comes into direct conflict with the overwhelming love of Yahweh—and has to concede (Jonah 4:2).

236. Calvin, *Institutes*, 2.16.8–12. Calvin acknowledged the *descensus* doctrine was only introduced to the creeds "after a time," and gradually. Nevertheless, Calvin insists it represented "common belief of all the godly." He believed the doctrine contained nothing but what was derived from "the pure word of God."

237. Holmes, "Justice of Hell," 401.

238. I acknowledge my debt to Pitstick for information on Balthasar's view. See, *Light in Darkness: Hans Urs von Balthasar and the Catholic Doctrine of Christ's Descent into Hell.* Pitstick believes Balthasar has placed his theology outside of Catholicism by his view. Also, Gardiner, "Balthasar."

damned in hell, offering them a second chance, in the hope of an ulti-mately empty hell.[239] The *descensus* view is not without problems. The biblical narratives strongly suggest that the atoning work was "finished" on Calvary.[240] Subsequent NT data imply the same, with the cross being central and final to actual atonement. But the *descensus*, being seen as an integral part of the atoning work, symbolized by the cross, cannot be rejected decisively, in my view, with the caveat that it must not endorse a second chance of salvation.[241]

Barth's retributive and remedial configuration of hell, necessary to make the gospel intelligible, configures with the seriousness of the cross of Christ—inclusive of his descent into hell. Barth argues everyone must face judgment, but there will be those who have not responded by faith to their election in Christ. These may incur the full wrath of God leading to possible annihilation. When refigured by Barth, this leads to a "reverend agnosticism" concerning an empty hell, similar to Balthasar's hope.

Birks argued that God displays his love and mercy toward the damned by delivering them from everlastingly sinning. The atonement delivers everyone from the first death—the curse of the law—and thereby allows the damned to share in the federal element of salvation. This per-mits the damned to glorify God, and thus gain some pleasure, from their recognition of the divine justice in their own punishment.[242] Blocher, on the other hand, would have more reserve about God showing mercy as such, but can concur with Fernando's claim that "judgment is essentially

---

239. It must be said that Balthasar was not a universalist, but this provision of a postmortem opportunity for repentance was his way of justifying the existence of hell by a good God and in view of human freedom. For him, it was the only way God could risk human freedom and yet guarantee the full opportunity for avoiding hell.

240. See John 19:30.

241. For Christ could not have publicly uttered, "It is finished," posthumously from the grave. See 1 Cor 1:17; Col 2:14. Acts 2:27 (Ps 16:8–11) indicates Christ descended only into *Hades*—the realm of the dead, not into *Gehenna*—hell, and that his deliver-ance from that realm was an aspect of his pre-resurrection triumph over death and *Gehenna*. Calvin, however, rejected this general understanding of the use of *hades*, as the realm of the dead, and argued strongly in favor of the *descensus*.

242. This "first death," refers to the wilful rebellion by humans against God, and their rejection of his love and glory. But for the atonement, this death would mean hell became eternally one of self-induced sinful misery and violence. For this to be eternally what hell is, would, in Birks' view, be ultimate defeat for God's goodness. Thus, hell is not now locked on the inside (à la C. S. Lewis, Kvanvig, Seymour). It is firmly and resolutely under the control of God and glorifies him.

a benevolent act," in that hell does not diminish the love God shows to believers.[243]

Volf argues a more essential morally direct conjunction between divine love and justice: "God will judge, not because God gives people what they deserve, but because some people refuse to receive what no one deserves; if evildoers experience God's terror, it will not be because they have done evil, but because they have resisted to the end the powerful lure of the open arms of the crucified Messiah."[244] This willful rejection of divine love is the evil God cannot forgive. That is, they have resisted the divine overtures of love, now heightened in the gospel of Christ, and, thus committed the greatest slight against God (Matt 21:33–44). The Lamb then becomes the "Faithful and True" who rides the white horse to judge in righteousness those who persecute the church.[245] Volf insists, "we must either reject the Rider's violence or find ways to make sense of it; we cannot deny it."[246] The requirement of the loving Lamb to execute justice is essential because nothing else is potent enough to change those bent upon remaining as beasts and false prophets, which, left to their violence, would impugn the divine love for his people.[247] Thus, "a nonindignant God would be an accomplice in injustice, deception, and violence."[248] Such a God would also be hard to reconcile with the intuitive phenomenon of human moral outrage toward evil acts within major incidents. Kvanvig, Walls, and Seymour all fail to do justice to this, in their resistance to the penal concept of hell. It is interesting that Volf's immersion in the injustices of the Balkans war gives him a different perspective.[249] God's wrath is the obverse of his love, responding to those who choose to remain implacably "caught in the self-generating

---

243. Ajith Fernando, *Crucial Questions About Hell*, quoted in Blocher, "Everlasting Punishment," 293.

244. Volf, *Exclusion and Embrace*, 298.

245. Which is to persecute God. Rev 19:11–21.

246. Volf, *Exclusion and Embrace*, 296. For Volf, the violence of the divine word is no less lethal than the violence of the literal sword.

247. Rev 6:10–11 reveals God keeps to his own calendar, even at the risk of giving the impression to the suffering saints that he will *never* bring justice to bear upon the plight they suffered on earth.

248. Volf, *Exclusion and Embrace*, 297.

249. Galen Strawson's hypothetical alternative to the Oklahoma bombing of the Alfred P. Murrah building, on April 19, 1995, by Timothy McVeigh makes intriguing reading. See "'The Buck Stops—Where?"

mechanism of evil."[250] Love could not be sustained as true love when God relates to those who freely, persistently choose to reject his loveliness. In situations of implacable violence it requires violence to stop the violence, in the interests of love. But that quality of violence belongs only to God, no one else.[251] This is why it is false to argue against the punishments of hell by utilizing the argument of nonviolence necessary within human restorative processes. Humans are not God, and their perspective upon human relations cannot be that of God. It cannot be penal; but God's can, and is, or love will cease to be moral.[252]

Is the doctrine of hell a part of the problem of evil or of the solution? While the traditional view would see the doctrine as a revelation of the solution, many others today imply it as intrinsic to the problem, including Marilyn Adams, Birks and Blocher, and Eric Stoddart.[253] Aspects of the traditional model are seen to be acutely problematic philosophically and morally, such as predestination and original sin.[254]

250. Volf, *Exclusion and Embrace*, 298.

251. Ibid., 303.

252. The exception being the divine mandate lying upon the state: Rom 13:4; 1 Pet 2:13–14. Volf's response to those who prefer concepts of hell, in the interests of the primacy of love, to the exclusion of the canonical linguistic narratives, is profound (*Exclusion and Embrace*, 304). The contemporary trend of judging God's attributes of love and justice by the criteria of largely, Western, suburban, phenomenalist, considerations is suspect, theologically. Contemporary modern or postmodern moral criteria are themselves being too commonly critiqued to assume they can be more superior, or healthier, than those at work in the canonical narratives.

253. See also Hick, *Death and Eternal Life*, 201, for his belief that the traditional view gives the evils of sin and suffering "an eternal lodgement within God's creation." For Hick the doctrine of hell is the major part to the problem of evil.

254. In this discussion I have chosen not to include the Calvinistic doctrine of election/predestination. The rationale for this choice is as follows: 1. Regarding Calvin's views on predestination and reprobation, there are very serious moral and ethical *sequelae*, an attempt at resolution of which would exceed my word count for this dissertation. The more thought I give to this Calvinistic doctrine of reprobation, the more uncomfortable I am with it when viewed from the praxis of major incident response. By it, among those who perished will be those non-elect who have been predestined to hell by eternal decree. 2. There are differences of perspective even within the Calvinist constituency, some of whom would attempt a get-out from the aporia above, by claiming Calvin did not teach predestination to hell. 3. The issues have been debated for centuries by finer intellects than mine and without resolution. 4. The issues are philosophically, theologically, and ethically complex, and lie outside of my research parameters for major incident response.

MARILYN ADAMS—Philosophically, on account of her metaphysical concept of God's transcendence and sovereignty, Adams maintains such a God would ensure no one comes to hell. For her, the traditional doctrine "is a paradigm horror, one which offers not merely prima facie, but conclusive reason to believe that the life of the damned cannot be a great good to them on the whole."[255] Because, for Adams, divine transcendence is so ontologically incommensurable with human beings, who deal only in commensurables, offered a genuinely free choice, such beings would never choose to enter hell. The moral standards set by the traditional view are unfair because humans develop only over time, by trial and error, and by developing strategies that are often inadequate but entrenched within them.[256] Humans evolve into adulthood with impaired freedom. Therefore, it would be cruelly unjust for God to expect humans with such naturally impaired freedom to be entrusted with deciding their eternal destiny.[257] However, Adams' philosophical reflection does not have a canonical fit. It accords neither with scriptural theology nor with an alternative, non-evolutionary, biblical anthropology.[258] Theodramatically, the Scripture narratives indicate that God, at creation, gave the first human beings an explicit responsibility for the most serious of decisions—life or death—and this is compatible with them being made in the divine image.[259] The tragedy is: those offered a genuinely free choice did choose a

255. Adams, "Problem of Hell," 304.

256. Adams' argument, however, needs to be understood against the primacy of her belief in the ontological gap between God and humans being incommensurable, so God is divinely antinomian. Yet she trusts implicitly in God's love for humans transcending any concept of divine obligation. In fact, in arguing thus, she "undermines the very pastoral confidence in the Creator that she wants to bolster" (Jackson, *Priority of Love*, 74).

257. Walls argues against this. He insists it is just of God to require humans to make such decisions on the basis that God has distributed optimal grace to all (*Hell*, 136–37). The OT states that God covenanted this responsibility to Adam and Eve (Gen 2:16–17), as they were created in God's image, thus closing the ontological gap far more than Adams assumes.

258. Adams' evolutionary presuppositions are also problematic for her view of evil/sin and her argument from justice, that human finite sin is disproportionate to the severity of a divine infinite punishment. Her view of sin seems to recognize sin resting in moral actions. This runs contrary to my view that sin rests with our status in Adam, and that being a rejection of God's covenantal love, it is now all the more vested in the gift of Christ, the Son. In this sense I think there is, at least, a theological argument for the infinite value of the nature of sin, worthy of an everlasting punishment, of degrees.

259. Gen 2:16–17; 1:27. I understand "life" to mean life in salvific relation to God.

course for "death." By the canonical linguistic narrative the consequences of this choice have been devastating for the whole creation, and for the human race in particular, given its union with Adam in "original sin."[260]

Birks and Blocher—Birks and Blocher also consider that the traditional view risks being a part of the problem of evil because it espouses a dualism that leaves hell eternally populated by the damned continually sinning against each other and God. Evil then remains eternally unresolved and, though exiled in hell, triumphant.[261] Neither annihilation nor universalism help, because the former means God destroys creatures made in his image, making destruction triumph over the *apokatastasis*, and the latter leaves outrageous evil unaccounted for. Thus, they insist, for the problem of evil to be fully resolved, it is important for evil to be conquered forever, so there can be no carry over of evil from this life into eternity, where only the divine glory of God's total goodness and loveliness, can exist. Thus, evil is not left with any "oxygen" of an ontological infamy.[262] This, resolution, they argue, has been achieved by the salvific cross and resurrection of Christ, and by the damned bowing their knee to the exalted Lord in an everlasting act of non-salvific *apokatastasis* and worship.[263] The punishment of the damned is, primarily, one of profound,

260. I am appealing here to the canonical linguistic narrative in both OT and NT (Gen 3:14–24; Rom 8:20–21). See my exploration of original sin in the context of evil in chapter 5, pages 112–15. Helm argues that so fundamental is the doctrine of original sin to the theodrama that themes of atonement and Christ as last Adam are unintelligible without it (Helm, *Faith and Understanding*, 153). Adams' evolutionist presuppositions make such a perspective impossible for her, of course.

261. This would be the case with all the traditional concepts, including the alternatives of Kvanvig, Walls, and Seymour. Strangely, Strong argues evil continuing in hell is a necessary aspect of God's benevolence, in that as evil is necessary to displaying human freedom and holiness in this life, so it will be for all eternity (*Systematic Theology*). In terms of the development of doctrine through the canon, Holland and Lorek's concept of exile leaves the problem of unresolved evil hanging. Adam's alienation and Israel's exile were never the end of the drama; Israel's exile was also restoratively motivated, as a discipline, though Adam's alienation was clearly retributive, but open to reversal via the Second Adam.

262. See chapter 5, p. 102.

263. Thus fulfilling Phil 2:10 and Col 1:20. Helm gives indication of his agreement with at least aspects of this view on hell. In the light of Phil 2:11, Helm concludes the damned will recognize the essential justice of their punishment, Christ's Lordship. Hell is, therefore, a place of pain not resistance. It "is not a demonic colony which has gained unilateral independence from God. Because there is full recognition of God's justice [I would add also, God's love is fully recognized even if in existential isolation

languishing regret at the "day" of salvation squandered, the divine love rejected, and the everlasting bliss forfeited—an experience wholly consistent with a body/soul created for the enjoyment of God's covenantal love.[264]

ORIGINAL SIN—Original sin and moral responsibility also create real moral dilemmas for modernity and the doctrine of hell: how can one be held eternally accountable for acts that spring from a nature that has, at its very core, a predisposition to sin, before ever any such acts are conceived or performed?[265] McFadyen's critical examination of the Augustinian/traditional doctrine of original sin exposes the weakness of modernity's assumption of human, personal autonomy. By testing against the extremities of trauma and violation, McFadyen argues personal moral choices are also consequences of different biological and social factors already in existence, which are themselves the products of a universal sinfulness originating in a federal solidarity with Adam in his original sin.[266] Without these concepts of evil, a realistic anthropological

from it], God's character is vindicated, and hence glorified, even by those who in this life have defied him and who suffer for it" (Helm, *Last Things*, 116–7).

264. It is in this sense that the tenebrous symbolic language of hell's torments is to be understood. See, for example, Matt 8:12, "cast into outer darkness" and "weeping and gnashing of teeth." Mark 9:43–44, "the flame that shall not be quenched"; "Their worm does not die."

265. McFadyen describes the assumption of modernity as: "For moral judgments are ultimately made, and can only be made, through the tracking of responsibility in the sense of will-contingent causation. That causation is personal, in the sense that it requires the additional supposition of freedom of will, such that the cause has free agency in relation to the effect. That is to say, one could have acted . . . otherwise in a way which would change the situation. Situations may only be judged moral if there are people who have brought them about or sustain them in being through their action or inaction where there is a possibility of doing otherwise" (*Bound to Sin*, 20, n. 7). Neuroscience also poses real challenges to the concept of will contingent autonomy, as Galen Strawson and Alan Torrance have argued. See Torrance, "Developments in Neuroscience."

266. McFadyen tested the doctrine of original sin with the traumatic evils of sexual abuse and the Holocaust, thus: "the personal power to make choices may be subject to a more powerful field of force which sequesters, colonises, and captures it" (*Bound to Sin*, 128). McFadyen is aware of the debate between science and morality over the interpretation of the Genesis account of Adam and Eve (*Bound to Sin*, 22–25). John Murray insists (contra C. H. Dodd's conclusion that the literalness of an Adam may not even have been in the apostle Paul's mind) that the whole theological argument of the Pauline argument would be wrecked if the datum is interfered with (*Epistle to the Romans*, 181). If Murray is right then it would seem difficult to believe the doctrine

understanding of such extremities is morally impossible. Original sin is, therefore, an essential for the diagnosis of evil on account of which hell is part of the solution. It is, therefore, strange that McFadyen has nothing to say regarding eternal judgment in his work on original sin.

Given that original sin is a valid aspect of anthropology and Christian ethics, what is its contribution to a doctrine of hell? Its fundamental contribution is that of the solidarity of the human race as a key focus in Christian theology.[267] We are all the problem of evil together. We are all guilty, and we are never truly free until freed from guilt and its consequences.[268] Apprehensions of individuality and autonomy must be conceived within the fundamental of solidarity, "in Adam." Freedom is only to be found within the loving relationship with God first offered to Adam and Eve, which was roundly rejected.[269] It is within the realm of

---

of original sin while holding to an evolutionary concept of human origins and development, given that evolution means progression from inferior to superior. Reinhold Niebuhr, however, made a great focus upon original sin, and yet believed the fall narrative to be a myth; since it "points to a true dimension or aspect of all our lives, not to an actual historical event" (Langdon B. Gilkey's introduction to Niebuhr, *Moral Man and Immoral Society*, xix–xx).

267. Rom 5:12 expounds this solidarity. But enormous dispute surrounds how it is interpreted. For the extensive reasonings for their interpretation of this phrase, see Hodge, *Commentary*, 148–55; Murray, *Epistle to the Romans*, 182–87. Holland interprets it in terms of a corporate solidarity "in Adam" and "in Christ," extending the theme of alienation, and captivity to satan, commenced, (theodramatically) back in the OT with Adam. (Holland, *Commentary*, chapter 5; Holland, *Contours*, chapter 5).

268. The concomitant of original sin being a fundamental bondage of the will, inclusive of our vulnerability to external influences—biological and social. Pure autonomy is an illusion of Pelagianism and modernity. For Pelagius it was important for the will to be autonomous and independent from any influencing sources. This made the will generic and impersonal however. Thus, Pelagianism saves the will but loses the person (McFadyen, *Bound to Sin*, 178). As a non-reductive physicalist, Nancey Murphy argues the most we can hope for is "*some measure* of autonomy from biological drives and social forces. But not a *great* deal" (*Bodies and Souls*, 108–9, emphasis author's). However, if we take serious account of the fall and original sin, then natural biological and environmental factors act upon us in fallen and dysfunctional ways, making concepts of total freedom even more suspect. I agree with Murphy, therefore, that the most we can hope for is a *certain level* of freedom, within the limited understanding of autonomy that we, as fallen creatures, can ever possess. Failure to accept this could lead us into delusions of autonomy (and grandeur) that are blasphemous.

269. Gen 2–3. Zizioulas argues that human freedom in the ontological/libertarian sense is impossible, given humanity's createdness. This ties humans to the necessity of their existence. He argues our only hope of becoming an authentically free person comes from the fact that God the Father, as person, wills communion with the Son and the Spirit. He assumes the monarchy of the Father, who begets the Son and the Spirit,

such solidarity that we are also held accountable for our personal choices.[270] We thus stand condemned "in Adam," but also because we choose to reject the free offer of divine love (salvific grace) that can deliver us from the curse of the original sin.[271] Just as the first sin resulted in death, persistence in the rejection of God's love can only result in the "second death."[272] Thus, I concur with McFadyen: only by taking into account the Augustinian doctrine of original sin are the pathologies of human life "given symbolic and explanatory power in relation to reality," including those of major incidents.[273] However, the doctrine also confirms the moral momentum of a doctrine of hell as an aspect of God's goodness— his loving justice.[274] By the canonical linguistic approach, the weight of human responsibility is consistent with the necessary moral endowment from divine love. The consequences are also proportional to the rejection of that love by human beings who have received optimal grace.[275] Given the "darkening" effect of evil, and the capacity for hardening the heart,

and it is through our regenerative person that we come to be authentically free persons through union with Christ.

270. These choices are critical, "for whoever shall keep the whole law, and yet stumble in one point, he is guilty of all" (Jas 2:10, also compare the apostle Paul's quote of Deut 27:26 in Gal 3:10, "Cursed is everyone who does not continue in all things which are written in the book of the law, to do them"). This is referring to legal guilt (that is: deserving the judgment of guilty as against not-guilty/acquittal) before God, in terms of a holistic concept of divine law. However, this is not stating that we are all equally guilty *to the same degree* for our own individual sins. There is scriptural warrant for believing there are degrees of sin/evil. For a helpful discussion on legal and relational sin, see Grudem, *Systematic Theology*, 501–4.

271. Hence the reference to Christ as a second Adam in Rom 5:12–21, where the first Adam's "offense" is counteracted by the second Adam's "righteousness."

272. Rev 20:11–15. This affirms that both death and Hades will be consigned to hell, along with Satan, the beast and the false prophet, and anyone not found written in the Book of Life. In this manner the curse is resolved justly and lovingly in the context of the Christian community.

273. McFadyen, *Bound to Sin*, 12.

274. McFadyen concludes, "universal solidarity is not something contingent in that sense on the empirical realisation of sin by all people; similarly, accountability for sin is not contingent on our free causation and moral culpability." The enjoyment of solidarity comes before freedom (*Bound to Sin*, 247–48). On God's justice being loving, see Rom 2:4–5, where divine wrath is incurred only following the extensive goodness of God in his forbearance and longsuffering, intended to lead to repentance, being rejected with hardness and impenitence of heart.

275. See Rom 1:18–20, where wrath is apportioned for those who have suppressed truth received since the creation, revealing God's attributes of eternal power and deity and also law (Rom 2:14).

a reaction against God can act as earplugs to the alarms of hell and as a blindfold to the attractiveness of Christ.[276]

ERIC STODDART—Stoddart also implies hell is a part of the problem of evil. His concern is aimed particularly at that part of the evangelical pastoral community that on the one hand claims to believe in eternal torment in hell and expounds on the doctrine in public preaching ministry, but on the other hand, applies considerable avoidance measures, and amelioration of the doctrine, in individual pastoral contexts.[277] Stoddart's concern is, the Evangelical doctrine of eschatological exclusion generates such unbearable emotional pain pastorally to clients, but also to practitioners, who then have to employ a variety of mitigation strategies to make their practice bearable. Thus, speaking of hell to the bereaved requires a cauterizing of the emotions that renders the practitioner immune to the hurt imposed upon the bereaved by his or her words and withdrawal from conveying the horror of the end their belief holds for the unbelievers before them. Stoddart explains: "I try not to make value judgments over the attitudes of fellow-pastors but am disturbed with the way an evangelical position on biblical authority can insulate us from hearing, and reflecting upon, the pain of those who hear our preaching on hell . . . When I hear about people who have lost a loved-one their community considers is likely to be heading to hell I think . . . their pain would be unbearable unless they can find some strategy for coping with it."[278] Stoddart believes this Evangelical stance lacks moral integrity (since it is not true to the actual belief in hell) and is unethical (since the actual belief, if conveyed, would cause unbearable hurt to the dying and

276. Matt 13:14–15, 17; John 3:19–20. Evil creates a hatred of "light" (God in Jesus Christ) and, therefore, of God's love.

277. Stoddart, "Hell"; Stoddart and Pryce, "Observed Aversion." See also Stoddart's more recent article, "Bespoke Theology?" Stoddart's research was conducted using a postal questionnaire survey of 750 randomly selected Scottish clergy during the autumn of 1998. Of the 346 useable returns, 50 percent believed in eternal separation from God; 20 percent believed the fate of such was the experience of physical torment in hell. See also Purcell, "Spiritual Terrorism." Both Stoddart and Purcell aim their complaints most against conservative Evangelicals who take more literal, and lurid, interpretations of the traditional doctrine of hell.

278. Stoddart, "Hell," 97. It is important to stress that Stoddart's research addresses the ethical problem he sees facing those conservative Evangelicals who believe in *everlasting torment* in hell. He rightly acknowledges there are those, recognized as evangelical, who believe in conditional immortality, or annihilation, and for whom the ethical dilemmas do not pertain.

bereaved). He rejects the applied theology approach, therefore, with its practice of starting with a given understanding of biblical propositions and imposing that grid onto the situations of the dying and bereaved.[279] For him, this method absolves pastoral responsibility by the imposition of a systematic theology of eschatological exclusion and stifles creative pastoral response, since it is locked into the method of "because the Bible says so." His preferred method is that of reflexive-*praxis*, where historical, social, situational, psychological, and communal contexts are allowed to interrogate the biblical text and inform the interpretation.[280] Hermeneutically, he concludes that hell is a verb, rather than a noun or adjective, for a definitive postmortem state.[281] Stoddart reacts against the evangelical predilection for the language of destination—"Where am I going?"

Adams and Stoddart both draw attention to the phenomenology of everlasting punishment as integral to hell being part of the problem of evil. While neither views these as conclusive aspects of their argument against eternal punishment, they are right to argue they are an aspect needing to be taken into account.[282] In view of Stoddart's primary concern being the emotional effect the doctrine can have upon the dying and bereaved (the fear, terror, hurt, and also the anger, it generates), in view of their extreme vulnerability, and nothing should be conveyed that risks exacerbating the state of the dying, I discuss his concerns in more detail. Since evangelical theology, if it is to be practiced with integrity, must take serious cognizance of the doctrine of hell and its tenebrous outcomes then the risks of such ill effects are probable. My discussion, therefore, gives particular focus to the case brought by Stoddart, and how alternative models of the doctrine can respond to it and still retain moral and ethical integrity, before concluding whether the doctrine is a part of the problem or of the solution to hell.

---

279. For a comparative perspective on the lack of integrity from evangelical practice, in the realm of American evangelical pressure for state religious education, see Marty, "Hell Disappeared," 381–98.

280. Stoddart's praxis-reflection methodology is a postliberal conflation of George Lindbeck's cultural linguistic theological model and Thomas Groome's shared praxis model.

281. This has similarities to Douglas Hall's integrative suffering, though Stoddart makes no reference to Hall. See above, chapter 5, pages 115–16.

282. Adams (but Stoddart and Purcell in particular) identifies the emotional impact of doctrinal models as significant in ways that the more philosophical explorations do not. For example, Swinburne and Craig dismiss the feelings aspect.

The Doctrine of Hell in Caring for the Dying and Bereaved—
A Response to Eric Stoddart

My concern here is to reflect upon those challenges to the doctrine of hell that have focused specifically upon pastoral care of the dying and the bereaved, believing that pastoral inclinations to warn people of exclusionary and tenebrous concepts represent a pathology from which pastors require curing (as well as their pastoral "victims"). These gain what may seem disproportionate attention, in the context of this dissertation, justified by the fact that they represent challenges to conservative Evangelical praxis in view of the negative effects the doctrine of hell can have upon the dying and bereaved. Such challenges also pose a real threat to evangelical pastoral carers becoming accredited for major incident response.

I reflect upon Stoddart's concerns from the perspectives of two different models: a medico-therapeutic, and a missiological, model.

MEDICO-THERAPEUTIC PERSPECTIVE—It is right and fair that the issues of exclusionary eschatology should be aired from a medico-therapeutic perspective because it does raise a real pastoral dilemma, largely because such concepts are alien to contemporary public discourse. In my view, this is one reason why the public is so disturbed when Christians raise them today.[283] A Western, Enlightenment medico-therapeutic outlook does not readily entertain concepts of ultimate accountability to God, and even less of eternal hell. These are alien concepts relative to the comforts of modern standards of living and the heightened expectations from medical palliatives for abolishing pain and suffering. Furthermore, when the vicissitudes of life are eventuated by a major incident the victims may protest they are already in "hell" and cannot stomach any additional tenebrosity. However, such psycho-social effects of the doctrine should not determine if the theology itself is valid. A public's susceptibility to the effects has already been preconditioned by an Enlightenment social and philosophical habituation that is alien to biblical teaching. Rather than encouraging a view of human *hubris* and an ability to fix life without pain, the biblical perspective is far more realistic in its anticipation of suffering.[284] Furthermore, Stoddart seems to overlook the biblical perspective

---

283. Of course it is not only Christian responders who may be inclined to raise issues of exclusionary judgment and punishment. Islamic responders may use them even more tenebrously.

284. See Gen 3:14–19; Rom 8:18–25; Matt 24:6–8. I am not reflecting any particular eschatological millennial view in my interpretation. From certain distinct millennial

of death itself being an event of divine judgment.[285] Theodramatically, human mortality, coupled with its dread, is the strongest empirical evidence of foreboding available.[286] Hence, Acolatse concludes, "There is also a recognizable and often unspoken aspect of death which often hinders the dying process from being the peaceable phenomenon it could be and throws it into a tortuous, agonizing experience: that is, justice."[287] The biblical emphasis is not upon redemption through physical health and freedom from suffering; for these, to varying degrees, are inevitable empirical precursors to dying; rather, it is upon finding holistic spiritual maturity in being able to live with suffering and triumph over the fears.[288] This represents good health as much as any injury-free or disease-free condition does. The task of life is to safely navigate a redemptive course that will take escaping from the corruption of sin and the wrath of God as seriously as trying to avoid incurring injury or falling sick.[289] Being made

---

perspectives, some eras of history would be more prone to disasters and violence than others. I am merely suggesting the biblical reflection, in nonspecific terms, presages disaster and suffering and is, therefore, also realistic. If practical theology is concerned to address the realities of life as a starting point for theological reflection then it ought to allow the biblical perspective of realism more validity than is common. In the end, however, Stoddart allows the pastoral contexts to take *full* control of the biblical text.

285. See Gen 2:17; 3:19; Rom 5:12; 1 Cor 15:21 as contributions to the doctrine that choreographs the theodrama. In subsequent conversation with me, Stoddart said he believes death is an evolutionary contingency. Stoddart's thesis suffers greatly, in my view, from confining itself to a practical theology methodology. He cannot engage with the dynamic challenges both biblical and systematic theologies pose. This demonstrates the weakness of pastoral reflection by the use of any single theological discipline.

286. Heb 2:15, "through fear of death." See Esther E. Acolatse, "Embracing and Resisting Death: A Theology of Justice and Hope for Care at End-of-Life" in Swinton and Payne, eds., *Living Well*, 257–58. It is for want of recognizing this that Kübler-Ross' model is deficient. It is important that pastoral carers do not sell out entirely to such models. Thus, the pastoral model can become non-distinguishable from any other model of care. Instead, our focus requires a deeper and more thorough theological foundation if it is to be authentically Christian. See Beuken, "Palliative Care," 40.

287. Esther E. Acolatse, "Embracing and Resisting Death: A Theology of Justice and Hope for Care at End-of-Life" in Swinton and Payne, eds., *Living Well*, 257–58.

288. This is part of what the Scriptures mean by the "testing" of faith. Anderson's reflections upon spiritual fitness are valid at this point, and in particular, his comment, on page 107 (*Spiritual Caregiving*, 105–12).

289. See Matt 10:28. This falls in the context of Jesus' instructions to the twelve in preparation for their ministry. The inevitability of suffering through persecution is spelled out (10:16–18, 21–23). So, too, is the dualistic anthropology of humans as embodied souls (v. 28) essential to a biblical eschatology that responds to terminal

aware of the ultimate consequences of failure to navigate safely is a part of the ethical process of ensuring safe travel. Thus, to destroy the divine warnings that assist safe navigation in the interests of not hurting an, albeit already hurting, public is neither ethical nor loving. To permit the effects to become the determining factor, therefore, is to allow sociology to trump theology. Effects I argue, are situational and highly subjective, and thereby unsafe, and for that reason, dubious to prioritize ethically. Stoddart's assumption that human sensitivity possesses the right to be shielded, reflects an Enlightenment influence, conflated with a postmodern secular medico-therapeutic reflection upon trauma, suffering, and dying, which gives priority to the problem of suffering and physical pain over death.[290]

Nevertheless, the fact that the doctrine of hell is by now so utterly alien a concept in the public square does have some significance for the manner in which theology is practiced. In Marty's words, there is now the "cultural unavailability of Hell"; there is no cultural matrix providing a framework for understanding.[291] For the concept to be understood it requires substantial introduction of the public to the theology of God, humans, and sin, in the overall light of divine goodness. In short, for the doctrine of hell to be pastorally meaningful requires a biblical worldview now almost extinct in the public square. There is little value in introducing someone to the concept of hell itself prior to such theological understanding by which it becomes at least morally accessible. Therefore, there is certainly an ethical issue where pastoral practice is motivated by little more than the discharging of duty (rhetorically termed "faithfulness") to pass on some concept of hell gleaned from systematic theology, but desensitized to effect. Due responsibility for the extinction of the biblical worldview must lie with the Christian community's failure in effective, long-term, holistic missiology. Mouw states the problem as, "our failure to speak about divine judgment is closely related to our refusal to face the reality of human evil. Even more important: it may have something to do

---

suffering. See my discussion in chapter 6, p. 139–50. For a discussion of Matt 10:28 in the context of a biblical anthropology, see Cooper, *Body, Soul*, 117–9.

290. For an alternative postliberal stance that would be very critical of Stoddart's sensitivities, see Hauerwas, *Naming the Silences*.

291. Marty's empirical observations were of the U.S. context, but they have even more relevance in the more secular UK context ("Hell Disappeared," 394).

with how much we actually feel the reality of human evil."[292] That failure also possibly has significant missiological consequences.

MISSIOLOGICAL PERSPECTIVE—I propose an alternative perspective to the medico-therapeutic model is worthy of exploration, and more suited to the theodrama. This is the missiological perspective. I do not explore this in isolation from the previous stance however, but seek to incorporate the emotional and ethical dilemmas that this perspective highlights.[293] This exploration is consistent with the canonical linguistic methodology I have adopted, one that incorporates systematic, biblical, and practical theological approaches.

By "missiological," I mean a handling of eschatological exclusion theology in routine pastoral care as an important aspect of gospel mission to the world. Eschatological exclusion is thus viewed as a necessary backdrop to the gospel of redemption. It is a part of what salvation, effected by Christ's life, death, and resurrection, is from. I have argued that a doctrine of hell is consistent with the primacy of divine goodness and the priority of love. Thus viewed, hell represents a significant reality (whether understood as place or experience, or both) in the divine cosmology. From a canonical perspective, the balance between emphases upon eschatological exclusion and salvation warrants serious attention—in particular, the surprising fact that most exclusionary emphases are found in Jesus' exhorting and encouraging of his disciples. In his reflection on the place of hell in Jesus' preaching, Eryl Davies concludes Jesus used the teaching on hell extremely sensitively, in keeping with his audience's condition and attitude. There was no indiscriminate preaching of hell, and the most tenebrous emphases fell upon those who exhibited most hardness of heart.[294] Jesus handled this theological balance impeccably.

---

292. Mouw, *Uncommon Decency*, 136. Klingbeil and Klingbeil argue for the Christian church recovering a prophetic voice in the public square where judgment and salvation need to be key factors ("Prophetic Voice"). They conclude, "In view of the magnitude and projected impact these messages [of judgment] have, what can be more relevant in the public square?" (182).

293. I am indebted to Professor John Swinton, University of Aberdeen, for drawing my attention to this distinction of perspectives, in email conversation with him.

294. Davies, "'An Angry God,'" 91. This emphasis would also concur with the views of Kvanvig, Walls, Seymour, as well as with those of Volf and myself. Warnings of hell seem most appropriate, theologically compatible, and ethical, when reserved for those who give indication of persistent hardness of heart toward the love of God in Christ Jesus.

The key to our missiological approach is mirroring that balance as best we can.[295]

Assuming a theology of eternal hell, there are excruciatingly difficult emotional and ethical dilemmas facing pastoral carers who operate with it in the context of major incident response, whether the particular theology regards hell as involving everlasting punishment or as annihilation.[296] Belief in hell, as everlasting punishment theoretically, does not mean that sharing this doctrine pastorally with unbelievers will be demonstrably more hell-explicit than it would be for those holding to a more inclusivist belief.[297] Stoddart and Pryce's research supported their hypothesis, that,

> the sensitivities surrounding the discussion of hell provide a strong motivation for the individual pastoral carer to seek (consciously or unconsciously) a doctrinal "loophole" in his/her beliefs on hell that will allow them to avoid raising the subject in pastoral contexts.[298]

In fact, the darker one's belief in hell the stronger this motivation can become. Their study shows that doctrinal conviction on the matter of eternal punishment, or the literality of hell, does not necessarily mean that the alarming threat of the doctrine will be shared to a proportional degree. Though some may feel that the conservative Evangelical view amounts to a theoretical doctrine that defies our human capacity to communicate, and thus a serious pathology to counter, I explore a real

---

295. This is not to suggest agreement with Rahner's view that the tenebrous threatening of the doctrine are only for antemortem life, intended to function in accordance with its literary character only as "threat discourse, not as a preview of an actual existence in the future" (Rahner, *Encyclopedia of Theology*, 603–4).

296. I am assuming here that the doctrine of annihilation is a consequence of scriptural evidence and exegesis, not an ameliorative to eternal punishment. Both hell and annihilation views carry profound eternal severity in their consequences for the unbeliever, which have formed a context for the need of the cross and resurrection. For a philosophical theological argument for the view that annihilationism represents a more tenebrous doctrine of hell than everlasting punishment, see Kvanvig, *Problem of Hell*, chapter 2; also, Hunsinger, *Disruptive Grace*, 234–42.

297. By "inclusivist" I mean a view that is more inclined to include unbelievers into salvation, and heaven, than to exclude them to hell.

298. Stoddart and Pryce, "Observed Aversion," 129–53. This study is significant empirical research because no previous studies have explored eschatological beliefs and their relationship to pastoral practice of clergy.

alternative that lies in the attitudes and practices of pastoral communication as much as with the doctrine itself.[299]

For Christians who are convinced inclusivists, the dilemmas are much less ethically problematic, and their focus will be more on assisting the living and dying processes than on postmortem consequences. For universalists there is no ethical dilemma whatsoever, apart from addressing the harm caused by what they may view as spiritual abuse by those who espouse a tenebrous view of hell. Thus, it is for Evangelicals, principally, that the doctrine of hell and its use can be a theological and practical dilemma. In contemporary death and bereavement care, the subject is regarded as a pathology warranting treatment rather than an important dimension to postmortem outcomes.[300] This has not been helped by the fact that virtually all Evangelical study of the subject has been within systematic, and not in practical, theology. This divorce between theology and praxis encourages an applied theology approach, which I am not convinced is commonly operated ethically or helpfully. I therefore explore, with a practical theology utilizing a canonical linguistic approach,

---

299. This is not to presume that there are no problematic aspects to the doctrine itself. Purcell's concern about the works of Gerstner and Dowsett have some validity in my view. Boyd C. Purcell identifies some in his, "Spiritual Terrorism." See also Dowsett, *God, That's Not Fair!*; Gerstner, *Repent or Perish*. Purcell reflects from within the US hospice care field, where he is a professionally accredited chaplain. While one respects those, like Purcell, who, every day, have to attend to the dying and bereaved, I take serious issue with his insistence that for sufferers to be able to entrust themselves to God, God must be portrayed (by pastoral carers) as wholly loving and accepting. He also caricatures evangelical theology as obsessed (to addictive levels) with tenebrous messages of hellfire. This again is both unfair and untrue to evangelical theology. In my view any focus upon taking the largely symbolic language of the Scriptures on hell, which conveys literal effects, is to be resisted. See how Kreider defends Jonathan Edwards' "Sinners in the Hands of an Angry God" sermon against the common tactic of caricature, in Kreider, "Sinners in the Hands of a Gracious God."

300. See Purcell, "Spiritual Terrorism." Recognizing his research needs to address the reality of conservative Evangelical theology remaining for the foreseeable future, Stoddart makes certain proposals, with a view to slowly challenging and influencing practitioners away from such tenebrous views and practices. He proposes that training in bereavement counseling, within the conservative Evangelical community, should incorporate detailed consideration of eschatological identity and its implications for eschatological exclusion. This would raise awareness of critical issues and facilitate healthy informed choice about operating with such beliefs. Stoddart concludes that it is so obvious that those operating from a conservative Evangelical theology of hell will not gain acceptance into current hospital or hospice chaplaincy, that he need make no recommendations ("Hell," 303).

the ethical and practical suitability of employing the doctrine of hell in pastoral response to major incidents.[301]

Missiological Communicative Praxis—I address two key missiological aspects for pastoral carers in a major incident:

- Communicating judgmental theology ethically to the dying
- Communicating judgmental theology ethically to the bereaved

Communicating Judgmental Theology to the Dying—Communicating judgmental theology to the dying is practically difficult and ethically complex. In major incidents, Christian responders may be faced with total strangers who have only hours or minutes to live and who are often impaired and vulnerable due to their injury and trauma.[302] By the applied-theology method it could be argued that the duty of imparting truth about hell overrides all other responsibilities, and one focuses upon discharging that duty as sensitively but as firmly and decisively as possible, on the basis that outcomes are God's responsibility not ours. However, Stoddart and Pryce are right to remind us that attitude is significant.[303] Also, credibility and believability are significant for effective mission and are a key ethical responsibility for pastoral carers. A significant aspect of this might be the "stranger" element: the fact that victim and responder are often total strangers to one another, thus heightening the ethical status for introducing such tenebrous communication.[304]

---

301. See Hilborn, "Nature of Hell." This work has a helpful bibliography.

302. Where an incident involves significant human impact on a local community, depending on the degree of public profile the church may have there, pastoral carers may find they know more of the people presenting. However, my point about "total strangers" still stands in the majority of cases, because even in local communities the public's relationship with the contemporary church community is often distant if not nonexistent. This fact highlights the importance of my missiological perspective, which encourages the church in operating a continuous pastoral agenda, through preaching and community engagement that helps the public prepare for trauma and death, risking the unpopularity that may bring in their ministry context.

303. Stoddart and Pryce, "Observed Aversion." Yet Phil 1:15–18 gives indication that God can use even suspect attitudes for good missiological ends.

304. The popular pulpit analogy of a stranger warning the sleeping inhabitants of a house on fire (as per Gerstner, *Repent or Perish*, 27) has grave moral deficiencies when it comes to the realities of interpersonal work in a major incident. Walls' response to the use of this analogy is that it breaks down with the reality of the fact that probably our neighbor has already heard of hell and yet does not think it much of a danger (*Hell*, 23).

However, teaching on hell is not the whole of our duty, only a part, and is only explicable in the context of the gospel of grace.[305] Thus, the over-arching emphasis upon the grace of God—that God is disposed to love us, even though we are non-deserving—is a priority. In the context of having only very limited time to communicate "leaving-of-life" issues, it seems in the best spirit of the gospel to concentrate upon the redemptive purposes of God in Christ and his willingness to accept the repentant believer in an instant.[306] This does not have to exemplify Stoddart's charge of taking advantage of a loophole, though. There are contexts that are suited to bringing out some aspects of theology and not others.[307] This is why pastoral care needs to administer truth sensitively. In the context of addressing traumatized unbelievers, Jesus' focus was primarily upon healing and imparting hope of salvation, though not at the expense of non-repentance. Unless, therefore, there is a specific request for counsel regarding hell, those who have little time left to live should be proffered the gospel in as digestible a form as possible, and in compassionate love, doing all to ensure the maximum physical and psychological comfort of their last moments. To do so need not communicate some kind of univer-salism to the dying, but it gives them a final offer of hope in Christ, before they die, and leaves the practitioner ethically humane.

Preparing people for dying and eternity is the duty, responsibility, and specialty, of the Christian community; there is a duty-of-care, be-fore God and out of love, to those who must die and face eternity, and the general public still have this assumption about pastoral carers, irre-spective of their own beliefs.[308] This duty can be neglected in pastoral

---

305. Helm, *Last Things*, 125–28.

306. Some claim the dying thief scenario (Luke 23:40–41) as a paradigm for the value of a gospel that assures one of instant access to paradise after death. However, this event cannot be taken as a generic paradigm for granting assurance of eternal safety to all the dying. The dying thief was already aware of his just "condemnation" and possessed his own consequential fear of God, and this could be why Jesus did not say a word of warning concerning hell to him, but gave him only the assurance of im-minent paradise (23:43). Nevertheless, the incident does serve to remind us that end of life crises and reconciliation with God is possible and indicative of grace operating in much less salvifically stringent ways than Evangelicals can often lay down.

307. Browning believes timing and practical relating theological-ethical issues are a significant concern for practical theology (Don Browning, "Pastoral Theology in a Pluralistic Age," in Woodward and Pattison, eds., *Blackwell*, 98).

308. Hauerwas draws attention to the belief of Alexander Solzhenitsyn, when he said, "the problem with our society and politics is its sinful presumption that man is born to be happy, when he clearly has to die" (quoted in Hauerwas, *Community*

ministry amidst the busyness of church management and the interests of maintaining popularity, or even one's job, in a culture that is all too often profoundly wary of negative images of God, or disdainful of the "paradise syndrome."[309] Rather than endorsing Stoddart's method that reinterprets teaching on hell to ensure no tenebrous meanings are intended and adapt to a contemporary culture now evacuated of hell concepts as they appear in Scripture, we could consider such an evacuation to be a tragic cultural consequence. The blame for this the Christian church ought to shoulder, for she has long lost the ear and heart of the public in her preaching, and thus lost the opportunity to be heard and to influence the culture in a way that re-sensitizes that culture to eternal postmortem eschatological meanings. It is the duty of Christian pastors to address eternal and "leaving-of-life" issues with congregants throughout their ministries and not to leave such issues until times of crisis. It is the most serious aspect of the Christian preaching and pastoral ministry. Sensitive addressing of eternal and judgment issues can be done in the course of routine pastoral duty in a way that can help people attend to their own duty-of-care regarding their death, but it becomes virtually useless if left until the shock and dying condition leave little energy for such critical end of life considerations.[310]

Communicating Judgmental Theology Ethically to the Bereaved— Communicating judgmental theology ethically to the bereaved can become very significant in a number of contexts:

If the bereaved question the postmortem status of their relative/ friend. This is not an uncommon request made to clergy/chaplains, and

---

of Character, 86). The more truthful task, therefore, is to teach people how to die, as much as how to live. See also Swinton and Payne, eds., *Living Well*. There is no addressing of hell, however, in Swinton and Payne's work, which Swinton puts down to the fact that most practical theologians tend to be liberals who would not find the doctrine salutary (email communication between Swinton and author, December 2009).

309. On the possible negative impacts upon theology and ministry that contemporary emphases upon management and technique can have (at least in the US context), see Wells, *No Place for Truth*.

310. In one sense this ethical dilemma in a major incident has similarities to those facing physicians over disclosure to patients of the terminal nature of an illness. Yet there is general opinion that this responsibility should not be shirked, but timed appropriately. It is a matter of honesty and ethical integrity. If more pastors attended to this responsibility routinely it would permit pastoral responders to major incidents to ask of the dying the natural questions, "Have you prepared for dying?" or "Are you ready to meet God?" more meaningfully.

can be heightened by antemortem trauma the deceased may have experienced because of their young age.[311]

When clergy/chaplains compose liturgies and sermons for funerals and memorial services, which are crafted from biblical data, to respond to anxieties concerning the deceased.

When those recently bereaved by a major incident are in attendance at Sunday services, hearing pastoral or evangelistic preaching.

For the bereaved there may be an understandable desire to be sure that a loved one is at peace and beyond the reach of further suffering. This is complicated by the commonplace assumption within contemporary Western culture that death always brings an end to suffering, whether by a blissful afterlife or by annihilation.[312] Unless there is an underlying awareness of postmortem belief in a heaven and hell, then raising the prospect of judgment and hell can be extremely controversial and offensive to the bereaved. The temptation therefore, to look for a "loophole" for facilitating avoidance of controversy and offense can be strong for pastoral carers. Context should influence wisdom and content. For those who hold to a belief in postmortem judgment and hell, it would be disingenuous to take advantage of any "loophole" in view of a direct or implied request for guidance from the bereaved, since the reality of judgment and hell, being so serious, would make avoidance unethical. Even so, one must be careful not to attempt to second-guess what the biblical data, often couched in symbolic metaphor, actually means in any great detail. What is there is sufficient to alert and warn us of a radical and serious consequence to persistent unbelief.[313] However, it need not represent a "cop out" to exercise due restraint in explicating details. This is only showing responsible care in the handling of biblical data in the pastoral context. The doctrine of hell is not the only doctrine requiring theologians and pastors to exercise some degree of agnosticism over the finer details.[314] Linfield has a point when he suggests, "At issue is not the

311. I can think of occasions in my own pastoral history where a set of parents has asked me concerning the possible postmortem whereabouts of their deceased child.

312. This is expressed publicly in the wording of messages and epitaphs left at local temporary shrines (in memory of murder, road traffic incident, or major incident victims), where those who would not profess any particular religion often express spiritual and religious assumptions regarding the nature of an afterlife or postmortem annihilation. See Eyre, "Remembering."

313. In the light of the biblical language of hell, Kvanvig's advice is prudent (*Problem of Hell*, 155).

314. Similar restraint and agnosticism would be due in explicating the doctrines of

ultimate reality of hell, but the way in which it should be understood."[315] Considerably more research is needed for the communication of a biblical or systematic theological reflection on hell in the light of contemporary cultural changes.

Given due restraint, there are ways of communicating the doctrine of hell generally, and sensitively, without making it the foremost focus of the communication, and without implying that it bears obviously on the deceased, about whom very little may be known by pastoral carers. What is more, all communication of the doctrine of hell should be woven into the gospel of Christ, accompanied with personal trepidation.[316] Indeed the greater emphasis of all Christian communication of solace to the bereaved should be in terms of the grace of God and the hope it holds out for the living bereaved.[317] In the context of public preaching on hell, it may be possible to alert the bereaved to the content of the sermon prior to attendance, so they may make an informed choice whether to exclude themselves for that occasion, and/or to offer to discuss the content privately; or, a pastor may adjust his/her message's weight as he perceives the need of the bereaved congregant. However, Stoddart has problems with the very principle of the evangelical doctrine of hell being expounded in the round of ordinary pulpit ministry at all, on the basis that the metaphors and imagery convey horrific concepts too unbearable for congregants (should they dwell upon them), making some kind of ameliorative inevitable.[318] His protest is not without some value. It is possible for the proclamatory rhetoric of the doctrine to be placed into the congregant's mind without them being given the pastoral support to ensure the sense can be digested appropriately.[319] There is usu-

---

providence, evil, and suffering, as my reflections of the severe limits of theodicy have shown.

315. Linfield, "Sheep and Goats," 63.

316. See Phil 3:18–19, where the apostle Paul, reflecting upon those who were enemies of Christ, speaks of his tears.

317. Even so Swinton and Payne, eds., *Living Well* is an impressive work that recommends refocusing attention on the dead at funerals and not escaping into memorials and celebrations of life.

318. Stoddart's research found that those holding to the more tenebrous views of hell tended to favor extenuating or inclusivist rationales for their own loved ones ("Hell").

319. Evangelicals may respond that it is the work of the Holy Spirit to provide the capacity to cope with the biblical rhetoric and concepts, concomitant upon the pastor's faithful carrying out of the duty to proclaim the truth. Stoddart's reminder of the

ally no opportunity for instant comeback or clarification in the context of public preaching nowadays, and hypersensitized hearts may become privately distraught in the aftermath of hearing the rhetoric, especially if the preacher has attempted to convey the wrath of God from a tenebrous mood. It is difficult to convey something so serious that has not been given prior reflection and where likely psychological impacts, both upon speaker and hearer alike, have not been anticipated.[320] The rhetoric of tenebrous preaching can flow much easier than can the emotional impact upon the hearers—especially those bereaved of unbelieving loved ones— and also upon the preacher in his/her subsequent reflective moments. Stoddart's response to this would be to suggest some kind of therapy for the guilt-ridden that helps them recognize that the source of the problem is the pathological doctrine of hell and its psychologically errant impact upon them as hearers or pastoral carers. One would not wish to rule out the possibility, with certain cases, that some need of pastoral detox or redirection may be required. However, to suggest this is the universal answer is based on the supposition that the doctrine of punishment in hell can only ever be pathologically conceived. Given the doctrine's platform in Scripture and through history, this supposition seems unjustified. That it can inspire high, and disabling, levels of fear in some may be due to predisposed personality tendencies, or negative upbringing permitting high levels of suggestibility to torturous hellfire imagery. Imparting, with tenebrous moodiness,[321] graphic, shocking imagery, with equally

---

ethical responsibility of the pastor in terms of both what and how rhetoric is used and concepts are delivered, is highly important.

320. Howard Davies goes beyond the reality, though, with his rhetorical flourish: "Of all the truths we must first preach this to our own hearts. We need to feel and see the utter tragedy of countless millions who rush blindly to perdition. Never will we preach it unless we first believe it ourselves" ("Judgement," 17). Stoddart is surely right to imply that a full realization of countless millions rushing to hell would be more than our human constitutions could bear.

321. Tenebrous moodiness is not the same as Godly solemnity, though. Marty contrasts the latter, represented in the moral seriousness of Jonathan Edwards, the Mathers, and Solomon Stoddard in their preaching on hell, and that of contemporary American televangelists who lose the message (of judgment in hell) in the medium of their "setting of material success, adaptation to worldly norms, and the glitter of entertainment and smiling camaraderie" ("Hell Disappeared," 395–96). See also Kreider's conclusion concerning the all-too-often caricatured preaching on hell of Jonathan Edwards, that Edwards' actual emphasis was very much upon the grace of God in Christ restraining divine wrath and extending certain hope of escape ("Sinners in the Hands of a Gracious God," 268–75).

horrific meanings, to victims who have been through literally horrific incidents, is both unethical and immoral. We should be cautious about believing a doctrinal concept of hell that actually renders Christians ethically disabled and emotionally dysfunctional when sharing it with those for whom they believe it is principally intended. Stoddart and Pryce's research identifies this as a real moral and ethical dilemma for those who hold to literal views of hell, but not an unassailable one.

CONCLUSION

In conclusion, the pastoral issues concerning reconciliation and justice before God are deeply problematic. I conclude these dilemmas are resolved by giving due place to the status of innocence, to the role of the emotions, and to a practical theodicy. The eschatological problematic should be addressed not by a medico-psychological approach, but more by a sensitive missiological one, where the Christian theodrama is choreographed by the doctrines of Christ's atonement and resurrection and by eschatological hope, which proffer enormous configurative imagination and potential for the aporias enunciated both in my own prefigured narrative and in this chapter.

However, a major practical problem remains in the form of how a Christian responder, enthused by such evangelical doctrines, can work in a multi-agency context of an ecumenical and interfaith nature, ensuring both an evangelical and catholic Christian response is contributed. I explore this in my next chapter.

10

Contribution—
Ecumenical and Interfaith Friendship

O NE ADDITIONAL THEOLOGICAL THEME for my configurative exploration remains. For my Evangelical constituency it represents the
most problematic—namely ecumenical and interfaith relations of friendship. In this chapter, utilizing my canonical linguistic approach, I wish to
explore a practical theological model that has potential for supporting
ecumenical and interfaith friendship. However, because it is so controversial an issue, some words of prefatory explanation are necessary.

PREFATORY COMMENTS

First, it is important to stress that my concern in this chapter is to explore
a model that is configured to major incident, ecumenical/multifaith response friendship, not to soteriological or worshipful practices. Salvation and worship have occupied ecumenical and interfaith dialogues
traditionally, and conservatives of different faiths have frequently ab-
sented themselves from such dialogues. These have also been the issues
around which the various categories of Christian theologies of religions
have been formed, the most common taxonomy being: pluralistic, in-
clusivistic, and exclusivistic (or particularistic).[1] However, my concern
is to explore a Christian model that facilitates social friendship between
key faith stakeholders in emergency response. It is concerned with how

1. Fackre has helpfully challenged this trilogy as inadequate, and has presented
his own, extended range. His pluralist perspectives are: Common Core; Common
Quest; Common Pool; Common Community; Common Range. Fackre's particularist perspectives are also helpful: Anonymous particularity; Revelatory particularity;
Pluralist particularity; Imperial particularity; Narrative particularity. He prefers the
last of these, and expounds his vision accordingly (see, "Claiming Jesus").

responding Christian communities relate to other faith communities more than what they think about their religions.[2]

Second, it is appropriate at this early stage to include a comment about the vocabulary that is currently predominant in the world of interfaith relations. The terms "religious others" or "others" have tended to replace "other religions." Similarly, we now hear of "faith communities" or "faiths."[3] The purpose of these shorthand collective terms is not necessarily due to a postliberal assumption that each faith has only its own tradition's concept of truth to accept as true, nor a modern secular assumption that all traditions can be subsumed under a religious universal. In reality, these terms are for ease of courteous collective reference rather than anything more theological. Such has been the meaning whenever I have employed these terms in this dissertation. Knight would contest the validity of such collective terms, in view of an implied theological consensus between all faiths complying with a secular agenda for a naked public square. I would agree if, and when, such were the actual rationale for the vocabulary. I certainly do not intend it in that sense. Inter Faith Network for the United Kingdom, a network of faith bodies set up in 1987, itself records,

> The terms "faith communities" and "people of faith" are sometimes used . . . as convenient shorthand collective terms to refer to the totality of people who follow or practise particular religious traditions. This can, though, convey the misleading impression that they form, together, some kind of homogenous entity. This would not do adequate justice to the distinctiveness, both in the past and today, of different religions.[4]

Significant intrafaith differences are also acknowledged. Given this usefulness as collective shorthand, I endorse it for my research.

RELEVANCE

Ecumenical and interfaith relationships are absolutely vital for pastoral carers in major incident response for many reasons.

First, they emerge from the theological themes I have explored already in this dissertation. They are both products and victims of a fallen,

2. Netland, *Encountering Religious Pluralism*, 311.

3. The interfaith-based *NYDIS Manual for NYC Religious Leaders*, prefers the term "houses of worship" (Harding, ed., *NYDIS Manual*).

4. Inter Faith Network for the United Kingdom, "Faith, Citizenship."

evil, suffering world. They represent concrete expressions of religion and spirituality in traumatization. They are also manifestations of common grace and are expressive, and deserving, of compassion. They are issues that concern reconciliation and justice.[5]

Second, the UK population now exposed to major incidents is multicultural and pluralist in nature.[6] Having summarized the history of Christianity's dominance in the West since the early church, Bosch concludes that with the collapse of colonialism Christianity lost its hegemony, and, therefore, "today has to compete for allegiance on the open market of religions and ideologies." Geographical separation of the nations has been superseded by diversity in the locale, so that, "In Western countries Christians, Muslims, Hindus, Sikhs, and Buddhists rub shoulders on every street. Serious Christians have also discovered that those 'other' religions are, incongruously, both more different from, and more similar to Christianity than they had thought."[7]

Third, emergency planning is, inevitably, of an ecumenical and interfaith nature. Many of the different faiths and ideologies would find themselves united in a desire for compassionate response.[8] Caring for the spiritual needs of victims of a major incident should be utterly indiscriminate in nature.[9] What is more, casualties are likely to outnumber pastoral carers so that the provision of a pastoral carer of the casualty's specific faith cannot be guaranteed.[10] Secular lead institutions, such as the NHS and Emergency Planning Departments, will tend to assume an ecumenical and interfaith concept in their demand for professionalism,

---

5. Mouw and Griffioen, *Pluralisms and Horizons,* 35.

6. In the 2001 census 76.8 percent of people in the UK identified themselves as having a religious faith, including 46 million Christians, 1.6 million Muslims, 0.56 million Hindus, 0.37 million Sikhs, 0.27 million Jews, 0.15 million Buddhists, and 0.18 million who describe their faith as "other" (UK Office of National Statistics, *Social Trends*).

7. Bosch, *Transforming Mission,* 475.

8. See Lyndon F. Harris, "Radical Hospitality: Houses of Worship Responding to Disaster," in Harding, ed., *NYDIS Manual,* 41.

9. "A tradition of caring for the sick and supporting those who care for them is common to all faiths" (South Yorkshire NHS Workforce Development Confederation, "Caring for the Spirit").

10. Although certain faiths may stipulate that only a pastoral carer of that faith is permitted to attend to the dead/injured under any circumstances. For general advice on attending to the deceased, see the relevant section in Blears and Goggins, "Needs of Faith Communities."

with the accompanying professional generic vocabulary, making the use of traditional, faith-specific language unprofessional and incomprehensible for other agencies.[11]

Fourth, interfaith relations for Evangelicals, on a theological as well as on a pastoral level, often have a reputation for indifference, isolation, or hostility, rather than for enthusiastic toleration, understanding, and friendship. This is due largely, in my view, to a serious lack of a visionary working model for pursuing positive relations between groups who know they have deep and distinct differences. Previous models for ecumenical and interfaith relations encouraged either a "stand off" or a sacrifice of important beliefs. However, more recent theological approaches (such as that of postliberalism) have seriously challenged the modernist notions that there is a foundational reason and an overarching universal that, transcending all religions, judges particular faiths. Today there is a far greater degree of honest realism in regard to the distinctive differences between the faiths. A model is required that can both accommodate such differences and their disagreements and at the same time stimulate understanding, trust, and constructive friendship for the sake of social friendship.[12]

Fifth, there are deeply felt disagreements of an intrafaith nature that could seriously jeopardize intra-Christian community relations in both the planning and response stages of a major incident that could have negative impacts upon an effective response.[13] Conservative Evangelical

11. Prof. John Swinton, in email discussion with me, makes the point that because within the NHS generic language is preferred (because of the particular understanding of professionalism the NHS has), this is influencing chaplaincy's drive toward professional standards and taking the eye off the significance of Scripture and tradition in chaplaincy. Such institutional pressures can weigh heavily in chaplaincy today (email correspondence in September 2008).

12. One group that has done a lot of academic research, and social interfaith engagement, is the Bradford Churches for Diversity and Dialogue (BCDD). See, in particular, the 2008 annual BCDD lecture by Professor Sebastian H. Kim, at Bradford University, entitled "Community Identity: Meaningful Engagement in Contemporary Society." Kim focuses on the significance of community identity in the wake of the 7/7 bombings and its contribution to peacemaking between communities.

13. Some of these disagreements have to do with differing stances, within Christian communities, on interfaith relations. For example, conservative Evangelicals (represented by affiliations such as Affinity; the FIEC, etc.) have objections to joining Churches Together in England and Wales and associating with the World Council of Churches. Other evangelical denominations and groups will not have such major conscientious differences (the Evangelical Alliance of the UK, for instance).

Christians are very sensitive to, and mainly negative toward, ecumenical/interfaith relations, as my own prefigured complicity has evidenced.[14] My configured grace and compassion theologies offer contributive value to a model that could help prevent interdenominational disagreements and theological differences impacting negatively upon interpersonal and social relations between responders. In pluralist cultures, the distinction between religious issues of salvation and worship and issues of social friendship must be recognized.

Sixth, traditional models of ecumenical and interfaith relations have proved inadequate for including the theological and pastoral contributions of Evangelical responders in particular. This is because those models have encouraged, consciously or otherwise, polarization and not convergence, leading to discrimination by all parties. Relations have been dogged either by relativism on the one hand or dogmatic absolutism on the other.

Seventh, one of the most serious threats to civil well-being today comes from violent religious extremism, particularly in the form of militant Islam. There is a body of opinion suggestive of such extremism influencing young British Muslims who are disillusioned by the current low moral state of the West and wars against Islamic enemies.[15] For pastoral carers involved in emergency planning and response, it is critical that some serious connection is made with Islam (even with extremists) through a model that can help give understanding of their grievances, and of the Qur'anic texts and theological interpretations that feed the sense of militancy.[16] Ford et al., seriously consider scriptural reasoning to be a way to challenge a rationale that views the clash between Islam and Judeo-Christianity to be a West versus the rest "clash of civilisations," which must risk violence.[17] Scriptural reasoning believes there is an in-

14. See chapter 4, above, pages 75, 75, 77, 81–82.

15. Principally, the Israeli-Palestinian crisis and the wars in Iraq and Afghanistan.

16. For an example of such a connection with militants see the experience in faith-based diplomacy by Doug Johnston, founder of the International Center for Religion and Diplomacy. In his article on Johnston, Rob Moll concludes, "While remaining committed to Jesus [Johnston is an Evangelical Christian, from Virginia] Johnston says he sees the image of God in all people. With that common ground, Johnston has shown that it is possible to make friends out of enemies" (Moll, "Father of Faith-Based Diplomacy"). For a more UK-based model, see Lewis, "For the Peace of the City."

17. Samuel P. Huntington, the Eaton Professor of the Science of Government and director of the John M. Olin Institute for Strategic Studies at Harvard University, in 1993 hypothesized that the future major conflicts of the world would center around

timate philosophical, cultural, and religious affinity between Islam and the Judeo-Christian West that can be demonstrated in those religions' commitment to scriptures and their study.[18]

These seven reasons signal ecumenical and interfaith relations as integral to contemporary emergency response for the evangelical catholic Christian community.

ROAD MAP

My road map for exploring a specific model for ecumenical and interfaith friendship takes me first of all to some essential definitions. I briefly survey other models that have been attempted (that, in my view, have largely failed). I then construct my own model by exploring a synergistic relationship between the socio-political practice of principled pluralism (PP) and two embryonic practices of ecumenical and interfaith relations: scriptural reasoning (SR) and civic networking (CN). I explore each to examine their individual value in the specific context of major incident response for Christian responders, before evaluating if there are sufficient points of convergence to indicate a probability of them forming a working model for ecumenical/interfaith friendship for major incident response.

DEFINITIONS

Pluralism

Pluralism has been described as the "religious supermarket," an "ism" about a plurality, and, "In this sense a pluralistic account gets set forth when someone is convinced that there is something important to say about a given 'manyness.'"[19] In one sense pluralism is a secular construct. From the point of view of Western modernism there is a view of religions,

---

cultures and civilizations (including their respective fundamentalist religions), not around economics or ideologies (Huntington, "Clash of Civilizations?").

18. Steven Kepnes, "A Handbook for Scriptural Reasoning," in Ford and Pecknold, eds., *Promise of Scriptural Reasoning*, 35. See below for criticism of the effectiveness of the current progress of SR in meeting this aim, p. 350. Lewis and Reid also query if SR has been very effective in the contexts of ordinary people in areas of conflict, p. 350.

19. Peter Berger, quoted in Netland, *Encountering Religious Pluralism*, 124. For three possible meanings of "pluralism" differing between what is and what ought to be, see Davie, "Pluralism, Tolerance, and Democracy," 224–41. Also, Mouw and Griffioen, *Pluralisms and Horizons*, 13.

that they are primarily general systems of beliefs, ideas and practices that can be "held" alongside each other in some overarching frame of reference, for example as instances of a category called "religion", or "religions" within a secular public sphere, thereby enabling them to be treated "equally" (as a "plurality") or encouraging them to engage with each other ("pluralism").[20]

Hauerwas argues that pluralism is a form for promoting a Western democratization that is insidiously Constantinian and a product of Enlightenment liberalism for maintaining Western global political hegemony.[21] Carson helpfully sets out the variety of perspectives on pluralism that may control definition.[22] He speaks of an empirical pluralism. That is, the observation of life as it is, with the reality of diversity resulting from migration for work and education, the concomitant influences of religious proselytism, disillusionment with homegrown religion, intermarriage, etc.[23] To these we might add Netland's reference to globalization and the "homogenization thesis," by which local events are influenced by events many miles away. Globalization has brought empirical interdependence, interconnectivity, and interrelatedness.[24] There is also a cherished pluralism that considers choice and diversity as essentially healthy for human societal existence—even an example of a Trinitarian diversity expressed throughout creation.[25] There is philosophical pluralism, which

20. Hardy, "Promise of Scriptural Reasoning," 186. Netland reminds us that pluralism is to be distinguished from "inclusivism," which is often confused with pluralism. Inclusivism entails the viewing and acceptance of other religions from the base point of one's own particular (*Encountering Religious Pluralism*, 218). Also, Baynes, "Habermas."

21. Hauerwas, "End of Religious Pluralism." For a similar conclusion, see Drane, "Globalization of Spirituality."

22. Carson, *Gagging of God*, 13–54. For a lucid, brief, summary of the history of pluralism, see Netland, *Encountering Religious Pluralism*, chapter 3.

23. For a discussion of the religious conflicts and challenges formed by migration into Britain, France, and the Netherlands, see Davie, "Pluralism, Tolerance, and Democracy." Also Casanova, "Immigration."

24. Netland, *Encountering Religious Pluralism*, 84.

25. Hauerwas supports Yoder's interpretation of the Babel account (Gen 11) as an act of divine endorsement for cultural (and religious) diversity ("The End of Religious Pluralism," 290–91). See the World Evangelical Fellowship Manila Declaration as a nuanced example of cherished pluralism. The declaration celebrates the fact that in many societies religion forms an important part of their identity. It also celebrates "certain aspects of the religions—may be affirmed as part of the richness of God's good creation," and as expressions of human longing for God and meaning. However, it also recognizes that people have sinfully used religions to create intimacy and superiority

is an epistemological stance, believing that interpretations of life are controlled by the broad and narrow cultures of the interpreter. We may conclude both modernist and postmodernist perspectives are "egalitarian and democratized" and hold "the same rough parity" for all religions concerning truth and salvific effectiveness. By this perspective religious pluralism is viewed as, "something inherently good, to be embraced enthusiastically" and forms the official orthodoxy in both academia and emergency planning.[26]

The real dilemma hinges on the philosophical kind, because here pluralism is viewed as the only legitimate way of knowing. It supposes that a normative, directional pluralism is a positive good that offers the only true path for a multifaith society. Modernist proponents identify a common core of divine being, disclosing, and delivering, of which particularist claims may be conceived as different "love-talk," not metaphysics, along the paths to this core reality.[27] Alternatively, particularist claims may be actual valid routes to salvation, each offering some unique aspect to ultimate truth that can be "pooled" to form a generic world faith. Postmodern philosophical pluralists, however, reject the concepts of any universal reality or world faith. For them every particular tradition and culture represents a valid communal contribution to a common quest.[28]

---

for their particular cultures and religious groups. The declaration concludes, "Here also, while always corrupted by sin in practice, we may affirm in principle the goodness of a diversity of some aspects of the religions" (in Netland, *Encountering Religious Pluralism*, 328–9). For the text see *The Unique Christ in our Pluralistic World: WEF Manila Declaration*.

26. Netland, *Encountering Religious Pluralism*, 12, 14.

27. Though the idea of "love-talk" was not John Hick's, he popularized a similar idea with the "Real." He propounded the idea that the key evidence for the existence of the Real was life transformation from self-centerdness to Reality-centerdness, which he considered to be present in roughly equal amounts among all the religions. Hick's model has been challenged on at least two fronts: 1. He is reductionist of religions, reducing them to a form offensive to their adherents. 2. He finds he is able to know more than his totally ineffable Real allows him to know. Thus Mavrodes concludes, "[Hick] postulates something which is neither good nor evil, neither purposive nor non-purposive. And of course Hick's Real is not loving, not powerful, not wise, not compassionate, not gentle, not forgiving. The Real does not know me (or anyone else), does not care about me (or anything else) and so on. The Real did not create the world, did not design the world, does not sustain the world, and will not bring the world to an end. What in the world does the Real have to do with anything which happens in the world?" (George I. Mavrodes, "Response to John Hick," quoted in Netland, *Encountering Religious Pluralism*, 244).

28. Fackre, "Claiming Jesus," 1–17.

Public Sphere

Public sphere is a concept of Jürgen Habermas. Baynes describes it as,

> like the closely related idea of civil society, the broad domain of "private" (non-governmental) associations in which citizens form debate, and revise variously shared interpretations of the world and its "meaning"; some of these interpretations will be shared among all citizens, but many others will be more sectarian in character.[29]

It is sometimes referred to as the "public square," which is a much older concept from ancient Hebrew, Greek, and Roman cultures. However, the public square is more situative, the site where information and discussion is brought into the public sphere.[30]

Dialogue

Dialogue is significant to relations in a pluralistic society. It is also the key form of engagement in PP, SR, and CN. Evangelical Christians are distinctly uncomfortable with the concept of interfaith dialogue.[31] Conservative Evangelicals emphasize proclamation and everyone else needing only to hear, not to dialogue. This presupposes the proclaimer alone possesses the authentic message. Preaching and proclamation are the traditional tools for Evangelical relationships with all non-Christians. That presumption should be open to critical evaluation.[32] The reason that dialogue is relevant lies in the fact that for major incident response, relating to religious others is unavoidable, and relationships are vital for cohesive cooperation and for avoiding additional trauma to that which will inevitably be incurred from responding to the incident itself. For establishing

29. Baynes, "Habermas," 495.

30. On "public square," see Klingbeil and Klingbeil, "Prophetic Voice of Amos," 161–4.

31. Not just Evangelicals though; it is also clear that Hauerwas has real concerns over the concept when he views it as a part of the rhetoric of Western imperialism ("End of Religious Pluralism," 287).

32. Hauerwas endorses Yoder's insistence that the Christian is always a herald—but never in a coercive manner ("End of Religious Pluralism," 289). I am not overlooking the fact that Evangelicals form friendships and parachurch alliances with non-Christians, of a social value. However, there is an overwhelming tendency for conservative Evangelicals to consider their essential duty, even in such relations, is to "proclaim" the gospel by invitations to hear preaching or by sharing their faith in a kerygmatic manner.

good working relationships, dialogue is constructive, preaching is not. Since my aim is to explore a model for interfaith friendship in a contemporary pluralist society for the benefit of major incident response, then this has to do with civil relations not salvific ones. Understanding and toleration, therefore, are equally significant to declaration and conversion in such a context.[33] For this reason, dialogue is essential. But it is also essential out of Christian humility and realism. By this I mean facing the reality that objectivity in understanding and interpretation of truth are achievable only in dialogue with a Christian community (ecumenical) and with communities of others (interfaith). Accepting this, Mouw and Griffioen propose a form of dialogue they call *dialogical theocentrism*. This is based on the Christian understanding of a non-negotiable objectivism, founded in an all-knowing God, for all that is rational, knowing, truth, reality, goodness, and rightness, which is manifest in Jesus Christ. However, non-Christians also share a cognitive longing for such virtues. Dialogical theocentrism, therefore, assumes this objective, transcendent reference point, but insists on the need to dialogue in community—both ecumenically and by interfaith relations. Claiming to possess the truth and proclaiming it is insufficient since, "The truths that we are given by God are provided as equipment to strengthen us on a pilgrimage whose distant destination is full maturity. One extremely important way to use that cognitive equipment properly is to engage in dialogue with others who are on the same journey."[34] Mouw et al., recognize the concern some Christians will have over this expansion to include non-Christian dialogic communities, but they justify such inclusiveness from the scriptural exhortations: to strive to live at peace with all, to honor all human beings.[35] Additionally, there is the Christian community's need to accept

33. I understand that the value of "witness" arising from personal attitudes, behavior, conversation, etc., is important for evangelical Christians. They inwardly hope, and pray, that there will be something from their passive witness that will provoke interest and inquiry from their non-Christian co-workers (1 Pet 2:12; 3:15). See also Swinton, *Raging with Compassion*, 241.

34. Mouw and Griffioen, *Pluralisms and Horizons*, 105. Their use of the expression "the same journey" seems unfortunate, in my view, even though the authors may have in mind simply the fact that both Christians and non-Christians are each on *a* pilgrimage, that is, *separate* pilgrimages. From an Evangelical particularist perspective, the pilgrimage a Christian is on is *not* the same as those of other faiths and none. Perhaps "mutual ambitions for maturity" would be more accurate. However, they may simply be using the expression as generically applicable among all faiths.

35. On the NT significance of intercultural and interpersonal relations, see Rom 12:18; Heb 12:14; 1 Pet 2:1.

rebuke and instruction from those features of common grace found in non-Christian communities when they exceed the Christian community in virtues such as the rational, knowing, truth, reality, goodness, and rightness.[36] Thus, Barnes refers to dialogue as critical generosity, where "Christians are called not just to speak of the God who is revealed in Christ but to listen critically yet with generosity to what is spoken about God by the other."[37] A Christian community under divine judgment may well find God speaking to her through the providential recourse to another culture and its faith, just as Israel and Judah were spoken to by the providential rise to prominence of her surrounding nations—Philistia, in the times of the judges; Assyria and Egypt with Israel; the Chaldeans and the Persians with Judah. Yet in all these precedents, the lessons learned were intended to serve the purpose of drawing the covenant community back to Yahweh, not to another deity or to an agglomeration of deities.[38]

MODELS OF INTERFAITH RELATIONS

A number of different models have been utilized in ecumenical and multifaith relations, which I want to survey briefly in order to demonstrate why they are unacceptable models for ecumenical and interfaith relations in major incident response. These are principally:

Secular

The secular model believes that faith is a private matter and should not be permitted to contribute sacredness to the public square. Faith should be excluded to ensure the square's nakedness (read secularity) and the participants' mutual tolerance.[39] Key twentieth-century academic influences on this model have been those of John Rawls and Jürgen Habermas.[40] Both believed that society could not be contained by a single set of convic-

---

36. This accords with my theology of common grace and compassion (see chapters 6 and 7). For hesitancy over the term "common grace," however, see Brock, *Singing*, 156.

37. Barnes, *Theology*, 23.

38. See Lorek's study of the exile motif in the Hebrew Bible, with the common themes of exile as expulsion, punishment, alienation, *return, and remnant* (emphasis mine) (*Motif of the Exile*).

39. Netland contends that the nakedness of the public square is starker in Europe than in the U.S., where religion (Christianity) still plays a significant role in public discussion (*Encountering Religious Pluralism*, 148–49).

40. Rawls, *Theory of Justice*; Adams, *Habermas and Theology*.

tions. Indeed, both considered that the imposition of such was dangerous and provocative. Because diversity is good, all public discourse, therefore, must be "thin" to achieve a working consensus. That is, it must be devoid of the particulars of any faith that may create a "thick" concept of the good. These are to be restricted to the private realm. The later Rawls and Habermas seemed to acknowledge the seriousness of pluralism, however, but again insisted that consensus was possible provided the "thick" discourse of particulars was not permitted in the public square.[41] This is the model that one suspects is still behind many current government and secular agency attitudes in emergency planning and response.[42] It is discouraging to find that secular agencies still think religion is to blame for civil disunity and is resistant to civil dialogue and the kinds of accommodation deemed necessary. Modernism still exerts a pressure for the view that "modernity's 'civilizing' project creates room for free-flowing public discourse and that religious dogma only serves to crowd and cramp that public space."[43] At very best, Rawls and Habermas believe Christians should convey their moral and social concepts using only the language common in the public sphere, and drop the "God talk."[44] Koenig has illustrated the kind of potential affront this can cause to faith groups and how their skills can be effectively stifled.[45] However, it is heartening that there is a real attempt to challenge this secular demand for metaphysical

41. In his *Political Liberalism*, Rawls takes into account the fixed diversity of religious and philosophical worldviews of contemporary pluralistic societies he overlooked in *A Theory of Justice*, and argues these must exist on terms of an equal reciprocity of morally acceptable doctrines that make for a reasonable pluralism. See also, Habermas, *Structural Transformation*. For Habermas, 9/11 was highly significant, as his acceptance speech for the award of the peace prize of the German Publishers and Booksellers Association, in the Paulskirche, in Frankfurt, on October 14, 2001 revealed. He conceded the importance of the religious in the public sphere, using a "translation model" of "democratically enlightened common sense." However, he insisted that religious arguments be communicated in secular, religiously-free language to gain credibility in the public sphere. For a description and critique of this shift in Habermas' thinking, see Carroll, "Secularisation."

42. A government document that could indicate otherwise is UK Department for Communities and Local Government, "Key Communities, Key Resources" (see chapter 1, p. 30–31). See also Obama, "President's Prayer."

43. Mouw and Griffioen, *Pluralisms and Horizons*, 159.

44. See Biggar, "Saving the Secular."

45. Koenig refers to the U.S. context when he highlights the federally mandated role of the American Red Cross (ARC), to provide health and mental health services for major incidents (*In the Wake of Disaster*, 106–7).

and ideological neutrality within the public square and the ironic agenda to dominate that square on secular terms. There is considerable academic literature that rejects the integrity of a naked public square, or indeed the neutrality of secularism.[46] I concur with Knight that radical secularism is the greatest foe to social cohesion because of its radical "religious" nature.[47] Because ideological liberal secular assertiveness is bent on keeping religion out of the public square, it denies society so many of the social and spiritual skills that religion has contributed historically. It also hacks at the academic roots of the university where so many social policies are seeded. Knight's judgment is telling:

> Secularism is a politics that does not admit that it is a politics, and thus it is an unaccountable exercise of power, that disallows any actual living tradition from being examined as a form of politics . . . Until it has got over its decision to be the arbiter that sits above all traditions, neither this ideological secularism that defines itself in opposition to religion, nor the discourse of "other religions" that flows from it, can contribute to public debate in good faith.[48]

I reject the secular model, therefore, because it is dishonest and unreasonably discriminating against religious life.

Liberal Christian

The liberal model is akin to the secular, principally because Christianity bought into secular Enlightenment modernism. The essential differences are: that it professes to be a Christian model and because of the way it has allowed modernism to shape its religious tenets. Liberalism teaches that all religions are reflections of a foundational universal religious reason or experience, by which they may be judged. It is fundamentally foundationalist but that foundation consists of human reason and rationality,

---

46. Examples are Taylor, "Living in a Secular Age,"; also, his *A Secular Age*. In 2007 Taylor won the prestigious Templeton Prize (£800,000) for promoting the message that the threat of terrorism could be solved by greater spiritual examination in Western and Islamic countries. His concern was prompted by the New York 9/11 and London 7/7 terrorist bombings (Akbar, "Philosopher Wins"); Spencer, "Doing God"; Biggar, "Saving the Secular"; Chaplin, "Talking God." For a brief discussion that questions the inevitability of secularization, see Coffey, "Secularisation?"

47. Reinhold Niebuhr had made the same point in his "The Christian in a Secular Age."

48. Knight, "Christ, Religion," n.p.

not Scripture. So, even the most incompatible particular narratives are silenced by the louder volume of the metanarrative of reason. This, of course, encourages the privatization of religion with only "thin" discourse in public being permissible. Thus, any particular religious contributions become selectively censored so that they do not offend the metanarrative. This "one-size-fits-all" concept of faith unity is both dishonest and dangerous.[49] It is dangerous because it is dishonest about the differences between Christianity and other faiths.[50] From an evangelical Christian perspective, Guinness states this reality as,

> Certainly, if the Eastern family of faiths is right, both the Western secularist family and the biblical family are wrong. Human rights are an illusion. Inalienable dignity is a conceit. The Eastern family contradicts the other two families sharply. Both sides cannot be right, and the consequences of their differences are plain.[51]

Repressing deep religious differences is not helpful to the kind of response to major incidents required of pastoral carers. Koenig, in his work on the religious responses to terrorism and catastrophe, notes that while all religions tend to be lumped together, in fact they need to be considered "idiosyncratically," each requiring a different approach.[52] Such a view confirms the urgent need for a model that will facilitate such. Liberalism's model has proven a failure.

---

49. For a brief summary of the Enlightenment case for pluralism, and the privatization of religion, and a convincing critique, see Hauerwas, "End of Religious Pluralism," 284–85.

50. Differences, both in theology and history, which, sadly, it has often taken terrorism to heighten. Thus, Davie concludes, "The cataclysmic shock of September 11, 2001, and the subsequent bombings in Bali (twice), Madrid, and London have altered our lives forever, and with them our understandings of the concepts in question. The war in Iraq has had a similar effect. Sadly, it is not only the Muslim communities in Europe that have suffered as a result; anyone 'not white' or 'not Christian' has been at the receiving end of prejudice and at times of physical violence. Post-9/11, it has become harder rather than easier to assume goodwill in our attempts to build an accepting and mutually considerate society" ("Pluralism, Tolerance," 38).

51. Guinness, *Unspeakable*, 123. This does not mean that there are no points of agreement on particular aspects. It means that the general metanarratives are incompatible.

52. Koenig, *In the Wake of Disaster*, 105.

Postmodern

The postmodern model, in contrast to the secular and liberal models, rejects all foundational, universal religious conceptuality. The only reality(ies) we have are particularist and culture-laden. The only way of interpreting reality and truth is through the lens of our own encultured vision. Since this is the only vision we possess, each individual/community's vision is true for them. For truth can only be "the way we see it." Thus, pluralism can be defined as multiple visions, each of which is true though they may all be incommensurable. Claims to be universally true are classed as idolatrous.[53] The primary difficulty with this model is its philosophical basis: all religions make their own claim to truth.[54] Assuming absolute claims to ultimate truth cannot be valid (according to postmodern thought) makes that absolute assumption itself invalid. Thus, postmodernism impales on its own sword and, therefore, cannot be safe for social cohesion.

Theocratic

The theocratic model is where a particular faith tradition believes society should be governed by the direct rule of that faith's deity(ies) alone. Some forms of current Islamic ideology come close to this (Talibanization), and, in the past, some forms of Christianity have been regarded as such (Calvin's Geneva; Puritan New England).[55] Some consider that "Dominion/Reconstruction theology, of the American far right, comes close to endorsing Christian theocratic rule today."[56] The basic tenets of dominion theology are: belief in the sovereignty of God, postmillennialism, presuppositional apologetics, and the concept of covenant as key to understanding the Bible and history. It aims for a reconstruction of social life under the dominion rule of biblical law. In his review of House and Ice's research, Geisler indicates, "They point out that a reconstructionist, decentralized, government working within a Christian theocratic context, would mean 'for non-Christians in a reconstructionist America the

---

53. McFadyen, "Truth as Mission."

54. For Evangelical challenges to the postmodern model see, Groothuis, *Truth Decay*; Carson, *Gagging of God*, 163–74.

55. Chaplin claims that the contemporary secular resistance to allowing religion into the public sphere of discussion stems from a suspicion of some agenda for imposing a theocracy ("Talking God," 13–19).

56. P. A. Marshall, "Theocracy," in Atkinson and Field, eds., *TNDCEPT*, 842–43.

free exercise of their religion *would be hazardous and unthinkable.* "[57] However, with theocratic models, understanding of what theocracy actually means in practical terms is often confused. In every form of theocracy there has been some human person or institution through which it has been interpreted and mediated, and this has usually resulted in dominance by some form of clericalism or ecclesiasticism.[58] Nazir-Ali judges, "but my own perspective is that, whenever people have promoted theocracy in Islam, they have found themselves on the margins."[59] I, therefore, do not consider the theocratic position to be biblically acceptable for today.

Alien

The alien model is how I describe that of Hauerwas and the Yale School. They stress the specificity of the Christian interpretive community as the context for God revealing his perspective on religious others. Interfaith dialogue, therefore, represents a democratization of difference, something Hauerwas sees as a form of Western idolatry he must resist.[60] Hauerwas reacts strongly to the notion of looking for commonality with the morality of others, and thus bartering away the distinctives of the Christian contribution. He insists discussion must be "thick" not thin. Hauerwas acknowledges he has no generic model for interfaith relations nor does

57. Quoted in House and Ice, *Dominion Theology*, 78. According to Geisler this book represents "the most thorough, comprehensive, and scholarly critique of Reconstructionism in print" (Geisler, review article in *Bibliotheca Sacra,* 226). Others nuance this plaudit, believing the book tends to focus most upon defending premillenialism against the postmillenial basis of dominion theology (Mare, review article in *Presbyterian*). See also, Barron and Shupe, "Reasons." Harold Cunningham debates the concept of "general equity" as per the Westminster Confession in light of the application of Old Testament law to today's world by the Reconstructionists (see "God's Law").

58. An evangelical movement in Northern Ireland (ECONI) argue that this has been the dominating position Paisleyism and Orangeism have assumed during the "Troubles," a position which ECONI decry as lying outside of *bona fide* confessional Evangelicalism. Yet, for pragmatic purposes they suggest that they do recognize both Paisleyism and Orangeism are within the Evangelical fold, even while disagreeing with them in distinctive ways. Mitchell concludes that ECONI's position in this matter is ambiguous, if not contradictory, due to different ways of defining "evangelical." He questions the capacity of ECONI to effectively erode the ideological base of the closed evangelicalism of Paisleyism and Orangeism in Northern Ireland (Mitchell, *Evangelicalism and National Identity*, 273, 278, compare 283–85, 294–96).

59. Nazir-Ali, "Global and Local," n.p.

60. Hauerwas, "End of Religious Pluralism," 287.

he think there should be one. He argues the case for complete disavowal of Constantinianism, with its subtle political agenda for power, in favor of Christological nonviolence that would have Christians believe they are simply exposed to the beliefs of others whom they can befriend and seek to show Jesus to, without the accoutrements of hubris and coercive dominance.[61] Kroeker expresses Yoder's resultant ecumenicity as "The rule of divine love and harmony represents a very different ecumenicity: a pattern of creative diversity, dialogue, a community that welcomes outsiders and that understands leadership as servanthood."[62] Both PP and SR could welcome this; however, it is the total pessimism regarding the possibility of any agreement on political justice that makes this model unworkable. There is no allowance for common grace providing legitimate points of contact for a public policy.[63] Furthermore, there are the complicating factors with Hauerwas' concept of the authority of Scripture in his post-liberal view of Christianity as a particularist tradition, to which Carson draws attention.[64]

Didactic

The didactic model has been the prevailing model for many Evangelicals. A key exponent of this is Professor Gerald McDermott. His work entitled, *Can Evangelicals Learn from World Religions? Jesus, Revelation, and Religious Tradition* is indicative.[65] McDermott suggests Christians can learn by seeing old ideas in new light cast by other religions and new perspectives, developing doctrines that are latent within the Bible. He sees biblical precedents for such learning in the forms of Melchizedek, pagan poets, and the "light" given to Gentiles.[66] McDermott concludes, "God's people were learning from those outside their traditions things

---

61. Hauerwas, "End of Religious Pluralism," 283–300. Hauerwas argues a return to a pre-Constantinian mode, where the Christian is a proclaimer of his/her particularist faith, sharing the vulnerability and weakness of their alliance to the Suffering Servant (289).

62. Kroeker, "Why O'Donovan's," 46.

63. See my discussion with Hauerwas and Stackhouse in chapter 7.

64. Carson, *Gagging of God*, 168–69. He has in mind Hauerwas' belief that the authority of the Bible lies in the interpretive community and the text's complete autonomy from any historical referent.

65. McDermott, *Can Evangelicals Learn?* McDermott is Professor of Religion at Roanoke College, Virginia.

66. See Gen 14; Acts 17:28; 2 Kings 5:1–14; Luke 4:24–26 respectively.

that helped them better understand their own religion."[67] Thus, in an-swer to the question, "What is the purpose of learning truth from other religions?" he helpfully avers, "learning from the religions can enhance ecumenical social action—or what some call missions of mercy."[68] While this didactic model is helpful in maintaining Christian humility and the mystery of God's providence in revelation, it is too unidirectional as a model for social cohesion.

Christian Nation

The Christian nation model (CNM) is one that has become seriously propounded in recent times. This model believes the core identity of the UK nation is Christian, even though explicit Christianity may no longer be in the ascendancy. Christianity has shaped its history, institutions, and public life, albeit with great imperfections.[69] Therefore,

> For public institutions to neglect or repudiate the legacy of Christian faith is to undermine the unique character of the na-tion and also to put at risk its main political achievements— freedom under law, accountable government, religious liberty, democracy, strong families, education committed to truth, and so forth.[70]

The Christian's task is to defend the Christian character of the nation and her institutions as far as possible and to seek extension of that char-acter by evangelism and social and political action. Because the church is a kind of "chaplain" to the secular powers, there should be an attempt to even monitor British legislation and case law to inform government of where these depart from biblical principles. Because it is important for the nation's laws to honor God, the Christian community has a duty to attempt ensuring Christ shapes the law.[71] I am sure the Christian nation

67. McDermott, *Can Evangelicals Learn?*, 89.

68. Ibid., 207.

69. O'Donovan, *Desire of the Nations*. This view, in essence, has also been supported by recent articles written by the evangelical former Anglican Bishop of Rochester, Michael Nazir-Ali and by para-church groups, the Christian Institute and Christian Concern For Our Nation (CCFON).

70. Chaplin, "The Bible, the State," n.p. Chaplin has developed his thinking in terms of religion and public discourse more fully in his *Talking God*. He acknowledges Rowan Williams' term, "procedural secularism" (in contrast to "programmatic secu-larism") as a secular equivalent for what he prefers as "Principled Pluralism."

71. Some would go further than this, to support the concept of a Christian

model could work SR effectively, and that it provides for a multifaith, pluralist society, where unbelievers may never be disadvantaged civilly and nothing need bar developing good interfaith relations. Yet, there are certain problems with it being the best model to work SR with, in my view.

My reasons for this conclusion are: The CNM assumes a nation, in a broadly unified manner, can enjoy some kind of covenantal relation to God, can yield political obedience to God, and can attempt to ensure these are enshrined in law. The theological basis for the CNM lies in certain combined readings of the Old and New Testaments, and assumes the Old Testament concept of a covenanted people has valid connections with the New Testament era, especially in the cases of peculiarly "God-blessed" nations. However, certain discontinuities are also recognized, such as religious uniformity must not be enforced and civil and religious liberties must be maintained. Furthermore, Old Testament civil laws are no longer binding upon the Christian nation. Granting such discontinuities, proponents still believe there is biblical endorsement for nations corporately embodying or professing a particular religious faith. However, principled pluralists contest this argument. While accepting that the nation of Israel was such a nation, it is theological and hermeneutical strangulation to extrude from this that any other nation should assume such a position in relation to God. Under the New Testament the covenant is made in Christ with peoples from all nations who, as God's elect, form a heavenly citizenship and a "holy nation" to be identified with no geographical area/land or natural nationality whatsoever.[72] It is transnational. Indeed, this specific feature of the holy nation is celebrated as a jewel in the crown of the New Testament.[73]

---

state—the difference being that the Christian state actually officially adopts Christianity in its constitution and/or by endorsing a national church.

72. See Phil 3:20 and 1 Pet 2:9 respectively.

73. See Eph 3:1–12. For a fuller discussion of O'Donovan's concept of Christendom and its conflict with the "free church" concept of Yoder and Hauerwas, see Kroeker, "Why O'Donovan's," 41–64. Kroeker critiques O'Donovan for not addressing the apocalyptic dimension and for his tendency toward institutionalizing and formalizing the role of the church as chaplain to the secular, whereas Yoder et al., view the church as an alternative eschatological community "free" from the state, though involved with its social politics. Yoder feared O'Donovan's concept left the church vulnerable to the temptation for power and dominance and moved away from the concept of the church as suffering servant, after the kenotic Christ.

Since the gospel is not to be forced upon any peoples by law, being a gospel of grace, it is hard to see how the Christendom concept cannot avoid encouraging nominal Christianity. Nominal Christians are not the kind of participants SR requires. At very least the CNM believes that where the majority community is Christian it should take advantage of that providential fact, to encapsulate Christianity into public and political life. However, the potential for clinging to faith dominance should ever a waning of such a Christian majority occur could be great, reinforcing a secular demand for a naked square.[74] Furthermore, there is great potential for intrafaith dispute—over which Christian community should form the national church, and for how long, and under what theological and ecclesiastical constrictions?[75] One of the benefits of PP would be its effective disestablishment of any single faith group/church.

Conclusion

My rejection of the above models has been encouraged by more recent postliberal challenges to modernism (and postmodernism) arguing for the religious community's right to inhabit the public square with their particular contributions to public discourse (a right defended as much by the CNM as by PP). A major advantage of postliberalism in this respect is that it provides a grammar for ecumenical dialogue and relationship because it believes a fixed doctrinal rule may require different expressions in different contexts. At the center of postliberal Christian theology is the non-negotiable status of Jesus Christ as Lord so that "either Christ confronts us with his exclusive claim as lord over all, or he does not confront us at all."[76] A credible academic challenge to liberal modernism has emerged, so that to suggest theology concerns the search for justifiable particularity is no longer deemed arrogant or imperialist.[77] Indeed, the situation is such that Volf can judge, "only those religious groups that

---

74. Yoder's suspicions of O'Donovan's concept of Christendom were connected to his fears of Christendom's tendency toward political struggles for power and ascendancy (Kroeker, "Why O'Donovan's").

75. As the history of conformity/nonconformity demonstrates only too well. Kroeger's exposition of Yoder's position, and his fears of where O'Donovan's Christendom concept could lead, echoes the fears nonconformists have had with conformity through the centuries (Kroeker, "Why O'Donovan's").

76. Philips and Okholm, eds., *Nature of Confession*, 11.

77. Ibid., 24.

make no apologies about their 'difference' will be able to survive and thrive."[78]

One notable contribution to religion's right to participate overtly in the public square that conflates liberal and postliberal thinking, is that of Professor Nigel Biggar's *Saving the Secular*.[79] He judges that current moral degeneration, and the consequent revulsion by young Muslims to this degeneration, in particular, makes the call for humble social interaction and dialogue essential. Radicalism can dignify people with a moral seriousness. He senses allies in the form of a "humane" liberalism of (the later) Habermas and Rawls and Stout. They envisage public consensus arising out of each citizen entering fully into the perspectives of all others. Biggar considers this academic ideal could well result in approximations within the Christian church, with the exception that Christians should not have to drop the 'God-talk,' while acknowledging religious contributions need to be reasonable. By this he means,

> religious believers won't cite authorities and make theological references without also proceeding to furnish explanations and reasons that have been crafted to persuade a skeptical audience. To consider how your auditors might receive what you say, and then to offer explanation, is to pay them a certain respect; and if love for one's neighbour involves more than respect, it doesn't involve less.[80]

The paradigm which Biggar sets out endorses a "humane polyglot liberalism" as akin to Christian moral theology. Thus, the Christian need not stop listening to and learning from liberalism, because, for theological reasons,

78. Volf quoted in Philips and Okholm, eds., *Nature of Confession*, 47. Ben Quash makes a similar affirmation: "As far as SR is concerned, there is no reason to apologise for speaking from a particular; there is every reason to acknowledge it" ("Heavenly Semantics: Some Literary-Critical Approaches to Scriptural Reasoning," in Ford and Pecknold, eds., *Promise of Scriptural Reasoning*, 66). Guinness insists, "To demand 'neutral discourse' in public life, as some still do [1988] should now be recognized as a way of coercing people to speak publicly in someone else's language and thus never to be true to their own" ("Making the World Safe," n.p.).

79. Biggar is Regius Professor of Moral and Pastoral Theology at Christchurch, Oxford. His views are set forth in his inaugural lecture delivered before the University of Oxford on April 22, 2008, entitled, "Saving the Secular: The Public Vocation of Moral Theology." References are taken from this edition. The address is now in *Journal of Religious Ethics* 37/1 (March 2009): 59–178, under the same title.

80. Biggar, "Saving the Secular," n.p.

he believes that the world is the creation of a single divine intelligence, he assumes that it is marked by a coherent order and is therefore comprehensible. And since he believes that the divine intelligence is benevolent, he assumes that the world's comprehensible order includes values as goods or forms of flourishing—that is, the basic elements of so-called "natural law."[81]

Biggar recognizes there are dangers with this paradigm, most notably in the abstracting of ethical concepts out of the biblical narrative and these becoming understood in ways alien to Christian presuppositions.[82] However, the contribution of the Christian moral theologian can interpret tolerance to be "an exercise in careful listening, and keep it from relaxing into slothful indifference."[83] Biggar argues that the introduction of citizens to foreign worlds, and teaching respect for those by the arts and humanities' departments, will

introduce us to worlds made strange by the passage of time, present worlds structured by the peculiar grip of unfamiliar languages, worlds alien to us in their social organisation and manners, their religious and philosophical convictions. They teach us to read strange and intractable texts with patience and care, to meet alien ideas and practices with humility, docility, and charity, to draw alongside foreign worlds before we set out— as we must—judging them.[84]

This serves to introduce us directly to the model of principled pluralism.

A NEW MODEL

Fueled by the postliberal challenges and Biggar's *apologia*, I construct a model of my own that pursues a synergy between a Christian socio-political theory called principled pluralism (PP) and two embryonic practices in ecumenical and interfaith relations, scriptural reasoning (SR) and civic networking (CN). I explore each of these in conjunction with my canonical linguistic method.[85]

81. Ibid.

82. A view Biggar shares along with Richard Hays.

83. Biggar, "Saving the Secular," n.p.

84. Ibid.

85. I am conscious that SR is driven predominantly by a postliberalism, but it can, in my view, be embraced under an evangelical theology of common grace such as I have propounded in chapter 6, above.

Principled Pluralism (PP)

Principled pluralism has been explored as a "stance towards the plural religious affiliations" of the state. Thus, "Its central aim is that the role of the state in a religiously diverse society is to maintain a public square equally open to contributions from many faiths rather than overtly prefer or privilege any one of them, even Christianity."[86] As an alternative to the Christian nation model, with its validation of Christianity as the preferred particular in the national public square, PP attempts to provide a theological justification for endorsing the square as neither naked (secular) nor sacred (Christian nation/state), but civil. This means that there are theological reasons for the public square giving equal rights to all religions and none—where every right one faith might assert is at once a right for the others too. Though, ultimately, my model is created out of Christian theology, it maintains fairness and equity for all.[87] It is not intended to constitute some breed of theocracy, though it acknowledges its Christian foundation, since foundational neutrality is not an option. In so far as it is a form of socio-political discourse it is peculiarly suited to an area of major incident response that has become highly politicized, namely interfaith relations. Though the term PP is not used, the concept has been propounded by a group of Evangelicals within the US in recent years, in the form of an "Evangelical Manifesto" (EM).[88] This acknowledges Christians are "resident aliens" on earth, called by God to be in the world but not of it. Contra the "alien" view critiqued above, EM fully endorses involvement with the world in public life as "a service to all, and to work with all who share these ideals and care for the common good."[89] Taking the EM as a model of PP, it rejects both the privatization and politicization of faith. PP is rooted in the belief that religious pluralism

86. Chaplin, "The Bible, the State." Chaplin has developed his ideas of PP (or Procedural Secularism) in his *Talking God*.

87. Jackson argues for the same out of his concept of "prophetic liberalism" in *Priority of Love*, 62–67. His arguments fit those of PP, as when he quotes William Galston, "Civic tolerance of deep differences is perfectly compatible with unswerving belief in the correctness of one's own way of life" (*Priority of Love*, 66).

88. Evangelical Manifesto Steering Group, "Evangelical Manifesto" The "Evangelical Manifesto" was a constructive progression from the 2004 landmark statement of the National Association of Evangelicals (U.S.) entitled, "For the Health of the Nation: An Evangelical Call to Civic Responsibility," led by Ron Sider and Jim Wallis. In broad terms, it is the model Barack Obama pleads for in his "The President's Prayer."

89. Evangelical Manifesto Steering Group, "Evangelical Manifesto," 14. See also Bretherton, *Hospitality as Holiness*, 111.

is something that Scripture actually endorses, and Christians, therefore, are under divine obligation to work within society. Therefore, Christian engagement in public life is from the perspective of the Christian faith while affording the same right to those of all faiths and none.[90]

Thus, PP endorses a hospitable, civil public square, where all can come and make their contribution, irrespective of how fervently religious or irreligious they are. PP values upholding strong truth claims (by all parties) while abandoning Constantinian programs of institutional coercion or enforcement. It does not mean an acceptance of the tenets of all faiths and none being truth, relative to their cultural context, above criticism or judgment. It is possible to endorse pluralism without relativism. The right to believe anything does not mean that anything believed is right. PP avers equally both the right to speak and the right to be criticized and judged. PP is about the provision of a civil public square and the rights of all, even those with whom we may fervently disagree. That the concept of pluralism is Christian in nature is openly avowed, but this does not require a Christendom to be operative.[91] Its application of the Golden Rule extends an open invitation to all faiths and none to cooperate in the public sphere to make religious liberty practical and religious persecution rare.[92] Such a Christian theology rejects the right of any one religion (including itself) or ideology to rule a society. PP adopts a confessional silence, which is not to be equated with confessional neutrality. PP's aim is not to transform society, nor to manage society bureaucratically, but to

90. The precise wording of EM is helpful at this point. Having rejected the extremes of privatization and politicization, EM states, "Our commitment is to a *civil public square—a vision for public life in which citizens of all faiths are free to enter and engage the public square on the basis of their faith, but within a framework of what is agreed to be just and free for other faiths too.* Thus, every right we assert for ourselves is at once a right we defend for others. A right for a Christian is a right for a Jew, and a right for a secularist, and a right for a Mormon, and [*sic*] right for a Muslim, and a right for a Scientologist, and [*sic*] right for all the believers in all the faiths across this wide world" (Evangelical Manifesto Steering Group, "Evangelical Manifesto," 17, emphasis original).

91. "An Evangelical Manifesto" is explicitly Christian, and broadly Evangelical, as its steering group membership exhibits. The steering group (US) comprises: Timothy George (Beeson Divinity School); Os Guinness (author/social critic); John Huffman (Christianity Today International); Richard Mouw (Fuller Seminary); Jesse Miranda (Vanguard University); David Neff (*Christianity Today*); Richard Ohman (businessman); Larry Ross (Larry Ross Communications); Dallas Willard (University of Southern California). Online: http://www.anevangelicalmanifesto.com/.

92. See Matt 7:12, "Therefore, whatever you want men to do to you, do also to them . . ."

render justice in the form of normative adjudications regarding the different religions and philosophies in a given nation or society. However, it can affirm deep commitment to Christian particularism, while accepting diversity and appropriate tolerance. A Christian principled pluralism will endorse a commitment to both truth and justice—"a gracious yet firm insistence upon Jesus Christ as the one Lord for all and a concern for justice that actively protests the rights of religious others to believe and practice as they do."[93]

To set my interest with PP in context, I am concerned that both national and local emergency planning tends to have an over-secular scope of reference in consulting with faith communities, which "fits" in with existing advisory interfaith bodies to only a limited degree.[94]

Advisory Interfaith Bodies

Inter Faith Network for the United Kingdom

The most reputable and representative of interfaith bodies is the Inter Faith Network for the United Kingdom (IFNUK). This was formed in 1987 to promote good relations between people of different faiths and is a network connecting many diverse faith-based traditions and organizations. It is often used in an advisory and facilitating capacity by national and local government emergency planning.[95] IFNUK methodology is based on the principle that, "dialogue and cooperation can only prosper if they are rooted in respectful relationships which do not blur or undermine the

---

93. Netland, *Encountering Religious Pluralism*, 347. See also Bader, "Religious Pluralism."

94. In other words, they are constrained by a secular agenda. This policy (or unconscious ideology) is potentially dangerous for the public that emergency planners are serving to protect, because it fails to seriously engage with the religious others, the particular needs of victims, and results of terrorist activities it makes plans to cope with.

95. Philip Lewis, 'For the Peace of the City." I am grateful to Dr. Lewis for sending me a copy of his chapter, and permitting me to quote and cite. Strictly speaking the organization that national and local government bodies will consult with most generally will be the Faith Communities Consultative Council (FCCC). This was set up in 2006 as a replacement for the Inner Cities Religious Council and the Working Together Steering Group. Among its objectives are: strengthening the links between government and faith communities and facilitating the faith communities' voice(s) being heard by government (Department of Communities and Local Government, "Faith Communities Consultative Council (FCCC)." The FCCC is mainly for the interests of social cohesion.

distinctiveness of different religious traditions."[96] This network promotes interfaith relations for the benefit of social cohesion within the UK, not theology *per se*. This is an important point for Evangelicals in particular, because it interrogates their public theology. Christianity's response to major incidents should include an expression of such theology. I suggest, therefore, there is nothing in the IFNUK guidance document for building good relations with different faiths and beliefs that does not harmonize with Christian common grace theologies also, which in turn resonate with PP. IFNUK guidance addresses the need for (Christian) respect and courtesy, for honesty, sensitivity, and straightforwardness. It also gives endorsement for persuasion and evangelism.[97] In the autumn of 2005 the IFNUK "Faith and Citizenship" project was initiated, partly in response to the London bombings in the summer of that year. The executive committee produced a consultative document entitled, "Faith, Citizenship, and Shared Life in Britain Today: A Discussion Document."[98] This was intended for wider discussion among the IFNUK's member bodies with a view to discovering what consensus there is between the different faiths in speaking with a joint voice on critical issues, while recognizing that each faith may wish to comment on such issues from their own distinctive faith perspective. This document helpfully summarizes the changing character of Britain's population and its diversity, the expressing of faith in public life, and it rejects any concept of a secular naked public square.[99] There is a healthy acceptance of robust debate about differences,

96. From the Inter Faith Network website. Online: http://www.interfaith.org.uk/.

97. See Inter Faith Network for the United Kingdom, "Building Good Relations." Evangelism is acknowledged within the requirements of self-restraint and concern for the other's liberty and dignity reflected by: respecting any expressed wish to be left alone; avoiding imposing oneself and one's views on any who are vulnerable to exploitation; avoidance of violent actions, language threats, manipulation, improper inducements, or the misuse of power; recognizing the right of others to disagree.

98. Inter Faith Network for the United Kingdom, "Faith, Citizenship," n.p. Comments were invited to this document by February 1, 2007. I am not aware of any sequel.

99. It also endorses Article 9 of the European Convention on Human Rights that states: 1. "Everyone has the right to freedom of thought, conscience and religion; this right includes freedom to change his religion or belief, and freedom, either alone or in community with others and in public or private, to manifest his religion or belief, in worship, teaching, practice and observance. 2. Freedom to manifest one's religion or beliefs shall be subject only to such limitations as are prescribed by law and are necessary in a democratic society in the interests of public safety, for the protection of public order, health or morals, or the protection of the rights and freedoms of others" (Council of Europe, "European Convention on Human Rights").

with a rejection of violence as a means of resolving those differences. The document regards vigorous, open dialogue as essential, and it rejects any attempt to "flatten out society into a featureless, characterless, 'politically correct' world in which we are all the same."[100]

The aims and objectives of the IFNUK seem to me to be wholly compliant with a PP milieu.[101] However, among its many member bodies there is no concerted Evangelical representation, an omission that seems theologically unnecessary and detrimental to an evangelical catholic Christian contribution to major incident response.[102] One reason for this omission could be that local expressions of the Inter Faith Network (local interfaith councils, forums, etc.) may not practice to the same precise parameters as the IFNUK itself endorses.[103]

Multifaith Group of Healthcare Chaplaincy

Though not a member of the IFNUK, the Multi-Faith Group of Health-care Chaplaincy (MFGHC) has become a highly influential body, working with the English *NHS* in an advisory role for health-care chaplaincy.[104] In so far as the *NHS* is a key player in the philosophy of major incident response, emergency planning can take a lead from *NHS* models. Since multifaith approaches to *NHS* health-care chaplaincy are now standard,

100. Inter Faith Network for the United Kingdom, "Faith, Citizenship," n.p.

101. Significantly for my research, the Cambridge Inter-Faith Programme: Judaism, Christianity, and Islam in Partnership *is* a member body of the Inter Faith Network for the United Kingdom.

102. There may be Evangelical representatives encompassed within Churches Together In Britain and Ireland and Churches Together in England, which both *are* member bodies of IFNUK.

103. For instance, my local Council of Faiths includes in its profile: "The Council is not bound by one faith but within it people of different faiths seek high spiritual values together: *peace, harmony and a spirit of unity* are at the top of our agenda," which is restrictive of the broader allowance for, and recognition of, faith difference, which the IFNUK endorses (see Loughborough Council of Faiths. Online: http://www.lboro-faiths.org.uk/.)

104. The MFGHC is in receipt of funding from the English Department of Health, and, therefore, would find it difficult to claim independence from their employers/ quasi-employers, a requirement of the 2007 white paper, UK Secretary of State for Health, "Trust, Assurance and Safety," chapter 1:1:5. See MFGHC website: http:// www.mfghc.com/index.htm, for extensive information. It should be noted that MFGHC's process of authorization of health care chaplains is exclusive, and their route, therefore, could exclude some faith groups (e.g., Kadampa Buddhists). The MFGHC is self-appointing and does not consist of those with experience of health care chaplaincy, strangely.

this weighs heavily in shaping Christian response to major incidents, alongside the drive to comply with *NHS* standards of professionalism. The MFGHC is committed to the advancement of multifaith chaplaincy health care in England and Wales.[105] To that end it provides, via its website, a substantial literature database of chaplaincy skills throughout health trusts in England, Wales, and Scotland.[106] These will provide valuable resources for chaplains in spiritual care for those who work in acute and specialist hospitals involving major incidents. However, there is substantial difference between the MFGHC and the IFNUK. IFNUK is primarily concerned with promoting social cohesion. MFGHC's primary concern is with promoting spiritual health care through a multifaith chaplaincy. It therefore impacts more upon the theology of pastoral care and worship, and in so doing will tend to run into conflict with distinctive Christian theology—certainly Evangelical theology, since there seems to be no mechanism for creating the common grace collegiality where differences are acknowledged and confronted with honesty and integrity.

UK Board of Healthcare Chaplaincy

The UK Board for Healthcare Chaplaincy (UKBHC) was established in 2008 and arose from a previous organization, the Chaplaincy Academic and Accreditation Board (CAAB). The UKBHC's purpose is to regulate health-care chaplains according to the principles of regulatory reform as described in the 2007 white paper, "Trust, Assurance and Safety."[107] This involves sustaining, improving, and assuring the professional standards of health-care chaplains, and also identifies and addresses poor practice or bad behavior. In its establishment, it has derived its authority from the professional membership organizations for health-care chaplains, name-

---

105. NHS (Scotland) has a somewhat separate existence under its own Act of Parliament (1948), which incorporates certain differences from preexisting health care arrangements in Scotland. This is becoming increasingly the case within the NHS in Wales. Wales is about to launch its own guidance on the provision of chaplaincy and spiritual care in NHS Wales and refers to its own arrangements for multifaith chaplaincy.

106. For example, see the MFGHC's index of resources on their website. Online: http://www.mfghc.com/resources/resources_docindex.htm.

107. UK Secretary of State for Health, "Trust, Assurance and Safety," especially when it states: "In order to assure a safe and high-quality experience for patients across the spectrum of their encounters with health professionals, we need to ensure proportionate arrangements for all the professions involved. There can be no weak links in the chain of care" (18).

ly: the Association of Hospice and Palliative Care Chaplains; the College of Health Care Chaplains; the Northern Ireland Healthcare Chaplains Association; and the Scottish Association of Chaplains in Healthcare, but aims to become independent of government, the professionals themselves, employers, educators, and all the other interest groups involved in health care according to the principles of the white paper.[108] It is interesting (and promising?) that Ford suggests SR's usefulness might be explored in the realm of chaplaincy.[109]

Applied in the context of major incident response for Christian responders, PP actually encourages a multifaith public response. That is to say, if Christians are acting as public citizens, they should be comfortable with a multifaith response in principle, and be distinctly uncomfortable if it is not present. However, PP alone is not sufficient for the close working relationships required within major incident response. Under PP, each faith representative could, in principle, function independently of the other, and, if that faith could not permit interdependence, PP would endorse his or her right to work independently.[110] On the realistic basis that society, and government, will require a great degree of interdependence in major incident response, it is necessary for PP to be achieved through some methodology that brings religions and ideologies together in a

108. I am grateful to Carol English for clarification regarding the UKBHC (email correspondence between author and Carol English, professional officer, Unite Health Sector in March 2010). This is illustrative of the extreme political difficulties inherent in forming interfaith friendship: the MFGHC and the UKBHC are currently embroiled in a dispute over which is to become the formal authorizing body in regard to health care chaplaincy in the UK.

109. Ford, *Christian Wisdom*, 291, n. 28. William Taylor, of The Grubb Institute of Behavioural Studies Ltd., London, and currently conducting a research project for the Cambridge Inter-Faith Programme: Judaism, Christianity, and Islam in Partnership, states that there has been no strategic work with health care chaplains thus far (2008), but there are a number of institutions in the prison and university chaplaincy sector where SR is being developed beyond its academic origins (email correspondence between author and Taylor, in September 2008).

110. This right is endorsed in the "Williamsburg Charter" (U.S.) in these words: "There must always be room for those who do not wish to participate in the public ordering of our common life, who desire to pursue their own religious witness separately as conscience dictates. But at the same time, for those who do wish to participate, it should be understood that those claiming the right to dissent should assume the responsibility to debate." The "Williamsburg Charter" is a reaffirmation of the First Amendment to the U.S. Constitution (effectively based on PP), endorsed on the bicentennial anniversary of that constitution in 1988. The Evangelical Os Guinness was a key driving force behind this charter and served as executive director.

form of cooperative understanding that is neither threatened by mythical neutrality, consensus, or veiled syncretism, but reflects transparency and integrity (both of which are Christian virtues).[111]

Given that all faiths are compelled by a spirit of compassion toward suffering, a methodology for co-working, which is honest, challenging to all, academically robust, and practical, is necessary. It needs to confront the possible problems PP can encounter before they arise. One problem is that of consensual repression, where each faith agrees itself, and with the others, to put their deepest differences aside in the interests of a united front. Human nature being what it is, this may cause the repression of profound disagreement that explodes later, given certain inflammatory circumstances. A model that will not minimize such disagreement, which will demand transparency of differences and commitment to open dialogue, is needed. Does such a model exist? I believe there are early beginnings, in forms called scriptural reasoning and civic networking.

Scriptural Reasoning (SR)

Background and General Purpose of SR

SR has emerged from the belief that the reasoning methods of the modern world are deeply flawed and dangerous in the multifaith reality of contemporary life, not least in theological methodologies that start by understanding the world before trying to understand what God is saying to the world. SR is a reaction against applying *a priori* forms of a secular ethical universalism to various scriptural traditions.[112] Modernity's failure to achieve its own goals receives the challenge from postmodernism that maybe there is no such thing, anywhere, as a neutral universal reason— the grand "baby" of Enlightenment modernism—that can rise above all religions and serve to judge them. That Western religion had sold out to such secular universals, and developed a religious orthodoxy based upon these, also contributed to the reaction from which SR has emerged. This "sell out" opened the door to critical scholarship moving further and further away from traditional uses of Scripture. Thus, "The literal sense of the scripture, and what it means to be a community of faith have been

---

111. Similarly, society and government need to acknowledge the moral and theological dilemmas that the secular dominated multifaith ideology forces upon the faith communities so that only those who have sold out to the secular terms are accepted.

112. Ochs, "Society of Scriptural Reasoning."

replaced by critical historical interpretations of scripture."[113] SR demonstrates the need to recognize that we are a multifaith and secular world, there are profound differences between the faiths, and secular neutrality does not work and therefore has no right to dominate the interfaith field. SR is an alternative to stifling diversity, and calls for a respectful seriousness toward religious others by making their scriptures an explicit theme for reflection.[114] SR requires dialogue with others in order to understand the Christian revelation more deeply, but even then SR avers there is a surplus that still awaits deeper discovery.

Ford locates the origins of SR in the early 1990s, when some Jewish text scholars and Jewish philosophers combined to connect textual studies with Western philosophy. In turn, this merged with the postliberal work being conducted by George Lindbeck and Hans Frei at the Yale Divinity School and their conclusion that faiths have their own tradition and cannot be subsumed under any single overarching rationale.[115] To date, SR is a largely joint American-British initiative and involves the three "Abrahamic" faiths: Judaism, Christianity, and Islam, but there is no particular reason why it cannot be expanded to involve other religions and philosophies as well.[116] SR is a flexible paradigm, carrying many definitions, and is resistant to authoritative overviews of the faiths and traditions involved. Thus, it is not a monologue but represents many voices.[117]

While SR is being explored as a methodology for a number of different areas of life, my interest is with its capacity for facilitating ecumenical and interfaith understanding and relations for major incident

---

113. Elkins, "Suffering Job," n.p.

114. Green, "Rules of Scriptural Reasoning," n.p. Adams suggests that there is a brand of "understanding" that goes on (and can be empirically demonstrated), that facilitates interfaith discussion, but that it is futile, and dangerous, to specify this understanding ("Making Deep Reasonings."

115. Ford, *Christian Wisdom*, 275–78. Ford points out that under the Jewish thinker, Peter Ochs, an embryonic form was developing at Drew University in the late 1980s.

116. SR has been a triadic discourse between the three "Abrahamic" faiths alone to date. The reasons for this triadic relationship are: their relation to Abraham, their core identities being scripture, their common focus upon scripture texts as the platform of primary discourse with God, and allied traditions, and the commitment to study the texts deeply. However, others have serious reservations about the use, and theological implications, of this term "*Abrahamic* faiths."

117. Ford, *Christian Wisdom*, 276.

response.[118] David Ford has been the principal explorer in the field of interfaith SR, and I am indebted to his major contribution in this field.[119] I, therefore, interact mainly with his rules of SR in the formation of my own exploratory model for major incident response.

Significant to my exploration for a suitable model for ecumenical and interfaith friendship in major incident response, is the fact that SR has been provoked by each religion having its own crises and sufferings. It assumes that moments of suffering are indications of failure in practice, which can become significant of new ways to repair these failures and to redeem and transform the world of suffering. SR is a form of "scriptural pragmatism," formed by the pragmatic connection between the goal of eliminating suffering and the interpretative practices of religious communities. Truth becomes identified and audited by its success in healing the sufferer. In his application of SR to the book of Job, Elkins concludes that the intention of the book is to move the reader to compassion for Job. This means being moved to action, to doing something to bring about relief. Job's "friends" failed, for all their theodicean tenacity, placing philosophical argument and defense before compassionate action.[120] SR could well be a constructive way forward to ecumenical and interfaith relationships in major incident response because it assumes the human world is broken, fallen, and filled with corruption, sickness, and trauma. It also brings together practitioners who jointly acknowledge their failure and impoverishment in providing healing for the world. In other

118. For example, see Jeff Bailey's exploration of SR for political practice ("Engaged Particularity"). The initiative beginning at the Thornbury Centre, Bradford, is conducting SR to enable deeper understanding of each participant's own faith (conversation with Dr. Helen Reid, at The Thornbury Centre, Bradford on October 22, 2008).

119. Especially chapter 8 in Ford, *Christian Wisdom*. This is a slightly altered version of "An Interfaith Wisdom: Scripture Reasoning between Jews, Christians and Muslims," in Ford and Pecknold, eds., *Promise of Scriptural Reasoning*, 1–22. Ford is Regius Professor of Divinity at the University of Cambridge. He stimulated my interest in SR by his paper at the 2007 Tyndale Fellowship Conference. See Ford, "God and Our Public Life."

120. Elkins, "Suffering Job" Elkins interacts with Cornel West's interpretation of Josiah Royce's pragmatism. Royce rejected the traditional view that the book of Job represents some kind of theodicy, in favor of the book highlighting the extent and depth of Job's suffering and the capacity to move the reader to action. Mouw proposes that every theological system also carries an associated sociology, "such that we can fully understand the claims of a theological perspective only if we attempt to see what it would look like if those claims were fleshed out in the life of the community" (Mouw, *He Shines*, 74).

words, "Scriptural reasoning is a way of wrestling with a deeply rooted and urgent twenty-first-century issue connected with the past, present and likely future traumas, and one inseparable from the possibility of long-term human peace and flourishing." And it is "a joint response by Jews, Christians, and Muslims, inspired by the reading of their scriptures, to the cries of a suffering world, including their own communities, and it is committed, for God's sake, to being part of God's compassionate response to those cries."[121]

It is this aspect of confessional humility that is so attractive about SR, which is important for Evangelicals. The crises that have contributed to the formation of SR include religious ones pertinent to the shame of all three "Abrahamic" faiths in terms of their historical engagements in persecution; therefore SR seeks to achieve an ethical relationship between the faiths.[122] SR demands a critical generosity whereby "Christians are called not just to speak of the God who is revealed in Christ but to listen critically and yet with generosity to what is spoken about God by the other."[123] Christians are to practice hospitality to the "strangers," yet with sensitivity not superiority, mindful of the haunting of prior attitudes towards Jews, Hindus, Muslims, etc. SR acts with an ethic of mutual responsibility. Accordingly, the Christian virtue of humility proves itself more open to tolerance of the stranger than the democratic liberalism that often severely criticizes it as a religion of intolerance. For Christian humility "cultivates a love for the particular in a way that does not negate the stranger or hide from itself its own temptation to coercion, its own lust for power, its own proclivities to sin."[124]

From this general introduction to SR, I shall become far more specific in my exploration.

What SR is Not

I start my focus by "clearing the ground" of possible misunderstandings. This is important given the propensity in all religious fundamentalists for intense suspicion of ecumenical, let alone interfaith, collaboration.

121. Ford, *Christian Wisdom*, 284, 382.
122. That is the *Shoah*, the Crusades, and Islamization/Talibanization.
123. Barnes, *Theology*, 23.
124. Fodor, *Christian Hermeneutics*, 20.

Abolition of Reason

SR is more a reform, than abolition, of reason and modernism.[125] SR is neither a fundamentalist nor a literalist practice, nor a deconstructivist postmodernism. Rather it is postliberal (or postconservative), sharing features of both liberalism and postmodernism.[126] Thus, SR represents a middle way between the particularism of modernism and the relativism of postmodernism. It is an attempt to make use of modernist intelligence to redeem intelligence with a compassionate postmodernism.[127] Above all, it prioritizes Scripture as the chief reformer of theological intelligence so that "our reading redeems the failings of modernity." Redeeming, and not replacing, modernity, this reading of Scripture will become a reasoning, just as modernity is a reasoning, but it will be a transformed reasoning.[128] Furthermore, this reading is done in society/community and thus breaks with the "charm" of Enlightenment modernism, namely primacy of the individual.

Consensus Faith

SR is not an attempt to arrive at a consensus faith.[129] Neither ecumenical nor interfaith groups are about establishing agreement between partners.[130] Bailey captures this when he states,

> The assumption behind each study is not that some underlying consensus exists beneath or behind the faiths represented—some kind of broad, "fourth way" that transcends the particularities of each faith with a kind of lowest-common denominator, all-roads-lead-to-the-same-place-consensus. The prevailing assumption is that each faith must go deeper into its own tradition, and not ignore the deep differences that exist—while, at the *same* time, believing that one must engage in

125. Green, "Rules of Scriptural Reasoning," n.p.

126. Kepnes, "A Handbook," in Ford and Pecknold, eds., *Promise of Scriptural Reasoning,* 37. Kepnes' resistance to identifying SR with traditional conservatism is on account of the latter's historic tendency to exploit theology for reasons of dominance and triumphalism.

127. Ochs, "Society of Scriptural Reasoning," n.p.

128. Ibid.

129. "A common pronouncement that means nothing because its words can be interpreted as meaning anything, should not be the goal of ecumenical dialogue" (Robbins, *Methods In The Madness,* 249).

130. Barnes, *Theology,* 226. Barnes is concerned to develop a theology *of* dialogue (as against a theology *for* dialogue). In this he overlaps with much of SR.

increasing depth with those of other faiths. These commitments are mutually not exclusive.[131]

Thus, resolution of differences is not important, understanding is. High quality argument is preferred to tolerance, and there is no need for apology for arguing from a particular place. Rather than avoiding points of textual, hermeneutical, theological, and philosophical confrontation, SR seeks a scriptural path directly to those points in dialogue with Scripture, and one often comes away more deeply conscious of the degree of difference than agreement. SR has been described as both midrashic and radically democratic, implying disagreement and argument can in fact be productive.[132]

What is SR?

SR is a particular interfaith engagement, which may also be applied to intrafaith deliberation. All the societies in SR are traditions/communities of redemptive inquiry, united in their realization that their modernist reasonings have failed (for Ochs, these are called B-reasonings). These conclusions about failed reasonings have been guided by a further set of reasonings, often unconsciously (A-reasonings). This process brings about a form of abductive reasoning (in addition to deductive and inductive). Abductive reasoning brings to consciousness the A-reasonings (which have been born in a crisis). Ochs explains:

> According to the theory of abduction, the very experience of the crisis that has brought us together will stimulate in us the capacity to bring to consciousness the rules of A-reasonings, in this case the logic of scripture that will enable us to make concrete hypotheses about how to repair the modern world that we all co-habit, animated as it is by all the failed B-reasonings of modernity.[133]

Thus, Scripture is brought back into the main frame of pragmatic reasoning for addressing a crisis.[134] Kepnes provides his definition of

131. Bailey, "Engaged Particularity," n.p. See also Hardy, "Rules of Scriptural Reasoning."

132. Bailey, "Engaged Particularity," n.p.

133. Ochs, "Society of Scriptural Reasoning," n.p.

134. Though I have not found any particular reference to Ricoeur in SR, these SR processes resonate with the Ricoeurian mimetic stages enunciated in chapter 3 above and followed throughout my dissertation. Mimesis$_1$ = B reasonings; Mimesis$_2$ = A Reasonings; Mimesis$_3$ = SR.

SR, focusing on contexts of suffering. He says, "SR is a practice of group reading of the scriptures of Judaism, Christianity, and Islam that builds sociality among its practitioners and releases sources of reason, compassion, and the divine spirit for healing our separate communities and for repair of the world."[135]

There are a number of important "rules" to SR, ensuring it works productively. These are:

TEXT BASED—SR is scripture-text based, not philosophical or cultural, though traditions and philosophical influences upon a faith text's interpretation will figure in the discussion.[136] Indeed, it is recognized that participants will bring their "internal libraries" with them that will include all they have learned through tradition (by study, prayer, and worship) but also through academic disciplines, culture, and contexts of art, politics, and economics.[137] Scripture is also taken very seriously because it is the language, or grammar, by which each faith tradition is known in-depth by thinking its language and immersing oneself in its tradition.[138] It is a basic assumption that each text is "taken as true" but without attempting to prove it. The sacredness of the other's scriptures is granted, without having to acknowledge their authority for oneself; each is assumed to be interpreting the text before God and for God's sake.[139] There is no patronizing of the others' texts.[140] Members can thereby learn from each other's chains of reasoning to discover both areas of convergence and divergence. Texts are studied seriously and assiduously, with the emphasis upon Scripture interpreting Scripture, primarily in the plain

135. Kepnes, "A Handbook," in Ford and Pecknold, eds., *Promise of Scriptural Reasoning*, 23.

136. In this emphasis SR has a direct fit with my mimetic canonical linguistic methodology.

137. Ford, "An Interfaith Wisdom," in Ford and Pecknold, eds., *Promise of Scriptural Reasoning*, 4–5.

138. Adams, "Making Deep Reasonings," 396. Yet, for the Christian the Bible/canon is not just a grammar, but the revealed Spirited theodrama itself (see chapter 3).

139. Ford, *Christian Wisdom*, 280. When the SR model is expanded to include non-textual faiths, or no-faith groups, then Ford suggests these must come under terms of "understanding and respect for how the others take their scriptures, willingness to be as vulnerable as the others in exposing their basic convictions to argument, and unwillingness to claim either an overview or a neutral vantage point" (*Christian Wisdom*, 280). See also Adams, "Making Deep Reasonings Public," in Ford and Pecknold, eds., *Promise of Scriptural Reasoning*, 44–46.

140. Hardy, "Rules of Scriptural Reasoning," n.p.

text sense.[141] A careful selection of texts is agreed upon by the SR group, which usually centers on a given topic/theme relevant to a crisis in view. Each faith representative explains their own faith text first, using its own rules of interpretation, and also revealing where intrafaith interpretations differ. Then, that text is open for interrogation and interpretation by the others in the group, attempting to understand what the passage is saying, and how it should be applied in today's context, to particular situations, at particular times, and in particular ways, past and present. The same process is followed with the other faiths, and the meanings are brought into (often lengthy and arduous) dialogue with each other—all this during both small group and plenary sessions.[142] This is in the belief that SR can enhance understanding of one's own faith in conversation with other religions.

SERIOUSLY ORTHODOX—SR takes orthodoxy seriously; it is not belittled, as was the case under modernism, but is the basis for a mutual understanding that "does not require participants to sacrifice the strong claims of their faith as the price of dialogue with others."[143]

DEEP REASONING—SR stresses depth, so the process of textual study is demanding and will not permit superficiality. Some of Ford's "maxims" for the wisdom of SR give indication of this feature. He suggests: time be allowed to read and reread; that one sticks with the text(s) and does not rush to premature conclusions; that participants draw upon shared academic resources, because members of different faiths may share training in a specific skills area. Also, participants must not fear argument conducted in courtesy and truth.[144] In fact, an assumption by the participants is that each faith must go deeper into its own tradition, not ignoring differences that exist, but engaging in ever greater depth with other faiths. Because of the emphasis upon depth, SR may not be the

141. For instance, see Elkins' rules for reading Scripture: 1. As a matter of practice, read scripture. 2. Read the text intertextually. 3. Read scripture in order to interpret scripture. 4. Read the text in order to redeem the signs of the times. 5. Read the text in order to interpret the signs of the times. 6. Read the text in order to bring people into community and communion (Elkins, "Rules of Scriptural Reasoning").

142. Bailey comments, "Often this requires slow, patient work, especially to unpack the underlying logic to the way a faith has historically interpreted a passage" ("Engaged Particularity," n.p.).

143. Green, "Rules of Scriptural Reasoning," n.p.

144. Ford, *Christian Wisdom*, 280.

most suitable forum for making deep reasonings public, but it may precede such publicity.[145]

Open-Endedness and Provisionality—SR operates with open-endedness and provisionality. As a practice, not a theory, SR thrives on "luck" more than careful planning and control. Thus, dialogues follow the leading of textual study in an endless flow of surprises made possible "by what ever makes such surprises possible (Texts? Persons? Relations? God?)."[146] There is an understanding that respects everyone's contribution is capable of change as time and discussion goes on. This provisionality is reflected in the meeting space, known as a "tent of meeting," where members of the faiths come to meet before returning to their own houses of faith (synagogues, churches, mosques).

Realistic—SR operates in the world as broken, corrupt, suffering, and sick, with a view to healing. It is thoroughly realistic, taking this from the texts in their exposition of the human state. Therefore, "SR is about faith, providence, hope, creation, judgment, mercy, salvation and redemption," in respect to God and suffering and the pursuit of healing.[147]

Community—SR operates in community/small groups (chevruta) and is never a process that can be engaged in personally and privately. The ambience is one of community and collegiality. SR requires the mutual aid of member communities. Faith communities are brought together, usually by invitation from one faith group, in groups of six to nine members per small group, but with time for plenary sessions where contributions from the small groups are shared and discussed together. To ensure mutual, and not neutral, space, the venue varies but is a space where all

---

145. Often public figures transmit their announcements through the media, who, in turn, operate by strict time scales, which SR cannot fit into, because SR cannot be rushed. Adams comments: "The problems bequeathed by rationalist philosophy are severe: it is still common for public figures to appeal to a basic identity that underlies the differences between religious traditions, and it is equally common for those public figures to attempt to describe that basic identity with the result that dissenting voices are viewed as an obstacle to peace, rather than as disconfirmation of the identity thesis" ("Making Deep Reasonings," 57).

146. Adams, "Making Deep Reasonings," 48.

147. Kepnes, "A Handbook," in Ford and Pecknold, eds., *Promise of Scriptural Reasoning,* 30. See also Ford's definition of SR on page 303 in his *Christian Wisdom.* The form of healing is the contribution SR can make to *transformation* under suffering, not suffering's elimination.

participants feel hospitable toward each other and not dominated or suspicious and is therefore often outside of the houses of the faiths.[148]

FRIENDSHIPS—More central to the aim of SR than the study of the texts is the forming of friendships. Though there are evident difficulties in bringing together participants who hold to their particular faith beliefs so seriously, SR requires friendship to be essential. Each faith group is both host and guest of the others in this context of mutual hospitality. Therefore, ethical respect for the other's integrity is key. Since SR provides for disagreements (both of an inter- and intrafaith kind) to be aired honestly and fully, the atmosphere can get "sharp." This is only possible in a context that places greater emphasis upon creating friendships than consensus. It also requires the kind of trust and group confidentiality that SR provides. As Adams states, "In a context which aims at consensus, disagreement is a problem to be overcome. In a context which values friendship, disagreement is a gift to be treasured."[149] This can only be achieved, however, when, no matter how strongly participants hold to their particular convictions, "each must *behave in the public arena as if* its truth was as tentative as an esthetic [*sic*] opinion or a scientific theory."[150]

DIALOGICAL—Because SR operates dialogically, not kerygmatically, the purpose of SR is not evangelistic. It is more a way of relating together in an often hostile, divided world and of forming friendships amid diversity upon principles of common grace.[151] It is a forum for serious intertextual and intratextual dialogue in the pursuit of spiritual wisdom for living in a multifaith world that is not assuming the public dominance of any faith. It addresses the dilemma facing pastoral carers in major incident response systems today, namely, "How to remain faithfully rooted in my own Christian vision of a time-honoured truth and yet become open to and respectful of those committed to sometimes very different beliefs

148. For a more detailed summary of how SR works, see Kepnes, "A Handbook," in Ford and Pecknold, eds., *Promise of Scriptural Reasoning*, 37–39. For a brief guide to operating a SR group, see Taylor, "Organising a Scriptural Reasoning Group."

149. Adams, "Making Deep Reasonings," in Ford and Pecknold, eds., *Promise of Scriptural Reasoning*, 54.

150. J. M. Cuddihy, *The Ordeal of Civility: Freud, Marx, Levi-Strauss, and the Jewish Struggle with Modernity*, in Mouw and Griffioen, *Pluralisms and Horizons*, 6.

151. Mouw, *Uncommon Decency*, 104, where he warns, "We mustn't set these relationships up in such a way that our efforts will be a failure if the relationships don't develop into evangelistic opportunities."

and values."[152] It is concerned with ethical cohabitation and friendship in the twenty-first century. It, therefore, assumes a principled pluralism. It also assumes that knowledge, contributively to helpful interpretations of Scripture, is not confined to the particular faith, but that "new insights can often be brought by a member of a different faith to the scripture being studied."[153] Additionally, as cultural and academic backgrounds do not follow religious affiliation necessarily, this means a Christian in the West may find closer affinity with a Muslim in the West than a Christian in the South. Barnes' concept of listening out for "seeds of the Word" is salient at this point, when he states, "the Church finds itself called not just to speak of what it knows in faith to be true, but it exercises a responsible discernment of the traces of God—seeds of the Word—in its own forgotten or occluded experience of the other," and thus, "what I [as a Christian] say of *Christ* questions the other, but I must also allow that what the other says may well be spoken about Christ, questioning me."[154] It is important to realize that SR resists forming static doctrinal propositions on the basis that the Scriptures resist total interpretation and the imposition of a "religion" as a totalizing logic (itself a secular construct).

Iɴᴛʀᴀғᴀɪᴛʜ Rᴇʟᴀᴛɪᴏɴs—SR can operate in intrafaith relations, which means that it can serve the interests of ecumenical relations within major incident response as well as interfaith relations.[155] Intrafaith problems can be as divisive as interfaith ones. SR provides a facility for profound dialogue and disagreement but also for cohabitation within the traumatic demands of a major incident response community. In fact, it is important within an interfaith SR context that such intrafaith differences are brought out, thus showing how a faith learns from making public its own internal disagreements that have shaped its tradition.

Critical Evaluation

Some critical evaluation of combining PP with SR as a model for ecumenical and interfaith relations is salient at this point. It is important

---

152. Barnes, *Theology*, 3.

153. Bailey, "Engaged Particularity," n.p.

154. Barnes, *Theology*, 182, 242.

155. An example of this could be the practice of the Evangelical organization in Northern Ireland, ECONI, in regard to relations between Evangelicals and Roman Catholics. ECONI's inclusivist identity is deemed as being a deliberately "porous" one (see Mitchell, *Evangelicalism and National Identity*, 287–8).

to repeat that my focus is upon the relational aspect, not the theologies or salvific values of respective faiths. I am cautious about cooperation between faith representatives at major incidents that requires responders "dumbing down" theological particulars in the interests of projecting a generic spirituality in the course of their work. My concern is to find a model that will sustain preserving faith particulars, with their corresponding particular methods of pastoral practice, but which will encourage *conscientious* friendship, respect, and practical cooperation in a collaborative response to major incidents.[156]

DIFFERENCES?—There are distinctive differences between PP and SR. SR is a practice more than a theory. PP is a socio-theological theory that has had practical expression mainly in the U.S. context.[157] The combination of PP and SR in the UK context would be novel and something that could be developed within the local micro-discourses of emergency planning and major incident preparedness.[158] Since PP is more of a "fit" for evangelical theology than SR is at the moment, it may be possible for Christian participants, in particular, to adopt PP as a working political philosophy for adapting the practice of SR. This has the potential for creating supportive friendships so critical in trauma response, but would not exclude Evangelical participation. It could also provide good mutual understanding between participating faiths in the planned major incident response. Most crucially, this model could facilitate key faith players having in-depth dialogue over significant issues such as evil and suffering, trauma, reconciliation, and justice. Additionally, it would be interesting to see if this model could practically incorporate secularist participants (e.g., from the NHS, social services, or emergency planning). Gaining understanding of each other's views on, and practical responses

---

156. My emphasis is deliberate in view of the premium Evangelicals place upon their appeal to the good conscience when it comes to ecumenical and interfaith relating. It is important for Christian responders to be able to relate to others by way of emotional and cognitive ease so that they can focus upon the traumas in hand.

157. In "Making the World Safe for Diversity," Os Guinness reflects exclusively upon the American context (choosing the term "chartered pluralism"). The Williamsburg Charter sets out a formal agreement for PP and reflects it as the peculiar genius of the historic U.S. contribution to the democratic world.

158. Bailey is currently exploring combining SR and radical democracy as a political methodology and, again, finding it must begin in small ways ("Engaged Particularity").

to, such issues, could benefit ecumenical and interfaith friendship and contribute significantly to an integrated emergency response.

Eғғᴇᴄᴛɪᴠᴇɴᴇss?—SR has been criticized—most notably in a clash between professors Ellis and Ford at the Christian "Greenbelt" event in 2007—for being ineffective. Ellis criticized SR for avoiding the Holocaust and Israeli-Palestinian land issues. In fact, Ellis concludes SR "should be called Avoidance Reasoning!" Ford's defense is that SR, in his experience, has addressed critical and practical points of difference, and experience of SR would bear this out.[159] Perhaps SR has to start somewhere less controversial to begin dialogue. Since contemporary major incidents may well be connected to religious violence, it is important that SR initiatives do grapple with the inflammatory issues if it is to be of practical value.[160] But, arguably, commencing good relations is not conducted effectively long-term by jumping in at the deep end. The critical point for SR is how long it will take to get to the inflammatory issues, for until it engages with such, it stands to be not only ineffective but possibly unethical. It is difficult to see why SR cannot move toward taking issues like the *Shoah*, Israel, and the Palestinians, more seriously in view of the ethical impact this event has had upon theology and interfaith relations.[161] Indeed, issues of ethical relationality between Christians and Jews demand this.[162] Lewis and Reid argue that SR is at too early a stage in its development to be applied directly to major incident planning programs, and for a number of reasons: first, because its current stage involves mainly academics, and these are at least one step removed from the "hands-on" level of localized pastoral carers.[163] Thus, SR still needs to percolate down through

159. Prof. Marc Ellis, is director of the Center for Jewish Studies, Baylor University. Prof. David F. Ford is Regius Professor of Divinity, Cambridge University. I am grateful to Ellis and Ford for confirming these details to me by email (September 30 and October 29, 2008 respectively; also between Simeon Zahl, research assistant, Faculty of Divinity, University of Cambridge, on October 24, 2008).

160. There is a case for believing the Israeli-Palestinian conflict had more than a passing impact with causing the Lockerbie, 9/11, and 7/7 murders. Lewis feels Ford is vulnerable as long as his practice of SR remains aloof from the practitioners on the ground.

161. For a discussion on the impact of the *Shoah* on interfaith relations (particularly between Jews and Christians) see Barnes, *Theology*, 50–54. He argues that all Christian theology needs to be pursued from within a Jewish matrix. Christian theological concepts are rooted in an "other" (Judaism), therefore.

162. A point I interpret Ellis as making about his clash with Ford (see above).

163. In fact, Lewis thinks that because SR tends to come out of a U.S. Jewish-Christian context, he is not sure that many Muslim scholars would accept its

the different social levels. Lewis doubts that SR has to be practiced only by academics, but there are particular difficulties, for instance in the way Muslims view their sacred scriptures and traditions with an exclusivity that does not permit valid contribution from non-Islamic sources.[164] There is considerable difference between the capabilities of Islamic scholars and local community imams. However, Lewis recognizes that there is a certain synergism between PP and SR that has promise for future development.[165]

"ABRAHAMIC" CONTRASTS?—Knight has suggested scriptural reasoning has made a mistake in contrasting the three scriptures of the "Abrahamic" faiths, and making them the focus of attention in isolation from secularism (a necessary fourth scripture, suggests Knight). The current status concedes to the secular accusation that these three religions are "intrinsically violent."[166] Also, Fackre questions those who "hold that God gives equal linguistic time to these three Near Eastern faiths," because in so doing they "demean the other religions they are seeking to honour."[167] SR can assume too great a theological similarity between Christianity and Judaism and Islam than Scripture would justify. Additionally, it might seem to contradict the theology of citizenship PP gives us, and by which we relate to each other—as religious or secular—as particular civic entities.[168] As indicated above, the "Abrahamic" dimension has simply provided SR with a convenient starting point. However, SR, practiced in isolation from PP, could be accused of failure to engage effectively with society and continue the divide between the secular and religious.

---

assumptions at the moment (email conversation between Dr. Philip Lewis, principal of the Bradford Churches for Dialogue and Diversity, and author, October 2008).

164. As with Christians, so with Muslims, Buddhists, Jews, and Hindus, etc., there will be different estimations of the relative authority of sacred texts and of their interpretation.

165. From discussion with Dr. Helen Reid, and Dr. Philip Lewis at the Thornbury Centre, Bradford Churches for Dialogue and Diversity in October 2008. Reid informed me that there is a small initiative for exploring with SR starting in Bradford, but it would be some way from being able to focus on major incident issues as yet.

166. Knight, "Christ, Religion," n.p.

167. Fackre, "Claiming Jesus," 1.

168. Knight, "Christ, Religion."

Suffering Repaired?—SR responds to suffering with a belief it can be repaired and audits its effectiveness by these ends.[169] This may be an unwarranted, idealistic aim for SR compared to Swinton's missiological perspective where Christian pastoral care focuses more on accepting, coping, and being transformed by suffering than with its eradication.[170] Also, Taylor cautions,

> In my experience, for Scriptural Reasoning to "work" you need to establish a robust container for the practice: you need to have a clear idea of the host institution and a clarity of agreed purpose between the Christians, Muslims and Jews taking part. The reason for this is that the practice can generate its own instabilities (and paranoias) and these need somehow to be held. Because of this I am not sure that it is a useful practice when trying to deal with trauma head on, or if you want to use it to "fix" a particular problem. It works at a much deeper and slower level. Having said that, I believe it can be transformative and can bring about deep repair over time.[171]

If the balance of scriptural emphasis is on transformation then a selecting of texts reflecting such could prove more realistic to SR's claim to be rooted in situations of suffering.

Inclusivist and Universalist?—SR is open to the criticism, from an Evangelical perspective at least, of being ultimately salvifically inclusivist and universalist. This potential is inherent within the postliberal methodology, where each particular tradition is truth in its own right and hermeneutical openness permits a multitude of meanings. Certainly Kepnes' concept sees the "tents of meeting" for SR as presaging the end time, and thus causing a "re-imagining of a new type of end-time in which universal peace is won through preserving the particularity of the other instead of obliterating it." For that reason, he avers, SR challenges some of the "exclusivist and triumphalist aspects of the traditional eschatologies of Judaism, Christianity, and Islam in which one religion triumphs over

---

169. Peter Ochs, "Philosophical Warrants for Scriptural Reasoning," in Ford and Pecknold, eds., *Promise of Scriptural Reasoning*, 128–9, 131–5.

170. See chapter 9 above, p. 299–308.

171. From email communication between William Taylor and author, October 2, 2008. Taylor is research fellow at the St Ethelburga's Centre for Reconciliation and Peace, London. Their website is: http://www.stethelburgas.org/index.htm.

the other two."[172] McFadyen's eschatological concept of truth is more nuanced. He is clear that Christianity is true. However, though its truth is universal, it requires faith and hope for the present. Christianity's monotheism signals the unity of truth, "even if that unity is an eschatological reality which allows pluralism the last word now, that turns out after all to be only the next-to-last word."[173] For McFadyen the kingdom of God is plurality concomitant with particularity, and redemption is both the transformation of every public world as well as a validation of the same.[174] Barnes acknowledges the great seductive "risk" of eschatological hope being "reduced to a prosaic and predictable expectation that 'all will be well.'"[175] From an evangelical perspective this overstates the postmodern dimension by espousing the overarching universal it avows to reject—namely, that it is not possible for any particular to form an authoritative judgment upon truth and falsehood in an other, or to conclude all religions will lead to eternal peace. At this point SR forsakes its emphasis upon being a practice more than a theory, and veers into ideology. There seems little purpose, therefore, in the deep reasoning SR prescribes other than to gain greater understanding of the others and of one's own faith. For what purpose, however, is the forceful arguing to be about, and practicing the overt evangelistic mandate Christian particularity commands, if, in the end time, Jews, Christians, and Muslims are all going to sit together in peace? Knight reminds us that Christians and Muslims "speak to one another as Christians and Muslims in the proper hope of converting one another: truth may not be left to one side for pragmatic

---

172. Kepnes, "A Handbook," in Ford and Pecknold, eds., *Promise of Scriptural Reasoning*, 37.

173. McFadyen, "Truth as Mission," 442.

174. Ibid., 437–56.

175. Barnes, *Theology*, 184–85. Barnes does not use the term SR; however, his focus upon a theology of religions is also formative of a theology *of* dialogue, not *for* dialogue. However, in most other respects he seems to be talking about what SR talks about.

purposes."[176] Nazir-Ali adds that it is a good thing for Christian-Muslim relations in the long run if they both confess their missionary nature.[177]

These criticisms of SR are not inconsequential. They seem to possess some validity for the form of SR practiced at the moment. However, SR is a very elastic embryo, and I need to explore whether there are sufficient points of convergence with PP, and with my exploratory theology so far, to consider if it can be adapted to an evangelical practical theology of ecumenical and interfaith friendship.

Compatibility

From my presentation of both principled pluralism and scriptural reasoning, certain clear similarities and overlaps emerge which could indicate possible compatibility for a suitable model. I identify these and how they sit with the practical theology I have enunciated so far.

SACRED-SECULAR/PRIVATE-PUBLIC—Both reject the sacred-secular and the private-public divides. My theological exploration has demonstrated a similar rejection while retaining the significance of the individual and of the legitimacy of the secular as socio-theological concepts. I have rejected secular paternalism and dominance. My anthropology esteems human beings as spiritual by virtue of the *imago Dei* prior to any other moral or religious considerations. Thus, his/her religion/spirituality is a part of his/her humanity. Therefore, when we meet a person of another religion we meet someone who is in relation to God through shared humanity and common grace, and someone who is ontologically spiritual/religious. From a Trinitarian perspective, they are also in community not just individuals.

REALITY—Both accept the reality of pluralism in a fallen and corrupt world. My explorations in a theology of evil and suffering accepted the theodramatic narrative of a universal fall of creation, from which the fact of pluralism stems, as does the necessity of confessing that any grasp of

---

176. Knight, "Christ, Religion," n.p. Fackre, on the other hand, argues for a possible salvific inclusion of the Jews, when he wonders, "Might it be that these heirs of Abraham, the 'father' of saving faith, will learn on that final Day that the identity of the agent of their Abrahamic faith is the Person of Jesus Christ? Not unlike what faithful Jews contend when they hold that Christians saved by their Noachic faith will learn of its source in the God of Abraham, Isaac, and Jacob" ("Claiming Jesus," 16).

177. Nazir-Ali, "Global and Local," n.p.

truth by any particular other is limited and subject to error and abuse.[178] My exploration has acknowledged, as non-innocents we hurt each other and are both victims and assailants. But this confession does not damage the conviction that Christianity is committed to addressing the suffering that a fallen life incurs. It just makes it messier. My focus upon a theology of compassion confirms this as an essential commitment. My exploration of common grace also convinces me that goodness is shared by other faiths and by secularism. Therefore a theology of ecumenical and interfaith friendship must seek commitments to peace and persuasion, not violence and coercion, in the interests of addressing suffering and trauma. For Christian participants in PP and SR, this means a necessary remembering of shared contributions to suffering and violence and dominance in which all have been implicated historically. No parties in ecumenical or interfaith relations can claim a pedigree of innocence or ethical righteousness. As a result, our theological reasonings must be tempered by humility and provisionality.

SACRED TEXTS AND TRADITIONS—Both value the retention of the particulars' sacred texts and traditions. Evangelical communities claim to be Bible communities, because of their passion for reading the Scriptures, and their scriptural foundationalism. Therefore, both the "permission" to study Scripture freely afforded by PP, and the discipline of deep study provided by SR are welcome. PP and SR provide the mandate to read widely and deeply, and to do so in community. Indeed, given the concerns over current evangelical scriptural illiteracy, we should be humbled by any commitment from those of other traditions.[179]

ESCHEWING POLARIZATION—Both eschew the polarity that upholding strong truth claims leads to intolerance and that tolerance requires the abandonment of strong truth claims. We are grateful for the contributions from postmodernism and postliberal theology for the dismantling of this once dominant view concerning interfaith relations. It is not a view my own theological exploration supports, due to the influences of

---

178. Netland, *Encountering Religious Pluralism*, 328. The same principle of recognizing the presence of religions and human corruption and fallibility is acknowledged in the World Evangelical Fellowship's Manila Declaration (1992). For the text see *The Unique Christ in our Pluralistic World: WEF Manila Declaration*. Netland also points out that the relationship between Christianity and another religion is often a relationship with that other's culture.

179. Witherington, "Ignorance is Bliss?," n.p.

my exploratory anthropology and grace. However, I have felt my own conservative presuppositions to be challenged on this point by my research. It is clear from the model of PP and SR, from an evangelical perspective, that it is possible (at least theologically) to uphold strong truth claims and to be tolerant.

A Meeting Place—Both endorse the meeting place for revelation, learning, and understanding. This is a concept that fits comfortably with my theology of Christological common grace, where general revelation can be found in all creative aspects, even at their most fallen. Fackre sees this through his narrative lens, in the context of pluralism, as the "sustaining largesse of the *Logos spermatikos* with a variety of gifts to know and do things that are true, good, beautiful and holy."[180] Such common grace is founded in the Noahic covenant and finds biblical expression in the meeting between Melchizedek and Abram.[181] All such marks of common grace are mediated by the Second Person of the Trinity; so, "Wherever truth is known or life made liveable, the hidden Christ is present."[182] There is now a "Noahic arc" over the entire world, of universal common grace, non-salvific but nonetheless inclusive of world religions as instruments of God's preserving purposes.[183] This gives credence to Barnes' concept of "seeds of the Word" that are to be looked for in other faiths.[184] It frees Christian responders to engage with religious others for more than just social or educational aims, but for general revelatory aims that may also be didactic, due to the similarities between aspects of Christianity and other religions.[185]

In this learning process it is important that Christians can live with both the passivity and activity necessary for PP and SR. Christians need to act as "guests" who are there to learn from the host(s), but also to be

180. Fackre, "Claiming Jesus," 8.

181. See Gen 9:1–7 and Gen 14:18–20 respectively.

182. Fackre, "Claiming Jesus," 10.

183. Ibid., 14. Also, McDermott, *Can Evangelicals Learn?*, 207. See also Jones' argument against those of Clark Pinnock, concerning Noahic covenant, and his rejection of the idea of "pagan saints," as construed by Pinnock's inclusivism (Jones, *Only One Way?*, 63–67).

184. Barnes, *Theology*, 203–4.

185. Netland, *Encountering Religious Pluralism*, 326.

contributors to the dialogue and learning process. This equates with Netland's concept of "theological modesty."[186]

MUTUAL HOSPITALITY—Both endorse the meeting place as a place for mutual hospitality. Welcoming the "stranger" and offering hospitality are central to the evangelical gospel life, and to the texts we inhabit.[187] God's people, from a Christian perspective, have a history rooted in their experience of strangerhood, but also of friendship.[188] Evangelical friendship is a "glue" for social cohesion, though all too often poorly practiced. It is inspired by grace and compassion.[189] Furthermore, the paradigm revealed in evangelical Trinitarian Christology leaves friendship as nonnegotiable, where Christ is "the friend of sinners," and who engages with the hospitality of religious others.[190] He could be friendly, hospitable, yet deeply embedded in his own convictions. Thus, my exploratory theology fully endorses hospitality with those of other faiths, and none, in the practice of endorsing friendship and understanding for the purposes of social cohesion in a world that Christians never regard as their true home anyway.

THE RIGHT TO DISAGREE—PP and SR endorse the right to disagree as well as the right to argue one's convictions. The issue with SR is, in friendship, to identify and confront the areas of disagreement that reality discloses are present between the faiths and ideologies. However, both PP and SR reject the continuation of dogmatic theological/ideological isolation, and consequent "stand-offs" as a way of resolving differences, but

---

186. Ibid., 314.

187. See Deut 10:18.

188. See Deut 10:19; Matt 25:35–36; Eph 2:19. This was the dual experience of Israel when he and his family first came into Egypt—as strangers, but friends (Gen 47). Swinton captures the characteristics of the stranger when he defines as: "Basically, a stranger is someone we do not know. She is an outsider who does not (or at least is not perceived to) share our environment, values, and assumptions about the world. The stranger is one who is perceived as significantly other than us. Strangers induce fear and uncertainty precisely because they emerge from environments and hold value systems that are, or are at least perceived to be, quite different from our own. Their presence challenges the boundaries of our safety zones. Strangers intrude on our security and raise issues that we may not want to address" (*Raging with Compassion*, 227).

189. That is: God's continuing "friendship" to those who reject his friendship; Luke 15—the continuous attitude and action of the "father" looking out for the "prodigal." See also Swinton's focus upon friendship in chapter 8, above, pp. 222–24.

190. See Matt 11:19; Luke 7:36–47; 10:28–37 respectively.

call for dialogue and respect. This represents a very welcome break from previous models of ecumenical and interfaith engagement, where issues of moral and theological disagreement are circumvented under the guise of respect. PP and SR can bring back honesty and integrity into social cohesion and reject avoidance and illusory compromises. It also breaks from the conservative tradition of isolation.

Conclusion

From this exploration I conclude that while there are difficulties with SR, and the criticisms hold some validity, yet the sheer elasticity of SR can permit adaptation. Without losing the core principles it is possible to respond to the criticisms with changes of the style and application that still leave the basic methodology intact. In this case the combination of PP and SR could have a key role in a practical theology of ecumenical relations, because here there is a greater degree of intrafaith openness and capability. However, certainly in the UK context, SR may be still too embryonic for facilitating interfaith relations in regard to major incident planning and response. It holds out hope for the longer term, but for the immediate future something is needed that fits with PP, which can create a foreground out of which SR can evolve. Such a model has been experimented with in the form of civic networking.

Civic Networking (CN)

Civic networking is a concept that has been pioneered in the UK, under Dr. Philip Lewis, in the metropolitan city of Bradford, between Christians and Muslims. Lewis offers Bradford City as a case study that argues the need for religion being a necessary focus for secular local authorities where religion is a part of the problem in social unrest/violence.[191] CN demonstrates how religious actors, embedded in the communities, can work with secular agencies to influence social cohesion in volatile/distressing situations of an interethnic nature.

In 2001 (before 9/11) a group of Christians and Muslims was convened—with Christian and Muslim representatives from European cities with large Muslim sectors—to share and discuss "convergences and divergences with regard to attitudes to politics, urban regeneration, local schooling, business and community building in the voluntary sector" and to encourage religious literacy among local policy makers. From this developed an Inter-Cultural Leadership School (ICLS), which runs a four

191. Lewis, "For the Peace of the City."

day course. This course aims to "begin a process of building a network of trust in Bradford and contribute to developing a new leadership at ease with religious and cultural diversity who can move across the major ethnic/religious divide in the city."[192] The model has been exported to other cities, such as Leicester.

One of the key problems CN has confronted is finding those in civic life who are capable of and willing to engage in this kind of social cohesion work in a seriously intellectual and practical way. However, in Bradford, they have seen the influence of respected faith scholars, through some of their postgraduate students, having significant percolating effect to religious and community leaders, making intelligent networking between faiths and secular agencies feasible. It has had some success in countering militant extremism, in particular, and in the areas of civil and family conflict resolution.

CN could find that PP provides a beneficial political and social framework.[193] It could also be helpful in creating the mutual social trust, at the interagency and community leader levels, which would create a social and intellectual foreground from which SR could evolve, and deepen the network of relations it requires to be in place before SR can operate outside of academia more meaningfully. In particular, since CN has had positive results in Bradford, in regard to situations where religion has been part of the problem, it would be worth exploring if it can also work beneficially in major incidents where spiritual and religious issues again are part of the problem, as explicated in my exploration of trauma, and where they are significant contributors to the solution. Thus, CN could provide a practical model for local interfaith forums in addressing the impacts of major incidents upon religiously and ethnically diverse communities.

Operational Forums

Given these three tools (PP, SR, CN), I would envisage them working in the interests of major incident response in the following forums:

- Formation of a proposal, consisting of a theoretical model (with the linkage of PP to SR via CN), for consideration by the UK government department responsible for emergency planning at the time.

---

192. Ibid., n.p.

193. It would challenge the negatives impacts of "turf wars" that bedevil major incident response so often (see chapter 1).

- Trialing of a CN model, adapted specifically to accommodate the needs of emergency planning and response, among a selection of local authorities and local and interfaith forums.[194]

- It would facilitate the inclusion of key category 1 and 2 responders, in the form of faith scholars, faith leaders, social service providers, police, health services, and local authorities, relating to one another positively.

- Exploring the use of my model in the field of mediation and conflict resolution in the aftermath of major incidents where religious factors have been significant.

- Encouraging the practice of SR at local intrafaith level among Christian leaders, or at least encouraging the practice of SR within theological and ministerial training institutions, to provide a pastoral responder base that is familiar with PP, SR, and CN.

- Stipulation that the ground rule for the functioning of CN or SR should be PP and the civic square.

- Careful monitoring of this policy would be important to ensure there is no weakening in resolve regarding PP.

I offer the model I explore in this chapter as a modest contribution to pastoral training institutions, as a model worthy of research piloting in their respective contexts.

This completes my configurative process, in which I have explored the doctrines of evil and suffering, trauma, and grace as configuratively legitimating major incident response from the evangelical catholic Christian community. I have then explored the doctrines of grace, compassion, reconciliation and justice, and ecumenical and interfaith friendship as significant configurations to a practical theology of response.

The final, conclusive, task is to evaluate if such a configuration offers potential for an improved response in the future. For this I subjected my prefigured narrative to mimesis$_3$.

---

194. I recognize there are funding issues involved here. However, given national government guidelines for involving the faith communities in emergency planning and the potential benefits for social cohesion arising from my model, this could be argued as money worth spending. Also there could be financial inputs from participating bodies and proposals for funding submitted to funding sources.

PART 3

Mimesis$_3$—Refiguration

THE CONCLUDING PART OF the methodological Ricoeurian mimetic process I am utilizing in my research project—mimesis$_3$—is designed to engage my configurative theological exploration with the realities of contemporary major incident response for the evangelical catholic Christian community. This is the stage where the theodrama meets the real world. At this point, to avoid the ills of both positivism and structuralism, as well as illusion, it is important that the reader must adhere to the language of praxis.[1] The theodrama must work. Thus, I conclude my book by having in mind my prefigured narrative, duly configured by my exploratory theology, along with that theology's applicability and serviceability in conjunction with the legislation and accompanied guidance in the secular culture of major incident planning. I also reflect from a practical theological perspective to evaluate, as a narrative reader, if this methodology proffers a theology of praxis for evangelical Christian responders to future major incidents. Given that my role, as dramaturge, "is to study the playscript and prepare it for performances that truthfully realize its truth,"[2] then, in particular, I revisit my prefigured narrative to assess if the work of configuration addresses the *aporias* identified, and whether it offers, in Vanhoozerian terms, a configured choreography to contemporary evangelical players in the theodrama of future major in-

1. Fodor, *Christian Hermeneutics*, 194–95.
2. Vanhoozer, *Drama of Doctrine*, 247.

cident response. Does it enable the theology to live and, in due time, to provide a greater level of coherence?[3]

The ideally decisive readership in this mimetic process should be objective readers.[4] However, I locate myself as a reader in view of the articulated subjectivity inherent in my research. I, therefore, seek as objectively as a subject can, to read my own narrative in the light of my configured theology to conclude if there is theological legitimation and contribution that challenges, and also helps, the evangelical catholic Christian community to provide a response of virtue and practical integrity in future major incidents. I present the refigurative process in the form of conclusions from my research; these should be read as forming the potentiality for a construction of a refigured narrative of major incident response for the evangelical catholic Christian community.

---

3. Fodor, *Christian Hermeneutics*, 260–61. Harak is right to remind us (in regard to passions, at least) that refiguration requires time to be effective (*Virtuous Passions*, 17).

4. That is, those who examine this project, and any future reader-responders.

11

Refigurative Conclusions

MY OVERALL PURPOSE FOR this research has been to explore a
practical theology of major incident response for the evangelical catholic Christian community that cultivates Christian personal and
community identity through the development of character in serving
God's redemptive transformative practices in a response of Christian
pastoral care. In order to achieve this purpose I have constructed and
implemented a practical theological methodology, combining the narrative approaches of Paul Ricoeur's threefold mimetic process with Kevin
Vanhoozer's canonical linguistic theology, in order to respond to three
research questions:

- What legitimates the Evangelical community responding to major
  incidents?

- What can a theologically informed community contribute to major
  incident response?

- What kind of Christian community is best placed to make such a
  response?

These questions are responding to the discordances and *aporias* of
my prefigured narrative, which I previously narrated and summarized.
For the refigurative process, I group these under three categories of aporias: the why, what, and can, questions.

WHY?

My prefiguration exposed a number of aporeatic *whys*, which I now subsume under three questions:

Why had this awful tragedy happened? [1] I conclude that such a question, though inevitably human, is pastorally useless, since the theodrama provides no specific answers. However, there are theological contributions that reveal the theodrama is wholly realistic in its emplotment. It does not avoid any discordant aspect even if it cannot provide all the answers. In particular, in regard to my prefigured conceptuality of evil and suffering, or at least in my capacity to view contours of evil in a major incident profoundly enough, I conclude that my conceptuality possessed a deficient perspective on the nature of, and relationship between, evil and suffering, due to a tendency to try and ontologize evil. A proper maturation of learning in regard to evil having no ontology encourages a transformed, refigured embracing of an ensuing suffering, which naturally repels. Nicholas Lash has expressed this concept of embracing suffering exquisitely: suffering teaches us our finitude before God, and maturation,

> thus construed, would be a matter of discovering that it is possible, without diminution of dignity, abdication of rationality, or loss of freedom, to yield to what we know and be commanded by it. Such discovery would, nonetheless, be both dark and painful, for its pattern was set in the garden of Gethsemane.[2]

The non-ontological nature of evil heightens this darkness and it enhances the sinful cruelty of all consequential suffering. I may never know the answer to the *why*, but, with Christ as the plot, I know the Answerer, who shines light into this darkness of evil.

Why is there the instinct to respond? I conclude that when viewed in the light of my configuration, responding to major incidents as situations of evil and suffering need not involve the kind of hesitation I exhibited, on two accounts: *First,* because common grace ensures that compassion

---

1. This question became increasingly acute as the investigation advanced. In fact, it took two further incidents, where engines of the same type failed, thankfully without further incapacitation of, or damage to, the aircraft or passengers concerned. The primary cause of the Kegworth/M1 had been due to an engine fan-blade sheer, which initially lodged in one of the engine housing's combustible linings. This gave a confused indication in the cockpit of a fire in one of the engines, which led the pilot and copilot to shut down the wrong engine. As this mistake was discovered coming into land at East Midlands Airport, the working engine, which was also now the damaged one, suffered catastrophic damage upon additional thrust, leaving the aircraft only able to glide until impact onto the motorway embankment, about 400 meters short of the runway.

2. Lash, *Beginning,* 243.

over the suffering of fellow human beings is irresistible in all and yet is heightened within the Christian community. For the special graced responder, therefore, the urge to respond is understandably so compulsive that an inclination to spontaneity is somewhat inevitable, and an absence of such compulsion is indicative of pathology. However, this compulsion must be trained wisely to ensure it does not become narcissistic or dysfunctional to a major incident response systematic call-out. *Second,* I conclude the degree of theological legitimation given to pastoral carers by my configuration means there is strong theological and pastoral foundation for my response and for the Christian community showing proactive enthusiasm for integration into the formal systems of major incident planning and response in the future, so they can already be part of the officially accredited, rehearsed, and tested response in advance of any incident happening.

Why did sudden death come as such an evil for the bereaved, irrespective of their religious beliefs? Why was death so indiscriminate and seemingly unfair? Again, there are no answers specific to any incident, but there is a helpful substrate in the doctrines of evil, the fall, and original sin, providing some pastoral coherence for these pathologies. Such substrata offer a worldview that resonates with the intensely realistic and pessimistic sequelae of the fall—such as, "natural" disasters, the negative impacts of trauma, disasters and non-innocence, and death as the last enemy—but also offering such Christocentric salvific grace and eschatological hope of reconciliation and justice. They also offer an anthropology that reveals humans as divinely created body/souls, finely "hard-wired" for relationship with God. These body/souls are also eschatologically configured.

WHAT?

I conclude the *what* questions become the more productive because my configured theology responds most at this point, and never more so than with the gospel of Christ's incarnate life, his atoning death, and his victorious resurrection providing a regenerative Spirited life that can prevent the tragic becoming evil and can furnish redemptive and transformative practices of God for his people. I subsume my *aporias* under three *what* questions:

What possible role can theology serve for Christian responders in the midst of such tragedy where the empirical reality often tests propositional theological dogmatics beyond its limits? I conclude, the perspective the theodrama gives to major incidents is: they are events revealing a profound spiritual/ religious substrate to human being, exposed by the traumatized nature, which requires a Christian theological perspicuity for comprehension and adequate pastoral care. In particular, major incidents are, theodramatically, the products of a cosmic fall and cursed sequelae, exacerbated through the subsequent sinful propensities of fallen human beings and the individual and corporate pathologies of such. I conclude that my theology provides a level of spiritual comprehension that responds to these causals of discordance from the priority of divine love that attends to the deepest needs of the traumatized being, providing a reconciliation of grace in Christ, with God, self, and others. Special grace provides, in the scriptural revelation, the narrative needed to provide, "the basis for a self appropriate to the unresolved, and often tragic, conflicts of this existence."[3] Special grace has potential for providing a population of responders who thrive on the adventure of contexts where we are being apprenticed to virtue in order to carry out whatever role our calling has appointed us.[4] The contributive value of such goods exceeds that which any professional, technical training programs can make.[5]

From biblical, historical, and systematic theological perspectives, common grace provides a more valid explanation for the self-evident phenomena of human and divine goodness than I prefigured. However, this vindicates my thesis that special grace does legitimate levels of partnership between Christian and non-Christian responding communities, but gives a unique contribution to the roles of Christian responders, not least of pastoral carers in terms of them operating under the virtues of grace, compassion, and reconciliation and justice.

In particular, the configurative discovery that compassion originates within a Trinitarian ontology of perichoretic self-dispossession, common graced to all human nature but made accessible to an enhanced degree by special grace, to and through the Christian community, offers much unique pastoral potential for major incident response. However,

---

3. See also Hauerwas, *Community of Character*, 149. Hauerwas bases this on the statement of St. Paul, in 1 Cor 15:10, "But by the grace of God I am what I am, and His grace toward me was not in vain; but I labored more abundantly than they all, yet not I, but the grace of God *which* was with me."

4. Ibid., 115.

5. Ibid., 126.

I conclude such a configuration is something that contradicts and challenges some current Evangelical cultures and their practices.

Such an overall configuration does not claim to provide a theology that gives all the answers, nor an anesthetic, for human trauma. However, it recognizes these realities as things we can fully confront and lament before God and which the immutable passions of God resonate with. As the Immanuel, he has fully indentified himself with these now in human flesh, yet without sin, thus providing himself as the unique savior.

I conclude my theology also offers a wisdom for Christian responders. Therefore, a Christian responder will have a unique Christocentric perspective upon what has happened and upon what constitutes best practice from the church community. Sapiential response, therefore, requires the virtues of humility—inclusive of personal awareness of one's own fallen and sinful propensity—and grace, to ensure avoidance of judgmentalism, and yet a realistic grasp of the seriousness of the situation, and for the application of Christ's salvific life, death, and resurrection to that plight with the compassion inherent in it. Thus, my thesis is valid—namely, in order to contribute Christianly in major incident response, I need to be a canonically configured sort of person/community, because the primary issue in major incident response is not how can I answer all the questions of incoherence and discordance, but how can I be the kind of person that is best placed to live with these issues, to operate the theological theodrama responsibly toward others.

Above all, my theology offers enormous potential for the provision of a community of virtue and character. Where most will be asking, "What is the right thing to do in this situation?" my theology seeks to address, "What kind of person do I need to be to identify, and then carry out, the right action?" I conclude that my theology has potential for maturation of the virtues of wisdom, grace, compassion, goodness, forgiveness, justice, and friendship. These should constitute the core virtues of the Christian responder/responding community and be essential aspects of the training the Christian community endorses most in her responders. However, my theology of common grace and friendship endorses levels of engagement with non-Christian agencies for aspects of major incident response they have the skills for training in. I believe it is at the community/church level that my theology provides the greatest challenge for the Evangelical community.

What can my theology serve for helping Christian responders recover from the traumas they have seen, smelled, and heard, with an enhanced sense of identity and purpose? A virtuous character is important for learning and discerning the evil pathological reality within a major incident. Holiness (not in the sense of a sanctimonious aloofness, belying personal fear of defilement by the pathology), can effect a wise grasp of the seriousness of evil within oneself, as well as its incoherent pathological impact upon human life generally, reducing a response being driven by lust for adventure or personal aggrandizement, but instead encouraging the urgency of humbly responding to an occasion where the impact of evil and suffering is so awful, while also having due recourse to self-care. I conclude my theology offers pastoral transformation through a Spirited empowerment that can ward off disabling victimhood. This will be largely supplied by the narrative we construct out of the effects events had on us at the time and the way these affect our memories of the past, which will, in turn, affect perception of our future. I conclude that my mimetic/canonical linguistic methodology holds great potential as a tool for pastoral configuration of traumatic experiences. This could be further explored in future research, in collaboration with existing fields of cognitive behavior therapy. Vanhoozer speaks in terms of canonical linguistic theology representing , "a kind of cognitive therapy that aims to replace distorted patterns of thinking with patterns that correspond to canonical practices, to the dramatic reality, and ultimately, to the mind of Christ."[6]

What can theology provide to help the evangelical catholic Christian community make more constructive progress in the areas of ecumenical and multifaith collaboration that contemporary major incident response demands? I conclude that current legislation and guidance mandates the need for ecumenical and interfaith friendship but does not require the additions of working with generic concepts of faith. It need not, therefore, exclude evangelical faith communities. However, events such as joint funerals and memorials can prove problematic as acts of worship. Though I conclude this is a vexatious area for evangelicals, it is one that requires more robust thought and a proactive approach. I conclude that my theology can provide a model for exploring ecumenical and interfaith

6. Vanhoozer, *Drama of Doctrine*, 256. In email conversation with me, Vanhoozer acknowledged, upon reflection, that mimesis could provide a tool for helping the traumatized to configure what has happened to them in a more meaningful way (September 16, 2009). Some engagement with Prof. Donald Capps' interest in the psychotherapeutic aspects of pastoral theology could also be appropriate.

friendship that is potentially groundbreaking, and which could place the evangelical catholic Christian community as a spearheading community in this significant field for further research in view of the increasing threat of civil tensions where religion could be the igniting issue for a major incident.

CAN?

Can responders from the evangelical catholic Christian community, working under my configured theology, legitimately work under current emergency planning regulations and guidance, in an inter-agency response to offer a valid pastoral care contribution? This will depend on how her role is defined. If the role is defined only in terms of a medico-therapeutic response, then I conclude the evangelical catholic Christian community should play no part, for she cannot commit, ethically, to providing a response to suffering that is primarily curative. Her theology neither calls her, nor equips her, as a trauma health care utility. I conclude that my thesis is vindicated—namely that a canonical linguistic practical theology of trauma requires the theodrama for pastoral configuration for maturation of a virtuous character, but which is not primarily concerned with therapeutic health care purposes. Similarly, if the role is defined in terms of operating with a generic concept of spirituality/religion, then my theology would balk against such. However, I conclude that my exploratory theology holds considerable potential for operating a role of specifically Christian pastoral care even within current multi-agency and multifaith remits, under a principled pluralist politic, which would also allow for the same pastoral rights being met by those of other faiths and none. If the role were defined in terms of a contribution to a holistic concept of care, then it would be valid. It is important to realize there is nothing in principle under current legislation or guidance that specifies pastoral care must be medico-therapeutic, or generic in nature, or prohibitive of the Christian particularist response my theology endorses, provided it is practiced wisely. However, local authorities and local faith leaders may prove obstructive to such evangelical participation where prior relations between evangelicals and others have not been constructive. In these cases it is down to the evangelical catholic Christian community to argue and demonstrate the case for the involvement that my research endorses. In fact, given my exploration's focus upon evil and suffering, grace, compassion, and reconciliation and justice especially, such a practical theology responds to so many of the core causals and intuitive fears and longings within the traumatized human being, irrespective of their spiritual/religious stance, indicating a Christian response as crucial. The key issue will be whether the evangelical catholic Christian community can collaboratively construct a professional, faith-community-accredited response plan that commands integrity. Certainly there is nothing in the systems of major incident planning to date to prevent this happening. However, such a task does not figure highly in the more immediate evangelistically orientated priorities of this community, and this is reflected in the absence of trauma response from the curricula of most Christian ministry training institutions. I conclude this gap in training needs to be urgently addressed, and I proffer my research as a working basis for a modular contribution to such training.[7] I conclude my configured theology can work collaboratively, offering mutual integrity, with other agencies holding to concepts of holistic care, where such collaboration offers mutual respect for parallel research methods and forms of working practice. I conclude, therefore, that the theology is evangelical and practical; what is critical, however, is how wisely and compassionately the theology is implemented by evangelical Christians. Some aspects of Evangelical theology and practice warrant being challenged in my view, in particular: ontologies of evil; strongly determinist theologies; platonic anthropologies; idealist ecclesiologies; and classically stated but underinformed and insensitively applied eschatologies. Also, the Evangelical take on ecumenical and interfaith relations needs to be far more constructive. I suggest a closer working within the discipline of practical theology in evangelical pastoral training institutions, even utilizing my own constructed method, would offer canonical grounds for safe change in such areas in the future. I believe my configurative work has had a tranformative effect upon me for any future pastoral response to a major incident. But, as an evangelical still, I conclude I can respond because I have a strong theological legitimation that "fits" with current major incident response requirements, within the parameters I have outlined.

Overall, I conclude that my research methodology has been a successful tool in demonstrating that there is a practical theology for major incident response that is both evangelical and catholic and which can service the Christian community in cultivating personal and community

---

7. Bearing in mind the realities of time constraints upon curricula formation such a module could address the pastoral care of trauma in broader terms, of which major incident response could be just one part.

identity through the development of character in serving God's redemptive, transformative practices in a response of Christian pastoral care within the current major incident planning systems. It remains to be seen if the Evangelical constituency will regard it as such, given the considerable theological and practical challenges it presents that constituency with, and the challenge for that constituency to become more engaged with the messiness of life wherein character and identity are formed. Finally, my approach has positive potential for ensuring that Christians/churches can fulfill their response as an adventure of maturation, ensuring a narrative of transformation not victimization.

In Ricoeurean terms, this research has been exploring theology linguistically—canonical linguistically—because language (which includes practices) is essential to the refigurative/transformative process. Let Fodor, summarizing Ricoeur, have the next-to-last word:

> We become, quite simply, refigured in and by the Word. The task of faithfully naming God, therefore, cannot help but be a fearful, awesome, dangerous enterprise, one which demands vigilance as much as it does courage. It requires that we be ever alert to our linguistic expressions, open and attentive in our listening, diligent in our habits of speech, circumspect in our discursive practices, courteous and faithful in our responses. [8]

The evangelical catholic Christian community requires refiguration for effective major incident responses. I conclude it has the canonical linguistic theology for such. I pray this research may play a small part in stimulating the mimetic process required. For me, personally, I am grateful to God for the "discovery" of a methodology and a theology that have helped me configure and refigure a discordant prefigured narrative in such a way that has left me feeling Kegworth/M1, for all its tragic and aporetic aspects, has provided me with a sense of profound honor at having been a Christian responder from the evangelical catholic Christian community. May there be many more, just as there will be many more major incidents.

---

8. Fodor, *Christian Hermeneutics*, 16.

Appendix 1

A Broad Survey of Major Incidents
from 1985 to 2005

From reading the literature, drawing on my own experience, and knowledge gained from my work on the Human Aspects Group (HAG),[1] I have selected incidents that fit the definition set out in the CCA 2004. I present a broad, chronological, survey of major incidents from 1985 to 2005. This period provides a concentration of disasters in the UK, including the so-called *decade of disasters* (1980–90) and takes into account the *International Decade for Natural Disaster Reduction* (1990–2000).[2] Extending the period for research beyond the 1980s allows for

1. My personal experience at Kegworth/M1 led on, from 1994, to developing a general interest in major incident response through the work of what has become known as the Human Aspects Group (HAG). The HAG is an ad hoc working party of the Professional Issues Group of the Emergency Planning Society (EPS). Because of my experience at Kegworth/M1, I was invited to join the HAG in 1994/5. Since that time we have produced a guidance document addressing the human aspects of major incident response and sought to disseminate this guidance among both statutory and voluntary bodies. We organized a national conference that brought together both responding agencies and those who had made use of them to discuss human rights issues. We have done work into the possibility of providing crisis support workers (CSWs), to supplement the work of police family liaison officers (FLOs). We have produced recommendations for coroners, police, and local authorities regarding the human aspects of dealing with mass fatalities. We also provided responses to the draft Civil Contingencies bill, during its preparation. In my involvement with all of this, I endeavored to bring a faith representation to bear upon the work issues. This has given me some experience into the challenges of working in a secular society from a faith community point of view.

2. Eyre, "In Remembrance." The International Decade for Natural Disaster Reduction (IDNDR) was declared for the decade of the 1990s by the United Nations. The aim of this "was and still remains to be the unacceptable and rising levels of losses which disasters continue to incur on the one hand, and the existence, on the other hand, of

consideration of the disaster response in the Omagh bombings (1998), the foot-and-mouth epidemic in the north of England (2001), the flooding in Carlisle (2005), the London bombings (July 2005), the 9/11 terrorist attacks (September 2001), and the Asian tsunami (December 2004) that impacted on UK nationals abroad. These incidents have provided an enhanced knowledge and learning-base for major incident response systems to date. I give indication of relevant sources in footnote form.

UK MAINLAND AND NORTHERN IRELAND

1985

Bradford football stadium fire[3]—56 died, many more seriously injured

Manchester airport air crash and fire[4]—55 died, 15 seriously injured

1987

King's Cross underground station fire[5]—31 died, many traumatized

Hungerford shootings[6]—17 died, 15 injured

The Enniskillen bombing[7]—11 died, 63 injured

---

a wealth of scientific and engineering know-how which could be effectively used to reduce losses resulting from disasters" ("International Strategy").

3. Harrison, *Bradford City*; Harrison, "After the Bradford Fire."

4. King, "8/1988 Boeing." It is ironic, in view of the neglect bereaved families experienced at the time, that twenty years later a memorial service was requested by British Airways senior executive staff and organized through the senior chaplain at Manchester International Airport. What is more, British Airways financed the development of a new chapel with the disaster memorialized in its stained glass windows. That memorial service after twenty years also demonstrated how deeply traumatized responding staff, as well as the bereaved, had been and how deeply they still felt the impact of the disaster.

5. Fennell, "Investigation." Also, Walker-Smith, "King's Cross Disaster."

6. Smith, "Shooting Incident at Hungerford."

7. Brown and Marshall, "Enniskillen Bomb"; Curran et al., "Psychological Consequences"; McDaniel, *Enniskillen*.

1988

Piper Alpha oil rig explosion[8]—167 died, many others horrifically injured

Clapham train crash[9]—35 died, nearly 500 injured

Lockerbie aircraft murders[10]—270 died, no passenger survivors

1989

Kegworth air crash[11]—47 died, 74 serious injuries

Hillsborough football stadium disaster[12]—95 died, many injured and traumatized

Marchioness Thames riverboat sinking[13]—51 died, many others traumatized

1994

Mull of Kintyre Chinook crash[14]—29 died, no survivors

1996

Dunblane school shootings[15]—16 died, 17 injured

8. Cullen, "Public Inquiry into the Piper Alpha Disaster"; "Piper Alpha's Legacy"; McGinty, *Fire in the Night*. Also personal conversations recalled with Rev. Fred Coutts, lead chaplain at Aberdeen Royal Infirmary when I visited him in January 2008. I am indebted to him also for various news cuttings and reports stemming from the involvement of his predecessor, Rev. Alan Swinton.

9. Hidden, "Investigation."

10. Details from my own conversations with Rev. Bill Scott, then pastor of the Free Church of Scotland in Dumfries; also, Charles, "Aircraft Accident Report"; McIntosh, "Lockerbie."

11. Paddock, "Air Crash M1 Motorway"; Trimble, "4/1990 Boeing"; Kirsh et al., "Nottingham, Leicester, Derby."

12. Taylor, "Hillsborough Stadium Disaster."

13. Clarke, *"Marchioness"/"Bowbelle"*. Also, literature provided to me by the Marchioness Action Group in November 2006, being a collection of timescales of events, reports, and correspondence pertaining to the Marchioness Action Group's activities between 1989 and 2006.

14. Committee to Review Chinook ZD 576 Crash, "Chinook ZD576—Report." Also, Edward, "Crash Victims Remembered."

15. Cullen, "Public Inquiry into the Shootings at Dunblane." For an interesting and informative perspective of the impact of this incident upon members of the reporting media, see Preston, "Dunblane."

1998

The Omagh bombing[16]—29 died, 220 injured

1999

Ladbroke Grove train crash[17]—31 died, over 400 injured

2000

Hatfield train crash[18]—4 died, 70 injured

2001

Foot-and-mouth epidemic[19]—No human deaths, many traumatized

2002

Potter's Bar train crash[20]—7 died, 76 injured

Soham murders[21]—2 died

2004

Morecambe Bay cockle pickers tragedy[22]—21 died

16. "The Omagh Bomb: 15 August, 1998."

17. Cullen, "Ladbroke Grove Rail Inquiry: Part 1 Report."

18. Rail Safety and Standards Board, "Hatfield Derailment Investigation."

19. Barclay, "Foot and Mouth Disease." See also Carruthers, "Farming Families." I have included this event in my research because it fits the criteria for a major incident even though there was no loss of human life from the infection itself, and also following reading a research paper. See Mort et al., "Psycho-Social Effects." Having read this, I contacted Dr. Mort by email, who referred me to Dr. Ian Convery, a fellow author of the paper. It was he who convinced me beyond doubt that this epidemic fit the criteria for a major incident in that it was an enormous threat to the human population in terms of its psycho-social effects and also to the environment. Also, a member of my church at the time, who was a vet, was seconded to work for DEFRA in the infected area, and he relayed to me details of the impact the epidemic was having upon local communities he was working in.

20. UK Health and Safety Commission, "Train Derailment at Potters Bar."

21. Information taken from Bichard, "Bichard Inquiry Report"; "Soham Trial"; Bell, "Soham Murders Trial." Also from a pilot semi-structured open interview with the local evangelical pastor in Soham at the time.

22. Gibson, "Ghosts"; Broomfield, *Ghosts*; Atkins, "Faith and Reason."

APPENDIX 3

Post-Traumatic Stress Disorder

POST-TRAUMATIC STRESS DISORDER (PTSD) was formally included as a recognized psychiatric disorder, in *The Diagnostic and Statistical Manual of Mental Disorders* (DSM-III).[1] The evaluation of PTSD as a clinical syndrome followed work with Vietnam War veterans and revision of concentration camp survivors' experiences in the first and second World Wars. At first, the diagnosis, "was not a result of careful factor-analytic studies of the symptom picture of people suffering from 'trauma neuroses,' but a compilation of symptoms that were arrived at on the basis of literature searches, scrutiny of clinical records, and a thoughtful political process."[2] By the time DSM-IV came out in 1994, clinical trials had produced scientifically conclusive evidence for the initial, more controversial, diagnosis being recognized as sound. There had been early suspicions of PTSD being an invention for the benefit of lawyers pursuing compensation claims for their clients. As early as the mid-twentieth century, German psychiatrists took the view that "traumatic neurosis was not an illusion, but an artifact of the insurance system . . ."[3] Herman notes,

> The study of psychological trauma must consistently contend with this tendency to discredit the victim or to render her invisible. Throughout the history of the field, dispute has raged over whether patients with post-traumatic conditions are entitled to care and respect or deserving of contempt . . . In spite of a vast literature documenting the phenomena of psychological

1. Revised in 1987 to take into account the stressor criterion and symptomology involving children, according to Robert J. Ursano et al., "Trauma and Disaster," in Raphael, et al., eds., *Individual and Community Responses*, 7.

2. Van der Kolk et al., eds, *Traumatic Stress*, 61.

3. Ibid., 51.

trauma, debate still centers on the basic question of whether these phenomena are credible and real.[4]

A first draft of DSM-V is currently available for public review, in which it is anticipated advancements in science and clinical knowledge will be taken into account. There is some fear that the diagnostic aspects seem to be fewer, thus making the actual clinical, and legal, diagnosis more difficult.[5]

4. Quoted in Bridgers, "Resurrected Life," 76–77, n. 25.
5. Online: http://www.dsm5.org/Pages/Default.aspx.

Bibliography

"7/7: The Angels of Edgware Road." Channel 4, July 13, 2008. Online: http://www .channel4.com/programmes/77-the-angels-of-edgware-road/4od.

"7/7: The Miracle of Carriage 346." Channel 4, July 7, 2008. Online: http://www .channel4.com/health/microsites/0-9/7-7/miracle.html.

Aberbach, David. "Trauma and Abstract Monotheism: Jewish Exile and Recovery in the Sixth Century B.C.E." *Judaism* 50/2 (Spring 2001): 211–21.

Achtemeier, Paul J. *Romans.* Interpretation: A Bible Commentary for Teaching and Preaching. Atlanta: John Knox, 1985.

Adams, Jay E. *Essays on Counseling.* Grand Rapids: Zondervan, 1972.

Adams, Marilyn McCord. "The Problem of Hell: A Problem of Evil for Christians," In *Reasoned Faith: Essays in Philosophical Theology in Honor of Norman Kretzmann,* edited by Eleonore Stump, 301–27. Ithaca: Cornell University Press, 1993.

Adams, Nicholas. *Habermas and Theology.* Cambridge: Cambridge University Press, 2006.

Adams, Nick. "Making Deep Reasonings." *Modern Theology* 22 (June 2006): 385–401.

"Addressing Lessons from the Emergency Response to the 7 July 2005 London Bombings: What We Learned and What We are Doing About It." Her Majesty's Government (HMG) report. September 22, 2006. Online: http://www.londonprepared.gov.uk/ downloads/homeoffice_lessonslearned.pdf

Ahmad, Eqbal. "Comprehending Terror." *MERIP Middle East Report* 140 (May–June 1986): 2–5.

Ahmed, Nafeez Mossadeq. *The London Bombings: An Independent Inquiry.* London: Duckworth, 2006.

Aichele, George. "The Slaughter of Innocents." *Christian Century* 95 (1978):1262–63.

Akbar, Arifa. "Philosopher Wins £800,000 Award for Spiritual Focus." *Independent,* March 15, 2007.

Al-Hasan, Bilal. "Who has the Right to Condemn Terrorism?" *Journal of Palestine Studies* 15 (Spring 1986): 150–51.

Allen, A. J. "Disasters: Planning For a Caring Response (Parts 1 and 2)." Disasters Working Party, report. London: HMSO, 1991.

———. "Disasters: Planning For A Caring Response." UK Home Office report, second impression. London: HMSO, 1992.

Almond, P. C. *Heaven and Hell in Enlightenment England.* Cambridge: Cambridge University Press, 1994.

Altschule, Mark D. "Acedia: Its Evolution from Deadly Sin to Psychiatric Syndrome." *British Journal of Psychiatry* 3 (1965): 117–19.

The Amnesty Committee. "Truth and Reconciliation Commission of South Africa." Report. March 21, 2003. Online: http://www.info.gov.za/otherdocs/2003/trc/.

Bibliography

Anderson, Ray S. "Barth and a New Direction for Natural Theology." In *Theology Beyond Christendom: Essays on the Centenary of the Birth of Karl Barth, May 10, 1886,* edited by John Thompson, 241–66. Princeton Theological Monograph Series. Allison Park, PA: Pickwick, 1987.

————. *The Shape of Practical Theology: Empowering Ministry with Theological Praxis.* Downers Grove, IL: InterVarsity, 2001.

————. *Spiritual Caregiving as Secular Sacrament: A Practical Theology for Professional Caregivers.* London: Jessica Kingsley, 2004.

Anees, Munawar A. "Salvation and Suicide: What Does Islamic Theology Say?" *Dialog: A Journal of Theology* 45 (Fall 2006): 275–79.

Aquinas, Thomas. *Summa Theologica.* Translated by the Fathers of the English Dominican Province. Benziger Bros. edition, 1947. Online: http://www.ccel.org/ccel/aquinas/summa.i.html.

Ariel, Yaakov. "Terror at the Holy of Holies: Christians and Jewish Builders of the Temple at the Turn of the Twenty-First Century." *Journal of Religion & Society,* Supplement 2, (2007): 63–82.

ariñes-voets, Ardi. "An Effective Humanitarian Supply Management System for Natural and Man-Made Disasters." Paper presented at the International Conference on Total Disaster Risk Management, December 3, 2003. Online: http://www.adrc.asia/publications/TDRM2003Dec/21_MS.%20ARDI%20VOETS.pdf.

Armstrong, Judith. "Emotional Issues and Ethical Aspects of Trauma Research." In *Trauma Research Methodology,* edited by Eva B. Carlson, 174–87. Lutherville, MD: Sidran, 1996.

Armstrong, Karen. *The Battle For God: A History of Fundamentalism.* New York: Random House, 2001.

Arndt, William F., and F. Wilbur Gingrich, eds. *A Greek-English Lexicon of the New Testament and Other Early Christian Literature: A Translation and Adaptation of Walter Bauer's Griechisch-Deutsches Wörterbuch zu den Schriften des Neuen Testaments und der übrigen urchristlichen Literatur. Fourth revised and Aug. Ed.,* 1952. Chicago: The University of Chicago Press, 1957.

Association of University Chief Security Officers. "Emergencies Planning and Management: A Good Practice Guide for Higher Education Institutions." Report. Higher Education Funding Council for England, 2008.

Atkins, Margaret. "Faith and Reason: Tolerance is Not Good Enough, as the Good Samaritan." *Independent,* February 5, 2005.

Atkinson, David J. *The Message of Job.* The Bible Speaks Today. Edited by J. A. Motyer. Leicester: InterVarsity, 1991.

Atkinson, David J., and David F. Field, eds. *The New Dictionary of Christian Ethics and Pastoral Theology.* Leicester: InterVarsity, 1995.

Augustine. *The Confessions of St. Augustine.* Translated by J. G. Pilkington. Edinburgh: T & T Clark, 1876.

Avgoustidis, Adamantios G. "Are Psychiatric Preconceptions Against Pastoral Care Scientifically Approved?" *Scottish Journal of Healthcare Chaplaincy* 7/1 (2004): 17–20.

Bader, Veit. "Religious Pluralism: Secularism or Priority for Democracy?" *Political Theory* 27:5 (October 1999): 597–633.

Bailey, Jeff. "Engaged Particularity: Interfaith Scriptural Reasoning and the Politics of Small Achievements." Paper presented to the Religion, Culture & Communication group of the Tyndale Fellowship, Cambridge, July 2008.

Ballard, Paul, and John Pritchard. *Practical Theology in Action: Christian Theology in the Service of Christ and Society.* 2nd ed. London: SPCK, 2006.

Barclay, Christopher. "Foot and Mouth Disease." Research Paper 01/35, Science and Environment Section House Of Commons Library, March 27, 2001. Online: http://www.parliament.uk/documents/commons/lib/research/rp2001/rp01-035 .pdf.

Barclay, Oliver R., ed. *Pacifism and War: 8 Prominent Christians Debate Today's Issues.* When Christians Disagree Series. Leicester: InterVarsity, 1984.

Barnes, Michael. *Theology and the Dialogue of Religions.* Cambridge Studies in Christian Doctrine. Cambridge: Cambridge University Press, 2002.

Barron, Bruce, and Anson Shupe. "Reasons for the Growing Popularity of Christian Reconstructionism: The Determination to Attain Dominion." In *Religion and Politics in Comparative Perspective: Revival of Religious Fundamentalism in East and West,* edited by Bronislaw Misztal and Anson Shupe, 83–96. Westport, CT: Praeger, 1992.

Barth, Karl. *Church Dogmatics.* 4 Vols. Edited by G. W. Bromiley and T. F. Torrance. Translated by A. T. MacKay, T. H. L. Parker, Harold Knight, Henry A. Kennedy, and John Marks. Edinburgh: T & T Clark, 1961.

———. *The Epistle to the Romans.* Translated by Edwyn C. Hokyns. 6th edition. Oxford: Oxford University Press, 1933.

———. *Ethics.* Edited by Dietrich Braun. Translated by G. W. Bromiley. Edinburgh: T & T Clark, 1981.

———. "Theological Declaration of Barmen." In *The Church's Confession Under Hitler,* by Arthur C. Cochrane, 237–42. Philadelphia: Westminster, 1962. Online: http://www.sacred-texts.com/chr/barmen.htm.

———. *The Word of God and the Word of Man.* Translated by D. Horton. Boston: Pilgrim, 1928.

Batson, C. Daniel. "Religion as Prosocial: Agent or Double Agent?" *Journal For the Scientific Study of Religion* 15 (March 1976): 29–45.

Batson, C. Daniel, A. Christine Harris, Kevin D. McCaul, Michael Davis, and Timothy Schmidt. "Compassion or Compliance: Alternative Dispositional Attributions of One's Helping Behavior." *Social Psychology Quarterly* 42 (1979): 405–9

Battle, Michael. "A Theology of Community: The Ubuntu Theology of Desmond Tutu." *Interpretation* 54 (April 2000): 173–82.

Bauckham, Richard. "Universalism: A Historical Survey." *Themelios* 4/2 (September 1978): 47–54.

Bavinck, Herman. "Common Grace." Translated by Raymond C. Van Leewen. *Calvin Theological Journal* 24:1 (April 1989): 35–66.

———. *The Doctrine of God.* Edinburgh: Banner of Truth Trust, 1977.

———. "Human Religions in God's Eyes: A Study of Romans 1:18–32." *Scottish Bulletin of Evangelical Theology* 12 (Spring 1994): 44–52.

Baynes, Kenneth. "Habermas." In *Political Thinkers from Socrates to the Present.* Edited by David Boucher and Paul Kelly, 480–95. Oxford: Oxford University Press, 2004.

Beales, Derek, and Geoffrey Best, eds. *History, Society and the Churches: Essays in Honour of Owen Chadwick.* Cambridge: Cambridge University Press, 1985.

Beardsley, Christina. "When the Glow Fades: The Chaplain's Role in Non-Religious Spiritual Rites for the Bereaved." *Practical Theology* 2/2 (2009): 231–40.

Bebbington, David W. *The Dominance of Evangelicalism: The Age of Spurgeon and Moody*. Leicester: InterVarsity, 2005.

———. *Evangelicalism in Modern Britain: A History from the 1730s to the 1980s*. New York: Routledge, 2005.

Becker, Stephen M. "Communicating Risk to the Public after Radiological Incidents." *BMJ* 335 (2007). Online: http://www.bmj.com/content/335/7630/1106.

Bell, Rachael. "The Soham Murders Trial." trueTV Crime Library: Criminal Minds and Methods. Online: http://www.trutv.com/library/crime/serial_killers/predators/ian_huntley/index.html.

Bergman, David. *The Case for Corporate Responsibility: Corporate Violence and the Criminal Justice System*. London: Disaster Action, 2000.

Bergmann, Gustav. *Logic and Reality*. Madison: University of Wisconsin Press, 1964.

Berkhof, Louis. *Systematic Theology*. London: Banner of Truth Trust, 1958.

Berkouwer, G. C. *General Revelation*. Studies in Dogmatics. Grand Rapids: Eerdmans, 1955.

———. *Man: The Image of God*. Studies in Dogmatics. Grand Rapids: Eerdmans, 1962.

———. *The Providence of God*. Studies in Dogmatics. Grand Rapids: Eerdmans, 1972.

Bessier, Dominique. "Transparency: A Two-Way Mirror?" *International Journal of Social Economics* 32 (2005): 424–38.

Beuken, George. "Palliative Care: A Theological Foundation: Sacrament of Anointing and Pastoral Care of the Sick." *Scottish Journal of Healthcare Chaplaincy* 5 (2002) 36–40.

Bichard, Michael. "The Bichard Inquiry Report." UK House of Commons. London: HMSO, June 22, 2004. Online: http://www.bichardinquiry.org.uk/10663/report.pdf.

Biggar, Nigel. "Saving the Secular: The Public Vocation of Moral Theology." An Inaugural Lecture delivered before the University of Oxford, April 22, 2008. Online: http://www.chch.ox.ac.uk/sites/default/files/njb%20inaugural%20university%20lecture%2008.pdf.

Billings, Todd. "After Tilley: The Sustaining Relevance of the Problem of Suffering as a Concrete Question." Paper presented at the American Academy of Religion National Meeting, Nashville, TN, Novermber 2000.

———. "Lived Question: Moving Beyond a Theoretical Approach to Theodicy." *Journal For Christian Theological Research* 5 (2000) n.p. Online: http://apu.edu/~CTRF/articles/2000_articles/billings.html.

———. "Theodicy as a 'Lived Question': Moving Beyond a Theoretical Approach to Theodicy." *Journal for Christian Theological Research* 5/2 (2000): n.p. Online: http://www2.luthersem.edu/ctrf/JCTR/Vol05/billings.htm.

Birks, T. R. *The Victory of Divine Goodness: Including I. Letters to an Inquirer on Various Doctrines of Scripture; II. Notes on Coleridge's Confessions of an Inquiring Spirit; III. Thoughts on the Nature of the Atonement and of Eternal Judgment*. London: Rivingtons, 1867.

———. *The Victory of Divine Goodness: Reply to Strictures in Two Recent Works*. London: Rivingtons, 1869.

Bittner, Patricia. "Disaster Management in the Digital Age: The Case for Latin America." Humanitarian Practice Network: A Forum for Improving Humanitarian Action. October 5, 2008. Online: http://www.odihpn.org/report.asp?id=1033.

Blears, Hazel, and Paul Goggins. "The Needs of Faith Communities in Major Emergencies: Some Guidelines." UK Home Office and Cabinet Office, July 2005.

Blocher, Henri. "Everlasting Punishment and the Problem of Evil." In *Universalism and the Doctrine of Hell: Papers Presented at the Fourth Edinburgh Conference in Church Dogmatics,* 1991, edited by Nigel M. de S. Cameron, 93–138. Carlisle, UK: Paternoster, 2000.

Bloom, Sandra. "Trauma and the Nature of Evil." Originally prepared for the 12th Annual Meeting for the International Society for Traumatic Stress Studies, November, 1996.

Bloomfield, Kenneth. "We Will Remember Them." Report of the Northern Ireland Victims' Commissioner. April, 1998. Online: http://www.nio.gov.uk/bloomfield_report.pdf.

Bolt, John. "Common Grace and the Christian Reformed Synod of Kalamazoo (1924): A Seventy-Fifth Anniversary Perspective." *Calvin Theological Journal* 35 (2000): 7–36.

Bosch, David J. *Transforming Mission: Paradigm Shifts in Theology of Mission.* Maryknoll, NY: Orbis, 2003.

Bosher, Lee. *Social and Institutional Elements of Disaster Vulnerability: The Case of South India.* Bethesda, MD: Academic Press, 2007.

Bowlby, John. *Attachment and Loss.* Vol. 3 of *Loss: Sadness and Depression.* London: Hogarth, 1980.

Bowpitt, G. "Evangelical Christianity, Secular Humanism, and the Genesis of British Social Work." *British Journal of Social Work* 28 (1998): 675–93.

Bradfield, Cecil, Mary Lou Wylie, and Lennis G. Echterling. "After the Flood: The Response of Ministers to a Natural Disaster." *Sociological Analysis* 49 (Winter 1989): 397–407.

Bray, Gerald. *The Doctrine of God.* Contours of Christian Theology. Edited by Gerald Bray. Leicester: InterVarsity, 1993.

Bretherton, Luke. *Hospitality as Holiness: Christian Witness amid Moral Diversity.* Aldershot, UK: Ashgate, 2006.

Bricker, Daniel P. "Innocent Suffering in Mesopotamia." *Tyndale Bulletin* 51 (2000): 193–214.

Bridgers, Lynn. "The Resurrected Life: Toward a Theology of Liberation for the Traumatized." *Journal of Religion & Abuse* 3 (2001): 61–80.

Brock, Brian. *Singing the Ethos of God: On the Place of Christian Ethics in Scripture.* Cambridge: Eerdmans, 2007.

———. "Why Genesis? Why Now?" Paper presented to the Religion, Culture & Communication group of the Tyndale Fellowship, Cambridge, July 2007.

Brooke, Heather. *Your Right to Know: How to Use the Freedom of Information Act and Other Access Laws.* London: Pluto, 2005.

Broomfield, Nick, director. *Ghosts.* London: Channel 4 Films, 2006.

Brown, Colin, ed. *New International Dictionary of New Testament Theology.* 4 vols. Translated, with additions and revisions, from the German *Theologisches Begriffslexikon Zum Neuen Testament,* edited by Lothar Coenen, Erich Beyreuther, and Hans Bietenhard. Carlisle, UK: Paternoster, 1986.

Brown, Harold O. J., et al. "The Communion of the Saints: A Statement of Evangelicals and Catholics Together." *First Things* (March 2003): n.p. Online: www.firstthings.com/article/2007/01/the-communion-of-saints-17.

Brown, M. G., and S. G. Marshall. "The Enniskillen Bomb: A Disaster Plan." *BMJ* 297 (6656) (October 29,1988): 1113–16. Online: http://www.ncbi.nlm.nih.gov/pmc/articles/PMC1834874/?page=1.

Brown, Robert McAfee, ed. *The Essential Reinhold Niebuhr: Selected Essays and Addresses*. New Haven, CT: Yale University Press, 1986.

Brown, Vincent, Philippe J. Guerin, Dominique Legros, Christophe Paquet, Bernard Pécoul, and Alain Moren. "Research in Complex Humanitarian Emergencies: The Médecins Sans Frontières/Epicentre Experience." *PloS Medicine* 5/4 (April 2008): n.p. Online: http://www.plosmedicine.org/article/info:doi/10.1371/journal.pmed.0050089.

Brown, Warren, Nancey Murphey, and H. Newton Malony, eds. *Whatever Happened to the Soul? Scientific and Theological Portraits of Human Nature*. Minneapolis: Fortress, 1998.

Bruce, Steve. *Fundamentalism*. Oxford: Blackwell, 2000.

———. *Paisley: Religion and Politics in Northern Ireland*. Oxford: Oxford University Press, 2007.

Brueggemann, Walter. *The Message of the Psalms*. Minneapolis: Augsburg, 1984.

———. *Praying the Psalms*. Winona, MN: Saint Mary's, 1986.

———. *The Psalms: The Life of Faith*. Edited by Patrick Miller. Minneapolis: Fortress 1995.

———. "Theodicy in a Social Dimension." *Journal for the Study of the Old Testament* 33 (1985): 3–35.

Buckley, James. "Invocation of Saints: A Theological Interpretation." *Pro Ecclesia* 13/4 (Fall 2004): 389–92.

Caldwell, William. "The Doctrine of Satan: I. In the Old Testament." *The Biblical World* 41 (January 1913): 29–33.

Calvin, John. *Calvin: Institutes of the Christian Religion*. Library of Christian Classics. Edited by John T. McNeill. Translated by Ford Lewis Battles, Volume 20. Philadelphia: Westminster, 1967.

———. *Calvin's Commentaries*. Translated by James Anderson. Grand Rapids: Baker, 1979.

———. *Sermons on Job*. Facs., 1574 ed. Edinburgh: Banner of Truth Trust, 1993.

Cameron, Nigel M. de. S., ed. *Universalism and the Doctrine of Hell*. Carlisle, UK: Paternoster, 1998.

Campbell, Donald. "'Downward Causation' in Hierarchically Organised Biological Systems." In *Studies in the Philosophy of Biology: Reduction and Related Problems*, edited by F. J. Ayala and T. Dobzhnsky, 179–86. Berkeley: University of California Press, 1974.

Capps, Donald, and Don S. Browning. *Pastoral Care and Hermeneutics*. Theology and Pastoral Care Series. Minneapolis: Fortress, 1984.

Carey, Peter. *Data Protection in the UK*. London: Blackstone, 2000.

Carley, S., K. Mackway-Jones, and S. Duncan. "Major Incidents in Britain Over the Past 28 Years: The Case for the Centralised Reporting of Major Uncidents." *Journal of Epidemiological Community Health* 52 (June 1998): 392–8. Online: doi:10.1136/jech.52.6.392.

Carlson, Eve B. *Trauma Research Methodology.* Lutherville, MD: Sidran, 1996.

Carroll, Tony. "Secularisation In Recent Social Theory." *Communio viatorium* 44 (2002): 250–65.

Carruthers, S. P. "Farming Families in Crisis: A Profile of the Recipients of RABI and ARC-Addington Fund Grants During the 2001 Foot-and-Mouth Disease Epidemic." A study commissioned and sponsored by the ARC-Addington Fund, Farm Crisis Network (FCN), the Royal Agricultural Benevolent Institution (RABI), and the Rural Stress Information Network (RSIN), April 2002.

Carson, D. A. *The Gagging of God: Christianity Confronts Pluralism.* Grand Rapids: Zondervan, 1996.

———. *How Long, O Lord? Reflecting on Suffering and Evil.* Leicester: InterVarsity, 1999.

Carson, D. A., and John D. Woodbridge, eds. *Scripture and Truth.* Grand Rapids: Baker, 1992.

Cartledge, Mark. *Practical Theology: Charismatic and Empirical Perspectives.* Studies in Pentecostal and Charismatic Issues. London: Paternoster, 2007.

Caruth, Cathy. "Unclaimed Experience: Trauma and the Possibility of History." *Yale French Studies* 79 (1991): 181–92.

Casanova, José. "Immigration and the New Religious Pluralism: A European Union/ United States Comparison." In *Democracy and the New Religious Pluralism*, edited by Thomas Banchoff, 59–83. New York: Oxford University Press, 2007.

Catholic Agency for Overseas Development (CAFOD). "Joining Together." Article about Asian tsunami. Online: http://www.cafod.org.uk.

Chadwick, Owen. *The Victorian Church: Part One* 1829–1859. 3rd ed. London: SCM, 1971.

Chalke, Steve, and Alan Mann. *The Lost Message of Jesus.* Grand Rapids: Zondervan, 2003.

Chaplin, Jonathan. "The Bible, the State and Religious Diversity: Theological Foundations for 'Principled Pluralism.'" Paper presented to the Religion, Culture & Communication group of the Tyndale Fellowship, Cambridge, July 2008.

———. "Talking God: The Legitimacy of Religious Public Reasoning." Report, Theos Public Theology Think Tank. London: Theos, 2008. Online: http://campaigndirector.moodia.com/Client/Theos/Files/TalkingGod1.pdf.

Chapman, Colin. "Christian Responses to Islam, Islamism, and 'Islamic terrorism.'" *Cambridge Papers* 162 (June 2007): n.p.

Charles, M. M. "Aircraft Accident Report No 2/90 (EW/C1094)." Report on the accident to Boeing 747-12, N739PA at Lockerbie, Dumfriesshire, Scotland, on 21 December 1988. UK Department of Transport, Air Accidents Investigation Branch. London: HMSO, 1990.

Chenard, Cynthia Jean. "Pastoral Care During Major Traumatic Events: Implications for Pastoral Care for Emergency Responders and Their Care-Givers." DMin diss., Vancouver School of Theology, 2004.

The Chernobyl Forum: 2003–2005. "Chernobyl's Legacy: Health, Environmental, and Socio-Economic Impacts and Recommendations to the Governments of Belarus, the Russian Federation and Ukraine." Report, 2nd rev. ed. Vienna: International Atomic Energy Agency, 2006. Online: http://www.iaea.org/Publications/Booklets/Chernobyl/chernobyl.pdf.

Chester, David K. "The 1755 Lisbon Earthquake." *Progress in Physical Geography* 25/3 (September 2001): 363–83.

———. "The Theodicy of Natural Disasters." *The Scottish Journal of Theology* 51 (1998): 485–505.

———. "Theology and Disaster Studies: The Need for Dialogue." *Journal of Volcanology and Geothermal Research* 146 (2005): 319–28.

Chester, David K and Angus M Duncan. "Geomythology, Theodicy and the Continuing Relevance of Religious Worldviews on Responses to Volcanic Eruptions." In *Living Under the Shadow: The Cultural Impacts of Volcanic Eruptions*, edited by John Gratten and Robin Torrence, 203–44. Walnut Creek, CA: Left Coast, 2007.

Chinnici, Rosemary. "The Role of the Theologian in Times of Terror: Seeking Life Among the Debris: The Public Role of Religious Scholars." Address to the Core Doctoral Faculty, Forum of the Graduate Theological Seminary, Berkeley, CA, February 20, 2002. Online: http://www.gtu.edu/page.php?nav=456.

Christenson, James A. "Religious Involvement, Values, and Social Compassion." *Sociological Analysis* 37 (Autumn 1976): 218–27.

Christie, Nils. "Restorative Justice—Answers to Deficits in Modernity." In *Crime, Social Control and Human Rights: From Moral Panics to States of Denial: Essays in Honour of Stanley Cohen*, edited by David Downes, et al., 368–78. Cullompton, UK: Willan, 2007.

Church World Service Emergency Response Program. "Church World Service Standard of Care for Disaster Spiritual Care Ministries." Online: http://www.cwserp.org/sitebuildercontent/sitebuilderfiles/spiritualcarestandards.pdf.

Churchill, Larry R. "The Dangers of Looking for the Health Benefits of Religion." *Lancet* 369 (May 2007): 1509–10.

Clarke, Adam D. "The Good and the Just in Romans 5:7." *Tyndale Bulletin* 41 (1990): 128–42.

Clarke, Anthony. *"Marchioness"/"Bowbelle": Formal Investigation under the Merchant Shipping Act* 1995 (Thames Safety Inquiry). HMSO, 2001.

———. "Public Inquiry into the Identification of Victims Following Major Transport Accidents." Report presented to Parliament. London: HMSO, 2001.

Clayton, Philip, ed. *The Oxford Handbook of Religion and Science*. Oxford: Oxford University Press, 2010.

Coakley, Sarah. "God and Evolution: A New Solution." *Harvard Divinity Bulletin* 35/2 & 3 (Spring/Summer 2007). Online: http://www.hds.harvard.edu/news-events/harvard-divinity-bulletin/articles/god-and-evolution-a-new-solution

Cobb, John. B., Jr. "Response to Mahayana Theology." *Buddhist-Christian Studies* 13 (1993): 44–47.

Cochrane, Elizabeth Agnew. "'At the Same Time Blessed and Lame': Ontology, Christology and Violence in Augustine and John Milbank." *Journal for Christian Theological Research* 11 (2006): 51–72.

Coffey, John. "Secularisation: Is it Inevitable?" *Cambridge Papers* 10/1 (March 2001): n.p. Online: http://www.jubilee-centre.org/document.php?id=31.

Cohen, Stanley. *States of Denial: Knowing about Atrocities and Suffering*. Cambridge: Polity, 2001.

Collett, Jessica, Tiffiny E. Guidry, Nancy J. Martin, and Rebecca Sager. "Faith-Based Decisions? The Consequences of Heightened Religious Salience in Social Service Referral Decisions." *Journal of Scientific Study of Religion* 45 (2006): 119–27.

Collins, C. John. "Psalm 139:14: 'Fearfully and Wonderfully Made'?" *Presbyterian* 25/2 (Autumn 1999): 115–20.

Collins, John J. "The Zeal of Phinehas: The Bible and the Legitimation of Violence." *Journal of Biblical Literature* 122/1 (Spring 2003): 3–21.

Committee to Review Chinook ZD 576 Crash. "Chinook ZD576—Report." UK House of Lords. London: HMSO, January 31, 2002. Online: http://www.publications. parliament.uk/pa/ld200102/ldselect/ldchin/25/2501.htm

Comstock, Gary. "Truth or Meaning: Ricoeur Versus Frei on Biblical Narrative." *The Journal of Religion* 66/2 (April 1986): 117–40.

Cook, Emma. "Crisis Support Volunteer Handbook." Report, Draft 7. Crisis Support Team Essex, Emergency Planning Unit, 2008.

———. "Essex Package of Care Strategy Document: Delivering Humanitarian Assistance in Essex—A People Focused Approach." Report. Version 3.0. Chelmsford, UK: Emergency Plans Unit, August 2007.

Cook, Paul E. G., and G. Harrison. *Christian Hymns*. Brigend, UK: Evangelical Movement of Wales, 1978.

Cooper, John W. *Body, Soul and Life Everlasting: Biblical Anthropology and the Monism-Dualism Debate*. Grand Rapids: Eerdmans, 2000.

Cottingham, John. "Philosophy and the Moral Virtues." Conference paper presented at Human Flourishing Through the Eyes of Faith and Reason, Blackfriars, Oxford, March 13, 2010.

Coulson, J., et al. *Oxford Illustrated Dictionary*. 2nd. ed. Rev. ed. London: Book Club Associates, 1981.

Council of Europe. "European Convention on Human Rights, Rome 4 November 1950 and its Five Protocols: Paris 20 March 1952; Strasbourg 6 May 1963; Strasbourg 6 May 1963; Strasbourg 16 September 1963: Strasbourg 20 January 1966." Online: http://www.hri.org/docs/ECHR50.html.

Cox, Leo G. "Prevenient Grace—A Wesleyan View." *Journal of the Evangelical Theological Society* 12/3 (Summer 1969): 143–49.

Crabb, Larry. *Shattered Dreams: God's Unexpected Pathway to Joy*. Colorado Springs: WaterBrook, 2001.

Crisp, Oliver D. "Problems with Perichoresis." *Tyndale Bulletin* 56/1 (2005): 119–40.

Crites, Stephen. "The Narrative Quality of Experience." In *Why Narrative? Readings in Narrative Theology*, edited by Stanley Hauerwas and Gregory Jones, 65–88. Grand Rapids: Eerdmans, 1989.

Crockett, William, ed. *Four Views on Hell*. Grand Rapids: Zondervan, 1992.

Cullen, William Douglas. "The Ladbroke Grove Rail Inquiry: Part 1 Report." UK Health & Safety Commission. HSE Books, 2001. Online: http://www.railwaysarchive .co.uk/documents/HSE_Lad_Cullen001.pdf.

———. "The Public Inquiry into the Piper Alpha Disaster." 2 vols. HMG report. London: HMSO, 1993.

———. "The Public Inquiry into the Shootings at Dunblane Primary School on 13 March 1996." Secretary of State for Scotland. London: HMSO October 16, 1996. Online: http://www.ssaa.org.au/research/1996/1996-10-16_public-inquiry-dunblane-lord-cullen.pdf.

Cunningham, Harold G. "God's Law, 'General Equity' and the Westminster Confession of Faith." *Tyndale Bulletin* 58/2 (2007): 289–312.

Bibliography

Curran, P. S., P. Bell, A. Murray, G. Loughrey, R. Roddy, and L. G. Rocke. "Psychological Consequences of the Enniskillen Bombing." *British Journal of Psychiatry* 156 (1990): 479–82.

Dante Alighieri. *The Divine Comedy*. Translated by H. F. Cary. N.P.: Plain Label Books, 1955. Online: http://books.google.com/books?id=eIsesnFvoqEC&printsec=frontcover&source=gbs_navlinks_s#v=onepage&q=&f=false.

Darzi, Ara. "NHS next stage review interim report," UK Department of Health, October 2007.

Davie, Grace. "Pluralism, Tolerance, and Democracy: Theory and Practice in Europe." In *Democracy and the New Religious Pluralism*, edited by Thomas Banchoff, 224–41. New York: Oxford University Press, 2007.

Davies, D. Eryl. "'An Angry God': The Place of Hell in Preaching." Paper read at the Westminster Conference, "Advancing in Adversity," London, 1991.

Davies, Douglas J. *Death, Ritual and Belief*. London: Cassell, 1997.

Davies, Gaius. *Stress: Sources and Solutions*. Fearn, Tain, UK: Christian Focus, 2005.

Davies, Howard. "Judgement: The Doctrine Lost to the Modern Pulpit." *The Banner of Truth Magazine* 364 (1994): 13–18.

Davies, Oliver. *A Theology of Compassion: Metaphysics of Difference and the Renewal of Tradition*. London: SCM, 2001.

Davis, Ian, and Michael Wall, eds. *Christian Perspectives on Disaster Management*. 2 vols. Teddington, UK: IRDA, 1991.

Day, John N. *Crying For Justice*. Leicester: InterVarsity, 2005.

Department of Communities and Local Government (UK). "Faith Communities Consultative Council (FCCC)."

Devji, Faisal. "Al-Qaeda, Specter of Globalization." *Journal of Religion & Society* Supplement Series 2, (2007): 103–9.

The Diagnostic and Statistical Manual of Mental Disorders (DSM-III). Washington DC: American Psychiatric Association, 1987.

Dixon, Thomas. "The Psychology of the Emotions In Britain and America in the Nineteenth Century: The Role of Religious and Antireligious Commitments." *Osiris*, 2nd Series, 16 (2001): 288–320.

Doctrine Commission of the General Synod of the Church of England. "The Mystery of Salvation: The Story of God's Gift." Report. London: Church House Pub., 1996.

Doka, Kenneth J. "What Makes a Tragedy Public?" n.p. Online: http://www.hospicefoundation.org/teleconference/2003/documents/doka4.pdf.

Dornisch, Loretta. "Ricoeur's Theory of Mimesis: Implications for Literature and Theology." *Journal of Literature and Theology* 3/3 (1989): 308–18.

———. "Symbolic Systems and the Interpretation of Scripture: An Introduction to the Work of Paul Ricoeur." *Seimia* 4 (1975): 1–21.

Dostoyevsky, Fyodor. *The Brothers Karamazov*. Translated by Constance Garnett. N.p: Plain Label, 1950. Online: http://books.google.com/books?id=nLEGs3YIbwAC&printsec=frontcover&source=gbs_navlinks_s#v=onepage&q=&f=false.

Downes, David, Paul Rock, Christine Chinkin, and Conor Gearty. *Crime, Social Control and Human Rights: From Moral Panics to States of Denial: Essays in Honour of Stanley Cohen*. Cullompton, UK: Willan, 2007.

Dowsett, Dick. *God, That's Not Fair! Understanding Punishment and the Christian's Urgent Mission*. Carlisle, UK: Paternoster, 1998.

Drane, John. "The Globalization of Spirituality." Paper presented to the Religion, Culture & Communication group of the Tyndale Fellowship, Cambridge, July 2007.

Drescher, Kent, and David Foy. "Spirituality and Trauma Treatment: Suggestions for Including Spirituality as a Coping Resource." *National Center for Trauma Clinical Quarterly* 5/1 (Winter 1995): n.p. Online: http://www.ncptsd.va.gov/publications/cq/v5/n1/drescher.html.

Dugan, Eileen. "Jerusalem In the Crusades: 'Crescent and Cross,' *Kingdom of Heaven*, and the Fall of the City in 1099 and 1187." *Journal of Religion and Society* Supplement Series 2 (2007): 4–13.

Dynes, Russell R. "The Dialogue Between Voltaire and Rousseau on the Lisbon Earthquake: The Emergence of a Social Science View." Preliminary Paper 293, University of Delaware Disaster Research Center, 1999.

———. "Noah and Disaster Planning: The Cultural Significance of the Flood Story." Preliminary Paper 265, University of Delaware Disaster Research Center, 1998.

Dyson, Michael Eric. *Come Hell or High Water: Hurricane Katrina and the Color of Disaster*. New York: Basic Civitas, 2006.

Eames, Robin. "Faith and Identity in Crisis." Paper delivered at St. Ethelburga's Centre for Reconciliation and Peace, London, May 26, 2004. Online: http://www.stethelburgas.org/documents/archbpeames.pdf.

Editorial. *Prophecy Today* 6 (September/October 1990).

Edward, Rhiannon. "Crash Victims Remembered Ten Years On." *Scotsman*, June 3, 2004. Online: http://tinyurl.com/3mxws3.

Edwards, Jonathan. "Christian Charity or the Duty of Charity to the Poor, Explained and Enforced." In *The Works of Jonathan Edwards*, vol. 2, revised and corrected by Edward Hickman, 163–73. Edinburgh: The Banner of Truth Trust, 1974.

———. "A Dissertation Concerning the Nature of True Virtue." In *The Works of Jonathan Edwards*, vol. 1, revised and corrected by Edward Hickman, 122–42. Edinburgh: The Banner of Truth Trust, 1974.

———. "Sinners in the Hands of an Angry God." In *The Works of Jonathan Edwards*, vol. 2, revised and corrected by Edward Hickman, 7–12. Edinburgh: The Banner of Truth Trust, 1974.

———. "A Treatise Concerning Religious Affections, In Three Parts," In *The Works of Jonathan Edwards*, vol. 1, revised and corrected by Edward Hickman, 234–343. Edinburgh: The Banner of Truth Trust, 1974.

Egan, John P. "Toward Trinitarian *Perichoresis*: Saint Gregory the Theologian, *Oration* 31.14." *The Greek Orthodox Theological Review* 39/1 (1994): 83–93.

Elkins, William Wesley. "Suffering Job: Scriptural Reasoning and the Problem of Evil." *The Journal of Scriptural Reasoning* 4/1 (July 2004): n.p.

Ellen, Paula, and Jane Shackman. *Building Resilience: Delivering Services to Victims of Terrorist Attacks*. Report. Victim Support Members' Services Dept. February 2007.

Elliott, Mark, ed. *The Dynamics of Human Life*. Carlisle, UK: Paternoster, 2001.

Ellul, Jacques. *Violence: Reflections from a Christian Perspective*. London: SCM, 1970.

Emergency Planning Society. "Responding to Disaster: The Human Aspects." Guidance document produced by Emergency Planning Society Professional Issues Group Public Information and Welfare Sub-Group, May 1998.

Ericksen, Richard, "Divine Injustice? Matthew and Narrative Strategy and the Slaughter of the Innocents (Matthew 2:13–23)." *Journal for the Study of the New Testament* 64D (1996): 5–27.

Bibliography

Etienne, Mill, Clydette Powell, and Brain Faux. "Disaster Relief in Haiti: a Perspective from the Neurologists on the USNS COMFORT." *The Lancet Neurology* 9 (2010): 461–63 Online: doi:10.1016/S1474-4422(10)70091-0.

Evangelical Manifesto Steering Group. "An Evangelical Manifesto: A Declaration of Evangelical Identity and Public Commitment." Washington DC, May 7, 2008.

Evans, G. R. *Augustine on Evil.* Cambridge: Cambridge University Press, 1990.

Everly, George S., Jr. "Pastoral Crisis Intervention: Toward a Definition." *International Journal of Emergency Mental Health* 2 (2000): 69–71. Online: http://www.icisf.org/acrobat%20documents/PCI.pdf#search=%22 George% 20everly%20 %22Pastoral%20Crisis%20Intervention%22%22.

Eveson, Philip. "The Inner or Psychological Life of Christ." Paper delivered at the Affinity Theological Study Conference, High Leigh, UK, January 30–February 1, 2007.

Eyre, Anne. "Community Support After Disasters." Report of a Winston Churchill travelling fellowship to the United States of America, 2006. n.p.

———. "In Remembrance: Post Disaster Rituals and Symbols." *Australian Journal of Emergency Management* 14 (Spring 1999): 23–29. Online: http://www.ema .gov.au/www/emaweb/rwpattach.nsf/VAP/(084A3429FD57AC0744737F8EA1 34BACB)~In_remembrance_post_disaster_rituals_and_symbols.pdf/$file/In_ remembrance_post_disaster_rituals_and_symbols.pdf.

———. "I've Learnt a Lot from Hillsborough." *Daily Telegraph*, April 15, 1999.

———. "Literature and Best Practice Review and Assessment: Identifying People's Needs in Major Emergencies and Best Practice in Humanitarian Response." Report. London: Department for Culture, Media and Sport, 2006.

———. "Remembering: Community Commemorations after Disaster." In *Springer Handbook of Disaster Research*, edited by H. Rodriguez, E. L. Quarantelli, and R. Dynes. New York: Springer, 2006.

Fackre, Gabriel. "Claiming Jesus as Savior in a Religiously Plural World." *Journal for Christian Theological Research* 8 (2003): 1–17.

Fennell, Desmond. "Investigation into the King's Cross Underground Fire." UK Department of Transport. London: Her Majesty's Stationary Office (HMSO), 1988.

Fernando, Ajith. *Crucial Questions About Hell.* Eastbourne, UK: Kingsway, 1991.

Fiering, Norman S. "Irresistible Compassion: An Aspect of Eighteenth-Century Sympathy and Humanitarianism." *Journal of the History of Ideas* 37 (April–June 1976): 195–218.

———. *Moral Philosophy at Seventeenth-Century Harvard: A Discipline in Transition.* Chapel Hill: University of North Carolina Press, 1981.

Figley, Charles R., ed. *Compassion Fatigue: Coping with Secondary Traumatic Stress Disorder in Those Who Treat the Traumatized.* New York: Routledge, 1995.

Fitzmeyer, Joseph A. *Romans: A New Translation and Introduction and Commentary.* Vol. 33 of The Anchor Bible. London: Geoffrey Chapman, 1992.

Flanagen, Kieran, and Peter C. Jupp, eds. *A Sociology of Spirituality.* Aldershot, UK: Ashgate, 2007.

Fodor, James. *Christian Hermeneutics: Paul Ricoeur and the Refiguring of Theology.* Oxford: Clarendon, 1995.

Ford, David F. *Christian Wisdom: Desiring God and Learning in Love.* Cambridge Studies in Christian Doctrine. Cambridge: Cambridge University Press, 2007.

Ford, David F., and C. C. Pecknold, eds. *The Promise of Scriptural Reasoning*. Oxford: Blackwell, 2006.

Forsyth, Peter Taylor. *The Justification of God: Lectures for War-Time*. Studies in Theology. London: Duckworth, 1916.

Fragos Townsend, Frances. "The Federal Response to Hurricane Katrina: Lessons Learned." White House Report. Washington DC, February 23, 2006.

Frame, John M. *The Doctrine of God: A Theology of Lordship*. Phillipsburg, NJ: P & R, 2002.

———. *No Other God: A Response to Open Theism*. Phillipsburg, NJ: P & R, 2001.

Frei, Hans. *The Eclipse of Biblical Narrative: A Study in Eighteenth and Nineteenth Century Hermeneutics*. New Haven, CT: Yale University Press, 1974.

Fretheim, Terence E. *The Suffering of God: An Old Testament Perspective*. Philadelphia: Fortress, 1984.

Furman, Leola Dyrud, Perry W. Benson, Edward R. Canda, and Cordelia Grimwood. "A Comparative International Analysis of Religion and Spirituality in Social Work: A Survey of UK and US Social Workers." *Social Work Education* 24 (2005): 813–39.

Fyall, Robert S. *Now My Eyes have Seen You: Images of Creation and Evil in the Book of Job*. New Studies in Biblical Theology. Edited by Don A. Carson. Downers Grove, IL: InterVarsity, 2002.

Ganzevoort, R. Ruard. "Scars and Stigmata: Trauma, Identity and Theology." *Practical Theology* 1 (2008): 19–31.

Gardiner, Anne Barbeau. "Balthasar, Christ's Descent, and the Empty Hell." Review of *Light in Darkness: Hans Urs von Balthasar and the Catholic Doctrine of Christ's Descent into Hell*, Alyssa Lyra Pitstick, in *New Oxford Review* 74/7 (July–August 2007). Online: http://www.newoxfordreview.org/reviews.jsp?did=0707-gardiner.

Gardner, E. Clinton. "Justice, Virtue, and Law." *Journal of Law and Religion* 2 (1984): 393–412.

Gardner, Frank. "Flu Pandemic 'Gravest Risk to UK.'" BBC News, August 8, 2008. Online: http://news.bbc.co.uk/2/hi/uk_news/politics/7548593.stm.

Gathercole, S. J. "A Law Unto Themselves: The Gentiles in Romans 2.14–15." *Journal for the Study of the New Testament* 24/3 (March 2002): 27–49.

Gavrilyuk, Paul L. *The Suffering of the Impassible God: The Dialectics of Patristic Thought*. Oxford: Oxford University Press, 2004.

Gay, Douglas C. "A Practical Theology of Church and World: Ecclesiology and Social Vision in 20th Century Scotland." PhD diss., University of Edinburgh, 2006.

Geach, Peter. *Providence and Evil*. Cambridge: Cambridge University Press, 1977.

Gearty, Conor, ed. *Terrorism*. Aldershot, UK: Dartmouth, 1996.

Geisler, Norman L. "The Significance of Christ's Physical Resurrection." *Bibliotheca Sacra* 146 (April–June 1989): 148–70.

Geldenhuys, Norval. *Commentary on the Gospel of Luke*. The New London Commentary on the New Testament. London: Marshall, Morgan & Scott, 1971.

George, Robert P. "Public Morality, Public Reason." *First Things* 167 (November 2006): 21–26.

Gerstner, John H. *Repent or Perish: With Specific Reference to the Conservative Attack on Hell*. Ligonier, PA: Soli Deo Gloria, 1990.

Gerteiny, Alfred G. *The Terrorist Conjunction: The United States, the Israeli-Palestinian Conflict, and al-Qā'ida*. London: Praeger Security, 2007.

Gibson, Alan. "Ghosts: A Haunting Portrayal of the Morecambe Bay Tragedy." *Socialist Worker Online*, Issue 2032, January 6, 2007. Online: http://www.socialistworker.co.uk/art.php?id=10385.

Gibson, David, and Daniel Strange, eds. *Engaging with Barth: Contemporary Evangelical Critiques*. Nottingham: InterVarsity Press, 2008.

Gibson, Marion. *Order from Chaos: Responding to Traumatic Events*. Birmingham, UK: Venture, 1991.

Gibson, Marion, and Dorota Iwaniec. "An Empirical Study into the Psychosocial Reactions of Staff Working as Helpers to those Affected in the Aftermath of Two Traumatic Incidents." *The British Journal of Social Work* 33 (2003): 851–70.

Gijsbers, Alan J. "The Dialogue Between Neuroscience and Theology." Paper originally presented at the Conference on Science and Christianity, Avondale College, Cooranbong, Australia, July 18–20, 2003.

Godet, Frederic Louis. *The Gospel of Luke*. 2 vols. Edinburgh: T & T Clark, 1976.

Graham, Elaine, Heather Walton, and Frances Ward. *Theological Reflection: Methods*. London: SCM, 2005.

Gray, Matt J., Brett T. Litz, and Shira Maguen. "Acute Psychological Impact of Disaster and Large-Scale Trauma: Limitations of Traditional Interventions and Future Practice Recommendations." *Prehospital Disaster Medicine* 19/1 (2004): 64–72.

Green, Garrett. "The Rules of Scriptural Reasoning." *The Journal of Scriptural Reasoning* 4 (July 2004): n.p. Online: http://etext.lib.virginia.edu/journals/ssr/issues/volume2/number1/.

Green, Joel B. *The Gospel of Luke*. The New International Commentary on the New Testament. Grand Rapids: Eerdmans, 1997.

Green, Joel B., and Mark Baker. *Recovering the Scandal of the Cross*. Downers Grove, IL: InterVarsity, 2000.

Green, Joel B., and Stuart L. Palmer, eds. *In Search of the Soul: Four Views of the Mind-Body Problem*. Downers Grove, IL: InterVarsity, 2005.

Greig, Gary S. "The Biblical Foundations of Identificational Repentance as One Prayer Pattern Useful to Advance God's Kingdom and Evangelism." The King's Seminary, Van Nuys, CA, April 2001.

Groothuis, Douglas. *Truth Decay: Defending Christianity against the Challenges of Postmodernism*. Leicester: InterVarsity, 2000.

Grudem, Wayne. *Systematic Theology: An Introduction to Biblical Doctrine*. Grand Rapids: Zondervan, 1994.

Guinness, Os. "Making the World Safe for Diversity: Religious Liberty and Social Harmony in a Pluralistic Age." Paper delivered at the International Christian Liberty Congress, London, July 23–26, 1989.

———. *Unspeakable: Facing Up to the Challenge of Evil*. New York: Harper, 2006.

Gundry, Stanley N., Dennis K. Okholm, and Timothy R. Philips, eds. *Four Views on Salvation in a Pluralistic World*. Grand Rapids: Zondervan, 1996.

Gushee, David P. "Remembering Rwanda." *Christian Century* 21/8 (April 20, 2004): 28–31.

Guthrie, Donald. *New Testament Theology*. Leicester: InterVarsity, 1981.

Haar, Gerrie ter, and James J. Busatti, eds. *The Freedom to Do God's Will: Religious Fundamentalism and Social Change*. London: Routledge, 2003.

Habermas, Jürgen. *The Structural Transformation of the Public Sphere: An Inquiry into a Category of Bourgeois Society*. Translated by Thomas Burger with Frederick Lawrence. Cambridge, MA: MIT Press, 1991.

Hahn, Lewis Edwin, ed. *The Philosophy of Paul Ricoeur.* The Library of Living Philosophers vol. 22. Chicago: Open Court, 1995.

Hall, Douglas John. *God and Human Suffering: An Exercise in the Theology of the Cross.* Minneapolis: Augsburg, 1986.

———. "Preaching Reconciliation in the World of Long Memories." *Journal for Preachers* 26 (Lent 2003): 9–14.

Haller, James E. "Deliver Us From Evil: Genocide and the Christian World." *Journal of Religion & Society* Supplement Series 2 (2007): 138–52.

Hancocks, Graeme, John Sherbourne, and Christopher Swift. "'Are They Refugees?' Why Church of England Male Clergy Enter Healthcare Chaplaincy." *Practical Theology* 1/2 (2008): 163–79.

Harak, G. Simon. *Virtuous Passions: the Formation of Christian Character.* New York: Paulist, 1993.

Harding, Stephen, ed. *NYDIS Manual for NYC Religious Leaders: Spiritual Care and Mental Health for Disaster Response and Recovery.* New York: NYDS, 2007. Online: http://www.nydis.org/nydis/downloads/manual/NYDIS_Disaster_SC-MH_Manual.pdf

Hardy, Daniel W. "'The Rules of Scriptural Reasoning." (A Response to Peter Ochs). *The Journal of Scriptural Reasoning* 2/1 (May 2002): n.p.

Harrison, Jemima. "Your Disaster, Our Story." *Independent,* December 11, 1991.

Harrison, Verna. "Perichoresis in the Greek Fathers." *St. Vladimir's Theological Quarterly* 35/1 (1991): 53–65.

Harrison, Wendy. "After the Bradford Fire—Steps Towards Recovery: A Summary of the Social Services Response and Recommendations for Future Involvement with those Affected by the Disaster." Bradford City Fire Disaster: Social Services Response Information Pack Report. Bradford, UK: Metropolitan Council, 1987.

———. *The Bradford City Fire Disaster: Social Services Response Information Pack.* Bradford, UK: Bradford Metropolitan Council, 1987.

Hart, David Bentley. *The Doors of the Sea: Where Was God in the Tsunami?* Grand Rapids: Eerdmans, 2005.

———. "Where Was God? An Interview with David Bentley Hart." *Christian Century* 123/1 (January 10, 2006): 26–29.

Hartley, H. J. "Disasters Never Walk Alone: A Socio-Legal Examination of the 1989 Hillsborough and Marchioness Disasters." PhD diss., University of Lancaster, 2000.

Hartley, John E. *The Book of Job.* The New International Commentary of the Old Testament. Grand Rapids: Eerdmans, 1998.

Hasker, William. *The Emergent Self.* Ithaca: Cornell University Press, 1999.

Hauerwas, Stanley. *Christian Existence Today: Essays on Church, World, and Living in Between.* Grand Rapids: Baker, 1988.

———. *A Community of Character: Towards a Constructive Social Ethic.* Notre Dame: University of Notre Dame Press, 1981.

———. *Dispatches from the Front: Theological Engagements with the Secular.* Durham, NC: Duke University Press, 1994.

———. "The End of Religious Pluralism: A Tribute to David Burrell." In *Democracy and the New Religious Pluralism,* edited by Thomas Banchoff, 283–300. New York: Oxford University Press, 2007.

———. "Love's Not All You Need." *Cross Currents* 24 (Summer–Fall 1972): 225–37.

Bibliography

————. *Naming the Silences: God, Medicine, and the Problem of Suffering*. London: T & T Clark, 2004.

————. *With the Grain of the Universe: the Church's Witness and Natural Theology*. London: SCM, 2002.

Hauerwas, Stanley, and Gregory Jones, eds. *Why Narratives? Readings in Narrative Theology*. Grand Rapids: Eerdmans, 1989.

Hauerwas, Stanley, and Samuel Wells. "Why Christian Ethics Was Invented." In *The Blackwell Companion to Christian Ethics*, edited by Stanley Hauerwas and Sanuel Wells, 28–39. Oxford: Blackwell, 2004.

Hauerwas, Stanley, and William H. Willimon. *Resident Aliens: Life in the Christian Colony*. Nashville: Abingdon, 1996.

————. *Where Resident Aliens Live: Exercises for Christian Practice*. Nashville: Abingdon, 1996.

Haughen, Gary A. *Good News About Injustice: A Witness of Courage in a Hurting World*. Downers Grove: InterVarsity, 1999.

Hayman, Andrew, and Margaret Gilmore. *The Terrorist Hunters: The Ultimate Inside Story of Britain's Fight Against Terror*. London: Bantom, 2009.

Hays, Richard B. *The Moral Vision of the New Testament: Community, Cross, New Creation: A Contemporary Introduction to New Testament Ethics*. New York: HarperCollins, 1994.

Head, Dominic. *The Cambridge Introduction to Modern British Fiction, 1950–2000*. Cambridge: Cambridge University Press, 2002.

Heald, Gordon. "The Soul of Britain." *The Tablet*, June 3, 2000. Online: http://tinyurl.com/ysc4zo.

"Health Care Chaplains: Code of Conduct." Association of Hospice and Palliative Care Chaplains; the College of Health Care Chaplains; the Scottish Association of Chaplains in Healthcare. 2nd ed. Amicus, 2005.

Heasman, Kathleen. *Evangelicals in Action: An Appraisal of their Social Work in the Victorian Era*. London: Geoffrey Bles, 1962.

Hecht, Richard D. "Writing Terror: The Representations and Interpretations of Terrorism in Eduardo Galeano, Cormac McCarthy, and William Vollmann." *Journal of Religion & Society* Supplement 2 (2007): 49–62.

Helm, Paul. "Analysis Extra: 'Inspiration and Incarnation' One More Time." *Helm's Deep: Philosophical Theology* blog, January 12, 2008. Online: http://paulhelmsdeep.blogspot.com/2008/01/analysis-extra-inspiration-and.html.

————. "B. B. Warfield on Divine Passion." *Westminster Theological Journal* 69 (2007): 95–104.

————. "Evil, Love and Silence." *Helm's Deep: Philosophical Theology* blog, February 1, 2008. Online: http://paulhelmsdeep.blogspot.com/2008/02/evil-love-and-silence_01.html.

————. *Faith and Understanding*. Reason and Religion. Edinburgh: Edinburgh University Press, 1997.

————. *John Calvin's Ideas*. Oxford: Oxford University Press, 2004. Online: http://dx.doi.org/10.1093/0199255695.001.0001

————. *The Last Things: Death, Judgment, Heaven and Hell*. Edinburgh: The Banner of Truth Trust, 1989.

————. "Natural Law and Common Grace." *Helm's Deep: Philosophical Theology* blog, November 1, 2008. Online: http://paulhelmsdeep.blogspot.com/2008/11/natural-law-and-common-grace.html.

————. "Propositions and Speech Acts." *Helm's Deep: Philosophical Theology* blog, May 1, 2007. Online: http://paulhelmsdeep.blogspot.com/2007/05/analysis-2-propositions-and-speech-acts.html.

————. *The Providence of God*. Contours of Christian Theology. Edited by Gerald Bray. Leicester: InterVarsity, 1993.

————. "Revealed Propositions and Timeless Truths." *Religious Studies* 8/2 (1972): 127–36.

Helminiak, Daniel A. "Neurology, Psychology, and Extraordinary Religious Experiences." *Journal of Religion and Health* 23/1 (Spring 1984): 33–46.

Hendriksen, William. *The Gospel of Mark*. New Testament Commentary. Edinburgh: The Banner of Truth Trust, 1975.

————. *The Gospel of Matthew*. New Testament Commentary. Edinburgh: The Banner of Truth Trust, 1974.

Henry, Carl F. H. *God Who Stands and Stays*. Vol. 6 of *God, Revelation and Authority*. Edited by Carl F. H. Henry. Carlisle, UK: Paternoster, 1999.

Herrmann, Jack. "Disaster Response Planning and Preparedness: Phases of Disaster." New York Disaster Interfaith Services; (DYDIS), (2007): 11. Online: www.nydis.org/nydid/downloads/manual/NYDIS_Disaster-SC-MH_SectionI-Chapter1.pdf.

Herzfeld, Noreen, "Lessons from Srebrenica: The Danger of Religious Nationalism." *Journal of Religion & Society* Supplement Series 2 (2007): 110–16.

Hick, John. *Death and Eternal Life*. London: Macmillan, 1990.

————. *Evil and the God of Love*. Rev. ed. San Francisco: Harper & Row, 1977.

Hickman, Edward, ed. *The Works of Jonathan Edwards*. 2 vols. Edinburgh: The Banner of Truth Trust, 1974.

Hicks, Peter. *The Message of Evil and Suffering: Light into Darkness*. Nottingham: InterVarsity, 2006.

Hidden, Anthony. "Investigation into the Clapham Junction Railway Accident." HMG report. London: HMSO, 1989.

Hilborn, David. "The Nature of Hell." Report by the Evangelical Alliance Commission on Unity and Truth among Evangelicals. Carlisle, UK: Paternoster, 2000.

Hill, Joseph. *Suffering—Understanding the Love of God: Selections from the Writings of John Calvin*. Darlington, UK: Evangelical, 2005.

Hinton, Boyd. "The Role of Providence in Evangelical Social Thought." In *History, Society and The Churches: Essays in Honour of Owen Chadwick*, edited by Derek Beales and Geoffrey Best, 215–33. Cambridge: Cambridge University Press, 1985.

Hittinger, Russell. "Justice." In *The Blackwell Encyclopedia of Modern Christian Thought*, edited by Alister E. McGrath, 289–93. Oxford: Blackwell, 1990.

Hodder, Lindsay Michelle. "An Exploration of Family Communication Style and Its Impact upon Post Traumatic Stress Disorder." PsyD thesis, University of Southampton, 2003.

Hodge, Charles. *Commentary on the Epistle to the Romans*. Reprint of revised edition, 1886. Grand Rapids: Eerdmans, 1950.

Hoekema, Anthony A. *Created in God's Image*. Grand Rapids: Eerdmans, 1994.

Holdt, Martin. "God's Terrible Voice in the Nation." Paper read at the Westminster Conference, "The Voice of God," London, 2002.

Holland, Tom. *Commentary: Letter to the Romans*. Forthcoming.

―――. *Contours of Pauline Theology: A Radical New Survey of the Influences on Paul's Biblical Writings*. Fearn, Tain, UK: Christian Focus, 2004.

Holmes, Stephen. "The Justice of Hell and the Display of God's Glory in the Thought of Jonathan Edwards." *Pro Ecclesia* 9/4 (Fall 2000): 389–403.

Hookway, C. J. Review of *Freedom and Belief* by Galen Strawson. *The Philosophical Quarterly* 38/153 (October 1988): 533–35. Online: http://www.jstor.org/ stable/2219717).

Horner, David J. "The Church and Disaster: The Role of the Church in Relation to Mass Emergency and Disaster Situations." MTh thesis, Oxford Brookes University, January 2002.

House, H. Wayne, and Thomas D. Ice. *Dominion Theology: Blessing or Curse?* Portland, OR: Multnomah, 1988.

Howarth, Glennys. "Viewing the Body after a Traumatic Death." *BMJ* 340/c2301 (April 30, 2010). Online: http://www.bmj.com/content/340/bmj.c2301.

Hughes, Philip E. *Hope for a Despairing World: The Christian Answer to the Problem of Evil*. Grand Rapids: Baker, 1979.

Hunsinger, George. *Disruptive Grace: Studies in the Theology of Karl Barth*. Grand Rapids: Eerdmans, 2000.

Huntington, Samuel P. "The Clash of Civilizations?" *Foreign Affairs* 72/3 (Summer 1993): n.p. Online: http://history.club.faith.edu.tr/103%20Huntington%20 Clash%20of%20Civilizations%20full%20text.htm.

Hutchison, Alison. "Christ Within Crisis." An adaptation of an address originally delivered at the Women's Guild National Conference, Church of Scotland National Assembly Hall, New College, Edinburgh, date not known. (Email correspondence from Alison Hutchison to Rev. Roger Abbot. Cited April 2008, with permission.)

Hutton, Sarah. "The Cambridge Platonists." *The Stanford Encyclopedia of Philosophy*, Spring 2007 edition, edited by Edward N. Zalta, January 23, 2007. Online: http:// plato.stanford.edu/archives/spr2007/entries/cambridge-platonists/.

Institute of Technology. "The Bichard Inquiry Report (Documentary Summary)." 2004. Online: http://www.napta.org.uk/resources/bichard_inquiry.pdf.

Inter Faith Network for the United Kingdom. "Building Good Relations with People of Different Faiths and Beliefs." Pamphlet. London: Inter Faith Network for the UK, 2010. Online: http://www.interfaith.org.uk/publications/buildinggoodrelations .pdf.

―――. "Faith, Citizenship, and the Shared Life in Britain Today: A Discussion Document." London: Inter Faith Network for the UK, 2006. Online: http://www .interfaith.org.uk/publications/faithcitizenship2.pdf.

International Decade for Natural Disaster Reduction (IDNDR). "International Strategy for Disaster Reduction (ISDR)." May 2006. Online: http://www.fire.uni-freiburg .de/programmes/un/idndr/idndr.html.

"Iranian Cleric Blames Quakes on Promiscuous Women." BBC News, April 19, 2010. Online: http://news.bbc.co.uk/1/hi/world/middle_east/8631775.stm.

Jackson, Timothy P. *The Priority of Love: Christian Charity and Social Justice*. Princeton: Princeton University Press, 2003.

James, William. *The Varieties of Religious Experience*. Liguori, MO: Triumph, 1991.

————. "What is an Emotion?" In *Collected Essays and Reviews*, 244–75. New York: Longmans, Green,1920.

Jervolino, Domenico. "The Depth and Breadth of Paul Ricoeur's Philosophy." In *The Philosophy of Paul Ricoeur*, edited by Lewis Edwin Hahn, 533–643. The Library of Living Philosophers, vol. 22. Chicago: Open Court, 1995.

Johnson, Dennis E. "Spiritual Antithesis: Common Grace and Practical Theology." *Westminster Theological Journal* 63 (2002): 73–74.

Johnston, Keith L. Review of *Barth on the Descent into Hell: God, Atonement, and the Christian Life* by David Lauber. *Perspectives in Religious Studies* 35/3 (Fall 2008): 338–43.

Jones, Hywel R. *Only One Way: Do You Have to Believe in Christ to be Saved?* Bromley, UK: DayOne, 1996.

Juergensmeyer, Mark. "Christian Violence in America." *Annals of the American Academy of Political and Social Science* 558 (July 1998): 88–100.

————. *The New Cold War? Religious Nationalism Confronts the Secular State*. Berkeley: University of California Press, 1994.

Kaiser, Walter C., Jr. *Towards an Old Testament Theology*. Grand Rapids: Zondervan, 1978.

Kane, Robert, ed. *The Oxford Handbook of Free Will*. Oxford: Oxford University Press, 2002.

Kasdorf, Julia Spicher. "To Pasture: 'Amish Forgiveness,' Silence, and the West Nickel Mines School Shooting." *Crosscurrents* 59/3 (Fall 2007): 328–47.

Kashan, Hilal, and Ibrahim Mousawi. "Hizbullah's Jihad Concept." *Journal of Religion & Society* 9 (2007): 1–19.

Kearsley, Roy. "The Impact of Greek Concepts of God on the Christology of Cyril of Alexandria." *Tyndale Bulletin* 43 (1992): 307–8.

Kegley, Charles W., Jr., ed. *The New Global Terrorism: Characteristics, Causes, Controls*. Upper Saddle River, NJ: Prentice Hall, 2003.

Keith, Graham. "Patristic Views on Hell—Part 1." *Evangelical Quarterly* 71/3 (1999): 217–32.

————. "Patristic Views on Hell—Part 2." *Evangelical Quarterly* 71/4 (1999): 291–310.

Keller, Timothy J. *Ministries of Mercy: The Call of the Jericho Road*. 2nd ed. Phillipsburg, NJ: P & R, 1997.

Kelly, J. N. D. *Early Christian Doctrines*. London: Adam and Charles Black, 1968.

Kelly, Joseph F. *The Problem of Evil in the Western Tradition: From the Book of Job to Modern Genetics*. Collegeville, MN: Liturgical Press, 2002.

Kent County Constabulary. "The Zeebrugge Ferry Disaster: Part 2." Kent County, UK: 1990.

Kettler, Christian D. "He Takes Back the Ticket . . . For Us: Providence, Evil, Suffering, and the Vicarious Humanity of Christ." *Journal of Christian Theological Research* 8 (2003): 32–57.

Kihlstrom, John F. "Trauma and Memory Revisited." Paper presented at the 6th Tsukuba International Conference on Memory, "Memory and Emotion," Tsukuba, Japan, March 15, 2005. Online: http://socrates.berkeley.edu/~kihlstrm/Tsukuba05.htm.

Kilpatrick, Margaret Ann. "Coping with Survival: Aircraft Disasters and Emergencies: Guidelines for Psycho-Emotional Recovery." 1985.

Kim, Jaegwon. *Supervenience and the Mind*. Cambridge: Cambridge University Press, 1993.

Kim, Sebastian H. "Community Identity: Meaningful Engagement in Contemporary Society." Bradford Churches for Diversity and Dialogue, annual lecture at Bradford University, March 10, 2008. Online: http://www.bcdd.org.uk/annuallecture.shtml .Kinchin, David. *Post Traumatic Stress Disorder: The Invisible Injury.* Wantage, UK: Wessex, 2001.

King, Anthony. "Britons' Belief in God Vanishing as Religion is Replaced by Apathy." *Telegraph,* December 12, 2004. Online: http://www.telegraph.co.uk/news/ uknews/1479811/Britons-belief-in-God-vanishing-as-religion-is-replaced-by-apathy.html.

King, D. F. "8/1988 Boeing 737-236, G-BGJL." Report on the accident to Boeing 737-236, G-BGJL at Manchester International Airport on 22 August 1985. UK Department of Transport, Air Accidents Investigation Branch, December 1988.

King, William McGuire. "'History in Revelation' in the Theology of the Social Gospel." *The Harvard Theological Review* 76/1 (January 1983): 109–29.

Kirsh, G., D. J. A. Learmonth, J. P. Martindale, and the Nottingham, Leicester, Derby Aircraft Accident Study Group. "The Nottingham, Leicester, Derby Aircraft Accident Study: Preliminary Report Three Weeks After the Accident." *British Medical Journal* 298/6672 (February 1989): 503–5.

Klingbeil, Gerald A., and Martin G. Klingbeil. "The Prophetic Voice of Amos as a Paradigm for Christians in the Public Square." *Tyndale Bulletin* 58/2 (2007):161–82.

Kloosterman, Nelson D. "A Biblical Case For Natural Law: A Response Essay." *Ordained Servant* 16 (December 2007): n.p. Online: http://www.opc.org/os.html?article_ id=77&issue_id=26.

———. Review of *A Biblical Case for Natural Law*, by David Vandrunen. *New Horizons* 28/6 (June 2007): 22–23. Online: http://auxesis.net/kloosterman/review_natural_ law.pdf.

Knight, Douglas. "Christ, Religion and 'Other Religions.'" Paper presented to the Religion, Culture & Communication group of the Tyndale Fellowship, Cambridge, July 2007.

———. "The Church, the State and the Archbishop: The Fretful Audiences of Rowan Williams." Paper presented to the Religion, Culture & Communication group of the Tyndale Fellowship, Cambridge, July 2008.

Koenig, Harold G. *In the Wake of Disaster: Religious Responses to Terrorism and Catastrophe.* Philadelphia: Templeton Foundation, 2006.

Koenig, Harold G., et al. "Religion, Spirituality, and Medicine: A Rebuttal to Skeptics." *International Journal of Psychiatry in Medicine* 29/2 (1999): 123–31.

Koenig, Harold G., Michael E. McCullough, and David B. Larson. *Handbook of Religion and Health.* Oxford: Oxford University Press, 2001.

Kreider, Glenn R. "Sinners in the Hands of a Gracious God." *Bibliotheca Sacra* 163/651 (July–September 2006): 259–75.

Kritzinger, J. J. "The Rwanda Tragedy As Public Indictment Against Christian Mission." *Missionalia: Journal of the Southern African Missiological Society* (2006): n.p. Online: http://www.oocities.org/missionalia/rwanda1.htm.

Kroeker, P. Travis. "Why O'Donovan's Christendom is not Constantinian and Why Yoder's Voluntariety is not Hobbesian: A Debate in Theological Politics Re-defined." *Annual of the Society of Christian Ethics* 20 (2000): 41–64.

Kroll-Smith, Stephen J., and Stephen Robert Crouch. "A Chronic Technical Disaster and the Irrelevance of Religious Meaning: The Case of Sentralia, Pennsylvania." *Journal for the Scientific Study of Religion* 1 (1987): 25–37.

Kübler-Ross, Elizabeth. *On Death and Dying.* London: Rutledge, 1970.

Kvanvig, Jonathan L. "Hell." In *The Oxford Handbook of Eschatology*, edited by Jerry L. Walls, 413–27. Oxford: Oxford University Press, 2008.

———. *The Problem of Hell.* Oxford: Oxford University Press, 1993.

———. "Resurrection, Heaven, and Hell." In *A Companion to Philosophy of Religion*, edited by Charles Taliaferro, Paul Draper, and Philip L. Quinn, 630–38. Boston: Blackwell, 2010.

Lacey, Nicola. "Denial and Responsibility." In *Crime, Social Control and Human Rights: From Moral Panics to States of Denial: Essays in Honour of Stanley Cohen*, edited by David Downes, et al., 255–69. Cullompton, UK: Willan, 2007.

Ladd, George Eldon. *A Theology of the New Testament.* Grand Rapids: Eerdmans, 1974.

Lane, Megan. "Grappling with Global Grief." BBC News, September 12, 2001. Online: http://news.bbc.co.uk/1/hi/uk/1539794.stm.

Lane, William L. *The Gospel According to Mark: The English Text With Introduction, Exposition and Notes.* London: Marshall, Morgan and Scott, 1974.

Larkin, G. L., and J. Arnold. "Ethical Considerations in Emergency Planning, Preparedness, and Response to Acts of Terrorism." *Prehospital Disaster Medicine* 18 (2003): 170–78.

Larsson, J. P. *Understanding Religious Violence: Thinking Outside the Boxes on Terrorism.* Aldershot, UK: Ashgate, 2004.

Lash, Nicholas. *The Beginning and the End of "Religion."* Cambridge: Cambridge University Press, 1996.

Leahy, Frederick S. *The Hand of God: The Comfort of Having a Sovereign God.* Edinburgh: The Banner of Truth Trust, 2006.

Leavelle, Tracy Neale. "Prophecy, Purity, and Progress: Religion and Violence in the Conquest of America." *Journal of Religion and Society* Supplement Series 2 (2007): 14–30.

Lenski, R. C. H. *The Interpretation of Luke's Gospel.* Minneapolis: Augsburg, 1961.

Leonardt, Jorg, and Joachim Vogt. "Critical Incident, Critical Incident Stress, Post Traumatic Stress Disorder—Definitions and Underlying Neurological Processes." In *Critical Incident Stress Management in Aviations*, edited by Jorg Leonardt and Joachim Vogt, 43–52. Aldershot, UK: Ashgate, 2006.

Lerner, Fred. "Searching the Traumatic Stress Literature." In *Trauma Research Methodology*, edited by Eva B. Carlson, 1–21. Lutherville, Maryland: Sidran, 1996.

Letham, Robert. *Through Western Eyes: Eastern Orthodoxy: A Reformed Perspective.* Fearn, Tain, UK: Mentor, 2007.

Levin, Jeffrey S., and Preston L. Schiller. "Is There a Religious Factor in Health?" *Journal of Religion and Health* 26/1 (Spring 1987): 9–36.

Lewis, C. S. *The Problem of Pain.* London: Fount, 1940.

Lewis, Philip. "For the Peace of the City: Bradford a Case-Study." In *World Christianity in Local Context and Muslim Encounter: Essays in Memory of David A. Kerr*, edited by Stephen B. Goodwin, 173–86. London: Continuum, 2009.

Lia, Brynjar. *Globalization and the Future of Terrorism: Patterns and Predictions.* London: Routledge, 2005.

Bibliography

Lifton, R. J. *Home from the War: Vietnam Veterans: Neither Victims nor Executioners.* New York: Basic Books, 1973.

Lindbeck, George. *The Nature of Doctrine: Religion and Theology in a Postliberal Age.* Philadelphia: Westminster, 1984.

Linfield, Alan M. "Sheep and Goats: Current Evangelical Thought on the Nature of Hell and the Scope of Salvation." *Vox Evangelica* 24 (1994): 63–75.

Lloyd-Jones, David Martyn. *Knowing the Times: Addresses Delivered on Various Occasions 1942–1977.* Edinburgh: Banner of Truth, 1989.

London Assembly. "Report of the 7 July Review Committee." London: Greater London Authority, June 2006. Online: http://legacy.london.gov.uk/assembly/reports/7july/report.pdf.

Lorek, Piotr. *The Motif of Exile in the Hebrew Bible: An Analysis of a Basic Literary and Theological Pattern.* Theologica Wratislaviensia: Monografie, vol. 1. Wroclaw, Poland: Ewangelikalna Wyższa Szkoła Teologiczna, 2006.

Loughlin, Gerard. "Persons and Replicas." *Modern Theology* 4/4 (July 1985): 303–19.

———. *Telling God's Story: Bible, Church, and Narrative Theology.* Cambridge: Cambridge University Press, 1996.

Lucas, J. R. "Justice." *Philosophy* 47 (July 1972): 229–48.

Lucie-Smith, Alexander. *Narrative Theology and Moral Theology: The Infinite Horizon.* Aldershot, UK: Ashgate, 2007.

Luhman, Reginald S. "Belief in God and the Problem of Suffering." Expanded version of a paper first published in the *Evangelical Quarterly* 57/4 (1985): 327–48. Online: http://www.theologicalstudies.org.uk/pdf/suffering_luhman.pdf.

Lyall, David. *The Integrity of Pastoral Care.* London: SPCK, 2001.

MacIntyre, Alasdair. *After Virtue: A Study in Moral Theory.* London: Duckworth, 1985.

———. *Whose Justice? Which Rationality?* London: Duckworth, 1998.

Macleod, Donald. *Behold Your God.* Fearn, Tain, UK: Christian Focus, 1990.

Mangina, Joseph L. *Karl Barth: Theologian of Christian Witness.* Aldershot, UK: Ashgate, 2004.

Mare, W. Harold. Review article. *Presbyterian* 15 (Spring 1989): 62–65.

Marsden, George M. *Understanding Fundamentalism and Evangelicalism.* Grand Rapids: Eerdmans, 1991.

Marsh, Clive. Review of *God is Not a Story: Realism Revisited* by Francesca Aran Murphy. *The Journal of Theological Studies* 60/1 (April 2009): 338–40.

Marsh, Michael. *Out-of-Body and Near-Death Experiences.* Oxford: Oxford University Press, 2010.

Marsh, William. "Healers or Hired Guns?" *R-Briefing* 25 (August 1999). Cambridge: The Relationships Foundation.

Marshall, Molly T. "Participating in the Life of God: A Trinitarian Pneumatology." Presidential address to the National Association of Baptist Professors of Religion. Toronto, CN. November 23, 2002.

Martin, Troy W. "*The Good* as God (Romans 5.7)." *Journal for the Study of the New Testament* 25 (2002): 55–70.

Marty, Martin E. "Hell Disappeared. No One Noticed: A Civic Argument." *The Harvard Theological Review* 78. (July–October 1985): 381–98.

Masonis, Jill. "Corporate Manslaughter Act—Do or Die." *Health Service Journal* 3 (September 2007): n.p. Online: http://www.hsj.co.uk/resource-centre/corporate-manslaughter-act-do-or-die/59537.article.

Mathewes, Charles. "Providence and Political Discernment." Conference paper presented for Deus Habet Consilium: The Career & Prospects of Providence in Modern Theology, School of Divinity, History and Philosophy, University of Aberdeen, January 2008.

————. *A Theology of Public Life*. Cambridge Studies in Christian Thought. Cambridge: Cambridge University Press, 2007.

May, Nicholas. "Job and Jeremiah: Understanding the Divine Moral Order through Lament and Response." *Journal of Biblical Studies* 3/1 (January 2003): 22–26.

McAllister, Therese, Jonathan Barnett, John Gross, Ronald Hamburger, and Jon Magnusson. "World Trade Center Building Performance Study: Data Collection, Preliminary Observations, and Recommendations." Chapter 1, FEMA 403, Federal Emergency Management Agency, May 2002.

McCann, J. Clinton. *A Theological Introduction to the Book of Psalms: The Psalms as Torah*. Nashville: Abingdon, 1993.

McClenahan, Muriel. "London Family Assistance Centre: Provisional Guidance Document." London Resilience Team. February 2006.

————. "Meeting the Needs of the People." The Emergency Services Show, Royal Horticultural Halls, London, October 19, 2006.

McDaniel, Denzil. *Enniskillen: The Remembrance Sunday Bombing*. Dublin: Wolfhound, 1997.

McDermott, Gerald R. *Can Evangelicals Learn From World Religions? Jesus, Revelation and Tradition*. Downers Grove, IL: InterVarsity, 2000.

McDowell, John C. "Much Ado about Nothing: Karl Barth's Being Unable to Do Nothing about Nothingness." *International Journal of Systematic Theology* 4/3 (November 2002): 319–35.

————. "Nothing Will Come of Nothing: Karl Barth on *Das Nichtige*." Unpublished paper.

McFadyen, Alistair. *Bound to Sin: Abuse, Holocaust and the Christian Doctrine of Sin*. Cambridge Studies in Christian Doctrine. Cambridge: Cambridge University Press, 2000.

————. "Truth as Mission: The Christian Claim to Universal Truth in a Pluralist Public World." *Scottish Journal of Theology* 46 (1993): 437–56.

McFadyen, Alistair, and Marcel Sarot, eds. *Forgiveness and Truth: Explorations in Contemporary Theology*. Edinburgh: T & T Clark, 2001.

McGinty, Steven. *Fire in the Night: The Piper Alpha Disaster*. London: Macmillan, 2009.

McGowan, Andrew. "Providence and Common Grace: A Reformed Perspective." Conference paper presented for Deus Habet Consilium: The Career & Prospects of Providence in Modern Theology, School of Divinity, History and Philosophy, University of Aberdeen, January 2008.

McGrath, Alister E., ed. *The Blackwell Encyclopedia of Modern Christian Thought*. Oxford: Blackwell, 1993.

————, ed. *Christian Theology: An Introduction*. 4th edition. Oxford: Blackwell, 2007.

————. *The Open Secret: A New Vision for Natural Theology*. Oxford: Blackwell, 2008.

————. *The Twilight of Atheism: The Rise and Fall of Disbelief in the Modern World*. New York: Doubleday, 2004.

McGrath, Joanna Collicutt. "Post-Traumatic Growth and the Origins of Early Christianity." *Mental Health, Religion & Culture* 9/3 (2006): 291–306.

McGrath, John, Ian Gray, and Kim Scriven. "Climate Alarm: Disasters Increase as Climate Change Bites." Oxfam Briefing Paper. November 2007.

McIntosh, Neil. "Lockerbie: A Local Authority Response to the Disaster." Report. Dumfries and Galloway Regional Council, 1989.

McTaggart, John. *Some Dogmas of Religion*. London: Edward Arnold, 1906.

Megoran, Nick Solly. *The War on Terror: How Should Christians Respond?* Nottingham: InterVarsity, 2007.

Meisenhelder, Janice Bell, and John P. Marcum. "Responses of Clergy to 9/11: Posttraumatic Stress, Coping, and Religious Outcomes." *Journal for the Scientific Study of Religion* 43/4 (2004): 547–54.

Mendus, Susan. "The Importance of Love in Rawl's Theory of Justice." *British Journal of Political Science* 29/1 (1999): 57–75.

Mennonite Disaster Service. "Early Response Team Manual." Revised edition, January 2008. Online: http://mds.mennonite.net/fileadmin/Resources/ERT_documents/Early_Response_Team_Manual_January__08_edition.pdf.

Meredith, Martin. *The State of Africa: A History of Fifty Years of Independence*. London: Free Press, 2005.

Milbank, John. *Theology and Social Theory: Beyond Secular Reason*. Oxford: Blackwell, 1993.

Misztal, Bronislav, and Anson Shupe. *Revival of Religious Fundamentalism in East and West*. Westport, CT: Praeger, 1992.

Mitchell, Jerry T. "The Hazards of One's Faith: Hazard Perceptions of South Carolina Christian Clergy." *Environmental Hazards* 2/1 (March 2000): 25–41.

Mitchell, Patrick. *Evangelicalism and National Identity in Ulster, 1921–1998*. Oxford: Oxford University Press, 2003. Online: http://www.oxfordscholarship.com/view/10.1093/0199256152.001.0001/acprof-9780199256150.

Moellor, Susan. *Compassion Fatigue: How the Media Sell Disaster, Famine, War and Death*. London: Routledge, 1999.

Moll, Rob. "The Father of Faith-Based Diplomacy." *Christianity Today* 52/9 (September 2008): n.p. Online: http://www.christianitytoday.com/ct/2008/september/29.54.html.

Moltmann, Jürgen. "The Crucified God." In *The Crucified God: The Cross of Christ as the Foundation and Criticism of Christian Theology*, edited by Jürgen Moltmann, 200–274 . London: SCM, 1974.

Moo, Douglas. *The Epistle to the Romans*. New International Commentary on the New Testament. Grand Rapids: Eerdmans, 1996.

Morris, Leon. *The Apostolic Preaching of the Cross*. 3rd edition. London: Tyndale, 1965.

———. *The Cross In The New Testament*. Exeter, UK: Paternoster, 1976.

———. *The Epistle to the Romans*. Leicester: InterVarsity, 1988.

———. *The Gospel According to John*. The New International Commentary on the New Testament. London: Marshall, Morgan and Scott, 1971.

Mort, Maggie, Ian Convery, Josephine Baxter, and Cathy Bailey. "Psycho-Social Effects of the 2001 UK Foot and Mouth Disease Epidemic in a Rural Population: Qualitative Diary Based Study." *BMJ* 331/7527 (November 24, 2005): n.p Online: http://www.bmj.com/content/331/7527/1234.

Mott, Stephen. *Jesus and Social Ethics*. Bramcote, UK: Grove, 1984.

Motyer, J. A. *The Prophecy of Isaiah*. Leicester: InterVarsity, 1993.

Mouw, Richard J. *He Shines In All That's Fair: Culture and Common Grace.* Grand Rapids: Eerdmans, 2001.

———. *Uncommon Decency: Christian Charity in an Uncivil World.* Downers Grove, IL: InterVarsity, 1992.

Mouw, Richard J., and Sander Griffioen. *Pluralisms and Horizons: An Essay in Christian Public Philosophy.* Grand Rapids: Eerdmans, 1993.

Mowat, Harriet. "The Potential for Efficacy of Healthcare Chaplaincy and Spiritual Care Provision in the NHS (UK): A Scoping Review of Recent Research." Report from NHS Yorkshire & Humber and Mowat Research, January 2008.

Mowat, Harriet, and John Swinton. "What Do Chaplains Do? The Role of the Chaplain in Meeting the Spiritual Needs of Patients." Report no. CSHD/MR001. University of Aberdeen; Mowat Research, February 2005.

Munday, Jack W. "A Ministry to a Pluralistic Community." Address given at Sharing Hope in Crisis, Billy Graham Rapid Response Team, Emmanuel Christian Centre, London, March 27, 2010.

Murphy, Francesca Aran. *God is Not a Story: Realism Revisited.* Oxford: Oxford University Press, 2007.

Murphy, Howard R. "The Ethical Revolt Against Orthodoxy in Early Victorian England." *The American Historical Review* 60/4 (July 1955): 800–817.

Murphy, Nancey. *Beyond Liberalism and Fundamentalism: How Modern and Postmodern Philosophy Set the Theological Agenda.* Valley Forge, PA: Trinity,1996.

———. *Bodies and Souls, or Spirited Bodies.* Cambridge: Cambridge University Press, 2006.

———. "A Non-Reductive Physicalist Account of Human Nature." Lecture presented at the Ethics, Values and Personhood in the 21st Century conference, Seattle Pacific University, January 2000.

Murray, John. *The Epistle to the Romans.* The New London Commentary on the New Testament. London: Marshall, Morgan & Scott, 1967.

Myers, Ken. "Christianity, Culture, and Common Grace." Berea Publications, 1994. Online: http://www.marshillaudio.org/resources/pdf/ComGrace.pdf.

Nader, Kathleen. "Guilt Following Traumatic Events." September 21, 2001. Online: http://www.giftfromwithin.org/html/firstaid.html.

Nazir-Ali, Michael. "Global and Local—Christian Muslim Relations, Here, There and Everywhere." Bradford Churches for Diversity and Dialogue, First Annual Lecture, March 22, 2007. Online: http://bcdd.org.uk/docstore/090307annual.pdf.

Netland, Harold. *Encountering Religious Pluralism: The Challenge to Christian Faith and Mission.* Downers Grove, IL: InterVarsity, 2001.

Neufeld, Tom Yoder. "'In the Middle:' Biblical Reflections on Restorative Justice." MCC Network Restorative Justice. Winnipeg, Canada, February 14–15, 2003. Online: http://mcc.org/canada/restorativejustice/resources/articles/neufeld.html.

Neuhaus, Richard John, ed. *Biblical Interpretation in Crisis: The Ratzinger Conference on Bible and Church.* Encounter Series. Grand Rapids: Eerdmans, 1989.

NHS Education for Scotland (NES). "A Multi-Faith Resource for Healthcare Staff." n.d. Online: http://www.mfghc.com/resources/resources_85.pdf.

NHS Management Executive. "Emergency Planning in the NHS: Health Services Arrangements for Dealing with Major Incidents." London: NHSME, 1990.

Nicetas. *Niceta of Remesiana: His Life and Works.* Elibron Classics. New York: Adamant Media, 2005.

Bibliography

Nichol, Armand M., Jr. *The Question of God: C. S. Lewis and Sigmund Freud Debate God, Love, Sex, and the Meaning of Life.* New York: Free Press, 2002.

Niebuhr, H. Richard. *Christ and Culture.* New York: Harper Collins, 2001.

———. "The Story of our Life." In *Why Narratives? Readings in Narrative Theology,* edited by Stanley Hauerwas and Gregory Jones, 21–44. Grand Rapids: Eerdmans, 1989.

Niebuhr, Reinhold. "The Christian in a Secular Age." In *The Essential Reinhold Niebuhr: Selected Essays and Addresses,* edited by Robert McAfee Brown, 79–92. New Haven, CT: Yale University Press, 1986.

———. *Moral Man and Immoral Society: A Study of Ethics and Politics.* Louisville: Westminster Knox, 2001.

Nock, O. S. *Historic Railway Disasters.* 4th edition. Revised by B. K. Cooper. London: BCA, 1992.

Noll, Mark A. *The Scandal of the Evangelical Mind.* Grand Rapids: Eerdmans, 1994.

"Non-Terrorist Related Disasters Affecting UK Nationals on Foreign Soil—The Bahrain Boat Disaster and the Tsunami." Part of a program for "Supporting Survivors: An Integrated Approach," Association of Train Operators, and Family Assistance Foundation, Dudley, West Midlands, UK, November 23–24, 2006.

North, Rachel. *Out of the Tunnel.* London: Friday, 2007.

Nugteren, Alertina. "Collective/Public Ritual Behaviours After Disasters: An Emerging Manifestation of Civil Religion?" Paper presented at the Spiritual Supermarket conference, London School of Economics, April 2001.

Nussbaum, Martha C. *Upheavals of Thought: The Intelligence of Emotions.* Cambridge: Cambridge University Press, 2001.

Obama, Barack. "The President's Prayer." *Third Way,* Winter, 2009. Online: http://www.thirdwaymagazine.co.uk/editions/winter-2009/features/the-president's-prayer.aspx

Ochs, Peter. "The Society of Scriptural Reasoning: The Rules of Scriptural Reasoning." *The Journal of Scriptural Reasoning* 21 (May 2002): n.p.

O'Donovan, Oliver. *Desire of the Nations: Rediscovering the Roots of Political Theology.* Cambridge: Cambridge University Press, 1996.

———. *Resurrection and The Moral Order: An Outline For Evangelical Ethics.* Leicester: InterVarsity, 1994.

Okholm, Dennis L., and Timothy R. Phillips, eds. *Four Views on Salvation in a Pluralistic World.* Grand Rapids: Zondervan, 1996.

Olsen, Stanley N. "Romans 5–8 as Pastoral Theology." *Word & World* 6/4 (Autumn 1986): 390–97.

O'Neill, Onora. "A Question of Trust." BBC Reith Lectures, 2002. Online: http://www.bbc.co.uk/radio4/reith2002/lecture1.shtml.

"The Omagh Bomb: 15 August, 1998." *Ireland Story* website. N.d. Online: http://www.wesleyjohnston.com/users/ireland/past/omagh/dead.html.

Orchard, Helen. *Hospital Chaplaincy: Modern, Dependable?* Sheffield: Lincoln Theological Institute, 2000.

Origen. *On the Principles.* Translated by Frederick Crombie. N.p. Online: http://www.ellopos.net/elpenor/greek-texts/fathers/origen/principia.asp.

Osborne, Grant. *The Hermeneutical Spiral.* Downers Grove, IL: InterVarsity, 1991.

Oswalt, John N. *The Book of Isaiah: Chapters 40–66.* New International Critical Commentary. Grand Rapids: Eerdmans, 1998.

Paddock, Gerald. "Air Crash M1 Motorway, Leicestershire, Sunday 8 January 1989." Report prepared by the ecumenical coordinator of church resources in the event of a major emergency, 1989.

Palm, Kathleen M, Melissa A. Polusney, and Victoria M. Follette. "Vicarious Traumatization: Potential Hazards and Interventions for Disaster and Trauma Workers." *Prehospital and Disaster Medicine* 19/1 (January–March 2004): 73–78.

"Panorama: Omagh—What the Police Were Never Told." *Panorama*, BBC One, 8:30–9:30 p.m., September 15, 2008. Online: http://tinyurl.com/4wy3uj.

Parkes, Colin Murray. *Bereavement: Studies of Grief in Adult Life*. Harmondsworth, UK: Penguin 1975.

Partridge, Christopher H., ed. *Fundamentalisms*. Carlisle, UK: Paternoster, 2001.

Peake, Gordon, Cathy Gormley-Heenan, and Mari Fitzduff. "From Warlords to Peacelords: Local Leadership Capacity in Peace Processes." Ulster: The United Nations University, 2004.

Peck, John, and Charles Strohmer. *Uncommon Sense: God's Wisdom for our Complex and Changing World*. London: SPCK, 2001.

Peels, Eric. "I Hate Them With Perfect Hatred (Psalm 139:21–22)." *Tyndale Bulletin* 59/1 (May 2008): 35–51.

Pellauer, David. *Ricoeur: A Guide for the Perplexed*. London: Continuum, 2007.

Philips, Timothy R., and Dennis Okholm, eds. *The Nature of Confession: Evangelicals and Postliberals in Conversation*. Downers Grove, IL: InterVarsity, 1996.

Pinnock, Clark. *A Wideness in God's Mercy: The Finality of Jesus Christ in a World of Religions*. Grand Rapids: Zondervan, 1992.

Pinnock, Clark, and Robert C. Brow, *Unbounded Love: A Good News Theology for the 21st Century*. Carlisle: Paternoster, 1994.

Pinnock, Clark, Richard Rice, John Saunders, William Hasker, and David Basinger. *The Openness of God: A Biblical Challenge to the Traditional Understanding of God*. Downers Grove, IL: InterVarsity, 1994.

"Piper Alpha Memorial." *Foresterhill News & Views*, August 1991.

"Piper Alpha's Legacy." *The Archive*, BBC Radio 4, 8:00–9:00 p.m., July 5, 2008.

Piper, John. "Putting My Daughter to Bed Two Hours After the Bridge Collapse." *Desiring God* blog, August 7, 2007. Online: http://www.desiringgod.org/Blog/745_putting_my_daughter_to_bed_two_hours_after_the_bridge_collapsed/.

———. "Tsunami and Repentance." *Desiring God* blog, January 5, 2005. Online: http://www.desiringgod.org/ResourceLibrary/TasteAndSee/ByDate/2005/1279_Tsunami_and_Repentance/.

Pitstick, Alyssa Lyra. *Light in Darkness: Hans Urs von Balthasar and the Catholic Doctrine of Christ's Descent into Hell*. Grand Rapids: Eerdmans, 2007.

Pitt, Michael. "The Pitt Review: Learning Lessons From The 2007 Floods: An Independent Review." HMG report. London: Crown Copyright, 2007.

Plantinga, Alvin C. *God, Freedom, and Evil*. Grand Rapids: Eerdmans 1999.

Plevak, David J. Review of *Heal Thyself: Spirituality, Medicine, and the Distortion of Christianity*, by James Shuman and Keith G. Meador. *Anesthesiology* 101/4 (October 2004): 1055. Online: http://journals.lww.com/anesthesiology/Fulltext/2004/10000/Heal_Thyself__Spirituality,_Medicine,_and_the.64.aspx

Plude, Frances Ford. "Coping With Disaster: How Media Audiences Process Grief." Article from *Media Development*, World Association for Christian Communication, London, 1992.

Plummer, A. *The Gospel According to St. Luke*. The International Critical Commentary on the Holy Scriptures of the Old and New Testaments. Edinburgh: T & T Clark, 1910.

Police Ombudsman for Northern Ireland. "Statement by the Police Ombudsman for Northern Ireland on her Investigation of Matters Relating to the Omagh Bomb on August 15, 1998." December 12, 2001. Online: http://cain.ulst.ac.uk/issues/police/ombudsman/po1212010omagh1.pdf.

Pollard, Laurence. "Art Attack (Part Two)." BBC Radio 4. November 3, 2009.

Pope Paul VI. *Lumen Gentium*. November 21, 1964.

Porter, Jean. "Recent Studies in Aquinas's Virtue Ethic—A Review Essay." *Journal of Religious Ethics* 26/1 (Spring 1998): 191–213.

Potter, Harry. "Rebel Against the Light: Job or God?" *Expository Times* 103/7 (April 1992): 198–201.

Pratz, Gunther. "The Relationship Between Incarnation and Atonement in the Theology of Thomas F. Torrance." *Journal for Christian Theological Research* 3/2 (1998): n.p. Online: http://apu.edu/~CTRF/articles/1998_articles/pratz.html.

Prestige, G. L. *God in Patristic Thought*. William Heinemann,1936; reprint London: SPCK, 1969.

Preston, Peter. "Dunblane: Reflecting Tragedy." Report from British Executive of the International Press Institute, September 1996.

Prochaska, Frank. *Christianity and Social Service in Modern Britain: The Distinguishing Spirit*. Oxford: Oxford University Press, 2006.

———. *Schools of Citizenship: Charity and Civic Virtue*. London: Civitas, 2002.

Proudfoot, Wayne. "From Theology to a Science of Religion: Jonathan Edwards and William James on Religious Affections." *The Harvard Theological Review* 82/2 (April 1989):149–68.

Purcell, Boyd C. "Spiritual Terrorism." *American Journal of Hospice and Palliative Medicine* 15/3 (May–June 1998): 167–73.

Purves, Andrew. *The Search for Compassion: Spirituality and Mission*. Louisville: John Knox, 1989.

Ra, Kyung-U. "An Investigation of the Influence of the Paschal-New Exodus Motif on the Description of Christ and His Work in the Gospel of John." PhD diss., University of Wales, 2009.

Raftery, John. "Doing Better than the Media: Ethical Issues in Trauma Research." *The Australasian Journal of Disaster and Trauma Studies* 2 (1997): n.p.

Rahner, Karl, ed. *Encyclopedia of Theology: A Concise Sacramentum Mundi*. London: Burns and Oates, 2004.

Rai, Milan. *7/7: The London Bombings, Islam, and the Iraq War*. London: Pluto, 2006.

Rail Safety and Standards Board. "Hatfield Derailment Investigation Interim Recommendations of the Investigation Board: Hatfield Report and Recommendations." November 16, 2004. Online: http://www.railwaysarchive.co.uk/documents/RSSB_Hatfield2000.pdf

Raines, John C. "Tools and Common Grace." *Cross Currents* 40/3 (Fall 1990): 314–27.

Rando, Therese A. *Treatment of Complicated Mourning*. Champaign, IL: Research, 1997.

Raphael, Beverly. *When Disaster Strikes: How Individuals and Communities Cope With Catastrophe*. London: Hutchinson, 1984.

Raphael, Beverley, Brian G. McCaughey, Robert J. Ursano, Carol S. Fullerton, eds. *Individual and Community Responses to Trauma and Disaster: The Structure of Human Chaos*. Cambridge: Cambridge University Press, 1994.

Rawls, John. *Political Liberalism*. New York: Columbia University Press, 1996.

———. *A Theory of Justice*. Oxford: Oxford University Press, 1999.

Ray, Charles. *The Life of Charles Haddon Spurgeon*. London: Passmore & Alabaster, 1903.

Redekop, Vern Neufeld, and Oscar Gasana. "Implication of Religious Leaders in Mimetic Structures of Violence: The Case of Rwanda." *Journal of Religion & Society* Supplement Series 2 (2007): 117–37.

Redmond, Anthony D. "Natural Disasters." *BMJ* 330/7502 (2005): 1259–61.

Reinders, Hans. "Providence and Ethics." Conference paper presented for Deus Habet Consilium: The Career & Prospects of Providence in Modern Theology, School of Divinity, History and Philosophy, University of Aberdeen, January 2008.

Ricoeur, Paul. "Evil: A Challenge to Philosophy and Theology." Translated by David Pellauer. *Journal of American Academy of Religion* 53/4 (December 1985): 635–48.

———. "Life in Quest of Narrative." In *On Paul Ricoeur: Narrative and Interpretation*, edited by David Wood, 20–33. London: Routledge, 1991.

———. *Time and Narrative*. Vol.1. Translated by Kathleen McLaughlin and David Pellauer. Chicago: University of Chicago Press, 1984.

Ridderbos, Herman. *Paul: An Outline of His Theology*. London: SPCK, 1977.

Ripley, Amanda. "A Survival Guide to Catastrophe." *Time*, May 29, 2008. Online: http://www.time.com/time/magazine/article/0,9171,1810315,00.html.

———. *The Unthinkable: Who Survives When Disaster Strikes—and Why*. New York: Crown, 2008.

Rittenhouse, Bruce P. "What Does It Mean to Tell the Truth about the Virginia Tech Killings?" *Currents in Theology and Mission* 34/5 (October 2007): 365–68.

Robbins, Anna M. *Methods In The Madness: Diversity in Twentieth-Century Christian Social Ethics*. Carlisle, UK: Paternoster, 2004.

Robbins, Thomas, and Susan J. Palmer, eds. *Millennium, Messiahs, and Mayhem: Contemporary Apocalyptic Movements*. London: Routledge, 1997.

Roberts, Richard. "Social Science and Christian Thought." In *The Blackwell Encyclopedia of Modern Christian Thought*, edited by Alistair E. McGrath, 608–16. Oxford: Blackwell, 1993.

Roberts, Stephen B., and William W. C. Ashley, eds. *Disaster Spiritual Care: Practical Clergy Responses to Community, Regional and National Tragedy*. Woodstock, VT: Skylight Paths, 2008.

Robinson, Anthony B. "The Church as Countercultural Enclave." *Christian Century* 107/23 (August 8–15, 1990): 739–41.

Robinson, Daniel Sommer. "The Critique of Meliorism." *International Journal of Ethics* 34/2 (January 1924): 175–94.

Rockwell, Teed. "Physicalism, Non-Reductive." In *Dictionary of the Philosophy of Mind*, edited by Elias Smith. Online: http://philosophy.uwaterloo.ca/MindDict/nonreductivephysicalism.html.

Rogers, Daphne Fuller. *Pastoral Care for Post-Traumatic Stress Disorder: Healing The Shattered Soul*. New York: Haworth Pastoral, 2002.

Bibliography

Roht-Arriaza, Naomi, and Javier Mariezcurrena, eds. *Transitional Justice in the Twenty-First Century: Beyond Truth versus Justice*. Cambridge: Cambridge University Press, 2006.

Rorty, Richard M., ed. *The Linguistic Turn: Essays in Philosophical Method*. Chicago: University of Chicago Press, 1967.

Rothstein, Edward. "Seeking Justice, of Gods or the Politicians." *New York Times*, September 8, 2005. Online: http://tinyurl.com/6f3tv8.

Rubin, G. James, Lisa Page, Oliver Morgan, et al. "Public Information Needs After the Poisoning of Alexander Litvinenko with Polonium-210 in London: Cross Sectional Telephone Survey and Qualitative Analysis." *BMJ* 335/7630 (2007). Online: http://www.bmj.com/cgi/content/full/335/7630/1143.

Runia, Klaas. *The Present-Day Christological Debate*. Leicester: InterVarsity, 1984.

Sage, William O. "The Faith Community as Intermediate and Long Term Caregiver: Stepping Forward in a Disaster." In New York Interfaith Service Disaster Manual, 2007: 15–21. Online: http://www.nydis.org/nydis/downloads/manual/NYDIS_Disaster_SC-MH_Manual_SectionI-Chapter2.pdf.

Sage, William W. "Spiritual and Emotional Care Resource." World Church Service. Online: http://www.churchpandemicresources.ca/files/SpiritualEmotionalCare.pdf.

Sahlin, Monte. "Waco: A Case Study in Crisis Management." In *Crisis Seminar Training Manual*. Crisis Management and Training Committee, 2002.

Sanday, William, and Arthur C. Headlam. *A Critical and Exegetical Commentary on The Epistle to the Romans*. 5th ed. The International Critical Commentary. Edinburgh: T & T Clark, 1902.

Sargant, William. *Battle for the Mind: A Physiology of Conversion and Brainwashing*. London: Heinemann, 1957.

Saville, Andy. "Reconciliationism—A Forgotten Evangelical Doctrine of Hell." *Evangelical Quarterly* 79/1 (January 2007): 35–51.

Schon, Donald A. *The Reflective Practitioner: How Professionals Think in Action*. Aldershot, UK: Ashgate, 1991.

Schreiner, Thomas R. *Paul, Apostle of God's Glory in Christ: A Pauline Theology*. Leicester: InterVarsity, 2001.

Schreiner, Thomas R., and Bruce R. Ware, eds. *Still Sovereign: Contemporary Perspectives on Election, Foreknowledge and Grace*. Grand Rapids: Baker, 2000.

Schuetze, Armin W. "The Church's Social Concerns: Scriptural Imperatives and Limitations." Wisconsin Lutheran Seminary. Online: http://www.wlessays.net/authors/S/SchuetzeSocial/SchuetzeSocial.PDF.

Seymour, Charles. "Hell, Justice, and Freedom." *Journal for Philosophy of Religion* 43/2 (April 1998): 69–86.

Sheehan, W., and J. Kroll. "Psychiatric Patient's Belief in General Health Factors and Sin as Causes of Illness." *American Journal of Psychiatry* 147/1 (1990): 112–13.

Sherman, Lawrence W., and Heather Strang. "Restorative Justice: The Evidence." London: The Smith Institute, 2007. Online: http://www.esmeefairbairn.org.uk/docs/RJ_exec_summary.pdf

"Show Issue." *Emergency Services Times* 7 (October 2006).

Shuman, Joel James, and Keith G. Meador. *Heal Thyself: Spirituality, Medicine, and the Distortion of Christianity*. Oxford: Oxford University Press, 2003.

Siemens, David F., Jr. "Neuroscience, Theology, and Unintended Consequences." *Perspectives on Science and Christian Faith* 57/3 (September 2005): 187–90.

Simkins, Ronald A., ed. "The Contexts of Religion and Violence." *Journal of Religion & Society* Supplement 2 (2007).

Simms, Karl. *Paul Ricoeur.* London: Routledge, 2003.

Sladden, David. "Identificational Repentance: Theology of Apology." Paper delivered at the Evangelical Alliance conference "Repenting for Others?" Sutton Coldfield Baptist Church, June, 2001.

Sloan, Richard P. *Blind Faith: The Unholy Alliance of Religion and Medicine.* New York: St. Martin's, 2008.

Sloan, R. P., E. Bagiella, and T. Powell. "Religion, Spirituality, and Medicine." *Lancet* 353/9153 (February 20, 1999): 664–67.

Sloan, R. P., et al. "Should Physicians Prescribe Religious Activities?" *New England Journal of Medicine* 342 (2000): 1913–16.

Smith, Colin. "Shooting Incident at Hungerford on 19 August 1987." Report to the Secretary of State for the UK Home Department. Online: http://www.economicexpert.com/a/Hungerford:Report.html.

Smith, David Horton. "Churches Are Generally Ignored in Contemporary Voluntary Action Research: Causes and Consequences." *Review of Religious Research* 24/4 (June 1983): 295–303.

Smith, Stacy. "Exploring the Interaction of Trauma and Spirituality." *Traumatology* 10/4 (December 2004): 231–43.

South Yorkshire NHS Workforce Development Confederation. "Caring for the Spirit: A Strategy for the Chaplaincy and Spiritual Healthcare Workforce." November 2003. Online: http://www.mfghc.com/cfts/cfts_strategy_03.pdf.

Southern, Neil. "Reconciliation in Londonderry: The Challenges and Constraints Experienced by Protestant Clergy." *Peace and Change* 31/4 (October 2004): 506–32.

Spencer, Nick. *Asylum and Immigration: A Christian Perspective on a Polarised Debate.* Bletchley, UK: Paternoster, 2004.

———. "Doing God: A Future for Faith in the Public Square." Report, Theos Public Theology Think Tank. London: Theos, 2006. Online: http://www.theosthinktank.co.uk/Files/MediaFiles/TheosBookletfinal.pdf.

Spurgeon, C. H. *C. H. Spurgeon Autobiography: The Early Years* 1834–1859. Vol. 1. Rev. ed. Originally compiled by his wife and private secretary. London: Banner of Truth Trust, 1962.

———. *The Park Street and Metropolitan Pulpit: Containing Sermons Preached and Revised by The Rev. C. H. Spurgeon During the Year* 1861. Vol. 7. London: Passmore & Alabaster, 1862.

Stackhouse, John G., Jr. *Can God Be Trusted? Faith and the Challenge of Evil.* 2nd ed. Downers Grove, IL : Intervarsity, 2009.

———. *Evangelical Futures: A Conversation on Theological Method.* Grand Rapids: Baker, 2000.

———. *Evangelical Landscapes: Facing Critical Issues of the Day.* Grand Rapids: Baker, 2002.

———. *Making the Best of It: Following Christ in the Real World.* Oxford: Oxford University Press, 2008.

Stackhouse, Max L. "In the Company of Hauerwas." *Journal of Christian Theological Research* 2/1 (1997): para. 1–30.

Stahlberg, Jeffrey. Review of *Democracy and Tradition* by Jeffrey Stout. *Journal of Cultural and Religious Theory* 8/2 (Spring 2007): 200–205.

Steinfels, Peter. "Scarcely Heard Question: How God Could Have Allowed Catastrophe to Occur." *New York Times*, September 8, 2005. Online: http://tinyurl.com/64hmfs.

Stoddart, Eric. "Bespoke Theology for the Bereaved?" *The Bible in Transmission* (Winter 2008): 20–22.

———. "Hell: A Practical Theological Inquiry." PhD diss., University of Aberdeen, 2001.

Stoddart, Eric, and Gwilym Pryce. "Observed Aversion to Raising Hell in Pastoral Care: The Conflict Between Doctrine and Practice." *Journal of Empirical Theology* 18/2 (2005): 129–53.

Stone, Lance. "Word and Sacrament as Paradigmatic for Pastoral Theology: In Search of a Definition via Brueggemann, Hauerwas and Ricoeur." *Scottish Journal of Theology* 56/4 (2003): 444–63.

Storkey, Alan. *A Christian Social Perspective*. Leicester: InterVarsity, 1979.

Stott, John. *The Cross of Christ*. 2nd ed. Leicester: InterVarsity, 1989.

Stott, John, and David L. Edwards. *Essentials: A Liberal-Evangelical Dialogue*. London: Hodder & Stoughton, 1988.

Stout, Jeffrey. *Democracy and Tradition*. Princeton: Princeton University Press, 2004.

Strawson, Galen. "The Buck Stops—Where? Living Without Ultimate Moral Responsibility." Interview by Tamler Sommers. February 10, 2003. Online: http://www.naturalism.org/strawson_interview.htm.

———. *Freedom and Belief*. Oxford: Oxford University Press, 1986.

Strong, Augustus Hopkins. *Systematic Theology: A Compendium Designed for the Use of Theological Students*. London: Pickering and Inglis, 1907.

Stroup, George W. *The Promise of Narrative Theology*. London: SCM, 1984.

Stump, Eleonore. "Dante's Hell, Aquinas' Moral Theory and the Love of God." *Canadian Journal of Philosophy* Vol. 16/2 (June 1986): 181–98.

Surin, Kenneth. "Evil, the Problem of." In *The Blackwell Encyclopedia of Modern Christian Thought*, edited by Alister E. McGrath, 192–99. Oxford: Blackwell, 1993.

Sutton, Jeannette. "A Complex Organizational Adaptation to the World Trade Center Disaster: An Analysis of Faith-Based Organizations." In *Beyond September 11th: An Account of Post-Disaster Research*, 405–28. Boulder, CO: Natural Hazards Center, 2003.

———. "The Response of Faith-Based Organizations in New York City Following the World Trade Center Attacks on September 11, 2001." Department of Sociology University of Colorado at Boulder. Quick Response Report 147 (2002): n.p. Online: http://www.colorado.edu/hazards/research/qr/qr147/qr147.html

Sweet, Melissa, and Cait McMahon. "Disaster & the Media." Presentation at the University of Sydney, Dart Centre for Journalism and Trauma, 2007.

Swinton, John. "Patience and Lament: Living Faithfully in the Presence of Suffering." Conference paper presented for Deus Habet Consilium: The Career & Prospects of Providence in Modern Theology, School of Divinity, History and Philosophy, University of Aberdeen, January 2008.

———. *Raging with Compassion: Pastoral Responses to the Problem of Evil*. Grand Rapids: Eerdmans, 2007.

Swinton, John, and Brian Brock. "Theses on the Aberdeen School of Practical Theology." University of Aberdeen website. October 16, 2006. Online: http://tinyurl.com/55f96u.

Swinton, John, and Harriet Mowat. *Practical Theology and Qualitative Research*. London: SCM, 2006.

Swinton, John, and Richard Payne, eds. *Living Well and Dying Faithfully: Christian Practices for End-of-Lif Care*. Grand Rapids: Eerdmans, 2009.

Tate, Marvin E. "Satan in the Old Testament." *Review & Expositor* 89 (Fall 1992): 461–74.

Taylor, A. J. W. "Spirituality and Personal Values: Neglected Components of Trauma Treatment." *Traumatology* 7/3 (September 2001): 111–19.

———. "Value Conflict Arising from a Disaster." *The Australasian Journal of Disaster and Trauma Studies* 1999/2 (1999): n.p. Online: http://www.massey.ac.nz/~trauma/issues/1999-2/taylor.htm.

Taylor, Charles. "Living in a Secular Age." Gifford Lectures at the University of Edinburgh, 1998–99.

———. *A Secular Age*. Cambridge, MA: Harvard University Press, 2007.

Taylor, Jennifer. "NHS Compensation Culture: Do Patients Justice." *Health Service Journal* (November 17, 2008): n.p. Online: http://www.hsj.co.uk/resource-centre/nhs-compensation-culture-do-patients-justice/1908796.article.

Taylor, Peter. "The Hillsborough Stadium Disaster." HMG final report. London: HMSO. January 1990.

Taylor, Terri Graves. Review of *Time and Narrative*, by Paul Ricoeur, trans. Kathleen McLaughlin and David Pellauer. *The Journal of Aesthetics and Art Criticism* 47/4 (Autumn 1989): 380–82.

Taylor, William. "How to Pitch a Tent: A Beginner's Guide to Scriptural Reasoning." London: St. Ethelburga's Centre for Reconciliation and Peace, 2008. Online: http://www.scripturalreasoning.org/pdfs/howtopitchatent.pdf.

———. "Organising a Scriptural Reasoning Group." London: St. Ethelburga's Centre for Reconciliation and Peace, May 2007. Online: http://www.scripturalreasoning.org/pdfs/organise.pdf.

Teichman, Jenny. "How To Define Terrorism." *Philosophy* 64/250 (October 1989): 505–17.

Thomas, Keith. "Providence: The Doctrine and Its Uses." In *Seventeenth-Century England: A Changing Culture*, edited by W. R. Owens, vol. 2, 24–31. London: Ward Lock Educational, 1984.

Thompson, John Bromilow. *The Ecclesiology of Stanley Hauerwas: a Christian Theology of Liberation*. Aldershot, UK: Ashgate, 2003.

Tinker, Melvin. "The Servant Solution: The Co-ordination of Evangelism and Social Action." *Themelios: An International Journal for Theological and Religious Studies Students* 32/2 (January 2007): 6–32.

Tipton, Lane G. "The Function of Perichoresis and the Divine Incomprehensibility." *Westminster Theological Journal* 64/2 (Fall 2002): 289–306.

Torrance, Alan. "Developments in Neuroscience and Human Freedom: Some Theological and Philosophical Questions." *Science & Christian Belief* 16/2 (October 2004): 23–37.

"Townsend Thoresen" *Kent Social Services Report*. Appendix 3b. n.d.

Trimble, E. J. "4/1990 Boeing 737-400, G-OBME." Report on the accident to Boeing 737-400 G-OBME Near Kegworth, Leicestershire on 8 January 1989. UK Department of Transport, Air Accidents Investigation Branch. London: HMSO, 1990.

Trueman, Carl R. "Heaven and Hell: 12 in Puritan Theology." *Epworth Review* 22/3 (September 1995): 75–85.

———. "What Can Miserable Christians Sing?" *Themelios* 25/2 (February 2000): 1–3.

Tutu, Desmond. *No Future Without Forgiveness*. London: Rider, 1999.

"UK Among the Most Secular of Nations." BBC News, February 26, 2004. Online: http://news.bbc.co.uk/1/hi/programmes/wtwtgod/3518375.stm.

UK Cabinet Office. "Civil Contingencies Act 2004 (Contingency Planning) Regulations 2005." Statutory Instruments 2005 No. 2042. London: HMSO, 2005.

UK Cabinet Office. "Civil Contingencies Act 2004: A Short Guide (Revised)." 2005. Online: http://www.cabinetoffice.gov.uk/resource-library/civil-contingencies-act-short-guide-revised.

UK Cabinet Office. "Emergency Preparedness: Guidance on Part 1 of the Civil Contingencies Act 2004, Its Associated Regulations and Non-Statutory Arrangements." November 2005. Online: http://www.cabinetoffice.gov.uk/resource-library/emergency-preparedness.

UK Civil Contingencies Secretariat. "Hurricanes Katrina and Rita: A Perspective." Report. March 2006.

UK Department for Communities and Local Government. "Key Communities, Key Resources: Engaging the Capacity and Capabilities of Faith Communities in Civil Resilience." Report. London: Communities and Local Government Pub., June 2008. Online: http://www.communities.gov.uk/documents/communities/pdf/846112.pdf.

UK Department for Culture, Media and Sport. "Humanitarian Assistance in Emergencies: Non-Statutory Guidance on Establishing Humanitarian Assistance Centres." HMG report. 2006.

UK Department of Health. "Pandemic Flu: A National Framework for Responding to an Influenza Pandemic." Report. London: Crown Copyright, 2007.

UK Foreign Affairs Committee. "Second Report." Section 4:93-97. February 2006.

UK Health and Safety Commission. "Train Derailment at Potters Bar 10 May 2002: A Progress Report by the HSE Investigation Board." Health & Safety Executive. May 2003. Online: http://www.railwaysarchive.co.uk/documents/HSE_Potters Repo52003.pdf.

UK Home Office and Cabinet Office. "Guidance on Dealing with Fatalities in Emergencies." Home Office Communication Directorate, 2004. Online: http://webarchive.nationalarchives.gov.uk/+/http://www.cabinetoffice.gov.uk/media/132748/fatalities.pdf

UK Home Office. "Planning for a Possible Influenza Pandemic: A Framework for Planners Preparing to Manage Deaths." HMG report, version 1:1. London: HMSO, 2007.

UK Home Office. "Working Together: Co-operation between Government and Faith Communities." UK Home Office Faith Communities Unit, August 2005.

"UK Majority Back Multiculturalism." BBC News, August 10, 2005. Online: http://news.bbc.co.uk/1/hi/uk/4137990.stm.

UK Ministry of Justice. "A Guide to the Corporate Manslaughter and Corporate Homicide Act 2007." October 2007. Online: http://www.justice.gov.uk/docs/guidetomanslaughterhomicide07.pdf.

UK Ministry of Justice. "Understanding the Corporate Manslaughter and Corporate Homicide Act 2007." October 2007. Online: http://www.justice.gov.uk/docs/manslaughterhomicideact07.pdf.

UK National Audit Office. "Review of the Experiences of United Kingdom Nationals Affected by the Indian Ocean Tsunami." NAO assisted by the Zito Trust. London: HMSO, 2006.

UK Office of National Statistics. *Social Trends* 38 (April 8, 2008). Online: http://www.ons.gov.uk/ons/rel/social-trends-rd/social-trends/no--38--2008-edition/social-trends-full-report.pdf.

UK Office of Public Sector Information. "Corporate Manslaughter and Corporate Homicide Act, 2007, c. 19." Online: http://www.opsi.gov.uk/acts/acts2007/ukpga_20070019_en_1.

UK Secretary of State for Health. "Trust, Assurance and Safety: The Regulation of Health Professionals in the 21st Century." London: HMSO, 2007. Online: http://www.official-documents.gov.uk/document/cm70/7013/7013.pdf.

Ullyart, M. "Cumbria Floods Technical Report: Factual Report on Meteorology, Hydrology and Impacts of January 2005 Flooding in Cumbria." UK Environment Agency, 2006. Online: http://publications.environment-agency.gov.uk/pdf/GENW1106BLSF-e-e.pdf.

The Unique Christ in our Pluralistic World: WEF Manila Declaration. Outreach and Identity: Evangelical Theological Monographs, 5. Seoul, Korea: World Evangelical Fellowship Theological Commission, 1993.

Valent, Paul. "Traumatology at the Turn of the Millennium." *Australasian Traumatic Stress Points* (2000): 2–4. Online: *http://www.paulvalent.com/publications/stress_trauma_maladaptive/stress_trauma_maladaptive_02.pdf*

Van der Kolk, Bessel A., Alexander C. McFarlane, and Lars Weisaeth, eds. *Traumatic Stress: The Effects of Overwhelming Experience on Mind, Body, and Society.* London: Guilford, 1996.

Van Gulick, Robert. "Who's in Charge Here? And Who's Doing All the Work?" In *Mental Causation*, edited by John Heil and Alfred Mele, 233–56. Oxford: Clarendon, 1995.

Van Holten, Wilko. "Hell and the Goodness of God." *Religious Studies* 35/1 (March 1999): 37–55.

Van Til, Cornelius. *Common Grace.* Philadelphia: P & R, 1954.

Vandrunen, David. *A Biblical Case for Natural Law.* Studies in Christian Social Ethics and Economics 1. Grand Rapids: Acton Institute, 2006.

———. "Vandrunen in the Hands of an Anxious Kloosterman: A Response to a Review of *A Biblical Case for Natural Law.*" *Ordained Servant* (December 2007). Online: http://opc.org/os.html?article_id=78.

VanGemeren, William A., ed. *New International of Old Testament Theology and Exegesis.* 5 vols. Carlisle: Paternoster, 1997.

Vanhoozer, Kevin J. *Biblical Narrative in the Philosophy of Paul Ricoeur: A Study in Hermeneutics and Theology.* Cambridge: Cambridge University Press, 1990.

———. *The Drama of Doctrine: A Canonical Linguistic Approach to Christian Theology.* Louisville: Westminster, 2005.

Bibliography

———. *Is There a Meaning in this Text? The Bible, the Reader, and the Morality of Literary Knowledge*. Leicester: Apollos, 1998.

———. "Philosophical Antecedents to Ricoeur's *Time and Narrative*." In *On Paul Ricoeur: Narrative and Interpretation*, edited by David Wood, 34–54. London: Routledge, 1991.

Venning, Ralph. *The Plague of Plagues*. Edinburgh: Banner of Truth Trust, 1965.

Villa-Vicencio, Charles, ed. *Theology and Violence: The South African Debate*. Grand Rapids: Eerdmans, 1988.

Vincent, Thomas. *God's Terrible Voice in the City*. London: George Calvert, 1667. Reprint, Morgan, PA: Soli Deo Gloria, 1997.

Volf, Miroslav. *Exclusion and Embrace: A Theological Exploration of Identity, Otherness, and Reconciliation*. Nashville: Abingdon, 1996.

Vriezen, Th. C. *An Outline of Old Testament Theology*. 2nd ed. Oxford: Blackwell, 1970.

Walker, D. P. *The Decline of Hell: Seventeenth-Century Discussions of Eternal Torment*. London: RKP, 1964.

Walker-Smith, Aileen. "The King's Cross Disaster Report: Assessing the Two Years of Coordinated Support." London: Camden Social Service Department, 1990.

Wallace, Mark I. "Can God Be Named Without Being Known? The Problem of Revelation in Thiemann, Ogden, and Ricoeur." *Journal of the American Academy of Religion* 59/2 (Summer 1991): 281–308.

Wallace, R. S. *Calvin's Doctrine of the Christian Life*. Edinburgh: Oliver & Boyd, 1959.

Waller, James E. "Deliver Us From Evil: Genocide and the Christian World." *Journal of Religion & Society* Supplement Series 2 (2007): 138–52.

Wallis, Patrick. "A Dreadful Heritage: Interpreting Epidemic Disease at Eyam, 1666–2000." Working papers on the "Nature of Evidence: How Well Do 'Facts' Travel?" No. 02/05, Department of Economic History, London School of Economics, May 2005. Online: http://www.lse.ac.uk/collections/economicHistory/pdf/FACTSPDF/FACTS2-Wallis.pdf.

Walls, Jerry L. *Hell: the Logic of Damnation*. London: University of Notre Dame Press, 1992.

Walsh, Bryan. "Picking Up the Pieces." In *Haiti: Tragedy and Hope*, edited by Michael Elliott, Jeffrey Kluger, and Richard Lacayo, 62–74. New York: Time, 2010.

Walters, Geoff. *Why Do Christians Find It Hard to Grieve?* Carlisle: Paternoster, 1997.

Walton, Heather. "Speaking in Signs: Narrative and Trauma in Pastoral Theology." *Scottish Journal of Healthcare Chaplaincy* 5/2 (October 2002): 2–5.

Warfield, Benjamin Breckinridge. "Imitating the Incarnation." In *The Person And Work of Christ*, edited by Samuel Craig, 563–75. Edinburgh: P & R, 1970.

Watson, Thomas. *A Body of Divinity: Contained in Sermons upon the Westminster Assembly's Catechism*. London: The Banner of Truth Trust, 1960.

Weaver, Andrew J. "Psychological Trauma: What Clergy Need to Know." *Pastoral Psychology* 41/6 (1993): 385–408.

Weaver Andrew J., Laura T. Flannelly, James Garbarino, Charles R. Figley, and Kevin J. Flannelly. "A Systematic Review of the Research on Religion and Spirituality in *The Journal of Traumatic Stress*: 1990–1999." *Mental Health, Religion and Culture* 6/3 (2003): 215–28.

Weaver, Andrew J., Laura T. Flannelly, John D. Preston. *Counseling Survivors of Traumatic Events: A Handbook for Pastors and Other Helping Professionals*. Nashville: Abingdon, 2003.

Weaver, Andrew J and Monica Furlong. *Reflections of Forgiveness and Spiritual Growth.* Nashville: Abingdon, 2000.

Weaver, Andrew J., Harold G. Koenig, and Frank M. Ochberg. "Posttraumatic Stress, Mental Health Professionals, and the Clergy: A Need for Collaboration, Training, and Research." *Journal of Traumatic Stress* 9/4 (1996): 847–56.

Webb, Barr W. "Ladbroke Grove Rail Crash, 5 October 1999: Review of Casualty, Bureau Procedures, Family Liaison Arrangements and Identification Process." Police report. March 30, 2000.

Webb, Gary R. "Individual and Organizational Response to Natural Disasters and Other Crisis Events: The Continuing Value of the DRC Typology." Preliminary paper 277, University of Delaware Disaster Research Center, 1999.

Webber, Robert E. *The Secular Saint: The Role of the Christian In The Secular World.* Grand Rapids: Zondervan, 1982.

Webster, John. "On the Theology of Providence." Conference paper presented for Deus Habet Consilium: The Career & Prospects of Providence in Modern Theology, School of Divinity, History and Philosophy, University of Aberdeen, January 2008.

———. "The Self-Organizing Power of the Gospel of Christ: Episcopacy and Community Formation." *International Journal of Systematic Theology* 3/1 (2001): 69–82.

Weinandy, Thomas G. *Does God Suffer?* Edinburgh: T & T Clark, 2000.

Weinberg, Leonard, and Ami Pedahzur, eds. *Religious Fundamentalism and Political Extremism.* London: Frank Class, 2004.

Weisaeth, Lars. "Preventing After-Effects of Disaster Trauma: The Information Support Centre." *Prehospital Disaster Medicine* 19/1 (2003): 86–89.

Wells, David F. *Above All Earthly Pow'rs: Christ in a Postmodern World.* Grand Rapids: Eerdmans, 2006.

———. *God In the Wasteland: The Reality of Truth In A World of Fading Dreams.* Leicester: InterVarsity, 1995.

———. *Losing Our Virtue: Why the Church Must Recover Its Moral Virtue.* Leicester: InterVarsity, 1998.

———. *No Place for Truth: Or Whatever Happened To Evangelical Theology?* Leicester: InterVarsity, 1993.

Wesley, John. *Serious Thoughts Occasioned by the Late Earthquake at Lisbon.* Photocopy of pages 1–13 in *The Works of the Rev. John Wesley, A. M.* 5th ed. Vol. 11. London: Wesleyan Conference Office, n.d.

Whitefield, George. *Whitefield at Lisbon: Being a detailed Account of the Blasphemy and Idolatry of Popery . . . With Mr. Whitefield's Remarks Thereon.* Photocopy. London: R. Groombridge & Sons, 1851.

Wiles, Maurice. "Scriptural Authority and Theological Construction: The Limitations of Narrative Interpretation." In *Scriptural Authority and Narrative Interpretation*, edited by Garrett Green, 42–58. Philadelphia: Fortress, 1987.

Williams, C. S. C. *The Acts of the Apostles.* 2nd ed. London: Adam & Charles Black, 1962.

Williams, Norman L. "Pastoral Ministry Following a Major Disaster." DMin diss., San Francisco Theological Seminary, 1998.

Williams, Rowan. "This Media Tribe Disfigures Public Life." *Guardian*, June 16, 2005. Online: http://www.guardian.co.uk/media/2005/jun/16/pressandpublishing. religion.

Bibliography

"The Williamsburg Charter, 1988: A Reaffirmation of the First Amendment." Online: http://religiousfreedom.lib.virginia.edu/const/Willburg.html.

Wilson, Bryan. "The Return of the Sacred." *Journal for the Scientific Study of Religion* 18/3 (September 1979): 268–80.

Wilson, Gordon L. *Dealing with Trauma: Some Guidelines for Clergy and Pastoral Workers Involved in Understanding and Caring for People with Traumatic Experiences.* N. p.: Avon & Somerset Constabulary, 2002.

Wisse, Maarten. "Narrative Theology and the Use of the Bible in Systematic Theology." *Ars Disputandi* 5 (2005): para. 1–30.

Witherington, Ben. "Ignorance is Bliss? Biblical Illiteracy in the West." Blog entry, August 25, 2007. Online: http://benwitherington.blogspot.com/2007/08/ignorance-is-bliss-biblical-illiteracy.html.

Witherington, Ben, III, with Darlene Hyatt. *Paul's Letter to the Romans: A Socio-Rhetorical Commentary.* Grand Rapids: Eerdmans, 2004.

Wolfe, Alan. *Moral Freedom: The Search for Virtue in a World of Choice.* New York: W. W. Norton, 2001.

Wolterstorff, Nicholas P. "Justice and Peace." In *New Dictionary of Christian Ethics and Pastoral Theology*, edited by David J. Atkinson and David H. Field, 15–21 Leicester: InterVarsity, 1995.

———. *Lament for a Son.* London: SPCK, 1987.

———. *Until Justice and Peace Embrace.* Grand Rapids: Eerdmans, 1987.

———. *What New Haven and Grand Rapids Have to Say to Each Other.* Stob Lectures. Grand Rapids: Calvin College, 1993.

Wong, Paul T. P. "Compassionate and Spiritual Care: A Vision of Positive Holistic Medicine." Keynote address at the Consultation on Holistic Healthcare for the Medical, Religious and Academic Professionals in Hong Kong, June 2004.

Woodward, James, and Stephen Pattison, eds. *The Blackwell Reader in Pastoral and Practical Theology.* Oxford: Blackwell, 2000.

Worden, J. William. *Grief Counselling and Grief Therapy.* New York: Routledge, 1992.

Wright, Bob. *Sudden Death: A Research Base for Practice.* 2nd ed. New York: Churchill Livingstone, 1996.

Wright, Christopher J. H. *The Use of the Bible in Social Ethics.* Bramcote, UK: Grove, 1983.

Wright, N. T. *Evil and the Justice of God.* London: SPCK, 2006.

Wright, Nigel. "The Reality and Origin of Evil." *The Bible in Transmission: A Forum for Change in Church and Culture* (Summer 2008): 5–7.

Wyatt, John. *Matters of Life and Death: Today's Healthcare Dilemmas in the Light of Christian Faith.* Leicester: InterVarsity, 1998.

Yancey, Philip. *Disappointment with God: Three Questions No One Asks Aloud.* London: Marshall Pickering, 1995.

———. *Soul Survivor: How My Faith Survived the Church.* London: Hodder & Stoughton, 2001.

———. *What's So Amazing About Grace.* Grand Rapids: Zondervan, 1997.

Young, Edward, J. *The Book of Isaiah: The English Text, With Introduction, Exposition, and Notes.* Vol. 3. Grand Rapids: Eerdmans, 1977.

Zapan, Daniel. *War, Morality, and Autonomy: An Investigation in Just War Theory.* Aldershot, UK: Ashgate, 2004.

Author/Name Index

Scripture Index

Subject Index